MOON

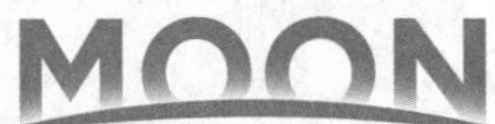

NORMANDY & BRITTANY

CHRIS NEWENS

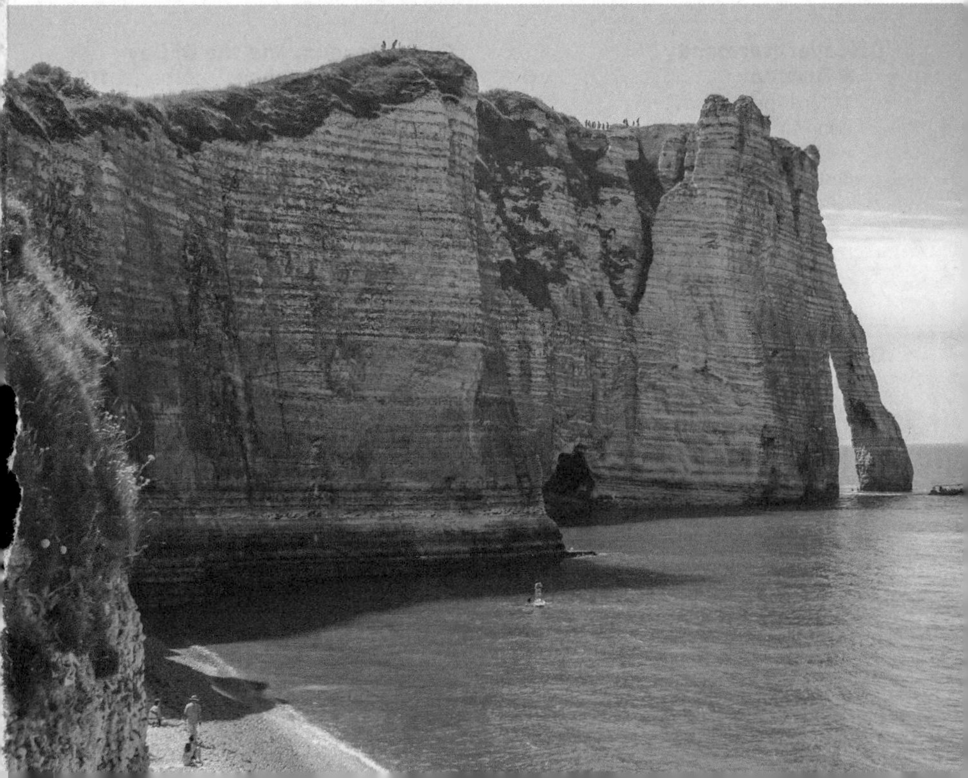

Contents

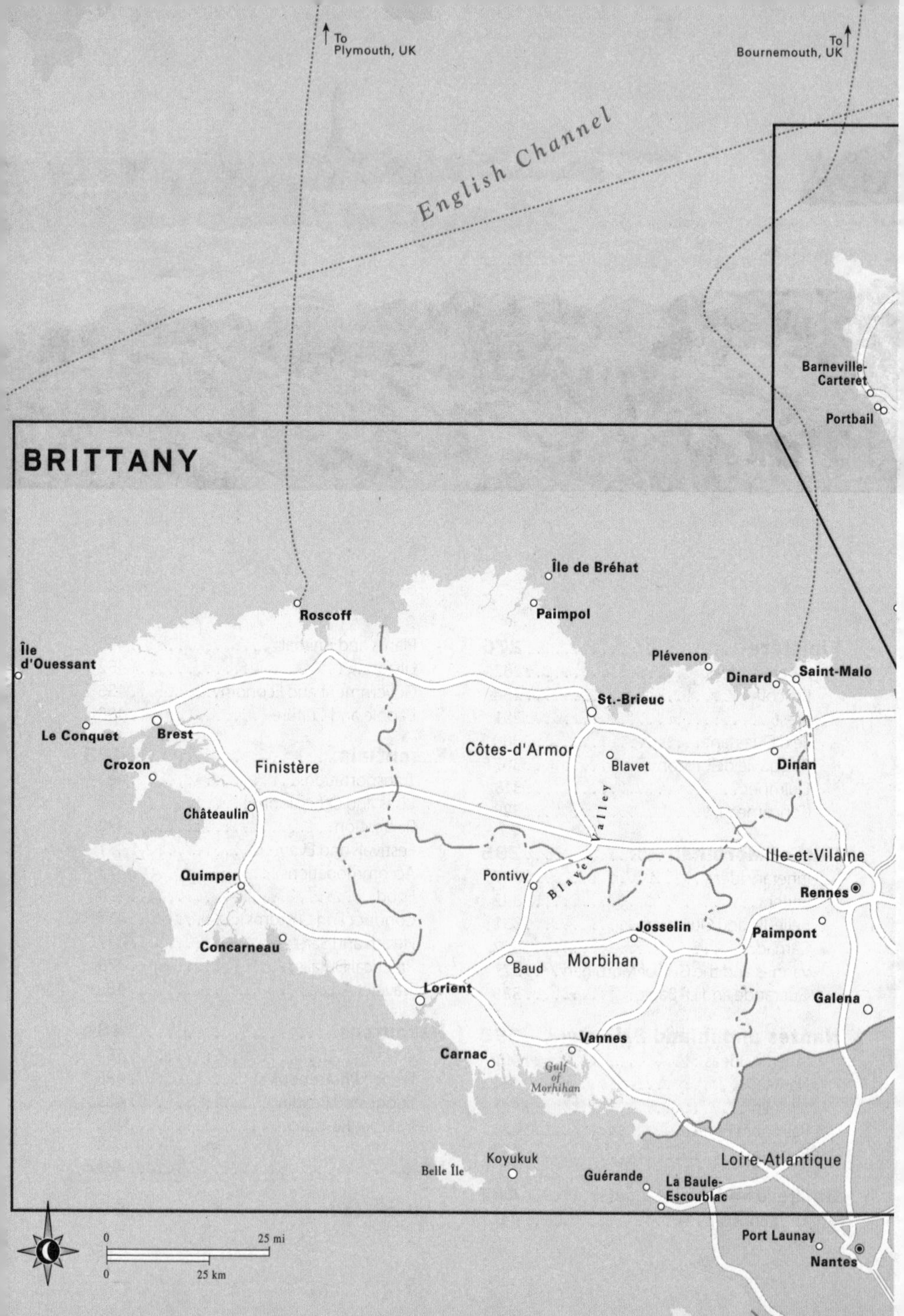

BRITTANY
To Plymouth, UK
To Bournemouth, UK
English Channel
Barneville-Carteret
Portbail
Île de Bréhat
Roscoff
Paimpol
Île d'Ouessant
Plévenon
Dinard
Saint-Malo
St.-Brieuc
Le Conquet
Brest
Côtes-d'Armor
Crozon
Finistère
Blavet
Dinan
Châteaulin
Blavet Valley
Ille-et-Vilaine
Quimper
Pontivy
Rennes
Josselin
Paimpont
Concarneau
Baud
Morbihan
Lorient
Galena
Vannes
Carnac
Gulf of Morbihan
Loire-Atlantique
Belle Île
Koyukuk
Guérande
La Baule-Escoublac
Port Launay
Nantes
0
25 mi
0
25 km

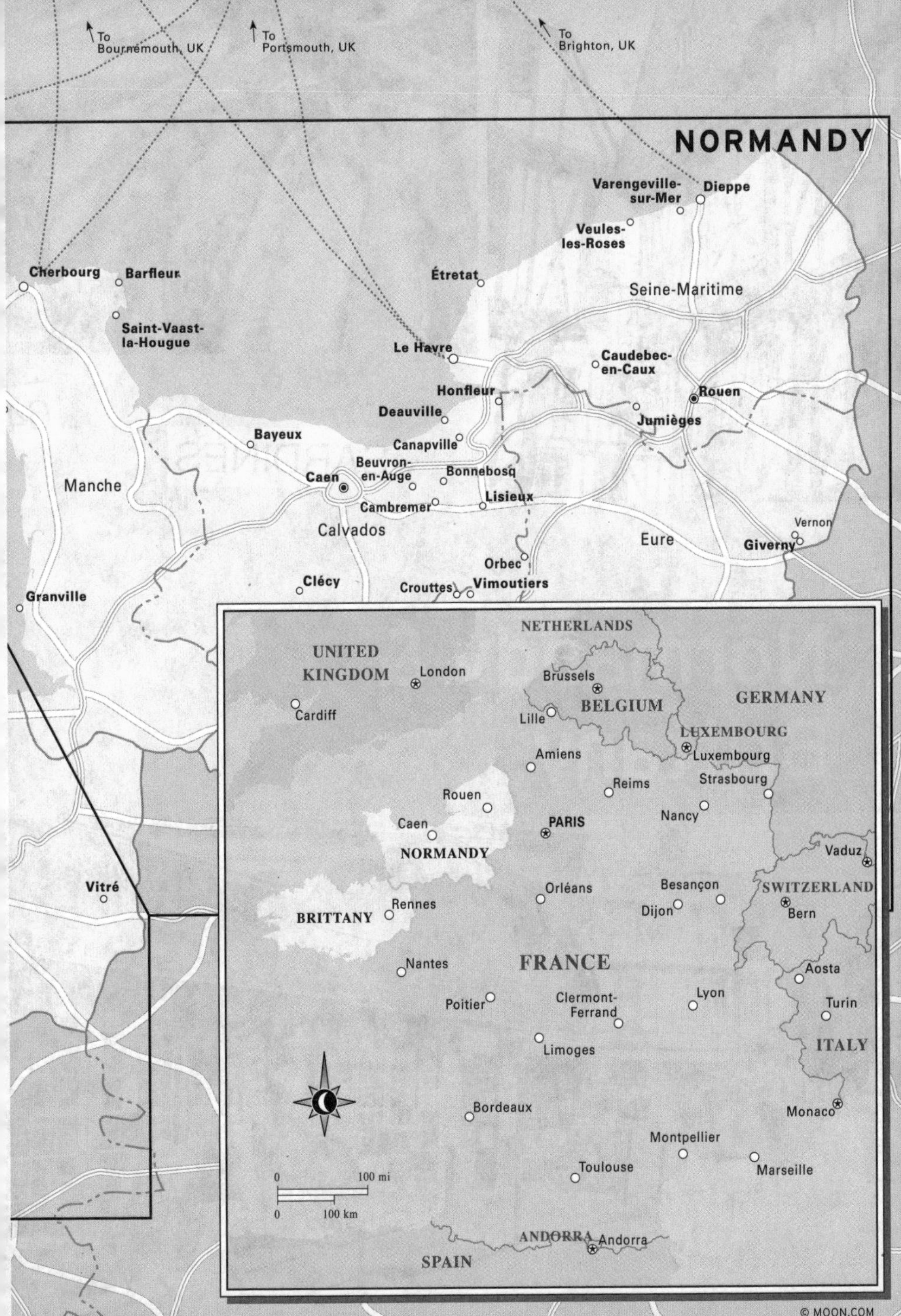

To Bournemouth, UK
To Portsmouth, UK
To Brighton, UK
NORMANDY
Varengeville-sur-Mer
Dieppe
Veules-les-Roses
Cherbourg
Barfleur
Étretat
Seine-Maritime
Saint-Vaast-la-Hougue
Le Havre
Caudebec-en-Caux
Honfleur
Rouen
Deauville
Jumièges
Bayeux
Canapville
Beuvron-en-Auge
Bonnebosq
Manche
Caen
Lisieux
Cambremer
Calvados
Vernon
Eure
Giverny
Orbec
Clécy
Crouttes
Vimoutiers
Granville
Vitré
NETHERLANDS
UNITED KINGDOM
London
Brussels
GERMANY
Cardiff
BELGIUM
Lille
LUXEMBOURG
Luxembourg
Amiens
Strasbourg
Reims
Rouen
Nancy
PARIS
Caen
NORMANDY
Vaduz
Orléans
Besançon
SWITZERLAND
Dijon
Bern
Rennes
BRITTANY
FRANCE
Nantes
Aosta
Lyon
Clermont-Ferrand
Poitier
Turin
Limoges
ITALY
Bordeaux
Monaco
Montpellier
Marseille
Toulouse
0
100 mi
0
100 km
ANDORRA
Andorra
SPAIN
© MOON.COM

DISCOVER

Normandy & Brittany

Seldom have two regions had more in common, yet more that divides them, than Normandy and Brittany.

On the one hand, there's their northern climate, their proximity to the sea, and the essentials of their cuisine—apples, dairy, and seafood—which they share. On the other, there's how both are so fiercely proud of their regional heritage, whether for the horse-riding exploits of Norman conquerors or the music and legends of the mysterious Celts.

And yet…

Normandy is a land of towering Gothic cathedrals, sedate farmland, and bourgeois seaside resorts, while Brittany has squat, almost pagan chapels, primordial woodland, and wind-lashed harbors that seem to exist in another time.

As one of the closest regions to Paris, Normandy has long been a weekend retreat for stylish urbanites looking for country air and exceptional rustic cooking. Its history is inextricably linked to that of the rest of France: It is long, deep, and known, and still feels like it can be touched. Joan of Arc was burned at the stake in Rouen; Impressionist painters roamed the cliffs of the Alabaster Coast;

Clockwise from top left: colorful medieval houses in Vannes; shimmering sardines from the day's catch; a statue depicting Joan of Arc's last minutes in Rouen Cathedral; umbrellas that launched a thousand photographs; a statue immortalizing a U.S. G.I. on Omaha Beach; the sprawling Taverne des Deux Augustins in Étretat.

and D-Day, the largest land invasion of all time, with implications not just for France but for the whole world, took place in living memory, at the base of the Cherbourg Peninsula.

Brittany, meanwhile, is otherworldly and distinct. Here are mysterious Neolithic monuments, legends of giants, and the forests where King Arthur and Merlin are said to have trod. Its coastline is salty and wild, spangled by hardy lighthouses and wondrous islands, a water-sports paradise crenelated with grand natural harbors and hidden coves. Then there are the Bretons themselves, whose culture swings to its own rhythm, drinking cider from earthenware bowls, telling folktales of the hinterland, and partying with Celtic dancing and song.

Bringing the two regions back together is that both offer remarkable rewards for the independent traveler. And whether your tastes run to the luxury sophistication of the casinos and elegant promenades of Deauville, or dancing into the night to the wail of bagpipes at a traditional *fest-noz* (night festival) in some little-known Breton village, there's more than a lifetime's worth of things to explore.

Clockwise from top left: just one of the many astonishing views hikers around Presqu'île de Crozon can enjoy; Notre Dame de Rouen; fresh, tasty clams; busy tables outside Café des Tribunaux.

Café des Tribunaux

33
PETONCLES BLANCS
7,80 €/kg
Zone de capture:
A.N.E

14 TOP EXPERIENCES

1 Feeling like you're inside an Impressionist painting in **Monet's garden at Giverny,** where the natural world has been tended into a living masterpiece (page 45).

2 Paying your respects at the **Normandy American Cemetery and Memorial,** a haunting sanctuary on the blustery Norman coast, where the massed ranks of silent graves tell the true cost of the D-Day landings (page 160).

3 Letting your imagination run away with you, exploring the abbey at **Mont-Saint-Michel,** the Gothic monument that soars high above a tidal plain and seems like it belongs more to fantasy fiction rather than the real world (page 199).

4 Experiencing the future as it was conceived of in the past in Le Havre's unique modernist downtown, especially in the **Église Saint-Joseph,** a concrete-and-glass kaleidoscope of a building (page 97).

5 Going back in time as you gaze at the **Bayeux Tapestry,** one of the most fascinating artifacts in Northern Europe that also tells the compelling story of the Norman conquest (page 144).

6 Enjoying the metallic taste of **Saint-Vaast oysters** at sunset, while overlooking the beds in which they were grown, and washing them down with a glass of chilled white wine (page 177).

7 Getting lost in the half-timber labyrinth of **Rouen's old town,** where every turn seems to reveal something beguiling, from the **Saint-Maclou Ossuary** to the elaborate carvings on the city's Gothic **cathedral** (page 51).

8 Pretending you're a French corsair as you tour the granite **ramparts of Saint-Malo,** which look like they've been carved from the ocean itself (page 232).

9 Learning to surf on **Goulien Beach** on the Crozon Peninsula, which is well shielded from the wind but still gets big waves: ideal for beginners and experts alike (page 311).

^
^
^

10 **Hiking** the jaw-dropping coastal route between **Fort la Latte** and the **Cap Fréhel**. When the sun's out and shimmering off the blue sea, the wildflowers are in bloom, and the air is dusted by a spring wind, you could be forgiven for thinking that there's no more beautiful walk in the whole world (page 253).

11 Discovering something truly unique at Nantes's sculpture-park-cum-theme-park for adults, the **Machines de l'Île,** where inventions straight from a Jules Verne novel are brought thrillingly to life. Conceived by Pierre Orefice and Francois Deleroziere (page 407).

12 Swilling cider and watching the dancing to bagpipes at a ***fest-noz.*** These Celtic night festivals take place in villages across Brittany and pulse with traditional food, dance, and song (page 440).

13 **Cycling** the narrow roads of Brittany's many different islands, from the genteel **Île-de-Bréhat** (page 258) to the windswept and ragged **Île d'Ouessant** (page 300), on the western edge of the European continent.

14 Marveling at the mysteries behind the **stones of Carnac** and questioning how early Bretons ever managed to drag into place the largest collection of prehistoric standing stones in the world (page 364).

Planning Your Trip

Where to Go

Normandy

GIVERNY, ROUEN, AND THE "IMPRESSIONIST COAST"

A region rich in history, holiday resorts, and natural beauty that has been attracting tourists and inspiring artists for generations, there's something here for all visitors. Architecture lovers and foodies will find much to enjoy in Normandy's capital, Rouen, with its elaborate Gothic churches such as **Saint-Maclou** and the **Notre Dame,** and its wide variety of **modern restaurants** updating the deep flavors of Norman cuisine for the 21st century. For those passionate about art, the landscape from the banks of the Seine to the **cliffs of the Alabaster Coast**—at their most jaw-dropping in Étretat—has been one of the greatest muses in the history of painting. Nowhere is this more the case than at Giverny, where for the latter years of his life Claude Monet set to work building one of the most glorious gardens anywhere in the world, making art from the landscape itself. People with a more contemporary eye in search of something unusual should head to the modernist marvel that is Le Havre, rebuilt after World War II in poured concrete, with buildings like **Église Saint-Joseph** and the **Vulcan theater** offering a view of the future as it might have been imagined in the past. Tourists wanting luxury should head straight for Deauville to relax on its **umbrella-dotted beach** or to get pampered in the ultra-plush **Normandy** hotel.

CAEN, BAYEUX, AND THE D-DAY LANDING BEACHES

The huge majority of visitors to this region will be here because of their interest in the events of June 1944, when the largest sea-to-land invasion of all time took place along its coastline. There

the abstract sides of Le Volcan theater

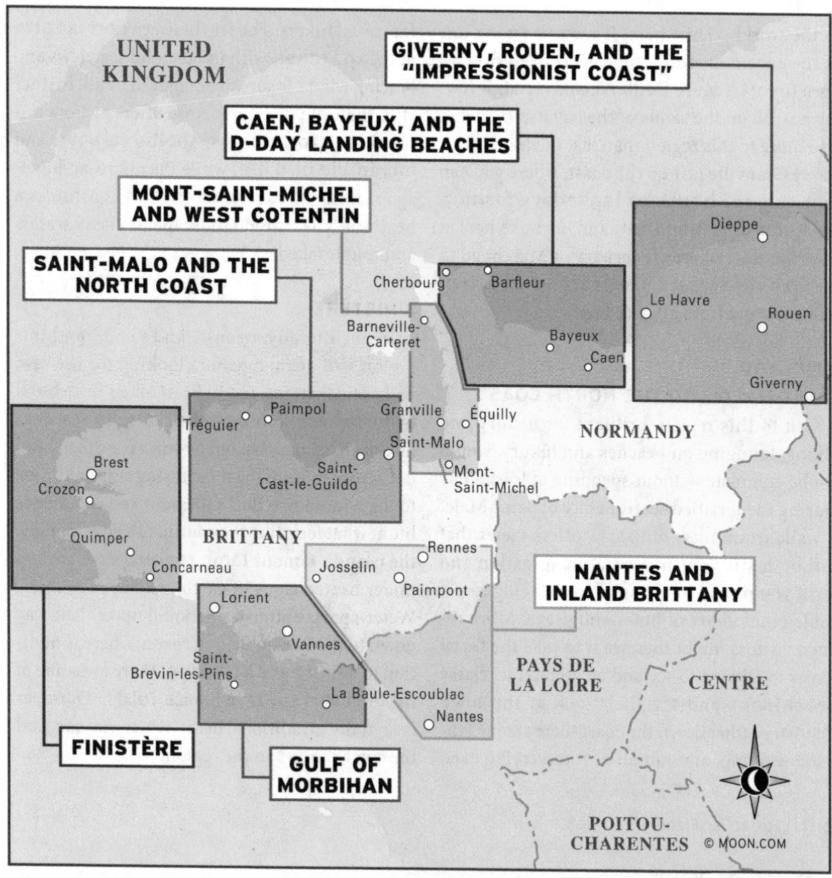

is so much to see that only the most die-hard World War II enthusiasts should try to take it all in. With that in mind, most people will create their own itinerary based on particular interests and often their nation of origin. Not to be missed, though, are the hauntingly grand **Normandy American Cemetery** and the dynamic remains of the **Pointe du Hoc,** where D-Day's impact on the landscape can be most clearly seen. Away from the beaches, the **Bayeux Tapestry** is a truly unmissable sight, being both an incredible artifact and an evocative visual story of another cross-channel invasion (this one in the other direction) almost 1,000 years ago. In Caen, the **Peace Museum** offers an excellent overview of the fighting that followed D-Day and far beyond. An entirely different and more pleasure-oriented experience can be found on the eastern side of the Cotentin Peninsula, where in the charming historic town of Saint-Vaast the **oysters** are some of the best in Normandy.

MONT-SAINT-MICHEL AND WEST COTENTIN

The **abbey** of Mont-Saint-Michel is an irresistible draw: The way its Gothic splendor rises with ethereal majesty out of the tidal plain makes it one of the most spectacular monuments anywhere in the world. While here, it's worth trying one of the enormous fluffy omelets cooked over an open fire at **La Mère Poulard,** and certainly having a stroll on the sands of the bay itself. There's also more to this region than just the Mont, with classy Granville just up the coast, where you can drop into the **house of legendary fashion designer Christian Dior,** and, if you're here at the right time of year (February or March) go to the town's lively **Mardi Gras carnival**, which attracts visitors from all over France.

Brittany

SAINT-MALO AND THE NORTH COAST

A visit to this region, brilliant for history and hiking, lounging on beaches and luxury, would not be complete without spending at least a day touring the fortified seafront city of Saint-Malo. A walk around its **ramparts** offers views that will both stir your historical imagination and thrill you purely in terms of color, being a veritable paint chart of blues and grays. More refined visitors might then want to take the **ferry** across to Dinard to see and be seen on its classy **beachfront** and try their luck at the town **casino.** Farther down the coast there's some fantastic walking, and not all of it too trying even for casual hikers: The trip between **Fort la Latte** and **Cap Frehel,** with its splendid sea views and bracing winds, is sure to be enjoyed by all. Farther still, the Côte de Granit Rose offers visitors unusual **rock formations, sheltered bays,** and **incredible bird life,** while the micro-archipelago making up the **Île-de-Bréhat** constitutes a beautifully textured landscape of glassy waters and rough-faced rock.

FINISTÈRE

Its name literally means "land's end," and this region will attract visitors looking for the raw, authentic Brittany. Go to Brest for its **laid-back atmosphere** and **bars** full of salty sea dogs looking to spin a yarn or buy you a pint, then head out across some of the most trying seas in Europe to the windblown Île d'Ouessant and experience life at what feels like the continent's edge. Sample the island's famous **lamb ragout,** slow-cooked under heated clods of earth, while you're there. Water-sports enthusiasts should make their way down to the Presqu'île de Crozon, where in addition to **sailing** and **kayaking,** there are some of the **best surf spots** in France. Inland, Quimper is Brittany's traditional heart, where you can find the **best crepes** in the region.

Fort la Latte at Cap Fréhel

GULF OF MORBIHAN

For those in search of magic, the area around the Gulf of Morbihan and the gulf itself are places of unanswered questions and bizarre but beautiful landscapes. The massed ranks of **standing stones** at Carnac are one of Brittany's greatest draws, being the largest Neolithic construction of their type anywhere in the world. The gulf, meanwhile, is almost an inland sea, pocked by mysterious private islands and plied by countless boats. A trip on its waters, whether by **kayak** or **pleasure cruise,** is a must. Nearby, a great place to base yourself is the walled city of **Vannes,** home to much **traditional half-timber architecture** and **ramparts** the equal of anywhere in Brittany. Farther down the coast are the striking **Guérande salt marshes,** a man-made landscape where Brittany's famous *fleur de sel* is produced. This area is also a great spot for **bird-watchers.** If you're around the Gulf of Morbihan in early August, feel like a party, and don't mind bagpipe music, check out the **Festival Interceltique de Lorient,** a vast, week-long celebration of Celtic culture.

NANTES AND INLAND BRITTANY

Boasting the region's two biggest cities in the form of its historic capital (Nantes) and current capital (Rennes), this area might be an obvious destination for urbanites. Nantes's unusual steam-punk-inspired sculpture park, the **Machines de l'Île de Nantes,** and Rennes's infamous **drinking scene** are just two of many elements that will keep such visitors happy. However, city attractions are far from the region's only draw. Even Nantes and Rennes are extremely green: Nantes was recently voted one of the best cities in the world in which to ride a bike, thanks to its **extensive system of bike paths** stretching deep into the surrounding countryside, while Rennes has powerful links with the farmers of the Breton hinterland, seen at its extensive town market, the **Marché des Lices,** and an **eco-museum**—effectively an open farm within the city limits. There's also the magnificent **Château in Josselin,** sure to delight history buffs, and the mystical Paimpont Forest, where many legends associated with **King Arthur** are said to have taken place, and where a simple bike tour takes you into the presence of such sights as the **tomb of Merlin** and a font said to be the original **fountain of youth.**

When to Go

With their mild climate, both Normandy and Brittany are perfectly hospitable for travelers whatever season they choose to visit, though there is a tendency for a number of hotels, campgrounds, museums, and other tourist sights to shut down and for local transport to run a skeleton service in the **winter** months, around November-March. Temperatures around this time average at about 50°F (10°C), though they can sometimes drop close to, and even just below, freezing in the very coldest months (December-February).

For both regions, things start to pick up in April, with average **spring** temperatures about 59°F (15°C). Though it's usually still too chilly for a beach holiday around this time, **April and May** are great months to enjoy walking through the landscape, and many of the top tourist sights are relatively undisturbed. Things don't get really crowded in the **summer** until July, when French kids break for school holidays, and August, when most workers take their annual leave in a tradition known throughout France as *la pause.* Temperatures around this time average at 72°F (22°C) and seaside resorts can get very busy. As such, these months are more or less the only two when booking ahead for most things is practically essential. At the same time, both Normandy and

If You Have...

FOUR DAYS

Head straight for Caen or Bayeux and use one of them as a base for the first couple of days in order to explore the D-Day landing grounds. You can organize a tour or take yourself around if you have your own transport; make sure to take in Caen's Peace Museum and the Bayeux Tapestry before you leave. Set off early to see Mont-Saint-Michel. Spend the day exploring the monument, then carry straight on to Saint-Malo. It sounds tiring, but it's worth it if you're limited on time. You'll then wake up in Saint-Malo and have a full day to explore the coastal citadel.

ONE WEEK

Before making the journey as above, start in Rouen, and follow the Seine to the coast to see Le Havre. This concrete masterpiece of urban planning is utterly different from anywhere else in either Normandy or Brittany. Cross the Pont de Normandie and drop in on Honfleur before spending the night in Deauville or Trouville for a day of relaxing and pampering. Then, carry on to Caen or Bayeux.

TWO WEEKS

Continuing on from the one-week itinerary, head east to spend a couple of days relaxing on the Emerald Coast and hike the Cap Fréhel. Then go farther east to Brest, where you can launch an overnight expedition to the Île d'Ouessant (staying the night on this remote island is highly recommended). When you return to the mainland, head down to Quimper, where the heart of Breton culture resides.

Pont de Normandie

Brittany are at their most convivial at this stage, and it's when they have the nicest weather—and best conditions for swimming. Moreover, museums, other sights, and water-sports centers will all be keeping their longest hours, with some opening only for this season.

June and September have almost as good weather, with average temperatures of around 68°F (20°C), but not being fueled by the school holidays, places can be surprisingly quiet, except on weekends. Note that the **D-Day Landing Anniversary** is on June 6, with events spanning the couple weeks before and after that date. By October, things have usually already started to wind down, particularly campsites, though the **fall colors** in both regions can be the equal of those in New England, especially if the summer has been hot.

Of course, there's also some appeal to heading out to the ragged edges of the regions in the middle of winter, renting a cottage on the Île d'Ouessant, say, and battening down the hatches, creating a cozy little isolated bunker against the Atlantic storms. Normandy is, on balance, the more "year-round" destination, having more big-name sights that can persist regular opening times throughout the year. Such sights include the Bayeux Tapestry, Mont-Saint-Michel, and most of the D-Day beaches and the museums associated with them. Note: Monet's house and garden at Giverny is not on this list, being largely outside and dying back in the winter.

Before You Go

Passports and Visas

UNITED STATES, CANADA, AUSTRALIA, AND NEW ZEALAND

A visa-waiver program allows individuals from all of the above countries to stay in France and the entire Schengen area (a group of 26 European nations with no border controls between them) for up to 90 days within a 180-day period, as long as they have a valid passport. In 2021, a pre-travel registration system (European Travel Information and Authorisation System or ETIAS) is expected to be implemented for entry to the Schengen area. Check with the state department or foreign affairs ministry in your home country for more information if traveling in 2021.

UNITED KINGDOM

At the time of writing, it's unclear what the rules will be for travelers to France from the United Kingdom due to Brexit. Most likely, laws similar to travelers from the United States, Canada, Australia, and New Zealand will apply, though of course you should check www.gov.uk/foreign-travel-advice/france closer to the date of travel.

EUROPE

Travelers from EU countries are allowed to travel in France for as long as they want without visas, though they should inform authorities should they plan to do so for more than 90 days at a time.

SOUTH AFRICA

South Africans must apply for a Schengen visa, which can be done via French authorities, no more than three months and no less than 15 days before their date of travel.

What to Pack

In general, traveling in Normandy and Brittany does not require specialized gear. Given that rain is likely in any season, packing a **waterproof jacket** and an **umbrella** is advised. Conversely, **sunscreen** is needed for protection against the strong coastal sun. Electrical sockets in France require round, two-pin plugs, so bring an **adapter** or two to keep your devices charged. Otherwise, what to bring depends on what you're planning to do, whether it's hiking (appropriate footwear) or just staying by the beach (swimsuit).

Transportation

By Air

Most people accessing Normandy and Brittany by air will be doing so by going via **Paris,** which is a major international hub with three separate airports, serviced by many of the world's biggest airlines. For visitors coming from outside of Europe, connecting through the French capital is pretty much the only option. Aside from that, several of Normandy's and Brittany's towns and cities have their own airports, including Rouen, Caen, Deauville, Rennes, Brest, and Nantes. Some of these even receive a handful of international flights. Internally, there are very few distances in the region that warrant a flight, either for economic reasons or in terms of saving time. Only if you're planning on going from Paris to the very western edge of Brittany is an internal flight worth considering, and even then, it usually makes more sense to take the train.

By Car

Traveling by car is the best way to get the most out of the two regions. Normandy and Brittany are well connected by a number of highways, some of which are toll routes, but the true depth of their charm lies in their many small roads that wind their way through every inch of the two regions' beautiful countryside.

By Train

There are no trains that run directly from abroad to either Normandy or Brittany. As with flights, you'll either have to travel via **Paris,** or, in the case of the Eurotunnel, **Calais.** The latter service is a good, fast way of getting a car to France from the United Kingdom, though a significant amount of driving is still required to get to Normandy or Brittany after that. Paris, meanwhile, is connected by train to numerous European countries. In Normandy and Brittany, all trains are run by the **SNCF.** The French are justifiably proud of their intercity national train service, which is one of the fastest and most efficient in the world. But prices can be high, with last-minute fares from Paris to most places in Brittany easily topping €140 return. Booking just a week in advance can significantly reduce the price, however, and most of Normandy, being much closer to the French capital, is cheaper to reach. A further disadvantage of rail, though, is that only large towns (Rouen, Caen, Saint-Malo, Rennes, Brest, Quimper, and Nantes) are easy to travel between, and not even all of them are directly linked. Branch lines, run by SNCF subsidiary **TER,** reaching out to smaller destinations do exist, but they do not always connect to one another, apart from at major transport hubs.

By Bus

Getting to Normandy and Brittany from abroad by bus is, again, impossible. However, services such as **Ouibus** and **Flixbus** offer intermittent service between Paris and some major towns, and for a fraction of the cost of the train (provided you book in advance). Local rural bus services linking villages are slow and run seldom, but are more reliable than their often-deserted stands and hard-to-read timetables might suggest.

By Ferry

Ferry is one of the more romantic ways of arriving in Normandy or Brittany. There are ferry ports along both coastlines, and boats run throughout the year—though more in summer—with crossing times from the **United Kingdom** ranging from 4-8 hours, or 14 from **Ireland.** Prices vary depending on which route, whether you're a foot or car passenger, size of vehicle, and time of year. Operators include Brittany Ferries, DFDS Ferries, and Irish Ferries. Traveling with a regular car in high season, booked in advance, will cost around €200 return. There are plenty of smaller boat services that connect Brittany's islands with its mainland; these are inexpensive and run throughout the year.

Best of Normandy & Brittany

There really is so much to see in Normandy and Brittany that being able to tackle it all in under 10 days is all but impossible. The tour below, then, is far from exhaustive. Instead, it concentrates on the most iconic sights and experiences of the regions, where history really seems to come alive before your eyes. It's also a reasonably easy journey to make all on public transport, which cannot be said for every trip you might plan here.

Day 1: Rouen

Start your trip in Rouen. Spend a morning exploring the sights of its **old town,** a sprawling network of lively roads overshadowed by half-timber houses, where highlights include the fascinating **Gros-Horloge,** an elaborately decorated 14th-century astronomical clock; the towering **Notre Dame de Rouen,** among the finest Gothic cathedrals in France; and the intricate sinister carvings in **Saint-Maclou Ossuary,** a perfectly preserved medieval courtyard that was the site where plague victims were buried in the 1500s. Have a light salad lunch in the playful **Zèbre à Pois,** then spend the afternoon exploring the **Musée des Beaux-Arts,** one of Normandy's most extensive art museums, with a large collection of Impressionist artworks as well as masterpieces from the Renaissance. Have dinner in one of Rouen's top-end restaurants, the two-Michelin-star **Restaurant Gill,** where traditional Norman cuisine is paired with flavors of Japan, to end your first day in style.

Day 2: Giverny

Leave Rouen for a day trip to Giverny (44 mi/72 km to the south, 1 hour driving, 40 minutes by train), the former home of Claude Monet, leading figure of the Impressionist art movement. Try to arrive as early as you can to beat the crowds and spend the morning exploring the **Fondation Monet.** Entering this house and garden that once belonged to the artist feels like stepping into a painting. There's an explosion of color, and, particularly around the famed lily pond, every aspect looks like a Monet masterpiece. Grab a sandwich lunch at **Au Coin du Pain'tre**—many

house and garden of Claude Monet with tourists

Best Beaches

The coast of Normandy and Brittany ranges from long, low-lying stretches of sand to dramatic white cliffs and craggy granite inlets. Brittany alone boasts a third of all of France's coastline, and so it's no surprise that there are beaches here that are perfect for various activities and tastes.

- **Plage de Deauville:** Best for people-watching and photo ops
- **Plage de Jonville (Saint-Vaast):** Best for escaping the crowds
- **Plage de Bon-Secours (Saint-Malo):** Best for a party atmosphere and stunning historical setting
- **Plage Saint-Guirec (Côte de Granit Rose):** Best for easy swimming and nearby bars
- **Plage de Goulien (Crozon):** Best for surfing (for beginners and experts alike)

Holiday makers enjoy the beach sands and rock pools at low tide at Saint-Malo beach.

of the other restaurants in Giverny village are overpriced. Then get some context on the Impressionist movement by having a look around the **Musée des Impressionnismes,** with its constantly changing collection. Have a look at Monet's grave at the **Église Sainte-Radegonde** before heading back to Rouen for a hearty, traditional dinner in the wood-beamed surrounds of **La Petite Auberge**—try the snails if you dare!

Day 3: Deauville

Head west toward the luxury seaside resort of Deauville (57 mi/92 km, 1 hour driving, 2 hours by local train) for a real change of pace. This town isn't really about taking in the sights so much as it is soaking up an atmosphere of luxury and class. If you've got the cash, book yourself into **Le Normandy** hotel, the flagship establishment of the luxury Barrière chain, which runs many high-end hotels, casinos, and spas along the Norman and Breton coasts. (If you're not feeling so flush, try the **Hotel Flaubert,** a classic seafront hotel straight from the 1950s, in Deauville's slightly earthier neighbor, Trouville.) A good day would include picking up some tasty paté and cheese at the **Breton Traiteur** in Deauville, then wandering casually to the town's art deco **Promenade des Planches**—rent a deck chair and an umbrella and relax on the fine sands of **Deauville Beach** while enjoying your snacks. Round off the day with a trip to **Les Vapeurs** for dinner; this always-bustling seafood brasserie in Trouville is one of the best in Normandy.

Day 4: Day Trip to Honfleur

Keeping Deauville/Trouville your base, make the half-hour trip, either driving yourself or boarding a local Bus Verts, out to beautiful Honfleur, 10 miles (17 kilometers) up the coast. Here, you can take in the town's stunning **old harbor** and the wooden church **L'Église Sainte-Catherine** that still looks something like a Viking drinking hall, and check to see if there's an exhibition on in the old salt warehouse, the **Greniers à Sel.** Keep lunch light at the **Café du Port,** one of the few non-tourist-trap restaurants in town, and which serves some excellent, inexpensive seafood. Then, spend the afternoon exploring one of Honfleur's museums; the **Musée de la Marine** is the most unusual, set inside an old church and boasting numerous scale models of ships, telling the story of the town's prosperous relationship with the sea. Head back to Deauville for dinner in **Le Drakkar,** excellent for carnivores and a good reprieve if you're feeling worn out by too much fish.

Day 5: Bayeux

Make for Bayeux (50 mi/80 km west, 1 hour driving, 2 hours by local train), a charming rural town west of Deauville famous for a certain tapestry. This is also an excellent base for visiting the D-Day landing beaches. Once there, the tapestry really should be your first port of call, housed in the **Musée de la Tapisserie de Bayeux.** This nearly 1,000-year-old length of embroidered fabric viscerally tells the story of the Norman conquest of England back in 1066 and is accompanied by a museum that elaborates on the era in which it was made. Once you're done, head straight outside the museum gates for the best crepes in town at the **Moulin de la Galette.** Spend the afternoon meandering through the **old town,** taking in the various half-timber buildings and splendid Gothic cathedral, then have a boozy evening in **Le Bouchon,** a wine bar that doubles as a restaurant, and does a fine line in finger food.

Day 6: D-Day Beaches

Still based in Bayeux, head north to spend the day exploring the D-Day beaches; if you don't have your own transport, by far the easiest way to do this is with a tour company. First make for **Omaha Beach** (about 13 mi/21 km northwest, 20 minutes driving), where the U.S. forces met the fiercest resistance of all the invading forces on that bloody day in 1944. On this blustery front you'll get a real sense of scale of the whole operation. Then go to nearby **Pointe du Hoc,** where some of the deepest scars of the battle can still be seen in the shape of blown-apart German bunkers and craters gouged out of the landscape. Have a light salad lunch at close by **La Sapinière,** then carry on just a short drive down the road to the almost impossibly moving **American Military Cemetery,** where the rows upon rows of sedate white gravestones offer a blistering reminder of just how many lives had to be sacrificed to secure Europe's freedom. After an emotionally draining day, return to Bayeux for a rich French dinner in one of the town's best restaurants, **La Rapière.**

Day 7: Mont-Saint-Michel

Leave Bayeux as early as you can to make a hit-and-run visit to Mont-Saint-Michel—staying near the monument itself tends to be overpriced. Getting there is a 73 mile (118 kilometer) journey, which should take about 1 hour 40 minutes driving, and two hours by train. (In order to experience this day as suggested, you'll have to take the 6:39am train direct from Bayeux station, which is early but worth it!) Before arriving in the Mont's parking lot, stop off in **La Bellevoisine** bakery in nearby Beauvoir to pick up a picnic. With that in hand, head for the monument. If you're still early enough to be ahead of the crowds, it's better to walk across the causeway than take the bus, allowing the dramatic details of Mont-Saint-Michel to emerge slowly and give you a chance to really appreciate its fantasy-novel form.

Once you're through its main gate, head straight up the **Grande Rue,** ignoring the trinket sellers, making direct for the **abbey,** which is the island's real draw: You want to have as much time as possible to appreciate its layering of historic detail and stunning views of the surrounding bay before the crowds arrive. After your tour is complete, settle down for your picnic lunch in the abbey's gardens—this is far more economically expedient and relaxing than visiting one of the island's many hyper tourist-trap restaurants. Take the **ramparts** to get back to the bay, reveling further in the excellent views, then dig your toes into the wet sands that surround the monument's walls before hopping back on the shuttle bus to get back to your car, or the train station. Push on to **Dinard,** a delightful town in its own right, and a good base from which to explore Saint-Malo. This is about 37 miles (60 kilometers) and should take just under one hour driving, and two hours by train. (If using public transport, you'll have to head to St-Malo first, then take the number 16 local bus into Dinard.) Have a lobster dinner at **La Gonelle,** spending your evening watching the crowds on the **promenade du Clair de Lune.**

Day 8: Saint-Malo

Take an early morning ferry, run by the Compagnie Corsaire, from Dinard to Saint-Malo, and enjoy your first real look at the famous walled citadel as it was meant to be seen, growing from out the waves. The first thing to do when you get there is go on an extended wander around its **ramparts.** These provide great views out to sea and across the yellow-lichen-spangled gray rooftops of the town itself. End this tour by popping inside **Saint Vincent Cathedral.** Its towering spire is one of the icons of Saint-Malo, while inside is a relatively quiet space, away from the town's sometimes-oppressive tourist crowds. When the sun is shining, the light that shines through its great rose window is nothing short of miraculous. Have lunch in the stylish and inventive **Breizh Café,** where Breton and Japanese cuisines are combined to make for some light, informal, nautically flavored dining. Spend the afternoon relaxing on the **Plage de Bon-Secours** under the shadow of Saint-Malo's walls. If you're feeling restless and the tide's out, you can always make a pilgrimage to one or both of the town's tidal islands, the **Grand** and **Petit Bé,** where there are again some excellent views. Take the ferry back to Dinard in the evening, and if you've got the energy, try your hand at gambling at the **Casino Barrière.**

Day 9: Rennes

Head down toward Rennes (42 mi/68 km, 1 hour driving and by train) as the final base for your journey. The modern capital of Brittany is a food lover's dream, and if you're lucky enough to be able to time your trip in order to arrive here on a Saturday, checking out the town's **Marché des Lices** is an absolute must. If it's not Saturday, a similar experience can be had at the town's **Halles Centrales,** where a covered market selling top-end local produce is open every day. Once you've spent a morning imagining all sorts of delicious local dishes, go treat yourself to a terrific, reasonable local lunch at the unpretentious **Chez Paul.** Spend your afternoon wandering the **old town,** which has an embarrassment of beautiful half-timber houses—the 16th-century **Maison Ti Koz** is a real highlight. Finally, take in a bit of urban culture at the **Opera de Rennes**—one of the smallest opera houses in France, it nevertheless boasts a very respectable program of national-quality shows.

Day 10: Day Trip to the Paimpont Forest

End your exploration of Normandy and Brittany with a day trip to the Paimpont Forest, (27 mi/44 km, 40 minutes driving, 1 hour by local bus 1a) from Rennes. Head out early to get a refresher on the myths of King Arthur at the **Centre de l'Imaginaire Arthurien** (many sights in the forest are associated with him). Then have a light meal at **La Fée Gourmande** and hire some bikes from the **Relais de Brocéliande.** After that, the forest is your playground, with plenty of intriguing spots to be explored: the **tomb of Merlin the Magician** and the **Fontaine de Barenton,** where he is said to have taught his spells to Morgan le Fay, are just a couple. Return to Rennes in the evening and spend the night drinking away and toasting the end of your trip on the town's infamous **Rue de Soif,** the street with more bars on it than any other in France.

Best Places to Hike and Bike

Normandy and Brittany are a walker's paradise, especially with that fabulous coastline. These regions are also excellent for those wishing to explore on two wheels and join in the general love that the French have for the humble bicycle: Here are a few of the best places to hike and bike:

HIKING

- **Étretat:** Walk the cliffs and beach to connect with a landscape that inspired many Impressionist painters yet remains surprisingly untouched by tourism. (Be aware, you'll have to wait for low tide.)
- **Crozon Peninsula:** Hike Pointe Pen Hir, Toulinguet, and Grand Gouin for dramatic, regularly changing landscape of cliffs and coves.
- **Emerald Coast:** Walk the section of the GR34 around Cap Fréhel, checking out the spectacular views along the coast and the fantasy-novel scale of the Fort la Latte.

BIKING

- **Rouen to Le Havre:** Cycle the banks of the Seine, from Rouen to Le Havre, enjoying the many abbeys nestled in the bucolic idyll of Normandy's hinterland, crossing the river on free ferries whenever you feel the need.
- **Nantes:** Cycle the greenery-filled routes around Nantes that have led it to being voted one of the best cities for cyclists anywhere in the world.
- **Île-de-Bréhat:** Cycle the beautiful silent and completely car-free island, where every turn yields a stunning vista of the archipelago of which it is a part, gracefully cradled by a silvery sea.

Four-Day Getaway to Brittany

Sitting on the edge of France, stretching out into the Atlantic, Brittany has long had an edge-of-the-world quality in the eyes of many. Indeed, Finistère literally means "land's end." This journey takes you from the urbane Nantes, through the region's increasingly magical landscape—the Gulf of Morbihan belongs in a fantasy novel—out to its most distant outcrop, the wild and windswept Île d'Ouessant. Like the above journey, it's easily possible to travel this route using public transport alone.

Day 1

Begin in **Nantes,** exploring the **Château des Ducs de Bretagne,** the ancient fortress that was once the home to the rulers of all Brittany. From the ramparts of this impressive building, you can get views out across much of this vibrant artistic city. Grab a crepe in the surprisingly trendy **Crêperie ker Breizh,** then get some shopping in at the spectacular, covered **Passage Pommeraye**—basically a mall from the 1840s. Then, visit one of the most unusual attractions in all of France at the sculpture-garden-cum-theme-park the **Machines de L'Île**. Then, have an indulgent flame-grilled steak for dinner at **La Vacherie.**

Day 2

Take the train or drive the 70 miles (113 kilometers) to the glorious walled city of **Vannes,** right on the Gulf of Morbihan—the journey should take about an hour and a half. The first thing to do there is join a boat tour of the Gulf with the **Compagnie du Golfe,** which takes in at least one of its major islands. If you choose the Île-aux-Moines, make sure to drop in at **Ets Martin,** where oysters are served fresh as they come, and

Historical Normandy and Brittany

From sites of epic battles to medieval trading hubs, Normandy and Brittany are extraordinarily dense with history. The list of places to explore for people with a passion for the past is innumerable, but here are a few spots not to miss:

- **Mont-Saint-Michel:** This utterly improbable Gothic abbey is perched on a tidal island, floating between sea and sky.
- **Rouen's Old Town:** History feels very present in Rouen's extensive labyrinth of medieval half-timber buildings.
- **Bayeux:** Normandy and Brittany's single most important historical artifact finds its home here. The Bayeux Tapestry, a 223-foot-long fabric embroidered almost 1,000 years ago, tells the story of the Norman conquest of England.
- **Honfleur Harbor:** Once one of France's most important ports, this harbor is still maintained in all its 17th-century glory, with multistore buildings from hundreds of years ago still teetering elegantly mere feet from the water's edge.
- **D-Day Landing Beaches:** Long stretches of low-lying, blustery coastline that were the stage of the world's largest ever sea-to-land invasion still remain powerfully evocative of the events that took place here.
- **Saint-Malo:** This brilliantly preserved walled city of formidable granite seems carved from the sea itself.
- **Standing Stones of Carnac:** Hundreds upon hundreds of neatly arranged standing stones, the largest megalithic monument of its type anywhere in the world, are still a mystery to archaeologists.
- **Ramparts of Vannes:** The well-maintained defenses of this prosperous town on the shores of the Gulf of Morbihan offer some excellent views of Vannes itself.
- **Château of Josselin:** This fairy-tale castle in the Breton countryside has been owned by the same family, the Rohans, for more than half a millennium.

in the most rudimentary surroundings, overlooking the beds where they're grown. Once you get back, treat yourself to dinner at **La Tête en l'Air,** an inventive restaurant that offers whole tasting menus of local flavor.

Day 3

Spend the morning exploring the medieval ramparts of **Vannes,** then go for a sumptuous but still reasonable lunch of lobster and fries at the aptly named **Homard Frites.** After that, hop on the train or drive the to Brest (114 mi/184 km, 2 hours driving or by train). You ought to arrive in the port town before nightfall, in time to sample some of its characterful street life—if you feel like an unusual end to the day, head to **Chez Kim,** where the owner and bartender serenades customers with pop classics on an acoustic guitar.

Day 4

Get up early and head for Brest's port to catch the boat out to the western edge of Brittany, France, and Northern Europe: the **Île d'Ouessant.** When you arrive after the leisurely two-hour journey, hire a bicycle at the harbor and start to explore—from the views of the famous **Jument** lighthouse to the raw power of waves crashing on the **Fromveur Passage,** there's plenty to see. At some point, you'll want to pause for lunch—the **Crêperie du Stang** is a good, not-too-touristy place to do this. To really get the most from the island, it's worth spending the night so that you'll get to see the beam of the **Créac'h Lighthouse,** the most powerful in Europe. Easily the best dinner you'll find is in **Chez Jacky.** There, you can get Ouessant's traditional dish: lamb ragout slow-cooked under heated clods of earth (this is a meal you have to prearrange, so reserve before you arrive).

Giverny, Rouen, and the "Impressionist Coast"

The area of Normandy closest to Paris and surrounding the sedate River Seine has long served as a kind of garden to the French capital, the first point of rural retreat for countless urbanites across generations.

This trend was made famous in the 19th century, when Claude Monet and other Impressionists from Sisley to Renoir began to adopt the Seine region and the Haute Normandie seaside as their "outdoor studio." Their paintings immortalized the lush farmland of these meandering valleys, the spectacular white cliffs of the Alabaster Coast, and the open skies over the mouth of the Seine. Indeed, such was the impact of this group of artists on the world imagination that when most people think of the French countryside, they are really thinking of here.

Highlights

Look for ★ to find recommended sights, activities, dining, and lodging.

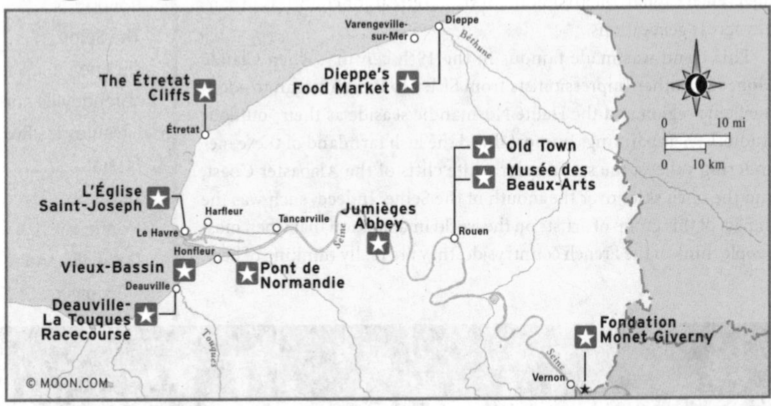

★ **Fondation Monet Giverny:** Visiting Claude Monet's former home and garden feels like walking into one of his paintings (page 45).

★ **Rouen's Old Town:** These timber-frame houses and cobbled streets allow a glimpse into Normandy's medieval past (page 51).

★ **Musée des Beaux-Arts:** Home to one of the largest Impressionist collections outside Paris, this Rouen museum includes some particularly impressive Monets depicting Rouen itself (page 58).

★ **Jumièges Abbey:** These majestic ruins of an enormous 11th-century abbey dominate an otherwise sleepy corner of the Seine valley (page 67).

★ **Dieppe's Food Market:** Bursting with human life and the freshest Norman produce, Dieppe's market is one of the best anywhere in France (page 75).

★ **Étretat Cliffs:** These iconic chalk cliff formations have been inspiring artists and visitors for centuries (page 87).

★ **L'Église Saint-Joseph:** Le Havre's jaw-dropping modernist cathedral is best described as a concrete kaleidoscope almost 400 feet (120 meters) high (page 97).

★ **Vieux-Bassin at Honfleur:** Once a major center of trade, this is now one of the most picturesque harbors in Normandy (page 103).

★ **Pont de Normandie:** The bridge built across the mouth of the Seine is an epic feat of civil engineering (page 106).

★ **Deauville-La Touques Racecourse:** A historic horse racetrack that was the making of Deauville and is still flocked to by French high society (page 113).

To be sure, the Impressionists drew inspiration from more than just the region's natural landscape: The cathedral of Rouen, the harbor at Honfleur, and the boardwalk in Deauville have all been captured by the artist's brush.

Long a crossroads of history, this part of Normandy grew rich off trade, and at one time boasted some of the great ports and cities of the medieval and Renaissance worlds. More recently, in the latter half of the 19th century, it was tourist traffic crisscrossing the region that prompted the creation of some of France's first resorts here.

HISTORY

A deep and easily navigable river, the Seine had been occupied for centuries by the time the Vikings started raiding the French coast in the 9th century. The banks of the river, and Rouen, which had been a settlement since Roman times, were all targets for the Norsemen.

After 851, the Vikings began to settle in the region of the Seine Valley, though they continued to carry out raids farther and farther south. The French King Charles the Simple signed a treaty in 911 with the Viking leader Rollo, which officially yielded Rouen and the lands already taken over to the Vikings on the proviso that they would guard the mouth of the Seine from further attacks. Under this deal the Viking leaders assumed the title Dukes of Normandy—Normandy being the land of the Norsemen.

Taking advantage in a crisis of succession to the Anglo-Norman throne, the French under Philip II wrested Rouen back into their power at the start of the 13th century, and the rest of Norman lands followed. The region was to see no small amount of war over the following centuries, though, as English kings sought to reclaim what they regarded as their ancestral lands.

During the Hundred Years' War (1337-1453), Rouen and its surrounding lands changed hands again, and it became the English capital in France. Not until the campaigns inspired by Joan of Arc in the 1430s did their grip on French territories begin fading, though not before they put the French martyr to death, burning her at the stake in Rouen's town square.

The centuries following the Hundred Years' War were prosperous times for this region, with some of its main port towns such as Dieppe and Honfleur finding themselves at the heart of France's trade empire, and leading the exploration of the New World. It was only really with the French Revolution and subsequent Napoleonic Wars (1789-1815), when the British set up a naval blockade, that these ports began to lose their prominence and find themselves replaced by others farther west.

On the upside, this meant such places were spared the worst ravages of the Industrial Revolution. They remained picturesque, and, along with their surrounding lands, were to provide inspiration for generations of artists in the 19th century. The advent of rail travel made Normandy more accessible than ever, and when Impressionist painters decided to leave their urban Paris home to paint the countryside, here was the obvious choice. Eventually, one even moved to make his own mark on the landscape, when Claude Monet established his house and garden at a small, unheard-of town called Giverny.

In the 20th century, war returned, and though this part of Normandy did not, in general, suffer as badly as the areas near the D-Day landing beaches, there were exceptions. In 1942, Dieppe was subject to a disastrous commando raid by the Allies, in which over 1,000 Canadian soldiers were killed; then during the eventual reconquest of France the harbor town of Le Havre was almost completely destroyed. It rose from the ashes, however, redesigned after the war out of poured concrete, a modernist city looking to the future.

Previous: inside the home of French impressionist painter Claude Monet; the cliffs at Étretat; view of the Rouen Cathedral from the park

Giverny, Rouen, and the "Impressionist Coast"

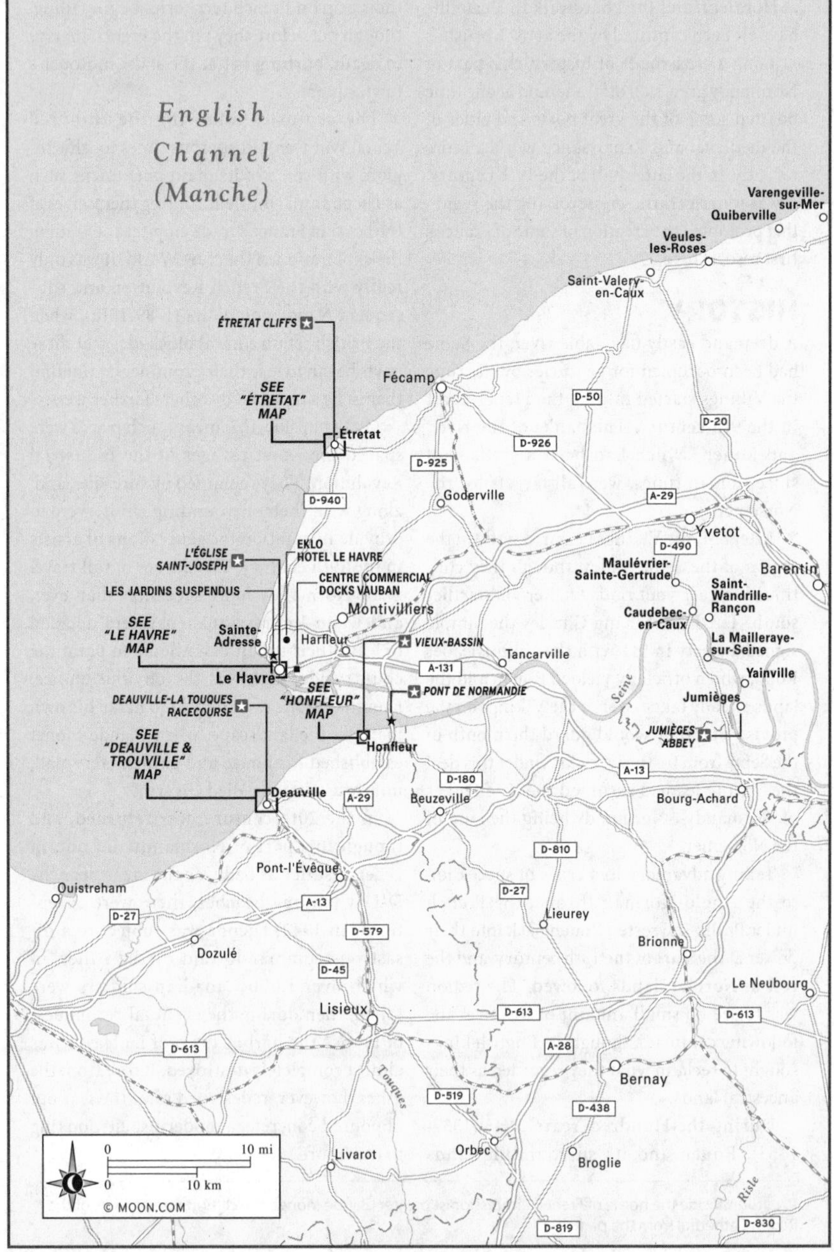

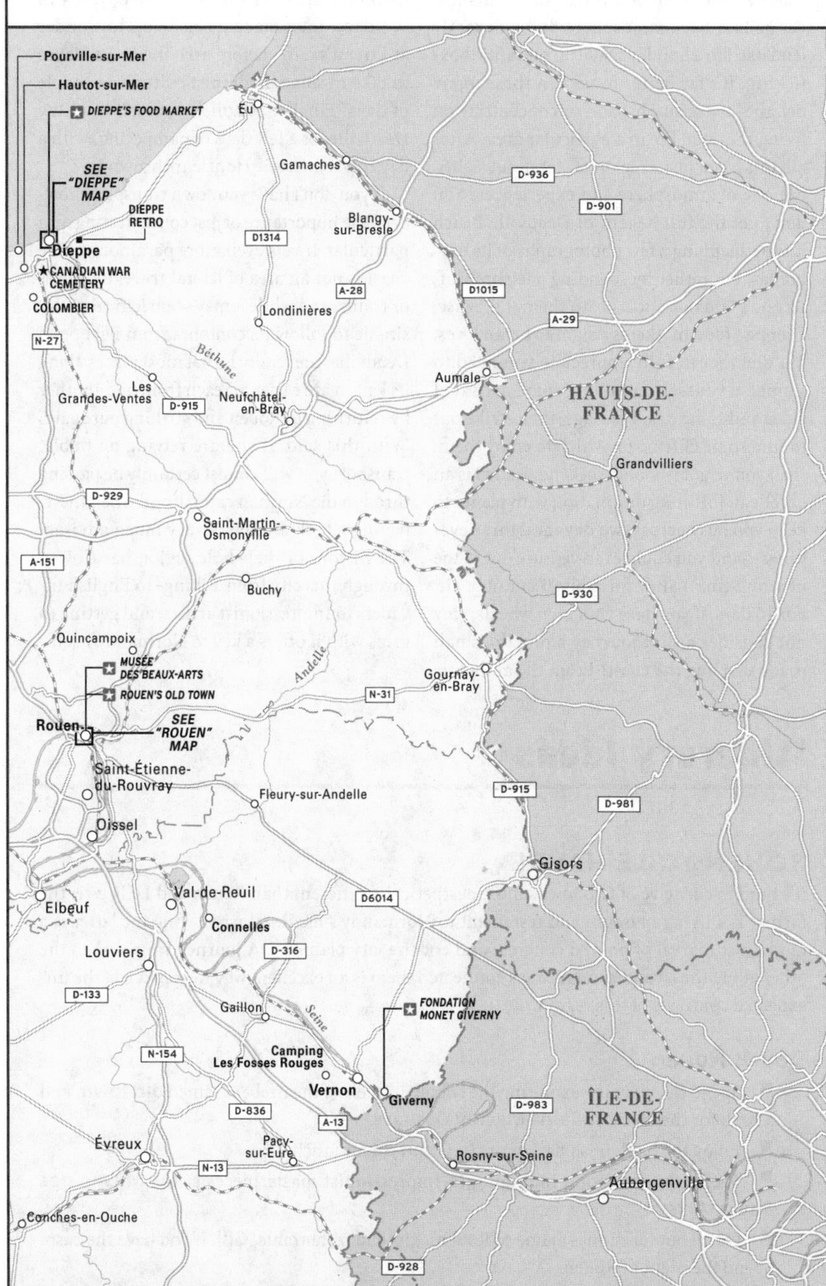

Pourville-sur-Mer
Hautot-sur-Mer
DIEPPE'S FOOD MARKET
SEE "DIEPPE" MAP
DIEPPE RETRO
Dieppe
CANADIAN WAR CEMETERY
COLOMBIER
Eu
Gamaches
Blangy-sur-Bresle
Londinières
Béthune
Les Grandes-Ventes
Neufchâtel-en-Bray
Aumale
HAUTS-DE-FRANCE
Grandvilliers
Saint-Martin-Osmonville
Buchy
Quincampoix
MUSÉE DES BEAUX-ARTS
ROUEN'S OLD TOWN
Rouen
SEE "ROUEN" MAP
Andelle
Gournay-en-Bray
Saint-Étienne-du-Rouvray
Fleury-sur-Andelle
Oissel
Gisors
Val-de-Reuil
Elbeuf
Connelles
Louviers
Gaillon
Seine
FONDATION MONET GIVERNY
Camping Les Fosses Rouges
Vernon
Giverny
ÎLE-DE-FRANCE
Évreux
Pacy-sur-Eure
Rosny-sur-Seine
Aubergenville
Conches-en-Ouche
D-936
D-901
D1314
A-28
D1015
A-29
N-27
D-915
D-929
A-151
D-930
N-31
D-981
D6014
D-316
D-133
N-154
D-836
A-13
D-983
N-13
D-928

PLANNING YOUR TIME

There's a lot to see in this part of Normandy, yet its laid-back atmosphere doesn't exactly lend itself to a holiday made up of frantic box-ticking. It's far better to take in these many delights at a leisurely pace, or concentrate on living the good life in a particular area. After all, this is not just a region of stand-out sights, but one of atmosphere and experiences: You don't get the full benefit of Deauville Beach just by snapping a few photographs of its umbrellas, but rather by spending a leisurely afternoon laid out underneath them. Likewise, Dieppe's food market is a sight to behold, yes, but one that to fully appreciate you need to immerse yourself in, to buy some artisanal cider and some dried sausage, then strike out to find some clifftop on which to enjoy them. If all you've got is a long weekend, Rouen is an excellent, fulfilling destination with plenty to keep you busy across two days and three evenings—and you could even venture out to the nearby Seine Valley for a bit of country air. For 10 days, if you have your own wheels, why not consider a slow journey along the small roads that hug the coast? From the authentic working port of Dieppe to the quaint seaside idyll of Veules-les-Roses can be covered in 3-4 days; then make a brief stop to wonder at Étretat's cliffs before arriving in Le Havre to take in some modernist culture—a couple of days. Finally, establish yourself in glitzy Deauville for a few days of pampering, with a day trip to historic Honfleur thrown in.

If you don't have your own transport, however, the importance of just concentrating on a particular area is even more paramount. The coast is not an area of lateral travel for buses or trains, and while it may seem logical or desirable to follow its contours from Dieppe to Deauville, the reality is that most places along its length are easier to reach from one another by returning to Rouen and striking out again. With this said, if you are relying on public transport you will almost certainly be passing through the Norman capital, and when there, having a look around is very much advised. The history of the whole region has flowed through this city from Vikings to English invaders to Impressionist artists, and getting to grips with it offers a key to Normandy itself.

Itinerary Ideas

ROUEN TO LE HAVRE

It's hard to conceive of two towns more aesthetically different than Rouen and Le Havre: the former is a living museum and testament to Normandy's medieval past, while the latter is a modernist marvel of poured concrete and concise city planning. A journey from one to the other along the river that has always connected them is an excellent way to appreciate the unexpected contrasts of this region.

Day 1: Rouen

- Spend the morning exploring the cobbled streets of the timber-framed **old town,** and search for the macabre **Saint-Maclou Ossuary.**
- Enjoy the bold, fresh flavors of **Un Grain de** for lunch.
- Spend the afternoon indulging in Impressionist masterpieces at the **Musée des Beaux-Arts**
- Go all out for dinner at one of Rouen's top-end restaurants, **Gill,** if you have the cash. Spend the night in Rouen.

Day 2: Along the Seine

- In the morning, make the 45-minute drive to Jumièges. Contemplate the passing of time while picking over the ruins of 11th-century **Jumièges Abbey.**
- Have a simple rustic lunch of garlicky potatoes and steak in pepper sauce at **Auberge du Bac.**
- Take the Jumièges ferry and travel the Seine's bucolic **Left Bank,** enjoying the contrast between its dramatic cliffs and the genteel fruit orchards, before using the Brotonne Bridge to cross back over to Caudebec-en-Caux.
- Wander around **Caudebec** peering into its gardens, and check out the **Notre-Dame de Caudebec-en-Caux,** which Henry IV called the finest in his kingdom.
- Have one of the best dinners anywhere in Normandy, served in the kitchens of the **Manoir de Rétival.**

Day 3: Le Havre

- It's less than an hour to drive from Caudebec to Le Havre. Spend your morning strolling around the modernist downtown, giving yourself at least 30 minutes to gawk at the interior of **L'Église Saint-Joseph.** You'll need it!
- Grab a great-value—but still high-class—lunch in the Lyonnais/Norman restaurant **Bistrot des Halles.**
- Get some further context on Le Havre's modernist history and see some excellent contemporary painting at **Musée d'Art Moderne.**
- Relax with dinner and drinks **La Taverne Paillette,** a local bistro that can trace its heritage back to the 16th century.

DIEPPE AND THE ALABASTER COAST

Often overlooked by tourists, Dieppe and its surroundings offer a great, authentic experience of the Norman coast. Rich in history and natural beauty, this is also a great area in which to interact with ordinary Norman people.

Day 1: Varengeville-sur-Mer

- Start the day in Dieppe, people-watching over breakfast at **Le Tribunaux**—even better if it's market day!
- Post-breakfast, take a quick stroll around **Dieppe's harbor,** and out onto the Pointe de la Jetée to see what the amateur fishermen have caught.
- Head to **Varengeville** to see Georges Braque's grave at **l'Église Saint-Valéry.**
- Drop into the **Auberge du Relais** and have some local oysters for lunch.
- After lunch, work off your meal with a wander through the **Bois des Moutiers** gardens.
- Indulge in a dinner of *fruits de mer* while looking out to sea at **Hôtel De La Terrasse,** then return to Dieppe.

Day 2: Dieppe

- In the morning, pay your respects to WWII heroes at the **Canadian War Cemetery.**
- Have a simple grilled lunch at **Le Sarajevo,** though hold off on the fries to make sure you've space for dinner.

Itinerary Ideas

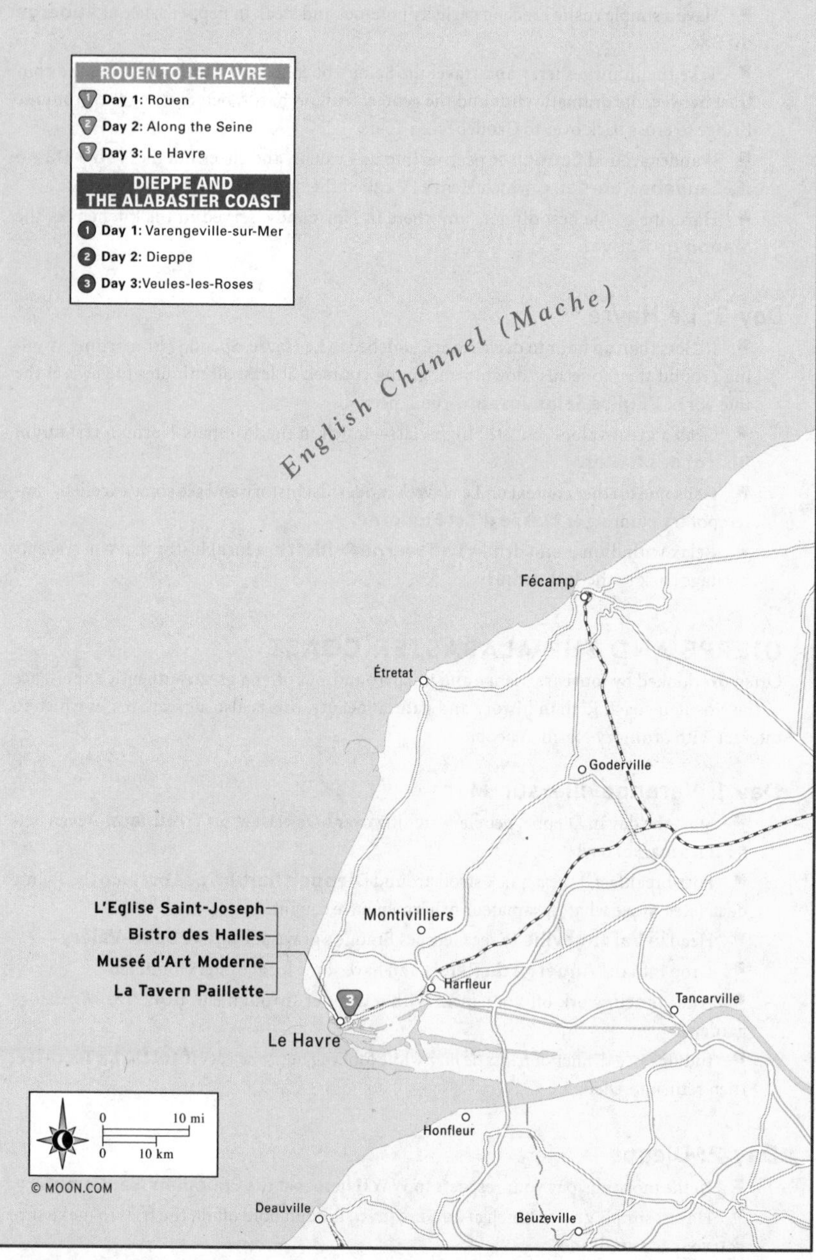

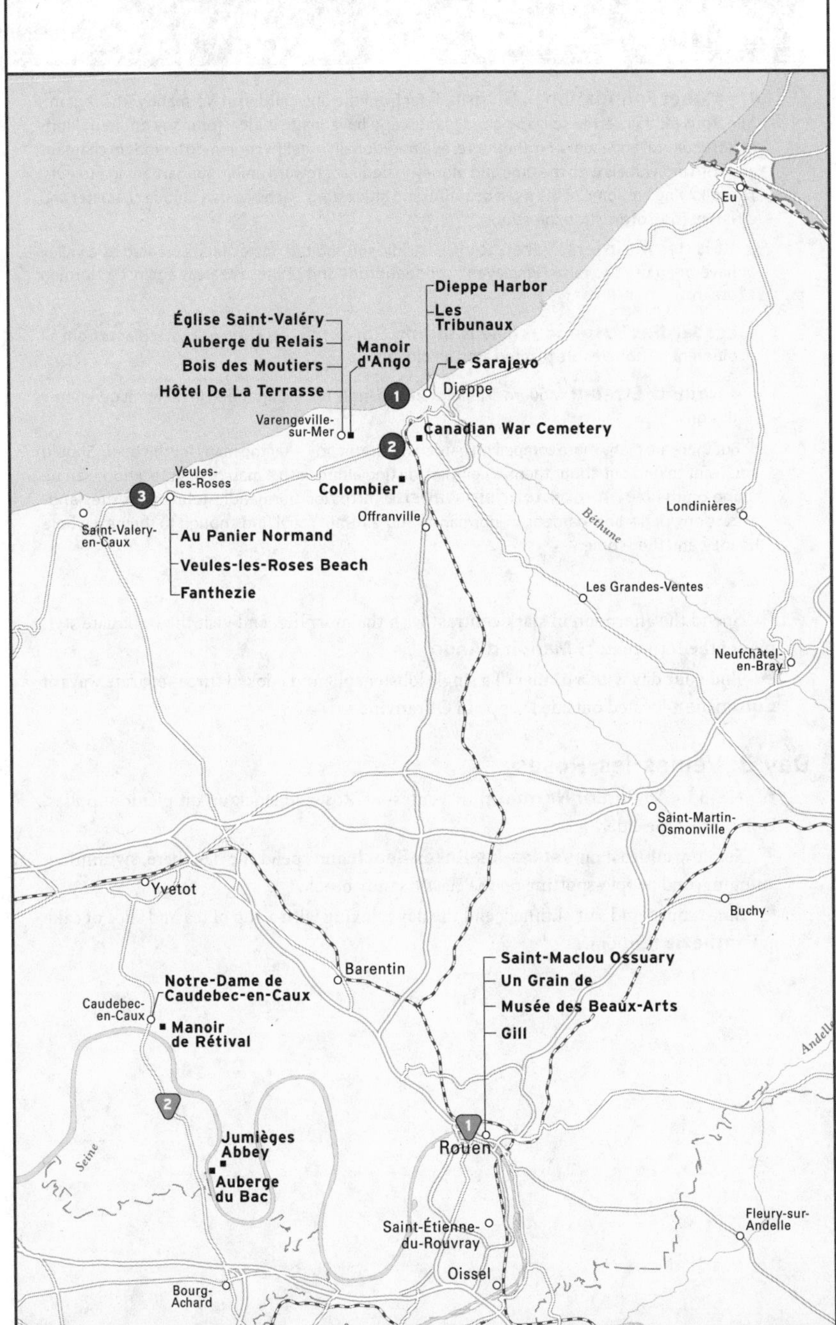
Eu
Dieppe Harbor
Les Tribunaux
Église Saint-Valéry
Auberge du Relais
Bois des Moutiers
Hôtel De La Terrasse
Manoir d'Ango
Le Sarajevo
Dieppe
1
Varengeville-sur-Mer
2
Canadian War Cemetery
Veules-les-Roses
3
Colombier
Saint-Valery-en-Caux
Offranville
Béthune
Londinières
Au Panier Normand
Veules-les-Roses Beach
Fanthezie
Les Grandes-Ventes
Neufchâtel-en-Bray
Saint-Martin-Osmonville
Yvetot
Buchy
Saint-Maclou Ossuary
Un Grain de
Musée des Beaux-Arts
Gill
Barentin
Notre-Dame de Caudebec-en-Caux
Caudebec-en-Caux
Manoir de Rétival
Andelle
2
1
Rouen
Jumièges Abbey
Auberge du Bac
Seine
Saint-Étienne-du-Rouvray
Fleury-sur-Andelle
Oissel
Bourg-Achard

Norman Gardens

The **Monet Foundation in Giverny** is far from the only garden in Normandy. The region's generous rainfall, fertile soil, and gentle landscape have made it ideal for many different kinds of horticultural endeavors. Furthermore, as a traditionally wealthy region it abounds in châteaus and with individuals with the time and money to dedicate toward ambitious gardening projects. The following are some of the most beautiful and interesting; each boasts a unique character and different form of artistic expression.

- **Bois des Moutiers, Varengeville:** Acidic soil and the microclimate created by a valley have been used to raise Himalayan rhododendrons and Chinese azaleas against a Norman green.
- **Les Jardins Suspendus (the Hanging Gardens), Le Havre:** Exotic plants from all different biospheres are planted atop an old fort.
- **Jardins d' Etretat:**. Modern art sculptures spangle foliage arranged in different geometric designs.

But there are many more compelling gardens in Normandy—far too many for this book. Should you want to find out about them, a complete listing along with a map of their locations can be found on the **Normandy tourism website** (http://en.normandie-tourisme.fr/sites-and-attractions/parks-and-gardens-in-normandy-300-2.html). You'll find enough to theme a whole holiday, and then some.

- Spend the afternoon in stark contrast with the morning, and visit the Italianate stylings of the 16th-century **Manoir d'Ango.**
- End your day with a dinner of a single lobster split and cooked three separate ways at **Colombier,** located outside Dieppe in Offranville.

Day 3: Veules-les-Roses

- Head to **Au Panier Normand** in Veules-les-Roses to stock up on picnic supplies. Don't forget the cider!
- Set up your feast on **Veules-les-Roses Beach** and spend the day there, swimming, lounging, and people-spotting on the classic sandy beach.
- Sun-tanned and salt-skinned, end the day relaxing with a cup of tea and slice of cake at **Fanthezie** tearoom.

Giverny

Located in a picturesque though otherwise fairly arbitrary corner of the French countryside, Giverny is famous for once being home to Impressionist Claude Monet and the garden that he regarded as his greatest masterpiece. For many of its visitors, though, Giverny is also their one exposure to the aesthetics of a French village and the texture of life in the country away from major cities.

The village was first noticed by Monet from a train window, and it made such an impression (sorry) that the artist came to live there shortly after, in 1883. His presence anointed Giverny in the eyes of the world as an artistic mecca, and it began to draw other Impressionists such as Willard Metcalf and Louis Ritman throughout the last decade of the 19th century and first decade of the 20th. Today, despite attracting more tourists than a village of its size should realistically be able to handle, it has retained much of what must have compelled Monet to settle here over a hundred years ago: fine half-timber housing, an isolated rural location, and fertile soil that lets a cornucopia of brightly colored flowers flourish in its gardens, streets, and surrounding fields. Visitors from all corners of the globe spend their time wandering around the picturesque village and its gardens, many playing artist themselves, shooting pictures in soft focus, so that when they get home they can almost claim to have a Monet of their own. If you can, visit in mid-spring, before tourist season hits its peak.

Orientation

Located on the Right Bank of the Seine, Giverny is about three miles from the town of Vernon, itself about 50 miles (80 kilometers) and 1 hour 20 minutes from Paris. This is where visitors coming by train will arrive—a regular shuttle service connects Vernon station with the village, though there's also a decent walking route, which takes about an hour. Giverny itself is hardly more than a single main high street (named, unsurprisingly, the rue Claude Monet) flanked by parking lots, restaurants, and hotels. Monet's garden, housed in the **Fondation Monet Giverny,** is at the far east end of this street, and includes within it a tunnel that takes you under the D5 (a main road) to the water garden, on the other side.

SIGHTS

TOP EXPERIENCE

★ Fondation Monet Giverny

84 rue Claude Monet, Giverny; tel. 02 32 51 28 21; http://fondation-monet.com; 9:30am-6pm daily Mar. 23-Nov. 1; adults €9.50, children and students €5.50, under 7 free, people with disabilities €4

Surely there's nowhere else on Earth for which the phrase "stepping into a painting" is a more accurate description. After moving here in 1883, Claude Monet made the development of this house and its surrounding gardens his central creative project. For the house, he retained its pink walls and used his own paintbox to color its interior. For the garden, meanwhile, he took on the employ of seven gardeners and saw it seperated into two distinct entities. The one nearest the house is referred to as the Clos Normand, and was expertly planned by Monet in the same way that he might have a painting, balancing light and shade and the colors of different plants along the geometric lines of a formal garden. The Water Garden, meanwhile, has an apparently wilder appearance, having been formed by the diversion of the River Epte. It was then designed to contain Japanese flourishes, such as the bridge—painted green as opposed to the traditional Japanese red—and became Monet's true pride and joy, where he liked to receive guests and spend hours in contemplation.

Today, all three spaces—the house and the two gardens—can be explored. With so many visitors, though, there's not a massive scope for aimless wandering. A fairly clear circuit exists that leads you first to the bottom of the formal garden, then under the road into the **Water Garden.** This is the real highlight of any visit: A looping circuit takes you around it, offering several iconic vantage points from which the view is almost identical to some of Monet's most famous paintings (especially if you squint). Monet's house, which sits at the top of the formal garden, is the way most visitors finish their tour. A traditionally maintained rural cottage, it gives a hint toward how Monet would have lived, and there are a number of original Japanese prints on display of the kind that inspired Monet in his work. At the end of the tour, you'll find Monet's old studio, which has been co-opted into a gift shop, where countless reproductions and prints on items from tea towels to pencil cases can be found at prices to suit all budgets. Expect to spend about 1-2 hours here in total.

Musée des Impressionnismes

99 rue Claude Monet, Giverny; tel. 02 32 51 28 21; www.mdig.fr; 10am-6pm daily late Mar.-Nov. 1 (closed one week in mid-July); adults €7.50, children 12-17 and students €5, children 7-11 €3.50, children under 7 free, people with disabilities €3.50

Shortly after Claude Monet came here to live and work on his garden and home, Giverny became a mecca for other Impressionist painters, particularly Americans, including Willard Metcalf and Louis Ritman, who came searching for inspiration both from the master himself and the village's surrounding countryside.

A museum was established here in 1992 as an ode to their experience. The museum evolved in 2009 into the Musée des Impressionnismes, which provides perspective on the artistic movement Monet was instrumental in creating. Here, talks, conferences, residencies for artists and art historians, and a regularly rotating exhibtion schedule offer visitors an appreciation of where Impressionism came from (Japanese prints, the outdoor studio movement, Manet) and what it went on to influence (pretty much all modern art!). Two temporary exhibitions here are featured every season, with the change between them occuring mid-July. Make sure to check the website for details.

Église Sainte-Radegonde de Giverny

53/55 rue Claude Monet, Giverny; 10 am-6 pm daily; free

Any true Monet pilgrimage should be rounded off by a visit to the painter's family tomb, which is found in the graveyard of this 11th-century Romanesque church. Fittingly bursting with flowers, the tomb became the artist's final resting place after he died in December 1926, by which time he was already firmly ensconced as a legendary innovator in the history of art. The church is worth looking in, too, and has the advantage of being a little way from the crowds, meaning you don't have to queue to get inside. Its interior is full of nice detailing accrued from across the centuries, including an altar of painted wood from the 1600s, and numerous statues of saints dating back to the 1300s—the 14th-century painted statue of Saint Louis of Anjou by the side entrance is particularly impressive.

FOOD

Local Cuisine

★ RESTAURANT BAUDY

81 rue Claude Monet, Giverny; tel. 02 32 21 10 03; www.restaurantbaudy.com; 10am-11pm daily; menus €30

The restaurant of the Hôtel Baudy, following Monet's arrival in Giverny, was fast elevated to a meeting place for some of the most famous names in the history of art. Cézanne, Renoir, Sisley, and Rodin were all known to have stayed and dined here. Today, the restaurant has done its best to maintain a glimmer

1: Restaurant Baudy, a former meeting place for artists **2:** inside the home of French impressionist painter Claude Monet **3:** Monet's water garden

1
2
3

of authenticity in the face of mass tourism, and its gingham-dominated interior and the wrought-iron chairs on its terrace remain passably 1900s, while its food is full of hearty rural flavors from duck to an excellent onion soup; there's also a good selection of salads if you want something lighter. Of course, you're about as likely to run into a contemporary French artist here as you are Monet himself, but for imagining yourself back into Giverny's past there's nowhere better.

LA GUINGUETTE

10 rue de Falaise, Giverny; tel. 06 72 76 03 66; 12pm-3pm and 6pm-12am daily; mains from €14

Good for lower-budget, fine-weather dining, this open-air restaurant makes the most of Giverny's rural setting, offering bucolic views from its rustic wooden terrace, which fronts onto the River Epte—an aspect that almost looks like an extra section of Monet's Water Garden, which makes it worth the visit alone. The food is not terrible, but also unlikely to set the world alight, consisting of fairly basic French classics such as steak and quiche, usually accompanied by salad and fries. The restaurant is also—as with just about everywhere in Giverny—only populated by tourists.

LE JARDIN DES PLUMES

1 rue du Milieu, Giverny; tel. 02 32 54 26 35; www.jardindesplumes.fr; 12pm-2pm and 7pm-10pm Wed.-Sun.; menu €52-98

Definite indulgence territory, this Michelin-starred restaurant offers high-end cooking of rich local flavors, delightfully prepared in ways that put a fresh spin on traditional dishes, from turning lobster into carpaccio or serving white fish in a cucumber sauce. The wine service is also excellent, with multilingual sommeliers making sure that you pair exactly the right drink with your meal. The building itself is half-timber in the classically Norman style, while the restaurant uses art deco flourishes to create an upmarket modern vibe. Such quality means that the whole place is elevated far above being a tourist trap; indeed, a trip to Giverny solely to sample its delights, that did not take in Monet's garden, would not be wasted.

Budget Options

AU COIN DU PAIN'TRE

73 rue Claude Monet, Giverny; tel. 02 32 71 01 70; 8am-7pm daily; €6-15

Its name's a pun; *pain* is French for bread, get it? And this bakery-cum-restaurant offers a fun setting and, above all, reasonably priced food, which makes it stand out from its many competitors along the rue Claude Monet. Granted, by the standards of a restaurant not in a mass-tourism site, it's a bit expensive, but that's a moot point. From takeaway sandwiches to a sit-down burger, this is the place in Giverny to beeline for if you don't want to break the bank.

ACCOMMODATIONS

€50-100

LE PETIT GIVERNY

41 chemin du Roy, Giverny; tel. 02 32 51 05 07; http://le-petit-giverny.com/fr-fr; from €90 d

Overflowing with rustic French charm and boasting a garden that's almost a rival to Monet's itself, every room here is differently styled, plush, and cozy, with traditional fittings as well as modern conveniences such as WiFi and flat-screen TVs. It's also right in the center of Giverny and boasts a decent on-site restaurant. The only issue is that it's not big and is very popular. If you want to stay here, be sure to book as early as possible.

€100-200

LE MOULIN DE CONNELLES

40 route d'Amfreville-Sous-les-Monts, Connelles; tel. 02 32 59 53 33; www.moulin-de-connelles.fr; from €180 d

A short drive away from Vernon and Giverny—you can only really stay here if you've got your own transport—this luxurious hotel in an old mill straddles an island on the Seine. The beautiful, classically Norman timber-frame building has spacious rooms with ultra-comfortable beds, and some balconies that award lovely views of the surrounding forest. The on-site restaurant seems to date from another time period, hushed and formal as it is, and serving locally sourced food that bursts with flavor. The foie gras crème brûlée is a sensation! There are also row boats, which are free for guests to take on a paddle up the river. It's best in autumn, just as the leaves are turning and the forest seems set aflame.

Camping

CAMPING LES FOSSES ROUGES

Chemin de Réanville, Saint-Marce; tel. 02 32 51 59 86; www.sna27.fr/Tourisme/Camping; Apr.-Sept.; €12 per night for two adults plus site, €33 per night for a cabin

A straightforward rural campsite in the western suburbs of Vernon, about four miles (six kilometers) from Giverny. There's nothing flashy here, but there are on-site showers, toilets, and a laundry service, as well as bike rental, which can be used to cycle into town and on to Giverny itself. The cabins are stylish eco-friendly "pods" made out of wood and complete with small terraces that blend into the natural environment and can house up to three people.

INFORMATION

MAISON DU TOURISME NORMANDIE-GIVERNY

80 rue Claude Monet, Giverny; tel. 02 32 64 45 0; www.giverny.fr; 10am-7pm daily late Mar.-early Nov.

Located between the Impressionist museum and the Claude Monet Foundation, Giverny's tourist office offers not just orientation in the town but the whole surrounding area. From Giverny along the Seine and out to the Alabaster Coast, this whole area of Normandy was perhaps the Impressionist movement's single greatest muse, and this tourist office is excellently suited to giving suggestions on how to continue a journey in their footsteps. It also offers WiFi and has English-speaking staff.

GETTING THERE AND AROUND

By Car

Vernon, the gateway town to Giverny, is around 50 miles (75 kilometers) and 1 hour 20 minutes by car from Paris and about 45 miles (70 kilometers) and 1 hour 10 minutes from Rouen. It is accessed from the A13 highway in either direction. This is partly a toll road, and to avoid the €3 fee when traveling from Paris, you can turn off onto the N15 at Mantes-la-Jolie, or from Rouen, take the D6014, followed by the D181. There is plenty of free parking in Giverny itself, though be prepared to spend some time looking for a space should you go in the height of summer. Should you be unwilling to take the risk, it's always possible to park in Vernon and take the shuttle bus the rest of the way.

By Train

Giverny may have caught Monet's eye from a train seat, but the hamlet itself is no longer serviced by rail. Instead you have to travel to the **train station** in Vernon, **Gare de Vernon-Giverny** (Place de la Gare, Vernon; tel. 36 35; 5:45am-9:05pm Mon. and Fri., 5:45am-8:55pm Tues.-Thurs., 6am-9:30pm Sat., 7:10am-10:10pm Sun.) from either Paris Saint Lazare or Rouen-Rive-Droit—the former was immortalized in a painting by Monet, which now hangs in the Musée d'Orsay in Paris. Most days there are around 10 trains leaving every 1-2 hours and costing about €10. Travel time is 45 minutes. From Vernon, a **shuttle bus** to Giverny completes the journey.

The Giverny shuttle bus leaves from the Vernon train station four times a day during the week and five on the weekend, with its first journey at 9:15am and its last at 3:15pm—it's not a massively efficient service. With round-trip tickets at €10, it's also not cheap for a journey that lasts barely 20 minutes. However, for independent travelers trying to get to Giverny without a car, it's either this or walking. There are seven return services to Vernon every day, with the last leaving Giverny at 7:10 pm. The service runs late March-early November.

Rouen

The capital of Normandy was once one of the great metropolises of medieval Europe. Astride the River Seine, which is far wider here than it is in Paris, and ringed by fertile hills, Rouen appears at once as the perfect location in which to found a city. Today, its former wealth bristles with Gothic abundance and can be seen in the teetering timber-frame houses that still line its streets in the old town, which still dominates the north bank of the Seine.

That so much of the town's medieval heritage remains intact distinguishes it substantially from its close urban neighbor, Paris, from which it is less than 80 miles (130 kilometers) away, as the crow flies. In France's capital, Baron Haussmann's mid-19th-century renovations buried much of the town's more distant history. In Rouen, this history still remains much on display. Because of that, the town can in places feel like walking through an older France, and indeed, an older Europe: pre-Revolutionary, dominated by the clergy and kings.

Of course, Rouen is also a thriving modern hub, with plenty of new architecture among its well-preserved heritage. Despite being only on a river, it is also one of the largest ports in France. It's restaurants and food are world class, while the thriving arts and theater scene offers great opportunities to go deeper into Norman culture, concentrating much of the surrounding region. Rouen's blend of old and new provides a striking contrast for visitors to explore. While there, make sure not to miss the splendid Gothic architecture of its churches, which are among the most spectacular anywhere in the world.

History

A Gaulish settlement first, then Roman, Rouen's Norman history really began when it was captured by Rollo, a Viking and the first ruler of Normandy, in 876. An inland city, which nevertheless had the potential to act as a major port, Rouen's qualities were fast apparent to its conquerors.

Despite losing favor to Caen under the reign of William the Conqueror (1060-1087), Rouen's prime position on the Seine meant it continued to prosper economically, becoming a center of trade for materials such as wine, wheat, wool, and tin. In that time, its culture too grew more cosmopolitan, attracting a large Jewish community, who at their height made up about a fifth of the city's entire population.

The fall of Rouen to the French at the beginning of the 13th century marked the end of the Norman state, and just over 200 years later the city changed hands again, being captured by King Henry V of England in 1419. It then regained its status as a capital, being the center of English power in occupied France during the final years of the Hundred Years' War, and in this time witnessed perhaps its most infamous historical event, when Joan of Arc was burned at the stake in the city's central square.

The 19th century saw the birth of Rouen's most famous son, the author Gustave Flaubert, who set a portion of his much-acclaimed debut novel, *Madame Bovary,* on the city's streets. It was also in this period that Rouen became muse to some of the Impressionist painters, notably Monet, who produced studies of the facade of Rouen Cathedral at different times of day.

About 45 percent of the city was destroyed during the Allied invasions of World War II, which though substantial was still considerably less damage than Normandy's other major centers, such as Caen and Le Havre. Though much of Rouen burned, over half remained, and its continued status as the closest major port to Paris gave it the economic strength to reestablish itself fairly quickly.

Orientation

Rouen is a large city of almost 110,000 people, though with a compact downtown. It is defined by the River Seine, which here is almost 650 feet (200 meters) across, and, as in Paris, splits the city into Right and Left Banks. The old town and central district, however, are defiantly on the Right one of these, along with the city's main train station and most of its major sights. This area is where most travelers will go. It is an easily walkable space of about a square mile, split almost in two by rue Jeanne d'Arc, which also leads to the station. Most major sights, including the cathedral, the ossuary of Saint-Maclou, and the Gros-Horloge, are to the east of this road. Along the river are wide thoroughfares, which make Rouen a surprisingly easy city to drive through—it doesn't have a ring road like many French towns. The docks, meanwhile, are spread over both the Right and Left Banks to the east of the city. These remain largely industrial, however, and so don't offer much for tourists.

SIGHTS

TOP EXPERIENCE

★ Old Town

Rouen's old town is one of the city's major draws, and yet it's also a surprisingly inconsistent place and hard to fully define where it starts or ends. Broadly speaking, it takes in the square mile or so, on Roeun's Right Bank, defined in the north by the train station and in the south by the D6015, and divided by rue Jeanne d'Arc. This is not a museum city, however, but rather has been a major center of trade and commerce for over a millennium. In that time, many buildings have gone up, and almost as many have come down, whether thanks to civic planning, fire, or military bombardment. Different eras of history now casually rub against one another here, with some modern buildings penetrating right into the heart of the old town, and other ancient houses spilling way into its outskirts.

Much gets treated with the kind of nonchalance bred by surplus: for a restaurant or a department store, a building is first and foremost just a place to run a business, which means there are many timber-frame buildings from the 1600s that now bear the scars of modern commerce. In a counterintuitive sense, though, this often adds to their authenticity. Without the deadening formaldehyde of overwrought civic preservation, the town's history feels very present, as though you might stumble into a couple of locals still chattering about what they should do with that Joan of Arc woman, who's still locked up down the road.

A lot of life in the old town focuses around the **Place du Vieux-Marché** in the west, which was in fact the same square in which Joan of Arc was burned at the stake. Today, this is ringed by half-timber buildings, many of which have been converted into restaurants, while the center is dominated by a modernist church, Église Sainte-Jeanne-d'Arc, and a market hall, the sweeping curves to the structure of which are meant to evoke both the flames that consumed the saint and the hull of an overturned longship—a reference to Rouen's Viking past.

East of here, crossing the thoroughfare of the rue Jeanne d'Arc (no, not everything's named after her in this city, but a lot is), you'll find most of the city's major sights, including the Gros-Horloge, the Saint-Maclou Ossuary, and several gothic churches, listed below. Besides these, keep an eye out for the rue Saint-Romain, the rue Martainville, and the rue Damiette, all of which boast some lovely, well-restored 15th- to 18th-century half-timber houses. No. 74 on Saint-Romain is particularly impressive, being Gothic in style with some fabulous 15th-century bay windows. Then there's the Renaissance fountain to look out for on Martainville, and the intriguing blind alley of Hauts-Mariages on the right of Damiette.

The rue Eue-de-Robec is also worth a look, lined as it is with more nicely restored

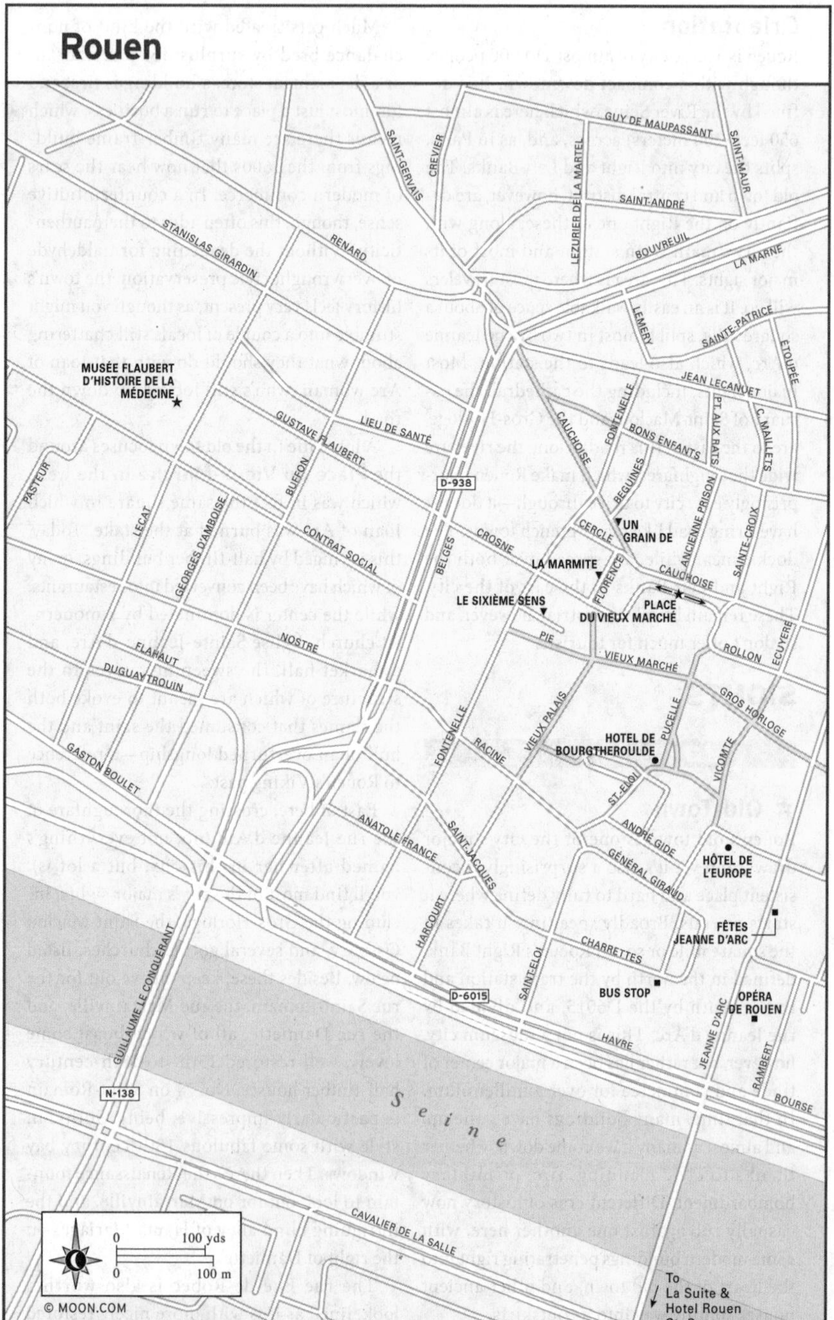

Rouen

GUY DE MAUPASSANT
SAINT-MAUR
SAINT-GERVAIS
CREVIER
LEZURIER DE LA MARTEL
SAINT-ANDRÉ
BOUVREUIL
LA MARNE
STANISLAS GIRARDIN
RENARD
LEMERY
SAINTE-PATRICE
ETOUPÉE
JEAN LECANUET
MUSÉE FLAUBERT D'HISTOIRE DE LA MÉDECINE
FONTENELLE
PL. AUX RATS
C. MALLETS
CAUCHOISE
BONS ENFANTS
GUSTAVE FLAUBERT
LIEU DE SANTÉ
PASTEUR
BUFFON
D-938
BEGUINES
ANCIENNE PRISON
SAINTE-CROIX
LECAT
GEORGES D'AMBOISE
CONTRAT SOCIAL
BELGES
CROSNE
CERCLE
UN GRAIN DE
LA MARMITE
FLORENCE
CAUCHOISE
PLACE DU VIEUX MARCHÉ
LE SIXIÈME SENS
ECUYÈRE
NOSTRE
PIE
ROLLON
VIEUX MARCHÉ
FLAHAUT
DUGUAY TROUIN
GROS HORLOGE
FONTENELLE
VIEUX PALAIS
PUCELLE
RACINE
HOTEL DE BOURGTHEROULDE
VICOMTE
GASTON BOULET
ST.-ELOI
ANDRÉ GIDE
HÔTEL DE L'EUROPE
ANATOLE FRANCE
SAINT-JACQUES
GÉNÉRAL GIRAUD
HARCOURT
FÊTES JEANNE D'ARC
CHARRETTES
GUILLAUME LE CONQUERANT
SAINT-ELOI
BUS STOP
D-6015
OPÉRA DE ROUEN
HAVRE
JEANNE D'ARC
RAMBERT
N-138
BOURSE
Seine
CAVALIER DE LA SALLE
0 100 yds
0 100 m
To La Suite & Hotel Rouen St.-Sever

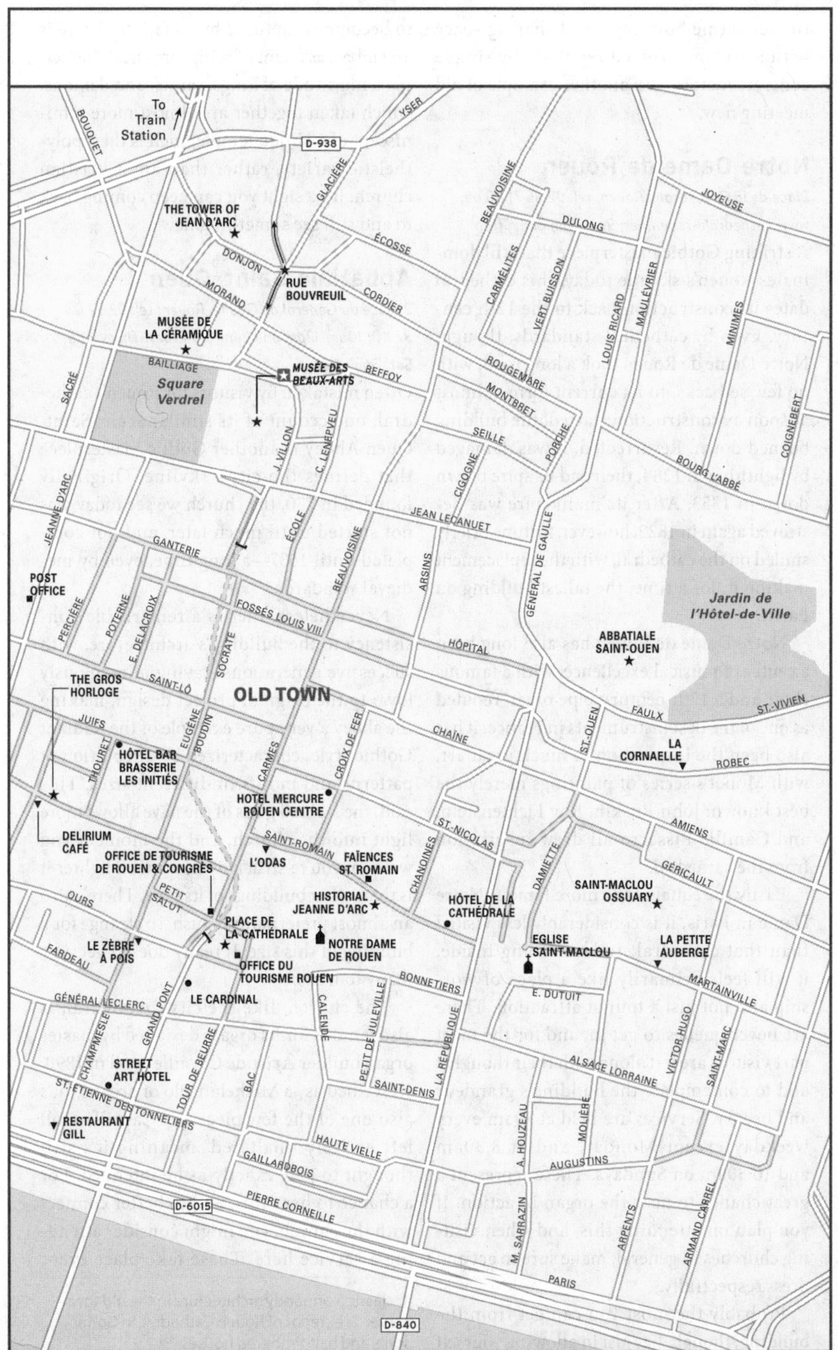
To Train Station
BOUQUET
YSER
D-938
THE TOWER OF JEAN D'ARC
GLACIÈRE
BEAUVOISINE
JOYEUSE
DULONG
ÉCOSSE
DONJON
RUE BOUVREUIL
MORAND
CORDIER
CARMÉLITES
VERT BUISSON
LOUIS RICARD
MAULÉVRIER
MINIMES
MUSÉE DE LA CÉRAMIQUE
BAILLIAGE
MUSÉE DES BEAUX-ARTS
BEFFOY
ROUGEMARE
MONTBRET
SACRÉ
Square Verdrel
SEILLE
COIGNEBERT
J. VILLON
C. LENEPVEU
CIGOGNE
PORCHE
BOURG L'ABBÉ
ÉCOLE
JEAN LECANUET
JEANNE D'ARC
GANTERIE
ARSINS
GÉNÉRAL DE GAULLE
POST OFFICE
PERCIÈRE
POTERNE
E. DELACROIX
FOSSÉS LOUIS VIII
Jardin de l'Hôtel-de-Ville
HÔPITAL
ABBATIALE SAINT-OUEN
SOCRATE
SAINT-LÔ
THE GROS HORLOGE
OLD TOWN
FAULX
ST.-VIVIEN
JUIFS
EUGÈNE BOUDIN
CARMES
CROIX DE FER
CHAÎNE
ST.-OUEN
LA CORNAELLE
ROBEC
HÔTEL BAR BRASSERIE LES INITIÉS
THOURET
HOTEL MERCURE ROUEN CENTRE
AMIENS
ST.-NICOLAS
DELIRIUM CAFÉ
SAINT-ROMAIN
CHANOINES
DAMIETTE
OFFICE DE TOURISME DE ROUEN & CONGRÈS
L'ODAS
FAÏENCES ST. ROMAIN
GÉRICAULT
OURS
PETIT SALUT
HISTORIAL JEANNE D'ARC
HÔTEL DE LA CATHÉDRALE
SAINT-MACLOU OSSUARY
PLACE DE LA CATHÉDRALE
FARDEAU
LE ZÈBRE À POIS
NOTRE DAME DE ROUEN
EGLISE SAINT-MACLOU
LA PETITE AUBERGE
OFFICE DU TOURISME ROUEN
BONNETIERS
MARTAINVILLE
GÉNÉRAL LECLERC
LE CARDINAL
E. DUTUIT
GRAND PONT
CALENDE
PETIT DE JULEVILLE
LA RÉPUBLIQUE
VICTOR HUGO
SAINT-MARC
CHAMPMESLÉ
STREET ART HOTEL
TOUR DE BEURRE
BAC
ALSACE LORRAINE
SAINT-DENIS
ST.-ETIENNE DES TONNELIERS
RESTAURANT GILL
HAUTE VIELLE
A. HOUZEAU
MOLIÈRE
GAILLARDBOIS
AUGUSTINS
D-6015
PIERRE CORNEILLE
M. SARRAZIN
ARPENTS
ARMAND CARREL
PARIS
D-840

timber-frame buildings, and sharing space with a stream, crossed regularly by simple concrete footbridges: another example of old meeting new.

Notre Dame de Rouen

Place de la Cathédrale, Rouen; tel. 02 35 71 85 65; www.cathedrale-rouen.net; 9am-7pm daily; free

A striking Gothic masterpiece that still dominates Rouen's skyline today, this cathedral dates its construction back to the 12th century. Even by cathedral standards, though, Notre Dame de Rouen took a long road, with no few setbacks, to its current form. Almost as soon as construction started, the building burned down. Resurrected, it was damaged by lightning in 1284, then had its spire blown down in 1353. After its main spire was destroyed again in 1822, however, fortune briefly smiled on the cathedral, with the replacement making it, for a time, the tallest building on Earth.

Notre Dame de Rouen has also long been a center of musical excellence, with a famous choir and a 17th-century pipe organ reputed as one of the best instruments in France. It has also been the inspiration to much great art, with Monet's series of paintings merely the best known: John Ruskin, Roy Lichtenstein, and Camille Pissarro all drew inspiration from the cathedral.

Easily the equal of the more famous Notre Dame in Paris, it is considerably less visited than that cathedral. Indeed, going inside, it still feels primarily like a place of worship and not just a tourist attraction. There are never queues to get in, and for the most part visitors are left alone with their thoughts and to contemplate the building's grandeur and beauty. Services are held at 10am every weekday except Monday, and at 8:30am and 10:30am on Sundays. These represent a great chance to hear the organ in action. If you plan on attending this, and when visiting churches in general, make sure to act and dress respectfully.

Probably the most you can get from the building, though, lies just in allowing yourself to become enraptured by its facade. There is an embarrassment of sculptures here, depicting a multitude of kings, saints, and demons, which taken together are almost more reminiscent of a Hindu temple, such is their polytheistic variety, rather than any Christian church. It's a sight you can keep coming back to and still see something new.

Abbatiale Saint-Ouen

3 place du Général de Gaulle, Rouen; tel. 02 32 08 32 40; 10am-12pm and 2pm-6pm Tues.-Thurs. and Sat.-Sun.; free

Often mistaken by visitors for Rouen's cathedral, on account of its similar scale, Saint-Ouen Abbey is another Gothic masterpiece that defines the city's skyline. Originally founded in 750, the church we see today was not started until much later, and not completed until 1537—a long time, even by medieval standards.

Nevertheless, there's a remarkable consistency to the building's architecture, with successive generations staying miraculously loyal to the original project design, making the abbey a very pure example of the Radiant Gothic style, characterized by a repitition of patterns and motifs in different sizes. This said, the stained glass of the nave allows more light into the church, and the moment you walk in, you're struck by how much lighter it is than other buildings of its type. There's also an almost preternatural hush, so strange for a building of this size: It really doesn't get very many tourists.

The church, like the city's cathedral, is also famous for its organ, designed by master organ builder Aristide Cavaillé-Coll in 1890. Described as "a Michelangelo of organs," it's also one of the few pieces by Cavaillé-Coll left entirely unaltered, meaning it's still thought to play exactly as he intended. For a chance to hear this, and to better connect with the church, you might consider attending a service here. These take place every

1: classic Normandy architecture in the old town center **2:** exterior of Rouen Cathedral, in Gothic style, and half-timbered houses

1

2

Sunday at 11am. If you decide to come to one, out of respect, you should be prepared to commit to its whole duration, which will be about an hour.

Église Saint-Maclou

7 place Barthélémy, Rouen; tel. 02 32 08 32 40; 10am-12pm and 2pm-6pm Sat.-Mon.; free

The third of Rouen's must-see Gothic churches, Saint-Maclou is also easily the smallest. It was built to replace the city's former Romanesque parish church that had fallen into disrepair. Construction began around 1435 and was funded by some of Rouen's wealthiest merchant families as the city went through a great economic boom.

Because of this, there's an interesting contradiction inherent in the church's style. On the one hand, it's a lavish display of the city's wealth, built in a basilica style, with four chapels positioned around its central octagonal choir, and on the other, its decoration is gruesome and morbid, being focused as it is on displaying scenes from the Black Death, which had killed an estimated three-quarters of Saint-Maclou parish in the 14th century, and led to an overcrowding in the graveyard of the original church.

Also much quieter than Rouen's Notre Dame, the added bonus to a visit here is that it's on a more human scale. There's still a big-city oppulance, but being smaller the building's story feels easier to read. It's also intimately connected with the nearby ossuary, and its decoration conjures similarly profound, occasionally dark thoughts.

Saint-Maclou Ossuary

186 rue de Martainville, Rouen; tel. 02 76 08 81 13; 9am-6pm Mon.-Fri.; free

One of Rouen's stranger, and certainly more macabre, sights, the cemetery Saint-Maclou Ossuary has its origins in the 14th century, when the Black Death was sweeping Europe and the continent's population were dying in their millions. Today, it remains an uncannily preserved medieval courtyard, which can be simply stepped into from the rue de Martainville.

Its design dates from the 1500s, when another outbreak of plague necessitated an expansion of the site and saw the building of the courtyard. The practice then was to bury bodies in its center, use quicklime to accelerate their decomposition, then collect their bones for storage in the attics of the courtyard buildings in order to make space for more victims.

Fitting its gruesome purpose, a lot of the decoration here has a deathly aspect: skeletons abound. Of course, it's no longer used for the same purpose, and indeed looked certain to slip into disrepair until Rouen's School of Fine Arts was moved to the building in 1940, which it still uses to this day, providing around 180 students higher education in the visual arts.

Several information boards add to the experience of the place, but this is not really a museum, just a fascinating corner of Rouen, imbued with the strange irony that a place so dedicated to commemorating death and decay should be one of the city's best preserved sights.

The Gros-Horloge

Rue du Gros Horloge, Rouen; tel. 02 32 08 01 90; 10am-1pm and 2pm-7pm Tues.-Sun. Apr.-Oct., 2pm-6pm Tues.-Sun. Nov.-Mar.; adults €7, reduced €3.50, under 6 free

This is one of the oldest astronomical clocks in Europe, showing the time and the phases of the moon. Its mechanism was built in 1389; the dial was added later, in the 1500s, when the clock was also moved to its current position in a Renaissance arch crossing an old town street that has come to bear the clock's name: the rue du Gros-Horloge.

Its facade is designed to look like a sun, with 24 golden rays pointing toward the hours of the day, and is gilded as extravagantly as

---

1: the door to Saint-Maclou **2:** a statue of Joan of Arc in Rouen Cathedral **3:** Rouen's Gros-Horloge

1
2
3

any religious artifact, reminiscent of an era when knowing the precise time was akin to magic, or being close to God. Long an emblem for the city, the entire building that the clock is housed in can now be visited, though its dial is now moved by an electric mechanism, with the original having been removed for posterity in 1928. The original mechanism still works, however, and indeed had barely missed a tick since the 14th century, something Rouen's tourist board points out as constituting more than five million hours of recording time.

★ Musée des Beaux-Arts

Espl. Marcel Duchamp, Rouen; tel. 02 35 71 28 40; http://mbarouen.fr; 10am-6pm Wed.-Mon.; permanent collections free, most temporary exhibits adults €6, reduced €3

Offering nothing less than one of the most comprehensive public art collections in France outside of Paris, Rouen's Musée des Beaux-Arts contains paintings and objet d'art from across Europe and from every major school from the 15th century to the present day. This includes works by such masters as Caravaggio, Rubens, and Velázquez, as well as more recent painters, including many Impressionists like Monet and Degas.

This wealth of content is housed over a relatively small space in comparison to some of the major Paris museums, making a visit here an altogether less intimidating experience than to one of its big-city cousins. Opened by Napoleon in 1801, the neoclassical building it is currently housed in was constructed in the 1880s and received an extensive renovation in 1994.

As well as the permanent collections, the museum hosts frequently changing exhibitions that showcase different artists and art periods to a world-beating standard. Particularly worth hunting down is Monet's painting of Rouen Cathedral in gray weather. Part of his extensive series on the building, depicting the cathedral at different times of the day and year, it represents an excellent communication between the Beaux-Arts museum and the city beyond its walls.

Musée de la Céramique

1 rue Faucon, Rouen; tel. 02 35 07 31 74; http://museedelaceramique.fr/fr; 2pm-6pm Wed.-Mon.; free

Rouen was a major center of pottery during the Renaissance, which is what this museum, located just next to the Musée des Beaux-Arts, is dedicated to. As well as boasting the world's largest collection of Rouen earthenware, it tells the story of ceramics across Europe and features works from many other centers of the trade, including Delft, Nevers, and Lille.

The collection of more than 5,000 individual pieces is eclectic and dates from the 16th to the late 18th century. It showcases the versatility and grandeur of ceramic art in everything from masterful paving by the Renaissance master Masséot Abaquesne to earthenware paintings and sculptures.

Situated in the 17th-century mansion the Hôtel d'Hocqueville, the museum interiors are in a fine neoclassical style, which offer a fitting complement to the ceramics.

Musée Flaubert d'Histoire de la Médecine

51 rue de Lecat, Rouen; tel. 02 35 15 59 95; www.chu-rouen.fr/le-chu/culture-et-patrimoine/le-musee-flaubert; 10am-5:30pm Tues., 2pm-5:30pm Wed.-Sat.; adults €4, reduced €2

Though it seems like a strange combination, this museum offers something for both literary pilgrims and those curious about French medical culture in the 19th century. It is housed in the childhood home of the famous Norman writer Gustave Flaubert, and while it certainly says something about his younger years, it's as much dedicated to the career of his father, who was a doctor with his own practice. The collections are eccentric and include objects from greatly varying fields, including medicine, fine arts, and furniture.

Tower of Jeanne d'Arc

Rue Bouvreuil, Rouen; www.donjonderouen.com; 2pm-4pm Tues.-Sun; free; escape room 4:30pm-10pm Sun., Tues., and Wed., 4:30pm-11:30pm Thurs.-Sat.; €105 for 3-8 players

Not actually the tower in which Joan of Arc

Joan of Arc

Most people know the outline of Joan of Arc's story: A peasant girl claiming visions of angels begs herself into the presence of the French King and then to the head of the French army, whom she leads to glorious victory against the odds, only to then be caught by her enemies and burned at the stake for her sins against them. In France, it's as good as a foundational myth, and it's such a compelling story that it's found its way into classrooms around the world. Often lost in our familiarity with it, though, is one quite staggering fact: that it's true. Such is its unlikeliness, so much of it reads like legend, that it can be hard to convince ourselves that Joan of Arc was a real person. But she was.

Imagine it: an illiterate 13-year-old in rural France, and a girl no less, who starts to believe she's being visited by the Archangel Michael telling her that she is the only person who can save her country against the rampant English armies who have been occupying French territory for the better part of a hundred years, and she makes it a reality.

Joan of Arc captured by the Burgundians at the Siege of Compiègne on a stained glass in the cathedral of Rouen, France

PETITIONING THE KING

To get an audience with the king meant starting at the bottom. Joan headed to the small town of Vaucouleurs near her village, where she petitioned the garrison commander for an armed escort to the French Royal court 300 miles (500 kilometers) away in Chinon. After months of trying, two soldiers were assigned to accompany her.

In a story full of miracles, that King Charles deigned to meet with her, and what's more, listen to what she had to say, might be the most astounding. But given the future of France was hanging by a thread, and that all rational recourses of action had been used up, the utterly irrational—trusting the army to the hands of an illiterate teenage farm girl—must have seemed worth trying.

SIEGE OF ORLEANS

After convicing the king, Joan was equipped for war and sent to Orleans, which the English had under siege, and where it was reasoned the fate of the whole Kingdom of France would be decided. Joan's precise military participation at Orleans is unclear, though the experienced soldiers running the city's defense did claim they listened to her, believing her advice divinely inspired. And after turning to a more aggressive strategy, they lifted the siege. Suddenly, after not having won a battle in a generation, victory followed victory, and with Joan of Arc before them, the French gradually drove the English off their lands.

TRIAL IN ROUEN

Joan was taken captive before the job was finished, and put on trial for heresy by the English in Rouen—the idea that God was on France's side understandably did not sit well with the English, who claimed Joan was inspired not by Him, but by the devil. The trial itself was as good as rigged, but even so Joan dazzled those watching with her eloquence and speed of mind. Some of the most learned men in Europe were left stupefied despite Joan's lack of any formal education, as she evaded trap after trap they set for her with their words. Indeed, the transcripts of the very same trial that condemned her were later used as evidence for her canonization. Nevertheless, condemned she was, and on May 30, 1431, she was burnt at the stake in the center of Rouen and her charred remains thrown into the Seine to prevent them becoming relics. By that stage, though, the tide of battle had turned, and 22 years later, the English had almost been expelled from France entirely, having lost the Hundred Years' War.

was imprisoned, this has nevertheless become representative of where she was held in Rouen Castle, being as it is the only part of that building left standing. Its impressive size gives some impression of the formidable fortification, built by Philippe Auguste and dismantled at the end of France's Wars of Religion (1562-1598). Today, in addition to being a historic monument, the tower is home to an interactive escape game in which teams of 3-8 people are locked into one of its rooms and have 60 minutes to answer several puzzles in order to find their way out. The game can be played in both French and English, and you'll need to book in advance, as there are limited spaces available. The earlier you reserve, the more likely you are of securing a place.

Historial Jeanne d'Arc

7 rue Saint-Romain, Rouen; tel. 02 35 52 48 00; www.historial-jeannedarc.fr/horaires-et-tarifs; 10am-7pm Tues.-Sun.; adults €10, reduced €7.50

An extensive nontraditional museum, located over five floors in the historic archdiocese of Rouen Cathedral, this offers an entirely new way to get to grips with the story of Joan of Arc. From her origins through the battles she helped win, and to her eventual trial and famous death in 1431, it provides visitors interactive tasks and 3D displays, and ultimately asks them to imagine what they might have done if they'd had to play judge to Joan of Arc's fate.

ENTERTAINMENT AND EVENTS

The Arts

OPÉRA DE ROUEN

7 rue du Dr Robert Rambert, Rouen; tel. 02 35 98 50 98; www.operaderouen.fr; ticket office 1pm-6pm Mon.-Fri., 2pm-5pm Sat., and one hour before showtime

Rouen has had three opera houses since the 1770s, with the first being gutted by fire in the 19th century and the second destroyed by Allied bombing in World War II. The current iteration is a brutalist building on the banks of the Seine constructed over 10 years and opened in 1962. It is home to the Rouen Philharmonic Orchestra and hosts a wide-ranging program that includes classical concerts, opera, and some plays. The season runs from September to June, when there is a show most evenings with earlier shows on Sundays. Five-euro tickets can be bought 15 minutes before showtime for those under 28 years old and are subject to availability.

Nightlife

DELIRIUM CAFÉ

30 rue des Vergetiers, Rouen; tel. 02 32 12 05 95; 3:30pm-2am Mon.-Sat., 6pm-2am Sun.

It can be hard in France to find decent beer; the country's dedication to wine tends to leave other alcoholic drinks a little neglected. Not so here. Delirium Café, situated in the shadow of the Gros-Horloge, is a veritable beer-drinker's paradise, with 20 varieties on tap and more than 200 in bottles (the 8.5% La Guillotine beer is a particular treat), and a cozy, if a little boozy, atmosphere to drink them in. It's popular with tourists and locals alike, and stays open into the small hours most nights.

LA SUITE

2 rue de Malherbe, Rouen; tel. 02 35 03 10 10; http://suiterouen.fr; 11pm-6am Thurs.-Sat.; entry €10

Right in the heart of Rouen, this nightclub complex is one of the biggest and liveliest in all of Normandy. With two different rooms boasting different atmospheres, there's also a rooftop snack bar. Nights are ostensibly themed, but in general expect the usual blend of dim lights, heavy beats, and dancing.

Festivals and Events

FÊTES JEANNE D'ARC

Place du Vieux-Marché, Rouen, and various locations; www.rouentourisme.com/agenda/fetes-jeanne-d-arc-3431; 9:30am-7pm last weekend in May; free

Commemorating the death of Joan of Arc, France's savior from the English, this is not just a festival put on for tourists. Were the country just slightly different, the day of this festival, rather than July 14, could be the

French national holiday, and commemorations of the saint are held with due seriousness, and a clear religious aspect. As well as lectures and performances, a mass is held in the Église Sainte-Jeanne-d'Arc (the modern church erected over the place where she was put to death), followed by a parade to the Abbatiale Saint-Ouen. Later, there is a service in Notre Dame, while the day is rounded off with a ceremony on the Boieldieu Bridge—symbolic of the saint's tomb, for her ashes were cast into the Seine to prevent them from becoming relics.

FÊTE DU VENTRE FESTIVAL

Place du Vieux Marché and rue Rollon, Rouen; http://en.rouentourisme.com/the-festival-of-gastronomy-of-the-stomach; third weekend in Oct.; free

Right at the end of harvest season, this "festival of the stomach," founded in 1935, is a showcase of the culinary delights that Normandy has to offer. Sellers descend on the town's central streets from the surrounding areas and offer up their very best produce as part of a festival that includes tastings, direct sales from producers, and demonstrations. The variety is nothing short of miraculous, with everything from root vegetables to artisanal cider to the best cheese that you'll ever eat on offer. If one of the best ways to understand a region is to sample its food, there can be few more instructive events than this.

SHOPPING

FAÏENCES SAINT ROMAIN

56 rue Saint-Romain, Rouen; tel. 02 35 07 12 30; www.faiences-rouen.com; 9am-7pm Mon.-Sat.

Straddling the line between museum and retail outlet, this ceramics-maker builds on Rouen's historic connection to the art form in its creation and selling of what seems almost every size and shape of chinaware imaginable. The shelves teem with mugs (from €30), bowls, plates (from €79), vases, china sculptures, and more. Shipping is available at an extra cost; they've also an extensive mail-order webpage, if you only decide you'd like something after you've arrived home.

FOOD

Local Cuisine

★ RESTAURANT GILL

8-9, quai de la Bourse, Rouen; tel. 02 35 71 16 14; www.gill.fr; 12pm-1:45pm and 7:30pm-9:45pm Tues.-Sat.; lunch menu €45, evening menus €75-135

Having been in possession of two Michelin stars since 1990, and being prominently located on the quayside of Rouen's Right Bank, Restaurant Gill has become an icon of Rouen's restaurant scene. The chef, Gilles Tournadre, is Norman by birth and dedicated to the flavors of his homeland, but he's also fascinated by Japanese cuisine, visiting the country every year, and constructing a menu that balances the two traditions in a way that goes way beyond oysters with a wasabi chaser: Many of Tournadre's meals build from Japanese treatment of broth, vegetable, and fish. This said, one of the restaurant's most iconic dishes is *pigeon à la Rouennaise,* a thoroughly juicy, intensely local creation. Prices are, justifiably, high, though with the lunchtime menu coming in at under €50, it is still possible to visit and not (entirely) break the bank. Booking is essential.

LE SIXIÈME SENS

2 rue Thomas Corneille, Rouen; tel. 02 35 88 43 97; https://le-sixiemesens.fr; 12pm-2pm and 7pm-10:30pm Sun.-Thurs., 12pm-2pm and 7pm-11pm Fri.-Sat.; lunch menu €23, evening menus €32-48

Offering food served to an extremely high aesthetic standard amid cutting-edge decoration, under a medieval vaulted ceiling, this is fine dining for the Instagram generation, and the flavors are excellent, too. Offering modern twists on French classics, such as scallops with fennel confit and lamb layered with a mille-feuille of potatoes, chef Hakim Benallal leads a young team in this restaurant, which is attracting an increasingly sophisticated crowd. The lunch menu represents a fantastic deal, though whenever you go booking is recommended.

LA MARMITE

3 rue de Florence, Rouen; tel. 02 35 71 75 55; www.lamarmiterouen.com; 12pm-2pm and 7pm-9:15pm Wed.-Sat., 12pm-2pm Sun.; menus €25-65

La Marmite is a high-quality, if slightly eccentric, restaurant with a dedication to fresh local flavors. They serve mostly French classics, but are also unafraid to bend the rules, introducing Asian tastes into traditional dishes—for example, mixing citrus-flavored yuzu seeds in with their langoustine risotto. Much of this is down to self-taught head chef Frédérique Antoine, whose personal story and willingness to experiment have made her something of a minor celebrity among the foodies of Rouen. Booking is recommended.

L'ODAS

Passage Maurice Lenfant, Rouen; tel. 02 35 73 83 24; https://lodas.fr; 12pm-2:30pm and 7:30pm-9:30pm Tues.-Sat., 10:30am-2:30pm Sun.; lunch menu €29, evening menus €49-135

This restaurant sets its own bar high. It's clear from the decor and the reverence of the waiters the moment you walk in that food here is treated as an art form. It's a formal, modern restaurant serving haute cuisine, from carpaccio of line-caught barfish to blue lobster with soy-glazed pork belly; all of the dishes look like mini works of abstract expressionism. On Sundays they also serve brunch, which is more traditional in its content and appearance. Booking is recommended.

LA PETITE AUBERGE

164 rue Martainville, Rouen; tel. 02 35 70 80 18; www.restaurant-petite-auberge.fr; 12pm-1:30pm and 7:15pm-9:30pm Tues.-Sun.; lunch menu €14.30, evening menus €19-37

Situated right in Rouen's town center and as traditionally French as a plate full of snails, this bustling, family-friendly restaurant specializes in rustic cuisine—including snails. For those whose mouths are not set watering by the thought of garlicky gastropods, however, there's also a wealth of less adventurous fare to choose from, and to eat in wood-beamed surrounds.

Budget Options

UN GRAIN DE

24 rue Cauchoise, Rouen; tel. 02 35 08 58 42; www.restaurant-rouen-ungraínde.fr; 12pm-2pm and 7pm-10pm Tues.-Sat.; lunch menus from €8.50, evening menus €16-20

Eschewing pretension, but nevertheless dedicated to bold, fresh flavors, Un Grain De is one of Rouen's less-expensive gems. They offer

La Petite Auberge

a rustic base of simple meat cuts, but are not afraid to seek inspiration from elsewhere in the world, with flavors such as curry and more exotic meats such as kangaroo. It's not overly formal, either, favoring conviviality over rigid presentation. Its colorful decor in a traditional building is a great symbol of its intent.

LE ZÈBRE À POIS

17 rue aux Ours, Rouen; tel. 02 35 70 42 00; 8am-7pm Tues.-Sun.; €8-20

Bursting with character, this local hangout specializes in salads, light snacks, and fueling the aperitif crowd after a day's work. The building it's located in is not much to write home about, but the owners have decorated the interior so that you wouldn't notice: Flowers and plants dominate, and then of course there's the large zebra model to remind customers where they are. It's not the kind of place you'd book ahead, but a great pit-stop if you stumble by.

LA CORNAELLE

174 rue Eau de Robec, Rouen; tel. 02 35 08 53 75; 12pm-2pm and 7pm-10pm Tues.-Sat.; €7.50-11.50

A good-quality inexpensive *crêperie* housed inside a traditional half-timber building. The dishes are filling and richly flavored, and the atmosphere is easy and informal, happy to accommodate families or lone travelers. When trying to figure out what dish to choose, simple and straightforward is best: The classic ham, egg, and cheese crepe here reminds you that it's a classic for a reason.

ACCOMMODATIONS

Under €50

HOTEL ROUEN ST. SEVER

8-20 place de l'Église Saint-Sever, Rouen; tel. 02 35 62 81 82; www.hotel-rouen-saint-sever.com; from €37 d

It's basic, and not exactly brilliantly located, being quite deep in Rouen's more residential Left Bank. But the rooms are clean and soundproof, and there's free WiFi, satellite TV, and a 24-hour reception desk. More than anything, though, it's the price that's going to keep people coming here; €37 for a double room anywhere in Normandy is a bargain, let alone close to the heart of one of the region's biggest cities.

€50-100

HÔTEL BAR BRASSERIE LES INITIÉS

45 rue aux Juifs, Rouen; tel. 02 35 71 50 93; http://lesinitiesrouen.fr; from €76 d

Centrally located and inside a half-timber building, the rooms are cozy and comfortable—if not especially large. There are, though, nice views from some of them of the other buildings of Rouen's medieval old town. WiFi is available throughout the property and there are satellite TVs in all the rooms. There's also a bar and restaurant located on-site.

HÔTEL DE L'EUROPE

87 rue aux Ours, Rouen; tel. 02 32 76 17 76; www.h-europe.fr; from €79 d

A hotel that's full of surprises. For while the basic rooms are fairly bland (though comfortable and clean), it also offers a series of themed rooms, from pop art to rock star. Aside from these, there's an executive feel to the place. It's in a modern building, meaning it's well insulated and relatively spacious, and there's even a small roof terrace where you can escape from Rouen's crowds and enjoy some great views of the city's fantastic churches.

LE CARDINAL

1 place de la Cathédrale, Rouen; tel. 02 35 70 24 42; www.cardinal-hotel.fr; from €88 d

The only hotel in Rouen with direct, unencumbered views of the city cathedral, this otherwise unremarkable place is elevated to a kind of luxury establishment simply because of what can be seen from its windows. Here, you can make like Monet from the comfort of your bed, and watch as the light changes on the Notre Dame's dramatic facade throughout the morning, day, and night. Or you can simply use the hotel as a well-located, reasonably priced base from which to explore the rest of Rouen's old town. WiFi is available throughout, and should you get bored of staring at the cathedral, there are also flat-screen TVs in all of its rooms.

STREET ART HOTEL

6 rue Saint-Étienne des Tonneliers, Rouen; tel. 02 35 88 11 44; https://streetarthotel.com; from €97 d

Undeniably different from every other kind of accommodation Rouen has to offer, this hotel turns on its head the sort of medieval stylings and traditional interiors one might expect from the city and instead provides a very modern vision. Every room is its own pop-art project, decked in collage images, graffiti, and nods to the Warhols, Harings, and Lichtensteins of the world. It also provides WiFi, and there's an on-site bar.

€100-200

HÔTEL DE LA CATHÉDRALE

12 rue Saint-Romain, Rouen; tel. 02 35 71 57 95; www.hotel-de-la-cathedrale.fr; from €105 d

Elegantly fitted inside a 17th-century half-timber house, the Hôtel de la Cathédrale offers a slice of old Rouen grandeur, with plush fittings and a sophisticated courtyard space in which to drink tea. It's close to all the major sights, and despite the building's age, there's no shortage of modern conveniences within, including WiFi and TVs.

HOTEL MERCURE ROUEN CENTRE

7 rue de la Croix de Fer, Rouen; tel. 02 35 52 69 52; www.accorhotels.com/fr/hotel-1301-hotel-mercure-rouen-centre-cathedrale/index.shtml; from €115 d

Offering the reliable executive feel of all Mercure hotels, a stay in this modern building means being in Rouen, but also being able to retreat into a well-insulated international environment at the end of the day. Rooms are air-conditioned and have WiFi and TVs, and some have excellent views out across the old town rooftops. There's also an equally reliable buffet breakfast every morning, and on-site parking is available.

Over €200

HOTEL DE BOURGTHEROULDE

15 place de la Pucelle, Rouen; tel. 02 35 14 50 50; www.marriott.com/hotels/travel/uroak-hotel-de-bourgtheroulde-autograph-collection; from €299 d

Housed within a Flamboyant Gothic 15th-century property, this boutique hotel by Marriott offers a spectacular courtyard, an on-site gym and sauna, and a swimming pool. The rooms are, naturally, fitted to the latest modern standards, while its massive central atrium and bar are renovated in such a way that blends up-to-the minute tastes with medieval extravagance.

INFORMATION

OFFICE DE TOURISME DE ROUEN

25 place de la Cathédrale, Rouen; tel. 02 32 08 32 40; www.rouentourisme.com; 9am-7pm Mon.-Sat., 9:30am-12:30pm and 2pm-6pm Sun.

A sizeable tourist office located in a Gothic-style building, this place provides extensive information on events going on in Rouen and its surrounds. Multiple languages are spoken, and no end of tourist literature is available.

SERVICES

Hospital

CHU DE ROUEN

37 boulevard Gambetta, Rouen; tel. 02 32 88 89 90; www.chu-rouen.fr; 24 hours

This large city hospital connected to Rouen University is located fairly centrally, on the Right Bank and slightly to the east. Waiting times, as with all hospitals, can be long, but it's an urbane enough setting that finding an English-speaking doctor is almost guaranteed.

Post Office

BUREAU DE POSTE

45b rue Jeanne d'Arc, Rouen; www.laposte.fr/particulier; 8am-6pm Mon.-Fri., 9:30am-12:30pm Sat.

There are plenty of post offices in Rouen, of which this is just one. Like most in France, sending or receiving a parcel here can seem intimidating, but in fact there's sleek system of helpers at hand to guide you through. Most of the time, they will approach you shortly after you arrive. There's no guarantee of English being spoken, but the setup is straightforward enough that you should be able to muddle through.

TRANSPORTATION

Getting There

BY CAR

A real transport hub, Rouen is well connected by road to both Paris and everywhere else in Normandy. From the French capital it's about 84 miles (135 kilometers) on the A13 highway, taking two hours. This is a toll road, which will set you back around €6. Avoiding tolls, it's possible to take the D6014, which adds about forty minutes to the journey, and is marginally, though not much, more picturesque. The A13 then carries on to Caen, with further toll charges of around another €6, and a journey time of 1.5 hours. Despite the number of roads that pass through it, Rouen doesn't have a ring road as such. Rather, the main arteries just thread directly through the town, so don't worry if you only mean to pass through and find yourself being directed into the center; it's all part of the system.

BY TRAIN

As much as it's a road hub, Rouen's main station, **Gare de Rouen-Rive-Droite** (place Bernard Tissot, Rouen; tel. 36 35; www.gares-sncf.com/fr/gare/frurd/rouen-rive-droite; 5am-11pm Mon.-Fri., 5:40am-10pm Sat., 6:30am-11:15pm Sun.) is even more important, with trains departing here for all over Normandy—vitally, it's not a terminus, but a junction. Indeed, for many journeys it's an essential connecting station from Paris, and if you are attempting to explore the whole region by train, don't be surprised if you keep having to return here to make connections between even seemingly close-together towns. There are 25 trains daily to Paris, with a journey time of about 1.5 hours and costing €10-24 (€13-18 on weekends); there five or six trains daily to Caen, taking 1 hour 45 minutes and costing around €28; and 16-20 trains daily to Le Havre, journey time one hour, costing €16.

The station sits just above the northern edge of Rouen's old town, with almost all major sights, hotels, and restaurants within a walkable distance.

BY BUS

It's now possible to reach Rouen by coach on the **Flixbus** (www.flixbus.com) from Paris, as it makes its way up to Dieppe. The buses leave from a variety of bus stations in Paris, though mostly Bercy, and stop in Rouen on the town's avenue Champlain, close to the quayside of the city's Left Bank. Prices vary depending on how early you book, but they can be as low as €5, and the journey time is just under two hours. There are between two and three coaches a day. As of yet, there is no direct coach to Caen.

BY AIR

Rouen does have an airport, **Aéroport Rouen Vallée de Seine** (Rue Maryse Bastié, Boos; 02 35 59 16 76 www.rouen.aeroport.fr), though there are only two direct flights coming in and out. One is to Lyon and the other to the city of Bastia in Corsica. Both are with Air France and will set you back around €200 one way.

Getting Around

For most tourists' purposes, Rouen is a fairly walkable city, with most of its main attractions and sights focused around its old town on the Right Bank. Nevertheless, it actually has one of the largest urban transit systems in France, with metro, trams, and buses all an option, run by a company called **Réseau Astuce.** Their website (reseau-astuce.fr/fr/horaires/23) gives you some idea of the extent of this network and its times. The cost of a single ticket on all networks is €1.60.

Another option is Rouen's bike rental network, **Cy'clic** (http://cyclic.rouen.fr), which has 22 stations and 220 bikes in service across the city. Subscriptions can be purchased for one day for €1, seven days for €5, six months for €15, or a year for €25, and the first half hour of cycling is always free regardless of your subscription. Following that, it's another €1 every half hour.

The Seine

Between Rouen and Le Havre, the River Seine meanders through a bucolic idyll of fields, forests, and fruit orchards in a landscape that boasts impressive cliffs rising from the water's edge. A tributary of mass commerce for literally thousands of years, leading eventually to the French capital, it's a historically wealthy area, with no small number of large churches and abbeys—some now lying in ruins—bristling from its towns. Even today, the river is dominated by frequent large barges, shipping the necessities of modern life toward the port at Rouen and beyond.

This said, it's today a fairly sleepy part of Normandy, especially as far as tourists are concerned—the kind of place one might call a backwater, if such a lable weren't so patently technically inaccurate. There's much to see here, and the lush countryside is a hiker's and cyclist's paradise, but many tourists pass over the area in a rush to the coast. It will profit those who pause, however, and allow themselves to get caught up in the leisurely pace of the area, as slow and calm as the Seine itself. A particular delight can be found in taking one of its many **car ferry crossings.** These are free, and very regular along the river's length between Rouen and Caudebec, offering a practical service and a wholly different perspective on the landscape at the same time.

Orientation

Twisting and turning along the path of least resistance, the Seine coils out toward the sea with the sights and major towns along its length nestled in its folds. Taking the small roads that hug the undulating banks of the river, it can take several hours to drive between the region's various towns, but a faster route can be found on the D982, which runs north of the river, linking Rouen directly to Caudebec-en-Caux in under 50 minutes. Of course, the farther you stray from this main artery, the sleepier and more bucolic the landscape becomes. Despite a general lack of bridges, the river can be crossed at various points along its length via free car ferry services, which run multiple times every day.

Crossing the Seine

The ferries, or *bacs,* along this part of the Seine help lend this region its unique character. These are simple roll-on roll-off boats that look a bit like floating platforms. They can fit roughly eight cars per crossing and multiple cyclists or pedestrians. There are numerous ports, making efficient substitutes for bridges between Rouen and Caudebec-en-Caux.

Crossings happen roughly every 15 minutes throughout the day, with an hour-long break for lunch, threading between the cargo-carrying barges on their way to Paris and Rouen. The services start at around 6am and continue until around 9pm, with slightly more limited hours on bank holidays and weekends. For precise timings, please consult the regional website: www.seinemaritime.fr/vos-services/transport-routes/se-deplacer-en-seine-maritime/les-bacs-et-horaires.html.

The ferries are free, and offer a relaxing, different perspective on the region. It's well worth taking one for more than just practical reasons.

- **Right Bank ports**: Yainville, Jumièges, Le Mesnil-sous-Jumièges, Duclair, Sahurs, Val-de-la-Haye, Dieppedalle
- **Left Bank ports**: Quillebeuf-sur-Seine, Heurteauville, Port-Jumièges, Yville-sur-Seine, Berville-sur-Seine, La Bouille, Port-Jérôme, Petit-Couronne, Le Grand-Quevilly

JUMIÈGES

A sleepy but very pleasant village along the banks of the Seine, Jumièges could easily have been overlooked by history were it not for the presence of a towering abbey built here in the 11th century. Dominating the landscape for miles around, Jumièges Abbey is this region's undisputed number-one tourist sight, and has awarded the village something of its own cottage industry. Tourist numbers are hardly overwhelming, but are enough to sustain several restaurants and hotels in the nearby area. The town is abundant with fruit orchards and threaded by narrow roads, making for a very pleasant drive, and also has a ferry service connecting it to the tiny hamlet of Heurteauville on the other side of the Seine.

Sights

★ JUMIÈGES ABBEY

24 rue Guillaume le Conquérant, Jumièges; tel. 02 35 37 24 02; www.abbayedejumieges.fr; 9:30am-6:30pm daily mid.-Apr.-mid.-Sept., 9:30am-1pm and 2:30pm-5:30pm daily mid-Sept.-mid-Apr.; adults €6.50, reduced €4

Jumièges Abbey is a rare example of a religious building in Normandy that lost its battle against the ravages of time, but nevertheless was still considered too impressive, too important, to pull down completely. Now, only the magnificent ruin of this place that was once a power center in medieval France remains, and is an affecting testament to the hubris of human endeavor.

Founded in 654, Jumièges quickly rose to prominence on account of good management and an enviable position on the banks of the Seine River, which then was one of the safest and fastest ways of traveling through France. It was built up on a massive scale, the new church being consecrated in 1067, in the presence of William the Conqueror himself. At its height, it was one of the most powerful institutions in the whole country. Its fall came slowly, suffering in the Hundred Years' War, and later France's Wars of Religion. It was only in the French Revolution, though, that it was sacked for good, and reduced to the ruin that we see today.

Now, to walk around it can feel something like exploring some forgotten temple of the ancient world. A substantial amount of the abbey's main Gothic church remains, with the crumbling facade visible from miles around. But this no longer has a roof, and covering its exposed floor is only grass. Scattered around the church's caracass, meanwhile, are substantial sections of archways, pillars, and walls, with the sight covering an area almost the size of a football pitch (soccer field)—big enough that visitor numbers seldom overwhelm, meaning you'll have space for contemplation. It can be rushed around in less

wandering the Jumièges Abbey ruins

than half an hour, but if the ruin captures your imagination, expect to stay longer, musing on how this place that was once one of the centers of European diplomacy and learning has been reduced to a lifeless but still affecting sculpture, incongruous in its domination of a sleepy village on the banks of the Seine. Note: There's no shelter in the ruins, so if it's raining, bring an umbrella, or you'll get wet!

Food

AUBERGE DU BAC

2 rue Alphonse Callais, Jumièges; tel. 02 35 37 24 16; www.aubergedubac.fr; 12pm-2pm and 7pm-9pm Wed.-Sun.; lunch menus €12.50-14.50, evening menus €18.50-37

A straightforward rural restaurant, this place serves decent, earthy, and rustic cuisine, such as steak and potatoes with rich sauce. The Auberge de Bac's real draw is its location, directly on the banks of the Seine, looking straight out to Jumièges's ferry dock, from which it gets its name. It's best on warm days when you can sit on its terrace and watch the ferry ship back and forth, while sipping a cool Muscadet and contemplating whether to opt for the cheese course or dessert (or both!).

AUBERGE DES RUINES

17 place de la Mairie, Jumièges; tel. 02 35 37 24 05; www.auberge-des-ruines.fr; 12pm-2pm and 7pm-9pm daily; menus €33-50

This is an upmarket restaurant in the shadow of Jumièges Abbey. The chef, Christophe Mauduit, works with local farms to offer his interpretation of Norman terroir, which changes with the seasons, from pan-fried scallops to generous cuts of local beef. Food is served in a stylish modern interior, decorated by the work of local artists. It's a relatively formal restaurant, attracting day-trippers from Rouen as much as tourists. Hours are liable to change out of season, so check before dining between September and June. Booking is essential, particularly for weekend lunchtimes. Expect fewer crowds in the evening midweek however.

Bicycling along the Seine

With many small roads and relatively little heavy traffic, the Seine region is prime cycling country, especially along the water's edge. Bike routes are well signposted and popular. Cycling the full 62-mile (100-kilometer) journey from Rouen to Le Havre is a well-traveled route, and a fit cyclist should be able to tackle it in 5-6 hours. It's possible to make the journey longer or shorter, either by really hugging the water's edge and crossing on ferries where you feel like it, or by cutting out some of the longer bends. For those wanting a shorter trip, from Rouen to Caudebec is about 22 miles (36 kilometers) and can be easily cycled in less than three hours. Jumièges to Caudebec is a little over 9 miles (15 kilometers) and should take under an hour.

Accommodations

DOMAINE LE CLOS DES FONTAINES

191 rue des Fontaines, Jumièges; tel. 02 35 33 96 96; www.leclosdesfontaines.com; from €197 d

Just a short walk from both the abbey and the Seine, this hotel occupies a traditional Norman half-timber building. Rooms are extremely cozy, decorated with a kind of rustic luxury, which includes wood or tile flooring and delicately patterned wallpaper. There are also TVs and minibars. Finally, there's an on-site spa and swimming pool, surrounded by Normandy green.

CAMPING DE LA FÔRET

582 rue Mainberte, Jumièges; tel. 02 35 37 93 43; www.campinglaforet.com; Apr.-Oct.; pitches from €30, cabins from €100

This straightforward though still well accommodated campsite in the rural surroundings of Jumièges offers services, such as the swimming pool and climbing frame, on a fairly small scale, but they are there, and there's a convivial, family-friendly atmosphere throughout. There's an on-site bar open 6pm-9pm, and both bikes and electric bikes can be hired for from €10 per day from the reception.

Getting There and Around

BY CAR

From Rouen, the D982 is the fastest way to get into the Seine region. For getting to Jumièges, turn off onto the D143 in Yainville, making for the river. It should take about 45 minutes and is a journey of around 17 miles (28 kilometers).

There are also multiple smaller roads around the region, some hardly more than a single lane, which can make for some very picturesque driving. The ferries that cross the Seine here are free and are designed to traffic cars.

BY BICYCLE

In Jumièges, the best place to hire bikes from is the **Camping de la Fôret** (582 rue Mainberte, Jumièges; tel. 02 35 37 93 43; www.campinglaforet.com), which can be done for from €10 a day.

BY BUS

The regional No. 30 bus route, which leaves from Rouen's Halte Routière (11 rue des Charrettes) for Caudebec-en-Caux multiple times a day, is the only way of getting to Jumièges by public transport. However, it only runs direct to the town during July and August, costing just €2, with a journey time of around 50 minutes. To get to Jumièges, it's necessary to take the same bus route to Yainville and walk the final kilometer. Full details of its schedule can be found at www.jumieges.fr/medias/File/transport/depliant_30.pdf.

The bus route is also the only public transport for getting around the Seine region.

BY FERRY

For the ferries (6am-9pm, one-hour break for lunch, about every 15 min., free) that shuttle cars, bicycles, and pedestrians across the Seine, there are Right Bank ports at Yainville, Jumièges, and Le Mesnil-sous-Jumièges, and Left Bank ports at Heurteauville, Port-Jumièges, and Yville-sur-Seine. For precise timings, please consult the regional website: www.seinemaritime.fr/vos-services/transport-routes/se-deplacer-en-seine-maritime/les-bacs-et-horaires.html.

CAUDEBEC-EN-CAUX

A picturesque and prosperous town hugging the banks of the Seine, Caudebec-en-Caux is well served by its geography. For a long time, it profited from being on the banks of the same river as Rouen and Paris, though as trade has become more mechanized and less inclined to pausing, the town has had to rely more on tourists to make its money.

Not a sight as such, but well worth peeking into as you wander around the town, are the residents' terraced gardens that decorate its elevations, creating almost a floral amphitheater looking out across the sweeping bend in the Seine on which Caudebec rests. The town also boasts a surprisingly fine church—Notre Dame de Caudebec-en-Caux, which King Henry IV dubbed the most beautiful in his kingdom. The town is also the site of a large modern bridge, the Pont de Brotonne, built in the 1970s, which represents a full stop to the ferry services that dot the river from Rouen. It can be seen clearly from the town. This also marks a point where the surroundings begin to get busier and more built up, and the last stretch of the Seine starts to merge into the suburbs of Le Havre.

If you've the money, this small town is also the unlikely home of one of the finest dining experiences in Normandy: the Manoir de Rétival invites guests to dine in its traditional kitchen, the food that comes out of which is intimately connected with the local terroir, playfully modern and relentlessly delicious.

Sights

NOTRE-DAME DE CAUDEBEC-EN-CAUX

Rue Jean Prévost, Caudebec-en-Caux; tel. 02 32 70 46 32; 9am-12pm and 2pm-6pm daily; free

One of the best things about Normandy is its wealth of authentic wonders in unexpected places. The Notre Dame de Caudebec-en-Caux is just one of these. Built in the Flamboyant Gothic style, it was described by King Henry IV as the most beautiful chapel in his kingdom (that, despite it not technically being a chapel). Literally covered in finely carved human figures (333 in total,) it is an endlessly beguiling "Where's Waldo" of a structure, and made even more impressive by the fact that there is seldom anyone else around, meaning visitors can appreciate its beauty in solitude and with plenty of time.

L'ABBAYE SAINT-WANDRILLE DE FONTENELLE

2 rue Saint-Jacques, Saint-Wandrille-Rançon; tel. 02 35 96 23 11; www.st-wandrille.com; 5:15am-1pm and 2pm-9:15pm daily; free

This still-functioning abbey built in the Carolingian style and added to over the years was founded in the almost impossibly distant AD 649. As with its neighbor at Jumièges, the monastery was at once very successful, both economically and spiritually—a number of saints emerged from its orders.

Its fortunes fluctuated over the ensuing centuries, as the Seine became less important in the running of France. Eventually, it, like Jumièges close by, could not withstand the trials of the French Revolution, being partially demolished and seemingly about to fall into complete disrepair. However, it was restored, and effectively re-founded by one George Sanislaus in the late 19th century, since when it has continued to prosper.

Today, its buildings remain an intriguing blend of different architectural epochs: Medieval cloisters taper into simple 19th-century housing and splendid intricate carvings punctuate its hallways, while its southeast corner remains as an unrestored but perfectly preserved ruin, the many thin vertical lines of its design looking almost like a petrified waterfall cascading from the craggy rocks of a Gothic mountain. Topping this off, one of the most compelling things about this abbey is that it remains fully in use, with monks wandering its grounds and hallways and performing several services throughout the day in the modest on-site church. These are technically free to attend, but donations are welcome. One of the most fascinating things is the chance to compare this living tradition to the gloriously ruined Jumièges Abbey down the road.

And for those who want to take their experience even deeper, it's possible to organize a retreat at the abbey, living among the monks. For single women or couples who wish to do this, contact st.joseph@st-wandrille.com; for men contact hotellerie@st-wandrille.com. Please be aware that this should be regarded as a spiritual service that they offer, and is not meant for casual tourists.

Food

★ MANOIR DE RÉTIVAL

2 rue Saint-Clair, Caudebec-en-Caux; tel. 06 50 23 43 63; http://restaurant-ga.fr; 12pm-2pm and 7:30pm-9pm Wed.-Sat., 12pm-2pm Sun., closed Jan.; menus €69-149

Sitting somewhere near the apex cuisine anywhere in the region, the Manoir de Rétival invites guests into its kitchen to sit around rustic wooden tables and watch its chef prepare dishes of the utmost quality. Choice is limited, and dietary requirements are not catered to, but the quality is resoundingly superb. There are few places that offer an experience as close to the Norman terroir, which they do almost counterintuitively by juxtaposing it with some unlikely international ingredients: Szechuan pepper accompanies local beef, truffles meet cream, oysters come baked in cheese and dusted with fish eggs. The restaurant is situated in a 12th-century manor, which is also a luxurious homestay, with views out across the Seine. Reservations are required.

AU FIL DU TEMPS

34 rue Saint-Clair, Caudebec-en-Caux; tel. 02 35 96 20 01; www.aufildutemps76.fr; 12pm-2:30pm Tues.-Wed., 12pm-2:30pm and 7pm-9:30pm Thurs.-Sat., 12pm-6pm Sun.; mains €13-23

Located under the shade of an old tree, and

1: a stream in Caudebec's floral backstreets 2: the grounds of the luxurious Manoir de Rétival

1

2

just back from the Seine, this is a straightforward French restaurant offering decent, tasty food, boasting Norman and French flavors: Think steak and fries washed down with cider, chased by a plate of cheese. It's particularly pleasant because of its terrace, even if the road that it sits on can get a little busy at times.

RENDEZ-VOUS DES CHASSEURS

1040 route de Sainte-Gertrude, Maulévrier-Sainte-Gertrude; tel. 02 35 96 20 30; 12pm-2pm and 7pm-9pm Tues. and Thurs.-Sat., 12pm-2pm Sun.; mains €21-30

With a name that literally means "the hunters' meeting place," this is a restaurant with strong links to the surrounding countryside. Off the beaten track—it's a little outside of Caudebec itself—it's very much in place for locals and has a friendly, welcoming atmosphere, with the proprietor often out front shaking the hands of his patrons. The food is full of rich flavor, including unapologetically generous slabs of foie gras, and in the winter months a log fire is lit, making it all the cozier. Booking, especially on the weekend, is recommended.

BRASSERIE DU BAC

4 quai Guilbaud, Caudebec-en-Caux; tel. 02 35 96 25 44; 9am-10:30pm Wed.-Thurs., 9am-11:30pm Fri.-Sun., 9am-5pm Mon.; mains €10-13

Not offering anything too flashy, this is a simple French brasserie that nevertheless provides food as good as you'd likely get elsewhere, but at a far lower price. The fish dishes come particularly highly recommended, with the usual combination of Normandy flavors all on display. It's on the riverfront too, which means you can watch the cargo barges slide by while enjoying your meal.

Accommodations

LOGIS HÔTEL LE CHEVAL BLANC

4 place René Coty, Caudebec-en-Caux; tel. 02 35 96 21 66; www.le-cheval-blanc.fr; from €65 d

Almost the archetypal budget hotel in the French countryside, this is a family-run place, the likes of which have been offering travelers places to lay their heads for generations. It's too tacky to really be called traditional, but you get the feeling that the kitsch has always been there in some iteration; it's simply moved with the times. There are hundreds of places like this across France, if not thousands; to anyone who's spent any time passing through the country, they form an essential part of its identity. The rooms are comfortable enough, and there's WiFi throughout.

MANOIR DE RÉTIVAL

2 rue Saint-Clair, Caudebec-en-Caux; tel. 06 50 23 43 63; http://restaurant-ga.fr; from €180 d

"The manor is not a hotel," announces Manoir de Rétival's own tourist literature, in what can only be described as a questionable marketing strategy designed to confuse potential guests. Because it *is* a hotel, an extremely luxurious one, set in the same 12th-century château that plays host to the exceptional restaurant. The pleading otherwise is intended to highlight the place's informality, that guests here are to feel more like family friends than paying customers, and indeed, the different designs of every room and the eccentric furniture certainly contribute to that effect. The château hasn't been planned like this, exactly; it just is. It has an excellent view out across the Seine and a charming terrace, and the on-site restaurant is second to very few.

CAMPING MUNICIPAL DU PARC

65 rue Victor Hugo, La Mailleraye-sur-Seine; tel. 02 35 37 12 04; from €9.50

France's municipal campsites are a godsend to the budget traveler. There's nothing remotely extraneous to this one. It offers, quite simply, well-tended patches of grass in a secluded spot, not too far out of town (not Caudebec, but La Mailleraye-sur-Seine), plus toilets and showers, and all for less than €10. An ideal base for exploring the Seine region on a shoestring.

Information

OFFICE DE TOURISME CAUX VALLÉE DE SEINE

Place du Général De Gaulle, Bord de Seine, Caudebec-en-Caux; tel. 02 32 70 46 32; www.normandie-caux-seine-tourisme.com; 10:30am-12:30pm and 1:30pm-5pm Mon.-Sat.

A modern, purpose-built tourist office on the banks of the Seine. It's full of leaflets about walks and bike trails in the region, and its staff can help with advice on what to do, or booking hotels. There's also a small gift shop inside. Most of the staff should speak some English.

Getting There and Around

BY CAR

For getting to Caudebec from Rouen, the D982 is the only road you need. The journey is around 23 miles (38 kilometers) and takes about 50 minutes. Outside Caudebec, the D982 continues out of town until Tancarville, where it turns into the A131 and can be followed all the way to Le Havre, which is 30 miles (51 kilometers) from Caudebec in the opposite direction. Thanks to faster roads, this journey should also take about 50 minutes.

There are also multiple smaller roads around the region, some hardly more than a single lane, which can make for some very picturesque driving.

The ferries that cross the Seine here are free and are designed to traffic cars.

BY BICYCLE

Caudebec sits along the popular 62-mile (100-kilometer) journey between Rouen and Le Havre along the Seine. In Caudebec, the best place to hire bikes from is **Velhano Sarl** (10 rue de la Vicomte, Caudebec-en-Caux; tel. 2 35 96 24 77), where having a bike for a full day is €11.50.

BY BUS

The regional No. 30 bus route leaves from Rouen's Halte Routière (11 rue des Charrettes) for Caudebec-en-Caux multiple times a day. However, it only runs direct to the town during July and August, costing just €2, with a journey time of around 50 minutes. Full details of its schedule can be found at www.jumieges.fr/medias/File/transport/depliant_30.pdf.

The bus route is also the only public transport for getting around the Seine region.

In the other direction, the similarly priced Line 20 connects Le Havre to Caudebec-en-Caux. It leaves multiple times a day from outside Le Havre train station (more in the summer) with a journey time of just under two hours. See this web page for full route details: www.caux-estuaire.fr/wp-content/uploads/2016/01/76-Ligne-20-Le-Havre-Caudebec-en-Caux-10p-ex8P.pdf.

Dieppe

More commonly passed through than stopped in, cross-Channel ferry port Dieppe is an underrated Norman gem. Though it's a little rough around the edges, and its seafront suffered in the Second World War, much of its old town remains intact and is very much a working center rather than one kept pristine for tourists. This is most apparent on Saturdays, when the town hosts one of the best and liveliest food markets in the region.

Dieppe has a prosperous history. Developing out of a fishing settlement in the 11th century, it spent much of the next thousand years with its eyes cast to the rest of the world. France's most advanced cartography school was based here during the golden age of exploration, and it was an important port for sending men on discovery missions to the Americas. This worldly quality can be seen in some of the town's indigenous cuisine; as well

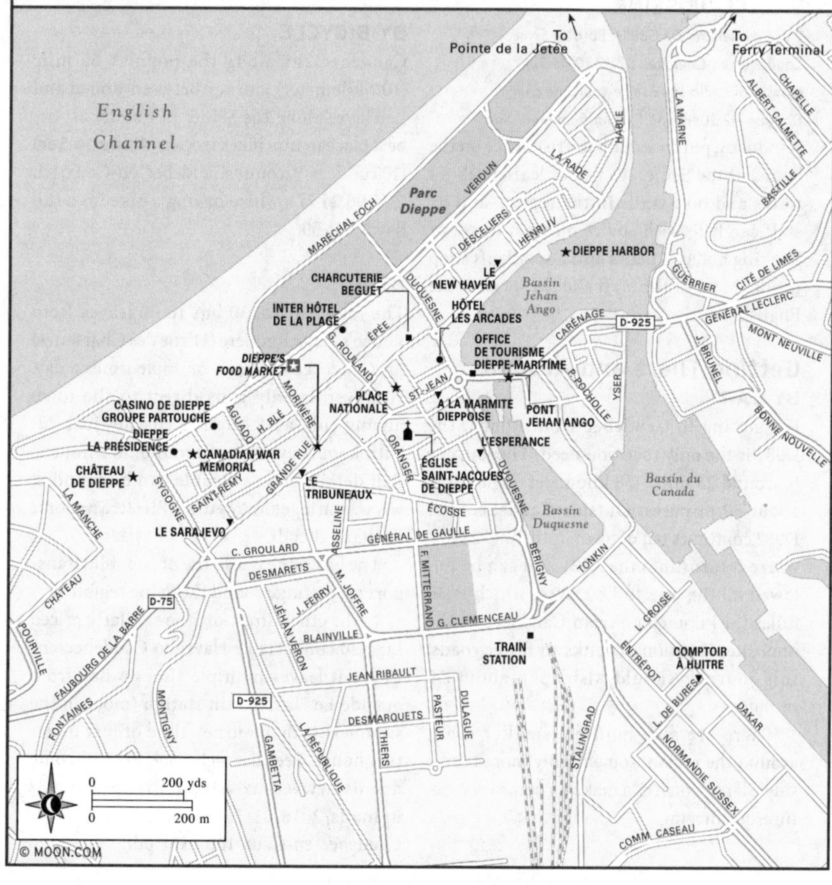

as being famous for its scallops, there is the *marmite Dieppoise*, a fish stew for which the exotic saffron is a key ingredient—this can be sampled in most of the town's excellent harbor-front restaurants.

In North America, meanwhile, Dieppe is best known for the disastrous commando raid that took place here in World War II. This happened in 1942 and resulted in the deaths of 1,400 Allied soldiers, most from the Second Canadian Infantry Division.

Orientation

A port town with a long pebbly beach, Dieppe's beating heart is its pedestrianized **Grande Rue,** which runs almost parallel to the beach, behind the first row of houses about 650 feet (200 meters) inland. This road skirts the north side of the Place National, on the other side of which is the town's main church, and ends in a harbor space, the banks of which are crowded by restaurants. The ferry port is a relatively small operation and can be found in the town's east. Outside of its center, Dieppe becomes hilly on all sides.

SIGHTS

★ Dieppe's Food Market

Grande Rue, Dieppe; 8am-12pm Sat.

A wonderful showcase of the produce that Normandy has to offer, this market assembles every Saturday morning for 4-5 bustling hours. There's everything from oozing cheeses to mud-covered potatoes to ripe Norman apples on display. Regularly voted the best market in Normandy, it's nevertheless utterly without pretense. Taking up the entirety of the Grande Rue, and spilling over onto some of Dieppe's other streets besides, this is where locals come every week to do their basic shopping. Follow the crowd to find the best stalls. If you're looking to buy ingredients for a picnic, keep your eyes peeled for dried meats, cheeses, and rotisserie chicken. There are also some stalls cooking fresh paella and *marmite Dieppoise* in large pots that can be ordered to go. After this, the seafront is a decent picnic spot, or if you've got a car, head out of town toward Pourville, where the beach is quieter and more picturesque.

Dieppe Harbor

Quai Henri IV, Dieppe

Back in the 17th century, Dieppe was one of the most important ports in all of France. Traces of its old riches remain, particularly along its harbor front, where a number of grand old buildings still teeter gracefully facing the water. Most are thin buildings, with tall, elegant windows, now with a row of bustling restaurants often occupying their ground floors. It was deemed sufficiently appealing to once have been painted by British artist J. M. W. Turner, whose 1826 painting attests that aside from the types of vessels that now occupy the harbor waters, not that much has changed since the 19th century. Keep an eye out for the neoclassical facade of the now-residential 1609 Hôtel D'Anvers at number 49—it bears the date 1697 over its door, though this was just when it received its first restoration.

On the weekend, particularly in the summer, it's well worth following the whole length of the harbor out onto the long concrete spit that is the **Pointe de la Jetée.** This manmade barrier against the sea is a popular fishing spot for locals, and can get very busy. The sight of 30, perhaps 50, Norman men stood in a long line tussling with their fishing rods or hauling in crab nets is as fine a sight as any in Dieppe, and speaks as much of the town's culture as any of its buildings.

Canadian War Memorial (Square du Canada)

900 rue de Sygogne, Dieppe; open year-round; free

Located at the far western end of Dieppe's beachfront and shadowed by the town's château, a simple garden emblazoned with two floral maple leaves and marked by a plaque commemorates the sacrifice of the Canadian commandos who perished during the disastrous raid on Dieppe during the Second World War (see callout). It remains a place of pilgrimage for Canadian tourists and is as important in their history books as any of the D-Day memorials farther down the coast.

Canadian War Cemetery

14 rue des 4 Vents, Hautot-sur-Mer; www.veterans.gc.ca/eng/remembrance/memorials/overseas/second-world-war/france/dieppe_cem; open year-round; free

This is the final resting place of 944 men from the Allied forces who were killed in 1942 during the Dieppe Raid, 707 of whom are Canadian. It is a unique cemetery, having been created during the war by the Germans—the military catastrophe of the Dieppe Raid necessitating that many dead should be left behind in enemy territory. As such, the headstones are back-to-back, and in long double rows in the German style. Nevertheless, when the Allies retook Dieppe in 1944, they felt it would be more respectful to leave the bodies undisturbed, and so left the cemetery as it was.

Église Saint-Jacques de Dieppe

10 rue Sainte-Catherine, Dieppe; tel. 02 35 84 21 65; 9am-7pm daily; free

A weather-beaten though still-imposing

1
2
3
BOULANGERIE
Patisserie
LA DANSE DES CRAYONS

church begun in the 13th century by Guillaume de Flavacourt, the then-Archbishop of Rouen. The choir, the nave, and the aisles date from the 14th century, and were followed by the tower in the 16th century, the finish of the church being Flamboyant Gothic in style. Its Chapelle du Trésor boasts a frieze portraying the various nations and cultures discovered by Dieppoise sailors, including Native American peoples. This was commisioned by one of the wealthiest Norman shipping maganates of the 16th century, Jean Ango, who was a patron of the church.

Dedicateed to Saint James, it was a stopping-off point for pilgrims making the trip to Santiago de Compostela by sea. Accordingly, the scallop shell of Saint James occurs regularly in its decoration—scallops also being, of course, a Dieppe specialty.

Today, the church still gets more use as an actual church than as a tourist attraction, which means that despite its size, outside of service times you're likely to find yourself enjoying it more or less alone. The flip side of this is that it also has a slightly neglected quality, which conversely offers it a more "authentic" feel. Mass takes place at 6:30pm on Monday, 7am on Tuesday, 8:30am on Friday, and 11am on Sunday.

Château de Dieppe

Rue de Chastes, Dieppe; tel. 02 35 06 61 99; 10am-6pm Wed.-Sun.; adults €4.50, under 25 free

Looming over the rest of the town, the exact origins of the Château de Dieppe are a mystery. Certainly, parts of it date back to the 12th century, such as a castle built by either Richard the Lionheart or Henry II of England. That castle, however, was mostly destroyed by the French in 1195, and it likely remained like that until a full restoration in 1433. Today, it still does a passable job of looking almost like a child's idea of a castle, and indeed its defensive capabilities were enhanced during the Second World War, when it was reinforced as part of Hitler's Atlantic Wall.

As well as its primary function, though, it has been used as a prison for counterrevolutionaries during the French Revolution, a barracks, and is today is home to the Dieppe Museum, with its collection of fine ivory sculptures, maritime exhibitions, and the effects of the composer Camille Saint-Saëns. The interiors are split between wood-paneled and early 19th century, some with exposed brick walls that hark back to the castle's more distant heritage. A number of rusting period canons line its battlements, from which some great views of Dieppe's seafront can be seen.

FESTIVALS AND EVENTS

DIEPPE RETRO

Grande Rue, Dieppe; tel. 02 35 82 49 29; www.dieppereretro.org; first weekend in Sept.; free for spectators

Among Dieppe's lesser-known claims to fame, it was the location of the very first motor Grand Prix. This was in 1907, back when the contest was a road race, and public roads surrounding the town were closed to make way for some hair-raising heroics on massively powerful, almost out-of-control, bygone machines. The Dieppe Retro commemorates this event, albeit sedately, with participants in classic cars from the 1950s and earlier parading around Dieppe and its surrounds. They stop in numerous towns and, on the Sunday, along Dieppe's Grande Rue, when spectators can closely inspect the cars.

LES FÊTES DES HARENGS

Quai Henri IV, Dieppe; 11am-4pm weekends in Nov.

Literally a movable feast, this festival, which takes place not just in Dieppe but in several other towns along the Alabaster Coast, coincides with, and celebrates, the migration of herrings toward the Atlantic. Each town's festivities occur when the shoals are said to be closest by, and therefore most easily fished from. In Dieppe, barbecues and tents are set up around the harbor, smoke rises into the

1: fishing off Dieppe harbor 2: strings of garlic and smoked garlic 3: root vegetables at Dieppe market

A Canadian Tragedy

A distant precursor to D-Day, the **Dieppe Raid** was one of the great Allied catastrophes of the Second World War. Ever since the evacuation from Dunkirk in 1940, the western Allies had been planning a route back into mainland Europe. The objective of assaulting Dieppe, however, was not to begin an invasion of enemy territory, but rather to explore the possibilities for doing so in the future. Dieppe was to be taken, intelligence was to be gathered, then it was to be relinquished and some German sea defenses to be destroyed in the retreat. None of these objectives were accomplished.

The assault consisted of around 6,000 men—5,000 from Canada, thanks to pressure from the Canadian government to make sure their troops saw some combat—landing on the beaches head-on, without aerial bombardment in support. There was minimal intelligence on enemy positions, with certain German gun emplacements dug into the headland cliffs not seen in reconnaissance photos. Meanwhile, the gradients of the landing beaches had to be worked out just by looking at holiday photos. To make matters worse, the Germans had been tipped off about the possibility of an assault on Dieppe by their spies, and so were on high alert.

As such, the raid was an almost complete disaster from the moment it began at 4:50am on August 19. Men were cut down by German machine gun fire at all six of the main landing beaches, with scenes of absolute carnage and confusion described across the front. Tanks became bogged in the shingle, and on one beach a smokescreen supposedly to shield Allied troops just blotted out their objectives and fed disarray. A retreat was issued at 11am the same day. But over half of the men who went ashore that day did not return; more than 3,600 of them were killed, wounded, or captured by the enemy. German casualties were 591.

The one glimmer of light the Allies were later able to take from this tragic fiasco was that it prepared them for D-Day, having offered bloody instruction of everything they ought not to do.

wintry sky, and endless herrings are served char-grilled on paper plates.

SHOPPING

CHARCUTERIE BEGUET

22 Grande Rue, Dieppe; tel. 02 32 14 08 20; www.traiteurcroyaldieppe.fr; 8:30am-1pm and 2:30pm-6:45pm Mon.-Fri., 8:30am-6:45pm Sat.

This excellent local charcuterie and general delicatessen offers a wide selection of meats, cheeses, and expertly crafted finger foods. A thoroughly local establishment, it's often dropped in on by the people of Dieppe after shopping at the Saturday food market in order to buy something special to finish off their planned meal. Prices reflect the quality, but the reliance on local custom keeps them competitive.

FOOD

Local Cuisine

★ LE TRIBUNAUX

1 place du Puits Salé, Dieppe; tel. 02 32 14 44 65; 9am-8pm daily; mains €8-20

Who cares that its Bavarian stylings don't make much sense? The Tribunaux is a landmark café in the traditional, community-hub style. With its two-level interior and terrace that aprons far out into the street, it has space for well over 100 customers at a time, and on market day the locals queue outside, waiting for a table. The food itself is seldom much more than acceptable, traditional French fare: a combination of meats, fries, and salads. But the café is so overflowing with life that it doesn't seem to matter. The best deal is on drinks, which usually come served with complimentary fries.

COMPTOIR À HUITRE

Cours de Dakar, Dieppe; tel. 02 35 84 19 37; 12pm-2pm and 7:30pm-9:30pm Tues.-Sat.; mains €21-35

A seafood eater's paradise. The interior is charmingly kitschy, though the tablecloths gleam white and always look freshly starched: One has a feeling it can't have changed much in years. The seafood and fish dishes are expertly prepared, and are often served without too much added, their flavors and freshness allowed to speak for themselves. It's justifiably popular among locals, especially on Friday and Saturday evenings, when booking is highly advised.

A LA MARMITE DIEPPOISE

8 rue Saint-Jean, Dieppe; tel. 02 35 84 24 26; https://marmitedieppoise.fr; 11am-2pm and 7pm-10pm Tues.-Sat., 11am-2pm Sun.; lunch menu €21, evening menus €33-44

Another excellent seafood restaurant, dedicated to making the absolute best of local flavors and freshly caught fish. The *marmite Dieppoise* itself, which is a lavish multifish stew flavored with cream and saffron, is particularly recommended. There are also plenty of good options on the menu for non-fish-eaters, and food comes served in a cozy, formal setting, usually full of local diners. Reservations, especially on the weekends, are advised.

LE NEW HAVEN

53 quai Henri IV, Dieppe; tel. 02 35 84 89 72; www.restaurantdieppe.fr; 11:45am-1:45pm and 6:30pm-9:15pm Thurs.-Mon., 11:45am-1:45pm Tues.; mains €16.50-33.90

The quai Henri IV on Dieppe's harbor front is full of decent bistros and restaurants, of which Le New Haven is just one. The food quality in all of them is of a similar fortifying and robust standard, making the most of local ingredients, particularly mussels, scallops, and turbot. Named for the British ferry port on the other side of the Channel to Dieppe, Le New Haven in particular offers a comfortable, light-filled dining experience, and there's a terrace for sunny days. Though it can get popular, especially on market day, there's not really too pressing a need to book, as should they be out of space, one of the neighboring restaurants can always be popped into instead for much the same kind of honest meal.

Budget Options

LE SARAJEVO

52 rue de la Barre, Dieppe; tel. 02 35 84 17 31; 7am-10pm Mon.-Thurs., 7am-11pm Fri.-Sat., 8am-7pm Sun., lunch service 12pm-2:30pm daily, dinner service 7pm-9:30pm Tues.-Sat.; mains €9-15

In theory, a Yugoslavian-themed restaurant; in practice, it serves lots of grilled meat on sticks. Nevertheless, it's a decent, friendly place, which offers a break from the many complex sauces of Normandy cooking in exchange for simpler fare. It remains open as a bar/café throughout the day, and is a good informal place to take a pause while exploring Dieppe.

L'ESPERANCE

50 quai Duquesne, Dieppe; tel. 02 35 06 19 34; 12pm-3pm and 7pm-10pm Thurs.-Mon., 12pm-3pm Tues.; mains €7-15

Its menu looks similar to many other places around town with the difference being the prices—the same dishes are about €3 cheaper across the board, and with little noticeable difference in quality from many of the other harbor-front eateries. Yes, the interior is fairly basic, but that's part of its charm.

ACCOMMODATIONS

€50-100

INTER HÔTEL DE LA PLAGE

20 boulevard de Verdun, Dieppe; tel. 02 35 84 18 28; www.plagehotel-dieppe.com; from €77 d (€107 with sea view)

On Dieppe's beachfront, which since its demolition during the Second World War has not been much to write home about, this is a large, relatively modern hotel with spacious rooms. Though the rooms are supposedly designed with a nautical theme, in reality they're fairly basic. Sea views are good, though, and

des Tribunaux
Café des Tribunaux
Café des Tribunaux
Le plat du marche
Dos de Cabillaud, linguine nero, émulsion de crustacés 16,90
La suggestion du jour
Choucroute de Jarret confit 16,50
1
2
RESTAURANT
de la mer
LE NEW HAVEN
LE NEW HAVEN
HAVEN
A EMPORTER
Plateaux de fruits de mer
METIER GLACIER

there are flat-screen TVs, bathtubs, and WiFi throughout the building.

HÔTEL LES ARCADES

1-3 arc de la Bourse, Dieppe; tel. 02 35 84 14 12; www.lesarcades-dieppe.fr; €85 d

Dieppe's harbor front boasts a number of elegant arcades, lending the town an almost Italianate flair. This hotel is located above them, with some nice views out across the harbor and toward the sea. The decoration of the rooms is pretty pedestrian, but many have floor-to-ceiling windows, which let in plenty of light. They also have flat-screen TVs and free Wi-Fi access throughout.

€100-200

CASINO DE DIEPPE GROUPE PARTOUCHE

3 boulevard de Verdun, Dieppe; tel. 02 32 14 48 00; www.casinodieppe.com; €133 d

A large hotel in a modern building with vast windows in most rooms, it offers good views out toward the sea. The rooms are clean, comfortable and adequately stylish. It also offers the kind of service one expects from a four-star establishment, and flat-screen TVs and WiFi are standard in all the rooms. Be warned, however, that the casino doubles as Dieppe's most popular nightclub, so there may be some noise outside on Friday and Saturday evenings.

DIEPPE LA PRÉSIDENCE

1 boulevard de Verdun, Dieppe; tel. 02 35 84 31 31; www.accorhotels.com/gb/hotel-7014-mercure-dieppe-la-presidence-hotel/index.shtml; €118 d

Part of the Mercure chain, this hotel provides a reliable kind of midrange luxury. Rooms are pleasant and clean, and many have good sea views. There's also an on-site aquatic thalassotherapy (sea-water therapy) center with an indoor pool and a heated outdoor one. It's right next door to the Casino de Dieppe Groupe Partouche, too, which is a double-edged sword: The casino doubles as Dieppe's most popular nightclub, so things can get noisy on Friday and Saturday nights.

Camping

CAMPING MARQUEVAL

1210 rue de la Mer, Hautot-sur-Mer; tel. 02 35 82 66 46; www.campinglemarqueval.com; open Mar. 20-Oct. 14; pitches from €27, cabins from €60

A lakeside campsite surrounded by rolling hills and just a short distance from the beach, barely 10 minutes' drive from Dieppe, it offers a variety of different cabin options, plus an on-site swimming pool and bar. Fishing is possible in the lake, and there's a petting zoo to keep kids entertained. Regular concerts are staged during the summer season for the benefit of campers.

INFORMATION

OFFICE DE TOURISME DIEPPE-MARITIME

Pont Jehan Ango, Dieppe; tel. 02 32 14 40 60; www.dieppetourisme.com; 9am-7pm Mon.-Sat., 9:30am-12:30pm and 2pm-5pm Sun.

Sitting on Jehan Ango Bridge, catching the eye of drivers traveling straight from the ferry port, this tourist office deals in information covering both Dieppe and much of the nearby Alabaster Coast. Its staff are multilingual and obliging in itinerary suggestions or linking you up with hotels.

TRANSPORTATION

By Car

Dieppe is about 2.5 hours (120 miles/193 kilometers) by car from Paris, taking the A13, then changing to the A150 after Rouen. Be warned, there are tolls on this route, which should set you back around €15. You can avoid these by taking the D915, which makes the total journey about 3 hours 15 minutes. From Rouen alone, Dieppe is about 45 minutes (40 miles/64 kilometers).

By Train

Dieppe is connected by train to the rest of France via Rouen. There are 10-16 trains

1: busy tables outside of Café des Tribunaux **2:** Named after Dieppe's sister port in the U.K., Le New Haven serves good local seafood.

daily departing from the train station, **Gare de Dieppe** (Dieppe; tel. 36 35; www.ter.sncf.com/normandie/gares/87415018/Dieppe; 5am-10:15pm Mon.-Fri., 5:45am-10:15pm Sat., 7:15am-10:15pm Sun.), to Rouen and vice versa. From Rouen, connections can be made on to Paris, Le Havre, and elsewhere. The journey time is about 40 minutes and it costs €12. Tickets all the way to Paris are €32.

By Bus

Dieppe is now connected directly to Paris by **Flixbus** (https://flixbus.com). Depending on how early you book, tickets for this cost €5-25. The journey takes just under three hours and goes via Rouen. There are usually between two and three journeys per day. There are no other national coach connections to or from Dieppe.

By Ferry

Putting Dieppe on the map for thousands of holidaying Brits every year, **DFDS Seaways ferry service** (7 quai Gaston Lalitte, Dieppe; tel. 800 65 01 00; www.dfdsseaways.fr) connects the town to the United Kingdom. It's a four-hour crossing each way that takes place twice a day in the summer and once a day in the winter. There is also a night crossing, which takes a little longer. Costs vary, but expect to pay around €100 for a car plus two passengers in high season.

Varengeville and Veules-les-Roses

Two towns along the stunning Alabaster Coast, both with their own unique charms, Varengeville and Veules-les-Roses make for a great paired day trip. Varengeville-sur-Mer is a small village with a rich, artistic heritage. It's the birthplace of Cubist artist Georges Braque, who is today buried in the graveyard of the village's spectacular cliff-top church. Impressionists Monet and Pissarro were also attracted here to capture its surrounding landscape in their painting. Add to that the only property designed by British Arts and Crafts architect Edwin Lutyens, and the Renaissance villa the Manoir d'Ango, and it's fair to say Varengeville has a deeper artistic history than towns many times its size.

Veules-les-Roses, meanwhile, has also been drawing writers and artists for years. In part, this is to do with its perfectly preserved old town, complete with a 13th-century church, three restored watermills, many old houses, and a profusion of flowers in keeping with its name. It also has a long beach, which is the only sandy one in the area that remains accessible at high tide.

Orientation

Just 5.5 miles (8.8 kilometers) west along the D75 from Dieppe, the center of Varengeville is not much to write home about, being just a simple main road flanked by a number of shops. It's the town's surroundings that really lend it character. The Manoir d'Ango, for example, is a turn to the left from the D75, just as you enter the town from Dieppe. And the cliff-top **Église Saint-Valéry** is a right turn at the roundabout once you've passed the shops. From there, there are plenty of forest walks, and a beach that can be accessed at low tide.

Veules-les-Roses is about a 20-minute drive west from Varengeville if you head inland to take the D925, or 30-40 minutes if you follow the undulating, and very beautiful, coastal road. It is a small town that's easier to drive around than walk, with lots of quaint backstreets. Nevertheless, the main road is a loop with three main exit points, two on the D925 and one on the D68 coastal road, which helps to ease traffic congestion in the high season. The north of the town is taken up by beach, which reaches along the coast to the east, gradually getting more rugged the farther from Veules-les-Roses it gets.

SIGHTS

L'Église Saint-Valéry

Route de l'Église, Varengeville-sur-Mer; 10am-6pm daily Mar. 20-Sept. 21, 10am-5pm daily Sept. 22-Dec. 31, 2:30pm-5pm daily Jan. 1-Mar.19; free

This stunningly located and hauntingly beautiful cliff-top church dates from the 12th and 13th centuries, with an entrance porch added in the 1500s. Inside is a cornucopia of modern and ancient art and sculpture, including several pillars that have been carved to depict Indian chiefs from distant lands, as well as a stained glass window designed by Cubist painter Georges Braque.

Born in Varengeville, Braque is buried in the church's graveyard, which is also the resting place of many mariners, forever looking out to the sea on whose waves they used to sail. A path just to the side of the church leads down to the sea. On the path there are several informative panels about Claude Monet, who used to come to this part of Varengeville to paint, and who included the church in several of his landscapes of the area.

Bois des Moutiers

Route de l'Église, Varengeville-sur-Mer; tel. 02 35 85 10 02; www.boisdesmoutiers.com; ticket office open 10am-12pm and 2pm-6pm daily Mar. 15-Nov.15, visits allowed 10am-8pm; adults €11, students €9, children 7-15 €5, under 7 free

Both a notable garden and manor house, the Bois des Moutiers is unique in France for being the work of a British partnership between architect Edwin Lutyens and garden designer Gertrude Jekyll. The pairing of gardener and architect, meanwhile, was brought together by a Frenchman, Guillaume Mallet, whose land it was, and who saw the plot's potential: It is located astride a large valley and overlooks the sea.

The manor was in fact preexistent at the time Lutyens was brought onto the project in 1898, but the Arts and Crafts designer substantially remodeled it in his characteristic style—aiming to highlight the materials used and to remind people that craft deserves to be recognized as art. The gardens, meanwhile, were separated into seven sections surrounding the house on the south and east sides. The layout of each garden was designed to reflect that of the house's rooms. The aim was always to bring a unification of the building and the garden, neither one taking dominance, but rather complementing each other fully.

Both the gardens and house can be visited. Neither tend to be particularly crowded, even on weekends, giving visitors a good

picturesque Église Saint-Valéry in Varengeville-sur-Mer

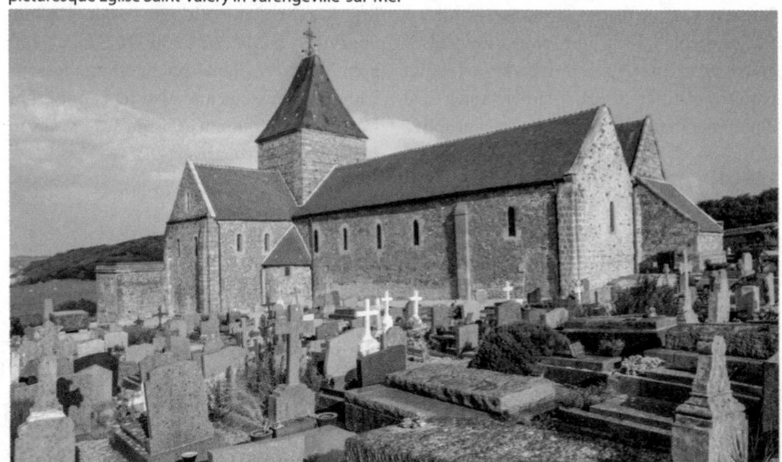

chance to fully appreciate the melding of architecture and landscape, the texture of which of course changes with the seasons throughout the year.

Manoir d'Ango

Route de la Cayenne, Varengeville-sur-Mer; tel. 02 35 83 61 56; www.manoirdango.fr; 10am-12pm and 2pm-6pm daily May 1-Sept. 30, 10am-12pm and 2pm-6pm Sat.-Sun. Apr. and Oct.; adults €5.50

The Manoir d'Ango was the private residence of Jehan Ango, a Norman ship owner born in 1480, who provided vessels to the French crown to aid with the exploration of the world. Born in Dieppe, in his younger years he went on many sailing voyages himself until taking over his family import-export business. Through this, he entered into the spice trade, where he began amassing a fortune.

The building was designed to incorporate architectural trends from the Italian Renaissance—Ango was, after all, nicknamed "the Medici of Dieppe." A low-lying complex of buildings, possibly its most remarkable quality is how few visitors it gets. Without other tourists walking into your line of sight, you can really believe you have traveled back in time. Though large and generally impressive, its most evocative features lie in its details: the stone flooring to its colonnades, the ancient exposed wood beams of its interiors. The most iconic feature here, meanwhile, is the dovecot, which dominates the central courtyard. It is characterized by arresting patterns of different colored bricks and a tiled dome roof that ascends into an elegant spire.

L'Église Saint-Martin

Centre du Village, Veules les Roses; tel. 02 35 97 63 05; 9am-6pm daily

Records state that the first church on this site was built in 1026. This was completely destroyed, however, only to be replaced by another church in the 13th century, which was also destroyed—this one in the Hundred Years' War—except for its tower, which continues to loom over the current church. The majority of the building, then, is a 16th-century construction, built while the area was prospering thanks to distant overseas trade. As such, as with many churches in the region, there are carvings in its stone pillars depicting symbols regarding the exploration of exotic lands, from ships to compasses to mermaids. The wood ceiling, too, is particularly impressive, looking for all the world like the hull of an upturned boat. A visit today is unlikely to be too crowded, unless it's a weekend in high season, when a number of the tourists who flock to Veules-les-Roses are likely to poke their noses in here, if only briefly. Nevertheless, don't expect queues!

BEACHES

VEULES-LES-ROSES BEACH

This long stretch of sand and shingle extending east out of Veules-les-Roses is one of the better beaches in the area, given that you can sit on it even at high tide—even if you do have to take to the stones. It's good for swimming, too, and can get very busy in the summer and on bank holiday weekends.

POURVILLE BEACH

Pourville-sur-Mer

Just down from Varengeville toward Dieppe, Pourville Beach may not have the largest waves in the world, but it's a fairly safe place for a beginner to try their hand at surfing. Surf'in Pourville (98 rue du Casino, Pourville-sur-Mer; tel. 06 30 59 02 76; 9:30am-6pm Tues.-Fri., 9am-7pm Sat.-Sun.; lessons €30) offers lessons and also rents out other water-sports equipment, from sea kayaks to stand-up paddleboards.

SHOPPING

LIN ET L'AUTRE

Place des Canadiens, Varengeville-sur-Mer; tel. 02 35 04 93 37; https://linetlautre-normandie.fr; 10am-1pm and 2pm-7pm daily

One of Normandy's less well-known crops is linen, which set the fields around Varengeville blazing blue every autumn. In Lin et L'Autre, it is converted into fabric and clothes. If it can be worn and made out of linen, chances are you'll find it here. Skirts, dresses, jackets, shirts (€50), trousers: All are on offer, and many with a trendier cut than you've any right to expect from a rural haberdashery. Different-patterned and -colored linen can also be bought here by the meter, and the shop sells plenty of buttons and beads.

AU PANIER NORMAND

14 rue Dr Pierre Girard, Veules-les-Roses; tel. 02 35 97 23 11; 8am-7:30pm Thurs.-Tues.

The genteel beach at Veules-les-Roses is a perfect spot for a picnic, and Au Panier Normand is a great place to pick up some local ingredients. Looking as quaint as anywhere else in town, its shelves are neatly stacked with attractively packaged conserves, spreads, and liquors. For beachside snacking you can pick up artisanal cider and Neufchâtel cheese, and they even sell bread from the local bakery for you to spread it on.

FESTIVALS AND EVENTS

LA ROSE EN FÊTE

Veules-les-Roses center; www.veules-les-roses.fr/event/la-rose-en-fete; June 16-17; free

Celebrating the flower in the town's name, La Rose en Fête is a festival of roses in which gardeners from the nearby region descend on the town to display their wares, both to delight the senses of passersby and for those who wish to purchase them. The already floral Veules-les-Roses becomes for a couple of days almost impossibly more so. There are also some talks (in French) and demonstrations put on by local gardeners.

FOOD

Local Cuisine

AUBERGE DE RELAIS

2 route de l'Église, Varengeville-sur-Mer; tel. 02 35 83 64 04; www.restaurant-varengeville.com; 9am-2:30pm and 6:30pm-9:30pm Wed.-Sun., 9am-3pm Mon.; menus €23-48

An old coaching inn repurposed as a restaurant, cozy in the winter and with an extensive garden terrace that can be used in the summer, this is a popular local restaurant that attracts customers from all around. Food is hearty and traditional and served in large portions. Should you be feeling extravagant, the *fruits de mer* platter comes highly recommended. If you're coming in the evening or Sunday lunchtime, make sure to book to be sure of a place.

COLOMBIER

1 rue Loucheur, Offranville; tel. 02 35 85 48 50; www.lecolombieroffranville.fr; 12pm-1:30pm and 7:30pm-9pm Thurs.-Mon., closed Sun. evening; lunch menu €32, evening menus €48-80

A really excellent, high-end local restaurant inside an old farm building. Unlike many restaurants of its class, it's oriented more toward tradition than modern experimentation, putting just enough of a spin on the classics that it remains up-to-date and innovative, such as serving a single lobster in three parts: one claw poached in vinaigrette, another as part of a layered paté, and the body grilled then covered by a garlic and sage sauce. The vast old hearth in the dining area is a great feature, too, which fits well among the white tablecloths and sparkling cutlery.

Budget Options

FANTHEZIE

12 rue Jean Lamy, Veules-les-Roses; tel. 02 77 24 60 72; 9am-6pm daily; mains €6-12

This simple café on a square makes for a good place to pause while exploring Veules-les-Roses. The inside is not that special, but the food (mostly salad and cheesy snacks) is made from fresh ingredients, comes quickly, and is inexpensive. The small terrace is a relaxing place to be.

ACCOMMODATIONS

★ HÔTEL DE LA TERASSE

Route de Vasterival, Varengeville-sur-Mer; tel. 02 35 85 12 54; www.hotel-restaurant-la-terrasse.com; Mar.-Oct.; from €75 d

A family-run hotel in the old style, this property boasts a stunning isolated location with uninterrupted views out to the English

Channel. With a tennis court, plenty of good nearby walks, and access to an often deserted, though beautiful stretch of beach, combined with the traditional restaurant on-site, it's possible to spend an entire holiday here without leaving once. The rooms, meanwhile, offer old-fashioned comfort, if not glamour. Early-evening cocktails on the hotel's eponymous terrace are a highlight.

RELAIS HÔTELIER DOUCE FRANCE

13 rue Dr Pierre Girard, Veules-les-Roses; tel. 02 35 57 85 30; www.doucefrance.fr; from €102 d

Less than 550 yards (500 meters) from the sea in a delightful 17th-century property, complete with timber-frame fittings and a turreted facade, this hotel's charms match those of Veules-les-Roses itself. The rooms are comfortable and traditional, and some have balcony views over Veules-les-Roses's small river. There's also an on-site tearoom with a river-fronting courtyard.

CAMPING DE LA PLAGE

Rue de la Saâne, Quiberville; tel. 02 35 83 01 04; http://campingplagequiberville.fr; Apr.-Oct.; two people for €25.50

Between Varengeville and Veules-les-Roses, this campsite is just a short walk from the beach and offers basic amenities as well as a snack bar, WiFi, and a tennis court. Quiberville also has the advantage of being where local fishermen sell their catch direct to the public every morning. If you've your own cooking equipment, this is certainly something worth taking advantage of.

TRANSPORTATION

By Car

Quite clearly the easiest way to get around the area, a car certainly helps you to see as much of the region as possible. There are effectively two options for making your way along the coast: either the direct and straight D925, or the winding, more picturesque D68. Taking the main road, Varengeville is about 20 minutes (five miles/eight kilometers) from Dieppe and a little over an hour (71 miles/114 kilometers) from Le Havre.

Varengeville itself rarely gets too busy, so parking near its sights shouldn't be a problem. In the height of summer, though, you might want to consider parking on the outskirts of Veules-les-Roses and walking the rest of the way into town.

By Bicycle

Picturesque and relatively free of traffic, this area is very popular among cyclists, and there are plenty of unspoiled backroads to explore. Be warned, though, along the coast can be relentlessly hilly, so make sure you're in shape before opting for this transport method. The Hôtel de la Terasse offers a good way around this, renting out electrically assisted bikes for €12 a day.

By Bus

Trying to negotiate the area by public transport is possible and fairly inexpensive, but buses are not regular, especially in the winter months. Line 61 is the one to look for, which leaves from Dieppe five times a day and takes around 20 minutes to get to Varengeville and 40 to Veules-les-Roses. A return service runs from Saint-Valery-en-Caux five times also, with the last buses of the day leaving not much later than 5pm. One ticket costs just €2, and full details of the timetable can be found here: www.vtni76.fr/ftp/FR_documents_vtni76/LIGNE%2061%202017-2018.pdf.

Étretat

Iconic across France because of its chalk cliff structures, Étretat has been drawing visitors for over a hundred years. The three natural arches and one stack formation known as l'Aiguille (the Needle) looks like an illustration in a geography textbook. Many come just to marvel at the landscape, and no few have set about trying to immortalize it in painting. Claude Monet, whose presence seems ubiquitous around this area of Normandy, was simply the most famous.

Thanks to its natural features being a tourist hot spot for so long, Étretat itself has evolved into something of a resort. As well as its long shingle beach, there are plenty of good long-standing restaurants and hotels, housed within purpose-built venerable old buildings that have been serving visitors for generations. So whether your intensions here are artistic or leisurely, whether you want to hike along the cliff tops or swim in the cool waters, there's plenty to occupy your time.

Orientation

Étretat' is in a shallow bay in between the famous rock formations, which can be seen from Étretat's beach. The town center itself is small and walkable, really less than 1,000 square feet (100 square meters) containing a jumble of streets that are easier to walk than to drive. Its border to the north by the sea and to the south by the D940, which leads into Le Havre. Beyond the D940, Étretat is more residential, and it's here you'll find parking. Follow the D39 out of town for free parking just outside Étretat's limits.

SIGHTS

★ Étretat Cliffs

Originally formed by an underground river running parallel to the coast, then further enlarged by the sea, the cliffs at Étretat are one of the most iconic sights in all of Normandy, if not all of France. Consisting of three natural arches and a stack known as l'Aiguille, they have inspired artists and writers for generations, finding their way into some of the most famous paintings of French art history and some memorable pieces of literature.

Three of the famous landforms can be seen from Étretat's beach: the smaller arch, the **Falaise Amont** to the northeast; the famous **Falaise Aval;** and the **Aiguille** to the southwest. Also to the southwest, the largest arch, the **Falaise Manneporte,** which French writer Guy de Maupassant described as looking like a great elephant draining its trunk into the ocean, cannot be seen from the town and requires walking up the western cliff-top paths to observe. An exploration of the cliff tops makes for a fuller experience and is recommended.

Paths up can be accessed at either end of the beach, and when out on the cliff tops, you'll find plenty of walkways and safety barriers to help guide you. The walks up can be trying, but if you take them slow, you should not have many problems, and you do not have to worry about specific footwear. That said, there is a parking lot near the top of the Falaise Amont. A full exploration of the cliff tops should take about two hours (an hour for each side of the beach), though it's recommended that you pause in the middle of that, when crossing back through the town, in order not to tire yourself out.

Do keep in mind that safety barriers are not everywhere, and you will often find yourself mere meters away from dramatic and potentially fatal drops, meaning caution is advised. Likewise, should you choose to walk out underneath the arch of the Falaise Aval at low tide, if you do not give yourself enough time to get back, the returning tide can cut you off from Étretat itself, leading to either a six-hour wait or an expensive boat ride.

Warnings notwithstanding, there can be few experiences where you'll feel yourself

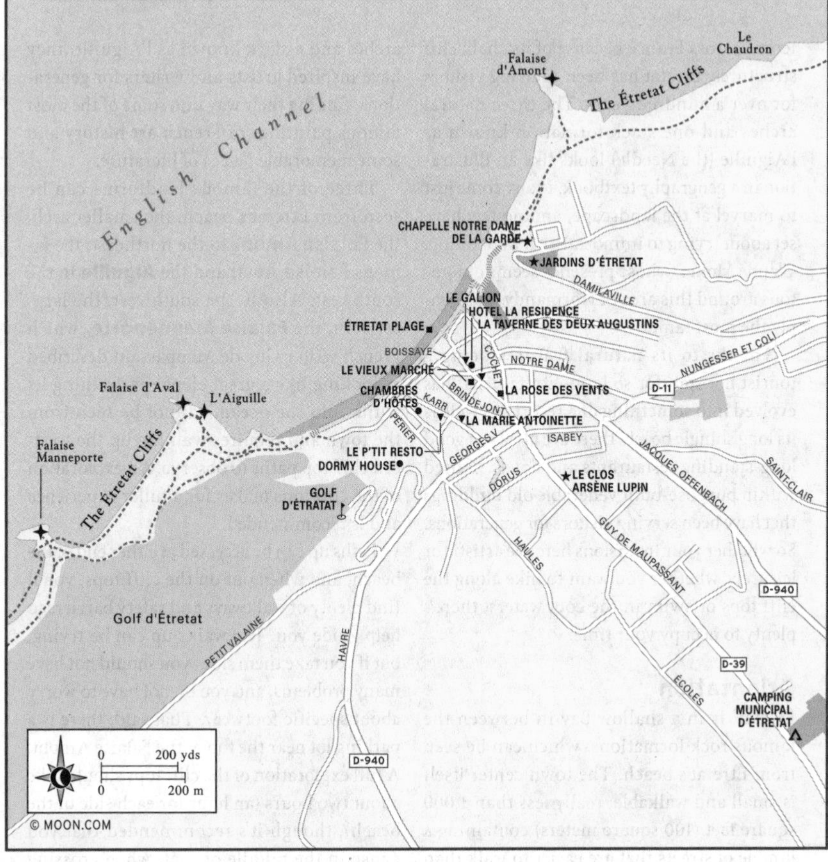

more in touch with how the landscape of France has informed its culture, whether seeing in your mind's eye Monet's depiction of the cliffs (or Gustave Courbet's or Eugène-Louis Boudin's) or considering Maupassant's elephant description.

Despite their world-renowned fame, the area around the cliffs has yet to be monetized, meaning they're entirely free to visit. It also means there's no specific visitors center. The tourist office in Étretat town, though, should be able to provide you with any extra information you need.

Jardins d'Étretat

Avenue Damilaville, Étretat; tel. 02 35 27 05 76; https://etretatgarden.fr; 10am-7pm daily; adults €8.80, children 2-12) €5.30

Only founded in 2016, these gardens have already been drawing many visitors and been subject to much praise. A landscaped area with views out over the famous cliffs, the gardens are divided into several sections, each with their own particular charm and purpose, but united by the same inspiration: to evoke

1: the cliffs at Étretat, one of Normandy's most iconic sights **2:** Chapelle Notre Dame de la Garde, looking out across Étretat

1
2

the history and landscape of Normandy. In general, it is unusual and very contemporary in feel, dotted by modern art sculptures by artists from all over the world. These include huge baby-like faces peering from the middle of bushes arranged to look like flower petals, box hedges planted in nautilus patterns, and wicker figures dressed to look like the clergy worshipping trees. They can get busy in the high season, but the expansive views and sky mean they seldom feel crowded, and a sense of calm pervades.

Chapelle Notre-Dame de la Garde

Chapelle des Marins, Étretat; tel. 02 35 20 72 76; mass 10am Weds.; free

Originally a 19th-century chapel dedicated to the protection of sailors on the sea, this clifftop neo-Gothic building was commissioned by a local Jesuit priest known as Père Michel in 1854 after he claimed to have come across a note on its current site written by the Virgin Mary requesting a church. Though this was met with suspicion among the locals, they nevertheless set about building the chapel, lugging much of its materials up to the clifftop by hand. This building was unfortunately largely destroyed by the Germans, and had to be rebuilt in the 1950s.

An important builiding among locals, it is nevertheless not often open—its isolated position and the heavy influx of tourists (everyone who visits the cliffs walks past it) meant that in the past, the shelter that it offered was abused. However, new owners are trying to change that, opening its doors for religious events and aiming to allow for more regular visits soon.

Le Clos Arsène Lupin

15 rue Guy de Maupassant, Étretat; tel. 02 35 10 59 53; 10am-12:30pm and 1:30pm-6pm Tues.-Sun. Apr.-Sept., 10:30am-12:30pm and 1:30pm-5:30pm weekends and school holidays Oct.-Mar.; adults: €7.50, reduced €8, children 6-18 €5, under 6 free

Gentleman thief and detective Arsène Lupin, often described as France's answer to Sherlock Holmes, was the creation of Maurice Leblanc, a Rouen native who owned this house in Étretat and famously set one of Lupin's stories here. The building actually changed hands several times after the author's death in 1941, but was repurchased by his granddaughter in 1999, who established it as a museum to both Leblanc and his most famous creation. The exhibits inside this half-timber mansion include the author's writings and other personal accessories, as well as clothing and other objects that could have belonged to his fictional hero.

BEACH

ÉTRETAT PLAGE

The beach at Étretat is a long, small-pebble beach in the center of town, backed onto by a boardwalk. It's good for swimming when the weather permits, and there's a barrier to prevent you from going too far out and a small pontoon that can be swum out to. Two of Étretat's natural arches can be seen from here.

SHOPPING

LE VIEUX MARCHÉ

16 place Maréchal Foch, Étretat; 11am-7pm daily

This covered market built in 1927 by the local architect Emile Mauge was originally used to cover produce sellers, but in more recent years has evolved into a space for artisan boutiques and antique sellers, as well as more classic tourist stalls. A great place to find souvenirs from old black and white postcards to panama hats, it gets quite bustling in the high season, but the rest of the year you'll have plenty of time and space to browse.

LA ROSE DES VENTS

2 rue Monge, Étretat; tel. 02 35 29 66 91; www.larosedesvents-etretat.com; 10am-7pm daily

Specializing in regional produce from all over Normandy, this is a great place to stock up on picnic snacks such as local patés, honey-glazed apples, and cider before heading to Étretat Beach, or indeed find nonperishables such as cider or calvados to take back home, some of which are sold in ready-made gift packs. Attractively presented in a rustic fashion, you

Impressionism and the Open Air Studio

These days, the work of the Impressionists has become so much a part of mainstream culture that it's hard to believe that when it first debuted, painting scenes in a manner that they didn't actually resemble was highly controversial and a subject for scorn. In fact, the very term "impressionism" was lifted from a satirical review of Claude Monet's famous *Impression Sunrise* painting, which kick-started the movement in 1873.

Among other Impressionists were Pierre-Auguste Renoir, Edgar Degas, and Camille Pissarro, all of whom took their cue from painters such as Eugène Delacroix and J. M. W. Turner, applying their paint freely, no longer giving as much care to line and contours of the image, creating just an impression of a scene that captured its essence rather than its precise reproduction. This also meant they could work faster than painters had in the past and set about using this technique in the open air, capturing the way that light is not a fixed entity, but rather one that flows and dances with time.

Anybody who's spent any time in a Normandy summer can attest to the restless quality of its weather and, by extension, light. Several seasons can at times seem crammed in the space of one day, and in such a way, the very region itself helped sculpt the artistic movement, offering the world an entirely new way of seeing. For as is now well known, the hostile public were soon won over by the vision that the Impressionists had created to such an extent that today, many of their depictions of Normandy are to some the very definition of classic art.

The movement remained at the forefront of artistic expression in France until the end of the 19th century, changing the art world irrevocably, and paving the way for increasingly more abstract techniques. The conceptual pieces that now decorate contemporary galleries around the world all have their most concrete origin in the paintbrushes of Monet and his contemporaries.

can also find wicker baskets and chinaware for sale.

FESTIVALS AND EVENTS

HELLO BIRDS

Étretat Plage, Étretat; https://etretat.hellobirdsfestival.fr; July 6-8; free

Linked to another festival of the same name in that other French iconic tourist destination, Saint-Malo, Hello Birds sees a young crowd taking to the beach and boardwalk of Étretat for contempory music concerts, drinking, and barbecues of Norman specialties. Obviously the weather plays a big part in the festival's success, but being free, no one has to take too much of a risk to attend.

FESTIVAL OFFENBACH

Multiple locations in Étretat; tel. 02 35 27 05 21 (tourist office number); www.etretat-festivaloffenbach.fr; August 3-12; concert prices from €17-25

This festival is actually a series of concerts taking place in various locations around Étretat by different musicians all playing compositions with some connection to the 19th-century French-German composer Jacques Offenbach, who once had a second home here. The festival was founded in 2003 and is growing year after year.

SPORTS AND RECREATION

GOLF D'ETRATAT

Route du Havre, Étretat; tel. 02 35 27 04 89; https://golfetretat.com; 8:30am-7pm daily Apr.-Oct., 9am-5pm daily Nov.-Mar.; nonmembers high season weekend fees from €80

One of the most spectacular golf clubs perhaps anywhere in the world, this 18-hole course rubs right up against Étretat's famous cliffs and offers plenty of impressive views as if designed to put you off your swing. Founded in 1908, it's got some serious heritage, while its club house is so positioned that it takes full of advantage of the location, too. It's a great place to pause for a meal, especially on days when the weather has stopped play.

FOOD

Local Cuisine

LA MARIE ANTOINETTE

12 rue Alphonse Karr, Étretat; tel. 06 09 40 57 66; www.marieantoinette-etretat.fr; 12pm-2:15pm and 6:30pm-9pm Wed., 11:30am-2:15pm and 6:30pm-9pm Mon.-Tues. and Thurs., 11:30am-2:15pm and 6:30pm-9:30pm Fri., 11:30am-3pm and 6:30pm-10pm Sat., 11:30am-3pm and 6:30pm-9pm Sun.; mains €12-20

Specializing in *fruits de mer,* but looking, as its name would suggest, like a restaurant designed by Marie Antoinette, this a great place to drop into for reasonably priced oysters, prawns, and other shellfish. As with most places in Étretat, its main clients are going to be tourists, but that doesn't mean there's a compromise in quality.

LA TAVERNE DES DEUX AUGUSTINS

Place Maréchal Foch, Étretat; tel. 02 35 27 06 99; www.les2augustins.com; 9am-10:30pm daily; menus €21-40

Founded in 1851, this restaurant and hotel has been serving visitors to Étretat for years. It wears this history on its sleeve, looking a bit like something you might find in the "Wild West" section of a theme park, and being so large that it's hard to miss. The food quality here is not very high for its price, consisting mainly of fast-food-style dishes cooked (and served) slowly. However, it does serve food throughout the day in its lively interior, and there are certainly enough chairs and tables that you'll not be in danger of not finding a seat.

LE GALION

Boulevard Président René Coty, Étretat; tel. 02 35 29 48 74; http://etretat-legalion.fr; 12pm-2pm and 7pm-9pm daily; mains €25-47

This attractive restaurant inside a beautiful old building cooks high-quality dishes of the region (think different kinds of white fish in rich sauces) and does a good cheese board, too. The atmosphere would be formal if the restaurant were located elsewhere in France, but given that it sits on the main street of a resort town, things are a little more relaxed. There's a small terrace outside, which is good for people-watching and enjoying the building's half-timber architecture, and during high season a special seafood selection gets added to the menu.

Budget Options

LE P'TIT RESTO

27 rue Alphonse Karr, Étretat; tel. 06 63 10 03 28; €5-10

Don't come here expecting a whole lot—it's not much more than a glorified fast-food outlet. However, if you want the cheapest sit-down meal in Étretat, this is your place. And frankly, there's not that much that can go wrong with fish and chips, or omelet and chips, or sausage sandwiches, which are the kinds of things Le P'tit Resto serves. Takeaways are also available.

ACCOMMODATIONS

€50-100

CHAMBRES D'HÔTES VILLA L'ESPÉRANCE

6 rue Anicet Bourgeois, Étretat; tel. 02 35 10 72 16; from €80 d

As a major tourist destination, there are a number of overpriced hotels in Étretat that don't necessarily have to try too hard to attract customers, and can feel a little soulless. One way around this is by opting to stay in one of the town's *chambres d'hôtes* (effectively bed-and-breakfasts). The Villa l'Espérance is a charming old-fashioned property with comfortable beds, a pleasant breakfast room, and claw-foot bathtubs. It's well located, too, just a short walk from the town's beach.

€100-200

DORMY HOUSE

Route du Havre, Étretat; tel. 02 35 27 07 88; www.dormy-house.com/accueil-falaise-etretat.html; from €117 d

Since being turned into a hotel in the 1950s,

Dormy House has become something of an Étretat legend. This is no doubt in large part due to its location, with a view out across Étretat itself and the Falaise Amont. The property itself is from the 19th century and boasts comfortable and colorful rooms, some of which have balconies. There are also TVs and WiFi throughout, and some of the en suite bathrooms have claw-foot tubs. Easy beach access and the hotel's own extensive gardens complete the picture.

HÔTEL LA RESIDENCE

4 boulevard Président René Coty, Étretat; tel. 02 35 27 02 87; from €129 d

Right in the center of Étretat, and located within a beautiful traditional building designed by the same architect who built the town's covered market, this is a surprisingly basic hotel that could easily have been turned into a four- or five-star establishment. It has clean, comfortable rooms that are both traditional in style but fairly minimalist in terms of clutter. Some have four-poster beds, others spa baths.

Camping

CAMPING MUNICIPAL D'ÉTRETAT

69 rue Guy de Maupassant, Étretat; tel. 02 35 27 07 67; open year-round; pitch for double tent with car €12

Easily the cheapest way to overnight near one of France's top tourist destinations, this basic campsite does the job it needs to, and then a little more. As well as the straightforward pitch setup and basic washing facilities, there's also a children's game room, table tennis, and a bocce ball court. It's just at Étretat's limits, and so is about a 15-minute walk from the beach and town center.

INFORMATION

OFFICE DE TOURISME D'ÉTRETAT

Place Maurice Guillard, Étretat; tel. 02 35 27 05 21; http://etretat.net/office-de-tourisme-etretat; 10am-12:30pm and 2pm-5:30pm Mon.-Sat.

In Étretat town, this tourist office is an excellent resource for providing maps and advice on how best to tackle sightseeing on and around the cliffs—there are no information points once you're up there, so coming here is good preparation. They speak English, and will also be able to help you with booking rooms in local hotels, while the website offers

the grand exterior of the Hôtel La Residence

some good advice and links on how to get to Étretat via public transport, which is not always the most straightforward thing to do.

TRANSPORTATION

Getting There

BY CAR

Driving is the easiest way to get to Étretat. The town is barely 20 minutes from Le Havre, 17 miles (28 kilometers) along the D940. From Paris, it is about three hours, 127 miles (205 kilometers) mostly along the A13 then the A131, until changing to a series of D roads gets you into town. This is a toll road, and the journey will set you back around €15.

There are plenty of parking options in Étretat, most of which require payment. More economical, and in the high season good for avoiding congestion, is to use the free parking lot out of town on the D39, and walk the last couple of kilometers.

BY BUS AND TAXI

For such a major tourist spot, Étretat is surprisingly hard to get to via public transport. Even in the high season there are only buses every weekend to the town, one a day, costing around €35 one way and taking about three hours. Otherwise, it's necessary to go to a larger town nearby, such as Le Havre, and take a local bus—Line 24, which is operated by the **Keolis bus service** (www.keolis-seine-maritime.com). Even this is not always possible, as the bus service does not run in school time. All this said, if you really are desperate to get to Étretat by public transport, a taxi from Le Havre is not going to cost much more than €40 for one direction. Some additional details of how to get to Étretat can be found on the town's tourist website (http://etretat.net/office-de-tourisme-etretat).

Le Havre

And now for something completely different. Le Havre is utterly distinct from the timber-frame houses and bucolic idylls of the rest of Normandy, as a poured-concrete, meticulously planned, modernist metropolis. Having seen so much of this historic harbor city destroyed in the Second World War, officials chose to build it up again in a way that broke completely with the past. The entire downtown area became a blank canvas for the firm of architect Auguste Perret, and a marvel of wide boulevards and towering concrete buildings began to grow. Le Havre was redesigned: a city of the future, as the future used to be conceived.

Of course, the brute facts of Le Havre life stayed much the same. Its very name means "the harbor," after all, and sitting on the Right Bank of the Seine estuary, as Paris's most obvious physical connection to the wider world, it has been one of the largest ports in France since the 18th century. As such, tourism here is very much a secondary concern in comparison to the shipping businesses with which a large portion of the town's citizenry are engaged. There are, though, plenty of things to do and see, not least of which is to explore the modernist downtown. There's also a well-used city beach, which though mostly shingle is sandy in parts, and a strong cultural scene, focused around the city's delightfully bizarre Volcan theater. Many might overlook Le Havre on their way to Normandy's more obvious attractions, but in that they're making a mistake, for the city offers not just something different from the rest of the region, but from the rest of the world.

Orientation

The biggest city in Upper Normandy, Le Havre's meticulously planned downtown is nevertheless very easy to find your way around—particularly if you're coming off the back of the winding medieval streets that make up many other Norman towns. The

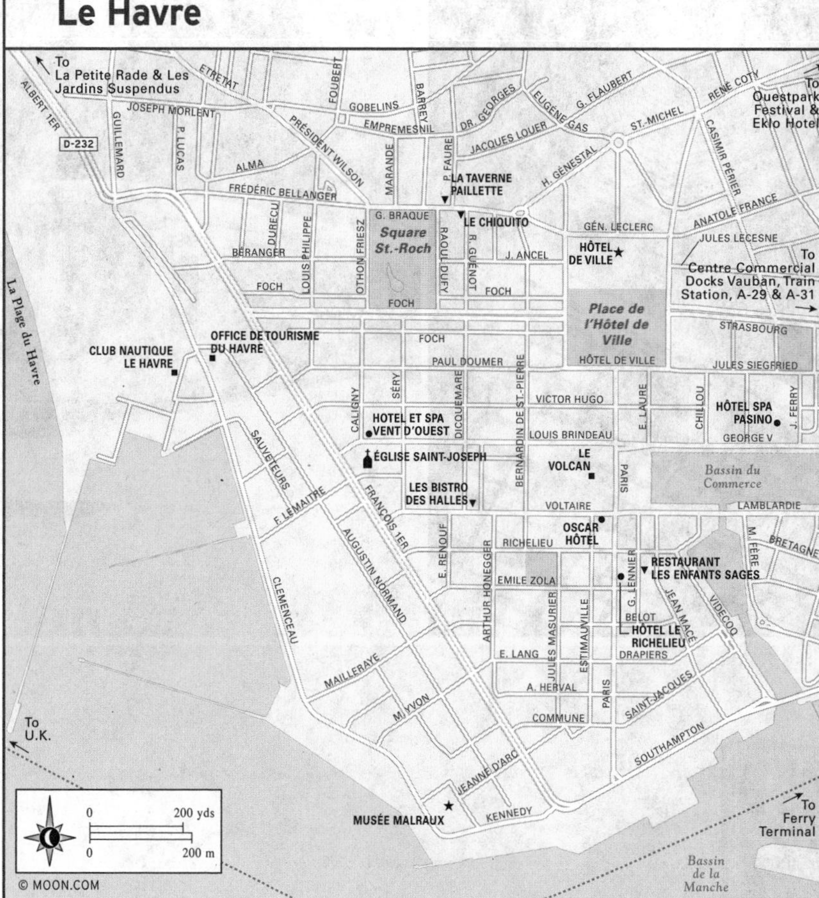

center is basically an upside-down triangle shape with its tip pointing toward the mouth of its harbor. The sea and beach are to its west and the extensive docks to east. Inside this is a grid system of some larger and some smaller blocks. Extending the pyramid metaphor, Le Havre's **town hall** sits in the very center of the pyramid's base. Unlike the extensive suburbs of the city, meanwhile, this central area is pretty walkable, covering less than a square mile in total. The **Jardins Suspendus** are the only real sight that you might need to take public transport to reach. They are in the northwest of the city, and accessible by Lines 3 and 5 on the city's **Lia bus service** (www.transports-lia.fr).

Most major roads approach the city from the east, and it is in this direction you need to head pretty much wherever it is you're trying to reach next, save for Étretat, which is connected by the D940 entering the northwest of the city.

1
2
3

SIGHTS

TOP EXPERIENCE

★ L'Église Saint-Joseph

130 boulevard Francois I, Le Havre; 10am-6pm daily; free

The emblem of Le Havre's reconstruction after WWII, this church was designed by Auguste Perret himself, whose studio had been given the job of rebuilding the whole city. Resembling something close to a lantern or lighthouse, the church's poured concrete form, at 350 feet (107 meters) high, continues to dominate the city skyline and is easily visible from the city's port. As well as being a functioning Roman Catholic church, it acts as a memorial to the 5,000 citizens of Le Havre killed as the city was flattened.

Even more impressive than its towering external appearance, however, is its interior. The tower is hollow inside, and patterned almost to its apex in stained glass designed by Marguerite Huré, the artist who introduced abstraction into French religious glassmaking. The effect of this is to bathe Saint-Joseph's alter and pews in a kaleidoscope of color—Huré's design made sure of a total of 50 different hues. The rest of the interior is a construction of bold, Gothic forms. Despite its unique splendor, the church sees comparitively few tourists, probably because Le Havre itself is—wrongfully—off most people's highlight list in France. This means you'll likely have it all to yourself, and can take all the space and time you need to fully immerse yourself in its marvels.

An undisputed masterpiece of 20th-century art and architecture, Saint-Joseph alone is enough to make any trip into Le Havre worthwhile.

Musée Malraux

2 boulevard Clemenceau, Le Havre; tel. 02 35 19 62 62; www.muma-lehavre.fr; 11am-6pm Tues.-Sun.; adults €7, reduced €4

A museum of firsts and superlatives: the first in France to be built after the war, and host to the country's largest collection of Impressionist paintings after Paris. The collection includes work by all the big names: Monet, Renoir, Pissarro, Manet, Degas, and more. If you've been traveling the nearby region already, you might be interested in Sisley's painting of the Seine, or Monet's depiction of the cliffs at Fécamp. Also notable is Gustave Courbet's painting *La Vague*, and one of Degas's studies of a woman drying herself after a bath.

This story of the building, too, is worthy of its own entry in the annals of art history. It was conceived in the 1950s as a place that would reinvent the very concept of what a museum could be, constructed to contain lecture halls and places for film screenings, which continue to be used until this day.

Though part of the reconstruction of Le Havre after the war, it was actually designed by a different architectural studio than Perret's. Guy Lagneau, Michel Weill, and Jean Dimitrijevic had broken away from Perret, and this sense of rebellion seemed to fit with the idea of what the museum wanted to achieve. Modern inside and out, it's without a doubt one of Normandy's finest museums.

Hôtel de Ville

1517 place de l'Hôtel de ville, Le Havre; tel. 02 35 19 45 45; www.lehavre.fr; 8am-4:50pm Mon.-Fri., 9am-11:50am Sat.

Representing the other architectural apex of Auguste Perret's rebuilding of Le Havre in the 1950s, its town hall ("hotel" in this context doesn't relate to a place where you can stay) evokes a regimented, almost Soviet aesthetic. Building work was begun in 1953, while the adjoining clock tower, which would grow to be 260 feet (80 meters) high, saw construction start a year later. The whole thing was inaugurated in 1958 and sits in the same location as the previous town hall. The vast square in front of it, also a Perret creation, feels almost

1: looking up into the glorious tower of St Joseph, the center point of this modernist city **2:** Le Havre tram **3:** Le Havre's town hall archetypal of a designed city, being large, though well proportioned, and breezy. It is now crisscrossed by trams and decorated by a large fountain.

Les Jardins Suspendus (The Hanging Gardens)

84 rue du Fort, Le Havre; tel. 02 35 19 61 27; 10:30am-8pm daily Apr.-Sept., 10:30am-5:30pm daily Oct.-Mar.; greenhouses adults €2, under 17 free

Occupying the ruins of Le Havre's 19th-century Fort Sainte-Adresse, the town's hanging gardens were inaugurated in 2008. As well as offering some excellent views out across Le Havre, they are home to plant species from around the world, from coffee plants to some weird and wonderful cacti. The greenhouse sections offer a botanical journey through different biospheres and pay tribute to famous botanists, many of whose travels began in Le Havre.

BEACH

LA PLAGE DU HAVRE

13-16 boulevard Albert 1er, Le Havre

Le Havre Beach is an unexpected delight. The city not being a beach destination, it is almost entirely occupied by locals, and thus has the relaxed atmosphere almost of a city park. In keeping with this, there are also a number of municipal facilities on offer, such as table tennis tables and beach volleyball courts. The beach itself is mostly shingle, though some walkways have been built for people to reach the water barefoot. As the tide goes out, more sand is revealed.

ENTERTAINMENT AND EVENTS

OUESTPARK FESTIVAL

55 rue du 329ème, Le Havre; tel. 02 35 19 00 38; www.ouestpark.com; Sept. 19-23; one-day pass €30, two-day pass €50

This music festival taking place in the north of the city brings together well-known groups as well as new musical discoveries of all different genres. A mainly young crowd attends, drawn from around Normandy. It's a smaller affair than many similar festivals around France, but the quality tends to be high.

LE VOLCAN

8 place Oscar Niemeyer, Le Havre; tel. 02 35 19 10 20; www.levolcan.com; Sept.-May; shows €5-€30

One of the more recent additions to the reconstruction of Le Havre, Le Volcan is the city's main theater house, and is considered one of the most important in France. So called because of its distinctive volcanic shape, its design was given over to Brazilian architect Oscar Niemeyer, while its construction took four years to complete and was finished in 1982. Originally named La Maison de la Culture, its volcano name became official in 1990 after a decision by the theater house's new director Alain Milianti. As well as theater, regular modern dance shows and classical concerts are also held here.

SHOPPING

CENTRE COMMERCIAL DOCKS VAUBAN

70 quai Frissard, Le Havre; tel. 02 35 11 33 60; www.docksvauban.com; 10am-8pm Mon.-Sat., 11am-7pm Sun.

A modern shopping complex crammed with high-street stores, restaurants, and movie theaters, the complex itself is routed firmly to Le Havre's history, having been built inside restored warehouses around the city's docks. Historically, these would have been home to a wide variety of trade goods, meaning there is some continuity with what they are used for today.

FOOD

Local Cuisine

LA TAVERNE PAILLETTE

22 rue Georges Braque, Le Havre; tel. 02 35 41 31 50; www.taverne-paillette.com; 12pm-12am daily; lunch menu €15.50-21.90, evening menu €31.20

Claiming an almost impossibly long heritage dating back to 1596, the Tavern Paillette is really a 1950s brasserie with links to Le Havre's historic brewing company Paillette. Boasting an interior and a menu that owes as much to Alsatian beer halls as it does Norman traditions, it's nevertheless considered a true Le Havre institution. Very popular with locals, especially on weekends, it's worth booking ahead; be prepared to wait for a table around lunchtime. Service runs late. Oh, and the in-house beer isn't half bad: a Pilsner served perfectly chilled, it's sparkling and crisp.

LES BISTROT DES HALLES

7 place des Halles Centrales, Le Havre; tel. 02 35 22 50 52; www.le-bistrot-des-halles-le-havre.com 12pm-2pm and 7pm-10:30pm Mon.-Sat., 12pm-2pm Sun.; menu €24.80

Complete with wooden floors and brass fixtures, this classic bistro takes its cue from Lyonnais cuisine, with certain nods to Norman cuisine: Try the coarse-grained sausage known as andouillette baked into a Camembert gratin. It's popular and bustles with locals and a good atmosphere. Aside from the high quality of food, what's most impressive here is the price. Spend any time in France, and a restaurant that looks like this, you'd be expecting to pay almost twice as much to what Les Bistrot des Halles demands. Booking's recommended, though not necessary.

RESTAURANT LES ENFANTS SAGES

20 rue Gustave Lennier, Le Havre; tel. 02 35 46 44 08; www.restaurant-lesenfantssages.com; 12pm-1:45pm and 7pm-9:30pm Mon.-Sat.; mains €19-23

In the nicest possible way, there seems something quite un-French about the Restaurant les Enfants Sages. Not in terms of the food, which is full of classic flavors, but in its casual ability to play fast and loose with tradition. The interior is a combination of the old and new, which so many aim for but don't easily achieve, and the dishes are uncomplicated and often zesty instead of swimming in cream. It also has a pleasant garden area, perfect for summer days.

Budget Options

LA PETITE RADE

3 bis chemin de la Mer, Prom. des Régates, Sainte-Adresse; tel. 02 35 48 33 05; 12pm-12am Tues.-Sun., 4pm-12am Mon.; €9-14

At the north end of Le Havre beach, and as much a bar as it is a restaurant, this is the place to be when the sun's going down and if you want to mix with the city's young crowd. Food is of the fast-food variety, including wraps, and the atmosphere strives toward that of a tropical paradise—when the Normandy weather complies (which is far from all the time), it succeeds.

LE CHIQUITO

47 rue Raymond Guénot, Le Havre; tel. 02 35 41 21 92; 7am-8pm Mon.-Sat.; menu €13.50

True, these kinds of brasseries exist all over France, and Le Chiquito isn't particularly exceptional. It is, though, a good example of its type, offering a friendly lunchtime environment and a higher-than-average quality of home-cooked food. If you want a simple lunchtime meal of, say, steak au poivre with fries that doesn't break the bank, you could do far worse.

ACCOMMODATIONS

Under €50

EKLO HOTEL LE HAVRE

466 avenue du Bois au Coq, Le Havre; tel. 02 35 42 27 33; www.eklohotels.com/hotels/le-havre; from €28 d

A good budget hotel, which manages a certain degree of style despite its otherwise basic amenities. The rooms may be small, but they're well insulated, and bathrooms are en suite. As with many establishments of its type, there are few gratuities; WiFi, access to the TVs, and even towels will cost you extra.

€50-100

HÔTEL LE RICHELIEU

132 rue de Paris, Le Havre; tel. 02 35 42 38 71; www.hotellerichelieu.fr; from €52 d

This is the hotel that time forgot sometime in the late 1990s, both in terms of what it looks like and its price. This may not be the most exciting place to stay, but it is clean and comfortable, with decent-size rooms. In theory it offers WiFi, but it can be patchy, as though it's trying to reach the hotel back from the 21st century. Nevertheless, for a centrally located place to lay your head, it's a strong choice.

OSCAR HÔTEL

106 rue Voltaire, Le Havre; tel. 02 35 42 39 77; www.hotel-oscar.fr; from €54 d

Well located, with some rooms that have views out over Le Volcan theater, and offering bright interiors that boast an almost 1950s theme (it's probably deliberate), this is another hotel with exceptional rates. There are televisions in all the rooms, and WiFi works throughout the building

€100-200

HOTEL ET SPA VENT D'OUEST

4 rue de Caligny, Le Havre; tel. 02 35 42 50 69; www.ventdouest.fr; from €104 d

A taste of the plusher, more traditional Normandy in midst of modernist Le Havre, this is a good hotel for those whose tastes run more toward the old fashioned—though it still is in a modern building, and the book wallpaper in its rooms may prove a little jarring to those with a more refined aesthetic eye. Still, it's very comfortable, and all mod-cons come as standard. And then, of course, there's the on-site spa with its steam room and offer of essential-oils massages in stylish, relaxing surrounds.

HÔTEL SPA PASINO

Place Jules Ferry, Le Havre; tel. 02 35 26 00 00; www.pasinohotellehavre.com/fr; from €117 d

A large, centrally located casino hotel, boasting comfortable rooms that just nudge the stylish side of bland. The floor-to-ceiling windows are an excellent feature, though, and offer some great views of downtown Le Havre. WiFi is available throughout the building, every room has a flat-screen TV and an en suite bathroom, and, as the hotel's name suggests, there's also an on-site spa with a swimming pool and a sauna.

INFORMATION

OFFICE DE TOURISME DU HAVRE

186 boulevard Clemenceau, 76600 Le Havre; tel. 02 32 74 04 04; www.lehavretourisme.com; 9:30am-1pm and 2pm-7pm daily

This modern tourist office with a boutique selling souvenirs from Le Havre-themed fridge magnets to waterproof jackets is located just back from the beach. They are happy to answer questions and distribute literature about Le Havre and its surrounding areas in a variety of languages.

TRANSPORTATION

Getting There

BY CAR

Unless you're coming from Étretat and the coast along the D940, driving into Le Havre means negotiating its motorway junctions in the east of the city, for this is where almost all roads toward (and out) of the city converge. Though efficient at funneling cars to and from the rest of France, the sheer number of slip roads can be a bit hairy, especially if you're not a confident driver. There's not much getting around this, of course, but just a word of warning!

Paris to Le Havre is 121 miles (195 kilometers) along the A13 and takes about 2.75 hours. Expect to pay around €15 in tolls. From Rouen it's about an hour, 55 miles (90 kilometers) on the A29, looping up over the meandering Seine, and to Caen you'll also want to link up with the A13, for a journey of about 60 miles (96 kilometers), taking around 1.5 hours with tolls of around €5.

BY TRAIN

The **Gare du Havre** (12 rue Magellan, Le Havre; tel. 36 35; www.gares-sncf.com/fr/gare/fraez/havre; 5am-12am Mon.-Thurs., 5am-11pm Fri., 5am – 11pm Sat., 6:15am-2:30am Sun.) receives trains from Paris's Gare St-Lazare 15 times every day, and 7-9 times on weekends. Journeys will cost €30 one way and take 2.25 hours. There are also 16-20 trains to and from Rouen every day, and 10 on Sunday, for €16, taking one hour. Finally, Fécamp on the Alabaster Coast is also served by 7-11 trains daily, costing €8 and taking 45-75 minutes.

BY BUS

Local buses connect Le Havre to a number of the tourist spots nearby. Look for the **Bus Verts** (www.busverts.fr) if you want to head south toward Honfleur or Deauville/Trouville. For both its Bus 20, of which there are 4-6 daily, costing €4.90. To Honfleur is 30 minutes; to Deauville/Trouville it's an hour. Heading north to Étretat take the **Keolis service** (www.keolis-seine-maritime.com), Bus 24. It costs €2 and takes an hour.

BY FERRY

Brittany Ferries (Terminal de la Citadelle, Le Havre; tel. 02 35 51 10 20; www.brittanyferries.de/article/33434/Fahrhafen-Le-Havre) connects Le Havre to the British port of Portsmouth. The service operates six times a week between March and October, and crossing takes around 5.5 hours. Prices can vary depending on the season and how early you book, but expect to pay over €300 for a return ticket with a car plus passengers.

Getting Around

While Le Havre is a decent-size city, most places that are likely to interest you as a tourist are in its very walkable center. Any farther than that and you can take the local bus service, the **Bus Oceane,** or the trams, all run by a company called **Lia** (www.transports-lia.fr). Tickets are the same for both and cost €1.70 for any journey, valid for an hour. They can be bought from bus drivers or the vending machines at tram stops.

Honfleur

Known for its famous harbor ringed by teetering, thin, and colorful buildings, and occupied by a constellation of fishing boats and small private yachts, Honfleur is perhaps the finest example of a small Norman port anywhere along the region's long coast. Its architecture and layout will be familiar to anyone who's already spent some time in Normandy, except that here its scale and state of preservation are unmatched.

Most present-day gems of European tourism were once boom towns, and so it was with Honfleur. Its position on the banks of the Seine estuary made it the Le Havre of its day—the town predates its larger neighbor by at least 400 years, the first mention of it being in the 11th century. It rose to prominence particularly after being conquered by the English in the Hundred Years' War, when it was set up as the main link between their French capital, Rouen, and the British Isles. It continued to prosper over the following centuries, becoming a major port first in terms of New World exploration and later New World trade. Its star began to fade, however, during the French Revolution and the following Napoleonic Wars, when it suffered because of a long-standing shipping blockade by the British. Ironically, this waning was probably the making of modern Honfleur, for it meant the port never fully industrialized and perhaps more importantly was not a major target in World War II, which it came through completely unscathed.

Today, it does have to withstand another kind of invasion, though: one of tourists, who come here in their droves, especially in the summer months. They've good reason, though, for there are few places in Normandy that still offer such an evocative insight into the region's past. It's a fantastic place for a slow wander among the old buildings, or to hunker

Honfleur

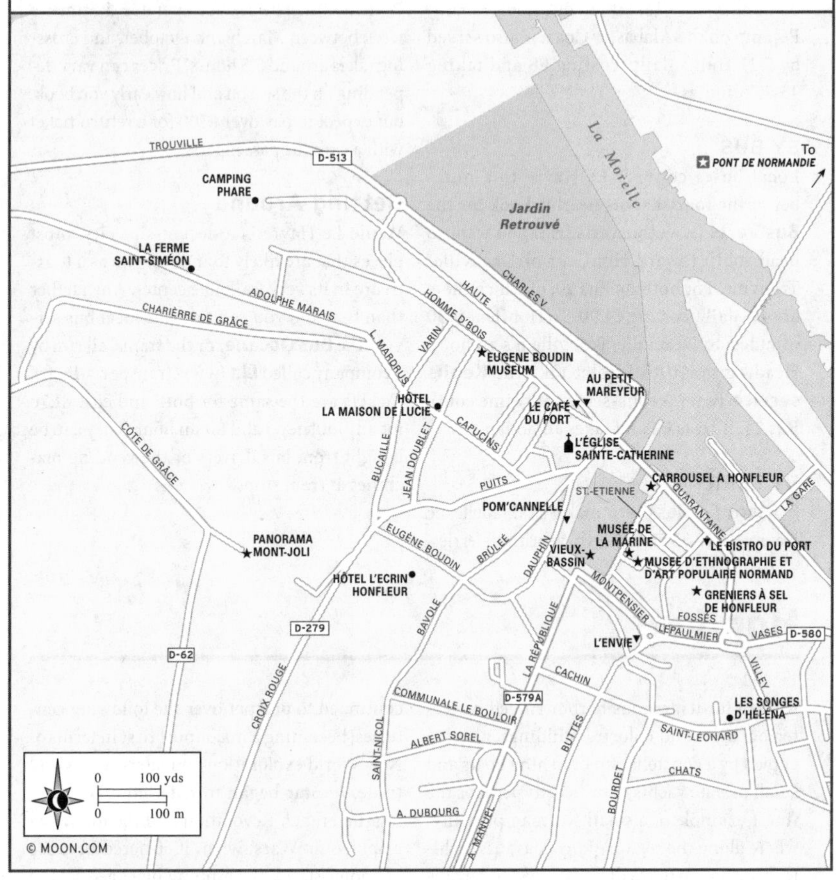

down for a long lunch of great seafood, and even better people-watching on the always-bustling old harbor.

Orientation

The old harbor in the center of Honfleur is broadly rectangular in shape, occupied by bobbing boats. As well as being ringed by colorful old houses, it's also home to numerous restaurants, many of which have terraces spilling out onto the harbor's edge. There are a few narrow backstreets leading from the harbor to more secluded sights, while Honfleur's famous wooden church, the **Église Sainte-Catherine,** is a street back from the harbor's northwest corner.

While it may have a picturesque center, the outskirts of Honfleur are given over to that altogether more humdrum example of urban architecture, the parking lot. The large numbers of visitors every year must be accommodated, and from the roundabout at the end of the D580, which is the most connected entry/exit road to the town, you find yourself very close to two large areas given over entirely to storing your vehicle. These are worth taking advantage of, though, as trying to find space in Honfleur center can be an expensive nightmare. In between these two parking lots is the town's main bus terminal, which in lieu of it having a train station gets a lot of traffic.

The harbor is just a five- to ten-minute walk from all of this, simply following the main road to the right.

SIGHTS

★ Vieux-Bassin

Honfleur's crowning glory, its harbor, is from whence all the explorers and traders who made the town's fortune once set out into the wider world—most notably Samuel de Champlain, who left Honfleur to found Quebec in the 17th century. It was remodeled in 1681 by Admiral Abraham Duqesne, who was actually born in Dieppe.

These days, the harbor is characterized by two different types of architectural style—large stone houses on the south quay and the more iconic narrow wooden ones on the north side—which have inspired the works of thousands of artists, amateur and professional alike. The entrance to the harbor is still guarded by the 18th-century lieutenancy building. This used to be home to the Governor of Honfleur. The harbor itself, meanwhile, is occupied by numerous yachts of different shapes, sizes, and ages. Some are antiques, making the harbor even more picturesque. Keep an eye out for the *Marie-Madeleine* from 1934, *Le Dehel* from 1931, and *Le Sheena* from 1916, which, though they can't be boarded, make for some lovely photo opportunities.

The space is great to casually wander around and take in the lovely architecture, though it can get extremely busy at the height of summer. During this time, the best experience is probably had by heading to one of the many restaurants that line its quays. Find yourself a seat in one of these and you can find almost as much enjoyment watching the crowds as you will looking at the architecture. To make sure this is as relaxing as it can be, try turning up toward the end of lunch (around 2pm); that way, you won't be pressured out to make way for the next serving. Note: Despite the crowds, there are so many restaurants, you'll almost certainly be able to find space in at least one of them.

L'Église Sainte-Catherine

l'Église Sainte-Catherine, Honfleur; tel. 02 31 89 11 83; 9am-7pm daily; free

It's a fact that not everyone might want to own up to, but traveling around Normandy for any length of time can spark a degree of Romanesque/Gothic cathedral fatigue: Once you've seen five awe-inspiring, gravity-defying structures of masonry and light in the space of a week, you may find yourself itching for something new. The wooden Église Sainte-Catherine is just that. Its oldest part dates from the 15th century, and its design and the material used in its construction speak elegantly of Honfleur's character and history.

Built on the model of a market hall, elements of shipbuilding were used in its construction, notably by the "masters of the axe" in Honfleur's shipyards, reputed for being able to sculpt and shape wood however they wanted with their axes. The ceiling and roof of the building were made to resemble an overturned hull (doubly reassuring for sailors, who, when returning to land to pray under its protection, would have perhaps found themselves reimagining their own craft as overturned churches).

Utterly different from other Norman churches, it perhaps inadvertently reminds one of the region's Viking past, looking as much like some great drinking hall as it does a place of worship, no doubt helped by the fact that it often throngs with tourists, especially in the high season. If you want to find a sense of contemplative spirituality in the place, arrive as early as you can, before the crowds.

Greniers à Sel de Honfleur

9B rue de la ville, Honfleur; tel. 02 31 81 88 00; www.ot-honfleur.fr/se-divertir/saison-culturelle/agenda

Constructed in 1670 out of stones from the ramparts of the city that had been taken down to make way for the expansion of the harbor, these buildings were used to store salt

1

2

3

collected from seawater and by cod fishers setting out for Newfoundland. Up to 10,000 tons of salt could be stored in these buildings at one time. These days, they are used as communal halls for regular concerts of all stripes, conferences, and art and photography exhibitions. Outside of these times they're closed. However, the exhibitions are very frequent. Check out Honfleur's cultural agenda, listed on its tourist website, to see what's on when.

Musee d'Ethnographie et d'Art Populaire Normand

Rue de la Prison, Honfleur; tel. 02 31 89 14 12; www.musees-honfleur.fr/musee-d-ethnographie.html; 10am-12pm and 2pm-6:30pm Tues.-Sun. Apr.-Oct., 2:30pm-5:30pm Tues.-Fri., 10am-12pm and 2:30pm-5:30 pm Sat.-Sun. Oct.-Nov. and Feb.-Mar.; adults €4.20, reduced €2.90

Located in a 16th-century timber-frame house and founded in 1896, this was the first ethnographic museum in France dedicated to one of the country's provinces, alongside one in the Provencal city of Arles. It consists of nine rooms, each dedicated to either a different trade or a different aspect of Norman life. Subjects include Norman furniture, clothing, headdresses, and earthenware.

Musée de la Marine

11 quai Saint-Etienne, Honfleur; tel. 02 31 89 14 12; 10am-12pm and 2pm-6:30pm Tues.-Sun. Apr.-Oct., 2:30pm-5:30pm Tues.-Fri., 10am-12 pm and 2:30pm-5:30pm Sat.-Sun. Oct.-Nov. and Feb.-Mar.; adults €4.20, reduced €2.90

Located in Honfleur's old Sainte-Etienne church, which gives it a strangely hallowed vibe and nods to how seriously the people of Honfleur take their relationship with the waves, this maritime museum was founded in 1976 when all collections pertaining to the sea from the ethnography museum were moved here. They tell the story of Honfleur's long and ultimately prosperous relationship with the waves. This includes information on its fishing and ship-building industries, as well as its history of maritime trade and certain folk crafts related to the sea. Best of all, though, is the profusion of scale models of old sailing galleons, sure to delight kids and imaginative adults. You can also find the history of the port here, alongside a collection of engravings and paintings that show how the town looked in the 18th and 19th centuries.

1: Honfleur Harbor **2:** the Musée de la Marine, inside an old church **3:** this classic carrousel on the harbor's edge delights children and nostalgic adults alike

Eugene Boudin Museum

Rue Homme de Bois, Honfleur; tel. 02 31 89 54 00; www.musees-honfleur.fr/musee-eugene-boudin; 10am-12pm and 2pm-6pm Wed.-Mon. Apr.-June and Sept., 10am-6pm Wed.-Mon. July-Aug., 2:30pm-5:30pm Mon. and Wed.-Fri., 10am-12pm and 2:30pm-5:30pm Sat.-Sun. Jan.-Mar. and Oct.-Dec., 10am-12pm and 2:30pm-5:30pm Wed.-Mon. Jan.-Mar. and Oct.-Dec.; adults €8, reduced €6.50

Honfleur was another great inspiration and meeting place for Impressionist painters. Part of the reason for the town's popularity among this group was that one of their great precursors was actually born here. Eugène Boudin, native of Honfleur, was a painter of landscapes and an innovator in terms of leaving his studio to work under the open sky. In Boudin's later years, he helped establish this museum in the town for his art and for other works by his famous contemporaries depicting the local area. The museum itself offers both old-fashioned and modern gallery space, and is seldom too crowded, on account of many not realizing the importance of Boudin in the history of art. There are also some great views of the Pont de Normandie from the top floors.

Carrousel a Honfleur

3 quai Saint-Etienne, Honfleur; May-Oct.; €2.50

Looking like it's always been here, or at least since the 19th century, the delightful two-tiered carousel by Honfleur's old harbor was actually only installed in 1995. Since then, though, it's become an icon of the waterfront, its classic design delighting adults and children alike.

★ Pont de Normandie

Pont de Normandie, Honfleur; www.pontsnormandietancarville.fr; visitors center free, crossing the bridge by car €5.40

Utterly apart from the quaint cobbles of central Honfleur, though visible from the town, is this epic work of civil engineering. Opened in 1995, at the time it was the longest cable-stayed bridge in the world, crossing the mouth of the Seine estuary and linking Le Havre with Honfleur.

As well as offering an incredibly practical function, cutting journeys down massively in this part of Normandy, it is also an awe-inspiring sight. The engineers obviously appreciated this, and although it's primarily a motorway bridge, it can also be crossed by foot, approached from a visitors center on the Le Havre side. It's just under 1.5 miles (2.4 kilometers) long, so to walk across should be about 40 minutes. An unusual tourist activity this may be, but it's rare to get such a close-up look at the kind of stresses and strains put on such structures and the awesome feats of engineering required to resist them. Crossing underneath the bridge and hearing the relentless traffic thunder above you is a both disconcerting and strangely thrilling experience.

The views it offers of the Seine estuary and Honfleur itself are also extremely impressive. Though if you're driving, do remember to keep your eyes on the road!

FOOD

Local Cuisine

LE BISTRO DU PORT

14 quai de la Quarantaine, Honfleur; tel. 02 31 14 11 14; www.bistro-la-grenouille.fr; 12pm-3pm and 7pm-10pm daily; menus €17.80-33

A bustling and nicely designed classic bistro facing Honfleur's outer harbor with a large covered terrace out front. The food is reasonably priced and of a decent quality, with plenty of locally sourced seafood dishes augmenting more terrestrial flavors. As with most places in Honfleur, the great majority of the clientele are tourists, which has its advantages in that English is widely spoken.

AU PETIT MAREYEUR

4 rue Haute, Honfleur; tel. 02 31 98 84 23; 9am-11pm Thurs.-Sun. Feb.-Dec.; set menus €28-70

A cozy restaurant, complete with a fireplace for chilly days. The food is crammed with local flavors, specifically lots of seafood, and is creatively presented in a way that sets apart the dishes from a lot of the surrounding restaurants. The bouillabaisse *Honfleuraise*, a lavish fish stew with what seems like half the contents of the English Channel served on your plate, is particularly recommended.

L'ENVIE

14 place de la Porte de Rouen, Honfleur; tel. 02 14 63 13 64; 11:30am-9:30pm Thurs.-Tues.; menus €17.90-28.50

Put simply, an excellent, unassuming restaurant. In a town like Honfleur, where the heavy tourist trade can permit a certain degree of cynicism to slip into restaurant attitudes, the Envie is a shining light. It offers straightforward local food, such as oysters and *moules frites,* done very well, and in an unpretentious, pleasant atmosphere. It even attracts locals. Booking ahead is recommended.

Budget Options

POM'CANNELLE

60 quai Sainte-Catherine, Honfleur; tel. 02 31 89 55 25; 9am-6pm daily; €3-12

There aren't that many budget eateries on the waterfront at Honfleur, and though the impressive lines of restaurants may have a good atmosphere, if you're watching your wallet or just planning on a light lunch then they won't be what you're after. This solid *crêperie* and ice cream parlor, moderately priced and in a good location, is a decent alternative.

LE CAFÉ DU PORT

7 rue Haute, Honfleur; tel. 02 31 87 33 45; 10am-6pm daily; menu €14.90

Despite its name, this is actually a little back from the port, and as such has slightly lower prices. A fairly basic bistro, the food is nevertheless tasty and well presented—the seafood is an especially good deal, being just as locally sourced as in any of the other restaurants nearby, but a little cheaper.

ACCOMMODATIONS

€50-100

LES SONGES D'HÉLÉNA

7 rue Saint-Léonard, Honfleur; www.chambres-hotes.fr/chambres-hotes_les-songes-d-helena_honfleur_h592939.htm; from €80 d

Chambres d'hôtes (bed-and-breakfasts) are always a good way to avoid expensive hotels, and they often offer just as pleasant an experience, giving you a better idea of how locals live. This is just such a place, located right in the center of town in a restored 18th-century townhouse. There are four separate rooms, all cozy and with private bathrooms. WiFi is available throughout the property. Contact via the Chambres d'Hôtes website.

€100-200

HÔTEL LA MAISON DE LUCIE

44 rue des Capucins, Honfleur; tel. 02 31 14 40 40; www.lamaisondelucie.com; from €170 d

A large 18th-century townhouse that's been lovingly maintained, its rooms offer polished wood floors, elegant furniture, and tasteful eclectic decoration. It's also a short walk from everywhere you might want to visit in Honfleur, and it offers WiFi and flat-screen TVs in all rooms. It was once lived in by the French poet and journalist Lucie Delarue-Mardrus, a writer primarily on the subject of lesbian relationships who was active in the first half of the 20th century. With only nine rooms available, book early if you want to stay here in high season.

HÔTEL L'ECRIN HONFLEUR

19 rue Eugène Boudin, Honfleur; tel. 02 31 14 43 45; www.hotel-ecrin-honfleur.com; from €170 d

"Lavish" is a word batted around a lot in guidebooks, but for this hotel it's an understatement. The Ecrin Honfleur, set within a neoclassical mansion, boasts a positively baroque interior, overflowing with fabric, color, and choice decoration. It nevertheless succeeds in presenting this opulence in a tasteful, classy manner. There is also an on-site spa with a sauna, hot tub, and hammam, and a peaceful outdoor swimming pool ringed by more traditional Norman buildings.

Over €200

LA FERME SAINT SIMÉON

20 route Adolphe Marais, Honfleur; tel. 02 31 81 78 00; https://fermesaintsimeon.fr; from €350 d

This 17th-century farmhouse played host to a number of young artists during the 1800s, and from them the Impressionist movement developed. It used to be a simpler inn, run by a woman called Mother Toutain, who provided exceptional hospitality to some of the greatest painters to ever hold a brush. Artists like Boudin, Corot, and Monet would then head out into the surrounding countryside and paint images that now hang on the walls of the world's most famous museums.

Needless to say, the hotel's way out of the price range of struggling artists today. But it continues to offer exceptional comfort and a relaxed, inspiring atmosphere within its renovated farmhouse buildings. There's also a deluxe spa on-site now, complete with sauna, hammam, hot tub, and massage options, and a top-end restaurant, which serves inventive modern updates of the kind of rustic fare that Mother Toutain would have fed the gathered artists all those years ago—they do a particularly strong line in lobsters. The hotel is just a short walk from Honfleur.

Camping

CAMPING PHARE

Boulevard Charles V, Honfleur; tel. 02 31 89 10 26; www.normandie-sur-mer.fr/25-nos-campings/125-camping-phare; open Apr.-Oct.; pitch €18

A no-frills campsite in a lush green environment that's excellently located, being just a short walk into the center of Honfleur and, in the other direction, to the beach. There are electricity outlets for camper vans, toilets, and showers. The atmosphere is friendly, as a number of people set up here for periods of one week or more. If you're planning on staying here in the high season (July and August), it's a good idea to book a pitch a good month or so ahead. Outside of that time, you should be OK just turning up.

TRANSPORTATION

By Car

From Paris, the fastest way to Honfleur is along the A13. It's a journey of about 120 miles (193 kilometers) that will take around 2.5 hours and will include some motorway tolls, totaling around €15. From Caen it's the same motorway in the opposite direction, with a journey length of about 40 miles (64 kilometers) and travel time of just under an hour. Tolls should be around €5. From Le Havre, take the epic Pont de Normandie, with a cost of just over €5. Be aware that the freeways leading to the Pont out of Le Havre can be hectic for an unconfident driver.

There are a couple of large parking lots on the main approach to the town along the D580. Both require payment. The one before the town center is a flat fee of €4 for the day, while the central parking lot has staggered prices starting at €1.40 for 30 minutes and going up to €22 for 24 hours. If you're planning on spending longer than a couple of hours in Honfleur, it's better to park before this central lot, as the walk from the other is only about five minutes more.

By Bus

Buses are the only form of public transport connected with Honfleur. Four to seven a day service Deauville/Trouville, taking 30 minutes at a cost of €2.50. Seven to 13 a day travel to Caen, taking around 2.5 hours and costing €4.90—there are also a couple of express services to Caen costing €12.10 and taking about an hour. Four to six buses serve Le Havre, costing €4.90 and taking around 30 minutes.

Getting to Honfleur from Paris means heading to one of these other transport hubs and connecting with one of their bus services.

Deauville and Trouville

Deauville and Trouville are two towns that share the same river but have different characters: That's the official line, at least. And while there remains a certain truth to it, chichi Deauville on the one side and working-class fishing port Trouville on the other, over the years there's been a definite spread of the high life. And now both communes are really just part of a single luxury destination, albeit one with a slightly more rugged architecture underneath, and the other that was always designed to gleam.

Deauville's ascent to becoming the "Queen of Norman beaches" began in the 1860s, with an investment by Duc Charles Auguste Louis Joseph de Morny, half-brother of Napoleon III. He built the train station that linked the town to Paris, a small casino, and a race course that would take advantage of this already famous horse-rearing region. High society began to flock to the town for their holidays, though it was only with the founding of the luxurious Normandy Barrière and Royal hotels in 1911 and 1913 respectively that Deauville reached its full renown as the "Parisian Riviera," and became lodged in French consciousness as a byword for all that is fashionable and chic. Trouville, meanwhile, which was still a small working fishing port, found itself pulled along on its neighbor's coattails, as better restaurants and bigger houses started to appear here, too.

Today, Deauville and Trouville are not so much towns full of sights that one comes to see as much as they are activities to be experienced. From staying in their top-end hotels, to gambling in their casinos, to wandering their elegant beachfront boardwalks, the holidays people take here have remained uncannily similar for the past 100 years.

Deauville and Trouville

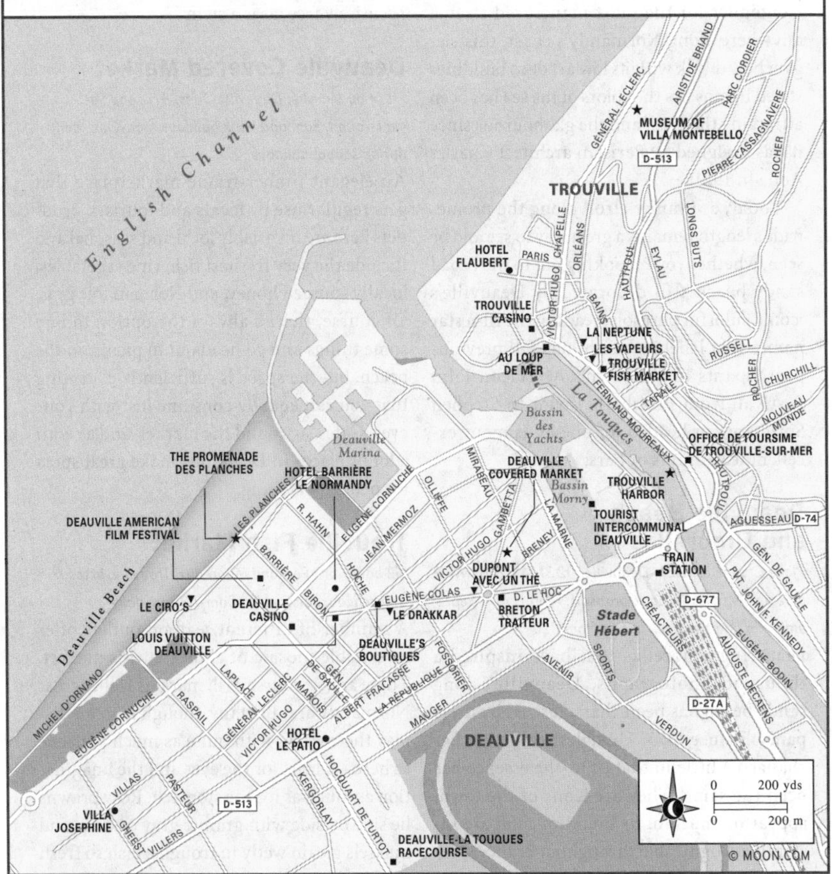

Orientation

Separated by the River Touques, the train station and the main road leading to both towns are just on the Deauville side. Arriving from either of them, turn right and you cross the bridge into Trouville. All of the town's main commerce lines the banks of the river that stretches about a third of a mile (half a kilometer) toward the town casino and beach. Just before them is the town's fish market and some of its better restaurants.

Turning left from the main road or station you enter Deauville proper, the spiritual heart of which is without a doubt the **Normandy Barrière** hotel and its adjoining casino. To reach that, cross the first roundabout you reach and make for the rue Désiré le Hoc. Follow this straight across the place de Morny until it turns into the rue Eugène Colas—both these roads are lined with top-end boutiques. The Normandy Barrière looms at the end of this street, a castle in the classic Norman half-timber style. On the other side of it is Deauville Beach and the **Promenade des Planches,** where movie-star names grace the beach huts, and seeing and being seen is elevated to an art form.

SIGHTS

Promenade des Planches

Contender for the most manicured stretch anywhere along Normandy's coast, this elegant boardwalk with its low art deco buildings styled in mosaics the colors of the sea has been attracting the great and the glamourous since it was designed by Parisian architect Charles Adda in 1921.

Today, a summer stroll along the promenade's length remains a great way to see and be seen, whether you're looking out to the broad sandy beach still decorated by Deauville's iconic colorful parasols, reading the film star names that label its beach huts (all previous participants in the town's American Film Festival, from Elizabeth Taylor to Stephen Spielberg), or headed for one of its many excellent restaurants or bars.

Deauville Beach and Umbrellas

Place Claude Lelouch, Deauville; 02 31 14 02 16; www.indeauville.fr/les-fameux-parasols; rentals Apr.-Sept.; umbrella and two deck chairs from €20

Featuring umbrellas that have inspired a thousand photographs, Deauville's long sandy beach has been characterized by these parasols since 1875. Though their design has changed a little in that time, the essence has been the same. They are icons of the town, appear on much of its branding, and are instantly recognizable throughout France.

Unfurled, too, they're much more than just parasols, each having a long skirt that hangs from its rear, hiding bathers from the prying eyes of people passing on the promenade. All this said, they are quite far from the sea, particularly at low tide, so if you're planning on going for a swim, be prepared for a decent walk.

Organize rentals on the Place Claude Lelouch, which is toward the north end of the Promenades des Planches. Someone will then take you out to your designated parasol and get you set up. Though it gets busy in the summer, it's rare that all places will be taken, so don't worry too much about having to arrive at the beach very early. Of course, if you don't want to pay for a deck chair, a seat on the sand is entirely free, as is a swim.

Deauville Covered Market

Place du Marché, Deauville; Tues., Fri., and Sat. year-round, Sun. and bank holidays Mar.-Oct., daily during school holidays

An elegant timber-frame marketplace that gets regular use by locals and tourists, products here are invariably local and seasonal and include the very freshest fish, ripe vegetables, locally sourced honey, and Norman foie gras. Of course, there's always the option to buy some things and go head out to picnic on the beach, but the space is sufficiently charming that you can equally consume just with your eyes. Cafés surround the market, and as with a lot of places in Deauville, make great spots for people-watching.

Trouville Fish Market

152 boulevard Fernand Moureaux, Trouville; https://lemarcheauxpoissons.fr; 8am-7:30pm daily

A number of different seafood outlets offer a veritable mosaic of choice at this market. There are, of course, fish markets right across Normandy and Brittany, though few can display their wares with quite as much panache as here—a feast for the eyes and the imagination as much as for the stomach. Rosy prawns lie side by side with granite gray oysters, and mussels gleam wetly in troughs. Fish so fresh they look still living stare at you with beady black eyes, and lobsters swim in their tanks, oblivious that they, too, are on the menu. All is offset by freshly chipped ice, white as snow; hand-drawn prices; and the sight of small fishing trawlers pulled up on the dock behind, a reminder that seafood does not come much fresher than this.

As well as selling fish wholesale, the outlets also have tasting options. So, if you feel like pulling up a chair and watching oysters freshly shucked for your benefit, then washing

---

1: the oft-photographed umbrellas of Deauville Beach 2: Deauville Casino

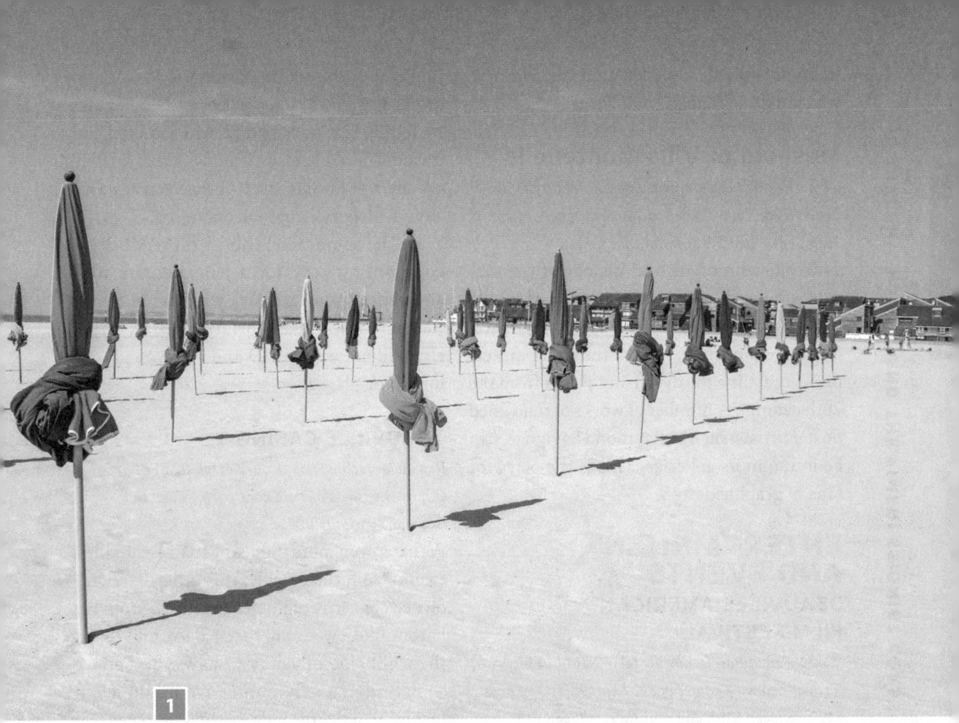

1

2

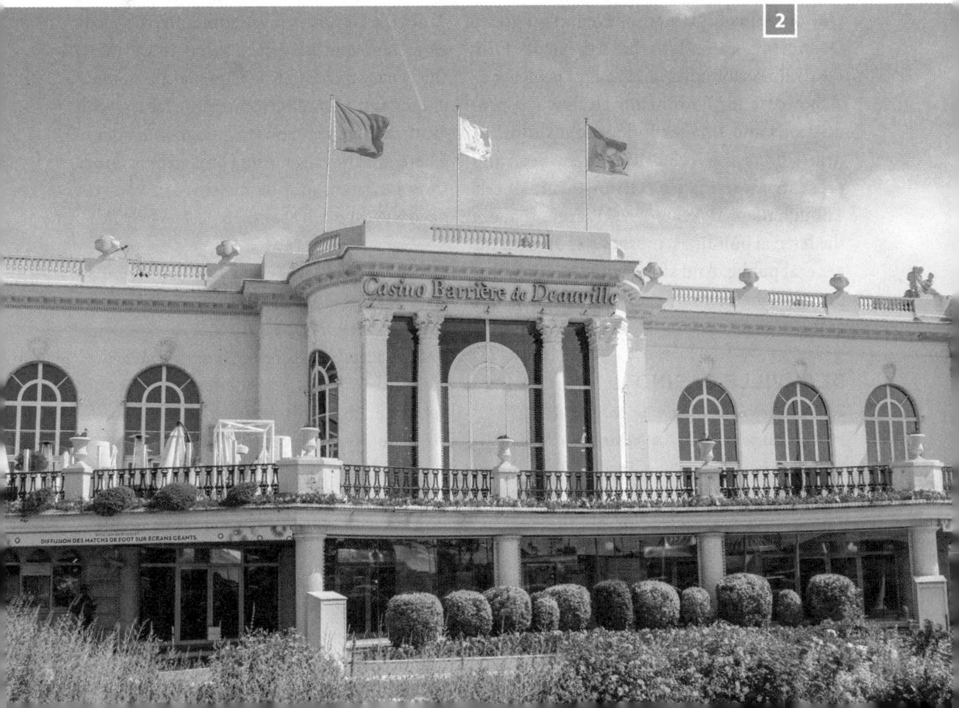

them down with some ice-cold Chardonnay, you can do so here.

Museum of Villa Montebello

64 rue Général Leclerc, Trouville-sur-Mer; tel. 02 31 88 16 26; 10am-12pm and 2pm-5:30pm daily June-Sept., 2pm-5:30pm daily Oct.-May

This museum of art and history of the seaside is housed in a spectacular mansion, one of several lining Trouville's boardwalk. Its collections span from some of the first painters of the coastline to advertising prints from the 20th century. A number of works of renowned poster artists, such as Raymond Savignac, can be found in its galleries. This is the place for fans of graphic design.

ENTERTAINMENT AND EVENTS

DEAUVILLE AMERICAN FILM FESTIVAL

Multiple locations, Deauville; tel. 02 31 14 14 14; www.festival-deauville.com; Aug. 31-Sept. 9; festival pass €160, reduced €110, day pass €35, reduced €16

One of the many glamorous events that graces Deauville's calendar, the American Film Festival was founded in 1975 and is meant as a showcase for both major Hollywood productions and smaller independent films. It draws bona fide celebrities every year and presents more than 100 films to audiences. Though there are certain V.I.P. areas that dot the festival buildings, most of it is open to the general public. And along with the films that premiere here, you never know who you're going to see.

DEAUVILLE CASINO

2 rue Edmond Blanc, Deauville; tel. 02 31 14 31 14; www.casinosbarriere.com/en/deauville.html; 10am-2am Mon.-Thurs., 10am-3am Fri., 10am-4am Sat.

This is the real deal. For all the shabby, pseudo-glamorous casinos that line the Normandy and Brittany coastlines, this one makes amends. Here, you are James Bond. Neoclassical stylings welcome you up a grand staircase to plush high-ceilinged halls, which jingle with the sound of money. The casino offers slot machines, a series of table games including blackjack and French roulette, and poker. There are also two on-site bars, three on-site restaurants, and a broad terrace area from which you can look out to sea.

At the same time, there's no strict dress code policy, save for a ban on tank tops and shorts; you can leave your tux at home. Remember your passport, though; anything else will not work as ID and you won't be allowed in.

TROUVILLE CASINO

Rue du Maréchal Foch, Trouville; tel. 02 31 87 75 00; www.casinosbarriere.com/fr/trouville.html; 9:30am-2am daily

Perhaps even more imposing than Deauville's casino from the outside, this other Barrière-owned concern dominates the end of Trouville harbor like a wedding cake palace, and is just the right side of gaudy to have you believe something equally impressive might await inside. To a degree it does, though in general Trouville Casino is more similar to the seedy establishments that can be found up and down the Norman coast. Inside are mainly slot machines and a few electronic game tables, with only a few cursory nods to human interaction. There are two restaurants and weekly dance shows. Also, it may be kitschy, but you still need a passport ID to enter.

SHOPPING

BRETON TRAITEUR

1 place de Morny, Deauville; tel. 02 31 88 22 90; www.breton-traiteur.com; 8:30am-7:30pm Tues.-Sun.

It's hard to know how delicatessens could get better than this family-run shop on the place de Morny. Every surface, it seems, is occupied by some freshly fabricated savory delight bursting with Norman flavor, or is stocked with expertly chosen wine, or is exuding the warmth and buttery rich scent of recently roasted chicken. Its mirrored ceiling and art deco stylings only enhance these effects. No wonder it's so frequently bustling with customers.

Lucien Barrière: The Business Behind Deauville

Aside from the Duke de Morny, there can be few individuals who have had more impact on Deauville as it is today than François André, progenitor of the Groupe Lucien Barrière, which today runs both the two largest hotels in town and its casino, as well as many other luxury establishments along both the Brittany and Normandy coasts.

THE BIRTH OF THE MODERN RESORT

Originally from Ardèche, André came up to Paris in the early years of the 20th century, and with his business partner began building the Hôtel Normandy and having the Deauville casino refitted. Indeed, repeating this process in the Brittany town of La Baule, it's argued that he invented the concept of the modern resort, drawing casinos, luxury hotels, and sports facilities together all on a single site. So successful was he at this that he set a tone for a certain kind of luxury experience that became respected right across the world. The **Hotel Normandy** in particular exemplifies this, having appeared in multiple pieces of French cinema and become well known throughout the country.

LUXURY HOTEL BRAND

The name Lucien Barrière was that of André's nephew and sole heir. Also from Ardèche and born to a family of goatherds, he founded the Lucien Barrière group in the 1950s off the back of his uncle's properties and continued to oversee its expansion. After his death in 1990, his daughter Diane Barrière-Desseigne took over the company, which then passed to her husband Dominique Desseigne after her death in 2001. The group now runs 18 luxury hotels and 37 casinos. The Normandy and Deauville, though, remain its undisputed spiritual home.

RUE EUGÈNE COLAS AND RUE DÉSIRÉ LE HOC

Several luxury brands have outlets lining the rues Eugène Colas and Désiré le Hoc. Frequented by many holidaying Parisians, these shops are as essential a part of Deauville as its boardwalk, beach umbrellas, or the Normandy Hotel. The shop for **Louis Vuitton** (103 rue Eugène Colas, 14800 Deauville; tel. 02 31 88 65 88; 10am-1pm and 3pm-7:30pm Mon.-Fri., 10am-7:30pm Sat., 10:30am-1pm and 3pm-7:30pm Sun.) is ostentatiously housed in a miniature version of a half-timber house, and nearby are outlets of Lacoste, Hermès, and Longchamp, to name just a few. A lot of the goods here tend to be aimed at the older market, who constitute most of Deauville's wealthier tourists. Don't come here looking for a good deal on luxury products, though; this town is all about conspicuous consumption.

SPECTATOR SPORTS

★ DEAUVILLE-LA TOUQUES RACECOURSE

45 avenue Hocquart de Turtot, Deauville; tel. 02 31 14 20 00; events throughout the year but most Grand Prix races in late July-Aug.; adults €8 weekends and €5 weekdays, reduced €5 weekends and €3 weekdays, Grand Prix adults €10, reduced €8

There's a fair claim to saying that this racecourse is where it all started for Deauville. Before the hotels, the casinos, the boardwalk, or the fashion boutiques, there were horses. Indeed, the area is and was historically the number-one thoroughbred-raising region in all of France, with stud farms still dotting the nearby countryside. This racecourse was part of the initial investment in the town by Charles Auguste Louis Joseph, duc de Morny back in 1862, which sparked its rise to prominence. Nothing, after all, attracts the wealthy quite like horse racing.

And though well over a hundred years have gone by since then, there's much that can be said to have stayed the same. The main horse racing season still takes place in August, when Parisians are taking a summer hiatus from their jobs. They descend on the racecourse to dress smartly and drink champagne, gossip and gamble, while some of the finest horses in the world take turns on the track in front of them.

The buildings of the course are cast in a faux-Norman style, meaning there's no mistaking where you are. With drinks for sale and plenty of things to look at, it's worth a visit, even if you're not interested in the racing itself.

FOOD

Local Cuisine

★ LES VAPEURS

160 boulevard Fernand Moureaux, Trouville; tel. 02 31 88 15 24; 9am-12am daily; menus €25-65

Improbably straddling the line between top-end seafood restaurant and working-man's bistro, this harbor-front establishment is a Trouville icon that has been packed out almost every night for more than 90 years, though dinner turn-over is fast, making reservations a precaution rather than a necessity. Penguin-suited waiters bustle between tightly packed tables both inside and on the terrace, hoisting mouthwatering dishes of everything from lobster to *moules frites*.

LE DRAKKAR

77 rue Eugène Colas, Deauville; tel. 02 31 88 71 24; www.restaurants-trouville.com/Drakkar-restaurant-deauville.html; 8:30am-12am daily; mains €17.70-40.10

A stalwart of Deauville's restaurant scene: In many respects, it's a fairly ordinary French restaurant of the kind that are seen from Brest to Nice, but this being Deauville, ordinary wouldn't quite cut it. The traditional interior is polished to a shine, the waiters do their jobs with a quiet intensity of purpose, and the food is of a rich, lavish quality. The dishes are classic Norman and classic French—go for the steak with Béarnaise sauce if you're feeling extravagant. It also doesn't have quite the same dedication to seafood as many places in town, meaning if you're a dedicated meat eater, here's a good place to indulge.

DUPONT AVEC UN THE

20 place de Morny, Deauville; tel. 02 31 88 20 79; www.dupontavecunthe.fr; 8am-7pm Thurs.-Tues.;

a bustling evening service at Les Vapeurs

menus €17.90-21.90

The more you look at it, the more you realize Deauville is a town of institutions. Businesses open here and they fast become part of the fabric of the place, and legends are born in the space of a century. Dupont Avec Un The is one of them. Founded in 1912, it is perfectly positioned, with a generous terrace spilling onto the place de Morny. This elegant tearoom serves a wide variety of French patisserie and hot drinks and is steeped in sophistication and good taste. As popular among locals as it is visitors, here you are both a watcher and watched. From the leather-skinned, white-haired men in chinos and pastel sweaters to the octogenarian ladies feeding their tiny dogs macarons, it can seem that things haven't changed here in a generation. The best breakfast spot in town.

LE CIRO'S

Promenades des Planches, Deauville; tel. 02 31 14 31 14; www.casinosbarriere.com/fr/deauville/le-ciro-s.html; 12pm-2pm and 7:30pm-10pm Mon., Thurs., and Fri., 12pm-2:30pm and 7:30pm-10:30pm Sat., 12pm-2:30pm and 7:30pm-10pm Sun.; menus €36-95

A restaurant affiliated with Deauville's casino, it sits picturesquely on the town boardwalk. Its design is pure belle epoque, and from certain angles you'd really think you were dining a hundred years ago. The food, which is of the classic Norman variety, is reliably superb. The seafood in particular does not just taste delicious but is beautifully presented as well. It's truly a feast for all the senses.

Budget Options

LA NEPTUNE

6 rue Amiral de Maigret, Trouville; tel. 02 31 88 10 25; mains €8-14

La Neptune probably doesn't make many guidebooks, tucked away as it is just behind Trouville's town hall, but it's a great reminder that for all the glitz and glamour of the two towns that there are some real people living here too. It's an authentic local bar with a great atmosphere and inexpensive food that isn't just cynically aimed at the tourist market. This is a good place to drop into if the whole scene is just starting to feel a bit *trop*, as the French would say.

ACCOMMODATIONS

€50-100

HÔTEL LE PATIO

180 avenue de la République, Deauville; tel. 02 31 88 25 07; www.hotel-lepatio.fr; from €82 d

A charming, inexpensive hotel in the faux-Normandy style hiding in Deauville's backstreets, rhe rooms are fairly basic but come well fitted out with all modern conveniences, such as WiFi, flat-screen TVs, and en suite bathrooms. If you want to come experience the luxury of Deauville without splurging on accommodations, this is a good choice. Its name, Le Patio, refers to a small sun-trap garden out back. It's a popular place, so make sure to book early.

€100-200

★ HOTEL FLAUBERT

Rue Gustave Flaubert, Trouville-sur-Mer; tel. 02 31 88 37 23; www.flaubert.fr; from €129 d

Named for the famous Norman writer, this is the kind of seaside hotel that belongs to a glamorous 1950s movie. With views out across Trouville's boardwalk and beyond that to the sea, the rooms are tasteful and well lit, decorated in light colors that make the most of their floor-to-ceiling windows. Some rooms have balconies wide enough to sit out on, and indeed one of the best experiences here is the offer of breakfast in your room, where it can be had out on the balcony watching the sea break and the people of Trouville greet the day. It's extremely popular, so you must book well in advance.

VILLA JOSEPHINE

23 rue des Villas, Deauville; tel. 02 31 14 18 00; www.villajosephine.fr; from €190 d

Looking something like a miniature version of the Hotel Normandy, this 19th-century half-timber villa in its own grounds is an excellent second-tier choice. Its rooms are luxuriously decorated with plenty of rich colored

1

2

fabric and individual features. There are only seven rooms, and as with most other hotels in Deauville and Trouville, demand is high, so the earlier you book the more likely you are to get a place.

Over €200

HOTEL BARRIÈRE LE NORMANDY

38 rue Jean Mermoz, Deauville; tel. 02 31 98 66 22; www.hotelsbarriere.com/fr/deauville/le-normandy.html; from €219 d

An icon of the town, just a short walk from Deauville's beachfront, Le Normandy, with its opulent traditional wood-frame exterior and paneled, softly furnished interior, is remarkably cozy for a five-star hotel. Its American bar is a particular gem, offering the comfort of a Victorian gentlemen's club combined with the efficiency and quality of French service. The founding hotel of the Barrière Group, which runs numerous other luxury establishments throughout Normandy and Brittany, rooms are big and bristle with wooden fittings and traditional details. There's also a small indoor pool and a spa on-site.

Camping

CAMPING CHANT DES OISEAUX

19 rue des Sansonnets, Royan; tel. 02 31 88 06 42; www.camping-royan-chantdesoiseaux.com; pitch €30, cabin from €525 per week

One of the most spectacular campsites anywhere in Normandy, laid out on a series of tiers in the cliff face, it offers unencumbered views out across the English Channel and toward Le Havre in the east. At night, the sea twinkles with the lights of ships, either large cargo ones as they queue to get into port, or fishermen out searching for the next day's *fruits de mer.* There's an on-site snack bar and basic facilities, but frankly it's the location that earns its high rates. A popular place for summering families, the cabins especially can book up fast in the high season. Also, make sure your tent is well secured; in the rare case of high winds, there's not much cover.

1: the lavish heart of the Hotel Normandy 2: the Hotel Flaubert: a perfect beachfront hotel

INFORMATION

TOURIST INTERCOMMUNAL DEAUVILLE

Quai de l'impératrice Eugénie, Deauville; tel. 02 31 14 40 00; www.indeauville.fr; 10am-6pm Mon.-Sat., 10am-1pm and 2pm-5pm Sun.

It's safe to say Deauville is well primed for tourism, and this is a top-end tourist office not far from the station, multilingual and brimming with ideas of things to do in the town and local area.

OFFICE DE TOURISME DE TROUVILLE-SUR-MER

32 boulevard Fernand Moureaux, Trouville-sur-Mer; tel. 02 31 14 60 70; www.trouvillesurmer.org/index.php/fr; 9:30am-7pm Mon.-Sat., 10am-6pm Sun.

Situated just over the bridge from Deauville in a one-story building, it's not quite as flashy as what its neighboring town has to offer, but that's hardly a surprise. Nevertheless, it's full of the same kind of extensive literature and informative staff. And there are longer opening hours, which must count for something!

TRANSPORTATION

Getting There

BY CAR

Most will arrive in town along the D677, which comes in just on the Deauville side of the River Touques next to its train station. This connects to the A13, from which Paris, Rouen, and Caen can be reached. Paris is about 123 miles (198 kilometers) away, and the journey from there takes about 2.5 hours. Expect to pay around €15 in tolls. From Rouen it's 57 miles (92 kilometers) taking about an hour, with tolls of around €5, and to Caen, 31 miles (50 kilometers) in the other direction, it's about 50 minutes. Expect €5 tolls.

Parking in Trouville and Deauville can be pricey with most spots costing about €1 every half hour, though if you persevere around their backstreets you may find some free parking.

BY TRAIN

Trains arrive at the **Gare de Trouville-Deauville** (Place Louis Armand, Deauville; tel. 36 35; www.gares-sncf.com/fr/gare/frtrd/trouville-deauville; 6:20am-9:45pm Mon.-Fri., 6:40am-9:45pm Sat., 7:20am-9:15pm Sun.). Most of the time, a train to Deauville means changing at Lisieux. This is 20 minutes away, costing €8. There are 9-12 trains daily. There are also two or three trains going straight to Paris every day, taking about 2.5 hours. These cost around €40, though it depends on how early you book. Farther destinations that can be reached from Lisieux include Caen, which is €16 and takes a little over an hour, with 6-11 connections running daily, and Rouen, which is €24, taking also a little more than an hour and running 5-8 times daily.

BY BUS

The **Bus Verts,** which leave from just outside the train station, can take you to Le Havre, Honfleur, and, in the other direction, Caen. Bus 20 is the one that serves all these towns. It takes two hours to Caen for €4.90 (7-12 buses every day), 1 hour 15 minutes to Le Havre for €4.90, and 30 minutes to Honfleur for €2.50—the same bus for these last two destinations, of which there are 4-7 every day.

Getting Around

Both Trouville and Deauville are fairly small, walkable towns in themselves, where you shouldn't have too much need for public transport. The farthest distance you're likely to go, on foot, is between Deauville and Trouville beach. Fortunately, there's a **foot passenger ferry** service crossing the harbor (Departure Quai Albert, 06 83 78 95 94; www.le-bac-de-trouville-deauville.fr), costing €1.20 each way. It's a very short crossing, and runs roughly every five minutes every day 9am-7pm March-May, and 8:30am-10:30pm June-September. There's also a foot bridge, only open at very low tide, that costs €0.50 to cross. The local bus service is the **Bus Verts** (www.busverts.fr), which also goes farther afield than just Trouville and Deauville, linking the towns to the surrounding countryside. A short journey on this service will only be €1.50 a ticket. Annoyingly, though, there's no single route that runs between Deauville and Trouville center, with buses from both terminating outside the railway station, which is effectively the midpoint between the two towns. Taxis can be booked with **Central Taxis Deauville-Trouville** (02 31 87 11 11; www.gie-central-taxis.fr). Expect a journey from Trouville to Deauville beach to cost about €10.

Caen, Bayeux, and the D-Day Landing Beaches

Calais may have seemed the more obvious choice, but when it came to staging the biggest sea invasion of all time and one of the most decisive battles of the Second World War, it was western Normandy that the Allies decided upon, and so the region became lodged in world consciousness forevermore.

Today, a whole industry exists to commemorate the soldiers who put to shore that blustery June day in 1944, and it draws visitors from all over the world to this low-lying stretch of coastline, characterized by long sandy beaches and a lush hinterland, so peaceful that in places, if it weren't for the occasional concrete remains of Nazi defensive positions, it would be hard to believe it had ever touched by war at all.

The region's towns often bear the scars of the invasion more openly.

Highlights

Look for ★ to find recommended sights, activities, dining, and lodging.

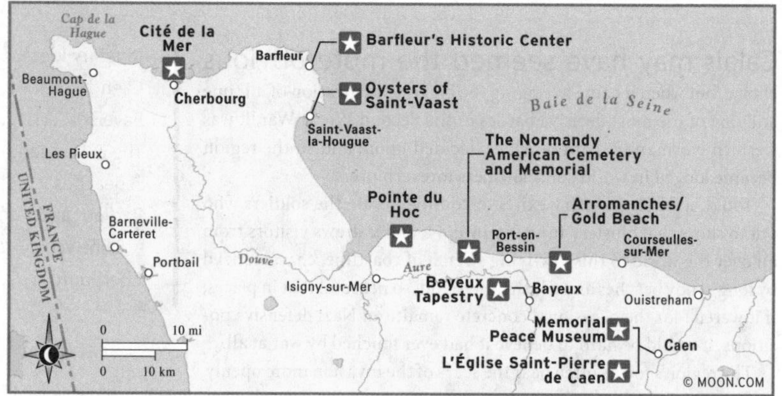

★ **Memorial Peace Museum:** The most extensive museum dedicated to military history in Normandy, it serves as a reminder of why nothing like World War II should ever be allowed to happen again (page 130).

★ **L'Église Saint-Pierre de Caen:** A lavishly decorated gothic church that survived the Siege of Caen remarkably intact. Not the town's biggest place of worship, but one of its most impressive (page 133).

★ **Bayeux Tapestry:** The world's most famous comic strip: a 164-foot (50-meter) embroidery depicting the events surrounding the Norman conquest of England in 1066 (page 144).

★ **Arromanches/Gold Beach:** One of the British landing grounds on D-Day, and the location of the remains of the massive man-made Mulberry harbor, essential to the war effort. Its scale is almost impossible to convey in photographs; only by being here do you really appreciate what an awesome accomplishment this was (page 157).

★ **The Normandy American Cemetery and Memorial:** Like a small patch of America in Normandy, a sea of white crosses and monuments both glorious and somber make this a powerful and poignant place to reflect (page 160).

★ **Pointe du Hoc:** One of the places where Normandy's topography was most affected by the D-Day battle, this landscape of craters and twisted metal has become its own memorial to the horrors of war (page 161).

★ **Barfleur's Historic Center:** A charming seaside village from which, in 1066, William the Conqueror made his original embarkation for England (page 173).

★ **Oysters of Saint-Vaast:** Some of the best oysters in France can be found here, and it's all the more pleasurable to eat them while overlooking the tidal reaches where they are farmed (page 177).

★ **Cité de la Mer:** An extensive museum dedicated to all things of or pertaining to the sea, housed inside Cherbourg's former ferry terminal, the largest art deco structure in the world (page 182).

With so much destroyed in the days that followed the Allied assault, many are now a mishmash of old and new. Nowhere is this more apparent than in Caen, the region's capital and once the favored city of William the Conqueror. The catastrophic damage suffered here during a month-long siege by Allied troops laid waste to its heritage, though many of the town's most impressive Romanesque monuments have now been restored, and they now bristle almost incongruously from its otherwise modern streets.

Just down the road, Bayeux was miraculously spared the ravages of the Allied advance, and now stands as a beautifully preserved reminder of Normandy's prosperous medieval past. Old watermills still turn in its river, and timber-frame houses teeter over its streets, while it draws tourists in with an artifact dedicated to another, far earlier, cross-Channel invasion: the Bayeux Tapestry, a 164-foot (50-meter) length of embroidered fabric depicting the events of William the Conqueror's 1066 conquest of England—perhaps the most famous comic strip in the world.

The region is more than just a museum to the monumental events of its history, however, and there remains a strong living culture here as well. This is true in Caen, with its lively student population, and in its many quaint villages, where local produce the equal of any in Normandy is prepared. Indeed, the oysters of Saint-Vaast, a little north of the landing beaches, are famous throughout France, and to eat one at sunset, overlooking the oyster beds, with a cool glass of white wine in hand, should be considered as much of a draw to this fascinating area as any of its bloody past.

HISTORY

Following a push west from the lands ceded to them by the Frankish king in the 9th century, the Normans soon began to make this fertile area in northern Calvados and on the sheltered coast of the Cotentin Peninsula the heart of their kingdom. Under the leadership of William the Conqueror and his brother Odo, the towns of Caen and Bayeux began to grow and soon boasted some of the most impressive architecture in Europe; they became thriving centers of commerce and trade.

In 1066, it was Barfleur in the northern Cotentin from where William first set out on his ultimate conquest of England. The shipwrights of that town were responsible for making his famous flagship, the *Mora*, and indeed, the port soon enjoyed a period of prosperity as one of the main crossing points for the Normans with their island kingdom over the sea. Many years later, this ease of access worked to its disadvantage when English King Edward III landed here, enacting a raid that was to become the start of England and France's Hundred Years' War.

The region was to remain on the frontlines of cross-Channel conflict over the centuries, including the Battles of Barfleur and La Hougue during the War of the English Succession in 1692. As a result, this coastal stretch became part of French military architect Vauban's project to secure the borders of France, which in turn led to the building of the largest artificially constructed harbor in the world, complete with fortifications, in Cherbourg 80 years later.

Not that these fortifications came in very useful in 1944, when the Allied forces united against Hitler to stage the greatest amphibious assault in all of history. The Germans had made this stretch of the Norman coastline part of their infamous Atlantic Wall defense system, the bunkers and gun emplacements of which can still be seen to this day. Nevertheless, the Allies persevered. After two months of fighting, despite much of its heritage being leveled, the region was free once again and able to rebuild.

Previous: Just a small remnant of Arromanches' Mulberry Harbor, which still rings the horizon; detail of the Bayeux Tapestry; eating St Vaast oysters with a cool white wine

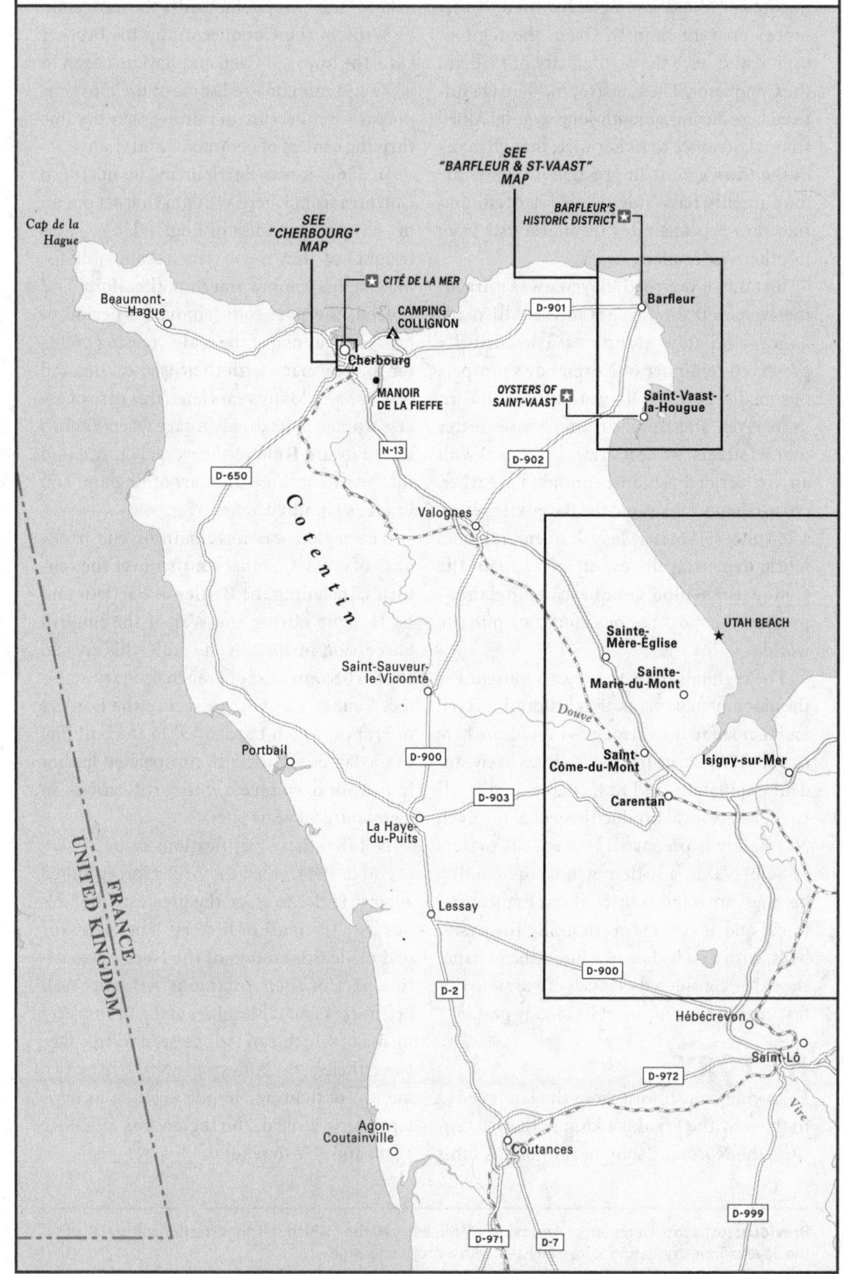
Caen, Bayeux, and the D-Day Landing Beaches
SEE "BARFLEUR & ST-VAAST" MAP
BARFLEUR'S HISTORIC DISTRICT
Cap de la Hague
SEE "CHERBOURG" MAP
CITÉ DE LA MER
Beaumont-Hague
CAMPING COLLIGNON
Barfleur
D-901
Cherbourg
MANOIR DE LA FIEFFE
OYSTERS OF SAINT-VAAST
Saint-Vaast-la-Hougue
N-13
D-902
D-650
Cotentin
Valognes
UTAH BEACH
Sainte-Mère-Église
Sainte-Marie-du-Mont
Saint-Sauveur-le-Vicomte
Douve
Portbail
D-900
Saint-Côme-du-Mont
Isigny-sur-Mer
Carentan
D-903
La Haye-du-Puits
FRANCE
UNITED KINGDOM
Lessay
D-900
D-2
Hébécrevon
Saint-Lô
D-972
Vire
Agon-Coutainville
Coutances
D-999
D-971
D-7

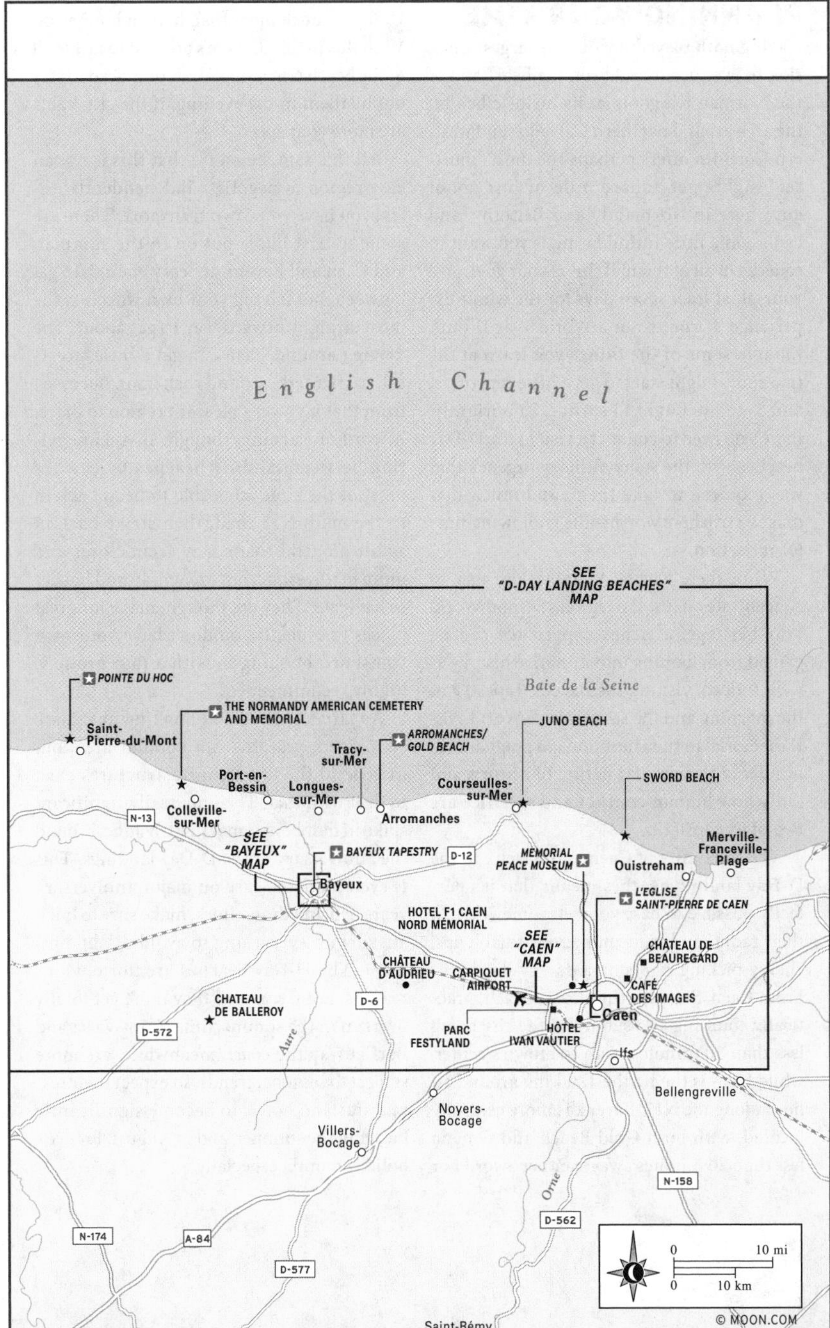
English Channel
SEE "D-DAY LANDING BEACHES" MAP
Baie de la Seine
POINTE DU HOC
THE NORMANDY AMERICAN CEMETERY AND MEMORIAL
Saint-Pierre-du-Mont
ARROMANCHES/ GOLD BEACH
JUNO BEACH
Tracy-sur-Mer
SWORD BEACH
Port-en-Bessin
Longues-sur-Mer
Courseulles-sur-Mer
Colleville-sur-Mer
Arromanches
N-13
SEE "BAYEUX" MAP
BAYEUX TAPESTRY
D-12
MEMORIAL PEACE MUSEUM
Merville-Franceville-Plage
Ouistreham
Bayeux
L'EGLISE SAINT-PIERRE DE CAEN
HOTEL F1 CAEN NORD MÉMORIAL
SEE "CAEN" MAP
CHÂTEAU DE BEAUREGARD
CHÂTEAU D'AUDRIEU
CARPIQUET AIRPORT
CAFÉ DES IMAGES
CHATEAU DE BALLEROY
D-6
Caen
D-572
PARC FESTYLAND
HÔTEL IVAN VAUTIER
Aure
Ifs
Bellengreville
Noyers-Bocage
Villers-Bocage
Orne
N-158
D-562
N-174
A-84
0
10 mi
0
10 km
D-577
© MOON.COM
Saint-Rémy

PLANNING YOUR TIME

Having both played host to the largest invasion to ever occur and been the heartland of the Norman Kingdom at its historic height, the area around northern Calvados and western Cotentin offers perhaps the most "must-see" sights per square mile of just about anywhere in Normandy and Brittany, and can seem a little intimidating if you want to squeeze in all of them. If this is your goal, give yourself at least seven days for the whole experience. If you're not a World War II buff, though, some of the things you learn at the museums might start to get a little repetitive, and 3-4 days ought to suffice. Importantly, there's no need to conduct a visit to the D-Day beaches with the same military urgency that was required to take them, and much that makes a trip here worthwhile is allowing time for reflection.

While there may be a temptation, also, to concentrate on just the region's Second World War heritage, a richer experience can be gained from looking into its native history as well. Indeed, visiting the Bayeux Tapestry in the morning and the same town's World War II memorial in the afternoon is a poignant reminder of the circular nature of history, and sadly how human conflict and sacrifice are two of its constants.

The proximity of Caen and Bayeux to the D-Day landing beaches means that it's perfectly possible to base yourself somewhere in their radius and make numerous small trips, cherry-picking sights on a day-by-day basis. From Caen, Sword is the closest beach, practically counting as a suburb of the city being less than 30 minutes from the town's center, while Utah is the furthest, taking around an hour along the N13. Bayeux is more centrally located, with both Gold Beach and Omaha less than 20 minutes away; neither Sword nor Utah are much more than half an hour away. With this in mind, there's no need to tackle all of the beaches in a single day, or indeed to stay out by them in the evening, if the city lights are more your speed.

All this said, be aware that this is not an easy region to negotiate independently unless you have your own transport. There are some tourist buses put on in the summer, and Caen and Bayeux are easy enough to get between, but having your own wheels is the most straightforward way to get about. The driving around Caen can get a little stressful, particularly around rush hour, but apart from that it's a very pleasant region to drive. A word of warning, though: If you are getting between landing beaches by car, it's most of the time advisable to head back in to the main N13 road, then strike back in again. Coastal roads may seem closer and more picturesque, but are windy and harder to navigate. They do, though, make for great places to cycle. If you don't have your own transport, booking in with a tour group is highly recommended.

As far as crowds and booking ahead are concerned, yes, this is a popular area, but in general the tourist infrastructures exist to deal with that. The only really significant spike in numbers comes in early June, around the anniversary of the D-Day landings. This is even more the case on major anniversary years. During those times, make sure to book ahead with everything to avoid disappointment. The D-Day beaches are, for obvious reasons, not resorts, so they don't get totally overrun in the summertime. Saint-Vaast and Barfleur up the coast, meanwhile, are more subject to seasonal trends, so expect their restaurants and hotels to become significantly busier in the summer, and in August, France's holiday month, especially.

Itinerary Ideas

DAY ONE

This is a day for trying to understand the American experience of D-Day, from windswept Omaha Beach to the reflective calm of the American Cemetery, full of truly moving experience. (Note: To follow this itinerary you're going to need either your own car or to splash out on a taxi.)

1 Assuming you're staying in Bayeux, consider forgoing the usual croissant and café au lait, and instead get yourself in the American mind-set with a simple U.S.-inspired breakfast from **Liberty Coffee.**

2 Drive to **Omaha Beach,** parking at the Monument des Braves, to get your first sense of the scale of the D-Day Landings: From that central point, the beach stretches almost two miles in either direction. Afterwards, make the short trip up to Pointe du Hoc, where the Allied bombardment left one of the most profound impacts on the landscape of Normandy anywhere along its coast.

3 Fortify with a light seafood lunch at **La Sapinière**—the mussels are great, if they're in season (October-March).

4 Pay your respects at the **American Cemetery and Memorial,** where the massed ranks of headstones offer a whole other sense of scale to the conflict, regarding the number of young soldiers who never made it home, while the memorial inscriptions talk not of victory for its own sake, but in order to free the world of tyranny, emphasizing the nobility of their sacrifice.

5 Follow the invasion inland to the small town of Carentan, where in the **Dead Man's Corner Museum** a simulation inside an actual paratrooper-carrying aircraft offers one of the more visceral experiences among D-Day's sights.

6 Head back to Bayeux for a traditional French dinner at **La Rapière** (don't forget to book ahead!).

DAY TWO

Even for the most die-hard D-Day enthusiasts, giving over some time to explore other aspects of Norman history is highly recommended. Half a day discovering Bayeux and the town's famous tapestry awards another view on the 1944 fighting, as just another event within this multifaceted region's history rather than the thing that will forever define it.

1 After breakfast at your hotel, take a stroll around Bayeux's picturesque old town, crossing the river from the rue Saint-Jean to the rue Saint-Martin, taking in the beautiful half-timber house and the wood sculptures of the **Hôtel d'Argouges,** then left to the enormous Romanesque/Gothic cathedral. This is where Harold Godwinson was said to have sworn an oath that he would support William of Normandy's claim to the throne of England, an event that precipitated the Norman conquest of England in 1066.

2 Telling the story of that invasion in astonishingly evocative detail is the **Bayeux Tapestry,** housed just a short walk from the cathedral down the rue de Nesmond. There can be few artifacts in the whole world that are quite as beautiful, educational, and

D-Day Beaches Itinerary

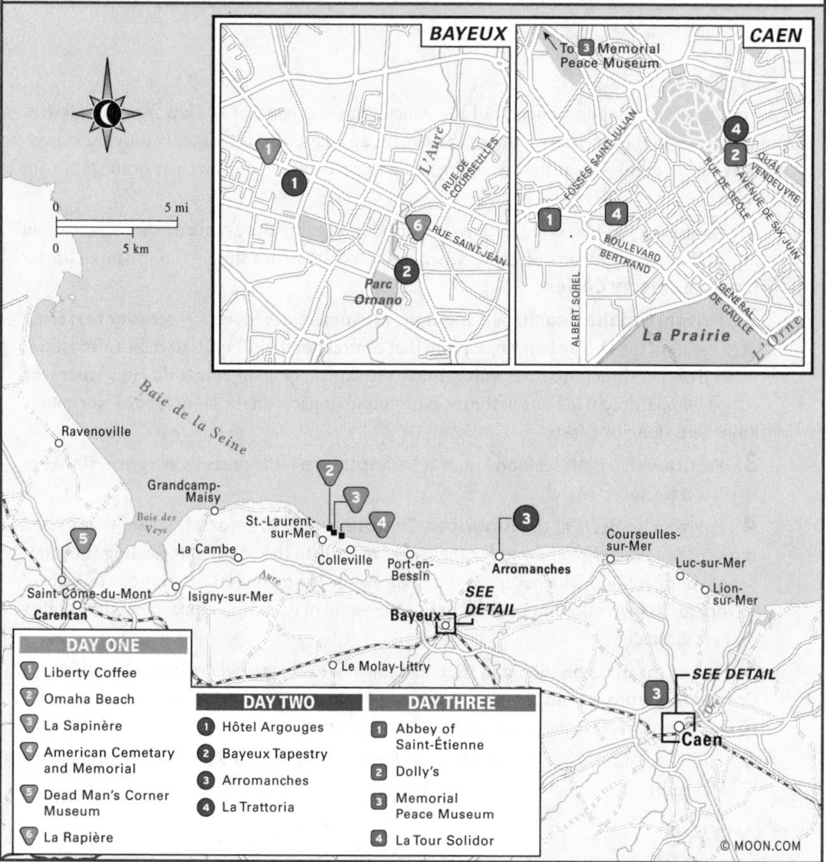

historically valuable all at the same time. An audio tour given free with the price of admission brings the tapestry even further to life by explaining the story of its various sections.

3 After that deep dive into European history, enjoy a crepe overlooking the River Aure at the Moulin de la Galette, then pack up and drive to **Arromanches.** Be sure to visit its artificial harbor and museum (the oldest on any of the D-Day beaches), which gives a good, if slightly old-fashioned, overview of the Allied invasion as a whole, complete with some scale models and military hardware being used as visual aids.

4 Head over to Caen to book into a new hotel and eat one of the best Italian dinners this side of Milan at **La Trattoria,** where the spaghetti dish made *inside* a wheel of Parmesan cheese is a show-stopping (and possibly heart-stopping) specialty.

DAY THREE

Caen was once the center of the Norman Empire, and while much of it was destroyed by fighting in the weeks that followed the D-Day invasion, many of the most majestic buildings from its heyday were either spared or have since been reconstructed, making it worth at least a day of your time. Its Memorial Peace Museum offers one of the most comprehensive public studies of 20th-century conflict anywhere in the world.

1 Grab an early breakfast at your hotel, then wander around central Caen, taking in William the Conqueror's crypt at the **Abbey of Saint-Étienne,** the **Église Saint-Pierre,** and the ramparts of the **château,** all Romanesque monuments that still bristle, almost incongruously, above the otherwise modern streets of the city, and serve as a reminder that Caen was once the center of power for one of the strongest dynasties in Europe.

2 Settle down for an early English lunch of fish and chips at the eccentric **Dolly's.**

3 Spend the whole afternoon exploring the **Memorial Peace Museum,** which offers a deeper perspective on the D-Day conflict, the fighting that came after it, and a look at other battles of the 20th century. The memorial gardens that surround it offer a chance to gather your thoughts and feelings on everything you have learned over the past few days.

4 Finally, unwind in the bars of rue Écuyère, grabbing a terrace table at **La Tour Solidor** if weather allows.

Caen

A testament to urban resilience, despite being massively damaged in the fighting that followed the D-Day landings, the capital of Basse-Normandie has risen from the ashes to become again a worthy destination in its own right, and not just a base from which to explore the coast.

William the Conqueror and his wife Matilda of Flanders saw this small marshy crossroads, once a minor Roman settlement called Cadomus, become one of the great cities of the 11th century. He supervised the building of several famous abbeys and churches, which attracted massive wealth and talent to the city. Many of these historical buildings escaped the Second World War remarkably unscathed or have since been meticulously restored.

Being located on a plain, combined with the damage the city underwent in WWII, means that Caen suffers from some particularly dispiriting suburban sprawl. But persevere through this and you'll find a well-restored heart of wide public spaces and historic Norman monuments of power, rising almost incongruously from otherwise modern streets. Despite the number of international tourists who pour through here every year on their way to the D-Day beaches, Caen has deftly sidestepped becoming a museum city. There's a real sense that Caen still belongs to its citizens, with a non-begrudging, easygoing atmosphere on its streets, and plenty of authentic restaurants and local bars to be explored. Still, the town's Memorial Peace Museum is one of the best and most extensive World War II museums anywhere in the world, and is not to be missed.

Orientation

The center of Caen remains its **château,** which has come to resemble what could be described as a gigantic roundabout feature, ringed as it is by a series of connecting roads, siphoning traffic to and from the rest of the city. The château itself is characterized by towering walls made of local Caen stone, inside of which is a largely open-air and grassy space, which is free to enter and contains several of the city's museums. Standing on the ramparts, you can get a pretty good sense of Caen in general and see all the major ancient landmarks, which still tower over this walkable city's modern streets.

Caen

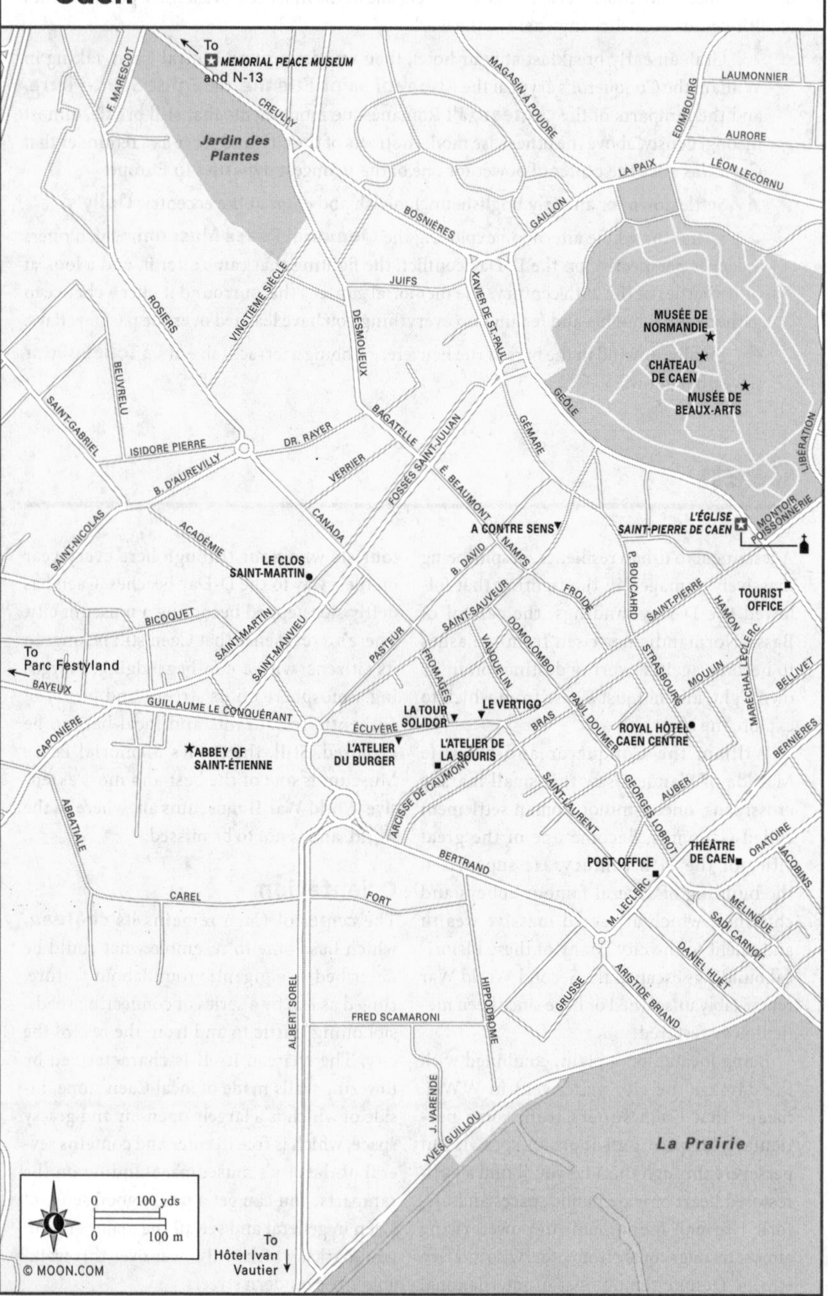
To
MEMORIAL PEACE MUSEUM
and N-13
Jardin des Plantes
F. MARESCOT
CREULLY
MAGASIN À POUDRE
LAUMONNIER
EDIMBOURG
AURORE
LA PAIX
LÉON LECORNU
GAILLON
BOSNIÈRES
JUIFS
XAVIER DE ST.-PAUL
ROSIERS
VINGTIÈME SIÈCLE
DESMOUEUX
MUSÉE DE NORMANDIE
CHÂTEAU DE CAEN
MUSÉE DE BEAUX-ARTS
BEUVRELU
SAINT-GABRIEL
ISIDORE PIERRE
B. D'AUREVILLY
DR. RAYER
BAGATELLE
FOSSÉS SAINT-JULIAN
GEÔLE
GÉMARE
LIBÉRATION
VERRIER
É. BEAUMONT
CANADA
ACADÉMIE
SAINT-NICOLAS
A CONTRE SENS
L'ÉGLISE SAINT-PIERRE DE CAEN
MONTOIR POISSONNERIE
LE CLOS SAINT-MARTIN
B. DAVID
NAMPS
FROIDE
P. BOUCAHRD
SAINT-PIERRE
TOURIST OFFICE
HAMON
BICOQUET
SAINT-MARTIN
SAINT-MANVIEU
PASTEUR
SAINT-SAUVEUR
DOMOLOMBO
VAUQUELIN
STRASBOURG
MOULIN
MARÉCHAL LECLERC
BELLIVET
To
Parc Festyland
BAYEUX
GUILLAUME LE CONQUÉRANT
FROMAGES
LA TOUR SOLIDOR
LE VERTIGO
BRAS
PAUL DOUMER
ROYAL HÔTEL CAEN CENTRE
BERNIÈRES
CAPONIÈRE
ÉCUYÈRE
ABBEY OF SAINT-ÉTIENNE
L'ATELIER DU BURGER
L'ATELIER DE LA SOURIS
ARCISSE DE CAUMONT
SAINT-LAURENT
AUBER
GEORGES LOBROT
ORATOIRE
ABBATIALE
BERTRAND
THÉÂTRE DE CAEN
POST OFFICE
JACOBINS
CAREL
FORT
M. LECLERC
MÉLINGUE
SADI CARNOT
DANIEL HUET
ARISTIDE BRIAND
GRUSSE
FRED SCAMARONI
ALBERT SOREL
HIPPODROME
J. VARENDE
YVES GUILLOU
La Prairie
0
100 yds
0
100 m
© MOON.COM
To
Hôtel Ivan
Vautier

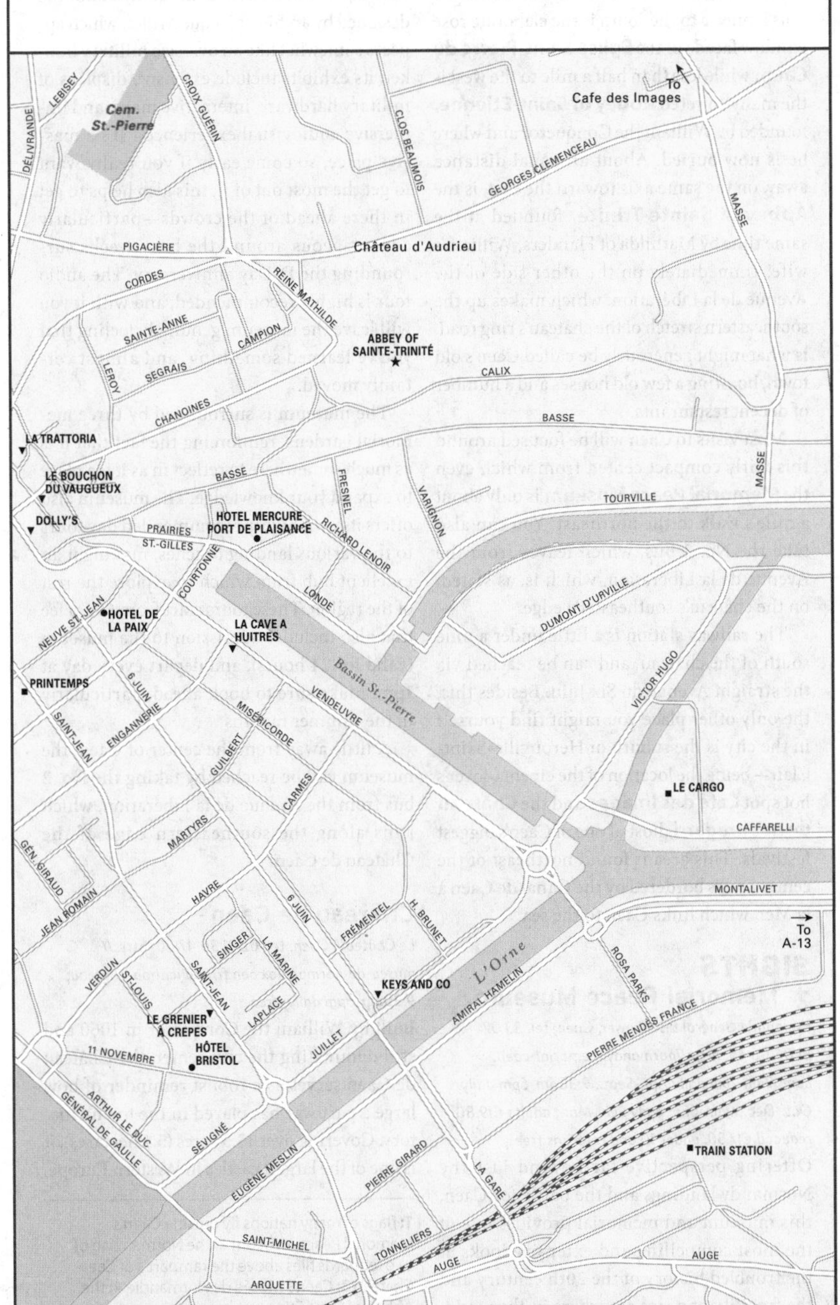
To
Cafe des Images
Cem.
St.-Pierre
LEBISEY
DÉLIVRANDE
CROIX GUÉRIN
CLOS BEAUMOIS
GEORGES CLEMENCEAU
MASSE
PIGACIÈRE
Château d'Audrieu
CORDES
REINE MATHILDE
SAINTE-ANNE
CAMPION
ABBEY OF
SAINTE-TRINITÉ
SEGRAIS
LEROY
CALIX
CHANOINES
BASSE
LA TRATTORIA
LE BOUCHON
DU VAUGUEUX
FRESNEL
VARIGNON
TOURVILLE
DOLLY'S
HOTEL MERCURE
PORT DE PLAISANCE
PRAIRIES
ST.-GILLES
RICHARD LENOIR
COURTONNE
LONDE
DUMONT D'URVILLE
NEUVE ST.-JEAN
HOTEL DE
LA PAIX
LA CAVE A
HUITRES
Bassin St.-Pierre
VICTOR HUGO
PRINTEMPS
6 JUIN
VENDEUVRE
SAINT-JEAN
ENGANNERIE
MISERICORDE
GUILBERT
CARMES
LE CARGO
MARTYRS
CAFFARELLI
GEN. GIRAUD
JEAN ROMAIN
HAVRE
6 JUIN
FREMENTEL
H. BRUNET
MONTALIVET
To
A-13
VERDUN
ST.-LOUIS
SINGER
LA MARINE
L'Orne
ROSA PARKS
SAINT-JEAN
KEYS AND CO
AMIRAL HAMELIN
LAPLACE
LE GRENIER
À CREPES
PIERRE MENDÈS FRANCE
JUILLET
11 NOVEMBRE
HÔTEL
BRISTOL
ARTHUR LE DUC
GÉNÉRAL DE GAULLE
SÉVIGNÉ
EUGENE MESLIN
PIERRE GIRARD
TRAIN STATION
LA GARE
SAINT-MICHEL
TONNELIERS
AUGE
AUGE
ARQUETTE

Just across the short rue Montoir Poissonnerie to the south is the elaborate rose window façade of the **Église Saint-Pierre de Caen,** while less than half a mile to the west is the many-towered **Abbey of Saint-Étienne,** founded by William the Conqueror and where he is now buried. About an equal distance away, on the same axis toward the east, is the **Abbey of Sainte-Trinité,** founded at the same time by Mathilda of Flanders, William's wife. Immediately on the other side of the Avenue de la Libération, which makes up the southeastern stretch of the château's ring road, is what might generously be called Caen's old town, boasting a few old houses and a number of decent restaurants.

Most visits to Caen will be focused around this fairly compact center, from which even the **Memorial Peace Museum** is only about a mile's walk to the northeast. You can also take the No. 2 bus, which leaves from the Avenue de la Libération, which is, as stated, on the château's southeastern edge.

The railway station is a little under a mile south of the château, and can be reached via the straight Avenue du Six Juin. Besides this, the only other place you might find yourself in the city is the suburb of Hérouville-Saint-Clair—being the location of the cinema-lover's hot spot **Café des Images** and the **Château de Beauregard,** host of one of Caen's biggest festivals. This area is found northeast of the center and is bordered by the Canal de Caen à la Mer, which links Caen to the sea.

SIGHTS

★ Memorial Peace Museum

Esplanade Général Eisenhower, Caen; tel. 33 02 31 06 06 45; http://normandy.memorial-caen.com; 9am-7pm daily Apr.-Sept., 9:30am-6pm daily Oct.-Dec., 9am-6pm daily Feb.-Mar.; adults €19.80, reduced €17.50, under 10 and veterans free

Offering perspective far beyond just the Normandy landings and the battle for Caen, this museum and memorial provides one of the most compelling and extensive looks at the troubled history of the 20th century and the fragility of peace anywhere in the world. Located within an austere modernist building designed by architect Jacque Millet, which appears somewhat like an oversize military bunker, its exhibits include extensive displays of military hardware, interactive maps, and immersive audiovisual experiences. It's a massive place, so come early if you really want to get the most out of it; this also helps to get in there ahead of the crowds—particularly advantageous around the busy weeks surrounding the D-Day anniversary. The audio tour is highly recommended, and with it you will leave the museum genuinely feeling that you've learned something, and almost certainly moved.

The museum is surrounded by three memorial gardens, reinforcing the fact that it is as much somewhere to reflect in as it is a place to expand your knowledge. The museum also offers its own highly recommended day tours to the various landing beaches, making it an excellent hub from which to explore the rest of the region. These tours start from €95, a fee that also includes admission to the museum (valid for 24 hours), and depart every day at 1pm. Make sure to book ahead, particularly in the summer months.

A little away from the center of Caen, the museum can be reached by taking the No. 2 bus from the Avenue de la Libération, which runs along the southeastern edge of the Château de Caen.

Château de Caen

Le Château, Caen; tel. 02 31 30 47 60; http://musee-de-normandie.caen.fr/application-chateau; 9:30am-6pm daily; free

Built by William the Conqueror in 1060 and still dominating the city center, the Château de Caen serves as a robust reminder of how large a part war has played in the town's history. Covering over 13.5 acres (5.5 hectares), it is one of the largest castles in Western Europe,

---

1: flags of many nations fly outside Caen's Memorial Peace Museum **2:** the Norman flag of two leopards flies above the rampart's of Caen Chateau **3:** Caen's Musée de Normandie **4:** the Abbey of Saint-Étienne

1
2
Musée de Normandie
3
4

and while unlikely to win any great prizes for beauty, its brutal practicality carries visitors directly back to the past; it's easy to imagine yourself a luckless medieval archer just by approaching its towering walls.

Despite these fortifications, the castle changed hands several times in its history. It was captured by Philip II during his conquest of Normandy in 1204, then swapped between the English and French a couple of times during the Hundred Years' War. Later periods left their mark, too: The castle's keep was pulled down during the French Revolution, and its ramparts sustained heavy damage during World War II, when it was used as a Nazi barracks.

Today, the castle has been repurposed as a home to museums, and it is host to unique sights, including a church, William's old parliament building, and a garden cultivated with the same plants it would have had in the Middle Ages. Entrance to the Château is free, and inside the walls it is mostly open-air, with plenty of grassy spaces, making it feel as much like a public park as a major historic monument. Indeed, it's almost as good for picnics as it is for sightseeing, and it is used as a daytime hangout spot by students from the nearby University of Caen Normandy—don't worry, though, it closes too early to ever get raucous. Even if you don't want to pay to go into its museums, the Château ramparts make for a great 15-minute wander, offering pleasant views across all of Caen and its many churches.

MUSÉE DE NORMANDIE

Le Château, Caen; tel. 02 31 30 47 60; http://musee-de-normandie.caen.fr; 9:30am-12:30pm and 2pm-6pm daily; adults €3.50, reduced €2.50, under 26 free

In the grounds of the Château de Caen, and housed in what used to be the home belonging to the city's governor—a building that can trace its history to the 13th century, though it has received extensive renovation over the years—stands this museum dedicated to the history and society of the Normandy region. It houses both rich archaeological and ethnological collections that chart the development of the Norman people from their Viking roots to their years as a medieval superpower. It also considers the place they hold in modern France, and what their culture, history, and cuisine have given to the nation as a whole. Displays include artifacts from Viking stone carvings to the delicate lace that the Norman people started manufacturing around the 16th century. Great for offering a more holistic view of the region, it's also not that big, and can be explored in little over an hour, leaving time to head to the Musée de Beaux-Arts, also on the château grounds—a reduced-price ticket for both is available for €8 (€6 reduced), which remains valid for two days.

MUSÉE DE BEAUX-ARTS

Le Château, Caen; tel. 02 31 30 47 70; http://mba.caen.fr; 9:30am-12:30pm and 2pm-6pm Tues.-Fri., 11am-6pm Sat.-Sun.; adults €5.50, reduced €3.50, under 26 free

Also in the château grounds, this art museum, housed in a modern building, boasts one of the finest collections of 16th- and 17th-century European painting anywhere in France. There are masterpieces here by Rubens, Brueghel, and Monet, among many others, as well as a fine collection of engravings and a contained sculpture park. Rotating exhibitions accompany the permanent collection, and numerous public events are hosted throughout the year.

The galleries are arranged over two floors, the ground floor dedicated to artworks from the 14th to 18th centuries and the lower level to pieces from the 18th century to the present day. There's certainly enough here to keep a dedicated art buff busy for a whole afternoon. For the more casual fan, an hour ought to suffice. A reduced-price ticket granting entry to both this museum and the Musée de Normandie is available for €8 (€6 reduced) and remains valid for two days.

★ L'Église Saint-Pierre de Caen

Place Saint-Pierre; tel. 02 31 27 14 14 (Caen tourist office); https://sites.google.com/site/saintpierrecaen; 8am-6pm Mon.-Sat., 9:30am-1pm Sun.; free

Facing the château, this Roman Catholic church may be diminutive, but it overflows with lavish, wedding cake-like architectural detail. Despite being constructed between the 13th and 15th centuries, there is a surprising unity to its design, with the Gothic style most prominent in its façade. Such is its striking quality, it is often mistakenly referred to by tourists as a cathedral, and indeed has been the site of most public ceremonies for the city. Notably, it was where Henry IV renounced Protestantism, bringing an end to the Wars of Religion, the French civil war that blighted the latter half of the 16th century. Aside from the bell tower being struck by a British shell during the siege of Caen in 1944, the church emerged from World War II remarkably unscathed, one of the few buildings in the city that can make that boast.

Inside, the opulence continues, with the church's chancel in particular boasting a stunning floral frieze in the Flamboyant Gothic style. There are also some interesting carvings decorating the top of some pillars: An unusual one to look out for depicts Aristotle being threatened by the whip of Alexander the Great's mistress (a reference to a 14th-century work by Norman poet Henri d'Andeli, where just that scenario occurs). The building is a space of quiet, contemplative beauty in the center of town.

Abbey of Saint-Étienne

Esplanade Jean-Marie Louvel, Caen; tel. 02 31 30 42 81; http://caen.fr/node/457; 9am-6pm Mon.-Sat., 2pm-6pm Sun.; free

This enormous church of a former Benedictine monastery is one of the finest examples of Romanesque architecture anywhere in Europe. It was founded by William the Conqueror back in the 1060s, when he was in the midst of his ambitious building project for Caen. Characterized by semicircular arches and its combination of ancient Roman and Byzantine architecture, the abbey was built from Caen stone and added to over the succeeding centuries with Gothic details, including the first ribbed vault in France, rosette windows, and flying buttresses.

It is believed that William founded the abbey after marrying Matilda of Flanders. This marriage had been formally forbidden by Pope Leo IX on the principle that William and Matilda were cousins and therefore too closely related. The abbey was William's penance for going through with it anyway. For the same reason, Matilda founded her own abbey, a Benedictine nunnery, the Abbey of Sainte-Trinité, which lies opposite Saint-Étienne, across the city. For these reasons Saint-Étienne is also frequently referred to as the Abbaye aux Hommes (the men's abbey), while Sainte-Trinité is known as the Abbaye aux Dames (the women's abbey).

William's tomb is found here, though most of his remains were lost in the French Wars of Religion, when the grave was opened and his bones scattered. To go inside the church is to be captivated by its size and solemnity. It has a relatively austere interior, and with William I's name displayed so prominently just before the alter, the whole place can feel as much like a monument to him and his dynasty as it does a house of God. Despite the building's centrality to Norman culture, it is seldom too crowded.

Abbey of Sainte-Trinité

Place Reine Mathilde, Caen; tel. 02 31 06 98 98; www.abbayes-normandes.com/abbaye/abbaye-aux-dames-caen; 8:30am-12:30pm and 1:30pm-6pm Mon.-Fri., 2pm-6pm Sat.-Sun.; free

The partner abbey to Saint-Étienne, this equally towering structure is often referred to as the Abbaye aux Dames (the women's abbey), as opposed to the former's the Abbaye aux Hommes (the men's abbey). This is because it was founded by William the Conqueror's wife, Matilda of Flanders, and because it was formerly run by Benedictine nuns. Work on the building was started at around the same time as Saint-Étienne, in

Herleva and Matilda: Women Behind the Conqueror

There's little doubt that William the Conqueror owed no small amount of his worldly success to two women in his life: his mother, Herleva, and his wife, Matilda of Flanders.

HERLEVA

Herleva, remarkably for a woman who would go on to mother the future King of England, began life as a tanner. It's said that it was in this role that she caught the eye of Robert, Duke of Normandy, and William's father. He saw her from the battlements of his castle, and she raised her skirts a little—but not too much—to further entice his lust. Won over, the Duke (as is a duke's wont) gave orders for Herleva to be brought up to him through the castle's back door. But Herleva played coy and said the only way she would go to him was on horseback through the front gate of the castle, like a noble, not a commoner. Still enchanted by the image of the young tanner-girl's legs, the Duke of Normandy agreed, and before long, William was conceived.

Another story of Herleva says that the night she became pregnant with the future king, she had a dream in which she saw a tree erupting from her stomach and growing so vast that its shadow was soon cast over all of Normandy, then over the English Channel, and finally over all of England. Whether or not the dream was true, there's little doubt that telling people of it would have served the ambitions of her and the duke's illegitimate son in the ruthless atmosphere of the Norman court.

MATILDA

Matilda of Flanders, meanwhile, came from the exact opposite end of the social spectrum. As a niece and granddaughter of French kings, Matilda was considered of far nobler heritage than William, her betrothed. Despite the obvious political gains of their marriage, though (she gained power; he social standing), it's believed to have been an affectionate union, and when William left for England in 1066, the ship in which he sailed, the *Mora,* was a gift paid for by Matilda's money.

She then governed Normandy in his absence and took a particular interest in the education of their children. She had her boys taught by the celebrated Italian scholar Lanfranc and she sent her girls to Caen's Saint-Trinité Abbey, which she herself had established.

1062, and was completed in 1130. Like its counterpart, the Abbaye aux Dames did not emerge from the intervening centuries entirely unscathed: Its original impressive spires were destroyed in France's Hundred Years' War with the English, and during the French Revolution, the nuns themselves were forced out and dispersed. Nevertheless, the abbey weathered most of what was thrown at it, and a restoration between 1990 and 1993 saw it returned to some of its former stature.

Romanesque in style, just as William's tomb dominates the altar of Saint-Étienne, so Matilda's tomb, marked by a single slab of black marble, sits in the chancel here in Sainte-Trinité. The church in general benefits from being slightly away from the main tourist circuit of Caen and tends to offer a quieter, more contemplative space than others in town, even while it may not boast quite the same opulence.

Parc Festyland

Route de Caumont, Bretteville-sur-Odon; tel. 02 31 75 04 04; http://festyland.com; 11am-6pm Sat.-Sun. Apr.-June and Sept., 10:30am-7pm daily Jul.-Aug., closed weekdays during school time; adults €20.50, under 12 and over 60 €17.50, children under 95cm (37in) free

Despite Parc Festyland touting itself as "the biggest theme park in Normandy," Euro Disney it is not. However, there are certainly enough attractions here to keep kids happy for an afternoon, if not quite the whole day. These include classics such as a roller coaster, waterslide, and pirate ship. Situated in the northern suburbs of the city, it's serviced by bus line 3, which can be caught from outside Caen's town hall or the main railway station. The park deserves some credit for its dedication to a theme: the time of the Norman conquests. As such, rides bristle with novelty-size Viking helmets; the "tea cups" have been rendered to seem like wooden barrels; and one ride promises kids a retracing of the footsteps of William the Conqueror. Food and drink can be bought on-site, though at slightly elevated prices. It's popular, but even in the height of the summer school holidays, queues are not as long as they can get in other theme parks.

ENTERTAINMENT AND EVENTS

Nightlife

A student town since the English founded a university here during their occupation in the 14th century, Caen has never been wanting for cheap, lively bars, the best of which can be found on the **rue Écuyère.** It's also a big enough urban center that most of these are not dominated by a younger crowd, welcoming locals and tourists alike.

LA TOUR SOLIDOR

24 rue Écuyère, Caen; tel. 02 31 86 10 35; 12pm-1am Mon., 9am-1am Tues.-Sat.

La Tour Solidor is one of the most popular bars in Caen. It is a veritable drinking institution with a large, traditional French brasserie interior, with a tiled floor and wood furniture. It also has a frequently packed terrace that lets the party spill out onto the street in the summer months. It tends to get busier as the night goes on, so the earlier you arrive the better chance you have of finding a seat. There's also a wide selection of cocktails on offer, made by competent servers.

LE VERTIGO

14 rue Écuyère, Caen; tel. 02 31 85 43 12; 11:30am-1am Mon.-Sat.

A kitschy, tightly packed drinking experience. The decorations here nod to Caen's medieval history, with replica suits of armor and heraldic shields lining the walls. The crowd is immensely friendly, and the drinks are very reasonable, though it is true that the music can be played a little too loud for some people's tastes. The drink selection is decent, with a few more beers on tap than you get elsewhere in France. It also claims to be the inventor of the truly original, if rather unappetizing, *embuscade* cocktail—half wine, half beer, topped up with a shot of calvados and black currant cordial: Try one once for the cultural experience! Finding a table is not always easy on a Friday or Saturday night, so unless you come early, be prepared to spend at least some of your night standing.

Performing Arts

THÉÂTRE DE CAEN

135 boulevard Maréchal Leclerc, Caen; tel. 02 31 30 48 00; http://theatre.caen.fr; seasons run from Sept.-June; basic adult tickets from €25

A city with a lively cultural scene, Caen has had a permanent theater since the mid-1700s. The current theater, however, was only built after the Second World War, following the destruction of the previous one in the 1944 battle for the city. An imposing modernist construction, it opened its doors in the late 1950s, and today offers a frequently changing schedule of high-quality acts. The huge majority of plays it puts on are, naturally, in French, though it also hosts opera, dance, and classical concerts throughout the year. As one of the central theater and music hubs for the whole Normandy region, if there's a show on here that seems accessible, it makes for a great and slightly different way to spend an evening, offering a great insight into the cultural life of Caen's population. Check the theater's website for the many different prices and deals.

LE CARGO

9 cours Caffarelli; tel. 02 31 86 79 31; www.lecargo.fr; box office 1:30pm-6:30pm Mon.-Thurs., 1:30pm-5pm Fri.

If you're looking for a live music fix, Le Cargo is a trendy waterfront venue and community hub that regularly puts on shows, both by local bands and international artists. All genres of music are featured, so check out the website for shows that might appeal. Most concerts start at 8pm and ticket prices vary; consult the website for details.

Cinema

CAFÉ DES IMAGES

4 square du Théâtre, Hérouville-Saint-Clair; tel. 02 31 45 34 70; https://cafedesimages.fr; screening times around 12pm-9pm daily; adults €7, reduced €6, under 14 €4

Caen is a town for cineasts, albeit with its more interesting cinemas outside of the center. The Café des Images is one of the best of these that specializes in putting out new arthouse films and retrospectives. And though of course many are in French, they've a dedication to original soundtracks, so if it's a British, North American, or Australian film then it will be in English with French subtitles. Situated in the north of the city, it is also home to a café where budding auteurs come to gather and discuss the latest releases. It regularly schedules an ever-changing roster of talks (in French) on all aspects of filmmaking.

Festivals and Events

FESTIVAL BEAUREGARD

568 Ancienne Route de Ouistreham, Hérouville-Saint-Clair; www.festivalbeauregard.com; Fri.-Mon. the first weekend in July; day pass €49 (with camping €56), full weekend €164 (with camping €184)

Festival Beauregard is an annual music festival that attracts some of the biggest pop acts from around the world and visitors from across northern France. Spread across three days in early July, it takes place on the grounds of the Château de Beauregard, in a northeastern suburb of Caen. Unpretentious and dedicated above all to music and fun, the festival has played host to bands such as Depeche Mode, Jack White, and the Pixies. There is onsite camping that can be purchased at only a slightly higher cost, while food and alcohol are sold at the festival too, though not cheap (you can't find a drink for less than €3). Beauregard is growing year after year; tickets for the 2018 edition, which, admittedly, was its 10-year anniversary) were sold out by early June of that year.

SHOPPING

PRINTEMPS

28 rue Saint-Jean; tel. 02 31 15 65 50; www.printemps.com/magasins/caen; 9:30am-7:30pm Mon.-Sat.

Imparting a Parisian glamour on Caen, this branch of one of the oldest department stores in the world offers a luxurious selection of the latest fashions, perfumes, makeup, and homewares, spread over several floors. But don't come expecting glorious Haussmann-style architecture of the kind that characterizes the French capital; this is still reconstructed Caen, after all. The store is situated in a resolutely modern, not especially flashy building. It's in what they sell, and how they sell it, that glamour is found.

L'ATELIER DE LA SOURIS

26 rue Arcisse de Caumont; tel. 9 83 20 13 64; www.atelierdelasouris.com; 11am-7pm Tues.-Sat.

At the other end of the shopping spectrum from Printemps, this craft boutique and haberdashery opened its doors in 2012 and specializes in bags, knickknacks, and decorations made from a colorful collection of different fabrics. You can also pick up cuddly-toy mice, which chime with the store's branding (*L'Atelier de la Souris* means The Mouse's Studio). The interior decor is on the charming side of twee, with fun, colorful patterned fabric festooning almost every surface, and floral chinaware on its shelves; the store is utterly unique to the city.

FOOD

Regional Cuisine

★ A CONTRE SENS

8-10 rue des Croisiers; tel. 02 31 97 44 48; www.acontresenscaen.fr/a-contre-sens; 12pm-1:15pm and 7:30pm-9:15pm Tues.-Sat.; mains €21-38, lunch menus €26-56, evening menus €56-64

When Anthony and Cindy Caillot established this restaurant in 2009, they did so with a bold, uncompromising vision, dedicated to surprising and contrasting flavors, and to taking diners on a journey of taste. Their ambition was rewarded in 2012 when A Contre Sens was judged worthy of a Michelin star. Though not cheap, the contemporary spin it puts on French and Norman classics, often tweaking them with Asian flavors such as coconut milk with langoustine or sauces made of coriander and leek, makes it worth every cent. Like the cuisine, the restaurant itself offers a blend of modern and traditional, with Caen stone walls and old wooden beams, contrasted with stylish new furniture, glassware, and plates. Popular among locals and visitors, it's worth booking in advance to secure a table, though midweek you might get lucky just turning up.

LE BOUCHON DU VAUGUEUX

12 rue Graindorge; tel. 02 31 44 26 26; www.bouchonduvaugueux.com; 12pm-2pm and 7pm-10pm Tues.-Sat.; lunch menus €17-25, evening menus €23-35

Catering to traditional tastes, and with close links to local producers, Le Bouchon Du Vaugueux expertly treads the line between formal and informal dining. It's as appropriate a place to pop into for a quick lunch as it is to set up in for a long drawn-out dinner. The flavors are as French as it gets, with excellent fish and meat options—adventurous diners should try the veal kidney, which is the chef's specialty. There is little on offer for vegetarian diners, however.

LA CAVE A HUITRES

24 quai Vendeuvre; tel. 02 31 75 58 65; www.la-cave-a-huitres.fr; 11am-2:30pm and 6:30pm-10:30pm Mon.-Sat.; six oysters from €9.10

A bright and lively oyster restaurant facing the port of Caen that's one of the best, and certainly the cheapest, places to get your hands on the mollusks anywhere in town. All different sizes are on offer, shipped fresh from the town of Asnelles, barely 10 miles (16 kilometers) to the north. The simplicity of the restaurant interior underlines that the food is the star of the show, though there is a pleasant terrace for warm Norman days. If oysters aren't to your taste, seafood platters are also on the menu. If you're not into seafood, well, this probably isn't the restaurant for you!

International

★ LA TRATTORIA

13 rue du Vaugueux, Caen; tel. 02 31 47 97 01; 12pm-1:45pm and 7:15pm-10:15pm Tues.-Thurs.,

Le Bouchon du Vaugueux

7:15pm-10:15pm Mon. and Fri.; lunch menus from €15, evening menus €25-31

High-quality Italian restaurants are few and far between in Normandy (and in all of France, for that matter), but La Trattoria is the real deal. It's connected to a delicatessen selling all manner of Italian antipasti and delicacies (open 10am-2pm and 4pm-7:30pm Tues.-Sat.). The quality of its produce is obvious before it's even been cooked. It's hard to choose a bad dish, but the hot pasta prepared inside a wheel of Parmesan cheese is a definite highlight, both for its taste and the performance in its preparation. For the quality of the food, it's an excellently priced place.

★ DOLLY'S

16 avenue de la Libération, Caen; tel. 02 31 94 03 29; 10am-1am Thurs.-Sat., 10am-11:30pm Sun., Wed., and Tues.; mains €9-15

Taking its cue from the old Somerset Maugham quip that "England is a country it's possible to eat well in provided one has breakfast three times a day," this British restaurant has rebranded the classic "full-English" breakfast of eggs, bacon, sausages, and more, as a "mixed grill du chef," which it is indeed possible to order whenever you feel the desire. There's also fish and chips, curry, and burgers on the menu, all reasonably priced and served in a space that looks something like an eccentric Brit's front room. Despite its sense of play, there's something strangely moving about dropping in for a meal here after a day on the British landing beaches. Considering the number of British servicemen whose blood watered the Norman soil, it's nice to find this corner of a foreign field which is forever England, where at least their ghosts would feel at home.

Budget Options

KEYS & CO

45 avenue du Six Juin, Caen; tel. 02 31 34 60 83; 9:30am-7pm Wed.-Sat., 10am-6pm Sun.; €6-11

A trendy café with an industrial chic interior that would not be out of place in Brooklyn or East London, Keys & Co can comfortably lay claim to offering some of the best coffee in Normandy. A joint French and New Zealander venture, it also does excellent healthy breakfasts and lunches in which international ingredients like quinoa and avocado feature heavily. It's a casual, welcoming place that could easily become a hub over a longer stay.

LE GRENIER À CREPES

182 rue Saint-Jean; tel. 02 31 83 79 44; www.legrenieracrepes.fr; 12pm-2pm and 7pm-10pm Mon.-Fri., 7:30pm-10pm Sat.; €6-11

Kitschy, quaint, and inexpensive, this is a great place for informal dining, run on the concept that if a food exists, you can probably put it inside a crepe: potatoes, mushrooms, bacon, salad, cherry tomatoes, the list goes on.... The polka-dot tablecloths and book-pattern wallpaper may not be to everyone's taste, but after a couple of bowls of cider and starting on your delicious crepe dessert after a delicious crepe main course, they hardly seem to matter.

L'ATELIER DU BURGER

27 rue Écuyère, Caen; tel. 02 31 50 13 44; www.latelier-duburger.fr; 12pm-2:30pm and 7pm-11:30pm Sun.-Fri., 12pm-11:30pm Sat.; €7.50-9

It may not be the most French of eateries, but sometimes all you want is a burger and nothing else will do. This burgeoning chain, with two outlets across Caen (the other is at 6 rue Buquet) and a food truck that moves about the city, specializes in the kind of gourmet burger experience that has become popular as an antidote to fast food in recent years. Think thick fries, high-quality meat, and an extensive number of toppings. The restaurants themselves are based on an upmarket diner style, with food served on trays, and plenty of condiments on hand. There are also vegetarian options.

ACCOMMODATIONS

Under €50

HÔTEL F1 CAEN NORD MÉMORIAL

Le Clos Barbey, Saint-Contest; tel. 891 70 52 04; https://www.accorhotels.com/gb/hotel-2229-

formule-1-hotelf1-caen-nord-memorial/index.shtml; from €35 d

F1 Hotels are found across France and are about as far from luxurious as you can get. But given that there really aren't many options for the shoestring traveler in Caen, you could do far worse. A decent level of cleanliness and basic comfort is guaranteed, with bathrooms en suite. Internet access is available throughout the building, and a straightforward continental buffet breakfast is provided. It's also excellently located for visiting the Memorial Peace Museum, from where it's possible to catch the No. 2 bus into town.

€50-100

HÔTEL DE LA PAIX

14 rue Neuve Saint-Jean; tel. 02 31 86 18 99; www.hoteldelapaix-caen.com; from €67 d

This is a centrally located, reasonably priced hotel. Its rooms may tend toward the basic, but they are airy, clean, and well lit, and the staff are very responsive to added needs and requests. Free WiFi is provided, even the most basic rooms have en suite bathrooms and TVs, and a continental breakfast is offered every morning.

HÔTEL BRISTOL

31 rue du 11 Novembre; tel. 02 31 84 59 76; www.hotelbristolcaen.com; from €85 d

Located near the train station, with clean and comfortable rooms, the Hôtel Bristol may not be overflowing with character, but as a trustworthy and reasonably priced location to lay your head for a few nights, it's unimpeachable. There's free WiFi throughout, cable TV in the rooms, and en suite bathrooms as standard. An on-site bar reserved only for guests is perfect for a nightcap after a long day seeing the sights.

€100-200

ROYAL HÔTEL CAEN CENTRE

1 place de la République, Caen; tel. 02 31 86 55 33; www.hotel-caen-centre.com; from €100 d

Comfort right in the center of town: As well as being extremely clean, this hotel boasts some excellent views of Caen's Place de la République from its rooms with floor-to-ceiling windows, and is good for those who want to wake up with the buzz of the city. Rooms are large and come fitted with satellite TVs, air-conditioning, and WiFi, as well as en suite bathrooms. For those driving, there's underground parking on-site.

HÔTEL IVAN VAUTIER

3 avenue Henry Chéron, Caen; tel. 02 31 73 32 71; http://ivanvautier.com; from €120 d

Specializing in modern luxury, as well as large, comfortable rooms, this hotel is home to a spa, offering a hammam, a sauna, and body treatments. More than anything that attracts guests, though, is the Michelin-starred restaurant, headed up by the chef Ivan Vautier himself, serving locally inspired dishes delicately presented so that they look like works of abstract art. This dedication to food permeates throughout the hotel and influences its character, with both the property's tearoom and its breakfast being influenced by the chef's touch.

HÔTEL MERCURE PORT DE PLAISANCE

1 rue de Courtonne, Caen; tel. 02 31 47 24 24; https://www.accorhotels.com/fr/hotel-0869-hotel-mercure-caen-centre-port-de-plaisance/index.shtml; from €124 d

Located on Caen's pleasant marina, this offers the slightly bland comfort of a chain hotel but is nevertheless a decent option if what you're after is a guarantee of a trouble-free stay at a still-reasonable cost. The rooms are large and accommodating, all with en suite facilities, and some rooms offer a view of the marina. There's also an on-site gym that guests are welcome to use free of charge, and a continental breakfast is served in the morning.

★ LE CLOS SAINT-MARTIN

18 bis place Saint-Martin, Caen; tel. 7 81 39 23 67; www.leclosaintmartin.fr/tarifs.html; from €150 d

For those wanting to connect with Caen's history, this bed-and-breakfast is housed in a renovated 16th-century mansion right in the city center, and every room has been uniquely decorated with luxurious antique furniture and trinkets. Alongside the exposed beams, however, there are modern touches, such as en suite bathrooms in every room and flat-screen TVs nestled discreetly amid the decor. It also offers a flowery courtyard, complete with outdoor furniture for relaxing after a long day seeing the sights. Continental breakfast is served on period silverware in an elegant dining room.

Over €200

★ CHÂTEAU D'AUDRIEU

Château d'Audrieu, Audrieu; tel. 02 31 80 21 52; www.chateaudaudrieu.com; from €330 d

In the countryside between Caen and Bayeux, this hotel and spa offers another level of luxury. Located within a beautifully maintained 18th-century château, its interior was designed by architect Philippe de Lanouvelle in a way that both pays homage to its history but allows for subtle touches of modern comfort, with spacious rooms that bring the lavish glamour of the past up-to-date. The restaurant and bar are top class, and the staff are bend-over-backward accommodating. Indeed, from its spa and swimming pool to its on-site gym and extensive grounds, there are very few areas in which the Château d'Audrieu does not excel. It also offers its own specialized tours of the region.

INFORMATION AND SERVICES

Information

TOURIST OFFICE

12 place Saint-Pierre, Caen; tel. 02 31 27 14 14; www.caenlamer-tourisme.fr; 9am-7pm Mon.-Sat., 10am-1pm and 2pm-5pm Sun.

Caen's well-accomodated tourist office is next door to Église Saint-Pierre. It's a tourism hub for more than just Caen, and it's possible to find out about trips and activities around all the surrounding area. This includes up toward Ouistreham on the coast, which in addition to being the location of Gold Beach landing ground also plays host to water sports centers—kayaks can be hired and sailing lessons organized here at the tourist office. English is, of course, spoken. It's also a great place to find out about guided tours of the landing beaches in general.

Emergencies

HOSPITAL CENTRE UNIVERSITY DE CAEN

Avenue de la Côte de Nacre, Caen; tel. 02 31 06 31 06; www.chu-caen.fr; 8:30am-8pm Mon.-Fri., 11am-7pm Sat.-Sun., ER open 24 hours

A large city hospital just north of the ring road, with a 24-hour emergency room service and numerous specialized departments. It makes no official promises of having English-speaking staff, but French doctors are often adept at the language, so you should be able to make yourself understood.

Post Office

LA POSTE

La Poste, 2 rue Georges Lebret, Caen; tel. 9 69 39 00 01; www.laposte.fr/particulier; 9am-6:30pm Mon., 8:30am-6:30pm Tues.-Fri., 1pm-6:30pm Sat.

One of the more centrally located of several post offices in Caen. Like most in France, sending or receiving a parcel here can seem intimidating, but in fact there's a sleek system of helpers at hand to guide you through. Most of the time, they will approach you shortly after you arrive. There's no guarantee of English being spoken, but the setup is straightforward enough that you should be able to muddle through.

TRANSPORTATION

Getting There

A transportation hub for almost all modes of travel, Caen is among the best-connected towns in all of Normandy and Brittany. Indeed, it has an almost vortex-like quality, which means however you're traveling, if you pass its line of longitude at any point during your visit to the two regions, then a trip via the city, or at least its ring road, will probably be the most efficient route. All this is also to say that it's very easy to get to: from Paris, from

Rennes, from Rouen, and in whichever way you see fit.

BY BOAT

Caen is linked to the British port of Portsmouth by **Brittany Ferries** (rue des Dunes, Ouistreham; tel. 02 31 36 36 36; www.brittany-ferries.fr; 6:45am-11:59pm daily), which sail into Ouistreham, northeast of the city. It is well signposted and can be reached from central Caen by car via the D515, and is connected by the Route 61 bus. Unfortunately, this bus does not run in the evening, so if you're on a boat arriving or departing then, you will have to get a taxi. These cost around €30 into Caen center between 7am and 7pm, and about €40 outside of those times.

The number of sailings a day changes depending on the time of year, with more in the summer months; check the website for up-to-date schedules. The journey takes just over five hours, and in high season, traveling with a car plus passengers you can expect to pay upwards of €400 for a return ticket, or around €100 if you're a foot passenger. Prices go up as the boat fills out, so book early for the better deal. This said, apart from in high season, it should be pretty easy to find a place on the crossing until fairly last-minute, especially if you're on foot.

BY CAR

Caen is well connected to the rest of France. The A13 links it to Paris, a journey of about 150 miles (241 kilometers), which should take just over three hours. Be aware that this is a toll road, and that you can expect to pay about €20 to complete the journey. From Bayeux, Caen can be reached via the N13, a journey of about half an hour, covering a little over 20 miles (32 kilometers). This is also the most efficient road to reach the city from if you are coming from most of the D-Day landing beaches—it's always worth driving in a little from the coast. From Utah—the farthest beach—the journey is 60 miles (96 kilometers) and should take about an hour. Sword Beach is the only exception, which could almost be described as a distant suburb of the city. From here take the D7 about 10 miles into Caen's center.

From Mont-Saint-Michel, take the A84, a journey of about 90 miles (145 kilometers), which should take 1.5 hours. From Rouen—which is en route from Paris—take the A13, a journey also of about 90 miles (145 kilometers) that should take 1.5 hours, with tolls of around €10.

To ease congestion, a ring road circles Caen. This can get busy during rush hours, between 5:30pm and 7:30pm, but most of the time it is fairly clear. Parking in the city is seldom free, apart from on some residential side streets; otherwise, there are plenty of underground central parking lots with prices starting at €1 per hour.

Several car rental companies are based out of the train station, including stalwarts such as **Europcar** (36 place de la Gare; tel. 9 77 40 32 74; www.europcar.fr) and **Hertz** (24 rue de la Gare, Caen; tel. 02 31 84 64 50; www.hertz.fr). Prices start at around €75 per 24 hours.

BY TRAIN

Caen's train station, **Gare de Caen** (tel. 36 35; www.gares-sncf.com/fr/gare/frcfr/caen; 2:45am-11:10pm Mon., 4:15am-11:10pm Tues.-Thurs., 4:15am-12:20am Fri., 5:15am-11:10pm Sat., 7am-12:10am Sun.), is in the southeast of the city, with trains arriving from other regional hubs such as Paris (13/day, two hours, €37), Cherbourg (8-15/day, 1.25 hours, around €24), Rouen (5-6/day, 1.75 hours, €28), Pontorson, which is the gateway to Mont-Saint-Michel (3/day, 2 hours, about €28). Getting to Bayeux takes about 20 minutes and costs €6 with trains running roughly every hour.

Many smaller towns, however, and specifically the D-Day landing grounds, are not connected by train.

BY BUS

France's nascent national coach network means that there are now around six arrivals from Paris a day, with companies **Flixbus** (www.flixbus.com) and **Ouibus** (www.ouibus.com) stopping just outside of Caen's train station. Prices vary depending on how far ahead you book, but provided you get in there early, expect to pay around €10 for a journey of three hours.

Regional journeys can be taken on board Calvados's own **Bus Verts** (tel. 09 70 83 00 14; www.busverts.fr). These link the city to other larger towns in Normandy, such as Deauville (4-7 a day, two hours, €4.90), Le Havre (6-10 daily, 2.75 hours, €4.90), and Honfleur (7-10/day, 2.5 hours, €4.20).

Buses run at least hourly connecting Bayeux to Caen for €4. The journey is less than half an hour.

The only D-Day beach connected directly to Caen by bus is Sword. From here you can take Line 61, a journey of about 35 minutes, costing €2. Otherwise, getting here from the D-Day beaches it's necessary to come via Bayeux.

BY AIR

Carpiquet Airport (route de Caumont, Carpiquet; tel. 02 31 71 20 10; www.caen.aeroport.fr), is located west of Caen, past the ring road. Though mainly focusing on domestic flights, with airlines such as Hop! and FlyBe, it is possible to reach Caen from London's Southend, as well as several towns in Italy. There are no direct flights from Paris, which really is too close to justify flying from anyway.

A city bus (Line 3) links the airport to the town center, running every 15 minutes Monday-Saturday (5:30am-12:30am) and Sundays (9am-12am). Journey time is 15 minutes and the cost is €1.50.

There's also on-site car rental by **Hertz** (tel. 02 31 84 64 50; www.hertz.fr) and **Europcar** (tel. 9 77 40 32 74; www.europcar.fr), from which you can continue your journey.

Taxis that line up outside the airport building cost between €25-30 to get into the city center.

Getting Around

Though a generally walkable city, Caen is also serviced by an urban bus service run by a company called **Twisto** (tel. 02 31 15 55 55; www.twisto.fr), while tramlines A and B link the train station and the town center. A word of warning for drivers and cyclists: Caen can prove a bit intimidating in parts, particularly near the train station, where a combination of bus lanes, tramlines, slip roads, and one-way streets make for a confusing mélange.

If you're interested in hiring a bicycle, **Maison du vélo** (54 quai Amiral Hamelin; tel. 02 31 34 45 70; www.maisonduvelocaen.fr/pid26/tarifs-location) is a good place to go, with rental packages starting out at €15 for a week.

There are several taxi companies in Caen, with **Taxis Abbeilles** being one of the largest (54 place de la Gare; tel. 02 31 52 17 89; www.taxis-abbeilles-caen.com). A trip to the airport will cost between €25-30 from the city center.

Bayeux

A town more famous for the artifact it contains than its own characteristics, charming Bayeux is nevertheless far more than just a home to the tapestry. Taken by British troops without a fight in 1944, it was spared the ravages of the Battle of Normandy and therefore has much of its medieval history still intact, and despite being home to one of the most famous artifacts in all of France, it's yet to be entirely ransacked by tourism; the town's relative fame awards it a clean-feeling prosperity that stops just short of kitsch.

A wander around the town offers one of the best insights into the glory years of Normandy, when William the Conqueror was still alive, and the bastions of Norman

Bayeux

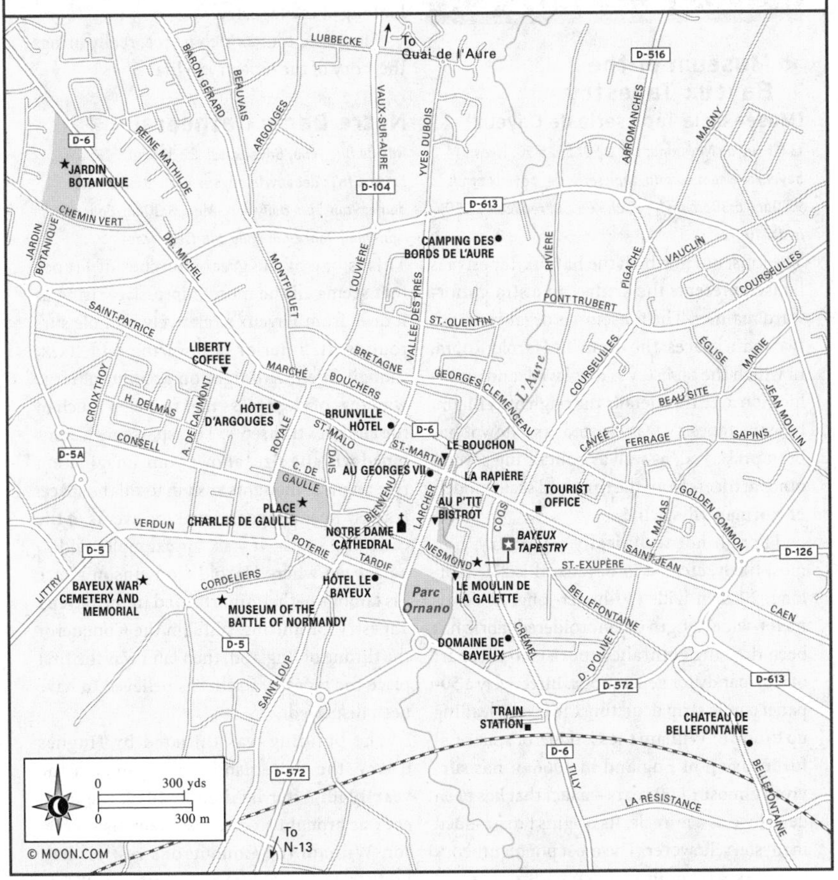

power were spread across all of Europe. Wooden waterwheels still turn in the river, half-timber houses loom over its streets, and medieval carvings decorate some of its masonry. Most striking of all is Bayeux's towering Romanesque cathedral, far bigger than you'd usually expect to find in a town of this size and which accordingly dominates its skyline and character. Bayeux was somewhat left behind following the Norman heyday, leaving it, for all its charm, a relatively small town that can be easily tackled in a day—tapestry included.

ORIENTATION

With a compact and perfectly preserved old-town center which contains all of the major sights, Bayeux is easily discoverable on foot. Running north to south, the River Aure splits this old center in two, and its banks are populated by elegantly restored mills and washhouses. Bayeux's main lateral access, meanwhile, is the pedestrianized rue Saint-Jean, which dates back to Roman times. Both the cathedral and the tapestry museum are south of this road; the former clings close to the west bank of the river, the latter to its east.

TOP EXPERIENCE

★ Museum of the Bayeux Tapestry (Musée de la Tapisserie de Bayeux)

13 bis rue de Nesmond; tel. 02 31 51 25 50; www.bayeuxmuseum.com/la_tapisserie_de_bayeux.html; 9:30am-6:30pm daily; adults €9.50, reduced €7.50, under 10 free

The museum in which the Bayeux Tapestry is housed presents the artifact in a straightforward manner. The museum is organized into two main spaces: the dimly lit Harold Room, in which the tapestry is displayed, and an exhibition area that details the reign of William, how the tapestry was created, and how it has been preserved, as well as containing several other artifacts from the time and scale models of Norman village life.

Though not technically a tapestry, nor, most likely, created in Bayeux, this 230-foot-long, 20-inch-wide (70-meter-long, 51-centimeter-wide) length of embroidered fabric has been drawing enthralled tourists to this part of Normandy for generations. Effectively a 50-panel comic strip depicting the events leading up to and of William the Conqueror's successful invasion of England in 1066, it has survived almost 1,000 years—a fact that has been described as a miracle. Its origins lie shrouded in mystery, however. The most popular theory is that it was commissioned by Bishop Odo, William's half brother, in order to coincide with the consecration of Bayeux Cathedral in 1077. Should this be the case, the tapestry would most probably have been embroidered in Kent, England, Odo's power-base, with local women responsible for the actual needlework of its design.

Today, it stands both as a remarkable work of art and a hugely instructive historical artifact, showing in visceral detail one of the most important events in European history. It also offers a stunning illustration of Norman and Anglo-Saxon culture at the time of the conquest: early-medieval hairstyles, ship types, and clothing can all be observed by looking at the tapestry.

The audio tour, which is free, really brings the story of the tapestry to life.

Notre Dame Cathedral

Rue du Bienvenu, Bayeux; tel. 02 31 92 48 48; www.bayeux.fr/fr/decouvrir-bayeux/cathedrale-notre-dame; 9am-5pm daily Jan.-Mar., 8:30am-6pm daily Apr.-Jun., 9am-6pm daily Jul.-Dec.; free

This is one of the great churches of France that seems all the more impressive, rising as it does from Bayeux's relatively humble surrounds. Its interior is towering and stark, though filled with light on account of large windows of clear glass that make up much of the church's transepts. This sparseness, combined with its size, allows your imagination free reign, as thoughts rush in to fill the space: it's easy to envisage the striking events of the cathedral's past. It was, for example, said to have been where Harold Godwinson swore his famous oath, immortalized in the Bayeux Tapestry, promising William the Conqueror the throne of England, then later was the first place the tapestry itself was believed to have been displayed.

The building was initiated by Hugues d'Ivry, the then-bishop of Bayeux, in the year 1040. After he died in 1049, the project was brought to conclusion by his successor, William the Conqueror's restless half brother, Bishop Odo. Consecrated in 1077 in the presence of William himself, the original structure was Romanesque, characterized by semicircular arches, but it has been added to over the years in various different architectural styles. The most sustained period of additional building took place in the mid-13th century, and indeed, it was this period that has lent the church most of its character: today, it is most accurately described as a Gothic cathedral on top of a Romanesque frame. Its central tower, meanwhile, was a 15th-century

1: detail of the Bayeux Tapestry depicting the Norman invasion of England in the 11th century
2: Notre-Dame de Bayeux

ENE RVNT
1
2

construction, with its "crown" remodeled in the 19th century.

Museum of the Battle of Normandy

Boulevard Fabian Ware, Bayeux; tel. 02 31 51 46 90; www.bayeuxmuseum.com/musee_memorial_bataille_de_normandie.html; 9:30am-6:30pm daily; adults €7.50, reduced €5.50, under 10 free

Notable for the fact that it escaped much of the fighting of D-Day, with the Germans preferring to make their stand in Caen 20 miles (32 kilometers) to the east, Bayeux nevertheless has an extensive museum dedicated to the invasion, and one that provides perhaps the best general overview anywhere in the region. With over 24,756 square feet (2,300 square meters) of floor space, visitors are invited to track the two-month progress of the Battle of Normandy, via themed areas and archive footage, from its preparation to August 29, 1944, when an Allied victory was official declared. The museum also plays host to some significant military hardware: an M3 Half-track, a Caterpillar D7 bulldozer, and a Willys Jeep, to name a few, as well as American, English, and German uniforms from the period. It's a little old-fashioned in appearance without some of the interactive displays you might find elsewhere, but very informative nonetheless.

Bayeux War Cemetery and Memorial

1945 boulevard Fabian Ware, Bayeux; www.cwgc.org; open 24 hours; free

Containing 4,648 burials, the Bayeux War Cemetery is the largest France-based cemetery of Commonwealth soldiers from the Second World War. Eleven different nationalities are represented, including 466 soldiers from Nazi Germany, most of whom died in the early days of the Battle of Normandy in 1944. Opposite the cemetery is the Bayeux Memorial, which bears the names of 1,802 soldiers who also lost their lives in the fighting that followed the D-Day landings but who have no known grave. Designed by the British architect P. D. Hepworth, this affecting monument to loss also pays homage to the Norman conquest of Britain with a Latin epitaph that reads, "We once conquered by William, have now set free the Conqueror's native land."

The space, characterized by the classic rows of cool white gravestones, between which bloom colorful flowers, was the inspiration behind a poem by Charles Causley, "At the British War Cemetery, Bayeux," the reading of which, if you can track it down before you go, is sure to lend an added poignancy to any visit. More prosaic advice is to keep aware that parking directly outside the Memorial is limited, and that it may be easier to find space down the nearby Chemin des Marettes.

For more details of who is buried here, you can consult the Commonwealth War Graves Commission website: www.cwgc.org.

Jardin Botanique

55 route de Port en Bessin, Bayeux; tel. 02 31 51 60 60; www.bayeux.fr/fr/lieu/le-jardin-botanique; 9am-8pm daily; free

Also referred to as the Jardin Public de Bayeux (Bayeux Public Garden), this tranquil and genteel municipal space of old trees and well-tended flower beds began life as a meadow gifted to the public in 1851 by Charlemagne Jean-Delamare, whose intent was to create a space for teaching horticulture. After a design by French landscape gardener Eugène Bühler, based around a main oval path, the space was opened to the public in 1864. Indeed, many trees from the original stock planted in the mid-19th century remain. Among them, and the garden's undisputed highlight, is a Weeping European Beech, with its explosion of gravity-defying branches all stretching wildly from a single trunk. This incredible tree, which is impossible to miss in this fairly small garden, was named one of the remarkable trees of France in the year 2000 by the A.R.B.R.E.S association, dedicated to protecting trees of historical importance throughout the country.

Bayeux's Old Town

Much like the cathedral, Bayeux's old town

1066 and All That

The opening chapter of modern English history, the Norman invasion of 1066, is a story of propaganda, deceit, and daring, which has divided historians for generations.

SUCCESSION TO THE ENGLISH THRONE

The Norman version of events begins with the English king, Edward the Confessor, declaring his distant cousin William of Normandy next in line to his throne. Edward then sends Harold Godwinson, an English noble with a clearer claim to the throne, across to Normandy. Once there, Harold swears on the holiest relics in Normandy that he will defer the throne to William when Edward dies. Other chroniclers (notably Anglo-Saxon ones) suggest that Edward made no such promise, and that Harold was taken prisoner by the Normans after his ship was blown off course and forced to swear the oath.

Whichever the case, upon Edward's death, Harold—who had returned to England by then—crowns himself king. William and the Normans make ready for war, mustering forces in Saint-Valery-sur-Somme, a coastal town several miles east of modern-day Normandy. Meanwhile, another pretender to the throne, King Harald Hardrada of Norway, invades the north of England. Harold successfully defeats and kills Harald Hardrada at the bloody Battle of Stamford Bridge, but he has no time to celebrate, or even lick his wounds, for word comes that the Normans have landed in the south.

THE BATTLE OF HASTINGS

The battle that decided English (and European) history took place on October 14, 1066, about nine miles (14 kilometers) northwest of the village of Hastings. There Harold and his battle- and road-weary troops take on William and the Normans. The battle lasts all day, from around nine in the morning until dusk, and is closely fought, despite the Anglo-Saxon army's lack of cavalry. Eventually, though, a tactic of feinting attacks from the Normans thins out Harold's lines; his heavily armored foot soldiers break their shield wall and are picked off. Then, Harold himself is struck by an arrow in the eye and dies. The day is William's; his epithet "the Conqueror" is secured. By Christmas Day 1066 he has crowned himself King of England, and thus began a dynasty that can still be seen on the throne to this day.

is a mishmash of architectural styles dating from the many epochs of its construction. There's a great deal to be gained from just a casual wander.

From the **Quai de l'Aure** there's a nice view of the river, specifically the old water mill, which harkens back to the days when Bayeux was a center of the tanning and dyeing trade. Farther along, on the corner of the rue Saint-Martin and rue Cuisiniers, teeters a 14th-century half-timber house. It's a design common throughout Normandy, though often only in reconstruction; this is an authentically medieval building. Unfortunately, it's not open to the public, though is well worth taking a look at from the outside.

There are then plenty of fine townhouses on the roads Franche, Ursulines, and Général-de-Dais, which are all worth a look on your way to the **Place Charles-de-Gaulle.** This refined public garden is so called because of the two speeches delivered in Bayeux by the French wartime leader, the first shortly after the battle of Normandy in 1944, and the second in 1946, when he outlined a number of ideas that would go on to inspire France's 1958 Constitution. An engraved column in the plaza commemorates the former of these speeches, and the area, surrounded by trees and centered on a fountain, is a pleasant place to relax after your walk around town.

Château de Balleroy

Rue du Sapin, Balleroy; www.chateau-balleroy.fr; 10:45am-6pm Wed.-Sun. Apr.-Jun. and Sept., 10:45am-6pm daily Jul.-Aug.; Château, Balloon

Museum, and Park: adults €9, reduced €6.50, Château and Park: adults €7, reduced €5.50, Balloon Museum and Park: adults €4.50, reduced €3.50, Park: adults €3, reduced free

A 15-minute drive to the southwest of Bayeux is this elegant trailblazing château from the early 17th century. Built by the revered architect François Mansart, the Château de Balleroy became a blueprint to many other similar buildings around France, including, most notably, Versailles.

Today, it remains an excellent place to visit, not least because of its stunning retention of original features, including the famous cantilevered staircase, which twists up around the central hallway with no support from beneath it. This apparently gravity-defying marvel was Mansart's innovation, and is the first of its design anywhere in the world. And speaking of defying gravity, one of the château's pavilions plays host to a museum of hot-air ballooning, covering the history of the activity right up to the present day.

FOOD

Regional Cuisine

AU P'TIT BISTROT

31 rue Larcher, Bayeux; tel. 02 31 92 30 08; 12pm-1:30pm and 7pm-9pm Tues.-Fri., 7pm-9pm Sat. and Mon.; lunch menu €16.90-19.90, evening menu €29-35

This bistro's interior can be a bit "provincial restaurant trying to be urbane," but the food is ambitious, well presented, and most importantly, delicious. The flavors are very much traditional French, with a focus on less popular meats such as duck and game tweaked in modern and inventive ways. Slightly formal, it's good for a long group dinner or a romantic evening, though relatively inexpensive for what it offers.

★ LA RAPIÈRE

53 rue Saint-Jean, Bayeux; tel. 02 31 21 05 45; www.larapiere.net; 6:30pm-9:15pm Mon.-Sat.; menus €36-49

This is one of Bayeux's undisputed dining gems. Nestled in a side alley, between ancient-looking walls, La Rapière offers the kind of rustic, home-cooked fare almost entirely sourced from local producers that people come to France in search of. With menus named after the Three Musketeers, expect rich and succulent variations on classic dishes of duck and veal, as well as the freshest local seafood. Ideal for evening dining, the restaurant is located in a building that dates from the 16th century, but has been decorated with just enough modern flourishes that it does not feel at all dingy or stuck in the past. Booking in advance is highly recommended.

★ LE MOULIN DE LA GALETTE

38 rue de Nesmond, Bayeux; tel. 02 31 22 47 75; 12:30pm-2:30pm and 7pm-9:30pm Fri.-Sat., 12:30pm-2:30pm and 7pm-9:30pm Sun.-Tues. and Thurs.; €5.60-16.80

With a terrace over the River Aure, there are few more picturesque places in town to drop in for a meal. Here the humble crepe is used as a base for any number of dishes: They come served heaped with everything from egg and bacon to pan-fried scallops. There are plenty of non-crepe-based options too, including salads and steak frites. Nothing's too expensive, though, making this a great little informal place to drop into for lunch or grab a quick dinner. Right next door to the tapestry museum, it can get very busy, so expect to wait for a table on warm summer days.

Budget Options

LE BOUCHON

15 rue Maréchal Foch, Bayeux; tel. 02 31 92 06 44; www.lebouchon-cavebistrot.fr; 10am-5:30pm Mon., 10am-7:30pm Tues.-Thurs., 10am-9pm Fri.-Sat.; menu €12

A wine shop and bar that doubles as an informal restaurant, Le Bouchon is a great place to drop in for a classy but inexpensive lunch of traditional French fare cooked in front of your eyes, or to grab an early evening drink

1: one of Bayeux's two old water wheels **2:** the Moulin de la Galette **3:** behind its houses Bayeux hides some spectacular old courtyards

1

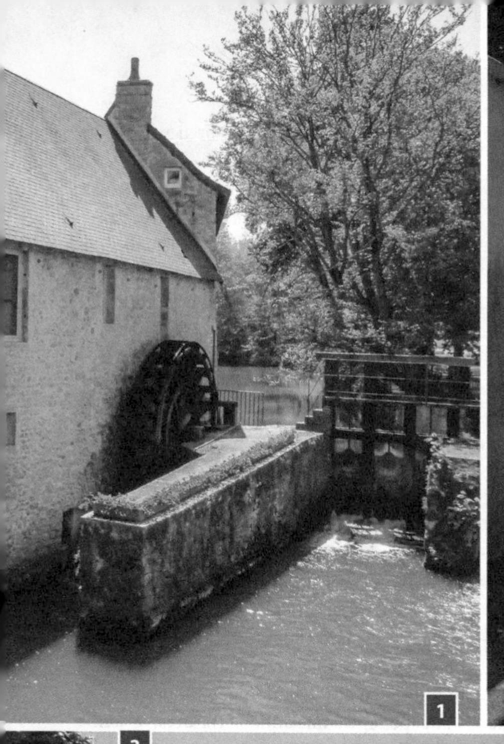

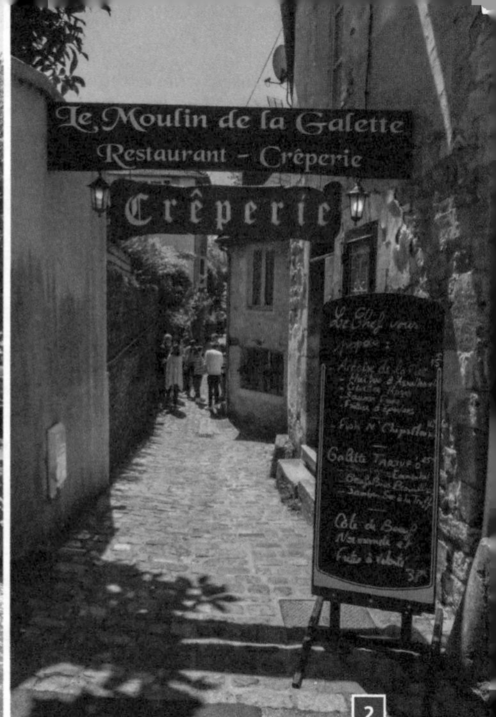

Le Moulin de la Galette
Restaurant - Crêperie
Crêperie

2

3

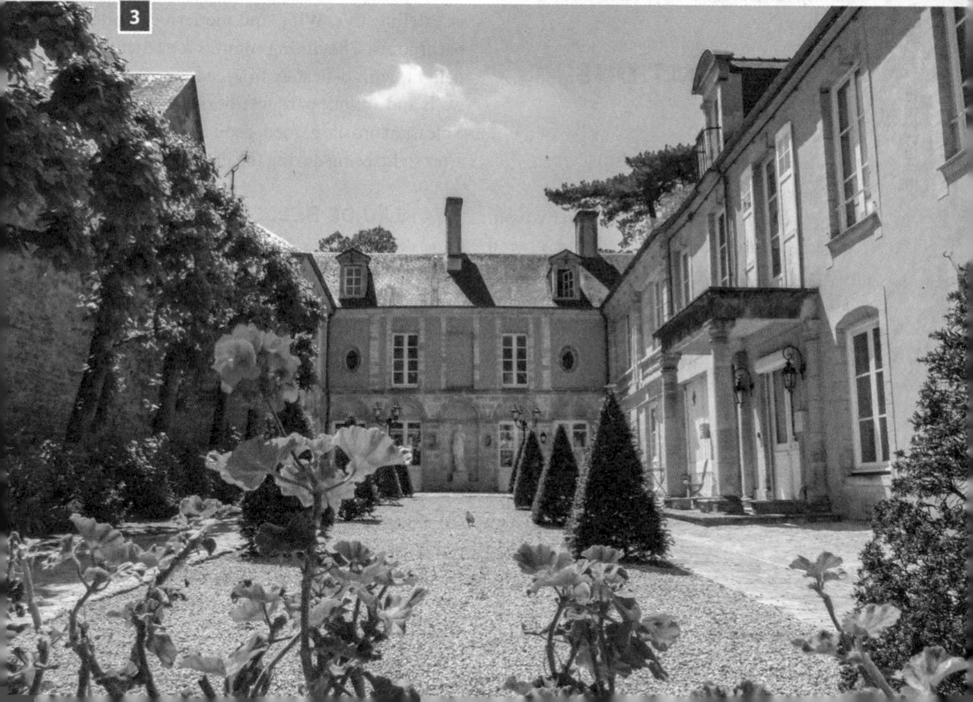

from their extensive wine selection paired with a platter of meat and cheese. The lunchtime menu is exceptionally good for the price; the only downside is there's next to no choice. The menu changes every day, and you get what you're given. Free wine tastings are offered too, so you might end up buying a couple of crates to savor when you get home. Unfortunately, it closes early most days, so it is not a place for dinner.

LIBERTY COFFEE

36 rue Saint-Patrice, Bayeux; tel. 02 31 22 06 03; 8am-6:30pm Mon.-Fri., 8am-3pm Sat.; €6-15

Catering to those in search of a taste of America, this café is a great place to drop into any time of day. There's a tasty burger and fries on offer, but perhaps the biggest draw is its dessert selection: colorful and icing- and sugar-heavy, they make a good reprieve from French patisserie. It's a good place to stop in for breakfast, serving yogurt, excellent coffee, and orange juice, as well as its sweet treats, making for a great way to fortify you for the day ahead.

ACCOMMODATIONS

€50-100

AU GEORGES VII

19 rue Saint-Martin, Bayeux; tel. 02 31 92 28 53; http://georges-7.com; from €50 d

This is a no-frills hotel in the Bayeux town center. And no-frills here really does mean no-frills—only some rooms have en suite bathrooms, none have TVs, and its promise of WiFi throughout cannot always be counted on. Nevertheless, if it's a cheap, well-located place you need to simply lay your head for the night, then this is as good a place as any. One could even say it has a kind of folksy French run-down charm. Also, the staff are extremely friendly, and the continental breakfasts are excellent.

€100-200

BRUNVILLE HÔTEL

9 rue Genas Duhomme, Bayeux; tel. 02 31 21 18 00; www.hotel-le-brunville-bayeux.com; from €105 d

Some questionable interior design decisions notwithstanding—the dining areas are decked out in full faux baroque style—this is a comfortable and clean place to stay in the very center of Bayeux. All rooms have en suite bathrooms, while the food served at the restaurant is locally sourced and of a high quality. The highlights are the heated outside pool and hot tub, which are open year-round.

HÔTEL D'ARGOUGES

21 rue Saint-Patrice, Bayeux; tel. 02 31 92 88 86; www.hotel-dargouges.com; from €141 d

This place is at the top end of Bayeux's town-center hotel scene. Located in an 18th-century townhouse, with all its original features perfectly restored and intact, the rooms offer plush comfort in a style that pays homage to the epoch of the building, with patterned wallpaper and some antique fixtures, as well as satellite TVs, WiFi, and modern en suite bathrooms. The dining room is a particular delight, with delicately filigreed wood panel walls and antique parquet floors. There's also a pleasant on-site garden, good for relaxing in after sightseeing during the day.

CHATEAU DE BELLEFONTAINE

49 rue de Bellefontaine, Bayeux; tel. 02 31 22 00 10; www.hotel-bellefontaine.com; €145 d

This beautiful 18th-century chateau on the outskirts of Bayeux is surrounded by its own calming and elegant grounds, with a large lawn area bordered by a canal, an on-site tennis court, and 200-year-old trees. It offers that rarest of things: reasonably priced luxury. Every room has its own unique period decoration and boasts WiFi access and a flat-screen TV. The sumptuous on-site dining room offers up traditional feasts with prior reservation. The only difficulty will be tearing yourself away to see the sights.

★ DOMAINE DE BAYEUX

20 rue de Crémel, Bayeux; tel. 02 31 21 36 15; www.domaine-de-bayeux.com; from €155 d

This is another grand old château with fabulous tree-lined grounds near the center of Bayeux. While the rooms are perhaps a touch more basic than one might assume from the outside, the building and its location more than make up for that. Staying here, it's easy to start believing yourself a Norman duke, especially given the friendliness of the staff. Despite the building's age, there's good WiFi throughout the property and TVs in all the rooms.

HÔTEL LE BAYEUX

9 rue Tardif, Bayeux; tel. 02 31 92 70 08; www.hotellebayeux.com; from €164 d

Housed within a pleasant period building, this comfortable and clean hotel provides all the necessary modern conveniences for a trouble-free stay in Bayeux, including WiFi and en suite bathrooms. It has several rooms that can accommodate up to five people, making it a great budget option for families or people traveling in larger groups. A large buffet breakfast is available every morning and the town center is a short walk away.

Camping

CAMPING DES BORDS DE L'AURE

Boulevard Eindhoven, Allée du Camping, RN 13; tel. 02 31 92 08 43; www.camping-bayeux.fr; high-season pitch for two people €22, high-season cabin for 2-4 people €96

With easy access to the town, though surrounded by greenery, this campsite is at the posh end of basic, situated in a clean, well-kept environment, with cabins on offer (complete with fully equipped kitchens and en suite bathrooms) as well as space to pitch tents. There's also a camp washing block, WiFi, and bike rental, and in the summer, food trucks regularly set up on the site and remain there into the evening. A swimming pool free to guests is the proverbial cherry on top.

INFORMATION AND SERVICES

Information

TOURIST OFFICE

Pont Saint Jean, Bayeux; tel. 02 31 51 28 28; www.bayeux-bessin-tourisme.com; 9am-7pm Mon.-Sat., 9am-1pm and 2pm-6pm Sun.

Right in the center of town, this tourist office deals with Bayeux and its surrounding areas. It's a good place to help you plan trips to the D-Day beaches, for where it organizes some tours, as well as find out about the more immediate town. Multiple languages are spoken by its staff, including English.

Emergencies

HOSPITAL CENTER DE BAYEUX

13 rue de Nesmond, Bayeux; tel. 02 31 51 51 51; www.ch-bayeux.fr; ER open 24 hours

A large hospital, very centrally located; it's just next to the Bayeux Tapestry museum. Like elsewhere in France, it makes no official promises of having English-speaking staff, but French doctors are often adept at the language, so you should be able to make yourself understood. The emergency room (*Urgences* in French) is open 24 hours.

TRANSPORTATION

Getting There

BY CAR

About 20 minutes (22 miles/35 kilometers) from Caen via the N13, and thereafter from Paris in about three hours down the A13, Bayeux is well connected by road. There's even a mini-ring road, which eases the stress of entering the town: Arrive from pretty much any direction and you'll soon see signs pointing where it is you need to go.

Being just inland from what was roughly the center point of the whole invasion, Bayeux is also the town closest to most of the sights along the D-Day beaches. From either Omaha or Gold Beach, it's less than a 20-minute drive into the town center. From Sword Beach, it is a 40-minute drive, and from Utah Beach, 45 minutes.

From Mont-Saint-Michel, the journey time is around 1.5 hours (a little over 70 miles/112 kilometers) along the A84.

You'll have to pay for most parking in the very center of Bayeux at a cost of €1 per hour. However, just one block out in any direction there are plenty of free spaces, still less than a 10-minute walk from most of the major attractions.

There are a couple of car rental places in Bayeux. But by far the most practical for most visitors will be **Bayeux BodemerAuto** (20 boulevard Sadi Carnot; tel. 02 31 51 18 34; www.bodemerauto.com/renault-bayeux) being right next to the railway station. Prices start from around €40 a day.

BY TRAIN

Via its train station, **Gare de Bayeux** (place de la Gare, Bayeux; tel. 36 35; www.gares-sncf.com/fr/gare/frcfr/bayeux; 5:35am-8:25pm Mon., 5:50am-8:25pm Tues.-Thurs., 5:50am-7:50pm Fri.-Sat., 8:05am-9:40pm Sun.) about 15 minutes southeast of the cathedral, Bayeux is serviced hourly from Caen, a 20-minute journey, costing €6, which passengers can reach from Paris and the rest of France.

Regular trains (about 15 a day) also come here from Cherbourg, with a journey time of one hour, costing about €20. Three trains a day make the 1.75-hour journey from that other Norman tourist hub, Mont-Saint-Michel, at a cost of around €24.

BY BUS

Calvados's **Bus Verts** service (www.busverts.fr) connects to Bayeux cheaply from Caen (€4, 30 minutes) and from the D-Day landing grounds. Of these, Bus 70 services Omaha Beach, Pointe du Hoc, and the American Cemetery, running the full route twice a day, more during July and August. Travel time between Omaha and Bayeux is about an hour. Bus 74, meanwhile, comes from Arromanches, runs three times a day, and takes 40 minutes. Tickets are €2.

Getting Around

Bayeux is a small, very walkable town, though should you need to get anywhere particularly fast, taxis can be called on (tel. 02 31 92 04 10). From the town center to the railway station shouldn't be much more than €5, and if you want to take one to Arromanches it'll be around €21, or the American Cemetery €36.

You can rent bikes, meanwhile, from **Vélos Location Bayeux** (impasse de l'Islet; tel. 02 31 92 89 16; https://velos-location-bayeux.business.site), with prices starting from around €7.50 for a half day.

The D-Day Landing Beaches

In June 1944, a 50-mile (80-kilometer) stretch of Normandy's coastline became the site of the largest military landing in history, as Allied forces gained a foothold on the European continent and began its bloody liberation, hastening the end of the Third Reich and the Second World War.

Today, the landscape remains sculpted by the brutality of war and everywhere you look there are reminders, both incidental and deliberate, of the price paid by thousands of American, British, Canadian, and other Allied soldiers, fighting for freedom far from home. A rich infrastructure dedicated to the landings themselves and the many battles that followed has developed, and from international cemeteries to museums, to the careful preservation of certain battle sites, there is much on this beautiful coastline to inspire reflection and to allow visitors to pay their respects.

Orientation

It should almost go without saying, but the D-Day beaches and the sights associated with Operation Overlord are spread across a very wide area. Indeed, just trying to cram all the major battlegrounds into a single day offers a striking idea of the operation's scale. **Sword Beach** is farthest east, just alongside the Orne Estuary, making up part of the front at Ouistreham, practically a suburb of Caen. **Utah Beach,** meanwhile, was the westernmost invasion point, and it sits at the base of the Cotentin Peninsula relatively far from any major towns. In the center are **Omaha, Gold,** and **Juno,** none much more than 30 minutes' drive from Bayeux, and which combined offer perhaps the best concentration of sights along the coast.

The fastest way between the beaches by car is to use the inland main road, the N13, though more picturesque coastal routes also exist, which are ideal for cyclists and those hiking their way between the battlefields, following the GR223 walking route.

It's worth pointing out, incidentally, that you shouldn't expect too much from the beaches themselves, or indeed, the towns that adjoin them. To put it bluntly, the landing grounds were not chosen for their physical beauty. In a sense, quite the opposite was true. Most consist of long, straight, fairly narrow stretches of sand, and are backed by flat countryside, all of which creates an atmosphere quite indifferent to history. The towns, meanwhile, are understandably almost entirely reconstructed, and of the ones actually on the coast, only **Arromanches** and **Ouistreham** have anything remotely to offer beyond tourist trappings. By all means, go stand on the beaches, and try to imagine yourself back in the chaotic and terrifying moments of June 6, 1944, but keep in mind that more evocative of the D-Day experience are often the places where smaller actions took place, the cemeteries, and the museums.

SIGHTS

Sword Beach

Lion Plage, Lion-sur-mer; Twisto Bus: Line 62

This easternmost of the five Allied landing beaches, and the one situated closest to Caen, was assaulted by the British Third Infantry Division on D-Day. It is today one of the most easily accessible of the beaches by public transport, with the small port town of Ouistreham, an effective suburb of Caen, situated at the beach's eastern limit, before it is full-stopped by the mouth of the River Orne. The liveliest spot along the D-Day coast, and the only one not entirely dominated by World War II memorabilia (though this is where Sword's museums are located), it's a living town with some nice reconstructed houses in the classic Norman timber-frame design. Heading west, along the beach out of town, the low-rise buildings clinging to its edge become more residential. There's a promenade that stretches three miles along its length, which is fairly featureless—better suited to getting invaded than picturesque walks.

The first Allied troops met fierce resistance as they came ashore, but they gradually made headway as they landed more armored vehicles on the beach. German beach defenses were overcome by the Royal Engineers and modified tanks, known as "Hobart's Funnies," which had been specifically designed for the assault, with additions such as mine ploughs and flamethrowers.

The most iconic image of Sword's invasion was that of Scottish war hero Lord Lovat's personal bagpiper, Bill Millin, wearing full Highland dress, playing the eccentric aristocrat's commando unit ashore. It's said the Germans long had Millin in their sights, but did not fire, assuming the kilt-wearing piper had gone mad. Today, a statue commemorates Millin's bravery, just along the promenade leading west along the beach at Ouistreham.

Musée du Mur de l'Atlantique le Bunker

Avenue du 6 Juin, Ouistreham; tel. 02 31 97 28 69; 9am-7pm daily; adults €7.50, reduced €5.50

This small museum offers a detailed look at the kinds of command bunkers that the Germans erected as part of their formidable Atlantic Wall, defending coastlines from northern Norway to the South of France. The museum itself is situated inside just such a

D-Day Landing Beaches

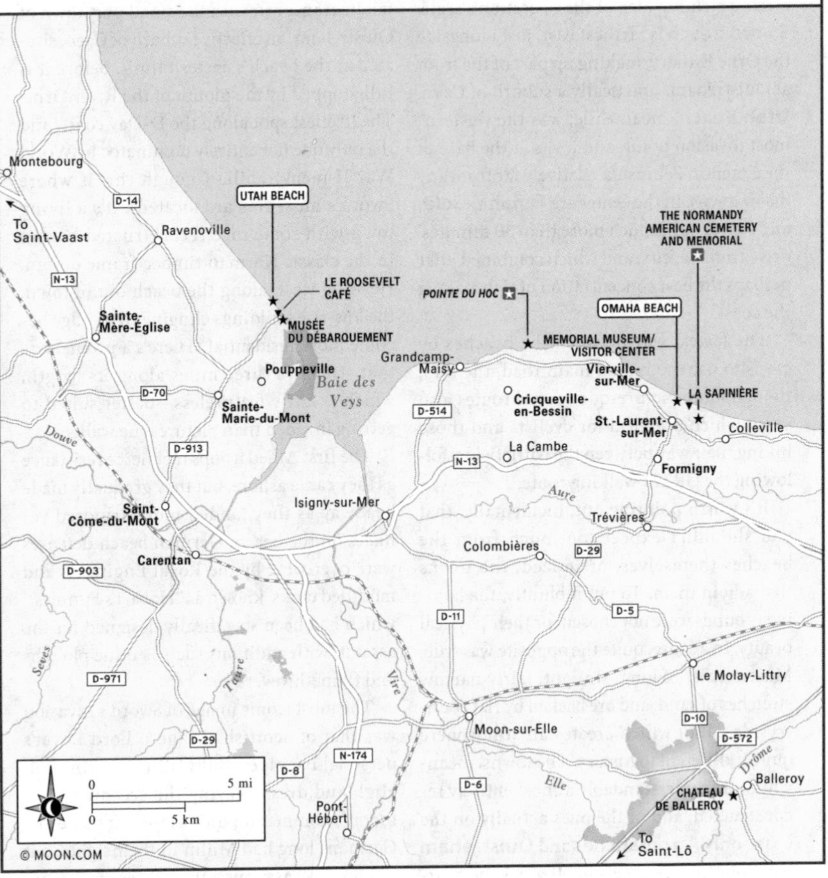

bunker, restored precisely to how it would have been on the eve of the D-Day landings. Visitors can tour the generator room, sick bay, and telephone switchboard among others, as well as stand at the observation post and look through the powerful ranger finder, imagining their own defense of Sword beach. There are many information boards in both French and English, though a visit shouldn't take much more than an hour.

Musée du No. 4 Commando

Avenue du 6 Juin, Ouistreham; tel. 02 31 97 28 69; www.museedugrandbunker.com; 9am-7pm daily; adults €7.50, reduced €5.50

This small museum tells the fascinating story of the French soldiers who joined Britain's elite No. 4 Commando unit and played a vital role securing the town of Ouistreham at the eastern end of Sword Beach. Theirs was one of the countless small-scale acts of heroism that ultimately won the day, the battle they fought over the wreckage of the town's casino being a particularly notable encounter. The museum is crammed with artifacts from the unit and brought alive by several life-size models. Wording for the exhibits is in French,

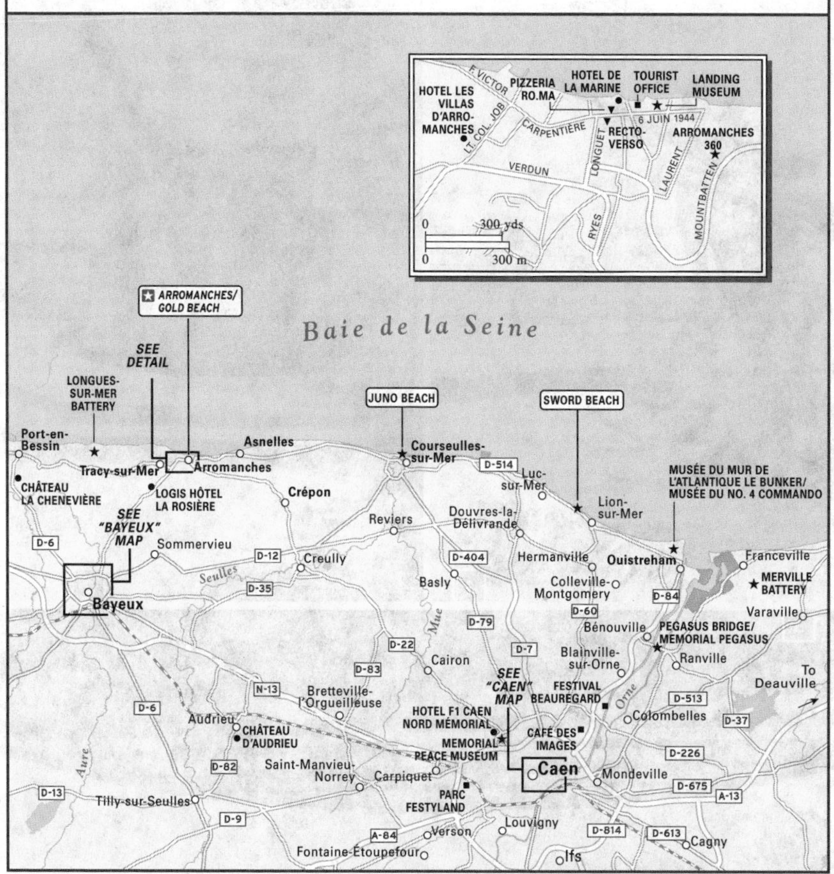

so it may be worth reading up on the story before your visit.

Merville Battery

Place du 9ème Bataillon, Merville-Franceville-Plage; tel. 02 31 91 47 53; www.batterie-merville.com; 9:30am-6:30pm mid-Mar.-Sept., 10am-5pm Oct.-mid-Nov.; adults €6.50, children 6-14 €3.50, under 6 free

This museum offers a display of a still-intact gun emplacement and an educational trail, complete with English and French information boards and military hardware, about what life was like for those who manned such stations, detailing how they were used strategically to defend the coast. The capture of Merville Battery itself was one of the first ground engagements of D-Day, taking place just after midnight on June 6 by an understrength force of British paratroopers. The exciting story of this battle is also detailed at the museum.

Memorial Pegasus

Avenue du Major Howard, Ranville; tel. 02 31 78 19 44; http://memorial-pegasus.fr; 9:30am-6:30pm daily Apr.-Sept., 10am-5pm Oct.-mid-Dec. and

1
2
3

Feb.-Mar.; adults €8, ages 8-17 €5, under 8 free

This museum and memorial dedicated to the 6th Airborne Division concentrates on the operation to capture Pegasus Bridge, a moveable bridge that was one of the first objectives to be seized by the Allies in the D-Day invasion. Under the title Operation Deadstick, 181 British soldiers landed here in six Horsa gliders and took the bridge with just two casualties. It was an essential strategic gain, for it limited the effectiveness of any German counterattack that might follow the Normandy invasion. The bridge itself, a Horsa glider, and other military hardware are all on display at this museum.

Juno Beach

2 avenue du Château, Courseulles-sur-Mer; Bus Verts: Lines 2 and 74

Juno Beach, located between the two British-attacked beaches of Sword and Gold, and running from the village of Courseulles in the west to Saint-Aubin-sur-Mer in the east, was assaulted by a largely Canadian force. Their objective was to cut off the Caen-Bayeux road, capture Caen's Carpiquet airport, and join up the two British armies from their respective landing grounds.

The beach itself is long and sandy, backed by houses and patches of scrub. Most things to see here are located in Courseulles, including the Juno Beach Centre, which gets its own parcel of land just west of Courseulles's small harbor, and on the seafront. Otherwise, Courseulles is an unassuming village filled with largely modern buildings, some of which have been constructed in the traditional timber-frame Norman style. Finding somewhere to park for free in this village should be simple enough, then you can walk wherever else you need.

Juno's code name, incidentally, was something of an anomaly to the rest of the operation. It was originally going to be called Jelly, in line with Gold and Sword as a type of fish, but Winston Churchill himself rejected this, insisting that a place where so many were likely to die deserved a more serious name, and so Juno was suggested.

Juno Beach Centre

Voie des Français Libres, Courseulles-sur-Mer; tel. 02 31 37 32 17; www.junobeach.org; 9:30am-7pm daily Apr.-Sept., 10am-6pm daily Mar. and Oct., 10am-5pm daily Feb. and Dec.; adults €7, reduced €5.50

This is not only a museum commemorating the events of Juno Beach, but a cultural center dedicated to the entire Canadian experience of the Second World War in France and beyond. The Juno Beach Centre offers a well-curated modern exhibition consisting of photographs, firsthand accounts, multimedia displays, maps, and military hardware to tell the uncompromising and moving stories of Canadian units from Sicily to Normandy and elsewhere. It also provides a memorial to the 45,000 Canadian soldiers who lost their lives in the war, as well as the 5,500 killed in the Battle of Normandy itself. As well as permanent displays, including one dedicated to re-creating arrival on the beach by landing craft and others looking at Canadian society as a whole in the 1930s, it plays host to regular public lectures about the Canadian experience of the war and social events on a Canadian theme. In general, it is one of the better funded and, as a result, higher-quality museums to be visited on the beaches themselves, and unmissable for anyone specifically interested in the Canadian experience.

★ Arromanches/Gold Beach

Gare, Arromanches les Bains; Bus Verts: Line 74

Located at the center of the five Normandy landing beaches and leading up to the old fishing port of Arromanches, Gold Beach was taken by the British Army, with the first wave of landings commencing at 07h25 followed by two hours of sustained naval bombardment to make way for the soldiers and landing craft. Today, Arromanches itself feels almost like an English seaside town, with pebble-dash walls

1: a statue just behind Omaha Beach commemorates the bravery of hundreds of G.I.s **2:** gun battery at Longues-sur-Mer **3:** from inside a bunker at Pointe du Hoc

The Longest Day

The Nazis had long expected an invasion of mainland Europe by the Allies, and in 1942 Hitler had ordered the construction of a vast line of coastal defenses dubbed the Atlantic Wall, stretching from Norway's polar reaches to France's Basque Coast. Where to penetrate this was the first question the Allies had to answer when they began preparations for D-Day back in 1943. Brittany, Cotentin, and Pas-de-Calais were all suggested, but the first two were dismissed for being peninsulas, and therefore easy for the Germans to cut off. Pas-de-Calais, meanwhile, seemed the most obvious point, being the closest sea crossing with the United Kingdom. But it was also the most heavily defended, and offered a hinterland meshed with difficult-to-cross canals. In the end, Normandy's western beaches were chosen, and thus they unknowingly began their wait to be written into history.

PREPARATIONS

As well as mustering massive troop numbers, a great game of deception needed to be played by the Allies in order to keep the Germans guessing where the ultimate strike would fall. Ordinary soldiers were kept in the dark, and great false displays of plywood military machinery were arranged near British ports that would suggest different points of invasion to confuse German spy planes. Perhaps the most daring element of this subterfuge, though, was provided by the double agent Juan Pujol García. The Allies first got him to send the Germans accurate information about some of their movements in order to secure the enemy's trust, then sell them a massive flat-out lie that the invasion was actually taking place in the Calais region.

The real D-Day was set for June 1944 in Normandy and proceeded by mass aerial bombardment, which succeeded in killing numerous French citizens as well as German soldiers—such was the price deemed necessary for winning the war. Atrocious weather delayed the operation by a couple of days and even saw it within a hair's breadth of being called off. But in the end, the American General Dwight D. Eisenhower gave the green light, and on June 6, 1944, the battle began.

THE FIRST WAVE

The first wave of more than 24,000 paratroopers and glider pilots deployed just after midnight.

rising from the beach and the smell of cotton candy and frying in the air, not to mention the many British tourists coming to pay their respects—don't worry, there's ample free parking off the François Carpentier, just to the west of the small town center and back from the coast.

Gold Beach is most notable for being the site of one of the artificial **Mulberry harbors** constructed soon after the invasion. With no deep-sea ports captured in the initial invasion, the Allies needed a way to immediately start bringing their military hardware ashore. They installed great buoyant concrete blocks that extended way out to sea, effectively creating a floating road that big ships could pull up alongside, and onto which tanks and troop carriers could be unloaded. Much of the floating harbor at Arromanches remains today. It is staggering in scale; several platforms ring the horizon like some vast art installation, while others remain dug in the sand of Arromanches beach, where they can be approached and seen up close. Shaggy with seaweed and abstract now divorced from whole harbor, they look like the forgotten monoliths of some alien civilization.

Photographs struggle to do the harbor's remains justice: One of the most impressive and unusual sights anywhere along the Normandy coast, they warrant a trip to see it with your own eyes, which is the only way you can truly appreciate the scale.

Arromanches 360

Rue du Calvaire, Arromanches-les-Bains; tel. 02 31 06 06 45; www.arromanches360.com; 10am-5:30pm daily Feb.-Dec.; adults €6, reduced €5.50, under 10

They went behind enemy lines in order to capture bridges and gun emplacements and thus ease the passage of the main force onto the beaches. Before sunrise, then, there had already been countless acts of extraordinary heroism along the coast, not least because the bad weather dissipated many of the paratroopers over wider drop zones than they had been intending, meaning that a number had to complete their missions under full strength. The storming of Merville Battery by the British is one of the main examples of this.

AMPHIBIOUS INVASION

The amphibious invasion began at 6:30am along five beaches of the Normandy coast, covering a combined length of around 50 miles. Each beach got its own code name, and was to be assaulted by different national armies: the British attacked Sword and Gold, named after fish, the Americans attacked Utah and Omaha, named after the states, while the Canadians attacked Juno, which was originally going to be called Jelly—also a fish—until that was deemed inappropriate for a place where it was known that so many would die; Juno was the name of the wife of a Canadian Wing Commander. The names were also chosen for all being phonetically distinct from one another, and for not giving away anything of the operations they referred to.

THE END OF THE DAY

Resistance was encountered along all the beaches, but nowhere was it fiercer than at Omaha, where high winds and cliffs also hampered the attack and led to around 2,000 casualties. Nevertheless, the Allied armies stuck to it, and by the end of the day had secured beachheads at all landing grounds along the coast. Though much more successful than it could have been, D-Day did not in fact reach any of its stated objectives within that first 24 hours: Caen, Carentan, Saint-Lô, and Bayeux were all still in German hands. At the same time, the Allies now had a foothold in France, and the ultimate German strategy based on holding them at the coast had been smashed. The battle for Normandy would go on to last another two months, but the events of D-Day now made an ultimate Allied victory all but inevitable.

free

This cinema features a 19-minute film about D-Day and the Battle for Normandy displayed on nine HD screens, which surround the viewer and immerse them fully in the action. While not necessarily the most informative of all exhibitions on the coast, it is certainly one of the most emotionally affecting. It is located on the cliffs above Arromanches, and there is a parking lot on-site for flat rate of €3, as opposed to parking in the rest of Arromanches, which is free.

Landing Museum

Place du 6 Juin 1944, Arromanches-les-Bains; tel. 02 31 22 34 31; www.musee-arromanches.fr; 9am-7pm daily May-Aug., 9am-6pm daily Sept., 9:30am-12:30pm and 1:30pm-5:30pm Oct.-Dec. and Feb.-Apr.; adults €8, reduced €5.90

Notable for being the very first museum dedicated to the Normandy landings anywhere along the coast (its doors opened June 5, 1954), this small establishment remains an excellent, digestible primer for teaching about D-Day. Some may consider its exhibits a little dated, though they still do a good job at getting information across. As may be expected, the Mulberry harbors are covered in detail. It's not a big place, but its location in the center of Arromanches makes it very popular. It can get busy in high season, so arrive early if you want to avoid the crowds.

Longues-sur-Mer Battery

39 rue de la Mer, Longues-sur-Mer

This is a well-preserved gun battery, with guns still intact, despite having been battered by around 1,500 tons of bombs the night before D-Day, then been subject to a bombardment by French, American, and British battleships throughout the day. Three of its four guns were eventually knocked out by British ships *Ajax* and *Argonaut,* while the emplacement itself fell to British soldiers on June 7. Indicative of the kind of men the Germans had guarding the Normandy coast: Of the 184 soldiers operating the battery, half were over 40 years old. Today, it's a peaceful area to wander around, teeming with coastal wildlife; even the ripped concrete and protruding iron from some of the damaged gun emplacements have taken on an almost organic quality. A visitors center offers more information on the battery.

Omaha Beach

Plage, Vierville-sur-Mer; Bus Verts: Line 70

If there is any operation that stands in the forefront of peoples' minds for the terrifying, bloody slaughter that took place on the beaches of Normandy on June 6, 1944, or contributes most to the images of cold, seasick servicemen, crammed together in amphibious landing craft about to risk everything in a maelstrom of bullets on gray, windswept sands, then Omaha is it. This was one of the two beaches assaulted by U.S. forces, where the waves were at their most severe, and where German resistance was strongest.

Immortalized by the photographs of Robert Capra, then later realized in all its frantic horror by Stephen Spielberg in his film *Saving Private Ryan,* the events of D-Day are chillingly palpable on Omaha, perhaps more than anywhere on the Normandy coast, though this is less to do with what the beach itself looks like—to all other intents and purposes it's just a long stretch of lonely beach—and more because of what visitors are inclined to bring to it. Perhaps imaginations are more easily fired, also, because Omaha is less built up than some of the other beaches; a row of houses line the coastal road, but they are well spaced. At either end of the beach there's a cluster of commerce, and a couple of memorials. The one at the western end consists of a classic sculpture of two American GIs advancing under fire, while at the eastern end is the *Monument des Braves* by French artist Anilore Banon. This is a more abstract sculpture of straight and curving metal that thrusts from the sand like waves or the blades of swords. At high tide, their bases are submerged by the sea, bringing to mind the many soldiers who would have had to wade waist-deep toward Nazi gun emplacements on shore.

There is free parking along the beach and in large parking lots at either end.

Memorial Museum

Avenue de la Libération, Saint-Laurent-sur-Mer; tel. 02 31 21 97 44; www.musee-memorial-omaha.com; 9:30am-6:30pm daily Apr.-May and Sept., 9:30am-7pm daily June, 9:30am-7:30pm daily July-Aug., 9:30am-6pm daily Oct.-mid-Nov. and Mar., 9:30am-5pm daily Feb.; adults €6.90, students €5.50, children 7-15 €3.90, under 7 free

With a floor plan that covers 12,917 square feet (1,200 square meters), this museum is specifically dedicated to detailing the events that took place on Omaha Beach on June 6, 1944. Life-size dioramas illustrate the battle in a wider context. There are also far more than just period weapons on display here: examples of 1940s ration packs, cigarettes, and more quotidian clothing and equipment give a real soldier's-eye view of D-Day, even if some of the displays can seem a little dated. Give yourself about an hour to take the whole thing in. There is parking on-site.

TOP EXPERIENCE

★ Normandy American Cemetery and Memorial

Colleville-sur-Mer; tel. 02 31 51 62 00; www.abmc.gov/cemeteries-memorials/europe/normandy-american-cemetery; 9am-6pm daily mid-Apr.-mid-Sept., 9am-5pm mid-Sept.-mid-Apr.; free

Effectively established just a couple of days after the initial D-Day assault, the Normandy American Cemetery and Memorial has become one of the most solemn and affecting pieces of land anywhere along this coast. Covering 172.5

acres (70 hectares), it is the final resting place of 9,385 American dead. The serene white crosses speak volumes to the sacrifice paid to liberate this part of France from the Nazi tyranny. Its close-cropped lawns, profusion of white marble, and uniforms of its staff add to a sensation that this is American rather than French territory, an appropriate resting place for the thousands of soldiers who never made it home. The memorial itself, which looks out from the head of the cemetery across the ranks of graves, is focused on the bronze statue of a lithe young man, ascending as though out of the waters toward heaven, titled *Spirit of American Youth Rising from the Waves.* It was designed by Donald de Lue and is framed by a semicircular limestone colonnade, the lintel of which is emblazoned with the words "This Embattled Shore, Portal of Freedom, Is Forever Hallowed by the Ideals, the Valor, and the Sacrifice of Our Fellow Countrymen."

A place of quiet contemplation, visitors move at a slow, respectful pace. Far more than just a tourist sight, visits here are liable to inspire all kinds of emotion, with some families making a pilgrimage to the grave of a departed relative, while other people search to make sense of the sacrifice in its striking totality. There is, of course, no single right way to visit the cemetery, though bringing flowers to lay at a grave, saying a prayer in the small, central chapel, or even just writing your feelings in the visitors center guestbook are all good ways to connect with the emotions it inspires.

The **visitors center**, meanwhile, houses a relatively new museum that opened its doors in 2007. It is dedicated more to the human stories of D-Day rather than the overall military tactics or historical context. Here, visitors are granted a personal look at the soldiers who fought the battle of Normandy, both those who came home and those who did not. The overall effect is deeply moving and serves to add further human context to the cemetery outside. Expect a visit to this center to take about 40 minutes, while visits to the cemetery will take as much time as you need.

There is extensive on-site parking.

★ Pointe du Hoc

Pointe du Hoc, Cricqueville-en-Bessin ; tel. 02 31 51 62 00; www.abmc.gov/cemeteries-memorials/europe/pointe-du-hoc-ranger-monument; 9am-6pm daily mid-Apr.-mid-Sept., 9am-5pm daily mid-Sept.-mid-Apr.; free; Bus Verts: Line 70

One of the most audacious assaults throughout all of D-Day, Pointe du Hoc was a fortified German area on top of a 98-foot-high (30-meter-high) cliff between Omaha and Utah Beaches, which the United States Army Ranger Assault Group captured by scaling the cliffs themselves. Today, the area retains the scars of the battle: An undulation of bomb craters and mangled defense bunkers, free for visitors to explore, serves as a haunting monument to the destructive powers of war. More chilling still are the bunkers that remain intact, their blackened wood ceilings a reminder of the flamethrowers that would have been used to clear them. It's a justifiably popular sight, and there's extensive on-site parking to cope with visitor numbers.

Utah Beach

Pouppeville, La Madeleine

An American landing zone, and the farthest west of all the D-Day beaches, Utah was the proverbial light to Omaha's dark with the assault here seeing the fewest casualties sustained anywhere along the coast that day. A full 21,000 men were put ashore on Utah, but just 197 casualties were sustained.

Even here, however, the invasion could not be celebrated as an unmitigated success. Strong winds blew numerous landing craft and airmen off course, and the ultimate goal of cutting off the Cotentin Peninsula and capturing the Cherbourg port would take the army a full 20 days to achieve.

Today, visits focus on the part of the beach nearest the Musée du Débarquement, where there is also the Roosevelt Café, plus space to park (there are no connections to public transport). There's not a massive amount to see on the beach itself, but the bit of barbed wiring near the dunes and a lack of housing in the nearby area means that this stretch of

1
2

beach today bears perhaps the greatest similarity to how it might have appeared back in 1944; it still seems an armada could arrive at any moment. A memorial, plus a number of statues of U.S. soldiers in action, help to center your visit.

Musée du Débarquement

La Madeleine, Sainte-Marie-du-Mont; tel. 02 33 71 53 35; www.utah-beach.com; 9:30am-7pm daily Jun.-Sept., 10am-6pm daily Oct.-May; adults €8, under 15 €4, under 7 and WWII veterans free

Set just back from Utah Beach, this museum unsurprisingly concentrates on the events of Utah. Still, it provides a broader perspective of the D-Day landings, with plenty of informative videos and displays guiding your visit. As well as the usual military hardware of tanks and amphibious landing craft, do not miss seeing the meticulously restored B26 Marauder plane, located in a hangar-like structure to the museum's side. This is among the best of the D-Day landing museums, particularly for its re-creation of German trenches, offering a chance to switch perspectives on the invasion and imagine how defending the Normandy beaches must have been as much of a hell as attacking them. It is well worth a look.

Musée Airborne

14 rue Eisenhower, Sainte-Mère-Église; tel. 02 33 41 41 35; www.airborne-museum.org; 9am-7pm daily May-Aug., 9:30am-6:30pm daily Apr. and Sept., 10am-6pm daily Oct.-Mar.; adults €9.90, children 6-16 €6, under 6 free

One of the region's best museums, the Musée Airborne is housed within a church in the village of Sainte-Mère-Église, just a short drive from Utah Beach. As with all the landing beaches, paratroopers descended behind enemy lines on Utah Beach in the wee hours of the morning on D-Day to further disrupt German defenses. Strong winds saw many miss their drop zone, and in no case more egregiously than John Steele of the Eighty-Second Airborne. His parachute got caught on the pinnacle of the church tower, where only by hanging limply and playing dead for two hours did he manage to survive. The museum offers an insight into paratroopers' experience of D-Day with several restored planes and lively exhibits, which, among other things, let you step inside one of the gliders used in the invasion, stand amid lifelike models of paratroopers being inspected by General Eisenhower just before takeoff, and, the real highlight, experience an educational simulation that offers intimate detail of what it would be like to fly out with the crew of a C-47 aircraft, then drop into Sainte-Mère-Église in the midst of fighting.

Carentan

A small town at the base of the Cotentin Peninsula, Carentan was an early strategic goal for the Allies in the immediate aftermath of D-Day, given that it would link Utah and Omaha Beaches and work as a staging post for the assault on Cherbourg later in the month. The responsibility fell to the 101st Airborne and the 2nd Armored Divisions, and resulted in several days of vicious house-to-house fighting. Then, after the town was taken, the Germans counterattacked in what became known as the Battle of Bloody Gulch—a nickname American soldiers had taken from a popular Western of the time.

The battle gained further notoriety recently when it was portrayed in the BBC/HBO series *Band of Brothers.* The town itself, meanwhile, despite the destruction wrought on it, remains a pleasant example of a fairly typical rural Norman town.

DEAD MAN'S CORNER MUSEUM

3 vierge de l'Amont, Saint-Côme-du-Mont; tel. 02 33 023 61 95; https://dday-experience.com; 10am-6pm daily Oct.-Mar., 9:30am-7pm daily Apr.-Sept.; adults €12, children 6-17 €9, under 6 free

This is another excellent museum experience, or rather two museum experiences, located in Carentan, a small rural town at the base of the

1: the American Cemetery **2:** the sands of Utah Beach

Contentin Peninsula. The Dead Man's Corner Museum is the restoration of a real property that was commandeered by Nazi paratroopers and used as a base of operations in the area. It is laid out exactly the way it would have been back in 1944, complete with guns and other hardware, plus some of the most lifelike models anywhere on the D-Day coast. Attached to it is the compelling and thought-provoking D-Day Experience, where a simulation of the events of D-Day from an American paratrooper's eyes is offered: You are invited to sit inside a genuine C-47 troop-carrying aircraft with video screens rigged up to its windows, displaying exactly what you would have seen were you to have flown that treacherous journey over the Normandy coast on June 6, 1944, while a nerve-jangling soundtrack plays the precise noise of the plane engines and flak from German antiaircraft guns trying to blow you out of the sky.

There is also an outdoor area where some of the surface-to-air weapons that the Allies would have been facing are displayed, while beyond the museum itself a historical trail is suggested for you to follow, stretching 25 miles (40 kilometers) in the footsteps of the 101st Airborne as they advanced on Carentan. The museum provides a map of this circuit, which, driving your own car, takes about three hours to fully complete.

FESTIVALS AND EVENTS

D-DAY LANDING ANNIVERSARY

Multiple locations; www.dday-overlord.com/en/normandy/commemorations; last week of May, first two weeks in June

As the most significant thing to ever happen along this coastline, D-Day is celebrated every year across the entire 50-mile (80-kilometer) stretch of invasion. Precise events are different each year and are bigger on round-number anniversaries, but in general expect the weeks either side of June 6 to be full of parachute-jump displays, the rumble of old military hardware, parades, and even the occasional 1940s-themed party. There's something to suit all tastes, but seeing almost-80-year-old aircraft take to the skies again is a sight to set alight the imagination and momentarily obliterate the distance between 1944 and now. Events take place in towns and fields near all the beaches and can even stretch to Caen and Bayeux as well. The great majority of celebrations are free; you just have to know where to be and at what time. Making this easier is the festival program released as much as a month before the festival and available for free in just about every bar, café, tourist office, and hotel foyer along the coast. Of course, this is also the area's most popular time of year, so it's worth booking your accommodations well ahead.

FOOD

Around Sword Beach

LES TISONS

74 avenue de la Mer, Ouistreham; tel. 02 31 96 20 17; 12pm-2:30pm and 7:15pm-9:30pm Wed.-Sat., 12pm-2:30pm Sun.; menus €14.90-24.90

A basic bustling bistro in Ouistreham, near Sword Beach, this spot is great for lunch and dinner, with very reasonably priced local food, strong on regional flavors of seafood, cheese, and apples (sometimes all in the same dish). There's also a great variety of options for mussels. It's popular with tourists and locals alike.

Around Juno Beach

LA MAISON BLEU

Rue de Marine Dunkerque, Courseulles-sur-Mer; tel. 02 31 37 45 48; 12:15pm-2pm and 7pm-9pm daily; menus €22.50-32.50

This sleek and stylish establishment sitting on Courseulles harbor has both a pleasant interior and a large terrace for warm summer days. The building may not be blue all over, but it does have traditional timber-frame detailing painted in that color. Family-run and family-friendly, they do a good job of being all things to all people; it's equally good for large groups as it is for couples wanting to keep to themselves. The *fruits de mer* (seafood platter) is a speciality, but there are also plenty of hearty meat dishes, too.

Around Arromanches/ Gold Beach

HÔTEL DE LA MARINE

Quai du Canada, Arromanches-les-Bains; tel. 02 31 22 34 19; www.hotel-de-la-marine.fr; 12pm-2:30pm and 7pm-9:30pm daily; menus €25-38

With a wonderful view looking out to the English Channel and the remains of Arromanches's Mulberry Harbor, this restaurant hardly has to try to offer a fine dining experience. Fortunately, the food is good, particularly the fish, which is fresh and allowed to speak for itself, rather than being drowned in rich sauces as can happen in some Normandy restaurants. The prices are a little higher than you might expect to pay for this kind of meal elsewhere, but the location makes it worth it.

RECTO-VERSO

17 rue Maréchal Joffre, Arromanches-les-Bains; tel. 02 31 51 82 61; 11am-11pm Mon.-Fri., 11am-10pm Sat.; €3-13

An unpretentious, family-friendly place on the backstreets of Arromanches, where the crepes are of an impressively high standard. Great for dropping into for a quick, inexpensive lunch to keep you fueled while touring the beaches. That their cider comes served in ceramic cups lends it an air of authenticity.

PIZZERIA RO.MA

12 rue Du Maréchal Joffre, Arromanches-les-Bains; tel. 02 31 22 30 16; 11:30am-2:30pm and 6pm-9:30pm Wed.-Sun.; €7.50-10

This is quite simply a great-value pizza place, with an authentic wood-fire oven to cook dough made on-site topped with fresh ingredients. The interior may not be anything special, but on a nice day there's nothing to stop you going for the takeaway option and eating your pizza on the beach itself.

Around Omaha Beach

LA SAPINIÈRE

100 rue de la 2ème Division Us, Saint-Laurent-sur-Mer; tel. 02 31 92 71 72; http://www.la-sapiniere.fr; 12:30pm-2:30pm and 7:30pm-10pm daily; mains €14-17

A bright and airy, none-too-flashy place that specializes in quality local food at a reasonable price. The seafood in particular is excellent and a very good value. Being a hotel, as well as having extreme proximity to Omaha Beach, means that "La Sap" attracts its fair share of tourists, but the upside of this is that they speak English and the menu is varied enough for most dietary requirements.

Around Utah Beach

LE ROOSEVELT CAFÉ

Rue Utah Beach, Sainte-Marie-du-Mont; tel. 02 33 71 53 47; www.leroosevelt.fr; 9:30am-6pm daily, menu €16.50

Sure, in a sense it's got tourist trap written all over it, catching visitors to Utah Beach in an area where they've literally nowhere else to go. But Le Roosevelt Café is better than it need be, and not as expensive as it could. A few mannequins in WWII dress line the bar and dot the tables—a decoration decision somewhere between fun and creepy—and the food, despite the establishment's name and general pretensions, is more French than American, including a highly recommended *moules cidre*—mussels in a cider sauce. Not worth a trip in itself, but acceptable in a pinch!

★ AUBERGE LE JOHN STEELE

4 rue du Cap de Laine, Sainte-Mère-Église; tel. 02 33 41 41 16; www.auberge-john-steele.com/restaurant; 12:15pm-1:45pm and 7:15pm-9pm Tues.-Sat., 12:15pm-1:45pm Sun.; menus €18.50-33.90

Near Utah Beach and named for the luckless American airman who found himself dangling from the church spire of Sainte-Mère-Église, this is nevertheless a French restaurant, albeit unafraid of adding a few zingy foreign touches to its otherwise local fare: The wasabi cream that it serves with its smoked salmon is a particularly pleasant surprise. The restaurant interior and appearance are on the formal side of rustic, and it's open all year-round, boasting an especially cozy fire in the cold winter months.

ACCOMMODATIONS

When exploring the D-Day landing beaches, many opt to base themselves out of the larger cities such as Caen or Bayeux. This can be a good idea, particularly should you want to join guided tours, which tend to operate out of the cities. The advantages of staying in a hotel closer to the coast, meanwhile, are both the standard ones for those who prefer the peace of the countryside over the bustle of the town, and that you can see the landing grounds themselves at less popular hours and often take more time exploring them. In short, a stay nearer the beaches can suit a more independently minded traveler. Most of the options below are near Gold Beach.

€50-100

GOLD BEACH HÔTEL

1 rue Devonshire Régiment, Asnelles; tel. 02 31 51 11 10; www.gold-beach-hotel.com; from €65 d

Modern and clean, this is an excellently located hotel close to—as its name suggests—Gold Beach. While it's not going to win any awards for character or design, it offers all the main amenities required by the modern traveler and at a very reasonable price. Visitors can expect rooms with WiFi, TVs, minibars, double-glazed windows, and safety deposit boxes. Some ground-floor rooms also have mini garden areas, while others have views of the sea. An on-site restaurant serves continental breakfast and daytime meals that combine Italian and Norman cuisine. An unlikely mix, the *moules alla Romana* (mussels Italian style) is nevertheless worth a try.

LA PECHERIE

7 place du Six Juin, Courseulles-sur-Mer; tel. 02 31 37 45 84; www.la-pecherie.fr; from €90 d

A lively hotel-restaurant near Juno Beach decorated in a colorful though still traditional style. The staff are friendly and used to international guests. Indeed, there's something of the flavor of a British pub to its common areas. WiFi is available throughout the property, and the restaurant offers solid local food for breakfast, lunch, and dinner. As well as regular rooms, bigger ones can be rented in the house opposite for a slightly higher price.

LOGIS HÔTEL LA ROSIÈRE

14 route de Bayeux, Tracy-sur-Mer; tel. 02 31 22 36 17; www.hotellarosierebayeux.com; from €93 d

This reasonably priced hotel a little inland from Arromanches, while not offering anything spectacular, is a perfectly acceptable place to rest your head for the night, or to use as a base to explore the beaches. Mostly just one story, rooms are spread motel-fashion across the property. The couple who run it are particularly friendly, and though there's no restaurant on-site (apart from a buffet breakfast of pastries and cereal), they are more than happy to give suggestions for places in the nearby area. WiFi is available throughout.

€100-200

HÔTEL LES VILLAS D'ARROMANCHES

1 rue du Lt Colonel Job, Arromanches-les-Bains; tel. 02 31 21 38 97; www.lesvillasdarromanches.fr; from €108 d

Set over several buildings on its own grounds, this stately, large hotel on the outskirts of Arromanches offers taste, tranquility, and comfort, as well as sea views for some. There aren't that many old structures left lining the D-Day coastline (on account of, well, D-Day), but Les Villas d'Arromanches would appear to be an exception. There's WiFi throughout, a good breakfast that can be brought to your room for a small extra cost of €5 per person, and the staff will even make up a picnic to be taken out with you when exploring the beaches during the day for €9.50 per person.

★ LA FERME DE LA RANCONNIERE

Route d'Arromanches, Crépon; tel. 02 31 22 21 73; www.ranconniere.fr; from €120 d

Located in a beautiful old farmhouse, this is the kind of place people dream about when they think of French countryside hotels. The rooms are clean and sumptuously furnished, offering 21st-century comfort in an old-fashioned setting. Meanwhile, its grounds are picturesque and pleasant to wander. A number of on-site services and activities are offered, including a tennis court and a small playground for kids. The restaurant is a terrific place for a no-expenses-spared feast: the *menu tradition* may be 44€, but the multiple-course Norman decadence will have you feeling you don't need to eat again for another week!

Over €200

CHÂTEAU LA CHENEVIÈRE

Escures-Commes 14520, Port-en-Bessin; tel. 02 31 51 25 25; http://lacheneviere.com; from €427 d

Five-star luxury in the Norman hinterland, this 18th-century mansion and former farm is also directly linked to the D-Day story, having been occupied first by the Germans and later by U.S. troops following the invasion. Restored in 1988, it now offers 29 uniquely designed rooms, all decorated with period furniture and modern accessories from WiFi to televisions. The English-style grounds are expertly manicured, and there's a swimming pool on-site. The hotel boasts two restaurants: the outdoor Le Petit Jardin, perfect for a light summer lunch, and the ultra-luxurious Le Botaniste, which promises no less than a "new Norman gastronomy."

Camping

CAMPING PORT'LAND

Chemin du Castel, Port-en-Bessin-Huppain; tel. 02 31 51 07 06; www.camping-portland.fr; pitch €38, cabins €125

Situated almost at the midpoint of the D-Day landings coast, this is a perfect campsite from which to base a full tour of the area. It's also in a beautiful, quiet area and offers so many services and activities (including on-site showers and toilets) that even if you've no intention of going near one of the famous beaches, there's plenty to keep you entertained. As well as some pleasant cabins that can be rented, there's a souvenir shop, a small bar, a couple of swimming pools (inside and outside), plus on-site fishing. WiFi is also available. The only word of warning: This area is popular with school trips, so it's not impossible in early season to find yourself sharing the campsite with a lot of children. If that doesn't put you off, just remember that during the weeks surrounding D-Day and in the month of August, campsites in this region can get very popular, so make sure to book ahead.

INFORMATION

Tourist information is rife throughout the D-Day landing beaches, whether in public information signs, regional tourist offices, or visitors centers. Even the gift shops of most museums are stuffed with leaflets and maps suggesting new experiences and other places to see. What's more, maps of the coast are literally everywhere. They may have military lines drawn over them, but will nevertheless leave you in no doubt as to where you are. All this said, the most comprehensive tourist offices for the region can be found in Caen and Bayeux, which are the effective gateway towns to the coast. Below represent a small sample of some of the official outlets found closer to the coast.

OFFICE DE TOURISME D'ISIGNY-OMAHA

Ancienne RN13, Formigny; tel. 02 31 21 46 00; www.isigny-grandcamp-intercom.fr; 9:30am-12:30pm and 2pm-6pm Mon.-Sat.

With its actual office looking not unlike an oversize bus shelter just back from Omaha Beach's *Monument des Braves,* this is nevertheless a good place to pick up literature about the surrounding area, and it has a good website to help guide your visit. The staff speak English.

OFFICE DE TOURISME DE LA BAIE DU COTENTIN

24 place de la République, Carentan; tel. 02 33 71 23 50; www.ot-baieducotentin.fr; 9am-6:30pm Mon.-Sat., 9:30am-1:30pm Sun.

A sizable tourist office in Carentan, good for providing information about the town, Utah Beach, and Sainte-Mère-Église. Looking beyond D-Day sights, there's also plenty to discover in here about things to do farther up the Cotentin Peninsula. English is spoken.

OFFICE DE TOURISME DE BAYEUX, ARROMANCHES OFFICE

2 rue Maréchal Joffre, Arromanches-les-Bains; tel. 02 31 22 36 45; www.bayeux-bessin-tourisme.com; 9:30am-7pm Mon.-Sat., 9:30am-1pm and 2pm-6:30pm Sun.

An outlet of the Bayeux tourist office, dedicated to the area immediately north of that town. Located right in the center of Arromanches, it's a large space filled with literature about local events and museums, and it's staffed by helpful fluent English-speakers.

TOURS

A massive industry of different tour companies service just about every sight along the D-Day coast, providing tours that last anywhere from a couple of hours to a whole week. They also come in all different sizes, from large group tours to bespoke and private tours, and leave from multiple different points, including Paris, though by far the most common departure point is Bayeux.

Because of the relative difficulty of getting between the beaches on public transport, guided tours are a popular option for those without their own means of travel, though they are recommended even for those with their own vehicles, as they offer perhaps the most direct way of connecting to the history of the landscape.

The variety of what's on offer is far too extensive to list in its entirety here, though as a basic yardstick, tours are separated into half-day experiences (four hours) or full-day ones (closer to nine), and tend to start at around €60 per person, though can be considerably more depending on what you want. The D-Day coast is far too extensive to see everything in a day, and indeed most tours don't even take you to all the beaches. There are some general tours that visit Arromanches, Omaha, and Utah, but more common is one taking in only the U.S. landing grounds or only the Canadian and British ones. Like this, there is at least a chance to end the day feeling as though you've learned a digestible story, rather than being overwhelmed by the sheer weight of information.

For the real enthusiast—and D-Day is a phenomenon with a lot of real enthusiasts—there are also plenty of more specialized tours, considering the day from the perspective of paratroopers, say, or that are conducted from the back of a vintage Jeep. Few tours take in the museums of the coast, which offer their own kind of guidance, instead concentrating on the actual locations of certain events, taking in cemeteries as well, where the graves of many soldiers who you will hear about still reside.

The quality of these tours often depends more on individual guides rather than whole companies, though the overall standard tends to be high. Below are a couple of the ones that come most highly recommended.

BAYEUX SHUTTLE

tel. 9 70 44 49 89; www.normandy-sightseeing-tours.com; half-day tours from €60, full-day tours from €110

A relative newcomer to the scene and based out of Bayeux, as the name suggests, it was created in 2012 by just a single driver and a single van. Within only six years it has upped its fleet to 15 vans and 15 drivers, offering one of the most applauded tours in the region with very enthusiastic, well-learned guides. As with all companies, it offers various different tours, from those providing a basic overview to ones that really grapple with specifics of D-Day history. Groups are also deliberately kept small (below 10 people), meaning guides are able to provide a personal service, while a particularly nice touch are the videos of archive footage of the invasion played in the van between locations. Expect to pay around €60 per person per half day and €110 per person per full day. Private tours are also available, starting from €500 for the group, for which a bespoke pickup point can be specified. Tours leave from either central Bayeux or Paris.

Be aware that the good reputation of this company is well known, and as such, booking way in advance is highly recommended.

DDAY HISTORIAN TOURS

6 place de Québec, Bayeux; tel. 02 31 22 28 82; www.ddayhistorian.com; private group tours €600-675

This is not so much a tour company as an individual tour guide with a reputation for being among the very best on the coast. Paul Woodage is a D-Day historian with an exceptional perspective and presentation style on all matters pertaining to the D-Day invasion. Such is his expertise, he even offers services to those on official research trips to the Normandy coast. A British national with over 15 years of experience touring the area, he now only offers private tours driving his own minivan. Prices start at €600 for a day-long group tour of up to four people, and €675 for up to seven, which is the maximum Woodage is willing to take. It's a little more than most other companies, but thoroughly worth it, as is evidenced by the fact that he starts getting booked out up to a year in advance. Children under 12 are not allowed on the tour.

TRANSPORTATION

Getting There and Around

With no real hub to the D-Day landing beaches themselves, many will use either Bayeux or Caen to base their excursions.

BY CAR

Driving is easily the simplest way to see the D-Day landing beaches. Though all the sights here often appear close together and are linked by small roads, by far the most efficient way of visiting them is to regularly return to the N13, a main road slightly inland, where driving is faster and the odds of getting lost greatly decreased, particularly because of copious signage. All the beaches and main sights are announced just ahead of the turnings you need to take for them from this highway with large illustrated tourist information signs.

From Caen the fastest way to Sword Beach is directly north up the D7 following signs to Ouistreham (about 20 minutes); to Juno it's also the D7, following signs to Courseulles-sur-Mer at the roundabout where you can change to the D404 (about 30 minutes); to Gold take the N13, taking the exit toward Arromanches along the D35 (about 40 minutes); to Omaha, also take the N13, passing Bayeux, and turning off about six miles (10 kilometers) afterward, taking the D517 following signs that point directly toward the beach (about 40 minutes); to Utah take the N13, passing Bayeux by about 18 miles (30 kilometers) and turning off on the D913, following signs for the beach itself (about one hour).

From Bayeux the fastest way to Sword Beach is heading east on the N13 all the way to Caen, then following the ring road to the north, leaving it on the D7, following signs to Ouistreham (about 40 minutes); to Juno take the D127, then the D12, following signs to Courseulles-sur-Mer (about 30 minutes); to Gold it's almost directly north on the D516 following signs to Arromanches all the way (about 20 minutes); to Omaha, take the N13 about six miles (10 kilometers) west, then take the D517 following signs that point directly toward the beach (about 20 minutes); to Utah take the N13 about 18 miles (30 kilometers) west, then turn off on the D913, following signs for the beach itself (about 45 minutes).

BY BICYCLE AND ON FOOT

Walking is a great option for those with more time and stamina. Unsurprisingly, the exact opposite advice applies to those wanting to take the car: the coastline here is a network of small roads and walking paths, many of which are well signposted and will take you efficiently and peacefully from one D-Day sight to another. The main track for this is the GR223, one of France's major walking routes. Look for the red and white symbol, which looks something like a Polish flag, to point this out to you. Though the main stretches of beach are, expectedly, flat, going is hilly in parts, particularly between the beaches.

Bikes can be hired in several places along the coast, including the hotel **Les Villas**

How to Visit the D-Day Beaches

A large area with more things to see and do than most will have time for in the space of a single visit, not to mention being emotionally draining, the D-Day beaches can seem an overwhelming prospect for a lot of visitors. Where to base yourself, which museums and sights to prioritize, and how to balance guided tours with independent travel are questions that need to be answered, and, of course, like with so much in travel, the answers depend on who you are and what exactly you are trying to get out of your D-Day experience.

WHERE TO BASE YOURSELF

For the broadest D-Day experience, the smart money and most popular choice is in Bayeux. A relatively small town that is easy enough to get in and out of, it's also full of hotels and good restaurants to go to in the evenings, is more-or-less located at the midpoint of all the D-Day landing grounds, and is where most (though not all) D-Day tour companies leave from and are based. At the same time, there's so much to be seen around specific beaches that if you have a particular interest in one of them, then staying nearby may be the right choice. An area so geared toward welcoming tourists, it can be easy to start to mistake the D-Day beaches and their "attractions" as a bunch of boxes that need to be ticked in a rush. But this is also a space that can be felt. Long walks on the beaches themselves and lingering at former gun emplacements can be just as informative as reading information signs or viewing multimedia exhibits, and sometimes to do that properly you need time, making a place to stay near the beaches essential.

WHICH MUSEUMS AND SIGHTS TO PRIORITIZE

Of course, this is a question of personal taste and interest—more often than not, it will be dictated by your nationality. Be aware, though, that most of the beaches themselves are not particularly spectacular (the exception being the beach at Arromanches with the remnants of the Mulberry

d'Arromanches (1 rue du Lt Colonel Job, 14117 Arromanches-les-Bains; tel. 02 31 21 38 97; www.lesvillasdarromanches.fr), or the **Office de Tourisme intercommunal d'Isigny-Omaha** (2 rue Maréchal Joffre, Arromanches-les-Bains; tel. 02 31 22 36 45; www.bayeux-bessin-tourisme.com). Both will set you back about €7 for the day, and it's worth calling ahead to check availability.

BUS

The whole area, apart from Utah Beach, is well connected by local bus services: **Twisto** (www.twisto.fr) runs Line 62 for Sword Beach, leaving from Caen roughly every half hour 7am-8pm, €1.50 one way; **Bus Verts** (www.busverts.fr) runs Line 74 for Juno and Gold, leaving from Bayeux at least twice a day, at around 12pm and 6pm, €2.50 one way. Line 70 by Bus Verts for Omaha leaves from Bayeux 3-4 times a day 7:45am-6pm, €3.70 one way. This option can be slow going, and apart from Juno and Gold the beaches are not connected to one another by bus. You'll have to plan to walk from the bus stops too, and don't expect to be able to see much more than the sights around a single beach in one day. It is at least cheap, however, never costing more than €4 for a single journey.

TAXI

Using a taxi to tour the D-Day beaches is certainly an option, though unless there are a few of you it's unlikely to be the most cost-effective method, costing a little more than just joining a guided tour on which transport is included. However, it is cheaper than most private tours, and of course such trips can be entirely bespoke—also, you may simply not be interested in listening to a guide. It's best to contact taxis online or over the telephone if you're planning on a full day, that way you can

harbor), and their impact relies more on what you bring to them than what is actually there. This said, there are some places where scars in the landscape tell the story of what happened here as profoundly as any images or words. Most extensive of these is **Pointe du Hoc,** where your imagination hardly needs any more help to visualize the horrors of war. The **American Cemetery** also is a must-see sight, even if you're not of that country. Besides anything else, it provides a very different way of commemorating victory than you will see elsewhere in Europe and across the world, not as the glory-filled success of individual men or abstract nations, but as the mass sacrifice of individuals fighting toward a necessary, noble goal.

In terms of museums, it's good to aim for a spread of those that emphasize experience and ones that are a little more fact-heavy. The **Landing Museum** at Arromanches is a good place for the latter, for while it may be a little old-school in its approach, a good overview aided with maps and battle dioramas is reached. **Dead Man's Corner,** meanwhile, is among the best for experiential exhibits—the paratroop simulation is so good, real veterans have left it shaking their heads, questioning how its designers could ever have known how precisely what flying over Normandy as part of Operation Overlord was like. Caen's **Peace Memorial,** meanwhile, stands either as an excellent primer or way to round off your trip.

GUIDED TOURS OR INDEPENDENT TRAVEL

Seriously consider going on a tour. They may be expensive, but the great majority are very professional and will bring the landscape to life in a way that without them you would never have thought possible. If you're planning on spending a number of days exploring the D-Day beaches, probably just a one-day or half-day tour will be enough. Making up your own mind and doing your own research about what you see can be just as important, too; not to mention that so much focus on war can be emotionally draining. Keeping at least in some way independent makes it far easier to call time when you feel you need a break.

establish rates beforehand, rather than just let the meter start running, as who knows where that might end up!

Les Taxis du Bessin are the most reliable company to go with (tel. 02 31 92 92 40; www.bayeux-taxis.com). Based out of Bayeux, they have been taking people around the coast for years and have a well-established pricing system: A trip from Bayeux to the American Cemetery, for example, will cost around €36 one way; a tour of the American Cemetery and Omaha beach lasting about 1 hour 45 minutes should be in the region of €70; and so it goes up, right to a full 6.5-hour tour of Arromanches, Longues-sur-Mer, the American Cemetery, Omaha Beach, Pointe du Hoc, Sainte-Mère-Église, and Utah Beach costing around €230.

Barfleur and Saint-Vaast

Two of the most charming small towns anywhere along Normandy's long coastline, Barfleur and Saint-Vaast are characterized by granite architecture, surrounded by pleasant sandy beaches, and backed by a lush hinterland. Their position on the comparatively sheltered east of the Cotentin Peninsula lends them a unique quality, pitched somewhere between Breton ruggedness and Norman gentility.

For two seemingly unassuming places, they've seen their share of world history: Barfleur is known for being the harbor where William the Conqueror's flagship, *Mora*, was

Barfleur and Saint-Vaast

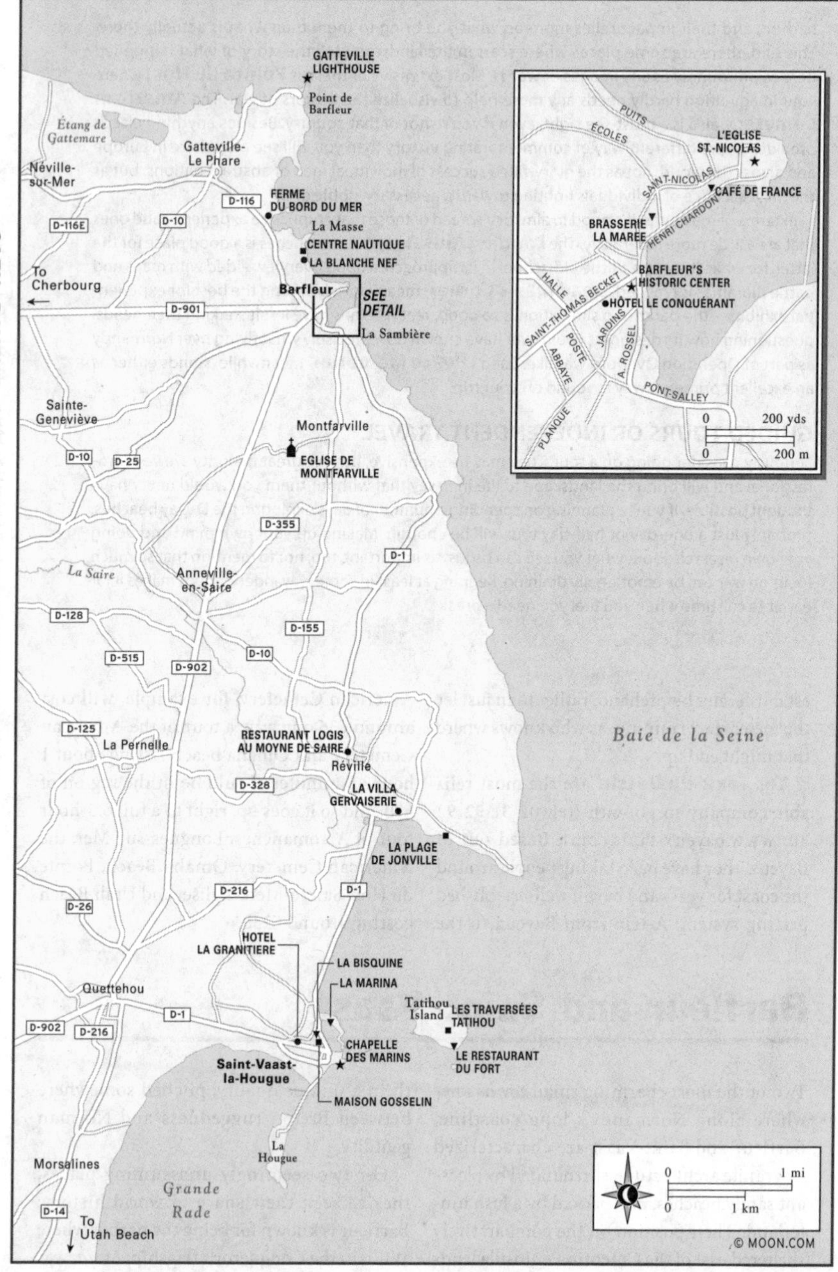

built, which he would later use to cross the Channel in his invasion of England, while Saint-Vaast was the landing point for an invasion in the other direction, that of English King Edward III in 1346, effectively starting the Hundred Years' War. Their reputation is not only for war and invasion, however; Saint-Vaast is also known far and wide for growing some of the best oysters in the region, a fact that dominates the very landscape of the town. As the tide slides back from its bay, so the oyster fisheries are revealed: endless ranks of meshed parcels, garnished by seaweed, and each containing delicious oceanic treasure.

Orientation

Saint-Vaast sits about 20 miles (32 kilometers) north of Utah Beach, along the coast of the Cotentin peninsula, while Barfleur is about seven miles (11 kilometers) farther north of that. The best way between the two is either the inland D902 or the more picturesque coastal route along the D1, which runs through the commune of Montfarville and connects to several smaller roads leading to nearby beaches.

Both Barfleur and Saint-Vaast are relatively small towns with most of their commerce focused around lively harbors. They are equally easy to navigate, being centered around their harbors, which the D1 leads to directly. For Barfleur, the other major center of action is the rue Thomas Beckett, which leads out of town west from the harbor, and is lined by some of the town's oldest houses, shops, and commerce. In Saint-Vaast, to a lesser extent, the rue de Verrue, just one street back from the harbor, plays this role. Both towns also have a network of smaller, charming backstreets populated by local artisans and artists, happy for you to come browse their wares.

The coastline here is characterized by a particularly long tidal range, and so it pays to keep wary should you want to go for a walk or set up on the sands. The **Île Tatihou** sits clearly opposite Saint-Vaast's harbor and can be reached on foot at low tide, but make sure to give yourself plenty of time.

The **Tour Vauban de la Hougue** sits on a spit of land stretching south from Saint-Vaast harbor, while **Gatteville Lighthouse** is just a short distance along the coast north of Barfleur.

SIGHTS

★ Barfleur's Historic Center

Rue Saint-Thomas Becket and quai Henri Chardon; www.barfleur.fr

Postcard perfect, with its long thin harbor lined with granite buildings built between the 16th and 19th centuries and covered with schist (a characterful finely textured rock), Barfleur's historic center has won recognition as one of the prestigious "Most Beautiful Villages of France." It's a lovely space to wander, or indeed to enjoy from one of the many restaurant terraces, where you can still observe the yachts mingle with commercial fishing boats in its waters, or watch the fishermen sell their fresh catch on the harbor's edge on Saturday mornings.

Start on the western end of the rue Saint-Thomas Becket and walk toward the harbor, admiring the ranked granite houses, dating from the 16th to the 19th centuries, though which taken together have a remarkable unity of form. Just before you reach the harbor, on the right you can slip through into the Coeur de Sainte Catherine surrounded by the town's oldest houses, from the 14th and 15th centuries.

Exiting onto the harbor, turn left to stroll along its northern edge, taking in the lapping water and more of the granite buildings that surround it. Then, at its far end, in the shadow of L'Église Saint-Nicolas, you will find a plaque commemorating the construction of *Mora,* the famous ship of William the Conqueror, gifted to him by his wife Matilda of Flanders in the summer of 1066. It was in this ship, the largest and fastest the Normans possessed, that William led his conquest of England, making Barfleur the effective starting point for that whole campaign.

L'Église St Nicolas

Rue Saint-Nicolas, Barfleur; 9am-6pm daily

At the far end of Barfleur harbor, this squat yet evocative 17th-century church is well worth a look inside. The first church on this site was built in the 11th century, but severely damaged by the invasion of Edward III and utterly destroyed in the Wars of Religion two centuries later. The current building's slightly inelegant hodgepodge of styles, ranging from neo-Gothic to Romanesque, is a result of it taking nearly 200 years to complete. This lack of elegance does not prevent it from being quite moving; however, its slightly cramped nature in parts offers a slightly different experience from many other churches. It now contains a relic of Saint Mary Magdalene Postel, who sheltered priests during the French Revolution.

Tatihou Island

Tatihou; tel. 02 33 23 19 92 ; www.manche.fr/tatihou; boat ticket office 9am-12:30pm and 1:15pm-5:30pm daily Apr.-Oct. 7; round-trip ticket adult €8, children 3-11 €4

This small tidal island in plain view of Saint-Vaast is accessible on foot at low tide by walking across the town's famous oyster beds. However, it is far safer to pay for the crossing by the amphibious vehicle (essentially a boat with wheels), tickets for which are bought on the quai Vauban, and which leaves from the breakwater on the far side of the harbor.

Easy to explore in about an hour, the island is barren, windswept, and barely populated; a world away from genteel Saint-Vaast. It is home to one of two towers built by engineer Sébastien Le Prestre de Vauban following the decisive naval battle of the Nine Years' War with the English in 1692 (the other is on La Hogue mount in Saint-Vaast). This can be visited, and going up it offers some great views back to the mainland and the bay. The island is also host to a bird sanctuary, for it's a popular stop-off for migrating birds, and a small but intellectually active **maritime museum** (tel. 02 33 54 33 33; www.manche.fr/tatihou; 10am-6pm daily Apr.-Oct.; adults €6, children €4; with round-trip boat tickets adult €10.50, children €8) containing nautical-themed paintings, information on how fishing was accomplished here in years gone by, and some artifacts of the area's natural history. The island has one restaurant, the **Restaurant du Fort,** which does fairly ordinary French lunches for a reasonable price (€16 for a menu). Small events take place here throughout the year, including the Traversées folk festival in August.

Chapelle des Marins

5585A place du Général Leclerc, Saint-Vaast-la-Hougue; 9am-6pm daily; free

Moving despite its small size, this "Sailors Chapel" is all that remains of a Romanesque church from the 11th century. Barely much more than a room under an arched roof, it is now dedicated to those who have died at sea, and is an evocative, meditative space, often filled with fresh dedications of flowers and candles flickering for the departed. Its walls are whitewashed, and above the altar stands a small statue of a Madonna and child, lending the space a shrine-like quality. Close to the shore, on windy days you can easily hear the perilous sea thrashing outside.

★ Église de Montfarville

Rue de la Poste, Montfarville; tel. 02 33 54 05 74; 9am-6pm daily; free

A delightful surprise in the town of Montfarville, which lies between Saint-Vaast and Barfleur, this church could very easily be passed through without a second thought. The 18th-century church was built around a 13th-century bell tower, but its real treasure is inside: a series of paintings by 19th-century artist Guillaume Fouace. A native to the area, with work now exhibited throughout France, including in the Musée d'Orsay in Paris, Fouace's work for the Église de Montfarville includes scenes of the Annunciation, the

1: Barfleur harbor, suspended between sea and sky **2:** looking out to Tatihou Island **3:** Chapelle des Marins **4:** Barfleur's Église St Nicolas

1
2
3
4

Flight from Egypt, the Journey of the Magi, and a copy of *The Last Supper* by Leonardo da Vinci that Fouace painted for the church's choir. The work may not be terribly original, but it is beautifully evocative of the Italian masters, and for the time you're looking at it, you could almost imagine yourself in the heart of some urbane Renaissance center, rather than in a village on the shores of the English Channel.

Gatteville Lighthouse

25c route du Phare, Gatteville-le-Phare; www.phare-de-gatteville.fr; 10am-12pm and 2pm-7pm May-Aug., 10am-12pm and 2pm-6pm Apr. and Sept., 10am-12pm and 2pm-5pm Mar. and Oct., 10am-12pm and 2pm-4pm Feb. and Nov.-Dec.; adults €3, under 13 €1

The waters around Barfleur and Saint-Vaast have always been perilous for ships—most notably the wrecking of the White Ship in 1120, when the heir to the English throne drowned, leading to a crisis of succession and a period of civil war in England—meaning there has always been the call for lighthouses to aid them. The first lighthouse on this site was built in 1774, though by the 1820s an update was deemed necessary. The new Gatteville lighthouse was first lit in 1835, and at 246 feet (75 meters), it was the tallest lighthouse in the world at that time. Even today it is the third-tallest lighthouse in the world. It remains functional, guiding ships around this still-treacherous coast, and is also open to the public as a lighthouse museum, the main exhibit of which is the lighthouse itself (aside from that, there is a small display detailing the history of lighthouses along the Norman coast, augmented by a few paintings of them and technical equipment they no longer use). Needless to say, there's a spectacular view from the top, though you have to work for it: there are a lot of steps and no elevator!

BEACHES

The coast around Barfleur and Saint-Vaast—and indeed the entire Cotentin Peninsula—is characterized by a long tidal range, which in plain terms means that sometimes the sea will be close to shore and that at other times it will be very, very far away. When it's farther away, this can make swimming difficult, not to mention that it exposes a lot of muddy sand, seaweed, and rocks. Obviously, tide times change throughout the year, so it's worth always consulting charts, which can be found in English at http://marine.meteoconsult.co.uk.

LA SAMBIÈRE

Barfleur

This sandy beach with grass tufts immediately south of Barfleur is almost a mile long. There are no amenities and it's not watched, but you can always grab a snack from the nearby Camping Indiana. When the tide is in it's good for swimming. It's popular in the height of summer, but it never really gets crowded.

LA MASSE

Barfleur

This long sandy beach with some rocks is around 656 feet (200 meters) long, and very much in the shadow of Gatteville Lighthouse. There's parking, and it's the location of Barfleur's water sports center. A lot of rocks get exposed at low tide, making it much better to come to when the sea is in, particularly for water sports. It can get busy in the high season, but not really crowded.

LA PLAGE DE JONVILLE

Reville

Located on the northern side of a bay, this is one of the very few south-facing beaches in all of Normandy. As such, it's pleasantly sheltered, as well as being near to a local municipal campground. The beach itself is a rough-and-ready combination of sand, grass, and rocks. It has a nice snack bar, **Le Goéland 1951,** to refuel at. It's good for swimming at high tide, and it's popular, though like the other beaches around here, it's never really what you would call crowded.

SPORTS AND RECREATION

CENTRE NAUTIQUE

10 chemin de la Masse, Gatteville-le-Phare; tel. 02 33 54 79 08; 9am-5pm Mon.-Fri.; kayak hire from €10, sailing courses from €70

This is a well-fitted water-sports center offering sea kayaking, stand-up paddle boarding, sailing, and catamaran sailing, as well as lessons, in the picturesque area just north of Barfleur harbor. It's only intermittently staffed in low season, however, with instructors spread along the coast at various other water-sport centers connected to this one. It's worth calling to check on hours before your visit, though English is not really spoken.

FESTIVALS AND EVENTS

LES TRAVERSÉES TATIHOU

Tatihou Island and Saint-Vaast; tel. 02 33 05 98 41; Aug. 6-15; free

There's a whiff of pilgrimage and magic to this unique world music festival that takes place every year on Tatihou Island. That's because tradition dictates that festivalgoers should make their way to the island at low tide. This can only be done at certain points of the day, meaning everyone arrives en masse, creating a festival atmosphere before they've even heard any music played. It's proved a popular formula; the festival was established in 1994 and is still going.

MUSIK EN SAIRE

Barfleur; http://musikensaire.fr; Sept. 1-2; free

Taking place the first weekend in September on Barfleur harbor, Musik en Saire is an eclectic gathering of the very best the Norman music scene has to offer. Bands from all over the region perform on outdoor stages, playing all different genres of music, from reggae to blues. A mixed-generational, largely local crowd attends.

SHOPPING

MAISON GOSSELIN

27 rue de Verrue, Saint-Vaast-la-Hougue; tel. 02 33 54 40 06; www.maison-gosselin.fr; 9:30am-12:30pm and 3pm-7pm Mon., 9am-12:30pm and 3pm-7pm Tues.-Fri., 9am-1pm and 3pm-7pm Sat., 9am-12:30pm Sun.

Founded in 1889, this delicatessen and boutique still seems to belong to another, more sophisticated time. As well as selling the highest-quality fresh local produce, it offers beautifully packaged (and excellent tasting) conserves, spices, liqueurs, and more. With Art Nouveau stylings and everything kept almost impossibly shiny and clean, it's worth dropping into just to see, even if you've no intent to buy. Though be warned, it's very difficult to leave with your hands empty. Great for stocking up on picnic food, souvenirs, and gifts alike.

FOOD

TOP EXPERIENCE

★ Oysters

LA BISQUINE

3 quai Vauban, Saint-Vaast-la-Hougue; tel. 02 33 023 95 82; www.labisquine-saintvaast.com; 12pm-2pm and 7pm-9pm Sat.-Wed.; mains €14.30-28.80

Dedicated to local produce and inventive, unpretentious cooking, this harbor-front restaurant is one of Saint-Vaast's undisputed gems. As with everywhere around here, their oysters are fantastic (it helps that they're sourced just a five-minute walk away), and you can have them prepared in three different ways: traditionally, accompanied by apple cider vinegar; more uniquely by hot pork crackling; or breaded and fried. The menu is laudably small, suggesting an absolute dedication toward freshness. And all this at an impressively reasonable cost.

The Oysters of Saint-Vaast

A food to inspire raptures, oysters have long stood in some ways apart from other cuisine. They are, after all, as the food writer Felipe Fernández-Armesto notes, one of the very few foods that we (should) eat entirely raw. That is to say, with no preparation whatsoever. Just remove the top of the shell put the creature to your lips, and in a gulp, you are "eating the sea," as another expert on the mollusk puts it, "only the sensation of a gulp of saltwater has been wafted out of it by some sorcery."

INDUSTRY

Oysters are produced in their thousands all along the Normandy and Brittany coast, though those from Saint-Vaast sit somewhere near the pinnacle of this industry with an unforgettable nutty taste valued across France. What causes this specific taste is down to endlessly complicated specifics about the precise salinity of Saint-Vaast's water and the length of its tides (which also means a regular cycling of water and strong currents), dubbed in some places the bay's "merroir" (a play on terroir, the French concept for how landscape forms food).

Home to oyster farming since ancient times, the business really got a boost here in the 1950s when the company **Huîtres Hélie** was established, which now is Saint-Vaast's main supplier to restaurants around France. It also has its own **store** in Saint-Vaast (23 place Belle Isle; tel. 33 0 33 54 42 13; 9am-12:30pm and 3pm-7pm daily Sept.-June, 9am-7pm daily July-Aug.). Aside from that, there is hardly a restaurant or bar in the town that does not have oysters somewhere on the menu.

WHEN AND HOW TO ENJOY THEM

The seasons for when they're at their best can easily be remembered as being any month with an R in it: January, February, March, etc., yes; May, June, July, August, no. Though don't let that put you off trying them in the hotter months; just know that if you come back at other times of year, the oysters might be even better!

Oysters are separated into numbered groupings depending on size, with 00 being the absolute biggest and 6 being the smallest. Standard thinking is that bigger is better, so the lower the number, the higher the cost. Debate on how to eat them differs: to swallow or chew? To add lemon or vinegar, or even Tabasco? With oysters the quality of Saint-Vaast's, however, if you're brave enough, you should, as Fernández-Armesto suggests, eat them entirely unprepared, allowing the full depth of their flavor to express itself. Press the morsel up to the roof of your mouth with your tongue, let the sensation of sea coat your taste buds, then wash it down with a sip of ice-cold dry white wine.

★ LA MARINA

8 quai du Commandant Albert Paris, Saint-Vaast-La-Hougue; tel. 02 33 43 75 62; www.lamarinasaintvaast.com; 8:30am-10pm Thurs.-Sat., 8:30am-8pm Sun.; mains €11.90-14.50

In a tranquil spot on the far side of Saint-Vaast harbor, with a terrace overlooking ranks of gently bobbing boats, and shielded from the wind, this is quite possibly the best place in town for an early evening drink, particularly in the summer. It's not quite as flashy as its name suggests, but it is modestly priced and has terrific double windows filling it with plenty of light. The food is tasty and local, and while there may not be any particular dish to write home about, there's always something special about eating seafood while listening to the lapping tide. Plus, as with everywhere in this town, the oysters are great.

Local Cuisine

★ LES FUCHSIAS

20 rue Maréchal Foch, Saint-Vaast-la-Hougue; tel. 02 33 54 40 41; www.france-fuchsias.com; 7:30pm-9pm Tues., 12pm-2pm and 7:30pm-9pm Wed.-Sun.; lunch menu €26, evening menus €32-42

Offering traditional elegance and charm, this hotel restaurant is well suited for a lavish meal.

With both an old-fashioned dining room and a peaceful courtyard to eat in, flavors here are rich and local, and the dishes come beautifully presented, including lamb raised on Tatihou Island. With the least-expensive evening menu coming in at €32, it's not cheap, but it is nevertheless popular with tourists and locals. Booking at least an evening ahead is recommended, and at peak times essential.

CAFÉ DE FRANCE

12 quai Henri Chardon, Barfleur; tel. 02 33 54 00 38; 8am-8pm Thurs.-Tues.; menus €19.50-23.90

Founded by a shipwright in 1901, this bistro has been a stalwart of Barfleur's harbor ever since, and is popular with tourists and locals alike. The food is of a consistently high quality—particularly the mussels, which surely get served up here by the ton—and the atmosphere is almost always lively and convivial. Its interior is pleasantly old-fashioned, too, and redolent of the sea.

BRASSERIE LA MAREE

25 quai Henri Chardon, Barfleur; tel. 02 33 020 81 88; 12pm-9:30pm daily; mains €8.70-21.50

Another solid harbor-front bistro specializing in flavors of the sea. It's frequently busy, and the mussels are as good as anywhere, though for a particularly reasonable price. There's a sheltered and heated terrace area, too, both for restaurant overspill and for customers who might want to dine outside, even when the weather's not behaving.

ACCOMMODATIONS

€50-100

RESTAURANT LOGIS AU MOYNE DE SAIRE

15 rue Général de Gaulle, Reville; tel. 02 33 54 46 06; www.au-moyne-de-saire.fr; from €77 d

Located in the little hamlet of Reville in between Saint-Vaast and Barfleur, this large house converted into a hotel offers comfortable, clean rooms styled in a modern, if slightly bland, way, and seclusion from the bustle of the town. More geared toward an extended stay than an overnight pit stop, it has a small garden and is just a few minutes' walk from the popular Jonville Beach. There's also a restaurant on-site, which is in a slightly higher-budget category than the hotel and offers good local food.

HÔTEL LA GRANITIERE

74 rue Maréchal Foch, Saint-Vaast-la-Hougue; tel. 02 33 44 89 50; www.hotel-la-granitiere.com; from €79 d

Granite by name, made of granite by nature; the slightly brutal façade of this building hides a surprisingly elegant interior. Comfortable and good value for money, it has a particularly pleasant lounge and breakfast room, decorated in a warm, traditional style. Rooms are cozy, if not especially exciting in their design. There's WiFi throughout the property and parking onsite. Though the hotel is not on the harbor, the sea is only a short walk away.

€100-200

HÔTEL LE CONQUÉRANT

18 rue Saint-Thomas Becket, Barfleur; tel. 02 33 54 00 82; www.hotel-leconquerant.com; from €129 d

A charming 18th-century manor house converted into a hotel that overlooks a pristinely maintained French garden, which was itself planted in 1910. Rooms are comfortable, with some antique features as well as the modern conveniences of WiFi and en suite bathrooms. Breakfast is served in a cozy old-fashioned room with a wood-beamed ceiling, or in the garden on nice days. Right in the heart of Barfleur, the town's harbor is just a couple minutes' walk from the front door.

★ LA VILLA GERVAISERIE

17 route des Monts, 50760 Reville; tel. 02 33 54 54 64; www.lagervaiserie.com; from €137 d

An out-of-the-way beachfront hotel (Jonville Beach) in which all rooms offer excellent views out across the Saire Bay, this is a stylish modern property with interiors to match. Rooms come fully equipped with WiFi, TVs, and minibars, and all have balcony spaces and en suite bathrooms. Breakfast is served here,

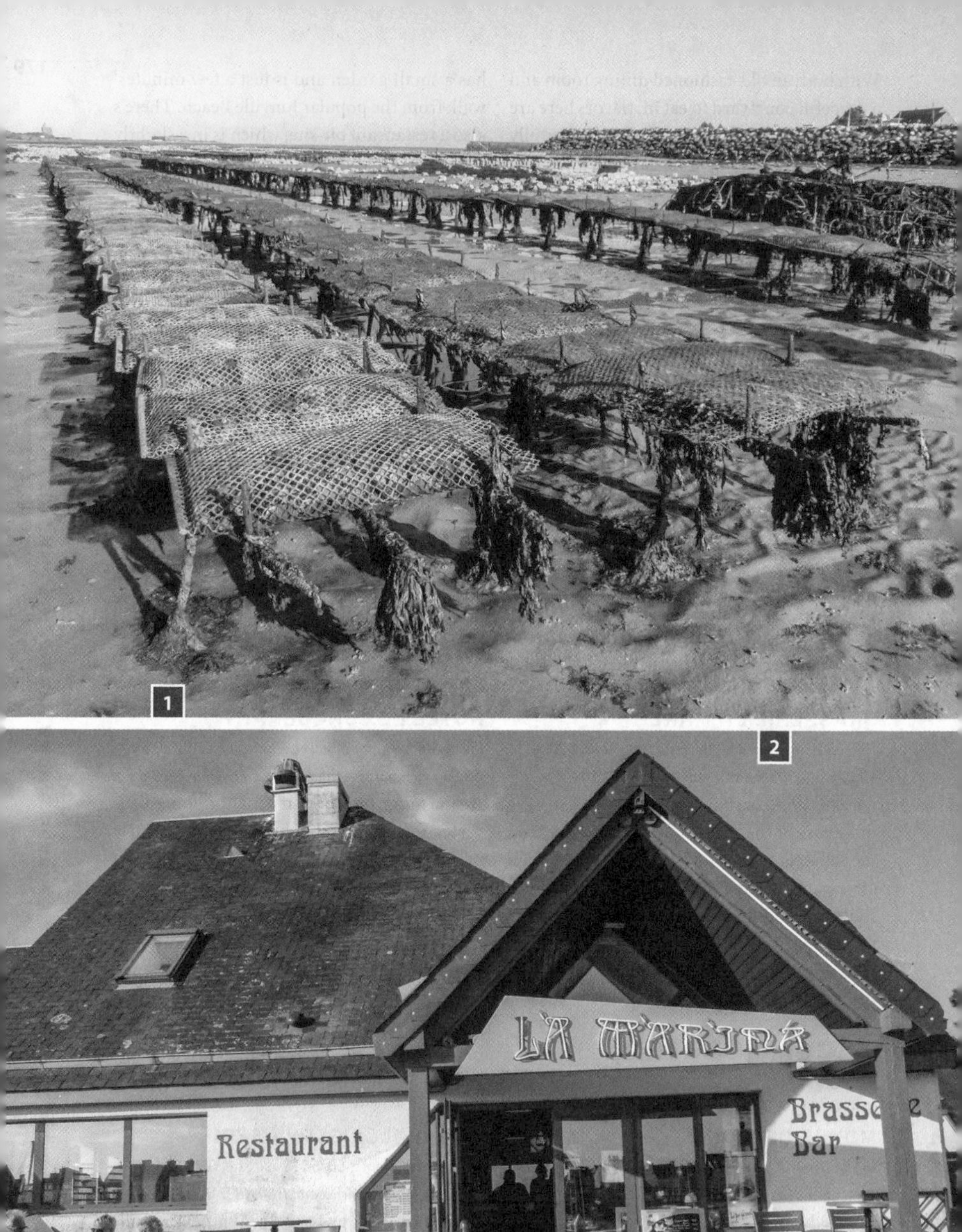
1
2
LA MARINA
Restaurant
Bar

but there's no on-site restaurant, so be prepared to venture out for food.

Camping

LA FERME DU BORD DU MER

43 route du Val de Saire, Gatteville-le-Phare; tel. 06 08 95 24 34; www.camping-gatteville.fr; pitch in high season €13.90, cabins €430 per week

A medium-size, fairly basic campsite in a great location with two shower blocks and disabled access. It's right next to a sheltered beach, in the shadow of Gatteville lighthouse, and just a few minutes' drive or walk from Barfleur. It gets its name from the small farm that also occupies the property, complete with rabbits, goats, a donkey, and chickens. As well as tent pitches, there are also cabins that can be rented, which come with full cooking facilities. A small shop and café offers breakfast and some food on-site, but for most meals, you'll probably want to head into town.

TRANSPORTATION

Getting There

BY CAR

By far the easiest way of getting to Barfleur and Saint-Vaast is by car. From Paris take the A13 to Caen, then the N13 via Bayeux, before splitting at Valgones to take the D902. It's a journey of almost four hours and 214 miles (328 kilometers). There will be toll charges from Paris to Caen of around €20.

The journey from Caen is about 1.5 hours and 70 miles (112 kilometers). From Bayeux it's about one hour, and 50 miles (80 kilometers).

The fastest way to Barfleur and Saint-Vaast from Sword, Juno, Gold, or Omaha Beaches is to drive down from the coast to join the N13, then follow that main road around. The journey is about 1.5 hours and 77 miles (124 kilometers) from the farthest east, Sword Beach, and one hour and 50 miles (80 kilometers) from the farthest west, Omaha Beach. From Utah Beach, which is actually on the Cotentin Peninsula, it's possible to take the coastal route, the D421, which gets you to Saint-Vaast in about 30 minutes, with a distance of just under 20 miles (32 kilometers).

From Cherbourg, it's about 30 minutes and 20 miles (32 kilometers) on the D901, arriving in Barfleur. Alternatively, you can take the very beautiful coastal road, the D116, which is about a 40-minute drive for roughly the same distance.

From Mont-Saint-Michel, Saint-Vaast is about two hours, taking the A84, then the N174. It's a journey of just over 100 miles (160 kilometers).

Parking in both towns is free, though in high season you may have to head into the backstreets to find a spot.

BY BUS

Buses to Barfleur, run by local service **Manéo** (tel. 02 33 055 550; www.manche.fr/transports/lignes-horaires-maneo-express.aspx), are available from Valognes or Cherbourg. Form Cherbourg, take Line 12, which runs between three and five times a day, takes about 45 minutes, and costs €2.30. The service does not run on Sundays. From Valognes, take Line 13, which runs between two and five times a day, takes just under an hour, and costs €2.30. This service also runs to Saint-Vaast, taking about 30 minutes for the same price, and accordingly connects the two towns. Buses stop in front of Barfleur's town hall, and on the harbor at Saint-Vaast.

BY TAXI

Similarly, taxis will take you from Valognes or Cherbourg, though expect to pay €30-40 plus. Most city taxis should take you, and you can just flag them down on the street—though certain individual drivers may not be willing to travel the whole distance. There are several companies you can call on, all of which offer much the same service. **Taxi Cherbourg Octeville** (tel. 02 33 53 36 38) is just one of them. Don't expect much English to be spoken.

1: oyster beds in Saint-Vaast, where the town's famous speciality is grown **2:** Saint-Vaast's La Marina, a great place for evening oyster eating

Getting Around

Both towns in themselves are very small and easily walkable. A trip between them by car will take about 10 minutes and is about a 30-40-minute cycle. Bikes can be hired at the municipal camping site **La Blanche Nef** in Barfleur (12 chemin de la Masse, Gatteville-le-Phare; tel. 02 33 023 15 40).

The Manéo bus, Line 13, runs between the two towns (tel. 02 33 055 550; www.manche.fr/transports/lignes-horaires-maneo-express.aspx), costing €2.30. It stops outside of Barfleur's town hall and at the north end of Saint-Vaast harbor. The journey takes about 25 minutes and also stops outside Montfarville church.

Cherbourg

France's great military architect Sébastien Le Prestre de Vauban (1633-1707) summed up modern Cherbourg best when he recognized it as one of "the keys to the (French) kingdom." Out of that observation grew all that would come to characterize the history and people of this salty deep-water port, which reaches out into the English Channel but remains sheltered from the worst of its storms. Cherbourg has been a gateway city of military conquest, trade, and tourism for generations.

It was in the 1770s, however, when Louis XVI really brought Vauban's observation to fruition by ordering the construction of what was to become (and still is) the largest artificial harbor in the world, thus bringing about an influx of money and people to the city. Though Cherbourg is often overlooked by tourists, who tend to pass through toward Normandy's more pastural delights, there's much to reward those who linger: an attractive downtown of winding lanes and stone buildings, civil structures that bristle with colorful umbrella decorations (a nod to the famous 1960s musical *The Umbrellas of Cherbourg*, which is still what the town is best known for in France), and above all, an authenticity: Tourism is largely inconsequential to Cherbourg, which means its restaurants and bars have been set up to serve locals first of all, and therefore cater to true Norman tastes.

Finally, in the Cité de la Mer, you will find one of the best maritime museums in all of France.

Orientation

Like a city with chunks bitten out of it by the sea, Cherbourg is characterized by its numerous harbors, the central and longest of which stretches right into the center of town, where it is called the Bassin du Commerce. The historic heart is to the west of this central dock, which is where you'll find the majority of restaurants and hotels, as well as the best district simply to wander. This is centered around the **Place Général-de-Gaulle,** a large square with a nice fountain and plenty of bars and cafés, off from which run winding lanes, along which there's plenty to explore.

The Cité de la Mer, which contains an aquarium and maritime museum, is the town's most visited attraction, on the central dock's eastern quay, slightly to the north. Around this area, the town takes on a different scale, as the evidence of heavy shipping is everywhere: The passenger **ferry port** is alongside the Cité de la Mer quay dominating the harbor to the east. Less than half a mile to the south rises the sandstone cliff of Montagne du Roule, which overlooks the town.

SIGHTS

★ Cité de la Mer

Allée du Président Menut, Cherbourg-Octeville; tel. 02 33 020 26 69; www.citedelamer.com; 9:30am-7pm daily July-Aug., 9:30am-6:30pm daily Apr.-May, 9:30am-6pm June and Sept., 10am-6pm Oct.-Feb.; adults €18, reduced €13

Cherbourg's undisputed main draw, this museum dedicated to all elements of the sea has

Cherbourg

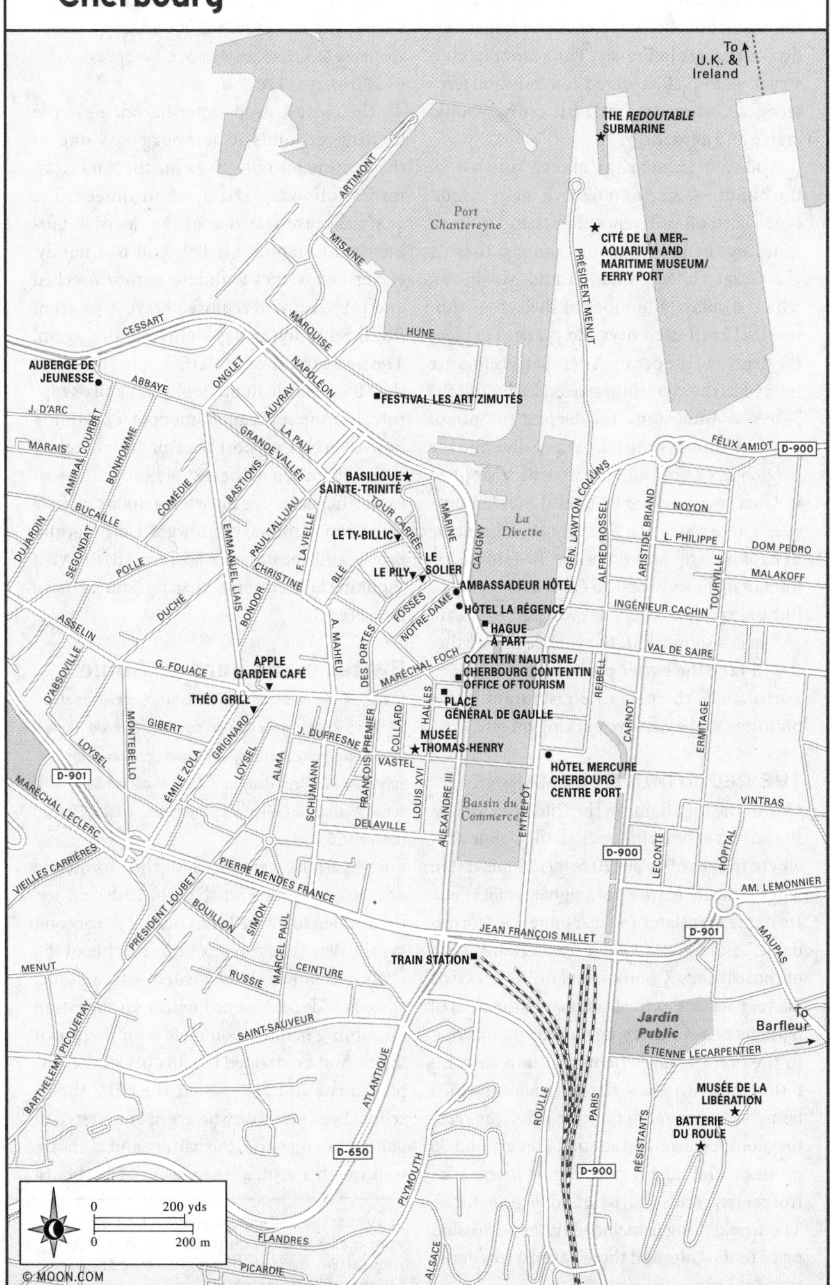
To U.K. & Ireland
THE REDOUTABLE SUBMARINE
Port Chantereyne
CITÉ DE LA MER-AQUARIUM AND MARITIME MUSEUM/FERRY PORT
PRÉSIDENT MENUT
ARTIMONT
MISAINE
MARQUISE
CESSART
HUNE
AUBERGE DE JEUNESSE
ABBAYE
ONGLET
NAPOLÉON
AUVRAY
FESTIVAL LES ART'ZIMUTÉS
J. D'ARC
MARAIS
AMIRAL COURBET
BONHOMME
GRANDE VALLÉE
LA PAIX
BASILIQUE SAINTE-TRINITÉ
FÉLIX AMIOT
D-900
BASTIONS
COMÉDIE
BUCAILLE
DUJARDIN
SEGONDAT
PAUL TALLUAU
F. LA VIELLE
TOUR CARRÉE
MARINE
CALIGNY
La Divette
GÉN. LAWTON COLLINS
ALFRED ROSSEL
ARISTIDE BRIAND
NOYON
L. PHILIPPE
DOM PEDRO
LE TY-BILLIC
LE SOLIER
LE PILY
POLLE
EMMANUEL LIAIS
CHRISTINE
BLÉ
AMBASSADEUR HÔTEL
MALAKOFF
TOURVILLE
DUCHÉ
BONDOR
FOSSES
NOTRE-DAME
HÔTEL LA RÉGENCE
INGÉNIEUR CACHIN
ASSELIN
A. MAHIEU
DES PORTES
HAGUE À PART
VAL DE SAIRE
D'ABSOVILLE
G. FOUACE
APPLE GARDEN CAFÉ
MARÉCHAL FOCH
COTENTIN NAUTISME/CHERBOURG CONTENTIN OFFICE OF TOURISM
REIBELL
THÉO GRILL
PLACE GÉNÉRAL DE GAULLE
MONTEBELLO
GIBERT
GRIGNARD
J. DUFRESNE
FRANÇOIS PREMIER
COLLARD
HALLES
MUSÉE THOMAS-HENRY
CARNOT
ERMITAGE
LOYSEL
D-901
ÉMILE ZOLA
ALMA
SCHUMANN
VASTEL
LOUIS XVI
ALEXANDRE III
HÔTEL MERCURE CHERBOURG CENTRE PORT
MARÉCHAL LECLERC
Bassin du Commerce
ENTREPÔT
VINTRAS
DELAVILLE
LECONTE
HÔPITAL
VIEILLES CARRIÈRES
PIERRE MENDES FRANCE
AM. LEMONNIER
PRÉSIDENT LOUBET
BOUILLON
SIMON
MARCEL PAUL
JEAN FRANÇOIS MILLET
D-901
MAUPAS
MENUT
TRAIN STATION
RUSSIE
CEINTURE
SAINT-SAUVEUR
Jardin Public
To Barfleur
ÉTIENNE LECARPENTIER
BARTHELEMY PICOUERAY
ATLANTIQUE
ROULLE
PARIS
RÉSISTANTS
MUSÉE DE LA LIBÉRATION
BATTERIE DU ROULE
D-650
PLYMOUTH
D-900
0 200 yds
0 200 m
FLANDRES
ALSACE
PICARDIE
© MOON.COM

been luring visitors from miles around ever since it opened in 2002. The enormous building was built in 1933 and is the largest art deco structure in France. The year of its construction to 1960, it served as a train and ferry terminal, where transatlantic cruises would arrive and depart.

Today, the museum makes full use of the building's size to offer five main exhibitions, each on different subjects and themes. Entering the building, for example, there is the Great Gallery of Men and Machines, which displays a number of the actual submarinal craft used over the years to explore the depths of the ocean. After that, visitors are invited to the aquarium spaces, including the "Abyssal Aquarium," the deepest column of water in Europe, or to take a deep dive into the tragic history of the *Titanic,* which stopped in Cherbourg before its fateful maiden voyage. There's also the *Redoutable* submarine to explore, and an immersive 50-minute exhibit that allows people to experience what it's like to explore the very deepest part of ocean.

There's so much in the Cité de la Mer that it will take the better part of a day to see it. Fortunately, there's a café/restaurant in the building, and extensive parking on-site.

THE *REDOUTABLE* SUBMARINE

One of the highlights of the Cité de la Mer, as the largest submarine open to the public anywhere in the world at 420 feet (128 meters) in length, the *Redoutable* is a sight all of its own. Its name translates to "fearsome" or "formidable," and the *Redoutable* was certainly both of those things. Comissioned in 1971, it saw a 20-year service as the lead boat in the class of ballistic missile-carrying nuclear submarines in the French Navy. Turning it into an exhibition took two years, the main task of which being the removal of the ship's nuclear reactor. Looking around the sub takes around 35 minutes, and takes in the engine room, control center, crew's quarters, and torpedo tubes. The whole thing is included in the admission price to the Cité, and there's even a free audio tour for kids.

Musée de la Libération

Fort du Roule, Montée des Résistants, Cherbourg-Octeville; tel. 02 33 020 14 12; 10am-12:30pm and 2pm-6pm Tues.-Fri., 1pm-6pm Sat.-Sun.; adults €3.20, reduced €1.70

As the closest deep-water harbor near the landing grounds, Cherbourg was one of the first major objectives for the American forces following D-Day. And indeed, the city's capture was one of the decisive moments throughout the Battle of Normandy. Nevertheless, they found the harbor wrecked and mined, and it required brave work from Royal Navy divers to get it functioning again. The museum, spectacularly located on top of the Montagne du Roule, looks at the city's capture and the subsequent months, explaining how Cherbourg's port became instrumental to the liberation of the rest of Europe. As well as terrific views, the museum exhibits include some period military hardware, clothing, and propaganda posters. It's fairly small, so a visit shouldn't take any more than an hour. Signage is in French.

Batterie and Fort du Roule

5 Montée des Résistants, Cherbourg-Octeville; tel. 06 31 45 25 80; www.exspen.com/batterie_du_roule.php; tours leave 2:30pm, 4pm, and 5:30pm daily July-Aug., 2:30pm daily and 4pm Wed. and Sat. June, 2:30pm Sat.-Sun. May and Sept.; adults €9, reduced €6

Fortifications were dug into the Momtagne de la Roule by the French in the 19th century, then added to by the Nazis during the Second World War. The tunnels that still thread the cliffs can now only be visited with a guide, who should speak some English. Groups strap on mining helmets complete with their own lights, and are treated to a history of the emplacement and facts about the cliffs themselves. Even for those who are not interested in going underground, the battery and cliffs are well worth a visit, as the views of Cherbourg

1: a visitor to Cherbourg harbor **2:** umbrellas appear all over Cherbourg in reference to 1950s musical film *The Umbrellas of Cherbourg* **3:** Cherbourg's Cité de la Mer

POGORIA
1
2
3
LA CITÉ
DE LA MER
CHERBOURG
Bienvenue
Welcome
Entrée
Entrance
Entrée à 150 m

are spectacular from the top, and are made even more so the way you are led to see them on this tour, emerging on the panorama from the darkness of the caves. Tours last a little under an hour; the guides suggest you turn up 15 minutes before they start to run through safety equipment. There's usually no need to book, apart from off-season where tours only take place on request. Tours can be organized by text any time of year, with a minimum price of €36.

Basilique Sainte-Trinité

1 rue de l'Église, Cherbourg-Octeville; tel. 02 33 53 10 63; 8:30am-7pm daily; free

A church that's a testament to its own fortitude, the Basilique Sainte-Trinité did not have an easy start. Construction of a gothic church started in 1412 to replace an older church at the same location, but was interrupted by a seige by the English, leading to famine and English rule. The building was eventually completed between 1450 and 1466, but was then ransacked during the French revolution. It underwent an extensive reconstruction in the 19th century, with architects adding a tower in the neo-Gothic style—likely the first time that style was used in France. The church, nevertheless, counts as one of the city's oldest monuments, and it has a richly decorated interior complete with gloriously patterned pillars covered in almost celtic designs, and an unusual altarpiece made largely of gold and boasting two fine marble statues against a bright painted backdrop of sky and clouds.

Musée Thomas-Henry

Centre Culturel Le Quasar, esplanade de la Laïcité, Cherbourg-Octeville; tel. 02 33 23 39 33; 10am-12:30pm and 2pm-6pm Tues.-Fri., 1pm-6pm Sat.-Sun.; €5

Founded by a series of anonymous donations in the early 19th century, this museum now contains around 300 artworks, including pieces by Fra Angelico, Brueghel, and Jean-François Millet, the last of whom used to come to the museum to copy paintings when he was a young artist. The donations that founded the museum were later revealed to have come from Thomas Henry, a town councillor and art critic who, having lost his two sons, wanted to help Cherbourg's youth to learn about art. Nicknamed the "Little Louvre," the museum can be a little intimidating to the non-expert. Among the highlights, though, are Angelico's *Conversion of Saint Augustine*; *Pieta,* a gut-wrenching deptiction of Mary mourning over the body of Jesus by 17th-century French master Nicolas Poussin; and the whole collection of Millet's paintings and drawings, typically moving scenes of peasant life, the largest in the world outside Paris.

SPORTS AND RECREATION

Water Sports

COTENTIN NAUTISME

14 quai Alexandre 3, Cherbourg-Octeville; tel. 02 33 53 92 05; www.cotentin-nautisme.fr; 9am-12:30pm and 1:30pm-5pm Mon.-Fri.

A central location that connects all the various water-sports centers in the Cherbourg area. Because instructors and supervisors can be spread thinly at off-peak times of the year, it is worth contacting this central body to check what's open and the activities that are available before just heading to a place on the coast. Cotentin is, of course, a great area for all sorts of sea-based activity, and everything from sea kayaking to small boat sailing is available. Such centers tend to be popular with locals and French tourists who visit Cotentin every year, but don't be intimidated: Outsiders are readily welcomed, and usually there will be enough English spoken for you to muddle through. Costs range from €10 to rent a sea kayak to €200-plus for sailing courses.

Boat Tours

HAGUE À PART

Pont Tournant, Cherbourg-en-Cotentin; tel. 6 61 14 03 32; hagueapart.com; tours adults €14.50, children €9.90, half-day boat rental from €130

Offering boat rental and tours of Cherbourg's remarkable harbor. The group tour of the harbor takes place in diesel-powered boats and explores the harbor's length and the small forts that dot it, and circles round Cherbourg's modern-day military port, taking about an hour with a maximum of 61 people on board. Farther flung excursions are also possible, such as along the coast to Port Racine, which stands in direct contradiction to Cherbourg, as it is the smallest harbor in France. Trips take place as part of a group in diesel-powered boats, though sailing deals and bespoke fishing trips are also available at a higher cost, starting at €30 per person.

ENTERTAINMENT AND EVENTS

Nightlife

LE SOLIER

52 rue Grande Rue; tel. 02 33 94 76 63; 8pm-2am Thurs.-Sat.; pints from €4

Cherbourg may not be the best city for nightlife, though there are some decent pub-like bars to be found on the backstreets of its old town. Le Solier is one of the best; it's got a celtic feel and frequent live music, which often devolves into lively sing-and-dance-alongs involving the entire bar.

Festivals and Events

FESTIVAL LES ART'ZIMUTÉS

Plage verte, Cherbourg-en-Cotentin; tel. 06 38 33 08 63; www.lesartzimutes.com; June 29-30; one-day pass €20; two-day pass €32

Held right in the center of town, this three-day, family-friendly festival brings together musicians, dancers, and craftspeople. Ongoing since 1999, the festival was conceived around the idea that festivalgoers are projected as the "heroes" of the festival. A series of tents are set up, along with several stages. In the tents, attendees are encouraged to meet their "hero" potential by taking part in craft activities. Later, even the singing along with musicians seems to bestow value on the festivalgoers themselves. It's a popular festival, and though family-focused in the day, it is more raucous at night. Book at least a month in advance to ensure tickets.

SHOPPING

CHERBOURG FLOWER MARKET

Place Centrale et place de Gaulle; www.cherbourgtourisme.com/node/214; 8am-12pm Sat.

This local institution is a beautifully colorful addition to Cherbourg's main market. Every Saturday, Place Centrale and Place de Gaulle are taken over by numerous small-scale flower sellers, selling both locally grown and more exotic plants. It's an exciting, fragrant space just to wander about and look at, and prices are sufficiently low that you might be tempted to pick up a bunch with which to decorate your hotel or B&B.

FOOD

Local Cuisine

LE PILY

39 rue Grande Rue, Cherbourg-Octeville; tel. 02 33 10 19 29; www.restaurant-le-pily.com; 12pm-1:45pm and 7pm-9pm Tues.-Sat. and 7pm-9pm Mon. Sept.-mid-June, 12pm-1:45pm and 7pm-9pm Tues.-Sat. and 12pm-1:45pm Sun. mid-June-Aug.; menus €45-114

Hiding in one of the backstreets of Cherbourg's old town, this one-Michelin-star restaurant concentrates on providing an intimate service to a small number of customers. It's a place characterized by control: Neither the food options nor the wine list is vast; rather, guests are invited to put themselves in the hands of the proprietor, Pierre Marion, who will guide them through a meal of fresh local flavors, presented in a stylish modern setting. Reservations are essential, particularly for weekends, which tend to fill up weeks in advance.

★ THÉO GRILL

12 rue Victor Grignard, Cherbourg-Octeville; tel. 02 33 01 27 97; 12pm-2pm and 7pm-10pm Tues.-Sat.; menus €16-20

Normandy may be known for its seafood, but sometimes, when you want to have a steak, nothing else will do. Théo Grill provides the perfect solution for such times, offering prime cuts of beef cooked over a charcoal grill. The smell of the restaurant is almost worth the—very reasonable—price alone. Perhaps it should go without saying, but this is not a place for vegetarians. And while the staff will do their best to accommodate, it can be hard to overlook the carnivorous atmosphere.

Budget Options

APPLE GARDEN CAFÉ

60 rue Gambetta, Cherbourg-Octeville; tel. 09 81 86 21 09; 12pm-2:30pm Mon., 12pm-6pm Tues.-Sat.; menu €10

A small, charming café run by an expat Welshman that has a real sense of community. It does a great line in baked potatoes, which come served with all manner of accompaniments, from tomato and feta to tuna salad. The homemade cakes are good too, and there's a lovely old courtyard garden out back to sit in on sunny days. Perfect for an inexpensive but filling lunch.

LE TY-BILLIC

73 rue au Blé, Cherbourg-Octeville; tel. 02 33 01 11 90; http://creperie-letybillic.fr; 12pm-2pm and 7pm-10pm; €6.50-8.90

A family-friendly *crêperie,* not afraid to dress crepes in some fairly luxury foodstuffs, such as duck breast and blood sausage. More conventional crepe toppings are also available, and prices are reasonable across the board. It's a fairly small place and popular, so reservations are a good idea if you don't want to wait around for a table.

ACCOMMODATIONS

Under €50

AUBERGE DE JEUNESSE

55 rue de l'Abbaye, Cherbourg-Octeville; tel. 02 33 78 15 15; www.hifrance.org/auberge-de-jeunesse/cherbourg-octeville.html; €22.60 per bed

A classic, clean youth hostel with decent on-site facilities, including a bar, a lounge, and TV area with a pool table, bike and bag storage, and even a barbecue grill. They also provide breakfast and lunch, and there's a personal cooking area, which is great either to save money or to try your own hand at preparing some of Cherbourg's excellent local produce. Rooms are fairly basic but clean, and not too enormous for a hostel. The biggest sleep 10, on five bunk beds. There are also smaller family rooms available, sleeping four, with en suite bathrooms, for the same price per bed. WiFi is available throughout the property.

€50-100

AMBASSADEUR HÔTEL

22 quai Caligny, Cherbourg-Octeville; tel. 02 33 43 10 00; www.ambassadeurhotel.com/en; from €64 d

Looking out over Cherbourg's harbor from the edges of its old town, this smart three-star hotel offers a clean modern design and bright unfussy rooms that come equipped with all the usual amenities for a property of this class. That means satellite TVs, private bathrooms, and WiFi. Private parking is available nearby and the reception is open 24 hours, happy to cater to your midnight needs. Its central location and its waterfront views, though, are its prime selling points.

HÔTEL MERCURE CHERBOURG CENTRE PORT

13 quai de l'Entrepôt, Cherbourg-Octeville; tel. 02 33 44 01 11 https://www.accorhotels.com/gb/hotel-9622-mercure-cherbourg-centre-port-hotel/index.shtml; from €91.20 d

A smart, modern hotel of the Mercure group with floor-to-ceiling windows offering some stunning views out over Cherbourg's harbor and towards its old town. The overall vibe is a little corporate, and the hotel is used frequently for conferences, but it's also packed with everything that you might expect and more from of a hotel of its price bracket. This includes an on-site gym, a roof terrace, and 24-hour reception.

★ HÔTEL LA RÉGENCE

42 quai Caligny, Cherbourg-Octeville; tel. 02 33 43 05 16; www.laregence.com; from €96 d

Offering the kind of cozy interior where it's easy to imagine sailors gathering in to share yarns of the sea, this hotel strays away from the modernity of others and caters to a holiday-maker more interested in tradition;

there's even something of the British pub to its communal areas. The rooms are comfy and clean, and crammed with modern features, including flat-screen TVs, WiFi, and en suite bathrooms. Some also offer excellent views of Cherbourg's harbor.

€100-200

★ MANOIR DE LA FIEFFE

La Fieffe La Glacerie; tel. 02 33 020 81 45; www.manoirdelafieffe.com; from €260 d

A little out of Cherbourg's center and feeling more isolated than it is, this 16th-century manor house is situated on four hectares (10 acres) of land and offers three sizeable rooms, plus a self-catered cottage. It's tastefully decorated in a bright and airy style and offers breakfasts to match. The grounds are excellent to wander around, and you can consult the owner about local walks. A concession to the hotel's difficulty to reach without a car, the owners will also come pick guests up from Cherbourg railway station, provided you let them know your time of arrival in advance—after that you'll either have to walk or take a taxi the two and a half miles into town (the taxi should set you back €10-15). A good countryside retreat.

Camping

CAMPING COLLIGNON

Rue des Algues, Tourlaville; tel. 02 33 41 85 70; http://camping-collignon.simdif.com; pitch for two people €18; cabin €49

Tourlaville is a resort-like suburb just to the east of Cherbourg's outer harbor wall, and this beachfront campsite offers cheap self-contained accommodations from which to enjoy all it has to offer. There's a food shop on-site, plus barbecue grills for fine weather and a well-maintained shower block. A swimming pool and easy access to the beach are pluses, plus a number of trendy and sturdy cabins for those willing to splash out a little more, and who don't want to spend their time in tents. Its biggest draw, though, is its proximity to Tourlaville's water-sports center where sea kayaks, sailboats, and stand-up paddleboards await.

INFORMATION

CHERBOURG CONTENTIN OFFICE OF TOURISM

14 quai Alexandre 3, Cherbourg-en-Cotentin; tel. 02 33 93 52 02; www.cherbourgtourism.com; 10am-12:30pm and 2pm-6pm Mon.-Sat.

Located at the northwestern corner of Cherbourg's central harbor, the tourist office is good for organizing accommodations and harbor trips and can help put you in touch with various water-sports facilities in the area around the town, as well as plan your onward journey.

TRANSPORTATION

Getting There

BY BOAT

One of France's major Channel ports, Cherbourg is linked to the British ports of Poole and Portsmouth via **Brittany Ferries** (Gare Maritime Transmanche, Cherbourg Octeville; tel. 08 25 82 88 28; www.brittany-ferries.fr) and to the Irish ports of Dublin and Rosslare by **Irish Ferries** (Gare Maritime Transmanche, Cherbourg Octeville; tel. 02 33 023 44 44; www.irishferries.com) and **Stena Line** (Terminal Transmanche, quai de Normandie, Cherbourg-en-Cotentin; tel. 02 33 43 23 87; www.stenaline.fr). The frequency of sailings changes from summer to winter months, though they are generally fairly regular. Prices also fluctuate depending on how far ahead you book and the season, though as a general yardstick expect to pay around €130 in either direction. Trips from Ireland are an overnight service taking 19-20 hours. From Portsmouth it's a six-hour trip, and from Poole around seven hours.

BY CAR

At one of the northernmost tips of France, Cherbourg is nevertheless well connected by road, and takes only four hours to reach from Paris, and is a journey of 220 miles (355 kilometers), first along the A13, then the N13. It is about 1.5 hours from Caen, 76 miles (123 kilometers) along the N13, and an hour from Bayeux, 58 miles (93 kilometers) along the same roads. It is about two hours and 110 miles (178 kilometers) from Mont-Saint-Michel starting on the A84, then connecting to the N174. On its either side the town boasts very beautiful coastal roads, reminiscent, on a bright day, of the Cote d'Azur.

BY TRAIN

Cherbourg's train station, **Gare de Cherbourg**, (avenue Jean François Millet, Cherbourg-en-Cotentin; tel. 08 92 35 35 35; www.gares-sncf.com/fr/gare/frack/cherbourg; 4:45am-12:30am Mon., 5:15am-12:30am Tues.-Fri., 5:15am-10:30pm Sat., 6:45am-12:45am Sun.), which sits at the southern end of its inner harbor, is well serviced from Bayeux, Caen, and Paris. Trains from all three run at least eight times a day. A one-way ticket from Paris will cost just over €50 and takes three hours. From Bayeux the journey is one hour, costing €20, with 8-15 trips daily; from Caen it's 1 hour 15 minutes, costing €24 with 8-15 trips daily. It's also possible to get there from Mont-Saint-Michel, with 3-5 trains running every day, taking 2.5-3.5 hours from the sight's nearby town Pontorson.

Getting Around

Cherbourg's center is very easy to walk around, while a free shuttle bus links it with the ferry terminal. This stops directly outside the ferry terminal and then outside the Cité de la Mer. Look for an ordinary-looking city bus with *navette* (shuttle bus) written as its destination. Taxis, meanwhile, can be called at 02 33 53 36 58, and to get between the train station and the ferry should cost around €10.

Mont-Saint-Michel and West Cotentin

A low-lying, windswept peninsula, stretching

out into the English Channel, the western Cotentin Peninsula is Normandy at its most elemental, where the proximity of Brittany and its wilder nature can be felt and seen. Defined as well by its impressive tidal reach, the longest in Europe, there is a scale at work here way beyond what is usually associated with the continent.

The pièce de résistance, and one of the most stunning sights in all of France, is of course the magnificent Mont-Saint-Michel: a Gothic abbey that rises with all the defiant improbability of the region itself from the Couesnon River estuary, and which has been attracting awestruck visitors for hundreds of years.

Talk of its epic qualities notwithstanding, this is also a region of

Highlights

Look for ★ to find recommended sights, activities, dining, and lodging.

★ **Mont-Saint-Michel Abbey:** One of the most awe-inspiring sights in the world, this abbey is known for its beautiful commingling of Romanesque and Gothic styles as well as its stunning location (page 199).

★ **Mont-Saint-Michel Bay:** A true natural wonder, this bay is home of the longest tidal reach in Europe: A veritable desert of sand is revealed every day as the sea departs from the ocean floor (page 203).

★ **Dunes of Hatainville:** Wander through these dunes rising 262 feet (80 meters) above the sea, a haven for all sorts of flora and fauna (page 210).

★ **Frescoes of Canville:** Ponder these compelling images discovered in a village church that depict a hidden gem of European history (page 211).

★ **Musée Christian Dior:** Visit the fashion legend's birthplace, now a museum, and marvel at the gorgeous belle epoque villa, expertly manicured English gardens, and the magnificent collection of Dior artifacts (page 218).

★ **Boat Tour of Îles Chausey:** Sail around the largest archipelago in Europe during high tide—an experience not unlike drifting over a map of the world (page 221).

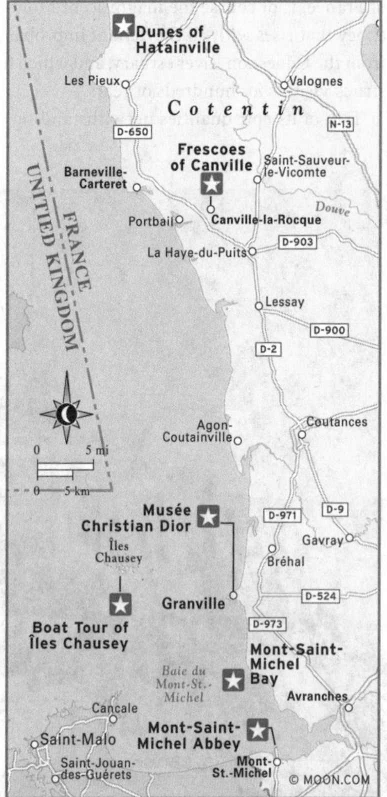

beach resorts, still serving weekend and summer crowds in much the same way it did during its heyday in the belle epoque at the end of the 19th century. A dusting of faded glamour remains, whether in the elegant cliff-top Musée Christian Dior—former residence of the great fashion designer—or in the blue and white beach cabins of Carteret, the civilized guardians to resort town Hatainville's spectacular dunes.

Whether it's to explore the epic landscape, get to grips with one of France's most famous historical monuments, or just relax on a stylish beach, there's something in this comparatively small region for everyone to enjoy.

HISTORY

Impressive though the monument is, it's hard to believe quite how much this part of Normandy has had its history defined by Mont-Saint-Michel, given the tidal island's very natural limitations in terms of size. Yet by being a pilgrimage center, an almost unassailable fortress, and most recently a world-beating tourist destination, that is exactly what has happened.

The modern history of the region begins with a legend, that of the great Scissy Forest, which is said to have covered what is today the massive tidal reach of Mont-Saint-Michel Bay. This was reputed to be a realm of pagan practices and dark magic, which the story holds was swept away and purified (in a Christian sense) by a vast tidal wave in 709.

In real-world terms, this was the year that Bishop Aubert of Avranches, supposedly at the instruction of the archangel Michael, established the first church on the enormous rock in midst of the bay's vast tidal reach, offering a desert-like isolation for North European hermits. At the time, this island was called Mont Tombe, but it soon became known as Mont-Saint-Michel, on account of the angel who had inspired Bishop Aubert to settle it. The abbey built upon it was thus the Abbaye du Mont-Saint-Michel. The Mont's remarkable natural location meant that it soon began to gather a reputation as a major pilgrimage destination. Money began to flow in, gradually more buildings were added to its contours, and a setting that was once simply stunning became something close to miraculous; an impossible jewel floating between the firmaments of sea and sky.

The surrounding region benefited from the money raised by Mont-Saint-Michel, making it a tasty prospect for invading English forces during the Hundred Years' War. Nevertheless, despite rampaging through the surrounding countryside for 30 years and two direct sieges in 1423-1424 and 1433-1434, the English were unable to take the Mont. This time did, however, see the English fortify the battlements of nearby Granville and extend their influence up and down the coast.

Even after they were defeated in that conflict, the area would continue to see battles between English and French armies for years to come, notably during the Nine Years' War in 1695, and again in 1803 during the Napoleonic wars.

In more recent years, the region has attracted more vacationers than it has conflict. The impressive coastline with good swimming and excellent water-sport potential transformed towns like Granville and Barneville-Carteret from medieval power centers into seaside resorts. The former, thanks to its rocky topography and glamorous associations, is becoming known as the Monaco of the North.

Mont-Saint-Michel remains the region's number one draw, however. Having weathered the French Revolution, when it was turned into a prison, it got a full-scale restoration in the 19th century, and now attracts more tourist-pilgrims than any other single location in France outside of Paris.

Previous: Mont-Saint-Michel from a distance; Mont-Saint-Michel Abbey Church; a bronze bust of Christian Dior by Félix Schivo 1976.

Mont-Saint-Michel and West Cotentin

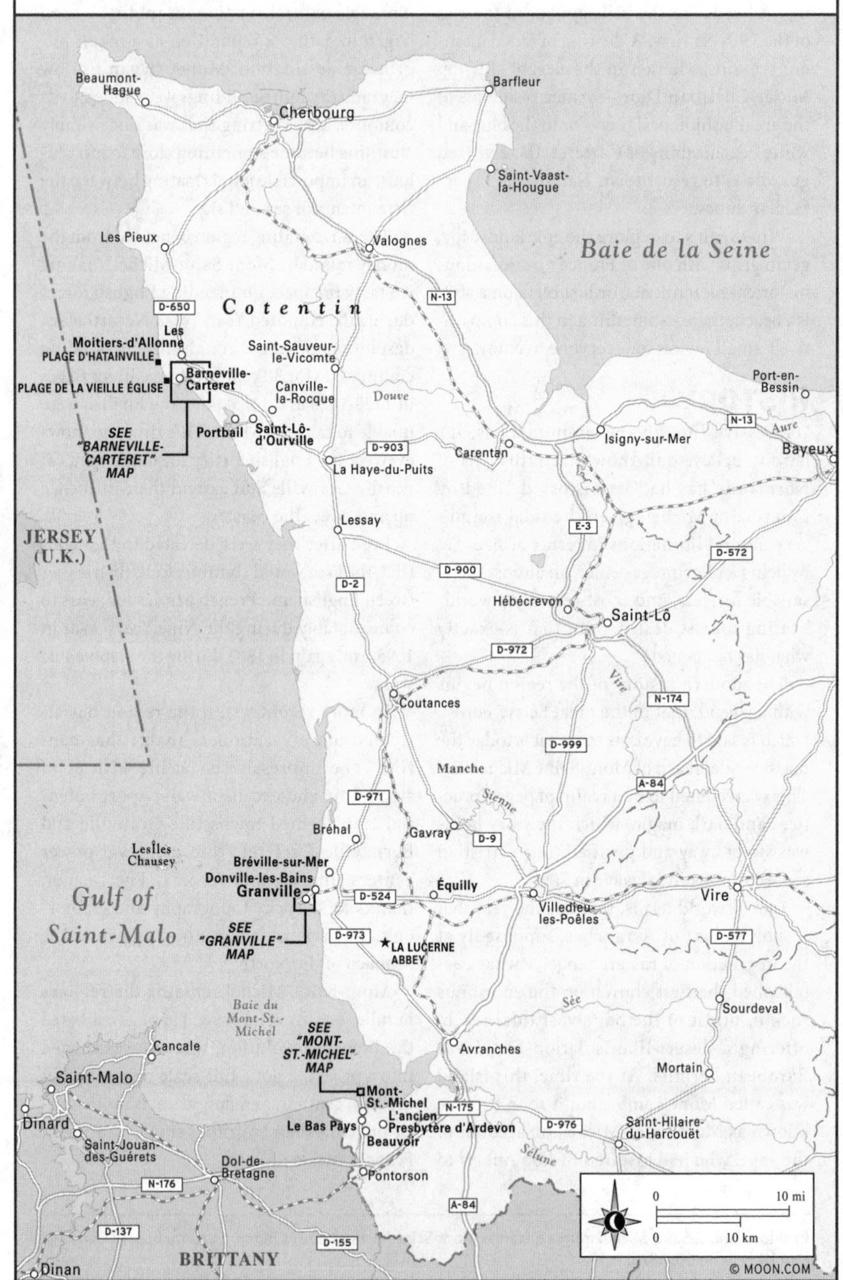

PLANNING YOUR TIME

As full of impressive sights and experiences as this region is, you may not feel the need to see and do all of them. Certainly Barneville-Carteret and to a lesser extent Granville are more suited to sedentary vacationing than excessive sightseeing. Notwithstanding that unless you've got a car, it's not the easiest region to travel around. This said, if your commitment is to sightseeing, then five days should be enough to get the measure of the place, including a hike on Hatainville's dunes and a boat trip to the islands of Chausey.

With Mont-Saint-Michel, it's possible to experience much of what the monument has to offer in a single day's visit—arriving early to beat the crowds, though, is highly recommended. There are obviously deeper experiences that can be gleaned by staying a little longer: walking the bay, for example, having a leisurely meal at La Mère Poulard, or indeed spending a night on the island itself.

A different and excellent way to experience the whole area, meanwhile, is to walk it. The GR223 hiking trail, which technically begins in Carentan in the east of La Manche, but that can be joined in Hatainville, just before its marvelous dunes, is a terrific way to take in many of the sights of this coast. Hiking from there to Mont-Saint-Michel takes nine days, with the Mont itself a regular ethereal sight on the horizon from Granville down.

Itinerary Ideas

TACKLING MONT-SAINT-MICHEL IN ONE DAY

1 Arrive early at Mont-Saint-Michel and grab a "to go" breakfast and some sandwiches for lunch at **La Bellevoisine** to fortify yourself for a day of walking and sightseeing.

2 Beat the crowds by heading directly to the **abbey** and spend the morning seeing the church, La Merveille, and the crypts.

3 Enjoy your picnic in Mont-Saint-Michel's comparatively secluded **gardens,** led up to by the La Truie Qui File.

4 Head up to the **ramparts** for glorious views of the bay, and if the tide is out, head back down for a meander around the bay—but stick close to the village walls!

5 Enjoy an early luxurious dinner at **La Mère Poulard**.

Mont-Saint-Michel

It's been called many things in its long history: "the jewel in France's crown," "the French pyramid," "wonder of the Western world." Its picture has graced the covers of a hundred guidebooks and it's been featured in thousands of magazines, but no description or image can do justice to its weirdness or its majesty. Fantastic in the purest sense of the word, it seems more than mere physics that allow Mont-Saint-Michel to rise like a lonely mountain from its tidal bay, and to any visitor it's hardly a surprise that this centuries-old pilgrimage sight is believed to be touched by God.

There's still a pinch-yourself quality to approaching the citadel, which is now connected to the mainland via a long, sweeping causeway, busy with free buses shipping visitors back and forth. But the Mont's iconic shape never quite seems to harden into reality; if

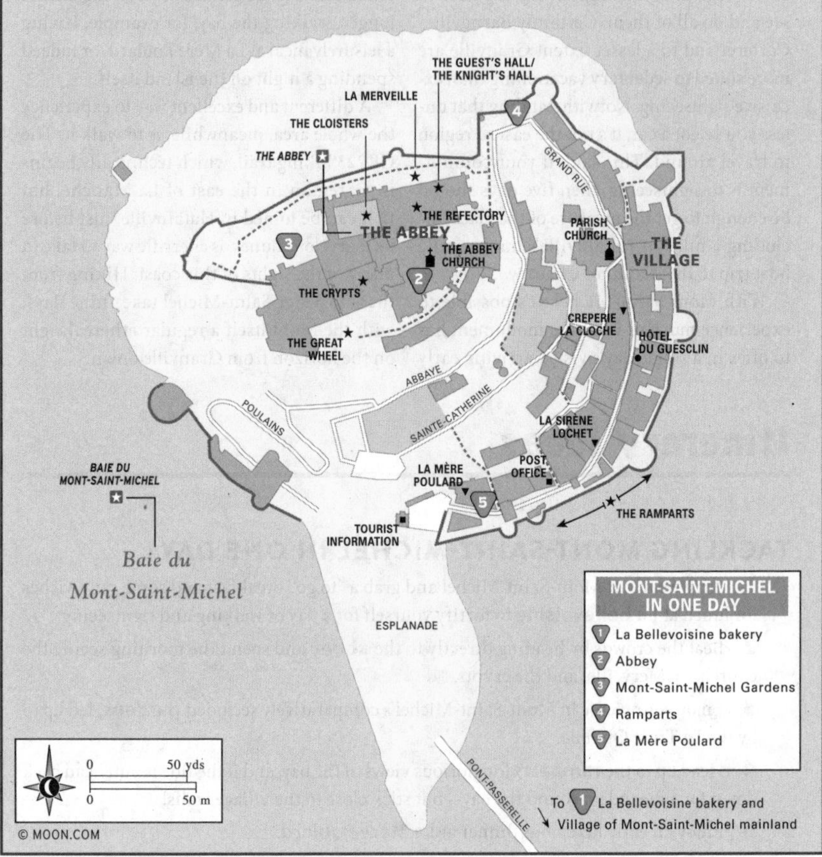

anything the dream just gets more impressive the closer you get, as the complex tangle of old domestic housing, fortifications, and transcendent religious building is revealed. Then, once you're inside and have climbed the medieval streets to the monastery that soars above it all, it's like you, too, are defying gravity. Standing in its cloisters, looking at turns up at the sky-etched steeple, then out across the shimmering bay, is to see achieved the ultimate goal of Gothic architecture: making stone seem lighter than air.

While global tourism has sunk its teeth deep into the organs of the Mont in recent decades, it's done little to undermine the monument's splendor. Consistently one of the most visited sights in all of France, an entire industry has evolved catering to the extraordinary demand from people all over the world to feast their senses on Mont-Saint-Michel's majesty. For the most part, this delivers a sleek visiting experience, and whether you join the day-trippers bused in from the mainland or choose to spend the night in a hotel nestled amid its ramparts, this is a world-renowned monument that does not disappoint.

HISTORY

With an easy-to-defend, dramatic aspect, the island was the site of fortifications and popular among religious hermits since ancient times. But it was Bishop Aubert of Avranches who cited it as spiritually important and who, claiming inspiration from the Archangel Michael, consecrated the first church here in 709.

Two hundred years later, at the request of the Duke of Normandy, a community of Benedictine monks settled on the Mont, though it was not until the 11th century that the first foundations of the Romanesque abbey were laid. This was added to over the following centuries with the Gothic stylings of the Merveille, constructed in the 1200s.

Notwithstanding its almost supernatural appearance, Mont-Saint-Michel really worked its way into the hearts of the French people during the Hundred Years' War, when, despite being in the heart of conquered territory, it managed to hold out against 30 years of English siege. It's even said that this remarkable story of resistance helped to inspire Joan of Arc to eventually lead the French to victory in the same conflict, concretizing Mont-Saint-Michel as a French talisman.

That did not prevent the island from being converted into a prison during the French Revolution, the monks being moved out, and the whole monument falling into a state of disrepair. In the 1830s, however, a group of French conservationists, including novelist Victor Hugo, led a campaign to restore the Mont. The prison was closed in 1863, and it was declared a historic monument in 1874, then a UNESCO World Heritage Site in 1979.

ORIENTATION

A tidal island built to reflect the strictly hierarchical medieval vision of the world, Mont-Saint-Michel becomes more impressive the closer you get to its center—and by implication its highest point. This vision is reflected in its modern-day layout. The mainland, which sits across the tidal bay about two miles south of the Mont itself, but still part of the same municipality, has become a kind of mass-tourism purgatory. This is where almost all visitors to Mont-Saint-Michel will arrive, whether by car, foot, bicycle, or the buses from Mont-Saint-Michel's "gateway" town, Pontorson, roughly six miles farther south.

In mainland Mont-Saint-Michel, private vehicles can't even be left in view of the monument. They can only get as far as an extensive parking area just south of the gaudy strip of restaurants and hotels. From there, a well signposted footpath takes you directly to a shuttle-bus service station, where free shuttle buses are constantly pulling in to provide lifts across the new causeway bridge, built in 2014, connecting the Mont to the mainland regardless of tides. It's also possible to just walk across the causeway, which if you've the time is highly recommended, for Mont-Saint-Michel is in your sightline for the entire walk, and it is a building that rewards a sustained study.

At low tide, the Mont can be reached without taking the causeway, but to do so is deceptively hazardous, thanks to quicksand and tides rushing in unexpectedly. You must find a guide if you want to take this route. There are several who offer this service, mentioned in the Information section below.

The shuttle bus drops you at the end of the causeway, just outside the main entrance in Mont-Saint-Michel's walls, the **King's Gate.** Step through here and you have the tourist office to your left, while the citadel's main and only thoroughfare, the **Grande Rue,** extends off to your right. This climbs up, spiraling left past hotels, restaurants, and souvenir shops, toward the abbey. It's fairly steep, and the trip to the abbey takes about 10-15 minutes depending on your level of fitness—keep an eye out for the Parish Church, which is on the left-hand side of the street, about three-quarters of the way up.

Fortunately, there's almost no chance of getting lost, given that the Grande Rue is the only big street in the whole place. Its walls, though, are pocked by numerous tiny side alleys and stairways, which burrow in other

Louis d'Estouteville and the Defense of Mont-Saint-Michel

The 1420s were a dark time for the French people. Decades of bloody fighting in the Hundred Years' War had seen them suffer defeat on top of defeat and pushed them deep into their ancestral homeland around Paris. The English occupied much of Normandy, and even the cathedral town of Reims was in their hands, leaving the French unable to officially crown their king. France's very existence was under threat.

THE RESISTANCE

And yet Mont-Saint-Michel resisted. Despite being deep in English-occupied territory, the treacherous tides and high walls of this abbey fortress meant the invaders were unable to break its resolve. And though the Mont was of very little strategic importance, it became a symbol of French resistance. Indeed, it's no exaggeration to say that the string from which the abbey hung in those volatile years was the same one suspending France itself: Had Mont-Saint-Michel fallen, it's very likely the whole country would have followed.

SECURING THE MONT

Enter Louis d'Estouteville, a name that should echo in the pantheon of French heroes almost as loud as Joan d'Arc herself. A member of old Norman nobility and named captain of Mont-Saint-Michel in 1424, he fast set to work implementing tactics and extreme measures that would eventu-

directions through the citadel, most taking you up to its ramparts, which rim the circumference of the monument—there's no real reason to take to these routes, though, as the ramparts are also directly accessible once you've seen the abbey. The entrance to the abbey itself, meanwhile, is unmissable at the end of the Grande Rue, and once you're inside the site, a route is clearly signposted.

At low tide, it's also possible to head back through the main entrance and tour the sands around Mont-Saint-Michel's walls before your return.

VISITING MONT-SAINT-MICHEL

Mont-Saint-Michel is a major international tourist site housed in the architecture of the Middle Ages, and frankly it's too small to have a particularly bespoke experience in. The best strategy for a visit is to come to terms with being part of the crowd. Everything has been set up as best it can to help funnel visitors from carpark to causeway to abbey and back again, and there's little sense going against the flow.

That said, a few tips on how to maximize your experience: Arrive as early as you can to avoid the worst of the crowds, walk across the causeway rather than take the bus to bask in the Mont's splendor for longer, and consider packing a picnic to enjoy in one of the small garden spaces that are just a tier below the abbey, and can be reached directly from the end of the Grande Rue, following La Truie Qui File. These gardens are usually a little quieter than the rest of the monument, and having your own food avoids the hiked prices of restaurants inside the citadel walls.

A visit to the abbey is a must—you can barely say you've been to Mont-Saint-Michel if you haven't seen its crowning glory! Tickets are sold at the door; there's a very efficient system, so don't expect to have to queue too long. Free guided tours in multiple languages leave from the western terrace of the abbey regularly. Don't feel too obliged to go on such a tour, however; the magic of the place is plain even without a deep understanding of its history.

ally turn the tide of battle. First, he strictly forbade the entrance of women and children into the citadel, deeming them extra mouths to feed, and also saying that they'd get in the way in the case of full frontal attack. Similarly, he then oversaw the transfer of prisoners of war elsewhere—no easy feat when you're deep in enemy territory, under siege, not to mention surrounded by miles and miles of temperamental tidal plain.

TURNING THE TIDE

He then began to win battles. In 1425, by giving the impression that Mont-Saint-Michel's garrison was more diminished than it in fact was, he lured an unsuspecting English battalion out onto the bay at low tide, then had the full weight of his forces assault them by surprise. The result was a massacre and a bloody tide, as the English stumbled through the mud and oncoming sea trying to escape.

Still the siege kept on, and it was not until 1434 that a truly decisive battle was fought, the English using rudimentary artillery to bring down some of Mont-Saint-Michel's walls. Knights and men-at-arms were soon fighting through the rubble, met in bloody hand-to-hand fighting by the Norman defenders under Louis d'Estouteville's command. It's reckoned close to 2,000 English were killed in that assault. This broke their spirit, and soon the French were able to ride forth, surprising the English garrison at Avranches, then taking the towns of Tombelaine and Granville soon after.

SIGHTS

TOP EXPERIENCE

★ The Abbey

Abbaye du Mont-Saint-Michel; www.abbaye-mont-saint-michel.fr; 9:30am-6pm daily Jan. 2-Apr. 30, 9am-7pm daily May 2-Aug. 31, 9:30am-6pm daily Sept. 1-Dec. 31; adults €10, non-EU residents 18-25 €8, EU residents under 26 and everyone under 18 free

Towering over the rest of the island like God in heaven, Mont-Saint-Michel's Romanesque and Gothic abbey had humble beginnings in the 8th-century dreams of Bishop Aubert d'Avranches. The holy figure claimed to have been visited by the archangel Michael, who instructed him three times to construct an oratory on what was then a tidal island called Mont Tombe.

The island soon became a pilgrimage center, and despite some wavering fortunes, over the next centuries its monks were able to exploit both this and Mont-Saint-Michel's natural advantages to accrue a corrupting level of wealth and power. Their decadence was recognized by Norman dukes, who forcibly replaced them with monks of the Benedictine order in the 10th century. The Benedictine monks steadily began developing the abbey structures, adding to it building by building, architectural style by architectural style, over the following centuries, creating a symphony in gray stone, which belongs as much to high fantasy fiction as it does the real world.

To visit today is like walking through history. Thanks to the large numbers who come here, there's a bit of a sense of being on railway tracks, and you can hardly be expected to confront every building in the strict chronological order in which it was built. But there's plenty of time to linger if you choose to take yourself around rather than follow one of the free guides (they leave regularly from the western terrace, and you needn't feel guilty tuning in if you see one passing).

The specific sights of the abbey are described below in the order that you encounter them, though the first place you will reach after buying your ticket, which gives access to the whole place, is the western terrace, a spectacular open space with commanding views out in every direction across Mont-Saint-Michel Bay, and down to the citadel ramparts.

A self-guided tour can take anywhere from 30 minutes to two hours, while one with a group should take about an hour. There are also audio tours available when you buy your tickets. These cost an extra €3, and should last about an hour.

THE ABBEY CHURCH

With its transept crossing at the very pinnacle of the mount and its spire reaching toward heaven, a total height of 557 feet (170 meters) above sea level, the abbey's church is Mont-Saint-Michel's symbolic heart and defines its iconic silhouette known around the world. Situated on a 262-foot-long (80-meter-long) platform, built over preexisting crypts built into the spur of the rock, the building has its origins in the early years of the 11th century and combines a Romanesque nave (central area) and Gothic chancel (the space around the altar). This mélange provides an arresting juxtaposition between somber and heavy, in the case of the former, and light-filled and uplifting, in the case of the latter. There's also a subtler magic that you feel stepping inside, just knowing how improbably high up all this weight of stone has been erected.

LA MERVEILLE

Given that its name literally means "the marvel," it's fair to say that the Gothic builders of the north side of Mont-Saint-Michel Abbey knew something of what they had achieved: one of the architectural masterpieces of the 13th century (a period that was not lacking in architectural masterpieces). Indeed, it's hard not to be impressed by the construction's scale and evident power. Built over 17 years, La Merveille consists of three layered levels, reaching up 115 feet (35 meters) from the rock, and is supported by no less than 16 buttresses. Though profoundly Gothic, there are hints here of the earlier Romanesque style on lower levels, where a somber simplicity still reigns. Comprising La Merveille are many of the abbey's most famous halls and spaces, including the cloisters, the Knight's Hall, and the refectory.

THE CLOISTERS

Cloisters, covered walkways that form a continuous quadrangle in the shadow of a cathedral or church, are an architectural design aimed to both symbolically and literally create a barrier between monks and the rest of the world (hence "cloistered life"). The cloisters at Mont-Saint-Michel are no exception. Designed in the 13th century, its gallery arcades are decorated in intricate carvings of both figures and foliage, while its central garden, festooned with herbaceous plants, is a good reminder despite the tourists that this was once a sanctuary and site of almost domestic calm. It's worth spending some time here to see if you can find a gap in the constant stream of visitors, in order to practice some quiet contemplation of your own. This said, if you do this in the high season, you might be waiting quite some time.

THE REFECTORY

Surely one of the most impressive cafeterias in the world, this hall is where Mont-Saint-Michel's monks sat down for their meals. Its Gothic credentials are clear from how light-filled it is—Gothic architecture is the architecture of light—with tall, thin windows between each of the many arches that run its flanks. A couple of long lines of austere wooden tables and benches offer a reminder of its original purpose, their simplicity providing a strong contrast with the rest of the space. Built between 1211 and 1218, it was among the first rooms of La Merveille to be constructed.

THE KNIGHTS' HALL

Boasting a somewhat militaristic name, this glorious space was in fact used by the monks

1: tourists walking Mont-Saint-Michel Bay **2:** the Cloisters **3**: The Mont's ramparts are little defense against some visitors.

1
2
3

for reading and study. Characterized by a forest of evenly spaced stone pillars which bloom into a canopy of intricate vaulting, the room has otherwise been left bare, meaning you can really appreciate its interior architecture. For a long time, it was also believed to be a space used for producing illuminated manuscripts, though this now is thought unlikely. The "knight" moniker, meanwhile, is believed to be a reference to the Order of Saint Michael, founded by Louis XI in 1469, with the abbey as its seat. Whatever its truths, the majesty of its appearance is indisputable.

THE GUESTS' HALL

Dating from 1213, there's something faintly unassuming about this room's name, given that the guests received here were only of the most important stripe, including several French kings, and the receptions took the form of banquets. A curtain of tapestries is hung in the room's center, designating half of it as a dining hall and the other half a kitchen—the latter is recognizable by its two enormous chimneys. Otherwise, it has been left bare.

THE CRYPTS

The oldest parts of the abbey—pre-Gothic, even pre-Romanesque—the three crypts were only rediscovered at the close of the 19th century. With no natural light, cramped, and pressured by the sediments of history layered above, stepping inside them, more than anywhere else on the Mont, feels like stepping back in time. All the stone that surrounds them also serves to deaden noise from the outside world, and often compels visitors into silence, as though suddenly reminded they are walking through a religious institution.

Particularly impressive is the Crypte des Gros Piliers, which, as its name would suggest, boasts 10 enormous granite pillars bearing the weight of the abbey above.

Adding to the evocative atmosphere, the humble chapel Notre-Dame-sous-Terre is also down here, an ancient space of rough-hewn stone, and arches that look like they could belong in Roman antiquity—it's a striking reminder of Christianity's humble foundations, which can otherwise be hard to recall in such a grandiose building. According to legend, this chapel was built in the same spot as the first church built here by Saint Aubert, founder of Mont-Saint-Michel in the 8th century, and was where the bishop's bones were laid after he died.

THE GREAT WHEEL

Sometimes, for all the majesty of world-famous monuments, it is their human-scale details that prove most evocative of their history. The Great Wheel is surely such a feature. This human-size wooden hamster wheel dates from when Mont-Saint-Michel abbey was being used as a prison, which it moonlighted as during the 15th-19th centuries. Inmates would stand inside of it and walk to turn a cog and haul provisions up to their place of incarceration. It stands behind barriers over an opening in the abbey walls, which leads to the ramp up which goods would be hauled.

The Village

www.ot-montsaintmichel.com

With a pedigree as old as the abbey, Mont-Saint-Michel's village is a tight medieval tangle of modern commerce, tourists, and none-too-few tourist-trap hotels. Despite the odds, it retains a glimmer of magic, in part because of the resilience of its picturesque half-timber and stone architecture, but mostly because, in many respects, this is exactly what it has always been. As a pilgrimage center, Mont-Saint-Michel has a long history of visitors outnumbering residents (currently, the ratio is around 2.5 million to 50), and of businesses cashing in on its popularity. Which means, if you're going to get fleeced anywhere, there are few places in France more authentic than here. In terms of size, the village is hardly much more than the Grande Rue high street, which coils scarcely more than a few hundred yards up toward Mont-Saint-Michel abbey; don't expect many practical amenities, aside from a post office. Otherwise, it's just restaurants, hotels, and souvenir stalls, which are mostly overpriced.

The Ramparts

As well as being a pilgrimage center, Mont-Saint-Michel's naturally isolated position made it a military stronghold. The sturdy granite fortifications that ring the Mont were built between the 13th and 16th centuries, coming in particularly important during the 100 Years' War, when the town held out for 30 years against besieging English forces—two rudimentary canons, called bombards, are left over from this time, and now displayed near the entrance to the Mont itself. The ramparts remain every inch the archetype of medieval defenses, consisting of long walkways, sections of evocative staircase, and fortified towers. Today, they make for a fine walk, offering great views out across the bay and indeed down into the scrum of Mont-Saint-Michel's streets. The best way to experience them is after a visit to the abbey. They are well signposted on the exit and make for a good route back down to the base of the citadel, avoiding the human traffic of tourists climbing up the Grande rue. You can get back to street level via a stairway, just before the King's Gate.

Parish Church

Église Saint-Pierre du Mont-Saint-Michel, Grande Rue, Le Mont-Saint-Michel; tel. 02 33 60 14 05; 9am-10pm daily; free

A small church built in the 11th century, then added to in the 15th and 16th, this makes for a nice stop off as you make your way up toward the abbey—it's on the left, about three-quarters of the way up the Grande Rue. It's a neat reminder that there is a human scale to religion as well as a majestic one. It is dedicated to Saint Peter, who among his many other roles was the patron saint of fishermen, a career that once would have occupied many of the island's residents. Though a bit of a mongrel in its design, it's a place of relative calm and contemplation amid the tourist crush and has some very pretty stained glass windows. It is furnished with art from the abbey, including a 15th-century statue of the Virgin and child, plus a stunning wood carving of Saint Michael.

★ The Bay

As important to Mont-Saint-Michel's grandeur and unique history as any other part of the monument, this remarkable tidal bay oscillates from sea to vast mud flat and back to sea again throughout the year. To walk out here is a surreal, almost extraterrestrial experience; it's a biosphere, after all, that few are familiar with, uncanny in its emptiness, and which feels at turns like some vast desert, or walking on the surface of a shallow sea.

In the past, this was considered a treacherous and almost mystical landscape, known for tides coming in "faster than a galloping horse," mysterious suddenly-descending fogs for which the abbey bells would peal in warning, and hidden quicksand—there's even a tale relayed by the Bayeux Tapestry about Harold Godwinson, the English king later defeated by William the Conqueror, rescuing someone from just this hazard.

These days, though still dangerous to the unprepared, the bay has been thoroughly mapped, and thus its tides are better understood and predicted. And of course the bridge to the mainland makes the Mont accessible high tide or low. Nevertheless, while a meander here close to the village walls should be trouble free, stray any farther than that and a guide is a necessary safety precaution. Keep in mind, too, that this is a wilderness area, with no deliberate concessions to tourists. That means that even right by the walls, there are no duck boards to walk on (so you might get sandy, wet shoes), and no handrails to steady your balance. This is another way of saying that there's no marked path; you simply step off the causeway onto the sand and start walking.

For further information about tides, consult with the tourist office, either in the citadel itself or on the mainland. Otherwise, look in the information section for suggestions on guides.

FOOD

Any island is a closed system where tourist traps can proliferate, and Mont-Saint-Michel is no exception. A large number of eateries here charge far too much for cynically bad cuisine, but here are a few options where you'll be able to find a decent meal. Another excellent way to avoid the many tourist traps of the island, though it requires a bit of forward planning due to the scarcity of supermarkets in the Mont-Saint-Michel area itself, is to prepare a picnic before coming, and settle down to eat it in one of the many picturesque gardens around the monument.

Local Cuisine

LA MÈRE POULARD

Grande Rue; www.merepoulard.com; tel. 02 33 89 68 68; 11am-10pm daily; menus €38-65

Unique and justifiably famous, even if the amount they charge for a few eggs may resemble daylight robbery for some, La Mère Poulard has been feeding visitors to Mont-Saint-Michel since 1888. The original Madame Poulard was born Anne Boutiaut, and she invented the restaurant's characteristic giant omelets cooked in copper pans over an open fire as a way of encouraging visitors to linger on the island a little longer rather than rush back to beat the tides. The resulting dish is more like a soufflé than a traditional omelet, and comes served with luxurious sides. If the price is not too much, you'll take your place among luminaries such as Ernest Hemingway and Yves Saint Laurent. It's located just the other side of the King's Gate to the Mont-Saint-Michel citadel.

HÔTEL DU GUESCLIN

Grande Rue; www.hotelduguesclin.com; 11:30am-2pm and 6:30pm-8:30pm daily; menu €20

The restaurant of Hôtel du Guesclin offers competitively priced hearty local flavors, including *agneau de pré-salé*—lamb raised in the surrounding salt marshes and therefore considered "pre-seasoned." One of the few good places to eat actually in the citadel itself, the dining area is bright and formal and has some fine views across the bay.

RESTAURANT LA RÔTISSERIE

Route du Mont-Saint-Michel; https://restaurants.le-mont-saint-michel.com/la-rotisserie; tel. 02 33 89 68 68; 12pm-2pm and 7pm-9:15pm daily; menu €21-27

Part of the strip of hotels and restaurants leading to the bridge that connects the mainland to Mont-Saint-Michel, this is a

The local lamb meat has a unique salty flavor from grazing on the tidal plain.

family-friendly, spacious, and comfortable restaurant. It may not boast much in terms of character or tradition, but for casual dining at a reasonable price and with decent local food, it's a good choice. If you're put off by the traditional selection of mussels or beef in a cider sauce, they do a solid hamburger, too.

RESTAURANT LE PRÉ SALÉ

Route du Mont-Saint-Michel; tel. 02 33 60 24 17; https://restaurants.le-mont-saint-michel.com/le-pre-sale; 12pm-2pm and 7pm-9:15pm daily; menus €18-35

This restaurant on the strip offers slightly classier cuisine in a more formal setting, and for a higher price than its competitors. *Pré-salé* lamb, raised on the nearby salt marshes, is, as the restaurant name suggests, its specialty, and can be ordered either as a grilled loin or a roasted rack.

LA FERME SAINT MICHEL

Lieu-dit, Le Bas Pays; tel. 02 33 58 46 79; www.restaurantfermesaintmichel.com; 12pm-2pm and 7pm-9pm Thurs.-Mon.; menus €22-45

An authentic, high-quality, rustic-style restaurant that can feel a welcome relief in comparison to the other polished, slightly soulless eateries on Mont-Saint-Michel's mainland. Family-run and located within an old farm building a little back from the main drag, the food is excellent and, where it can be, locally sourced. Group dining and a less expensive snack bar are also options.

Budget Options

LA SIRÈNE LOCHET

Grande Rue; tel. 02 33 60 08 60; 11:45am-3pm daily; €10

A straightforward *crêperie* nestled in the tight lanes of Mont-Saint-Michel village's Grande Rue. To be sure, it doesn't set the world alight, but the prices are low given its location, and there are several vegetarian options on the menu. It can get busy in high season.

CRÊPERIE LA CLOCHE

Grande Rue, Le Mont-Saint-Michel; tel. 02 33 68 80 26; 11:45am-3pm daily; €10

Another decent, inexpensive *crêperie* on Mont-Saint-Michel island itself. The point here is not so much that you'll get a great meal; more that you'll avoid a bad one. The staff are efficient and it's a clean, pleasant setting. Great for a fortifying meal after walking across to the island and exploring the ramparts in preparation for a visit to the abbey.

LA BELLEVOISINE

40 route du Mont-Saint-Michel, Beauvoir; tel. 02 33 48 04 72; 7am-7pm Thurs.-Tues.; baguettes from €1

A colorful bakery, just back from the main Mont-Saint-Michel compound, and a good place to load up on bread, patisseries, or sandwiches, which you can then bring with you to the citadel for a picnic on one of its green spaces. It's not going to win any awards compared to some bakeries in France, but the bread is nevertheless baked fresh every day, and shopping here is both a way to keep costs down and to feel satisfied that you're somehow beating the system.

ACCOMMODATIONS

€50-100

HÔTEL SAINT AUBERT

Lieu-dit La Caserne, Le Bas Pays; tel. 02 33 60 08 74; www.saint-aubert.com; from €67 d

Named after the founder of the famous abbey, this is one of the less-expensive hotels in the immediate vicinity of Mont-Saint-Michel. Located in a restored farmhouse, it is comfortable, clean, and cozy, and has a large terrace garden space for relaxing in after a long day exploring the Mont. A breakfast buffet is served on-site, and there's free WiFi throughout.

AUBERGE DE LA BAIE

44 route de la Rive Ardevon, Pontorson; tel. 02 33 68 26 70; https://hotels.le-mont-saint-michel.com/auberge-de-baie; from €69 d

Being a short drive from the Mont-Saint-Michel complex of hotels means that this place is priced lower than much of its competition. It's a straightforward hotel with few bells and whistles, but is nevertheless comfortable and clean, making it perfectly acceptable if all you're looking for is a place to rest your head for the night, especially if you want to be a little outside the tourist crush. Mont-Saint-Michel can be seen from some of its rooms, and all have WiFi and flat-screen TVs. There's also an on-site restaurant, which makes up for the somewhat isolated location.

€100-200

HÔTEL DU GUESCLIN

Grande Rue; tel. 02 33 60 14 10; www.hotelduguesclin.com; from €105 d

One of the best-value deals on the island, though that being said, don't expect too much for your money. The rooms are clean, and comfortable in a somewhat twee way, though not especially big. Of course, the real luxury is being able to go to sleep and wake up on Mont-Saint-Michel itself, getting the island at its best times, when there are the fewest tourists about. WiFi is available throughout, and the on-site restaurant comes recommended.

L'ANCIEN PRESBYTÈRE D'ARDEVON

1 route de la Rive, Bourg d'Ardevon; tel. 07 81 24 35 78; from €150 d

Though hardly four miles (six kilometers) from Mont-Saint-Michel, L'Ancien Presbytère d'Ardevon offers the feeling of being almost anywhere in the idyll of rural France, unspoiled by the massive crowds arriving from Paris every day. Located in a sturdy old country mansion, this bed-and-breakfast is a study in rustic luxury, with a beautiful garden terrace and a log fire in the winter. Bicycles can be borrowed directly from the property to bike the nearby area, and even across to Mont-Saint-Michel itself should you feel like it. WiFi is available throughout.

Over €200

LA MÈRE POULARD

Grande Rue, Mont-Saint-Michel; tel. 02 33 89 68 68; www.lamerepoulard.com; from €200 d

This 19th-century hotel, like the famous omelet restaurant it's attached to, can feel overpriced to some. The rooms are old-fashioned and, especially in the lowest price bracket, not especially large, but you do feel like you're staying in a piece of living history, and it's hard to put a price on the experience of spending the night on Mont-Saint-Michel itself. WiFi, minibars, and flat-screen TVs are in all rooms.

L'ERMITAGE MONT-SAINT-MICHEL

14 route du Mont-Saint-Michel, Beauvoir; tel. 02 33 50 60 00; www.lemsm.com; from €370 d

Five-star luxury in a beautifully restored old building, just outside of the main Mont-Saint-Michel complex. Plush is the best way to describe the interiors here, which overflow with sumptuous furniture and decoration: The bathrooms are a particular highlight. For such an obviously high-class establishment, there's also a surprisingly personal touch, with the owners being hands-on, friendly, and accommodating. There is a top-end restaurant on-site, and a garden terrace. Free WiFi is available throughout, and all rooms have not one, but two flat-screen TVs.

INFORMATION AND SERVICES

Tourist Information

Boulevard Avancée, Le Mont-Saint-Michel; tel. 02 33 60 14 30; www.ot-montsaintmichel.com; 10am-5:30pm daily

Unsurprisingly, there is no shortage of tourist information at Mont-Saint-Michel, with all hotels and hotel staff very accommodating in terms of offering advice and brochures on tours to take and activities to partake in. Furthermore, there is probably more English spoken here than any one single place in Normandy. The official tourist office is just to the left as you enter the walls of Mont-Saint-Michel village, and it is open every day of the year between 10am and 5:30pm, with a pause for lunch and slightly longer opening hours in the summer. It is a great place to organize tours of the island. Another tourist information center is on the mainland (Le Bas Pays, Beauvoir; tel. 02 33 70 74 65; 9am-7pm daily). This modern building offers a good way to familiarize yourself with some of the history and natural surroundings of Mont-Saint-Michel before your visit.

Bay Tour Guides

Because of aggressive tides, quicksand, and fast-changing weather conditions, Mont-Saint-Michel's bay is too treacherous to venture out onto without a guide. Naturally enough, then, given its popularity among tourists, a decent number of companies have sprung up to cater to the demand of people wanting to explore this strange landscape and learn more about its wildlife and geology. Good ones to get in contact with are **Découverte de la Baie** (tel. 02 33 70 83 49; www.decouvertebaie.com) and **François Lamotte d'Argy** (tel. 02 33 48 93 38; www.traversee-montsaintmichel.com). Both offer several different tours, which do not all leave from the main Mont-Saint-Michel compound. The specific company will let you know where to meet, depending on the tour you book; all departure points though, are, of course, fairly close by to the Mont.

Post Office

Grande Rue, 50170 Le Mont-Saint-Michel; 9:30am-12pm and 1:30pm-4:30pm Mon.-Fri., 9:30am-12pm Sat.

Despite its small size, Mont-Saint-Michel has a fully functioning post office squeezed on the Grande Rue. It's perfect for sending off postcards just bought in stores nearby, and it also offers a money exchange and an ATM.

TRANSPORTATION

Getting There

BY CAR

As one of the most popular monuments in France, Mont-Saint-Michel is as well signposted as a major city, with road signs across Brittany and Normandy pointing you in the right direction. Mont-Saint-Michel sits at the northern end of the D976, which comes from the D175 at Pontorson, which is about six miles (10 kilometers) and 20 minutes away.

From Paris to Mont-Saint-Michel, take the A13, then the A84. It's a journey of about 220 miles (354 kilometers) and takes around four hours. Expect to pay some toll charges on the freeways, which cost about €20.

From Caen, it's around 80 miles (128 kilometers) west along the A84 and takes about 1.5 hours. From Rennes in Brittany, it's about 50 miles (80 kilometers) north, also along the A84 and takes about an hour.

From Saint-Malo, meanwhile, the journey is 30 miles (48 kilometers) and involves heading south first to join up with the N176, then heading east. It's a journey that should take 40 minutes. Similarly, from Granville, head inland a bit, taking the D973 until it meets up with the N175. This is a journey also of about 30 miles (48 kilometers), though it will likely take a little longer, thanks to the roads being smaller—around 50 minutes.

The parking lots at Mont-Saint-Michel are €12.50 for 24 hours. Free parking can be found in the village of Beauvoir, but the walk to the monument is farther.

BY TRAIN

Run by France's national operator SNCF (www.sncf.com/fr), trains from the rest of the country arrive at the station (place de la Gare, Pontorson; tel. 02 33 60 00 35) in the town of **Pontorson**, six miles (10 kilometers) south of Mont-Saint-Michel. These include three services per day from Caen (€28, 1.75 hours) and 3-4 from Rennes (€15, 50 minutes). There are an average of five departures from Paris every day that will reach Pontorson, requiring changes at either Rennes or Villedieu-les-Poêles (€70, four hours). Though it's very unlikely any of the trains will sell out, for the longer journeys (i.e., from Paris) it's worth booking in advance to keep prices down.

From Pontorson, a **shuttle bus** completes

The Channel Islands

Representing a strange echo of European history, despite their extreme proximity to France, the Channel Islands, just off La Manche's western coast, remain a protectorate of the British crown. The reasons for this are, unsurprisingly, complex, though effectively can be boiled down to the islands being fought over a lot between the English and French in the 14th century, and the English under Edward III ultimately emerging victorious.

Their status remains curious, however, never having been fully absorbed as part of the United Kingdom of Great Britain, but rather existing as dependencies of the Crown. This circumstance means they have remained separate from the British Commonwealth and the European Union.

What they are considered is remnants of the Duchy of Normandy; for this Queen Elizabeth II is still frequently referred to there by her traditional title, the Duke of Normandy. Indeed, the systems of government on the Islands still date from the Norman era, with legislative bodies there still being termed States, derived from the Norman Etats. These days, these are run democratically.

Despite all this, the feel of the islands is distinctly British, with the TV, radio, and newspapers all in English, and pubs outnumbering cafés. The two largest islands are Jersey and Guernsey, with populations of around 100,000 and 60,000, respectively. Of the rest, only six are inhabited, while many are no much more than rocks, making up a large archipelago.

the journey to Mont-Saint-Michel. This shuttle bus runs 11 times a day between 7:35am and 9:45pm, costs €2.90 for a one-way journey, and drops you right outside of Mont-Saint-Michel citadel itself, with stops in the Mont-Saint-Michel mainland site, as well. Journey times are about 20 minutes. Stopping immediately outside Pontorson station, this bus is identifiable because it will have "Mont-Saint-Michel" written clearly as its destination in its frontal display. Buy tickets onboard.

BY BUS

Four buses run all the way to Mont-Saint-Michel every day from Rennes (€15; 1 hour 15 minutes), and around two from Paris (€30; 4.5 hours). These are run alternately by **Ouibus** (www.ouibus.com) and **Flixbus** (www.flixbus.com), two relative newcomers to France's intercity travel game. From Paris, the Ouibus leaves from Clichy in the city's north, while Flixbus leaves from Bercy in the west. From Rennes all buses leave from outside the station. At Mont-Saint-Michel, they stop right next to the shuttle bus station.

Getting Around

Traffic is heavily restricted in the Mont-Saint-Michel area itself, and unless staying in one of the hotels, visitors are expected to park their cars before they even reach the mainland village (parking is €12.50 per day). If you are staying at that village, the closest you can get to the Mont by car is still only your hotel parking lot.

There are several options for getting to the island, however. The most common is to take the regular shuttle buses, which are free and leave very regularly from just after the parking lot area, taking about 10 minutes. The more romantically inclined might want to get on board one of the wagons drawn by a couple of sturdy horses. These are sheltered and usually carry 10-20 people at a time. They leave almost as regularly and from the same place as the shuttle buses, with the 45-minute ride costing €5.30 per person (you pay onboard). The final option is to walk.

A general tip is the slower you approach the better, for it allows for a full appreciation of the view of the Mont and of the subtle changes it undergoes the closer you get. The walk from the parking lot is a little under two miles (three kilometers) and should take less than an hour. Once in the village walls, everything must be explored on foot.

Barneville-Carteret and the Côte des Îles

The western coast of the Cotentin Peninsula is a land of long sandy beaches, impressive tidal reach, and old-fashioned seaside resorts that still cling to the spirit of the belle epoque. Rubbing alongside the British-owned Channel Islands, there's a sense of intertwined culture and history between France and its overseas neighbor here, too. British radio stations dominate the airwaves and regular ferry services leave for Jersey and Guernsey every day; even the name Carteret comes from a famous English family, who once ran the town and many other places along the coast.

Though the towns can get busy in the summer, they are well-prepped for all visitors, meaning hotels, restaurants, and activities are plentiful. Beyond the resorts, there's also a feel of rugged wildness to the landscape here. Facing west toward the Atlantic, storms can be more severe than in the sheltered east of the peninsula, and there's something quite awe-inspiring about the vast stretches of sand and large dunes, which are on an almost New World scale.

ORIENTATION

The Côte des Îles extends along 20 miles (32 kilometers) of coastline, from the commune of Baubigny in the north to Denneville in the south. It faces west, toward the Channel Islands, hence its name. The towns and beaches along the coast are connected by the arterial D650, which has plenty of turnoffs.

Barneville-Carteret is the largest of these towns and is located more or less at the midpoint of the coast. As its name would suggest, it is effectively two towns, which came together to form a single commune in 1964. They are split by the mouth of the Gerfleur River, with north bank Carteret being the livelier, more resort-like of the two, and more restaurants and hotels bordering its harbor and close to its beach; it's also home to the Channel Islands ferry port. The Cap de Carteret is at the far western edge of the town, and takes the form of a rocky headland from which you can look north across the Hatainville Dunes. There's a large parking lot just behind it, which is also convenient for Carteret's Plage de la Potinière.

Barneville, meanwhile, centers away from the sea, originally built on a hill just back from the coast. Its beachfront is primarily residential and consists of campsites and vacation homes. Despite sitting right next to each other, getting between Barneville and Carteret requires heading inland and driving about 10 minutes.

The area's other major town, **Portbail,** is about seven miles farther south. It is also fastest reached by the D650. Similar to Barneville, its center is away from the sea, hugging a large inlet, which is entirely sandy when the tide is low. It has a beachfront, made up entirely of vacation housing, which can be reached by taking the Route de la Plage west, across the fine old bridge out of town.

SIGHTS

Beach Cabins of Carteret

Plage de la Potinière, 6 rue du Port, Barneville-Carteret

The simple pleasure of bathing in the sea began to take hold in France in the 19th century, with Carteret being among the first towns recommissioned as a resort to serve that purpose. Beach huts were assembled to protect beachgoers' modesty when they wanted to change into their swimming costumes. Prettily colored in white and blue, 67 of them still remain standing on La Potinière beach today, positioned in one long line at the far north end of the Plage de la Potinière, facing the sea. They are a reminder of a more

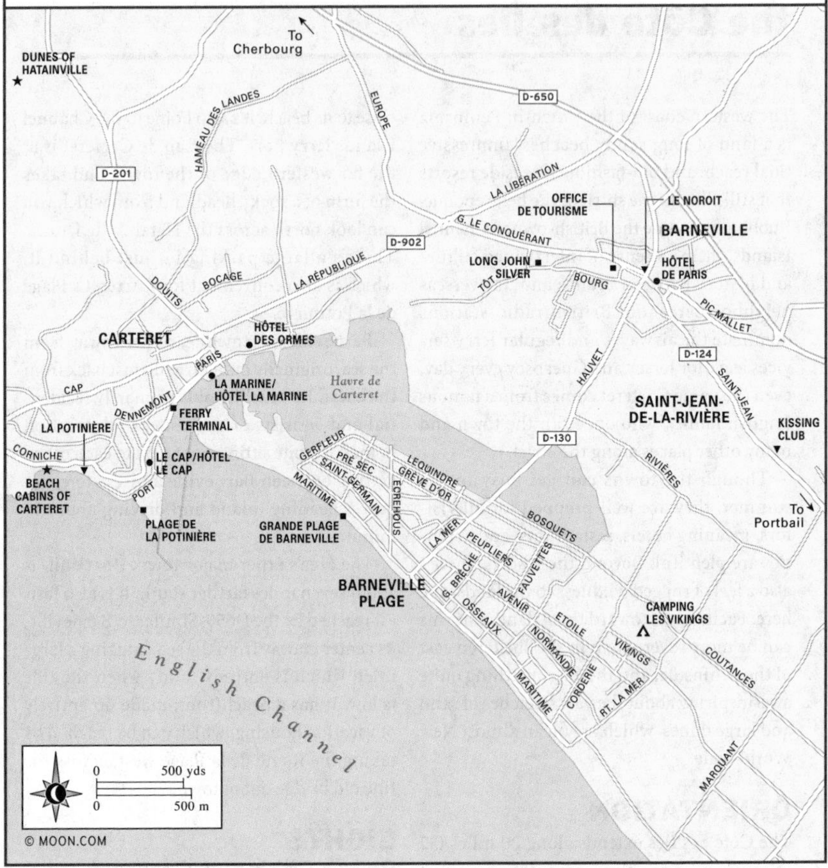

conservative world and lend a civilized atmosphere to Carteret's otherwise quite wild-feeling beach. They are still in use by individuals who lease them over an extended period (think decades) from the Barneville-Carteret municipality. The waiting list to lease a cabin for yourself is understandably very long: You pretty much need to have your name down since childhood to stand a chance.

★ Dunes of Hatainville

Plage d'Hatainville, D242, Les Moitiers-d'Allonne

North of Cape Carteret runs an undulating field of dunes, peaking 262 feet (80 meters) above sea level and stretching a couple of miles back from the shore. Previously mobile, the dunes have been stabilized in recent years by the construction of wooden fences and the deliberate planting of grasses across their surface. Varying in color and form, they offer a mosaic of vegetation, from the pinks of orchids to the yellow-brown of ophrys to the mauve of thyme, and are a haven for rare wildlife, including cormorants, warblers, and even dolphins offshore. They also make for a spectacular area to explore on foot and are crossed by the GR223 hiking trail. Paths are obvious, and well signposted, and there are a couple of parking lots at the far western end of Carteret from which you can begin. The one slightly to the north is closer to the dunes and therefore slightly more convenient. Walking paths lead directly from this parking lot—make sure to keep to these as you explore the area, so as not to damage the natural environment.

Portbail's Old Town

An ancient port town that, thanks to the five Roman roads connected to it, is believed to have once been a major stopover in the ancient tin trade between Cornwall and the Mediterranean, it is also, according to legend, where the relics of Saint George arrived in France. Today, it remains a charming jumble of gray stone buildings, sat on the edge of a large tidal inlet. The town has several sights worth seeking out.

Evidence of the its Roman heritage, for example, is seen in a 6th-century baptistery, built at the very start of the Christianization of Cotentin. Only the foundations of this building are left: hexagonal and 30 feet (9 meters) wide, they look almost like a fossil of social history, with the remnants of the font itself a 23-inch-deep (60-centimeter-deep) indention in the floor. The site is now protected by a modern roof.

Portbail's main church, Notre-Dame de Portbail, overlooks the inlet and dates partly from the 11th century. Inside, it is austere with worn stone slabs for the floor and a ceiling of 15th-century timber still visible. Look out for the painted statue of Saint James that dates from the 16th century.

Another highlight of the town is a long stone bridge built in 1873, which leads out across the town's tidal inlet and is notable for having an unlucky number of arches—thirteen. At high tides, this bridge can be flush with the sea level, which means when you walk over it it feels like walking on water.

★ Frescoes of Canville

L'Église Saint-Malo, Canville-la-Rocque; tel. 11 86 12 (town hall); 9am-6pm daily

Nestled in the Côte des Îles hinterland, the charming old town of Canville la Rocque guards one of the region's most beguiling treasures. Restorations of the town's Église Saint Malo in 1984 uncovered a series of Renaissance frescoes, painted on its walls in around 1520, depicting the legend of the "Pendu Dépendu" ("The Hanged Man Unhanged"), a story of a German family on the pilgrimage to Santiago de Compostela. While staying at an inn, their son refused the advances of a serving girl, who out of spite then accused him of theft. This led to the son being hanged. The rest of the family nevertheless continued on their pilgrimage, and on their return discovered him still alive, saved by a miracle from Saint James.

The frescoes are naïve and almost cartoonish in their design. But taken together, they are colorfully beautiful, and speak of an ordinary human devotion to Christianity and storytelling that was present across western Europe 500 years ago. A quiet tourist sight, it offers an intimate contemplation on the history of the region.

BEACHES

PLAGE DE LA POTINIÈRE

6 rue du Port, Barneville-Carteret

A clean beach, just past Carteret's town center, well defined by cliffs to one end and the mouth of Gerfleur River to the other. It's popular and quite built up, with its famous blue and white cabins and La Potinière bar and restaurant. Nevertheless, the main activities here are sunbathing and swimming. It can get extremely popular in the summer months, when there are lifeguards looking out for swimmers.

PLAGE DE LA VIEILLE ÉGLISE

Barneville-Carteret

Up past Cape Carteret, this is easily the wildest beach in the area, and it is backed by the impressive wilderness of the Dunes of Hatainville. The beach is ideal for surfers thanks to its sometimes turbulent waters. Be cautioned, though, that it is not monitored. The small ruined church that gives the beach its name, meanwhile, was built in honor of

1
2
LE CAP
RESTAURANT
HÔTEL★★
Logis
H
3
4

Germain à la Rouelle, an Irish saint who was said to have arrived on this coast using just the wheel of a chariot as a raft. The ruins evocatively overlook the southern end of the beach, and you can get up close to them if you want to.

GRANDE PLAGE DE BARNEVILLE

Boulevard Maritime, Barneville-Carteret

Another long, sandy beach, bordered by an esplanade, vacation homes, and campsites, it is good for swimming, with a small lifeguard post set up opposite Avenue de la Mer in the summer months. Away from Barneville center, there are fewer amenities here than might be expected, especially later into the evening, with the only café and bar closing at around sundown.

LINDBERGH-PLAGE

Lindbergh Plage, Saint-Lô-d'Ourville

South of Portbail and named after Charles Lindberg (somewhat tenuously; a local farmer claimed to have heard the American aviator flying overhead as he completed his first-ever flight the Atlantic). It's a long sandy beach, which is good for swimming. Unbuilt-up and un-monitored, there is, nevertheless, a small café just behind its dunes.

WATER SPORTS

ÉCOLE DU VENT

5 la Caillourie, Portbail; tel. 02 33 10 10 96; www.ecoledevoile-portbail.fr; kayak rental from €10 per hour; sailing courses from €130 for five days

Tucked away just the other side of the bridge leading out of Portbail, this "school of wind" specializes in kayaking, sailing, and sand surfing. The last of these makes a lot of sense when you see how it is located. Due to the area's long tidal reach, this water-sports club spends much of its time surrounded by dry land. Rental equipment, lessons, and week-long courses are available.

1: Portbail's bridge leading to the sea **2:** Le Cap Hotel and Restaurant **3:** some of the recently discovered frescoes in Canville church **4:** Plage de la Potinière in Carteret

LONG JOHN SILVER

8 chemin du Tôt, Barneville-Carteret; tel. 02 33 04 71 51; www.long-john-silver.com; cruises from €80

Located right next to the archipelago, Barneville-Carteret is an excellent place from which to launch a sailing adventure. *Long John Silver* is a 40-foot sailing boat, skippered by Jean Geurin, which can be chartered for just that. Anything from day outings to week-long cruises are available, for groups and individuals, but make sure to book ahead early as supply is limited, and demand in the summer months can be high.

ENTERTAINMENT AND EVENTS

GLISS FESTIVAL

1 place de la Mairie, Barneville-Carteret; http://glissfestival.fr; July 21-22; free

For two days every July, the beach of Barneville takes on an almost Californian aspect, when this family-friendly board-sports festival sets up along its length. As well as half-pipe and surfing competitions, kite displays and concerts augment the fun.

NIGHTLIFE

LA POTINIÈRE

16 rue du Port, Barneville-Carteret; tel. 02 33 53 75 99; http://la-potiniere-carteret.com; 11am-1:30am daily

A faultlessly located bar and restaurant on Potinière beach itself. With views straight onto the waves, it's the ideal place to grab a drink before dinner on a sunny evening. The food is excellent, too, with fresh local produce used to make straightforward, family-friendly meals at a reasonable cost. The only issue is finding a table in high season. They don't take reservations, so you'll either have to arrive early or queue.

KISSING CLUB

33 route de Barneville Portbail, Saint-Jean-de-la-Rivière; tel. 08 11 26 29 29; www.kissing-club.fr; 12pm-7am Fri.-Sun.

What self-respecting resort town could exist without a nightclub? The Kissing Club is

Barneville-Carteret's, and it offers a reasonably priced evening, complete with themed nights and a little more style than places like this tend to have outside of major urban centers. Naturally enough, its busiest times are in the high season, when young out-of-towners flock to its dance floor. It also offers free shuttles to get people there from distant areas.

FOOD

Local Cuisine

AU RENDEZ-VOUS DES PECHEURS

2 place Edmond Laquaine, Portbail; tel. 02 33 04 81 37; 9am-12am Thurs.-Mon.; mains €15

A cozy pub-like restaurant just next to Portbail's 13-arched bridge, food here is full of hearty local flavors, and there's a great friendly buzz as it also functions as a bar. There's a terrace for sunny days, too, and while it's popular, there's also extra seating upstairs, which means you'll usually be able to find a table without too much of a wait.

LE CAP

6 rue du Port, Barneville-Carteret; tel. 02 33 53 85 89; www.hotel-le-cap.fr; 12pm-1:30pm and 7pm-9:30pm daily; menus €20-41

Located just back from La Potinière beach, this hotel restaurant offers fresh local produce cooked in a straightforward manner in a semiformal setting, with interior design redolent of the sea. Where better to opt for a full seafood platter? Here it's a real showstopper. The restaurant is justly popular, even midweek, so booking ahead is always worthwhile.

LA MARINE

11 rue de Paris, Barneville-Carteret; tel. 02 33 53 83 31; www.hotelmarine.com/le-restaurant; 12pm-2pm and 7:30pm-10pm daily; menus €46-66

This top-end hotel restaurant has a Michelin star, a clean, bright dining area, and a wonderful view looking out directly on Carteret harbor. The food is elegantly presented, boasting locally sourced produce and flavors—it's strongest on fish and seafood, with the scallop soup a particular delight. The restaurant's prices and popularity reflects all this, though lunchtime menus at just €29 are an extremely good value. Booking ahead is necessary.

Budget Options

LE NOROIT

10 place du Dr Auvret, Barneville-Carteret; tel. 02 33 53 86 42; 7:30am-8pm Mon.-Sat. daily; mains €10

In Barneville's center, away from the beaches, this is a lively local restaurant and bar, which does a good line in inexpensive home-cooked food of French basics such as lightly grilled steak and roast chicken, usually with lashings of tasty fries on the side. It's a good place to head to get away from the thickest crowds.

LE TRAITEUR DU COTENTIN

Place Edmond Laquaine, Portbail; tel. 02 33 93 87 00; 8:30am-12pm most days; €10

This rudimentary charcoal-powered rotisserie stall sets up most mornings in Portbail's Place Edmond Laquaine and offers terrific take-away roast meats at a brilliantly reasonable cost—enjoy them on the beachfront or on a town square bench. They have no internet presence and can seem to make their own hours, so can't necessarily be counted on, but are well worth keeping your eyes peeled for when you're in town.

ACCOMMODATIONS

€50-100

HÔTEL LE CAP

6 rue du Port, Barneville-Carteret; tel. 02 33 53 85 89; www.hotel-le-cap.fr; from €80 d

Just a few steps back from Potinière beach, this colorful, traditional hotel offers great views of Carteret harbor from its un-trendy but comfortable rooms. There's a good on-site bar with a flower-filled terrace and a recommended restaurant. There's also on-site parking, which can prove very useful in the summer rush for spaces, and WiFi throughout.

HÔTEL DE PARIS

8 place de l'Église, Barneville-Carteret; tel. 02 33 93 17 60; http://hoteldeparis.barnevillecarteret.com; from €50 d

In Barneville center, this is a good budget

place to lay your head for the night if you're just passing through town. It's a good 20-minute walk from the beach, though there is free on-site parking, so if you want to drive the journey, you can be guaranteed space to return to. The hotel itself is fairly basic, its one concession to character being that all the rooms are named after districts of Paris. There is also an on-site bar and restaurant, and the staff are friendly.

€100-200

HÔTEL DES ORMES

Prom. J. Barbey d'Aurevilly, Barneville-Carteret; tel. 02 33 52 23 50; www.hotel-restaurant-les-ormes.fr; from €99 d

Located in an ivy-clad 19th-century property, in its own well-kept garden, this hotel offers comfort and a fresh seaside style. There are also pleasant communal spaces, which make it feel like a home away from home. Rooms with sea or harbor views come complete with satellite TVs and bathtubs. Potinière beach, meanwhile, is less than a 10-minute walk away.

HÔTEL LA MARINE

11 rue de Paris, Barneville-Carteret; tel. 02 33 53 83 31; http://www.hotelmarine.com; from €149 d

Enviably located right on Carteret harbor, this is a light-filled, modern hotel offering stylish comfortable rooms. Its white color scheme gives it a pervasive freshness precisely in tune with seaside holiday expectations. There's also the on-site Michelin-starred restaurant, and a sunny terrace area. Many of the rooms have large private balconies; all come equipped with the expected mod cons: TV, WiFi, minibars, etc.

Camping

CAMPING LES VIKINGS

4 rue les Vikings, Saint-Jean-de-la-Rivière; tel. 02 33 53 84 13; www.camping-lesvikings.com/fr; pitches from €130 per week

"Campsite" barely does justice to this complex of cabins, shops, and water slides situated a third of a mile back from Barneville Beach; it's practically its own town. For budget travelers, though, there are places to pitch tents amid the copious services. Primarily, this is a space for family holidays, so expect the kids to be in control during the busy summer months.

INFORMATION

OFFICE DE TOURISME DE LA CÔTE DES ISLES–BARNEVILLE-CARTERET

15 rue Guillaume le Conquérant, Barneville-Carteret; tel. 02 33 04 90 58; www.otcdi.com; 9:30am-1:30pm Mon. and Thurs., 9:30am-12:30pm and 2pm-5pm Fri. and Wed.

Located inland, along the main street of Barneville's town center, the main Côte des Îles tourist office is perhaps not that convenient for those making a direct line for the beaches, but it is a good place from which to plan activities and excursions up and down the coast, talking with the English-speaking staff.

TRANSPORTATION

Getting There

BY CAR

Driving yourself is by far the easiest way to get to Barneville-Carteret. From Paris take the A13 via Caen, then the N13 up to Valognes, and finally the D902 to the coast. The journey takes around four hours and is just under 230 miles (370 kilometers).

The town is also connected to the D650, to Cherbourg in the north (23 miles/37 kilometers, 40 minutes) and Granville in the south (50 miles/80 kilometers, 1 hour 15 minutes). If you're driving here from Mont-Saint-Michel, meanwhile, it's faster to take a slightly more inland route, first heading toward Avranches on the N175, then joining the A84 briefly toward Villedieu-les-Poêles, where you change for the D9 and head again for the coast. It's a journey that is roughly 80 miles (128 kilometers) and takes about 1.75 hours.

Keep aware that while there's ample parking in Carteret specifically, the reliance everyone has on cars to get here means that it can get very busy in the high season. Getting in is seldom a problem, though getting out can be a bit of a nightmare, what with Carteret's largest parking lot being a very deep cul-de-sac. If you want to avoid the worst of the traffic jams after a day at the beach, consider leaving a little earlier than you otherwise might to beat the rush. Traffic and parking in Portbail and Barneville is less of an issue, being both better connected and marginally less popular than their neighbor.

BY FERRY

The closest French port to the Channel Islands, there is one ferry a day from Jersey to Barneville-Carteret, usually leaving between 6pm and 7pm. It is run by **Manche Îles Express** (www.manche-iles.com/en), costs around €65 one-way, and takes about an hour.

BY BUS

Local buses from Cherbourg train station leave for Barneville-Carteret and Portbail around twice a day. They are run by Transports Manche and are referred to as the **Manéo Express** (www.manche.fr/transports/maneo-service-express.aspx). The line is No. 10, and the journey takes about an hour from Cherbourg, costing just €3. No buses service the town from the south.

Getting Around

Due to its proliferation of harbors and long tides, the Côte des Îles is not an easy place to get around. Both Carteret and Portbail's beaches exist in effective cul-de-sacs, and in the high season, traffic can get heavy. While there's plenty of free parking just behind La Potinière, be ready to join a long traffic jam if you leave at sunset with the rest of the day-trip crowds. Distances between the towns, though—even between Barneville and Carteret—are significant enough that walking is an endeavor.

Two buses run every day between the town hall in Barneville and Portbail and back again. One ticket for this route will cost you €2.30. Incidentally, it is the same route that starts in Cherbourg, Line 10, which is run by Transport Manches, and known as **Manéo Express** (https://www.manche.fr/transports/maneo-service-express.aspx). In the summer, a **tourist train** (www.train-touristique-du-cotentin.com; adults €5, ages 5-12 €2.50, under 5 free) runs back and forth once a day between Carteret and Portbail on Tuesdays and Thursdays when it leaves Carteret at 3pm and starts the return journey from Portbail at 5pm; and on Wednesdays and Sundays when it leaves Carteret at 10am and makes the return journey at 12:30pm. Journey time is 35 minutes.

Granville

A historic resort town and the birthplace of fashion designer Christian Dior, Granville has an air of old-fashioned elegance about it that remains today, with its prominent casino, long seaside promenade, and elegant mansions clinging to the rocky cliffs that define the town's topography.

But as with so many towns that now seem dedicated only to the good things in life, Granville also has a long and serious history. Those same cliffs that now offer such great views were once formidable fortifications, and the harbor now given over to pleasure cruises used to arm warships—the town itself provided no fewer than 15 admirals in the French navy. This past lends present-day Granville a serious quality alongside its resort-town reputation.

Nevertheless, most visitors are drawn here today by its faded glamour—the town's still regarded by some as a Monaco of the north. Easy to reach by train, it offers a city break with beaches, and just on its horizon are the famed Îles Chausey, Europe's largest archipelago, a mesmerizing sea landscape of granite islands that represent some of the

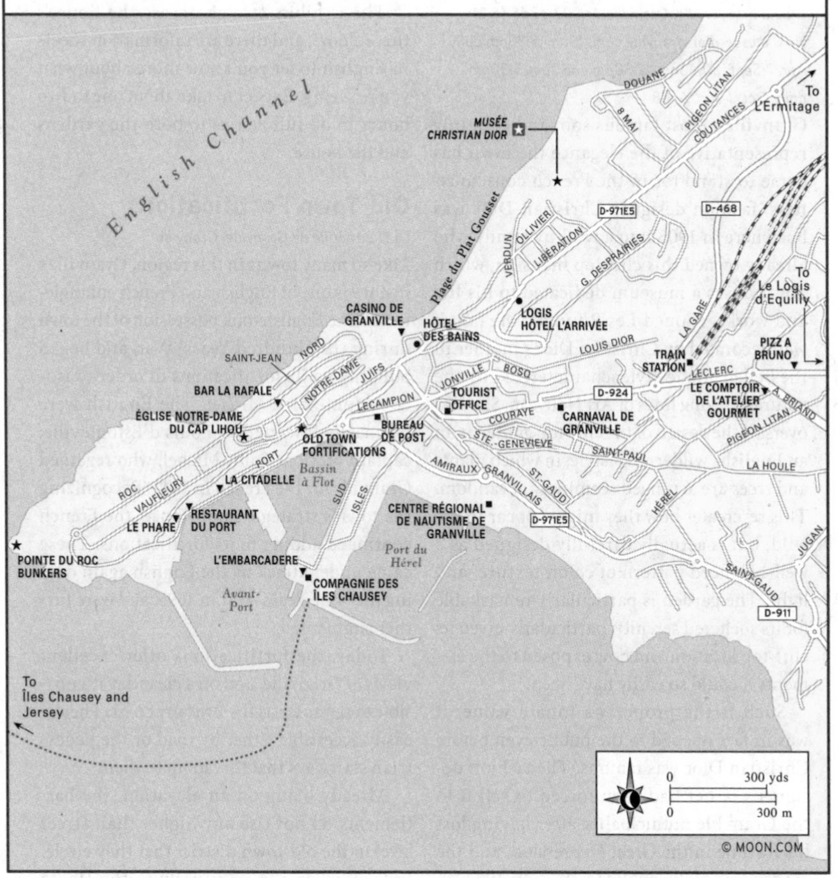

most fascinating waters anywhere along the Norman coast.

ORIENTATION

Characterized by cliffs, harbors, and the sea, Granville is a walkable town in a broadly triangular shape, converging on a small peninsula, the tip of which is the **Pointe du Roc.** On top of the peninsula sits the old "high town" or "haute ville" the hill where Granville's original fortifications can be explored. Running the south side of this peninsula and wrapping along the coast inland are a couple of harbors and a dry dock, plus the arterial D911, one of the main roads out of town.

On the north side of the peninsula, along the coast, is the beachfront Promenade du Plat Gousset. This is overshadowed by cliffs, upon which the **Musée Christian Dior** is found—with a steep climb, this can be accessed from the promenade.

Granville's downtown, where most shops and commerce are, is on the relative flat, directly east from the high town. Slightly farther east of here is the town's railway station.

SIGHTS

★ Musée Christian Dior

1 rue d'Estouteville, Granville; tel. 02 33 61 48 21; www.musee-dior-granville.com; 10am-6:30pm daily Apr. 7-Sept. 30, 10am-12:30pm and 2pm-5:30pm daily Oct. 1-Jan. 6; €8

Granville's most famous son, and certainly representative of the elegance the town has come to stand for in the French consciousness, fashion designer Christian Dior was born here in 1905 into a wealthy family who already owned this cliff-top mansion, which now houses a museum dedicated to his life and works. Named Les Rhumbs, the house was decorated by Christian Dior's mother in the belle epoque style, characterized by the natural curving lines of Art Nouveau. She also oversaw the design of the cliff-top garden in in an English "wilderness" style, in which plants and trees are arranged seemingly at random. This re-creates how they might appear in the wild, but is actually carefully designed as a well-balanced pattern of color, texture, and light. The garden is particularly remarkable for its sheltered serenity, particularly given its cliff-top location and how exposed to the elements it could so easily have been.

Such is the property's innate value, it was in fact opened to the public even before Christian Dior was famous. The fashion designer's father had been forced to sell it to the Granville municipality after having lost his fortune in the Great Depression, and the garden was made public in 1938. In 1997, 40 years after Christian Dior's death, it became a museum dedicated to the designer himself. Since its inception, the museum has acquired more Dior-related artifacts than it can possibly display at one time. These include original outfits he designed and hundreds of photographs from his life and shows. The excess of material means that the precise nature of the exhibitions differs every year. What is constant, though, is the elegance of the building's interior. Much of the furniture may be gone, but the doors, windows, and fireplaces still remain: their design a turn-of-the-century juxtaposition of organic curves and plotted straight lines.

The exhibits stretch across the house's three floors, and there are information sheets in English to let you know more about what you're seeing. Expect to take about one to two hours to do full justice to both the gardens and the house.

Old-Town Fortifications

La Haute Ville de Granville, Granville

Like so many towns in this region, Granville's history is one of English and French entanglement. The English took possession of the town during the Hundred Years' War, and began building up its fortifications in order to isolate Mont-Saint-Michel. The English were ultimately thwarted by Louis d'Estouteville, captain of Mont-Saint-Michel, who regained Granville for the French in 1442. Recognizing the town's strategic importance, the French continued adding to its fortifications. These came under attack by the English again during the Nine Years' War in 1695, and were further augmented.

Today, the fortifications offer excellent views of Granville, and on a clear day it's possible to see as far as the Brittany coast. They're easily accessible either by road or the pedestrian stairways that thread up to them.

Already being on an elevation, the battlements do not rise any higher than street level in the old-town district that they circle. Indeed, when you're actually in the Haute Ville, as this area is called, without paying attention, you may not notice the ramparts at all. It's only looking from below that their true size can be fully appreciated.

The Haute Ville itself is a charming maze of narrow alleys and old stone houses. Mostly residential, and surprisingly untouched by tourism, there is a museum here dedicated to the town's past and culture: the **Musee d'Art et d'Histoire de Granville** (2 rue Lecarpentier, Granville; tel. 02 33 50 44 10), which offers a surprising wealth of artifacts over three floors of a historic stone building. These include things from multiple different

Christian Dior

Born in Granville in 1905, Christian Dior would go on to head one of the most famous fashion houses in the world. Despite family pressure for him to become a diplomat, Dior was insistent on more artistic pursuits. He sold his own fashion sketches to make money, then with family assistance founded a small gallery in 1920s Paris, where he bought and sold work by some of the most respected artists of the time, including Pablo Picasso.

Nevertheless, financial disaster in his family forced him to close the gallery, leading him into fashion: In 1937 he began to work for the designer Robert Piguet. He had to leave when he was called up to fight in the war, but France's swift capitulation meant he was back in fashion houses by 1942, working for Lucien Lelong, and in fact creating designs for the wives of Nazi officers—this while Dior's sister, Catherine, fought for the French Resistance.

In 1946, under the patronage of the entrepreneur Marcel Boussac, Dior established his own brand, concentrating on curves and excess in fabric—a complete break from the box-like, necessarily minimal designs that because of fabric rationing had dominated the war years. Despite courting a certain degree of controversy, not least because fabric was still hard to come by, the floral excess of these designs was soon embraced, reinvigorating the French fashion scene.

The designer died in Italy in 1957, and though most reports suggested it was of a heart attack after choking on a fishbone, rumor at the time blamed something altogether more in keeping with the life of a famous designer of fashion: that Dior's heart attack was brought on from strenuous sexual activity.

eras, from historic Norman headdresses to kitchen utensils to radios from the 1930s. There's also a scale model of Granville to enjoy. Previously only €2, the museum was excellent value. At the time of writing, however, it has recently closed for renovations, so check ahead to see if it's reopened, and for the new hours and admission cost.

Pointe du Roc Bunkers

Pointe du Roc

Due to its position, harbor, and preexisting military fortifications, Granville remained a tactical goal throughout the Second World War. As with everywhere along the Normandy coast, remnants of Hitler's famous Atlantic Wall, a system of coastal defenses stretching from Norway to Southern France aimed to prevent an invasion of continental Europe, are still visible here. These take the form of small-to-large bunkers that surround the Haute Ville on Pointe du Roc. Effectively, they are the most recent ramparts built to protect the city—though somehow they seem far more incongruous and surreal, made from reinforced concrete rather than granite, most looking like huge gray motorbike helmets thrust seemingly at random around the peninsula. There are 11 emplacements in total, which have today simply been imbibed into the street furniture, squeezed between parking spaces or recommissioned as flower beds. Unlike elsewhere along the coast, most have now been boarded up due to questions of safety.

The Pointe du Roc itself is a green space, just west of the Haute Ville. The peninsula's tip, it tapers into some jagged-looking cliffs regularly thrashed by the sea. A rare place where you can be awed by nature in the midst of a town; on a clear day you can see out to the Îles Chausey.

Notre Dame du Cap Lihou

3 place du Parvis Notre Dame, Granville; tel. 02 33 50 03 55; 9am-6pm daily

The first chapel here was built by sailors in 1113 after finding a statue of the Virgin Mary in their nets. The current church, though, has its origins in the 1440s, when Granville was under control of the English—while adding to the ramparts of the high town, they built the

1
2
3

bell tower. Mostly, though, it was constructed in the early 17th century, going on to be declared a historic monument of France in 1930. Particularly noteworthy is the organ, which was also made in the 17th century and boasts about 2,500 pipes. These seem to spread like Gothic wings above the main entrance, dominating the spirit of the place. Aside from that, the interior is characterized by large sturdy pillars, setting the church powerfully against the elements blowing in from off the sea. Masses take place 9:30am on Sundays, and offer a good chance to hear the organ being played. This was also the church where Christian Dior was baptized.

La Lucerne Abbey

L'Abbaye, La Lucerne-d'Outremer; tel. 02 33 60 58 98; www.abbaye-lucerne.fr; 10am-12pm and 2pm-6:30pm Mon.-Sat. Mar. 31-Sept. 20, 10am-12pm and 2pm-5pm Mon.-Sat. Oct. 20-Nov. 4, 10am-12pm and 2pm-5pm Mon.-Sat. Dec. 22-Dec.31; adults €7, reduced €4

A world away from the resort life of Granville, this Premonstratensian monastery in the forests of the Thar Valley was founded in 1143 by Hasculf de Subligny, the son of Othoerne de Subligny who had tutored William Adelin, the would-be future King of England. Built largely in the Romanesque style, like so many religious institutions it suffered greatly during the French Revolution, and was effectively a ruin until 1959, when a massive reconstruction project was begun.

Today, the abbey church boasts a minimalist though well-lit interior—a bit like if Ikea did the high Gothic—while the gardens still show evidence of the ruin it used to be, with piles of old masonry and some evocatively crumbling arches that speak of a distant time. There's also a beautiful old dovecote on-site.

The abbey still functions as a working monastery, though individual visits are permitted in fairly narrow time windows. There are also guided tours of its buildings, which allow you to better see how the monks live. Check out the website for a list of the regular concerts, craft courses, and acts of worship that the public can attend.

★ Les Îles Chausey

www.manchetourisme.com/chausey

Legend has it that once this area of the French coast was covered in the mysterious Scissy Forest. It was believed to be a place of pagan devotion and dark magic; then, in 709, it was engulfed in a tidal wave, the forest was washed away, and the distant tidal plain that characterizes the area today was created. Several islands were said to have remained above the wave's reach (Mont-Saint-Michel being the most famous), and the Îles Chausey are among them. Though modern science may have disproved the tidal wave story, the islands are real, low-lying amalgamations of sand, grass, and dark rock.

Just an hour away from Granville, a boat trip out to Europe's largest archipelago is an unforgettable experience. At high tide, with so many granite islands all so close together, the journey is like floating over a map of the world, and there's every chance of seeing dolphins, while on a clear day out in the distance you can make out the pinprick of Mont-Saint-Michel. Take a tour to the archipelago with a company like **Compagnie Îles Chausey** (Gare Maritime, rue des Îles, www.vedettesjoliefrance.com, from €20), which offers one trip a day in the winter, and two or three a day in the summer. Their modern boats are skippered by captains who know these treacherous waters intimately, and this is the most trouble-free way of seeing these marvelous islands. They also provide a commentary on what you're seeing, though unfortunately only in French. Sailors planning their own trips should exercise caution: many islands can get hidden by the tide and this can be very hazardous.

You can also take a boat with the Compagnie Îles Chausey directly to the largest island, Le Grand Île, where there are beaches, a

1: the front of the Musée Christian Dior **2:** Biking up to Granville's "haute ville" is not a task for the faint hearted **3:** the roof of Granville Casino

lighthouse, and a 19th-century fort. Despite its name, this island is actually pretty small, and can easily be explored in a few hours. In the high season there are around four sailings there and back every day. In the lowest season, there's only one.

BEACHES

PLAGE DU PLAT GOUSSET

Place Maréchal Foch, Granville

Granville's Plage du Plat Gousset is the town's most central beach, and is accordingly very close to a number of bars and restaurants. Located along the northern shore of the seaside resort next to the casino, it has good views up toward the Haute Ville and is bordered by a long promenade. Somewhat surprisingly, there are no lifeguards, though at low tide a concrete basin catches the retreating waters, so swimming is still possible.

WATER SPORTS

CENTRE RÉGIONAL DE NAUTISME DE GRANVILLE

Boulevard des Amiraux Granvillais, Granville; tel. 02 33 91 22 60; http://centre-regional-nautisme-granville.fr; 9am-12pm and 2pm-6pm Mon.-Sat.,; kayak and paddleboard rental from €15/hour

If it can be experienced on the water, chances are that Granville's Centre Régional de Nautisme, one of the largest water-sports clubs in the region, will offer it. This means catamarans, sailing, paddleboards, kayaks, and more. In addition to rentals, there are also plenty of courses available—though they will be in French. The one restricting factor is Mont-Saint-Michel Bay's massive tides, which means the sea is not always available. In such situations, though, sand sailing is always an option.

FESTIVALS AND EVENTS

GRANVILLE CARNIVAL

Various locations; www.carnaval-de-granville.fr; Feb./Mar.; free

One of the longest-running and important Mardi Gras carnivals in France, this five-day festival that sees over 100,000 people descend on Granville at the end of winter has its origins in the town's history of cod fishing. It used to coincide with the departure of Granville's fishermen to the fishing grounds around Canada's Newfoundland; the carnival was their last party on shore before going to sea. The celebration consists of massive street parties, concerts, and parades. It opens with the mayor handing the keys of the city to the Carnival King (a papier-mâché figure), which leads to a procession of floats interspersed with marching bands. Over the next few days there are various ticketed social balls that take place around town, each aimed at different age groups, and a "confetti battle" in the town square—which is just what it sounds like.

One unusual tradition are the "intrigues," in which certain citizens disguise themselves, then begin to spread rumors and tell anecdotes in local bars, goading others to guess their true identity. The carnival ends with the King being cremated in the town port, at which point things return to normal.

NIGHTLIFE

CASINO DE GRANVILLE

Place Maréchal Foch, Granville; tel. 02 33 50 00 79; www.casino-granville.com; 10am-4am daily

An essential element of any French seaside resort, Granville's casino was built in 1910, located just before the city's main beachfront promenade. Its architecture is intended to be reminiscent of Indian palaces, while art nouveau dominates the interior. The establishment itself, however, doesn't quite live up to these glamorous stylings; rather, it is very much just a somewhat gaudy, functioning casino, complete with ranks of slot machines, blackjack tables, and electronic roulette.

BAR LA RAFALE

6 place Cambernon, Granville; tel. 02 33 50 10 01; www.la-rafale.com; 10am-1am Wed.-Sun.

A great old-fashioned bar, nestled among the twisting streets of Granville's high town. Perfect for predinner drinks, it also has an extensive beer selection and throws regular evening concerts. On certain special occasions, the music even spills out onto the road outside.

FOOD

Local Cuisine

LA CITADELLE

34 rue du Port, Granville; tel. 02 33 50 34 10; www.restaurant-la-citadelle.fr; 12:15pm-2pm and 7:15pm-9:30pm Thurs.-Tues.; mains €32

An excellent quality, higher-end restaurant on Granville's port. Dishes are lavish and generous, and burst with fresh seafood flavors. Its specialty is the lobster menu, the *menu homard*, which though certainly not cheap at €80 uses only the freshest, most locally caught ingredients: The lobsters come straight from the waters around the Îles Chausey and are served grilled. Booking ahead is recommended.

LE COMPTOIR DE L'ATELIER GOURMET

13 avenue Aristide Briand, Granville; tel. 02 14 13 64 32; 12pm-1:15pm and 7pm-9:30pm Tues.-Sat.; mains €22

A laid-back, modern little restaurant where the menu combines traditional local ingredients into imaginative dishes that play with flavor in new ways. In addition to the excellent food, the staff are very accommodating, and most have a good grasp on English. Either come early, or book ahead, as word of its quality is well known.

RESTAURANT DU PORT

19 rue du Port, Granville; tel. 02 33 50 00 55; http://restaurantduport-granville.com; 12pm-2pm and 7pm-10pm Tues.-Wed. and Fri.-Sun., 12pm-2pm Thurs.; mains €19

Family-run and among the best of several restaurants surrounding Granville's port. Like most places in town, seafood is its specialty, with head chef Laurent Delchard cooking up a variety of interesting flavors, and not being too limited by local traditions as he does so; the paella is one of his most-recommended dishes. With an upstairs, downstairs, and a terrace, there's plenty of room.

LE PHARE

11 rue du Port, Granville; tel. 02 33 50 12 94; www.restaurant-lephare-granville.com; 12pm-2pm and 7pm-9:30pm Fri.-Tues., 12pm-2pm Wed.; mains €14

A straightforward seafood restaurant, decorated in a nautical theme with some excellent views of Granville harbor, this place thrives as much on local trade as it does with tourists. The *soupe de poisson* (fish soup) in particular comes highly recommended. You can probably get away without booking, but at high season and on weekends it's worth the precaution.

Budget Options

L'EMBARCADERE

Quai S, Granville; tel. 02 33 51 83 84; 9am-9:30pm Tues.-Sat., 2pm-9:30pm Sun.; €10

With a view out across the harbor, this brasserie offers simple, bold-flavored food, offering some local classics like mussels and other shellfish as well as international favorites like burgers and fries and British-style fish and chips. It's solid, inexpensive place for a lunch pit-stop on a sunny day.

PIZZ A BRUNO

35 avenue des Matignon, Granville; tel. 02 33 91 92 30; www.pizzabrunogranville.com; 12pm-2pm and 6pm-10pm Thurs.-Mon.; €10

Primarily a take-away joint, though there are a few inside tables, this inexpensive pizza place bucks the trend for France and serves up excellent, well-cooked variations on the Italian dish, some of them with fresh local seafood ingredients on top. It's a bit awkwardly located, but plan ahead, and taxi with your pizza to the seafront for a delicious, al fresco evening meal.

ACCOMMODATIONS

€50-100

HÔTEL L'ARRIVÉE

110 avenue de la Libération, Granville; tel. 02 33 50 03 00; www.hotelarrivee.com; from €77 d

In a great location, just a short walk from Granville's main promenade, beach, and the Christian Dior Museum, the Hôtel l'Arrivée is meticulously clean and comfortable with friendly, accommodating staff. The interior design in some of the rooms may not be to everyone's taste, favoring as it does bright primary colors, but with free WiFi and an on-site restaurant and bar, this is certainly a good value spot. There is parking on-site.

L'HÔTEL DES BAINS

19 rue Georges Clemenceau, Granville; tel. 02 33 50 17 31; www.hoteldesbains-granville.com; from €80 d

Purpose-built in 1881, this elegant, large hotel is now associated with Granville Casino, which it stands opposite, and has fair claim to representing Granville's heart. Its 54 rooms are comfortable, and though they offer a slightly uneven blend of modern and traditional, many have spectacular views of the sea. There are also several communal rooms, including an on-site bar.

€100-200

LE LOGIS D'EQUILLY

Le Château, Le Logis d'Equilly, Équilly; tel. 02 33 61 04 71; www.lelogisdequilly.fr; from €140 d

About six miles (10 kilometers) outside of Granville, away from the coast, this 13th-century manor still seems locked in a beautiful dream of the past. The rooms are sumptuous and wood-paneled, and the communal areas are warmed by roaring log-fires in the winter months. With extensive grounds and an on-site tennis court, it's an excellent long-term holiday base for exploring the whole Mont-Saint-Michel Bay area. There is extensive on-site parking.

Camping

CAMPING L'ERMITAGE

12 allée des Costillets, Donville-les-Bains; tel. 02 33 50 09 01; www.camping-ermitage.com; pitch for two adults from €17

Just a short journey to the north of Granville, only 54 yards (50 meters) from Donville Beach, this is a well-accommodated three-star campsite. A bar/restaurant and boulangerie are on-site, there's free WiFi throughout, and in the summer there are plenty of events and numerous shows put on for both adults and kids.

CAMPING LA ROUTE BLANCHE

6 la route Blanche, Bréville-sur-Mer; tel. 02 33 50 23 31; http://campinglarouteblanchenormandie.business.site; cabins from €540

A five-star campsite also to the north of Granville, this offers self-catered cabins for those who don't want to spend the night in tents, as well as a swimming pool, a multi-sports area, and a children's playground. In the summer months, you barely have to leave the property, as a bar, pizzeria, and grocery store open on-site, though if you do, Bréville-sur-Mer Beach is less than a 10-minute walk away.

TOURIST INFORMATION

4 cours Jonville, Granville; tel. 02 33 91 30 03; www.tourisme-granville-terre-mer.com; 9:30am-12:30pm and 2pm-5:30pm Mon.-Sat.

Granville's tourist office is right in its modern town center and is extensively stocked with leaflets, and it has a multilingual staff happy to help orient you and aid in your plans of how to tackle the town and surrounding region, including giving information about the vast tidal reach and how to plan trips to the Chausey Islands.

SERVICES

Hospital

LE CENTRE HOSPITALIER AVRANCHES GRANVILLE

849, rue des Menneries-BP 629-50 406 Granville; tel. 02 33 91 50 00; www.ch-avranches-granville.fr; ER open 24 hours

Located to the southwest of the town, this is a large, modern hospital complex with a fully staffed emergency room open 24 hours a day. It's likely you will be able to find English speakers on the staff.

Post Office

BUREAU DE POST GRANVILLE

8 cours Jonville, Granville; tel. 36 31; 9am-12:45pm and 2:30pm-5:45 Mon.-Fri., 9am-12pm Sat.

Found in the center of town, though French post offices keep decidedly "public service" hours—shutting every day for lunch—they are also efficient and surprisingly easy to use. Though it's unlikely you'll find many people speaking fluent English, the color-coded systems and multitude of staff should make sending or receiving packages from here relatively easy.

TRANSPORTATION

Getting There

BY CAR

Granville is well connected by road. From Paris, take the A13 to Caen and then change to the A84, which will take you all the way to Granville. The total journey takes about 3.5 hours. From Mont-Saint-Michel, the journey is about 30 miles (48 kilometers) and takes an hour along the N175 and the D973. From Barneville-Cateret it's about 50 miles (80 kilometers) along the D650, with a journey time of roughly 1 hour 15 minutes. Parking can be difficult to find in town, so the large, free parking lot, Parking Herel on Boulevard des Amiraux Granvillais, is your best option.

BY FERRY

Granville is reachable by ferry from Jersey. **Manche Iles Express** (Gare Maritime, Granville; tel. 08 25 13 10 50; www.manche-iles.com/en) runs a service up to six times each week, and the trip takes around 1 hour 25 minutes. The cost can vary, but can be as much as €60.

BY TRAIN

Arriving at Granville's train station, **Gare de Granville** (tel. 36 35; 4:15am-11:20pm Mon., 5:15am-11:20pm Tues.-Sat., 6:15am-11:20pm Sun.) are around three trains every day direct from Paris Montparnasse at a cost of €50-70—prices will be cheaper the earlier you book. Travel time is about three hours. From Caen's main station, there are five direct trains a day. This costs around €25 and takes about 1 hour 40 minutes.

There are also two direct trains every day from the main station of Rennes in Brittany, costing around €20 and taking about 1.75 hours.

From Mont-Saint-Michel, there are an average of two trains a day taking about 40 minutes and costing about €12.

Getting Around

Despite its topography, Granville is a fairly easy town to walk around. There is a city bus service, though, called **Neva** (tel. 02 33 91 30 24), and there are two lines, servicing the far west (Line 1) and far south (Line 2) of the city. Line 1 is more useful for tourists, as it services the harbor and the high town. Buses run 7:30am-8pm Mon.-Sat., with a single journey costing €1. There should be a bus roughly every 40 minutes.

Saint-Malo and the North Coast

Brittany's north coast is a paint box of dramatically changing color and light. Toward the east are the sharp gray ramparts of Saint-Malo, then the striking yellow sands of its nearby beaches alongside capricious cobalt seas. These are met by rolling green fields of gentle countryside, forming an idyllic setting for a number of coastal resorts, which have prospered here from the 19th century until now.

Then, after a series of headlands, as Brittany stretches toward the Atlantic, the sand turns to rocks, which become pink and orange in turn, making up the remarkable Côte de Granit Rose. This is both intensely beautiful and alive with coves, harbor towns, and resorts. Brittany's north coast makes ideal holiday territory regardless of

Highlights

Look for ★ to find recommended sights, activities, dining, and lodging.

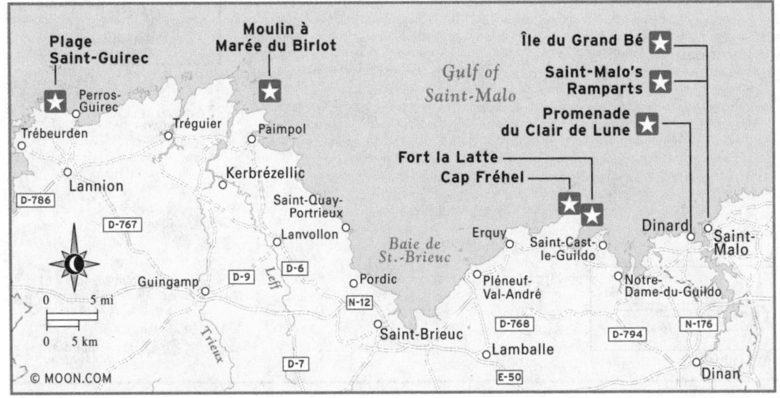

★ **Saint-Malo's Ramparts:** There's no better introduction to Saint-Malo than a stroll atop the town's fortifications (page 232).

★ **Île du Grand Bé, Saint-Malo:** At low tide, walk out to this tidal island to explore the ruins of an ancient fort and for majestic views of the walled town (page 234).

★ **Promenade du Clair de Lune, Dinard:** Walk along this boardwalk for a safe way to explore Dinard's rocky coastline (page 238).

★ **Fort la Latte, Côte d'Émeraude:** Be awed by this fantasy-novel-style castle in a stunning setting (page 251).

★ **Cap Fréhel, Côte d'Émeraude:** Hike this magnificent peninsula for a dose of fresh sea air, a landscape of wild moorland, and excellent bird-watching (page 253).

★ **Moulin à Marée du Birlot, Île de Bréhat:** This humble water mill framed by blue sea and islands is one of the most iconic scenes in Brittany (page 260).

★ **Plage Saint-Guirec, Côte de Granit Rose:** Go swimming at this beach at sunset, when its rocks blush the most gorgeous shade of pink (page 271).

Saint-Malo and the North Coast

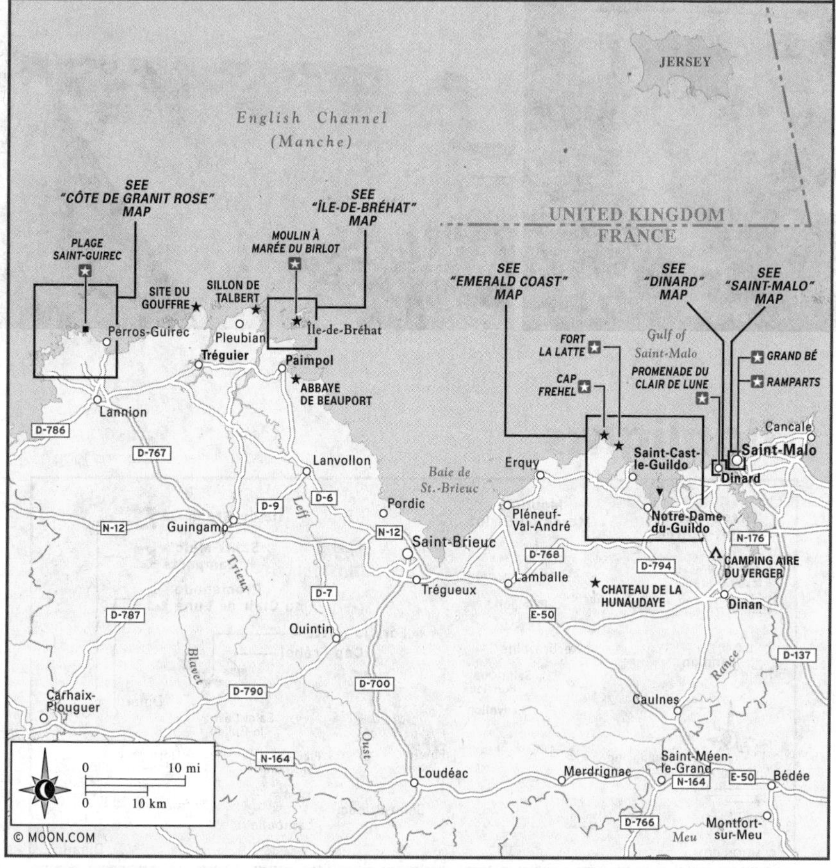

whether you want to seek out the crowds or get away from them to commune with nature alone.

HISTORY

The towns along the north coast of Brittany can sound less like urban centers and more just like a list of names: Saint-Malo is the best known, and there's also Saint-Briac, Saint-Jacut, Saint-Cast, and Saint-Guirec—and those are just the towns covered in this guide.

All are named for immigrant monks and missionaries, most from Wales, who arrived in Brittany in the 6th century running from the Saxon invasion of their homeland. They arrived here, spreading the word of the gospels and establishing monasteries and towns. Many were drawn to Brittany's northern granite coast for its offering of isolated peninsulas and islands, both easily defendable and isolated from the distractions of hinterland life.

The now-famous fortified port town

Previous: Saint-Malo is a walled port city in Brittany in northwestern France on the English Channel; the walking route to Cap Fréhel; Saint-Malo's ramparts.

Saint-Malo certainly sees its modern history start like this. There was already a major fort in this area, protecting the entrance of the River Rance against invaders from the sea, when the hermit Saint Aaron established a hermitage in nearby Aleth. He was joined there by one Saint Maclou, who took over running the hermitage following Aaron's death. Saint Maclou's name became changed over time to Saint Malo; when the hermitage was forced to migrate to the nearby fort for its own safety, it adopted the name too.

Much of the history of this coast and its surrounds is either connected directly to Saint-Malo or reads something like a version of the port town's story in miniature. Tales of successful seaward expansion combined with a fierce independent streak occur again and again, as well as the need to weather waves of foreign aggression, the coastal setting making attractive targets for the navies and pirates of the world.

Saint-Malo was warred over by the dukes of Brittany and the kings of France for many years of the 14th and 15th centuries, switching hands three times. During the 16th century, the town even claimed its own independence, chancing its own prosperity over the anarchy rife in France at that time. It's probably from this brief time as a republic that the town owes its unofficial motto: "*Malouin* (of Saint-Malo) first, Breton perhaps… then French if there's anything left over."

Saint-Malo eventually returned to France, but the value for independence remained, and the town became known for its privateers—effectively pirates sanctioned by the French crown. Thanks to them, trade, and fishing, Saint-Malo prospered. One of the town's most famous sons, Jacques Cartier, discovered Canada in the 16th century, and many sailors from Brittany's north coast headed out in his wake to seek their fortune. This led to particular success centuries later for the fishermen of Paimpol, who brought great wealth back to their town from the fisheries around Iceland and Newfoundland.

As with the rest of France, the region suffered under the Germans in the Second World War, and was particularly damaged during its reconquest by the Allies. The town of Saint-Malo itself was almost completely destroyed by American shells, with the Allies mistakenly believing that it was being used to harbor thousands of German troops, a major stockpile of armaments behind its walls. The town was meticulously restored in the years after the war.

PLANNING YOUR TIME

The north coast of Brittany offers a multitude of delights for the traveler, not to say a few conundrums. Save from Saint-Malo and Dinan, its highlights are mostly natural, and for many it is the kind of place where you just pick a single beach area or resort and spend most of your trip in its immediate surrounds. There is nothing wrong with this, of course, though it is worth pointing out that while the various stretches of this coastline may appear to offer similar experiences—walking, swimming, water sports, to name a few—their natural landscape is quite stunningly varied, and there's much to be gained by visiting more than one.

This said, it's not an easy coast to get around. Most of the interesting places are tucked away at the top of peninsulas, and traveling around by car here can feel a bit like swimming through molasses. But treasures await the persistent traveler. Of course, perhaps the best way of all to experience this coastline is to walk it. The GR34 walking path runs right along the coast, and thanks to the crazy profusion of bays and islands here, there's something new to see almost every couple of miles.

In general, though, if you explore a bit of the history of Saint-Malo, find a good beach at which to go swimming, take a couple of hikes, and mark out time to ride on some kind of water transport, you're going to be getting most of what this region has to offer.

The Breton Sweater: A History

Iconic not just of Brittany but of France all over, the Breton sweater represents an unexpected fashion success story of extraordinary proportions. From the very humblest beginnings, Breton sailors in the early 19th century would wear tops made of tightly knit wool worn close to the skin as an extra layer to keep them warm as they braved cold sea winds to wrest their catch. This form of top was officially adopted into the French naval uniform in 1858, which also introduced the iconic striped design. The precise measurements and number of hoops that are still used today by the best-known sweater brand, Saint James, was set in stone then: 21 white stripes and 21 blue stripes on the body, 15 white stripes and 14 blue stripes on the sleeve. Legend says that the number of stripes are supposed to represent Napoleon's victories against the British. The design became known as Breton, more by coincidence than any active role that Brittany had in its design. The fact was that as a seafaring region, Brittany provided most of the manpower to the French Navy and had a large number of large ports within its borders; a big part of its population therefore wore the striped top of its official uniform.

It was the fashion designer Coco Chanel who really propelled the top to true icon status. Holidaying in Brittany, she noticed its potential, and in 1913 invested in making it a popular choice for women's beachside fashion, liberating them from the heavy, hot dresses that otherwise got in the way of their relaxation. From then on, the top was picked up by stars and fashion icons all over the world, from Brigitte Bardot to Jean-Paul Gaultier, who even made the stripes part of his brand. Even so, it still remains worn by some Breton sailors today, and why not? It's practical, fashionable, and an indelible badge of their identity.

Itinerary Ideas

One of the best things about the north coast of Brittany is how close spectacular historic monuments are to wonderful wilderness and landscape. This tour allows the fit tourist to take in both, and gives some time to enjoy the luxurious delights of Dinard as well.

Day 1: Saint-Malo

1 Take a morning walk around the historical **ramparts,** and admire the panoramic views of Saint-Malo and its beaches.

2 Grab a Japanese-inspired galette at **Breizh Café** for lunch.

3 After lunch, if the tide is low, walk out to **Île du Grand Bé**. Check out the ruins, and take in the views of the town.

4 Walk to the **Fort National** if you have time and explore the museum there.

5 Dine in style at Michelin-starred **Le Chalut.**

Day 2: Dinard

1 Take the scenic **ferry** across the Rance estuary from Saint-Malo to **Dinard.**

2 Have a gentle meander around the **Promenade du Clair de Lune.**

3 Enjoy a seafood lunch right on the promenade at **Restaurant La Gonelle.**

4 Spend the afternoon relaxing, getting a suntan, and swimming at the **Plage de l'Écluse.**

Itinerary Ideas

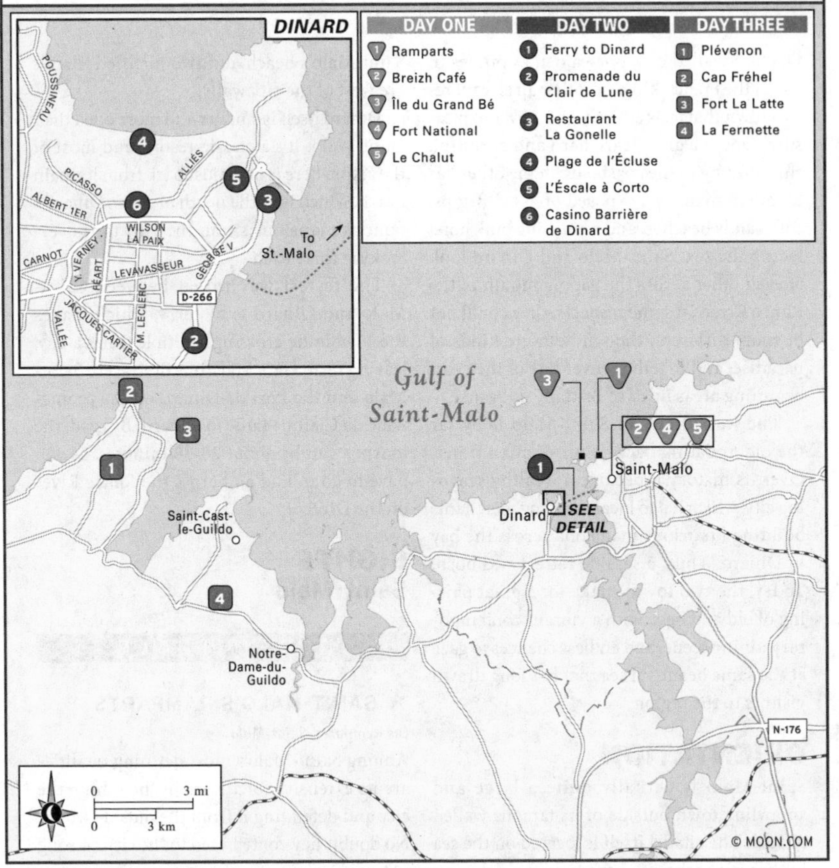

5 Unwind with dinner and drinks at the village-pub-like **L'Escale à Corto.**

6 Then, if you're feeling lucky, hit the **Casino Barrière de Dinard.**

Day 3: Cap Fréhel

1 Park your car in **Plévenon** and buy sandwiches and other snacks for lunch at **Aux Délices du Cap** boulangerie.

2 Hike out to **Cap Fréhel** to check out the awesome views of the ocean and the cliffs and do a spot of bird-watching, while you settle down for picnic lunch.

3 Then head to **Fort la Latte** for more stunning coastal views and an afternoon of exploring the nooks and crannies of this fairy-tale castle.

4 Drive back to Saint-Cast for dinner at **La Fermette.**

Saint-Malo and Dinard

One is a walled city, once a den of pirates in pay of the French king; the other an elegant resort town that feels entirely given over to pleasure. One is a gray pearl, hard and beautiful, shimmering in the coastal light; the other has decadent mansions exposed on its cliff-tops, soft, sandy beaches, and a blushing pink hotel facing the sea. Saint-Malo and Dinard look at each other across the gaping mouth of the Rance River. In some respects, they could not be more different, though both are kinds of paradise, and together cover one of the most beguiling areas in all of Brittany or France.

The walled city of Saint-Malo is by far the older, dating back to pre-Roman times. Over its history it became a wealthy seagoing city, which led to local shipping merchants building luxurious mansions across the bay in Dinard. Thus, a seaside retreat was born. Today, the two towns make for a great pairing of old and new, with a vibrant contemporary dining scene, and endless chances to gaze at the same beautiful sea that has long drawn visitors to the region.

ORIENTATION

Saint-Malo is actually quite a large and sprawling town outside of its famous walled citadel. The citadel itself is located on the sea in the west of the city, separated from the rest of the town by a large dockland area. It's serviced by several roads, but the D126 is most efficient and links with the main road systems of Brittany's northern coast. The town's railway station is just over half a mile outside the citadel, stopping just before the city docks. Inside the citadel is a network of small to large streets, which can be driven down, though many are one-way—they're also often quite busy with people on foot, so it pays to keep vigilant. There are also several large parking lots just outside the ramparts, and it's advised you use them, then continue on foot. Saint-Malo's beach and two fortified islands are west of the city walls.

Dinard itself is smaller and more open than Saint-Malo. It's a classic resort, and most of the action here is on or just back from its main beach, which is in the north of town. Dinard's famous mansions sit on the cliff tops overlooking this beach.

The fastest way to get between Saint-Malo and Dinard is by ferry, which makes the 10-minute crossing multiple times a day, leaving from Gare Maritime du Nayein Saint-Malo and the Port de Dinard on the promenade du Clair de Lune in Dinard. By road, the journey can be about 20-30 minutes, as you have to go inland and cross the Rance River on the D168.

SIGHTS

Saint-Malo

TOP EXPERIENCE

★ SAINT-MALO'S RAMPARTS

Les Remparts, Saint-Malo

Among Saint-Malo's most defining qualities are its extensive fortifications, hemming the city and defending it from the outside world. No doubt they contributed to the city's strong sense of isolation, not just from France, but from Brittany as well—especially from 1590 to 1593, when Saint-Malo declared itself an independent republic.

The ramparts themselves started to be erected in 1144 at the instruction of the Bishop of Aleth Jean de la Grille, and continued to be added to over the centuries. Much of these original ramparts are now lost, however, with the oldest sections remaining the Grand'Porte and the section of the Petit Murs by the Biduoan tower, both of which date from the 15th century. Three-quarters of the medieval walls were replaced between 1708 and 1742, while the last addition was made in the

Saint-Malo

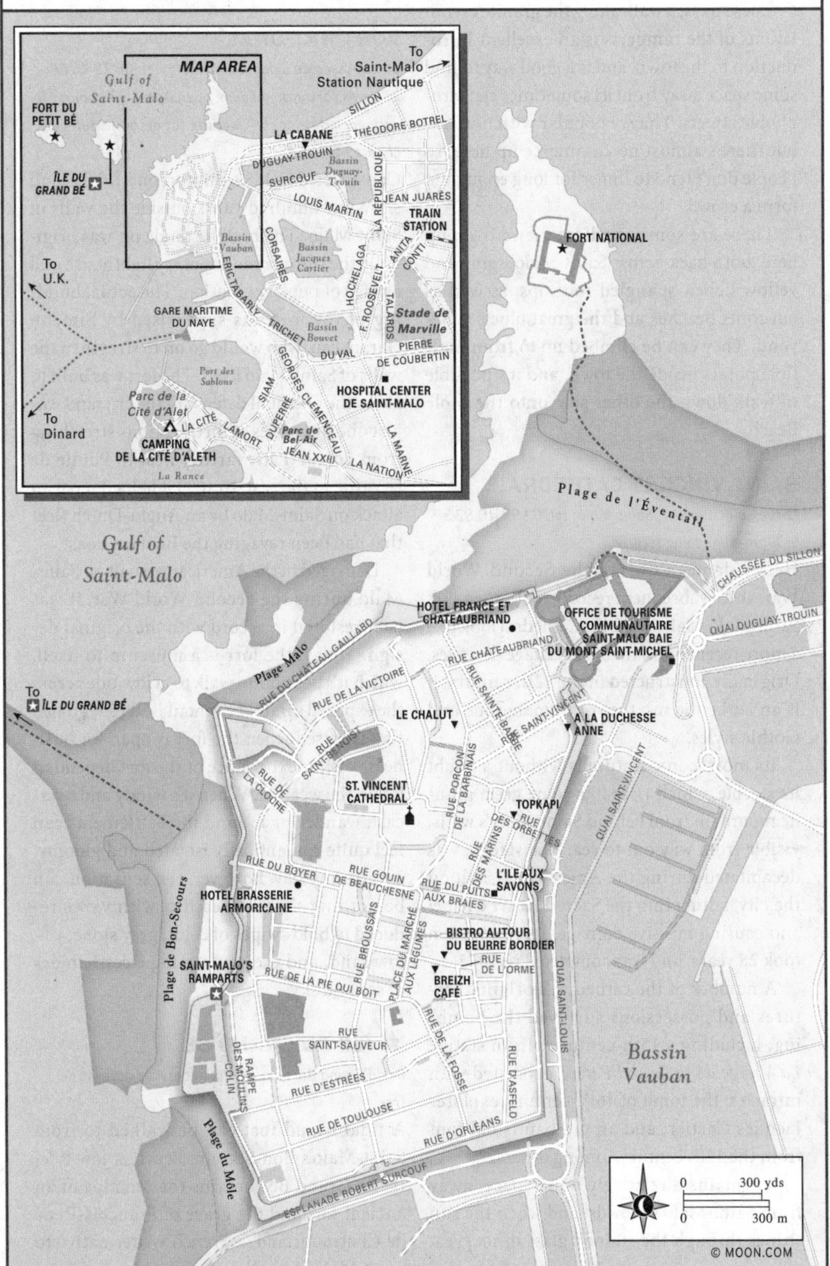
MAP AREA
Gulf of Saint-Malo
FORT DU PETIT BÉ
ÎLE DU GRAND BÉ
To Saint-Malo Station Nautique
SILLON
LA CABANE
THÉODORE BOTREL
DUGUAY-TROUIN
Bassin Duguay-Trouin
SURCOUF
LOUIS MARTIN
JEAN JUARÈS
LA RÉPUBLIQUE
TRAIN STATION
Bassin Vauban
CORSAIRES
Bassin Jacques Cartier
HOCHELAGA
ANITA
CONTI
To U.K.
ERICTABARLY
F. ROOSEVELT
TALARDS
Stade de Marville
GARE MARITIME DU NAYE
TRICHET
Bassin Bouvet
DU VAL
PIERRE DE COUBERTIN
GEORGES CLEMENCEAU
Port des Sablons
Parc de la Cité d'Alet
SIAM
HOSPITAL CENTER DE SAINT-MALO
To Dinard
LA CITÉ
DUPERRÉ
Parc de Bel-Air
LAMORT
CAMPING DE LA CITÉ D'ALETH
JEAN XXIII
LA MARINE
LA NATION
La Rance
FORT NATIONAL
Plage de l'Éventail
Gulf of Saint-Malo
CHAUSSÉE DU SILLON
HOTEL FRANCE ET CHATEAUBRIAND
OFFICE DE TOURISME COMMUNAUTAIRE SAINT-MALO BAIE DU MONT SAINT-MICHEL
QUAI DUGUAY-TROUIN
Plage Malo
RUE DU CHÂTEAU GAILLARD
RUE CHÂTEAUBRIAND
To ÎLE DU GRAND BÉ
RUE DE LA VICTOIRE
RUE SAINTE BARBE
RUE SAINT-VINCENT
LE CHALUT
A LA DUCHESSE ANNE
RUE SAINT-BENOIST
RUE PORCON DE LA BARBINAIS
QUAI SAINT-VINCENT
RUE DE LA CLOCHE
ST. VINCENT CATHEDRAL
TOPKAPI
RUE DES MARINS
RUE DES ORBETTES
RUE DU BOYER
RUE GOUIN DE BEAUCHESNE
RUE DU PUITS AUX BRAIES
L'ILE AUX SAVONS
Plage de Bon-Secours
HOTEL BRASSERIE ARMORICAINE
BISTRO AUTOUR DU BEURRE BORDIER
RUE BROUSSAIS
PLACE DU MARCHÉ AUX LÉGUMES
RUE DE L'ORME
SAINT-MALO'S RAMPARTS
RUE DE LA PIE QUI BOIT
BREIZH CAFÉ
QUAI SAINT-LOUIS
RUE DE LA FOSSE
RUE SAINT-SAUVEUR
RAMPE DES MOULINS COLIN
Bassin Vauban
RUE D'ESTRÉES
RUE D'ASFELD
Plage du Môle
RUE DE TOULOUSE
RUE D'ORLÉANS
ESPLANADE ROBERT SURCOUF
0 300 yds
0 300 m
© MOON.COM

19th century between La Reine Fort and the cavalier des Champs-Vauverts.

These days, a walk along the granite crenulations of the ramparts is an excellent introduction to the town, and is a good way to find some space away from its sometimes claustrophobic streets. They're popular with tourists, but there's almost no commerce up here, so people don't tend to linger for long enough to form a crowd.

There are some excellent views from up here, both back across Saint-Malo's gray and yellow lichen-spangled rooftops, as well as out to its beaches and the great blue sea beyond. They can be climbed up to from multiple points inside the town, and it's possible to walk down the other side onto the Mole Beach.

SAINT VINCENT CATHEDRAL

12 rue Saint-Benoist, Saint-Malo; tel. 02 99 40 82 31; 9:30am-6pm daily; free

Heavy damage during the Second World War, and a subsequent reconstruction, makes Saint-Malo's Saint Vincent Cathedral look like a more recent build than its heritage deserves. Originally constructed in the 12th century, it is an authentic mixture of Romanesque and Gothic styles.

Its most iconic feature is without a doubt its steeple, which rises like some great granite mountain from behind Saint-Malo's walls, visible from way out to sea. The steeple was decapitated during the American assault on the city, falling into the Sacred Heart Chapel and causing massive damage. Its restoration took 28 years, and was completed in 1972.

A number of the cathedral's original features and possessions survived the bombing, including a 15th-century virgin statue, *La Vierge de la Grand'Porte,* associated with miracles; the tomb of 16th-century explorer Jacques Cartier; and an old baptismal font from the 12th century, among others.

It remains a relatively quiet space, away from Saint-Malo's crowds, and when the sun shines through the stained glass of its great rose window, a stunning kaleidoscope of dappled color is thrown on its gray floors.

FORT NATIONAL

60 chaussée du Sillon, Saint-Malo; tel. 06 72 46 66 26; www.fortnational.com; open Apr.-Sept., hours vary each day; consult website for details; adults €5, children 6-16 €3

Constructed in 1689, this fort on a tidal island sits a few hundred yards outside the walls of Saint-Malo. The rock it stands on was originally the site of a rudimentary lighthouse and a place of public execution. The actual building of the fort was supervised by Siméon Garangeau, who would go on to stregthen the walls of Saint-Malo itself. The fort was built to aid in the potential defense of the city, and was just one in a series of fortifications stretching from Fort-le-Latte farther west to Pointe de la Varde in the east. In 1693 it helped repel an attack on Saint-Malo by an Anglo-Dutch fleet that had been ravaging the Brittany coast.

Damaged in the American assault on Saint-Malo during the Second World War, it was later restored in accord with the original design. Today, the fort is a museum to itself, which it's possible to walk to at low tide across the exposed sands of Eventail Beach. A French flag is raised when the fort is open for business. Visitor experience of the fort depends a lot on the weather. When it's windy and overcast, wandering around the battlements can feel quite romantically isolated and gloomy; on a sunny day, however, the sensation can be nothing short of beatific, with views reduced to bold swipes of color: gray stone, yellow sand, and the contrasting electric blues of sea and sky.

★ ÎLE DU GRAND BÉ

Île du Grand Bé, Saint-Malo; accessible at low tide; free

A tidal island that can be walked to from Saint-Malo's Bon-Secours Beach at low tide, Île du Grand Bé contains the remains of an ancient fort and the grave of François-René de Chateaubriand, a French writer native to Saint-Malo. As well as these sights, the island

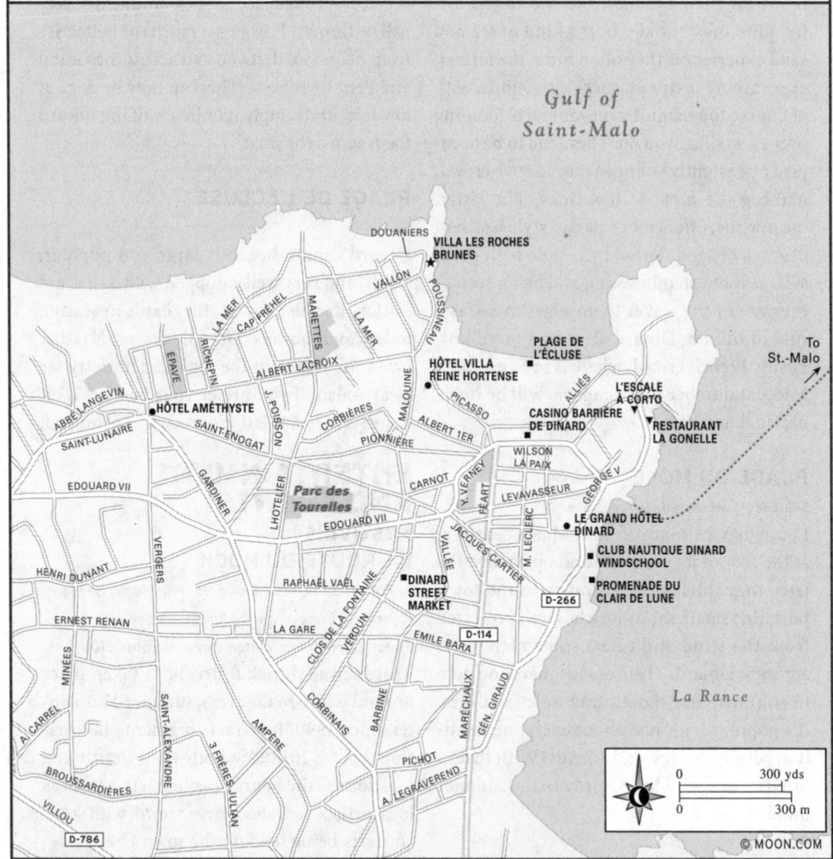

offers a good view of the **Fort du Petit Bé,** but really earns its place as a highlight for being one of the best places from which to take in the full scope of Saint-Malo's ramparts.

At low tide—which is the only time you can reach the island—in the foreground there's the exposed sand, seaweed, and rock, which glistens like a jewel box. Then there are the two gray walls, converging to a point, and behind them the rank and file of Saint-Malo itself, a granite symphony centered by the sharp spire of Saint Vincent's pointing into a miraculous expanse of empty sky. It's the perfect view for holiday snaps or your Instagram story.

Dinard

VILLA LES ROCHES BRUNES

3 allée des Douaniers, Dinard; tel. 02 99 16 30 63; 2pm-7pm Wed.-Mon.; €7

Looming prominently over Dinard's bay, this seaside villa became an emblem of the resort town, referred to as "the Pearl of the Emerald Coast." Constructed between 1893 and 1896 for the Parisian fashion designer Emile Poussineau, the Villa les Roches Brunes is among the most magnificent of Dinard's belle epoque-style houses. The house, along with its gardens, is open to the public, preserved as a time capsule of a more glamorous age.

BEACHES

While both Saint-Malo and Dinard are famous for their beaches, the two towns differ quite substantially in the kind of sea and sand experiences they offer. From the former, expect more textured, rocky surrounds, with of course the magnificent ramparts looming over everything you do. They tend to be occupied by a slightly younger, more active crowd, making the most of low tides. The latter, meanwhile, offers more classic-style beaches, of acres of sand dotted by people with parasols, as interested in seeing and being seen as they are in the waves themselves. Also, as a rule of thumb, Dinard attracts a more uniformly French crowd, whereas in Saint-Malo a decent number of beachgoers will be international tourists.

PLAGE DU MOLE

Saint-Malo, accessed via rue Louvel

Located to the south of Saint-Malo's old town, at the foot of its ramparts and up against the jetty that shields the entrance to the town port, this small, sandy beach is well protected from the wind and offers some nice views across to Dinard. There are lifeguards on duty in summer, and shower and toilet facilities. It's popular with just about everyone: families, young couples, and friends. With that in mind, it can get a little rowdy in the summer months.

PLAGE DE BON-SECOURS

Saint-Malo, accessed via la porte des Champs Vauverts

Saint-Malo's most beautiful beach offers great views back toward the old town behind and the two Îles de Bé ahead. Also, it's very well equipped. There's sea kayak rental here at **Le Spot Nautique Saint Malo Bon-Secours** (10am-6pm July-Aug.; kayaks €8 per hour), disabled access, a first-aid station, and a saltwater pool, plus a diving board filled by the tide. There are also showers and toilets, and the beach is supervised by lifeguards in the summer. With all these facilities, needless to say, it can get pretty crowded, especially in the summer, and is not what anyone would call a relaxing beach. However, there's plenty of fun to be had, and if you can find space to kick around a soccer ball or throw a Frisbee, so much the better. It's from here, too, that you can access the Grand and Petit Bé islands. This can only be done at low tide, and simply requires walking toward them across the sand.

PLAGE DE L'ÉCLUSE

Dinard

Dinard's main beach is large and popular, sandy, and very well equipped with a first-aid station, disabled access, lifeguards in season, toilets, and showers. The only downside is that when the tide's out the sea can get pretty far away—also, if you prefer your beaches a bit more secluded, this one's probably not for you.

ENTERTAINMENT AND EVENTS

Festivals

LA ROUTE DU ROCK

Le Fort de Saint-Père and la Nouvelle Vague and la Plage Arte Concerts; www.laroutedurock.com; twice a year, summer and winter; three-day pass €108

This biannual rock festival has taken place around Saint-Malo every summer and winter since 1990. It attracts big-name international acts: 2018 saw both Patti Smith and Charlotte Gainsbourgh playing sets, as well as local artists. It draws a large crowd, with some concerts being held on the town's beaches—spectators stand, and the atmosphere can get pretty rowdy. The "winter collection," which is smaller than the summer event, is a play off the fashion world trend for celebrating the different seasons.

FOLKLORES DU MONDE

Saint-Malo, multiple locations; tel. 02 99 48 29 93; www.folkloresdumonde.bzh; July; two-day pass €32

Taking place in locations all over Saint-Malo for a week in July, this festival attracts folk

1: Saint-Malo in all its splendor **2:** Dinard boasts several sandy beaches. **3:** A swimming pool filled by the sea dominates Saint-Malo's main beach.

1
2
3

musicians from all over the world. Founded in 1996, it features Balinese dancers, Mexican mariachis, Spanish flamenco guitarists, and more among the regular mix of Irish and other Celtic flautists. A colorful "march of the nations" parade down boulevard Rochebonne to the Parc des Chênes caps the event each year.

DINARD FESTIVAL OF BRITISH CINEMA

28 boulevard Féart, Dinard; tel. 02 99 88 19 04; www.dinardfilmfestival.fr; Sept.; festival pass €80, film screenings adults €7, reduced €5

Film festivals offer a certain glamor to beachside resort towns, luring stars and giving a good excuse for a flashy party. In a move directly copied from the American cinema festival in Deauville, in 1989 Dinard set up its own, the Festival of British Cinema, showcasing both major British releases and independent prodcutions. Director Alfred Hitchcock has become the festival's emblem, due to local claims that he used to visit the town and based the house in *Psycho* on the villa above the Plage de l'Écluse.

Casinos

CASINO BARRIÈRE DE DINARD

4 boulevard Wilson, Dinard; tel. 02 99 16 30 30; www.casinosbarriere.com/fr/dinard.html; 10am-2am daily

Well-located with views out across Dinard's main beach, this straddles the line between seedy and glamorous. There are more actual croupiers here than at other casinos, though, which is something, offering a wider variety of face-to-face table games. There is a bar and restaurant on-site, and no strict dress code—shorts and tank tops aren't allowed, but don't worry about the tux. Remember to bring your passport as an ID, as nothing else will be accepted.

SHOPPING

St. Malo

L'ÎLE AUX SAVONS

5 rue du Puits aux Braies; tel. 02 99 46 60 59; http://lileauxsavons.com; 11am-1pm and 3pm-7pm Tues.-Sat.

This quaint soap store on Saint-Malo's backstreets offers both local products and those from around the world. A number are already prettily wrapped up and make for good gifts or souvenirs.

Dinard

DINARD STREET MARKET

Les Halles de la Concorde, Dinard; 7:30am-1:30pm Tues., Thurs., and Sat.

One of the largest in the region, this largely covered market offers up the usual combination of local produce, seafood, and cheap clothing. Almost 300 merchants set up every Tuesday, Thursday, and Saturday morning around the area of Les Halles de la Concorde. It can also stand as an earthy relief from the glamour of a Dinard holiday.

SPORTS AND RECREATION

Walks

★ PROMENADE DU CLAIR DE LUNE

Promenade du Clair de Lune, Dinard; free

This boardwalk, wrapping around Dinard's rocky coastline and protected from prevailing winds, offers a gentle appreciation of the town's grandiose and slightly surreal landscape, as well as its multitude of differently designed villas, balanced on cliffs and buttressed with faux-medieval foundations. There is a mix of vegetation here, too, mainly Mediterranean, but also including Moroccan cedars, eucalyptus trees, and Himalayan pine. These perfume the air with the whiff of distant lands, all mixed up with Brittany's salt wind.

It may sound unlikely, but a walk here offers a small sense of adventure and whiff of the exotic. It's a combination of the unusual plant life and the city defenses, probably, that almost makes you imagine yourself on the set of *Pirates of the Caribbean*. So what if the other people you're sharing your walk with are not wearing tricorns and eye patches, but rather pastel jumpers and boat shoes? The promenade can get busy in the evenings, but most visitors to Dinard stick to the beach.

The promenade itself is only around 300 feet (about a hundred meters) long, but to continue the experience, cross the Plage de l'Écluse and pick up the Chemin de Ronde de la Malouine, which wraps around the rocky outcrops of the town for another mile. A nice easy circuit is to walk this route until the first small beach you come to, from whence you can climb some steps onto the boulevard de la Mer and walk back among the fancy residential villas to the center of town.

Water Sports

CLUB NAUTIQUE DINARD WINDSCHOOL

Plage de Saint Enogat, rue Roger Vercel, Dinard; tel. 06 35 96 18 55; http://windschool.free.fr; 10am-6pm daily Apr.-Sept.; courses from €120, kayak rental €12 per hour

Despite its name, this water-sports center offers far more than just wind-based activities. As well as windsurfing and catamaran rental and lessons, there are also stand-up paddleboards and sea kayaks available. It's a friendly place, used to dealing with out-of-towners, and has great access to the waters around Dinard, which are a delightfully picturesque place to splash about in. Keep aware that Dinard is a very popular tourist venue, so if you're planning on making use of this club, it might do to reserve a spot in a course before you arrive.

FOOD

Saint-Malo

LE CHALUT

8 rue de la Corne de Cerf, Saint-Malo; tel. 02 99 56 71 58; 12:15pm-1:15pm and 7:15pm-9:15pm Wed.-Sun.; menus €25-75

An extremely good, somewhat classy seafood restaurant. Here, they take real time and effort over the catch, preparing it beautifully with well-balanced sauces. The menu also includes the offer of a whole lobster, which is sure to delight many. Popular among locals and tourists alike, it's a reasonably formal dining experience, and booking is recommended for both lunch and dinner.

LA CABANE

Quai Duguay-Trouin, Saint-Malo; tel. 02 23 15 32 63; www.lacabane-saintmalo.com; 7pm-9:30pm Thurs.-Fri.; 12pm-2:30pm and 7pm-9:30pm Sat.-Sun., menus €29.80-48.80

Feeling fishy? La Cabane is definitely the place to go. Its no-nonsense menus offer an almost overwhelming assault of denizens of the deep (all locally sourced, of course):

wandering around the rocks in Dinard

a starter of fish soup, followed by a heaving tray of *fruits de mer*, then half a grilled lobster to finish it all off. The interior is similarly stripped for purpose, being nautical-themed but not overwhelmingly so, and it's as much for locals as for tourists.

BISTRO AUTOUR DU BEURRE BORDIER

7 rue de l'Orme, Saint-Malo; tel. 02 23 18 25 81; www.lebeurrebordier.com/bistrot-autour-du-beurre; 12pm-2pm and 7pm-10pm Tues.-Sun.; mains €19-32

Wonder of wonders! This restaurant builds its entire meal selection from the highest-quality artisanal butter and cheese. Most dishes have some mouthwatering base, from fennel-infused to smoked-salt butter. Yes, it's rich, but it's also delicious. On top of the butter, meals are fairly traditional French with a mixture of fish, meat, and game on the menu, while the restaurant interior is of old rock walls, eclectic decorations, and modern furniture design.

A LA DUCHESSE ANNE

3-5 place Guy la Chambre, Saint-Malo; tel. 02 99 40 85 33; 12pm-2pm and 7pm-9:30pm Thurs.-Tues.; menus €22-35

A classy-looking place, where the food is well presented and served with some flare by white-jacketed waiters. There's a relatively large terrace, too, which is good for warm nights. The food itself is of fairly classic French/Breton variety: a good number of seafood options, plus red meat such as *agneau de pré-salé* (lamb whose flesh is considered "pre-salted" having been raised on nearby tidal plains). Being right in the center of town, it can feel a bit touristy, but it is still a good bet.

BREIZH CAFÉ

6 rue de l'Orme, Saint-Malo; tel. 02 99 56 96 08; https://breizhcafe.com; 12pm-2pm and 7pm-10pm Wed.-Sun.; €10-17

Pushing the humble crepe to quite extraordinary heights, this is a terrific place to stop for a light lunch or even a full evening meal. Recognizing a certain kinship between Japanese and Breton cuisine—specifically in their appreciation of fish—this restaurant brings the two together in terrifically tasty ways. There are also plenty of more traditional dishes on the menu, borrowing heavily on apple flavors. The presentation, too, is slick and stylish. You'll never look at a crepe the same way again.

TOPKAPI

1 rue des Orbettes, Saint-Malo; tel. 09 50 20 11 64; 11am-11:30pm daily; €10-€13

A place in which the French take on the traditional English dish of fish and chips, Topkapi manages it brilliantly. There's nothing flashy going on here, but the fish is fresh and it's served as it ought to be, wrapped in newspaper and alongside brilliant green mushy peas. A happening place for people to pop into on a night out, it's popular not just with visiting Brits but locals as well.

Dinard

L'ESCALE À CORTO

12 avenue George V, Dinard; tel. 02 99 46 78 57; 7:30pm-1am Tues.-Sun.; mains €17-27

With a friendly owner and staff and feeling something like a village pub, this place is the perfect antidote to a lot of the posher restaurants around town, offering top-quality local cooking at honest prices. The scallops are a particular delight. It's popular year-round, so book ahead.

RESTAURANT LA GONELLE

Promenade du Clair de Lune, Dinard; tel. 02 99 16 40 47; www.lagonelle.com; 12:30pm-1:30pm and 7:30pm-9:30pm Thurs.-Mon.; menus €16-35

Sitting right on Dinard's beautiful promenade du Clair de Lune and looking out to the water, this restaurant is great both for people-watching and its views. There's copious seafood available on the menu, interestingly prepared and well-presented—they're not afraid to use plenty of cheese and cream! Lobster, fish, and crab tanks are found inside.

ACCOMMODATIONS

Saint-Malo

HÔTEL BRASSERIE ARMORICAINE

6 rue du Boyer, Saint-Malo; tel. 02 99 40 89 13; www.hotel-armoricaine.com; from €95 d

Right in the center of Saint-Malo's old town, this is a convenient and cozy hotel that won't break the bank. Rooms may seem small for some, but squeezed between the walls of Saint-Malo, it's hard to expect much more for this price. Most importantly, the Bon-Secours Beach is just a short walk away. There's also WiFi throughout and an on-site restaurant serving local cuisine.

HÔTEL FRANCE ET CHATEAUBRIAND

12 place Chateaubriand, Saint-Malo; tel. 02 99 56 66 52; www.hotel-chateaubriand-st-malo.com; from €132 d

Named for François-René de Chateaubriand, the Saint-Malo writer buried on the Grand Bé, this large, elegant hotel housed in a Napoleon III-era building has high-ceilinged, comfortable rooms, some of which have balconies looking out onto Saint-Malo's ramparts. It's also just a short walk from the town's Grande Plage du Sillon, and naturally comes fully equipped with all the expected mod cons. Public spaces are also impressive, with hints of the 19th century in their decor, and appear filled with life.

Dinard

HÔTEL AMÉTHYSTE

2 rue des Bains, Dinard; tel. 02 99 46 61 81; https://amethyste.popinns.com; from €76 d

Brightly lit, this budget hotel spans three floors in a traditional Dinard house. Don't expect anything too much, but it's clean and passably comfortable, a very short walk from the beach, and not too far from the center of town either. WiFi is available throughout. For pricey Dinard, this is a good deal.

HÔTEL VILLA REINE HORTENSE

19 rue de la Malouine, Dinard; tel. 02 99 46 54 31; www.villa-reine-hortense.com; from €180 d

Here's your opportunity to stay in one of the icons of Dinard's beachfront. This majestic belle epoque hotel was built by the Russian prince Vlassov in honour of Queen Hortense de Beauharnais of Holland in the early 19th century. It remains just as elegant as it ever was today, with rooms and views fit for royalty. As a luxury establishment, you can expect all the modern conveniences. The terrace, too, is one of its high points, reserved only for

luxury hotel and beachfront icon Villa Reine Hortense

guests, perfectly located and with easy access to the sea. If you want to stay here, make sure you book well in advance, as rooms fill up with alarming speed.

LE GRAND HÔTEL DINARD

46 avenue George V, Dinard; tel. 02 99 88 26 26; www.hotelsbarriere.com/fr/dinard/le-grand-hotel.html; from €330 d

Part of the high-end Barrière group with all the classic features of luxury: indecently soft bedding, scented hallways, minibars, and incredibly attentive staff. A large terrace bounded on three sides and looking out to the sea awards an almost cloistered feel, like the beautiful view of Dinard's bay belongs only to you. Decorated with furniture from the time of Napoleon III and infused with a belle epoque charm, this hotel provides service of the highest standard.

Camping

CAMPING DE LA CITÉ D'ALETH

Allée Gaston Buy, Saint-Malo; tel. 02 99 81 60 91; www.ville-saint-malo.fr/camping-la-cite-dalet; open Mar. 31-May 21 and July 1-Sept.; pitch for two people in high season from €17.10

This is a remarkably well-located campsite, a walkable distance (just) from Saint-Malo's citadel and close to the ferry port—great if you're shipping out the next day. It boasts some amazing views straight out onto the Rance estuary and to Dinard. It's fairly basic, mind, without even showers or toilets, but it does have a water supply, and electricity hookups are available for an additional price. In other words, it's more for motor homes than those with tents, unless you're willing to rough it.

INFORMATION

OFFICE DE TOURISME COMMUNAUTAIRE SAINT-MALO BAIE DU MONT SAINT-MICHEL

Espl. Saint-Vincent, Saint-Malo; tel. 08 25 13 52 00; www.saint-malo-tourisme.com; 9:30am-7:30pm Mon.-Sat., 10am-7pm Sun.

With the number of tourists coming through Saint-Malo, it's hardly surprising that this is a sleek operation with well-trained, multilingual staff. They're happy to give advice about activities and events both in Saint-Malo and the wider area.

DINARD ÉMERAUDE TOURISME

2 bis boulevard Féart, Dinard; tel. 08 21 23 55 00; www.dinardemeraudetourisme.com; 9:30am-6:45pm daily

Located in a stunning art deco building, this is a large tourist office that, as well as covering Dinard, can also give you plenty of advice about excursions farther along the Emerald Coast. Staff are multilingual.

SERVICES

HOSPITAL CENTER DE SAINT-MALO

1 rue de la Marne, Saint-Malo; tel. 02 99 21 21 21; www.cht-ranceemeraude.fr; ER open 24 hours

A good-size hospital with an emergency unit located very close to Saint-Malo's old town center. You'll likely find English-speaking doctors if you need them.

TRANSPORTATION

Getting There and Around

BY CAR

Having a car is a mixed blessing for Saint-Malo. The town is not serviced directly by a freeway, and the fastest way in or out is the D137, which connects with the N176—the freeway that runs laterally across this part of northern Brittany, and is, despite how things may look on the map, the fastest way of moving along this coast. It in turn connects to Pontorson (30 miles/48 kilometers, 40 minutes), Caen (105 miles/169 kilometers, 1 hour 50 minutes), and in the other direction Dinan (20 miles/32 kilometers, 30 minutes). Rennes is directly to the south along the D137 (40 miles/64 kilometers, 50 minutes).

Saint-Malo can also be approached from the east along the coast, which may be tempting if you're coming from Mont-Saint-Michel. This is a very attractive drive but takes considerably longer than the inland route (45 miles/72 kilometers, about 1 hour

40 minutes), being around on slow roads—it may take even longer if you stop for photos, and there are ample chances to do that along the way, with the iconic shape of Mont-Saint-Michel often winking in the distance. From Paris, the drive is around four hours, leaving the French capital on the A11, which takes you via Rennes and is a toll road. Expect to pay around €20. From Rennes the drive is about an hour along the D137.

Once arriving in Saint-Malo, you'll have to find somewhere to park. Be aware that if you are not prepared or willing to compromise that this hunt may become one of your defining memories of the city. Most visitors will search for a space in one of the large parking lots just outside the city walls. These fill up early, however, and so should you if you don't want to spend an hour looking. Prices are €1.20 for two hours in the low season €3 for two hours in the high season, with every additional 15 minutes being charged at €0.20 and €0.40, respectively.

Cheaper and less stress is the park-and-ride option in the Paul Féval parking lot, about a mile east of the old town. This is €3.30 for the whole day, and is connected to the old town by the Line 2 bus service, which is free with the price of a parking ticket. For those planning ahead, meanwhile, there's the Saint-Vincent underground parking lot option (www.q-park-resa.fr/fr/parking/saint-malo/saint-vincent-23.html?). This has 481 spaces, and is intended more for long-stay visitors to the town. Importantly, you can reserve a spot from just under €14 a day.

Those feeling ambitious might want to try parking inside the city walls. Costs are €2 per two hours in low season and €4 per two hours in high season, with prices going up €0.30 and €0.60 respectively every 15 minutes after that. Conversely, so many people are so certain they won't find a space in the old town, you may actually have more a chance looking here than outside the walls if you turn up late or without planning. It can be good if you're there for a shorter stay.

Getting to Dinard is much the same as Saint-Malo, though the town is more forgiving once you arrive. Free parking there is available in residential areas if you're willing to look for it. Even the center of town has quite reasonable parking prices: The first half hour is free throughout the year, then it's €0.40 per hour in low season and €1.20 per hour in high season.

Any town with a tourist office that looks as good as the one in Dinard, you know is well set up for visitors.

BY TRAIN

Trains to Saint-Malo include three a day from Paris, costing around €74 one way and taking just under three hours; nine every day from Dinan for €10, taking an hour; and 16 from Rennes, taking about an hour and costing around €15. The station, **Gare de Saint-Malo** (avenue Anita Conti, Saint-Malo; tel. 08 92 35 35 35; www.gares-sncf.com/fr/gare/frxsb/saint-malo; 5:40am-9:30pm Mon.-Thurs., 5:40am-11:10pm Fri., 7am-9:50pm Sat., 8:10am-9:50pm Sun.) is less than a mile away from the old town, and should be an easy walk. There are no trains to Dinard.

BY BUS

To reach Saint-Malo and Dinard from Paris by coach, there are two services a day, one run by **Flixbus** (www.flixbus.com), the other by **Ouibus** (www.ouibus.com). Both will cost around €25 provided you book at least a couple of days in advance. Buying a ticket on the day from the bus itself will cost about €60. Departure times are early, around 7:30am, and the journey lasts about 5.5 hours. From Rennes, the Illenoo service runs 3-6 services every day to Saint-Malo and Dinard for about €7. They also run between the two towns.

In all likelihood, your time in Saint-Malo will be spent mostly in the old town without the need for buses. However, should you have to catch one for whatever reason, they cost €1.30 and run until about 8pm, with some running later in the summer. The service is run by a company called **Mat** (www.reseau-mat.fr). From the train station, Buses 1, 2, and 3 run to the old town, as does a shuttle called the Cœur de Ville, which runs 7:40am-7pm Monday-Saturday. For a bus into Dinard, take the **Illenoo** (www.illenoo-services.fr) service, which leaves from the train station every hour and takes about 30 minutes, costing €2.70, depositing you close to the center of town.

Dinard, meanwhile, is a very walkable town.

BY FERRY

Saint-Malo is an international port town, and there are sailings to Saint-Malo from Portsmouth, U.K., by **Brittany Ferries** (tel. 02 99 40 64 41; www.brittany-ferries.fr), with one sailing a day costing around €240 each way for a vehicle plus passengers in high season, with a sailing time of around 11 hours (foot passengers are €45 each way). **Condor Ferries** (www.condorferries.co.uk), meanwhile, sails from Poole in the U.K. via the Channel Islands for about the same price, with journey times of about 12 hours. The port, **Gare Maritime du Naye, Saint-Malo,** is less than a mile from the old town, and connected by a free shuttle bus: Signs for this should be obvious once you disembark.

The ferry between Saint-Malo and Dinard is run by the **Compagnie Corsaire** (www.compagniecorsaire.com), and leaves in high season at least every 30 minutes, costing €8.60 return for an adult and €5.60 for a child. The journey time is about 10 minutes. Off season, there are fewer crossings and they are less expensive.

Dinan

An impeccably preserved hill town of half-timber houses, narrow cobbled streets, and a lively river port, Dinan seems to have changed little since the Middle Ages. Much of its prosperity grew from its connection by river to the busy trading port of Saint-Malo, less than 20 miles (32 kilometers) away to the north. As an inland conduit to that town, Dinan earned the money to spend on expanding its ramparts and building municipal vanity projects, such as the Tour de l'Horloge.

The wealth of its past, combined with a degree of luck for weathering the storms of war and never growing so much as to be swamped by ugly suburbs, means that Dinan today remains a tourist gem, resembling a porthole into history that allows us to see what Brittany must have been like years ago.

Like many such towns, Dinan plays home to a cottage industry looking to cash in on its medieval past. There is a degree more authenticity to the trinket sellers here than in many of the other old forts of Europe, however. The affection Bretons have toward history shines through, and working glass blowers, book binders, and engravers still operate in Dinan's streets. Every year the town throws a medieval-themed festival called the Fête des Remperts, which seems perhaps less for visitors and more for the locals to celebrate their heritage themselves.

ORIENTATION

There are really two parts of Dinan worth visiting: its port and the old town behind its walls. The former is a stretch of quayside bordering the River Rance, lined by old houses and crossed by a 15th-century bridge. From here, the steep rue de Petit-Fort leads you uphill into the old town. Should you continue following this road, which was the main way into Dinan up until the 18th century, it turns into the Grande rue, which though not especially "grand" eventually brings you out the other side of the old town, where a parking lot and most of the major roads leading into Dinan converge. The town center itself is a maze of cobbled streets and old houses, which are delightful enough just to walk around at random. **Ramparts** encircle the old town and offer excellent views of the countryside beyond.

SIGHTS

Tour de l'Horloge

23 rue de l'Horloge; tel. 02 96 87 69 76; 10am-6:30pm daily May-Sept.; adults €4, reduced €2

Originally a meeting place for the town council, this 15th-century tower also served as a lookout for fires that were common among Dinan's wooden houses. It became a clock tower at the turn of the 16th century. A gift from Duchess Anne of Brittany, its largest bell, which weighed about 2.5 tons, was called Anne. Anne was melted down in 1907 and recast into a bell called Duchess Anne, which still rings today. There are five bells in the tower in total, though one does not ring. The smaller ones chime out every quarter hour, leaving the powerful sounding Duchess Anne to mark the hour. The original clock mechanism was made in 1498 in Nantes and is one of the oldest in Europe.

A 150-foot-high (45-meter-high) tower was opened to the public in 1932 by the then mayor of Dinan, Michel Geistdoerfer. Today, it hosts a small museum about old Dinan, and the views from the top remain spectacular—on a clear day you can see Mont Saint-Michel from its heights.

The Ramparts

Les Remperts, Dinan

Erected at the end of the 13th century, the town ramparts are 8,800 feet (2,700 meters) all the way around and include no less than 14 guard towers and four gates, plus the town's castle from which its defenses would have

THE CLO K TOWER
1
2
3

been organized, and which now houses the town museum. When they were built, these ramparts were the third largest in Brittany, with only those in Nantes and Rennes being more extensive. The ramparts of those towns have now disappeared, however, while Dinan's continued to be added to in small ways across the centuries, leaving it now with the biggest medieval fortifications of the region.

Today, a walk around them offers some great views out across the surrounding countryside and is an excellent way to get the measure of Dinan itself. They are also punctuated by information boards, in French, offering up facts about particular towers and the history of the town.

Château de Dinan

Rue du Château, Dinan; tel. 02 96 39 45 20; www.dinan-capfrehel.com/culture-patrimoine/chateau-de-dinan; 1:30pm-6:30pm daily Mar.-May, 10:30am-7pm daily May-Sept.; adults €5.90, reduced €2.90

The crowning glory of Dinan's fortifications, this castle was the command center for the defense of the city. Now known as the Donjon de la Duchesse Anne, after Brittany's famous 15th-century ruler, it was actually constructed on the order of John IV, Duke of Brittany in the late 14th century. It stands 111 feet (34 meters) high.

After Dinan began to lose its strategic importance in the 17th century, the château, along with some of its rampart towers, were largely converted into a jail. For a time after that, the building played host to the Musée d'Histoire de la Ville de Dinan, but that recently closed as the building's naturally damp interior was damaging the artifacts. Now, its interiors can seem a little bare, though this is probably a more acurate representation of how they would have been kept historically.

1: Dinan's striking clock tower **2:** Dominating the town ramparts is Dinan's château, which today doubles as the town museum **3:** a view from Dinan's ramparts out across the town's old river port

Basilique Saint-Sauveur de Dinan

14 place Saint-Sauveur, Dinan; tel. 02 96 87 69 76; free

The story of this church begins in the 12th century, when one of the lords of Dinan, Rivallon Le Roux, on crusade in the holy land was taken prisoner by the Saracens and imprisoned for years. While there, he vowed that if he ever escaped and saw Dinan again he would build a church in the town dedicated to the Holy Trinity and the Holy Savior. He did make it back to Dinan, and the Basilique Saint-Sauveur was the result.

Begun in 1123, its design bears an imprint of this story and of the crusades themselves. Conceived in the Romanesque style, it has hints of Byzantine and even Persian designs. The details in its carvings have no equivalant in Brittany, some depicting very un-Breton creatures such as camels and lions, far more appropriate to Middle Eastern art. Little of the original church remains today, work to expand it having begun in the 15th century and finally completed in the 17th with an addition of a bell tower, which took over from the Tour de l'Horloge as the tallest building in Dinan.

Despite its history and unusual interior, the church remains more a space for worship than it does for tourism, and is a comparatively undervisited part of the town. The atmosphere inside is one of hushed reverence, giving visitors the space and time to deeply contemplate its carvings and other artifacts. Mass is held every Sunday at 9am, should you want to attend.

Château de la Hunaudaye

La Hunaudaye; tel. 02 96 34 82 10; www.la-hunaudaye.com; 2pm-6pm daily Apr.-June and Oct.-Apr., 10:30am-6:30pm daily July-Sept.; adults €5.50, reduced €3.50

About 12 miles (20 kilometers) west of Dinan lay these still-spectacular ruins of a medieval castle as you might imagine medieval castles would look. Constructed around 1220, Château de la Hunaudaye was intended to defend the territory of the town of Lamballe, and did so until being destroyed during Brittany's vicious civil war in the 1300s. It was rebuilt in the 15th century and experienced a long period of prosperity, which only really began to fade in the 18th century. A hundred years later and weeds were beginning to grow between its masonry, and local villagers had started to use it as a quarry for their own building needs. The rot was stopped when the château was declared a historic monument in 1930. Today, visitors are invited to explore the ruins, which include a drawbridge, five towers, the courtyard, and various living areas. As you do this, despite its ruined state, it doesn't take long to start imagining marauding armies barely beyond the horizon, or envisioning the kind of strangely cloistered lives the medieval nobles who slept in these rooms must have lived. It's also surrounded by a moat, which helps add to the unexpectedly living quality of this ruin, and makes for good photographs.

Abbaye de Lehon

18 le Bourg; tel. 02 96 87 40 40; 10:30am-12:30pm and 2:30pm-6:30pm daily July-Aug., 2:30pm-6:30pm daily Sept.; guided tours €5, reduced €3

Legend has it that this abbey was founded by six traveling monks from Wales in the 9th century. They had settled on the banks of the River Rance and were praying to find land on which to build a monastery. By chance, Nominoe, the first duke of Brittany, was at that time hunting nearby. He heard prayers and made the offer that he would grant them land provided they acquired the relics of a true Breton saint.

Norman invaders destroyed this first abbey not long after, and the buildings were reconstructed in the 12th and 13th centuries. As with many other religious buildings in France, it suffered during the French Revolution, being used as an ammunition dump, and by the 1890s was falling into ruins until local villagers took it upon themselves to restore the structure. From there, throughout the 20th century, larger restoration projects took place, making now for a fascinating place to visit, where the architecture, some of which has been left in an evocatively ruined state, speaks of centuries of stories and undulating prosperity. There are also some lovely small gardens to see, including one used for growing herbs and vegetables, which really hearkens back to the days when abbeys would have needed to be almost self-sufficient to survive. The abbey can be reached by walking along the towpath of the River Rance, about half a mile to the south of Dinan.

FOOD

Local Cuisine

LA COURTINE

6 rue de la Croix, Dinan; tel. 02 96 39 74 41; 12:15pm-9pm Tues.-Sat.; mains €18-24

Hidden away on one of Dinan's side streets, this is an excellent local restaurant serving locally inspired dishes that include lots of fresh white fish from the coast at a very reasonable cost. Run by two young men who are unafraid to experiment in combining flavors, it has an uncomplicated, broadly traditional interior and is frequently busy. Booking is recommended, especially on weekends. Earlier in the week, it should be easier to find a spot.

LA LYCORNE

6 rue de la Poissonnerie; tel. 02 96 39 08 13; www.restaurant-lycorne-dinan.com; 12pm-2pm and 7pm-11pm Tues.-Sat.; mains €10-24

With a name that translates to "the unicorn" in English, there is something if not quite magical then at least very playful about this popular local hangout. Its extensive seafood selection reminds you that Dinan is a port and not all that far from the sea, while the offer of hot plates on which to cook your own food is sure to bring a smile to most people's faces (Note: this is not obligitory; if you want food precooked, they do that too). Food is locally sourced; there's even a blackboard on which they've chalked up the nearby producers they rely upon. Booking is recommended.

CHEZ ODETTE BONGRAIN

9 rue du Quai; tel. 02 96 87 57 51; 12pm-2:30pm and 6pm-9:30pmFri.-Tues., 6pm-9:30pm Wed.; mains €20-40

Chez Odette Bongrain serves up hearty regional cuisine of steak and seafood from which lashings of cream, cheese, or butter are seldom far away. Dishes come on wooden boards or in earthenware bowls, and this traditionally decorated quayside place has a friendly atmosphere and very welcoming staff. It could easily be cynically touristy, but in fact is quite the opposite. It attracts plenty of locals, as well, so make sure to book ahead.

Budget Options

CRÊPERIE AU COIN DE LA BREIZH

18 rue de la Poissonnerie; tel. 02 96 87 01 47; 12pm-2pm and 7pm-10pm daily; menus €10-12

This is a friendly crepe establishment with strong local community vibes despite its location in the heart of touristy Dinan. A wide variety of crepes is on offer: try some with scallops as the main ingredient. All are delicious and excellent value. The staff are attentive and speak some English.

ACCOMMODATIONS

€50-100

HÔTEL ARVOR DINAN

5 rue Auguste Pavie; tel. 02 96 39 21 22; www.hotelarvordinan.com; from €80 d

Housed in an elegant 18th-century property, converted from a Dominican convent, this is a cozy, charming hotel in the town center. It benefitted from a major renovation program in 2014 and 2015, and offers rooms for up to six people. Its public spaces are furnished with antique furniture, while its individually decorated rooms offer WiFi and flat-screen TVs.

€100-200

LA MAISON PAVIE

10 place Saint-Sauveur; tel. 02 96 84 45 37; www.lamaisonpavie.com; from €105 d

Looking out to the Basilique Saint-Sauveur and located within a classic 15th-century townhouse, this hotel offers guests an excellent view of Dinan from the other side of the timber-frames. Decorated with the utmost taste in bold colors and varnished wood surfaces, it makes the most of its heritage, keeping it on display but in a manner which is undoubtedly far more comfortable than it would have been during its medieval years. The hotel takes its name from a former

Restaurants today make up the ground floor of many old buildings in Dinan's center.

resident, Auguste Pavie, a French explorer of Southeast Asia who was born here in 1847. WiFi and flat-screen TVs are found throughout. An excellent deal.

LE 27 À DINAN

27 place Duguesclin; tel. 06 15 53 55 97; www.le27-bbb.fr; from €145 d

This bright and colorful bed-and-breakfast crammed with stylish original features is located inside a 19th-century building, which backs onto the town's ramparts. There's a comfy shared lounge, a garden for sunny days, and even a billiards room to unwind in in the evenings—this can also be a good place to strike up conversation with fellow guests. Breakfast is a sumptuous buffet of meats and pastries. Make sure to book early, as it can be popular.

Camping

CAMPING AIRE DU VERGER

La Gromillais; tel. 06 12 13 44 04; www.aireduverger.com; open May-Sept.; camping for two people €15, cabins from €28

A little out of town, near the village of Pleslin-Trigavou, which is about a 15-minute drive to Dinan, this charming, secluded spot is set in a forested patch of the Breton countryside. It can seem almost too anarchic to be an official campsite, with pitches rough-and-ready and not clearly defined. However, there's definite curation at work here, with some interesting vintage cabins, plus on-site showers, toilets, and cooking facilities.

TRANSPORTATION

Getting There and Around

BY CAR

By car, Dinan is about 20 miles (32 kilometers, 40 minutes) south of Saint-Malo, first taking the D137, then crossing the River Rance on the N176. From Rennes, take the D137 north, turning off on the D794. This journey is also about 40 minutes, though a little further—30 miles (48 kilometers). Should you be traveling from Paris (250 miles/402 kilometers total), the fastest way is to go via Rennes along the A11, and total journey time is about four hours.

There are plenty of parking lots around town, but you have to pay for them (€0.50 per hour). The lot at the Place du Marché is the only one inside the ramparts, but it's both a little more expensive (€0.80 per hour) and very popular, especially in the high season. In general, you're better off parking just outside the town walls and walking in.

BY TRAIN

Trains to and from the Dinan train station, **Gare de Dinan** (place du 11 Novembre 1918, Dinan; tel. 36 35; www.ter.sncf.com/bretagne/gares/87478164/Dinan/pratique; 6am-7:30pm Mon.-Fri., 6:50am-7:30pm Sat., 9:45am-7:30pm Sun.), run laterally along the Lison to Laballe line. This means that if you want to get here from Saint-Malo or Rennes, you'll have to change at Dol de Bretagne. You can make the trip nine times a day from Rennes, costing from €15.70, taking 1 hour 15 minutes, and nine times daily from Saint-Malo, costing from €10 and taking about an hour. The station itself is located about 300 yards northwest of the old town.

BY BUS

The **Illenoo bus service** (www.illenoo-services.fr) leaves from place Duclos and from the train station bus stop, running several times a day to Dinard for €3.90 and taking 30 minutes, and to Rennes costing €6.20 and taking around 1 hour 15 minutes.

BY FERRY

For a scenic journey and timeless approach to Dinan, take a ferry boat from Saint-Malo or Dinard along the Rance River. The landscape along its banks is at once romantic and stunning, passing perfectly preserved fishing villages, old castles, and sheer cliffs. The arrival in Dinan's port is then something quite special all of its own, as you pull up along the timber-frame houses, being gifted a close-up experience of how most people would have arrived in the town throughout its history.

The journey is run by **Compagnie Corsaire** (www.compagniecorsaire.com) and costs adults €33.50 return and €27.50 one-way. Children are €20.20 return and €16.50 one-way. The journey time is 2 hours 45 minutes. The ferry itself, meanwhile, is a fairly small boat, though it still has room for two decks, plus an inside and outside space. When it's full, which it is often in the summer, it can get a little cramped, so dreams of spreading out a leisurely picnic rug for the duration of the trip will have to be put on hold. If you think you're likely to get hungry, though, do pack a sandwich—while there is a snack bar on board, the quality is not massively high.

Côte d'Émeraude

A land of small fishing villages, resort towns, and stunning promontories east of Dinard, the Côte d'Émeraude (Emerald Coast) is so called because of the occasionally emerald-green color of its sea. This remarkable stretch of the region's coastline caters to all tastes.

For those wanting to relax, there are the communes of Saint-Jacut and Saint-Cast, situated on capes on either side of the Arguenon estuary. Historically isolated, the two once had to compete fiercely over the year's mackerel catch just to survive. Fortunately, times move on, and with their profusion of beaches, friendly atmosphere, and quaint local architecture, now neither town has trouble attracting enough tourists for all.

For the more energetic, this is prime hiking country. Cliff-top trails wrap dramatically around the coastline, spangled by a kaleidoscope of wildflowers in the summer and with views out to the blazing sea beyond. The terrain is ideal both for extended rambles and short walks to help build an appetite for dinner.

ORIENTATION

Made up of a series of capes, the Côte d'Émeraude is not a place where you'll be getting around anywhere too quickly. Saint-Jacut, Saint-Cast, and Cap Fréhel are not directly linked by road. The capes are laid out like three jagged teeth: to get between them, you have to keep returning to the jawline. In practical terms, this means the fastest way between towns is to head back to the main D786, which runs inland just behind where any of the capes begin to reach out to sea.

On foot, the same of course applies, though chances are you won't mind taking the long way, with the easy-to-navigate GR34 walking route linking the capes both beautifully and efficiently. Be aware that there's a long tidal reach in these parts, with long sandy bays exposed when it's low. On the one hand, this means shortcuts between outcrops are possible, but be careful not to get caught by the incoming sea! It also makes for an ever-changing, very beautiful landscape.

SIGHTS

★ Fort la Latte

Plévenon; tel. 02 96 41 57 11; www.lefortlalatte.com; 10:30am-6pm daily Apr.-June and Sept., 10:30am-7pm daily July-Aug., 1pm-5pm daily Oct., 1pm-5pm Sat.-Sun. and bank holidays Nov.-Dec.; adults €5.70, students €4.70, under 12 €3.70, under 5 free

There are a number of storybook castles throughout Brittany, but few are more impressive in scale or setting than Fort la Latte. Looking like something that wouldn't be out of place in fantasy fiction, it's an unforgettable sight, thrusting out on a promontory high above the waters of the English Channel. A visit here will leave you wondering why Fort la Latte isn't better known—it's popular, yes, but this could easily be thought of as one of Brittany's most iconic sights.

Built in the 14th century by Étienne III de Goüyon, the fort allowed for control of the

The Emerald Coast

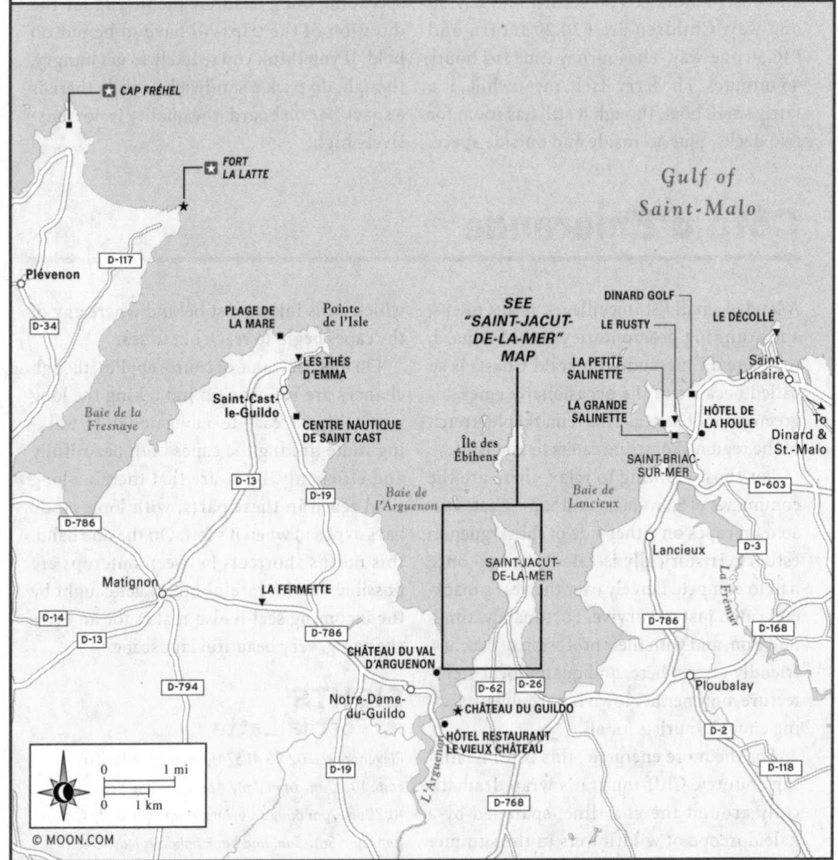

Fresnay Bay, an anchorage for ships waiting to put into Saint-Malo. The castle was besieged several times in its history, for a time was left abandoned, and was later used as a military base until Napoleonic times, when eventually advancements in military technology left it unfit for purpose.

Now, it's a tourist site, having been restored in the 1950s. The fort cannot be approached directly by car. Instead, the parking lot is about 15 minutes' walk from its entrance. The walk is through some stunning scenery, and you do not have to pay admission until the fort gate. Wandering around the castle grounds is both a giddy trip back through history—it feels as if a medieval garrison has just left—and a stunning visual experience, as incredible views are presented at near every turn. Replicas of certain siege defenses still dot the grounds, giving your imagination even more of a nudge, while the 360-degree panorama from the main tower is the peak of any visit.

Château du Guildo

52 boulevard du Vieux Château, Saint-Jacut; open 24/7; free

This evocative castle ruin occupies a

Saint-Jacut-de-la-Mer

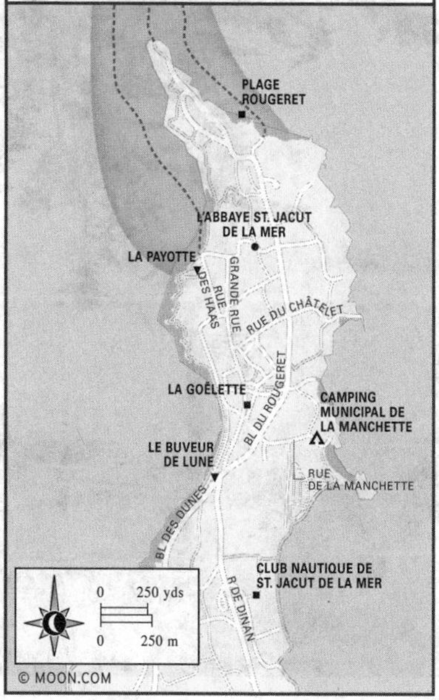

dramatic spot. Here, unlike in much of the fastidiously restored heritage of the region, the ravages of time are clear to see. As such, it's a more melancholic sight, less awe-inspiring, a testament to the transience of history rather than resilience. The castle itself was built in the 13th century and suffered through many sieges throughout its existence, finally being abandoned in the 16th century following an attack. It's recently been subject to extensive archaeological research, the evidence of which is plain among the ruins, which are accordingly, if paradoxically, well preserved.

With no entrance fee and no barriers, it's a freeing experience, and a place to let your imagination run wild. There's also plenty of room to park about 50 yards away from the castle itself.

ENTERTAINMENT AND EVENTS

Festivals

RENDEZ-VOUS À SAINT-BRIAC

Saint-Briac (multiple locations); https://festivartsaintbriac.fr; Ascension weekend

This contemporary art festival dedicated to local and national artists takes place in Saint-Briac over the Ascension weekend—usually toward the end of May. Held in municipal buildings around Saint-Briac since 2014, the festival is getting bigger every year, attracting visitors with a series of talks and exhibitions. The association running the festival also stages smaller shows and talks throughout the year.

Bars

LA GOËLETTE

31 Grande Rue, Saint-Jacut; tel. 02 96 27 75 23; 8:30pm-1am Wed.-Mon.; half pint of beer from €3

A lively pub and restaurant in one of Saint-Jacut's inland streets, this local hangout also caters to a lot of tourists who might congregate in the evening for a drink. There's a terrace, and free WiFi is offered (not always easy to find in Breton bars). There are themed nights on Thursdays in the summer, and the food's not bad, either, consisting of multiple simple seafood dishes, pizza, and steak frites.

SPORTS AND RECREATION

Hikes

TOP EXPERIENCE

★ CAP FRÉHEL

Pointing like some vast and craggy finger from the Côte d'Émeraude into the capricious waters of the English Channel, this imposing windswept peninsula is a hiker's dream. It's an area of authentic wilderness, with no towns or villages, just a couple of lighthouses, including one from the 17th century.

Views from tip reach as far as the Channel Islands on a clear day, while the peninsula underfoot is covered in protected moorland. Its

flashings of heather and gorse have attracted artists and scientists, and dazzled ramblers for centuries. This is also an excellent area for bird-watchers, with an estimated 700 pairs of native and migratory species roosting on the many cliff faces and islands off the coast.

Walkers can begin their trip in the west from Pléhérel Plage (about four miles/six kilometers, 1 hour 15 minutes to the Cap) or Sables-d'Or-les-Pins (about six miles/nine kilometers, taking two hours), or in the east from Fort la Latte (three miles/four kilometers, 1 hour). Most journeys take you along the well-signposted GR34 walking path, providing walkers good orientation—for the most part, it's a fairly narrow dirt track, bounded by foliage or fields. At the same time, bringing a map is highly recommended. Be aware too that the weather can change suddenly, so come prepared with waterproof gear. There's also a parking lot about 500 yards from the peninsula itself, if you don't fancy exerting yourself. That said, most of the walking is fairly tame and passes through some beautiful protected moorland, where you'll be too distracted by flora and fauna, as well as the great views out to sea, to get tired!

Water Sports

CLUB NAUTIQUE DE SAINT-JACUT DE LA MER

Z.A. les Basses Terres; tel. 02 96 27 79 13; www.cn-saintjacut.com; 9am-4:30pm Mon.-Fri.; 2pm-5pm Sat.; stand-up paddleboard rental from €15, course of sailing lessons from €200

This terrific and unintimidating water-sports club is ideally located on the tip of Saint-Jacut. It's well stocked with equipment of all sorts for rent, and offers lessons to all ages. Be aware, though, that the tidal reach is very long here, and when it's low the bay is all but dried up, which means that it may not always be possible to take to the water.

1: looking out to sea from Saint-Jacut **2:** A castle straight from the pages of a fantasy novel, Fort la Latte has watched over this coastline for centuries.

Golf

DINARD GOLF

53 boulevard de la Houle, Saint-Briac; tel. 02 99 88 32 07; http://dinardgolf.com; 9am-7:30pm daily; high-season green fee €100

One of the oldest golf courses in continental Europe, this was founded by a small group of British people living in Dinard at the end of the 19th century. A links course in a spectacular setting, it soon became justifiably famous throughout the golfing world. The clubhouse is a stylish art deco building designed by Marcel Oudin, a pioneer in using concrete in architecture, and finished in 1927. Despite the course's name, it's actually found in Saint-Briac.

BEACHES

LA PETITE SALINETTE

Saint-Briac

This slightly hidden sandy beach to the north of Saint-Briac is relatively quiet. It's got a nice view out across the Bay of Lancieux, though the many rocks here make swimming tricky at low tide. There's no easy access by car, either, so you'll have to walk. The beach is accessible from rue des Essarts, from which a pedestrian track takes you the rest of the way. It's close to town, but it lacks services, and there are no lifeguards.

LA GRANDE SALINETTE

Saint-Briac

La Grande Salinette is a truly classic beach. Ringed by white beach cabins, which unfortunately can't be rented on a daily basis, it looks out to Saint-Briac Bay, with Saint-Cast glinting off in the distance. With soft powdery sand, supervision in the summer, nearby parking, and free showers, it ticks a lot of boxes and is accordingly popular.

PLAGE ROUGERET

Saint-Jacut

A sandy beach, with great views out toward the Ebihens Archipelago, there are beach cabins to rent and it's supervised in the summer—by the local fire brigade, no less!

Somewhat exposed, it can get a little windy, which is at least good news for the water-sports center that adjoins it, and which does not stop it from getting crowded, especially in summer. There are beach volleyball nets, showers, nearby restaurants, and more. Access is via the boulevard du Rougeret, with parking nearby.

PLAGE DE LA MARE

Saint-Cast

A large, wild, and sandy beach facing north, which puts it in the way of some larger waves than other places. Perhaps its most seductive factor is the view it boasts of the Fort la Latte, which looms over the sea to the west. Access from Saint-Cast is along the D19, and it's easy to park nearby.

FOOD

Saint-Briac

LE DÉCOLLÉ

1 le Décolle, Saint-Briac; tel. 02 99 46 01 70; www.restaurantdudecolle.com; 12pm-2pm and 7pm-9:30pm Fri.-Sun. Feb.-Mar., 12pm-2pm and 7pm-9:30pm Wed.-Sun. Apr.-June and Sept.-Oct., 12pm-2pm and 7pm-9:30pm Tues.-Sun. July-Aug.; menus €33-45

Located in a fantastic spot, just at the end of the Décollé cape not far from Dinard, this simply designed restaurant with large windows allows its views out across the bay to do most of the talking. Table decoration is tasteful and uncomplicated, and the food, which unsurprisingly consists of a lot of fish, is wonderful. It's particularly good on sunny days, and booking is recommended.

LE RUSTY

27 rue du Port Hue, Saint-Briac; tel. 02 99 40 00 79; www.lerusty-stbriac.com; 9:30am-2am daily (lunch 10am-2pm and dinner 5pm-11pm); mains €18-24

This family-run restaurant is situated in a large, traditional-looking building with a big garden area surrounding it. Specializing in seafood, Le Rusty boasts a modern aesthetic in its interior and in the presentation of its food—try the *assiette apéritive,* a surf-and-turf tasting platter of smoked salmon, white fish carpaccio, Iberian ham, and homemade foie gras. Booking is reccomended, though with its long service hours, you may get a table if you're willing to wait.

Saint-Jacut

★ LA PAYOTTE

Rue des Haas, Saint-Jacut; tel. 06 31 23 70 34; 10am-9pm daily; mains €6-12

Not much more than a beach shack cobbled together on the cliffs overlooking Saint-Jacut's Plage des Haas, this spot has great views and a laid-back vibe, sometimes with live music in the summer. With its well-stocked bar, it's good for just a drink, for a snack of croque monsieur, or for splurging on a bowl of steaming mussels and fries.

LE BUVEUR DE LUNE

1 boulevard des Dunes, Saint-Jacut; tel. 02 96 27 74 20; www.lebuveurdelune.com; 6pm-11pm Tues.-Wed., 12:30pm-11pm Thurs.-Sun.; mains €6-20

With a great view out toward the sea and a Hawaiian theme inside, this fun café has a covered terrace, an uncovered terrace, and a garden. Bright colors and fun staff make it a great hangout, and they host regular parties. The food is also of decent quality, with seafood flavors and crepes the norm.

Saint-Cast

LA FERMETTE

L'Hôpital, Saint-Cast; tel. 02 96 41 00 95; www.restaurant-la-fermette.fr; 12pm-2pm and 6:45pm-9pm Thurs.-Mon., 12pm-2pm Tues.; mains €19.50-45

The Maître Cuisiniers de France (Master Chefs of France) is an association with a very elite membership. La Fermette is run by such a master, Thierry Blandin. Inside an old stone building in Saint-Cast, the restaurant's exceptional local flavors, such as its lobster and salmon tartare and exquisitely grilled steak, will give you an idea why. Food is served in a crisp, light-filled interior for which booking is highly recommended.

LES THÉS D'EMMA

15-17 rue de la Feuillade, Saint-Cast; tel. 02 96 41 88 21; www.lesthesdemma.com; 3pm-7pm daily; teas from €3.70, a plate of patisseries €5.50

Boasting a wonderful terrace with a quite spectacular panoramic view out across Saint-Cast harbor, this tearoom featuring delicate homemade patisseries is an excellent, refined place to relax away from the beach crowds. Its garden is bursting with flowers, while its interior is homey and fun.

Plévenon

AUX DÉLICES DU CAP

Rue du Vieux Bourg, Plévenon; tel. 02 96 41 50 51; 7:30am-1pm and 4pm-7pm Wed.-Sat., 7:30am-1pm Sun., 7:30am-1:30pm and 3pm-6:30pm Mon.; sandwiches €4.10

A decent French bakery, it's well placed for hikers wanting to pick up food for picnics before they head out walking on the Cap Fréhel. The sandwiches are substantial and tasty, with classic fillers from tuna to chicken, while the patisserie selection is actually really good: Of course, whether you think packing an elegant baba au rhum fits with a hike onto a windswept cape is a matter of opinion.

ACCOMMODATIONS

Saint-Briac

HÔTEL DE LA HOULE

14 boulevard de la Houle, Saint-Briac; tel. 02 99 88 32 17; www.hoteldelahoule.com; from €179 d

Just a short walk from Saint-Briac's beach, this hotel in a traditional stone building offers comfortable rooms, tastefully decorated in marine colors with nautical touches. Some have sea views. There's also a sun terrace and an on-site bar and restaurant for the evenings. All rooms have en suite bathrooms, some of which have bathtubs.

Saint-Jacut and Around

HÔTEL RESTAURANT LE VIEUX CHÂTEAU

9 place Gilles de Bretagne, Guildo; tel. 02 96 41 07 28; www.hotel-restaurant-le-vieux-chateau.fr; from €53 d

This very reasonably priced hotel typifies a French country inn, with old-fashioned decor and friendly staff. It's in a picturesque location on Guildo's harbor, just down the road from Saint-Cast. Of the 15 rooms available, a number have sea views, while the premises also provide an on-site restaurant serving traditional flavors (try the *moules frites*) and a bar. There are two terraces, one with a view of the sea and the ruined Château du Guildo.

L'ABBAYE SAINT-JACUT DE LA MER

3 rue de l'Abbaye, Saint-Jacut; tel. 02 96 27 71 19; www.abbaye-st-jacut.com; shared room from €71.10

Providing a very different kind of beach holiday, Saint-Jacut's abbey offers quiet contemplation in a beautiful natural setting. Here you are a guest in a place that draws its values from the Gospels rather than the tourist board, cultivating a diverse meeting point of many different people either searching for spiritual harmony or just a break from the stresses and strains of modern life. The access points the abbey offers for doing this are multiple. At its most straightforward, you can attend the many services, and remain quietly contemplative outside of them, but there are also discussion groups to attend and minibus trips to go on around the local area. You can even combine your spiritual retreat with wind-surfing lessons on the beach nearby. Booking at least 24 hours ahead is essential, and mealtimes are shared.

CHÂTEAU DU VAL D'ARGUENON

Rue du val, Notre-Dame du Guildo; tel. 02 96 41 07 03; www.chateauduval.com; from €170 d

This château guesthouse not far from Saint-Cast is an excellent deal. With plush, old-fashioned interiors and extensive grounds, and just a short walk from a private beach area, it's the kind of place where you could spend a whole holiday and never leave. On site are a billiards room, a tennis court, and a table tennis table. There's also a shared lounge, and breakfast is provided.

Camping

CAMPING MUNICIPAL DE LA MANCHETTE

24 rue de la Manchette, Saint-Jacut; tel. 02 96 27 70 33; www.mairie-saintjacutdelamer.com/page.php?id=29; open Apr.-Sept.; pitch for two people in high season €13.70

At this large municipal campsite right next to the sea, features are basic, but all the necessities are here: toilet and shower blocks, washing machine access, and even a small outside games area. WiFi is available at an extra cost.

TRANSPORTATION

Getting There and Around

BY CAR

Car travel is by far the easiest way to get around this region, though be aware that Saint-Jacut, Saint-Cast, and Cap Fréhel are all capes, meaning to get in and out is often the same road. The fastest way between them is to head back to the main D786, which runs inland just behind where any of the capes begin to reach out to sea. It comes from Saint-Malo and Dinard in the east (10 miles/16 kilometers, taking 20 minutes) and Saint-Brieuc in the west (40 miles/64 kilometers, taking one hour). Parking is mostly free, and though it may take a moment or two to find a spot, tourists tend to spread out enough that mostly you can. Should you want to hug the coast all the way from Saint-Briac to Cap Fréhel, the journey will last roughly 1 hour 15 minutes, covering 15 miles (24 kilometers).

BY BUS

There is a bus service, which runs from Saint-Malo to Saint-Cast via close to Saint-Briac and Saint-Jacut four times a day in the summer. This is part of the **Tibus** company (www.tibus.fr), costing €2 for a single journey and taking about an hour to go all the way. Bus 14 is the one to take. There are 19 buses of the **Illenoo** company (www.illenoo-services.fr/en) throughout the day running from Saint-Malo direct to Saint-Briac, with a journey time of about 40 minutes. Be aware, nine leave before 9am to cater to the morning rush. Cost is €3, and it takes about an hour. The best place to catch these buses is outside Saint-Malo train station.

Paimpol and the Île-de-Bréhat

TOP EXPERIENCE

The coastline near Paimpol is a place of hardy fishing villages and picturesque ports, while just out to sea glimmers the Île-de-Bréhat, an undulating, carless paradise where land and sea seem to be playing a constantly surprising game of give and take, and which is surely one of the most beautiful islands in Brittany.

Developing around Beauport Abbey, Paimpol established itself as one of the great fishing ports of the Breton coast, sending ships to search for cod off the coast of Iceland. This trade reached it peak in the late 19th century, with the town paying a heavy toll for such prosperity—it's estimated that at least 2,000 fishermen from Paimpol drowned between 1852 and 1932. Its main trade now is tourism, which is far less perilous.

The Île-de-Bréhat is actually an archipelago consisting of two main islands and many smaller ones. The view from its elevated points looks like some great living map of a fantasy world. Blessed by a warm microclimate, it also plays home to many Mediterranean plants, and much of its coastline is formed of dazzling pink granite rocks. Settled since at least the early Middle Ages, the island's beauty did not spare it from a turbulent history. It's been

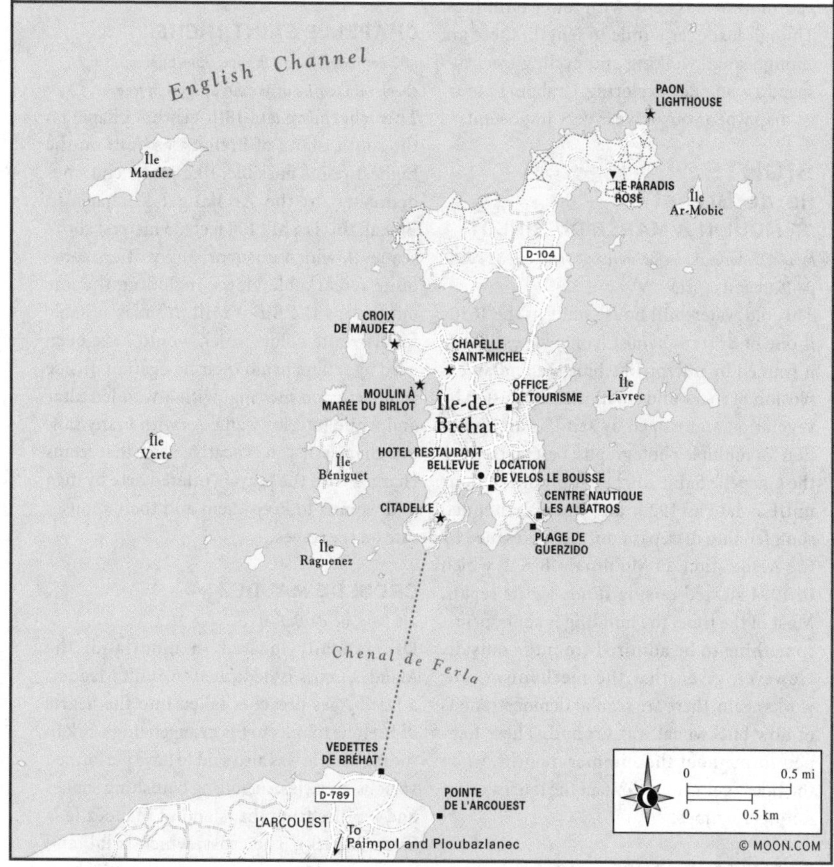

invaded many times by foreign powers—the English and even the Spaniards—and later was a base for French pirates. Things have calmed down today, however, while many of the encroachments of modern society have been kept away from the island, most notably cars, meaning it's still possible to explore its wild natural beauty in peace.

ORIENTATION

Paimpol itself is a relatively small harbor town at the heart of a long, narrow bay. It has a few pleasant backstreets, but most of its action takes place around its port. The closest beach to town is the **Plage de la Tossen,** just a short walk to the west of the center toward the Pointe Brividic. The **Abbaye de Beauport** is about a half a mile down the coast on the D786.

Taking this road north out the other side of Paimpol for about three miles will bring you to the Pointe de L'Arcouest, where the ferries for the **Île-de-Bréhat** depart. This "island" is actually an archipelago made out of two main islands linked by a causeway, and many other islands surrounding it. There's a small town-center-like area about 540 yards north of the port, on the east of the south island. As you go farther north from here, crossing the causeway, so the Île de Bréhat becomes wilder and more windswept, with fewer buildings. Though just over a mile in length, there are enough small walking and cycling tracks to spend a whole day exploring. Grabbing a tourist map when you arrive is very important.

SIGHTS

Île-de-Bréhat

★ MOULIN À MARÉE DU BIRLOT

Moulin à Marée du Birlot, Île-de-Bréhat; tel. 02 96 20 04 15 (tourist office)

This old water-mill house built in the 1630s is one of Brittany's most iconic views. To see it framed by mirror-like blue sea and an explosion of rocks and small islands, dusted by vegetation and ringed by sand, is an invitation for multiple photographs, best taken from the Chapelle Saint-Michel. It produced flour until as late as 1920, and once abandoned soon fell into disrepair, only to be rescued by the Association du Moulin du Birlot, which in 1994 started raising funds for its repair. Most of the time, the building is shut up, just something to be admired from the outside. However, given that the mechanism now works again, there are regular demonstrations of how buckwheat was ground. These happen throughout the summer months, when the tide is going out. Contact the tourist office for precise times.

PAON LIGHTHOUSE

Phare du Paon, Île-de-Bréhat; tel. 02 96 20 04 15 (tourist office)

In the windswept reaches of Bréhat's north island, towering from a promontory of pink granite rocks, this lighthouse makes for a good destination point during any exploration of the island. The first lighthouse was built here between 1855 and 1860, replaced in 1880, and then given an electric light in 1942. Occupying German troops dynamited the lighthouse in 1944, and the one that's seen today was erected in 1952. It's an automated lighthouse, with some good views back along Bréhat's coast. You can't go inside, but there's a platform surrounding it, which you can access to get as close as you want any time of day.

CHAPELLE SAINT-MICHEL

202 Kermique, Île-de-Bréhat; 9am-6pm most days, check with tourist office out of season; free

This charming late-18th-century chapel on the south island of Bréhat was built on the highest point possible, like many churches dedicated to the Archangel Michael. In Bréhat, this is a hill 108 feet (33 meters) above sea level, which unsurprisingly offers some quite remarkable views, including the one out toward the Birlot Mill. It's also notable for its white color, which would have been used by sailors to aid their navigation. Inside is austere and moving, with a wooden altar and white interior walls. As with many sailors' chapels, it's an evocative place that seems charged with the prayers uttered here by men and women to keep them and their spouses safe on the waves.

CROIX DE MAUDEZ

218 Birlo, Île-de-Bréhat

Dramatically located in moorland, the Maudez Cross is dedicated to Saint Maudez, a Dark Ages preacher taken into the hearts of Bretons thanks to his evangelizing work in the region. He was also said to have performed various miracles, including banishing snakes and reptiles from the island of Maudez (à la Saint Patrick). The cross, which is tall and narrow and carved from weathered stone, looks out to that island, which Maudez is also said to have built a monastery on in 570, of which no clearly visible evidence now remains. The cross was erected by locals in 1788.

CITADELLE

La Citadelle, Île-de-Bréhat, tel. 02 96 20 09 09; 10am-4:45pm Mon.-Fri.; free

Built during France's "second Empire" from 1860-1862, but abandoned by troops less than 15 years later, this squat fortress was lived in

1: the kind of tranquil vista around every corner on the Ile de Bréhat **2:** Bréhat's mill draws a line through an undulating landscape.

1
2

by island locals until the late 1980s. Before it could fall into ruin, however, restoration was carried out, and a center dedicated to glass blowing was formed. Now, you can visit during the week and see the glassblowers in action. It's a mezmorizing experience, at once dramatic and calming, as the superheated glass is made to look like toffee, or the bubbles in a lava lamp, while it's being deftly manipulated at the end of the glassmith's metal pole. Once you're done seeing how they're made, it's hard not to want to buy some of the glassware yourself to take home.

Paimpol

ABBAYE DE BEAUPORT

Place de Kérity; tel. 02 96 55 18 58; http://abbayebeauport.com; 2pm-6pm daily Mar., Oct., and Nov., 10:30am-12:30pm and 2pm-6pm daily Apr.-June, 10:30am-7pm daily July- Sept.; adults €6, reduced €3, under 5 free

The institution that drove the development of Paimpol and brought money into the area, Beauport Abbey is both the well-preserved ruins of a monastery and a functioning one founded in the 13th century. It was built at the request of powerful Breton noble Count Alain de Goeelo, and grew to become one of the most prosperous monasteries in Brittany.

Going into a long state of decline during the 16th and 17th centuries, the abbey was abandoned during the French Revolution, and the building itself begin to fall apart and was looted for stone. Only after it was classified as a historic monument in 1862 was the rot halted and the looting stopped.

Today, visitors come to see the fascinating architecture of the building itself, which is a combination of Gothic and 19th-century construction, including the meticulously tidied-up ruins of the original buildings. They also come for the well-tended gardens and orchards, of which some of the old ruins, given that they lack a roof, could be considered a magnificent feature. The institution still promotes many of the traditions of cloistered life, with talks and exhibitions dedicated toward intellectual improvement being held here throughout the year.

MUSÉE DE LA MER

11 rue de Labenne; tel. 02 96 22 02 19; http://museemerpaimpol.fr; 2pm-6:30pm daily Apr. 15-Nov.4; adults €4.10, under 18 free

Built in 1990 in a former cod-drying factory from the 19th century, this museum traces Paimpol's great history as a center of fishing, looking at the ups and downs of life here

Paimpol's "museum of the sea"

during the late 1800s, when most of the town's men would have sought their fortunes off the icy seas of Iceland and Newfoundland. A more extensive museum than you might expect for what is now a quiet port town, many different aspects of maritime life are explored here through a collection that includes a number of scale models of different boats, as well as old photographs and maps. If you want to understand more, there are information cards written in several languages (including English) that accompany the displays.

SILLON DE TALBERT

Rue du Sillon de Talbert, Pleubian

A surreal, almost ephemeral geological feature, this thin spit of land, just over 114 feet (35 meters) across, reaches out from the Breton coastline a full 1.8 miles (three kilometers) into the English Channel, farther north than anywhere else in mainland Brittany. Scientists would say it was pushed into existence by the competing currents of the Trieux and Jaudy estuaries, but folklore suggests tales of either King Arthur building it to reach the enchantress Morgan le Fay, or the wizard Merlin to get to the Lady of the Lake.

Whatever you choose to believe, when you can access it, the walk out here is thrilling and exposed, an experience unlike anywhere else along the coast: elemental, and whipped by a lashing force of coastal wind. If you're brave enough to come here in the winter, keep an eye peeled for migratory birds, such as geese, which spend the colder months here.

ENTERTAINMENT AND EVENTS

FESTIVAL DU CHANT DE MARIN DE PAIMPOL

Paimpol, multiple locations; www.paimpol-festival.bzh/fr; Aug.; three-day pass: adults €42, children 6-14 €4, one-day pass: adults €21, children 6-14 €2

A far bigger event than its name might imply, this sea shanty festival is more than a few old men in a pub crooning over a wheezy accordion. Rather, it's a massive three-day extravaganza full of world music, Breton music, brass bands, and, yes, sea shanties. There are also exhibitions and local produce tastings, while the town harbor is taken over by hundreds of traditional ships.

SHOPPING

LIBRAIRIE DE L'ONCLE PAUL

6 rue du 18 Juin, Paimpol; tel. 02 96 22 67 33; 10:15am-12:30pm and 2:30pm-7pm Tues.-Sat.

A charming used bookstore just back from Paimpol harbor, it's well worth a little browsing. Given the town's popularity on the tourist circuit, you should be able to find a few English-language books here, if you're lucky.

BOAT TRIPS AND WATER SPORTS

CENTRE NAUTIQUE LES ALBATROS

371 Guerzido, Île de Bréhat; tel. 02 96 20 07 24; www.les-albatros.com/accueil; 9:30am-6:30pm daily Apr.-Oct., 9am-6pm Mon.-Fri. Oct.-Apr.; kayak rental from €15, week-long sailing course from €195

Found in a secluded location, on a beach 20 minutes' walk away from Bréhat's main port, this is a great water-sports center at which to spend a decent period in order to really master a craft. With its own lodgings and restaurant on-site, and diving lessons on offer too, it's a friendly spot, and not intimidatingly inundated by locals as a number of such centers can be.

VEDETTES DE BRÉHAT

6 route de l'Embarcadère, Ploubazlanec; tel. 02 96 55 79 50; www.vedettesdebrehat.com; 10am-12pm and 2pm-6:30 Tues.-Sat.; adults from €16, under 11 from €11

The boat company that gets you to and from Bréhat also offers some great cruises around the island, taking you to locations that are otherwise inaccessible, floating through a veritable solar system of rocks and small islands. On a clear day there can be few things more worthwhile, as the sea around Bréhat fizzes an electric blue, beautiful as it splashes against the pink granite of the island's coast. If you're lucky, you may even see dolphins. They also offer trips down the historically picturesque

Trieux River, providing a very different view of the Breton countryside in all its green abundance. There's plenty of wildlife to see wherever you go, and the boats help with this, providing binoculars to passengers.

BEACHES

PLAGE DE GUERZIDO

Île de Bréhat

The main beach on Bréhat and where the island's water-sports club is located. It's a beautiful spot of find sand and a few pebbles cradled by the island's characteristic pink granite rocks. However, it's not that big, so it can get quite busy in the summer. It's unsupervised, but there are bathrooms nearby.

PLAGE DE LA TOSSEN

Paimpol

A pleasant sandy beach, which is supervised in summer. There's a seawater pool and a view to the left of Paimpol, and in front to some smaller islands. Free parking on the rue de la Tossen is about 275 yards from the beach itself.

FOOD

Île-de-Bréhat

LE PARADIS ROSE

Le Paon, Île-de-Bréhat; tel. 02 96 20 03 89; 11am-5pm daily; from €5

Situated in a delightful garden on the north island of Bréhat, this makes for a great place to punctuate your day. It serves mainly crepes, and while they're nothing particularly special, it's a lovely floral location. They also serve local cider, should you really want to take it easy.

Paimpol

LE BALTHAZAR

26 rue des Huit Patriotes, Paimpol; tel. 02 96 20 08 85; http://lebalthazar.fr; 12pm-2pm and 7pm-10pm Wed.-Sat., 7pm-10pm Sun.; lunch menu €12.50, evening menu €29

For those tired of all the seafood specialty restaurants lining the Breton coast, this carnivore's paradise provides a real antidote. Look no further than the large indoor grill dedicated to steak, usually served with a baked potato. The interior, meanwhile, is as rustic and seductive as the food. (And for those still insistent on finding flavors from the sea, they grill scallops and fish, too.)

LE 18 CUISINE BISTRO

18 rue des Huit Patriotes, Paimpol; tel. 09 72 82 82 13; 12pm-2pm and 7pm-10pm Thurs.-Mon., 7pm-10pm Tues.; menu €32.50

With the kind of interior design that could only really appear in a family-run restaurant—walls and spare surfaces covered in a profusion of pictures, porcelain, and plates—this is a characterful and comfortable place, which serves some excellent, unpretentious French food with a hearty, home-cooked quality. It's well worth ordering from the daily specials, which are chalked up across a blackboard that dominates one wall of the restaurant, though they also offer an epic cut of steak, which can be hard to resist.

L'ISLANDAIS RESTAURANT

19 quai Morand, Paimpol; tel. 02 96 20 93 80; www.hotel-kloys.com/restaurant/l-islandais-paimpol; 12pm-10pm daily; menus €23.30-€40

A stylish restaurant on Paimpol's port, it mixes traditional and modern design and contains many nods to the town's rich fishing history. The dishes are mostly refined, with an emphasis on seafood and local flavors, while the menu evolves depending on the catch on sale at the market that day, but they also do a very tasty take on British-style fish and chips.

ACCOMMODATIONS

Île-de-Bréhat

HÔTEL RESTAURANT BELLEVUE

Le Port Clos, Île de Bréhat; tel. 02 96 20 00 05; www.hotel-bellevue-brehat.fr; from €149 d

Built in 1904, though completely renovated in 2013, this hotel stares visitors in the face the moment that they arrive from the mainland. A couple of terraces make for excellent places to unwind from and watch the sunset, while there can be few experiences that compare with staying in the tranquility of Bréhat overnight. Some rooms are fairly spacious and get a lot of light, though others are a little more cramped. There's WiFi throughout and a restaurant on-site.

Paimpol

HÔTEL LE K'LOYS

21 quai Morand, Paimpol; tel. 02 96 20 40 01; www.hotel-kloys.com; from €65 d

Featuring an eclectic design in its different rooms, this hotel on Paimpol's harbor is in a building from the 19th century. Some rooms are quite modern-looking, while others have a more traditional quality, and can include rather colorful wallpaper. Nevertheless, it's comfortable throughout, and there's a decent restaurant on-site, with smoked trout part of the buffet breakfast in the morning.

HÔTEL LE GOËLO

4 quai Duguay Trouin, Paimpol; tel. 02 96 20 82 74; www.legoelo.com; from €72 d

It's not exactly the Ritz, but with a convenient location and low prices, this inexpensive hotel on Paimpol's harbor is still worth a night if you're just passing through. There are flat-screen TVs in all the rooms and free WiFi throughout the building. Buffet breakfast is a little extra.

Camping

CAMPING DE CRUCKIN

Rue de Cruckin, Paimpol; tel. 02 96 20 78 47; www.camping-paimpol.com; Apr.-Sept.; pitch for two people in high season €16, cabins from €250 per week

Very well-located, with 115 pitches, this campsite is just a short walk outside of Paimpol center, with easy access to the beach and basic amenities such as a shower block and free WiFi. There would be some great views, but they're mostly obscured by hedges, which is about the only negative thing that can be said about this very reasonable facility. It can get very busy in high season, so make sure to book early.

INFORMATION

OFFICE DE TOURISME DE GUINGAMP–BAIE DE PAIMPOL

Place de la République, Paimpol; tel. 02 96 20 83 16; www.guingamp-paimpol.com; 9:30am-7:30pm Mon.-Sat., 10am-12:30pm and 4:30pm-6:30pm Sun.

A modern, well-equipped tourist office just next to Paimpol's harbor. You can get plenty of information here about the town and the surrounding region, as well as the Île-de-Bréhat if you need it.

OFFICE DE TOURISME DE L'ÎLE-DE-BRÉHAT

Place du Bourg, Île-de-Bréhat; tel. 02 96 20 04 15; www.brehat-infos.fr; 10am-1pm and 2pm-5pm Mon.-Tues and Thurs.-Sat.

Found in the small built-up area toward the middle of the island, the Île-de-Bréhat's tourist office will help with accommodations, bike rental, and more. It's also a source of the all-important maps of the island, though to be honest, if you haven't picked one up from the port already, the tourist office itself may not be that easy to find.

TRANSPORTATION

Getting There and Around

BY CAR

Out on a promontory, Paimpol always seems to take longer to get to by car than one might imagine. From Rennes (90 miles/144 kilometers, 1 hour 40 minutes), take the N12 to Saint-Briac and change to the D7 to climb up the coast. From Paris, the drive goes via Rennes and is just over a total 300 miles (482 kilometers), a total journey time of almost five hours.

From Brest (90 miles/144 kilometers, 1 hour and 40 minutes), take the N12 in the other direction, until turning north around Guingamp along the D9.

In Paimpol itself, there is usually space to park that you won't have to pay for. For the Île-de-Bréhat, where cars are not allowed, you will have to park in the nearby parking lot. Prices here start at a flat rate of €6.50 for the day.

Hôtel ** BelleVue
1
2

BY TRAIN

The Guingamp station, **Gare de Guingamp** (place de la Gare, Guingamp; tel. 36 35; www.gares-sncf.com/fr/gare/frggp/guingamp; 4:25am-10pm Mon., 6am-10pm Tues.-Thurs., 6:30am-11:40pm Fri., 6:15am-9:50pm Sat., 9:55am-10:50pm Sun.) is the hub for getting to Paimpol from elsewhere in France. There are five trains per day from Guingamp to Paimpol. They cost €7.90 and take about an hour.

There are 10 trains per day from Rennes to Guingamp (1 hour, €25) and around 13 trains per day from Brest (1 hour, €25).

BY BUS

Line 24 of the **Tibus** bus service (www.tibus.fr) runs seven services a day between Paimpol and the Pointe de L'Arcouest, from where the ferry for Bréhat departs. These cost €2 each direction and take about 15 minutes.

BY FERRY

The boat company that takes you between the mainland and the Île-de-Bréhat is the **Vedettes de Bréhat** (6 Route de l'Embarcadère, Ploubazlanec; tel. 02 96 55 79 50; www.vedettesdebrehat.com). It's a short crossing of about 10 minutes, but they're still able to charge €10.30 for an adult return and €8.80 for children under 11. There are 13 outward sailings a day (14 from July 15-August 31), and 12 return sailings (13 from July 15-August 31). The last outward sailing is at 7:30pm (8pm from July 15-August 31) and the last return sailing is at 7pm (7:45pm from July 15-August 31).

Be aware, low tide means walking about five minutes farther to the boat than high tide. So, unless you're sure, always give yourself time to spare.

BY BIKE

With no cars on the island, bike is the fastest way to get around Bréhat. There are a number of bike rental companies on the island, all shopping a similar deal (around €14 for the day), with several types of bike on offer, including ones that are electrically assisted. However, the island is not that big, and biking is not necessary if you want to see most, if not all, of it in a single day. The first company you'll come to is the **Location de Velos le Bousse** (tel. 06 89 09 95 34; http://velosbrehat.fr), which is directly opposite where the ferry arrives.

Côte de Granit Rose

Colors often find their way into the names of coastlines. All too often, though, this is just the work of the overactive imaginations of a particular tourist board. Not so here. The Pink Granite Coast, as this area's name translates to, is just that: a coast of pink granite. It blushes in the sunlight quite unlike anywhere else in Brittany, and is nearly unique in the world. Not only that, but the formations that this rock has been sculpted into over the years are strangely beautiful: large boulders balance on top of one another, while others seem petrified into solid pink waves.

There's a prehistoric quality to the landscape, made even more so by the lush vegetation that thrives in the coast's mild climate and is offset by its sandy beaches. Full of bays, resorts, and calm waters, there's much to occupy your time here. And like so many other places in Brittany, this coast is a paradise for ramblers, with the GR34 walking trail continuing its relentless journey west, across the Côte de Granit Rose's rocky pathways and sandy shores, toward the Atlantic Ocean.

1: The Hotel Bellevue is one of the first buildings you'll see when you put ashore Île-de-Bréhat.
2: In a land without cars, bicycles make for the fastest way to explore Bréhat.

Côte de Granit Rose

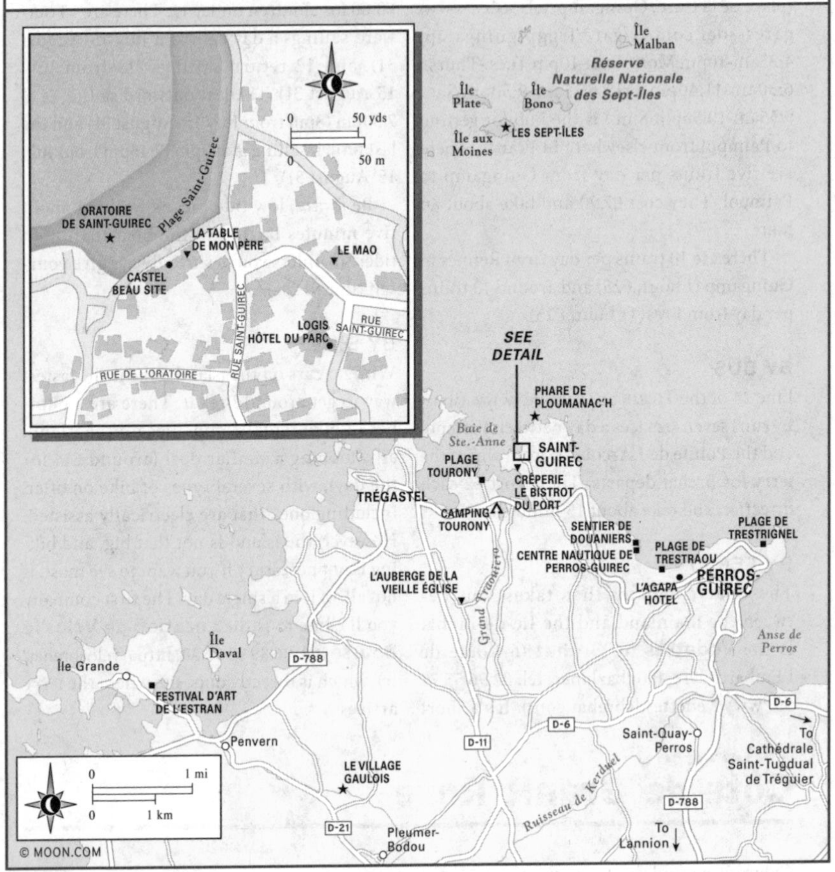

ORIENTATION

The Côte de Granit Rose is effectively the area of coastline starting from Perros-Guireca, a medium-size harbor town in the east, and running to the area around Ploumanac'h in the west, where there are a number of small coves and promontories to be explored. The main road threading through the area is the D788, though most of the time you will have to take smaller roads to reach your destination. Ploumanac'h is a cape, so be prepared to take the same route back that you took on your way in.

SIGHTS

Oratoire de Saint-Guirec

137 rue Saint-Guirec, Saint-Guirec

Located right in the heart of Saint-Guirec cove, this small religious monument is proof that sights do not have to be big to inspire awe. It looks something like a small temple cast from red stone, under which stands a smaller than life-size statue of Saint Guirec, who was said to have founded a Christian community on this coastline in the 6th century. What really makes it special, though, is how the monument sits perched on top of one of the many rocks in the bay, so you can walk out to it at low tide; when the sea is high, translucent water surrounds its base.

The structure is thought to date from around the end of the 11th century, though the wooden statue that used to stand here in the 14th century has since been moved to the nearby Saint-Guirec chapel, having been replaced by a granite one in 1904.

There are several legends related to the oratory, the best known being that if a young single woman can stitch a needle on the nose of the statue, then she will be married by the end of the year.

Phare de Ploumanac'h

Perros-Guirec

This beguiling lighthouse was made from the very pink granite that so characterizes the coast itself. The original from 1860 was destroyed by German troops in 1944, but the current building appeared just two years later—an exact copy of the first, designed to harmonize with the surrounding landscape. It was first lit in October 1948.

You can't go inside the fully automated lighthouse, but you can wander around this stretch of the Granit Rose coastline, where the surrounding rocks, sculpted by the wind and waves, look like vast modern art sculptures standing against the sea.

Les Sept-Îles

Seven islands that over the years have defied most attempts at human settlement, these offshore outcroppings seem to wink at you from the horizon as seen from the Côte de Granit Rose. These days, it's mainly seabirds that occupy them, and a dazzling array of species make their nests here. Puffins are perhaps the most famous, but there are also guillemots, fulmars, and kittiwakes, and from spring to September a veritable avalanche of gannets descends. There are boat tours to the islands run by **Armor Navigation** (tel. 02 96 91 10 00; www.armor-navigation.com) that depart either from Perros-Guirec or Port Blanc. There are an average of five trips a day leaving from around 9am to 4pm every day from April to September, and the tours last from 1 hour 45 minutes to 2.5 hours. Adults pay €18, and children under 12 can go for €12.

During the right seasons, a trip here is to be awed by magic of nature. The birds caw and screech, and take to the air and land again, their sheer numbers making them seem almost a moving landscape rather than individual creatures. It is possible to book a tour that lands for a short time on the largest of the islands, the Île Aux Moines, where there's an old fort and a lighthouse—mostly, though, it's just a good way of stretching your legs mid-journey.

Note: This is a popular trip to take in the high season, so it can be worth reserving tickets in advance, and if you want to be sure of a good view, arrive early to secure a top-deck seat.

Cathédrale Saint-Tugdual de Tréguier

1 place du Général Leclerc, Tréguier; tel. 02 96 92 30 51; 10:30am-6:30pm July-Aug., 10:30am-12:30pm and 2:30pm-6:30pm Apr.-June and Sept.-Oct.; free

Situated a little inland from the Côte de Granit Rose, in the town of Tréguier, this masterpiece of Gothic architecture is arguably a little incongruous in what is otherwise a fairly small town. It was the place of exile and pilgrimage for Saint Tugdual, who fled Wales from Anglo-Saxon invasions in the 6th century. Thought of as one of the founding saints of Brittany, he founded a monastery here in around 532 and was made a bishop by the then Breton king Childebert.

Norman invasions in the 9th century saw the monastery ransacked. When the raiders were forced out 90 years later, building began on a new Romanesque cathedral, of which today only the north transept remains. The main structure now dates from the 14th century, when a Gothic building was started. The church was added to continuously over the intervening centuries. Today, it is no longer the seat of a bishop, but its great size and

1

2

the splendor of its architectural blend remains an unexpected big-city-like delight in such an unassuming town.

When inside, keep an eye out for the wood carving of 14th-century Breton saint Saint Yves mediating between a poor man and a rich man, as well as the portraits of 14 former bishops. The cathedral's calm cloisters are also well worth a visit. Built in the Gothic style in the 16th century, they have a row of eerie funerary sculptures along their west aisle.

Le Village Gaulois

Parc du Radôme, Pleumeur-Bodou; tel. 02 96 91 83 95; www.levillagegaulois.org; 10:30am-7pm daily; adults €6, children €5

There is a feeling in Brittany that you're closer to France's ancient roots than just about anywhere else in the country. This Gallic-style village certainly makes that even more of a reality, offering an opportunity to see how people would have lived before the days of the Roman invasion on a grand scale. Interactive displays, shows, and actors populate the village to make for both an educational and entertaining time.

ENTERTAINMENT AND EVENTS

FESTIVAL D'ART DE L'ESTRAN

Along the Côte de Granit Rose; www.festivaldelestran.com; Sept.; free

The Côte de Granit Rose can feel like an open-air sculpture park at all times of the year, given the strange and abstract shapes blown into its various colorful rock formations. This art festival takes that fact and runs with it, inviting artists to compete with and work alongside the incredible backdrop and place their works along its beachfronts and cliff tops for appreciation by all.

1: the Oratoire de Saint-Guirec, proving there's more to spectacle than mere size **2:** the Phare de Ploumanac'h, made from the pink rocks of the coast itself

BEACHES

★ PLAGE SAINT-GUIREC

Saint-Guirec

The beach of the small seaside resort Saint-Guirec features a small, half-moon bay loomed over at either end by the coast's characteristic pink rocks, which can be fun to clamber around on. It's where the oratory is located, and swimming is easy regardless of whether the tide is in or out. The beach is supervised in summer, and there are plenty of restaurants and hotels, plus a parking lot nearby.

It gets busy but seldom is completely packed, and when the sun shines the atmosphere is one of almost tropical relaxation. This beautiful spot is great for families as well as young people, given the nearby bars. Swimming here at sunset or sunrise, when the orange light blazes from the pink rocks, is almost achingly magnificent, and you can feel comfortable swimming quite some distance out, as the sea seldom gets that rough. With that in mind, it's not really a beach for the more bracing water sports.

PLAGE DE TRESTRIGNEL

Rue de Trestrignel

This decent-size sandy beach is backed by a long boardwalk in a town. It's a good place to see and be seen, with attractive villas looking over one end of it, and a real resort vibe. The beach is supervised in season, and there are showers and toilets, good parking options, and lots of restaurants nearby.

PLAGE DE TRESTRAOU

Boulevard Joseph le Bihan

The main beach of Perros-Guirec is long and sandy. Bathing cabins occupy it at both ends, while on the left end as you face the sea there's a nautical center. It's a beach with plenty of amenities, including beach volleyball and showers; it's also supervised in the summer.

PLAGE TOURONY

Rue de Tourony

A beautiful cove away from any town

centers—though close to extensive free parking. Sandy and dotted with characteristic pink granite rocks, it also offers a view out to the private Château de Coastéres, looking like a Bond villain's lair out in the shimmering waters of the bay.

WATER SPORTS

CENTRE NAUTIQUE DE PERROS-GUIREC

Plage de Trestraou; tel. 02 96 49 81 21; http://nautisme.perros-guirec.com/decouvrez-le-centre-nautique.html; 9am-12pm and 2pm-5pmMon.-Sat.; sea kayak rental from €14, one hour of coaching €61

This commercially geared water-sports center makes a real effort to speak English, and coaching is sold by the hour rather than by the lesson. The usual list of water sports is on offer, from sailing to stand-up paddleboard. There's also the option to be taken out sailing on a regular boat or a catamaran.

FOOD

Local Cuisine

LA CRÉMAILLÈRE

13 place de l'Église, Perros-Guirec; tel. 02 96 23 22 08; 12pm-2pm and 7pm-9:30pm Tues.-Sun., 7pm-9:30pm Mon.; menus €24.90- €45.20

Located over two floors in a traditional stone building, this pleasant and friendly establishment serves up tasty, unpretentious French food, including a great prawn and mussel stew and some fantastic fish soup. The atmosphere gets quite lively, and it's well worth booking in high season.

LA TABLE DE MON PÈRE

137 rue Saint-Guirec, Perros-Guirec; tel. 02 96 91 40 87; www.castelbeausite.com/fr/restaurant-perros-guirec.html; 7:30pm-12am daily; menus €49-64

A top-end restaurant that plays elegantly with traditional Breton flavors (for example, cannelloni filled with spider crab and mango, and John Dory fish with carrots and cardamom) offering impeccable presentation in a brightly lit room with some stunning views out over Saint-Guirec Bay. Eating here while the sun sets, blazing over the pink rocks that turn even pinker, is an experience hard to match. It's worth booking ahead.

L'AUBERGE DE LA VIEILLE ÉGLISE

9 place de l'Église, Trégastel; tel. 02 96 23 88 31; www.aubergedelavieilleeglise.fr; 12pm-2pm and 7pm-9:30pm Tues.-Sun.; menus €27-45

This traditional French seafood restaurant offers freshly caught food cooked in a straightforward manner. The interior's neither

stand-up paddleboarding in the waters of the Côte de Granit Rose

particularly exciting nor unattractive, but the atmosphere is welcoming, cozy, and traditional. They're particularly proud of their lobster, which can be ordered in a variety of delicious ways: the lobster in a cider sauce is a particularly tasty, not to mention, extremely Breton dish. Book ahead in high season.

Budget Options

CRÊPERIE LE BISTROT DU PORT

56 chemin de la Pointe, Ploumanac'h; tel. 02 96 91 44 52; www.creperie-bistrotduport.fr; 10am-9:15pm daily; menus €12.50

A bustling *crêperie* on Ploumanac'h port, with a nice outside terrace, good for when the sun's shining. They have mussels on the menu as well as crepes, which can come served with all manner of seafood accompaniment if you want. It gets busy in the summer, but its continual service means that even if it's completely full to bursting, you won't have to wait too long for a table.

LE MAO

147 rue Saint-Guirec; tel. 02 96 91 40 92; 12pm-9pm Tues.-Sun.; crepes €9

There's a feeling that this large restaurant just back from Saint-Guirec Beach belongs farther south—in the Mediterranean, say, or even in Southeast Asia. Perhaps it's the large tree in its courtyard, or its thatched roofing. However, the food's pretty representative of the region. That goes for the crepes and the *fruits de mer* options, though there's also fish and chips on the menu, for those feeling more British than Breton.

ACCOMMODATIONS

€50-100

LOGIS HÔTEL DU PARC

174 rue Saint-Guirec, Perros-Guirec; tel. 02 96 91 40 80; www.logishotels.com/fr/hotel/hotel-du-parc-3190?partid=661; closed Jan.; from €70 d

This inexpensive hotel is set in an old-fashioned-looking building with a modern interior. It's well located, just a short walk from the Plage Saint-Guirec, and would make for a good place to base a holiday for which most of the time is spent outside. There's WiFi throughout the building, and a decent restaurant on-site with a nice terrace area.

€100-200

L'AGAPA HOTEL

12 rue des Bons Enfants, Perros-Guirec; tel. 02 96 49 01 10; www.lagapa.com; from €120 d

Looking a little space-age from the outside, this hotel's design is really about letting in the maximum amount of light and awarding the best views out across the Côte de Granit Rose. Being purposefully built, it's spacious and well insulated when it needs to be, and the rooms are a lot more stylish than you might expect from the hotel frontage. Then there's also the on-site spa, complete with swimming pool, sauna, hammam, and hot tub. The less expensive rooms are the first to go, so book early to avoid exorbitant rates.

CASTEL BEAU SITE

137 rue Saint-Guirec, Perros-Guirec; tel. 02 96 91 40 87; www.castelbeausite.com; from €139 d

A hotel in as beautiful a location as its name would suggest, this is a modern, stylish, high-end establishment. Dominating one end of Saint-Guirec Beach, the rooms have a modern interior design with a purple-gray color scheme, and floor-to-ceiling windows looking out over the bay. Expect all modern conveniences to come as standard. There's also the exceptional on-site restaurant, La Table de mon Père. The less expensive rooms go first, so book early if you want to avoid paying huge fees.

Camping

CAMPING TOURONY

105 rue de Poul Palud, Trégastel; tel. 02 96 23 86 61; camping-tourony.com; Apr.-Oct. 22; high-season pitches from €20.90

Well located for trips into town and to the beach, the campsite occupies a quiet few acres in Tourony village, situated in an inlet of the bay. There are toilets and shower facilities, plus a small bar and restaurant with a terrace on-site—though it is only intermittently open.

Parish Closes: Monuments to a Celtic Christianity

Enclos paroissiaux, or "parish closes," as they're called in English, are unique and flamboyantly beguiling walled-in church complexes in some towns along the Breton coast. They were directly linked to economic prosperity here in the 16th and 17th centuries, thanks to the money brought in by the manufacture of sailing goods such as rope and sails. Newly wealthy towns became competitive with one another about producing the most impressive churches they could, often overloading them with sculptures, religious furniture, and stained glass.

As well as a church, the walled-in area had to include an ossuary, a stone cross, a triumphant gateway, a fountain, and a chapel for storing relics. The expansive parish close idea was more than just a convenient way to excuse more lavish spending. It had its origins in the region's Celtic culture and its preoccupation with well-defined sacred features, such as springs or groves. On top of this, there was a great borrowing from Celtic tradition in telling about the lives of local saints, many of which are elucidated by sculptures in parish closes, often following the same storyline of ancient myths. This said, Brittany was a defiantly Christian region by the time the closes were built.

In practical terms, the more money towns earned, the more they expanded their parish close, and some of the largest ones today are really quite staggering explosions of oversize wedding-cake-like decoration, even while they appear in what may seem now fairly small, out-of-the-way towns.

Regardless, there are plenty of other bars and restaurants nearby.

INFORMATION

OFFICE DE TOURISME DE PERROS-GUIREC

21 place de l'Hôtel de Ville, Perros-Guirec; tel. 02 96 23 21 15; 9am-7pm Mon.-Sat., 10am-12:30pm and 4pm-7pm Sun.

A friendly staff works throughout the year to offer plenty of information about activities, walks, and transport right across the Côte de Granit Rose. There's ample literature on offer here, advertising restaurants, hotels, and things you might want to do.

TRANSPORTATION

Getting There and Around

BY CAR

Out on a promontory, the Côte de Granit Rose can take longer to get to by car than you might expect. **Perros-Guirec** is the region's gateway town, fed by the D788, and unless you are making your way slowly along coastal roads, you will likely approach from the south.

From Rennes (109 miles/175 kilometers, 2 hours), take the N12 as far as transport hub Guingamp, then change to the D767 to climb up the coast. From Paris you want to go via Rennes; the total journey is 324 miles (522 kilometers) and a little more than five hours.

From Brest (74 miles/119 kilometers, 1 hour 40 minutes), take the N12 in the other direction, though heading north before Guingamp along the D11.

BY TRAIN

The closest train station to the Côte de Granit Rose is in Lannion, where trains arrive and depart from **Gare de Lannion** (1 avenue du Général de Gaulle, Lannion; www.gares-sncf.com/fr/gare/frlai/lannion; 4:45am-9:20pm Mon.-Thurs., 4:45am-10:15pm Fri., 6:35am-8:50pm Sat., 8:40am-10:30pm Sun.). From Lannion, you'll have to travel the rest of the journey by bus. **TILT** (www.lannion-tregor.com/fr/deplacements/le-reseau-tilt.html) runs five buses (Line E) a day in high season from Lannion toward the Côte de Granit Rose. They leave from Lannion train station and arrive in Perros-Guirec after about 40 minutes. (The line then carries on along the coast to Trégastel.) The cost is around €3.

There is one direct train to Lannion from

Paris daily (3.5 hours, €73). There are around eight local trains a day from **Guingamp** (Gare de Guingamp; place de la Gare, Guingamp; tel. 36 35; www.gares-sncf.com/fr/gare/frggp/guingamp; 4:25am-10pm Mon., 6am-10pm Tues.-Thurs., 6:30am-11:40pm Fri., 6:15am-9:50pm Sat., 9:55am-10:50pm Sun.) to Lannion, costing about €9 and taking half an hour. Trains arrive in Guingamp from Brest and Rennes every hour (the journeys take about an hour, too, and cost around €20). There are also five direct trains from Paris that come to Guingamp, taking about three hours and costing around €60. From here you'll have to take the **Tibus** (www.tibus.fr/horaires/?rub_code=23) Line 6 bus to Lannion. The journey is about an hour long.

BY BUS

From Perros-Guirec, in the summer there are also two shuttle bus lines, called **Le Macareux** (http://tourisme.perros-guirec.com/perros-guirec-pratique/se-deplacer-a-perros-guirec/en-navette-le-macareux.html), which take you all around the coastal area. They run from the Plage de Saint-Guirec in the west to the Esplanade de la Douane in the east, going close to both the Plage de Trestraou and the Plage de Trestrignel. It costs €1.20 for a ticket, and the buses are circling constantly, so there should be one roughly every half hour.

Finistère

The remote character of Finistère is so pervasive, it even extends to its name: *fin* being French for end, and *terre* for the earth. The most westerly outcrop of mainland France, stretching deep into the icy Atlantic, its coastal waters are some of the most viciously dramatic anywhere in Europe, and are frequently churned to a boiling intensity by winter storms.

It probably should come as no surprise, then, that Finistère is a region of great natural beauty; of warm, life-loving people; and of lighthouses. Lots of lighthouses. Not as touristy as other parts of Brittany, it nevertheless offers some of the region's most dramatic walking trails, surf spots, and sailing schools in the Crozon peninsula, and in Concarneau, some of the best seafood in all of France.

Highlights

Look for ★ to find recommended sights, activities, dining, and lodging.

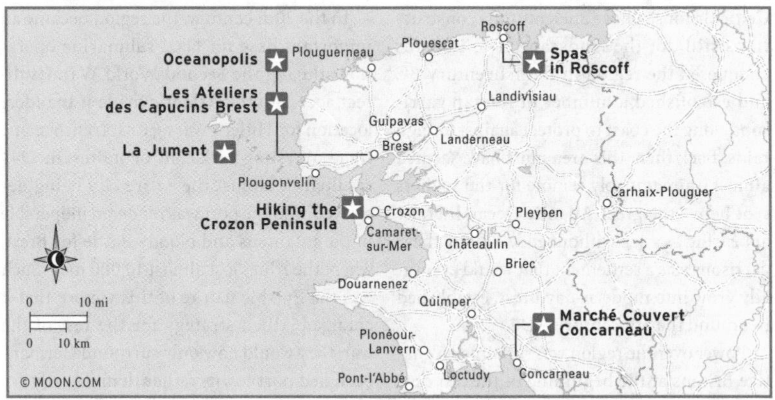

★ **Spas in Roscoff:** This charming coastal town specializes in seawater therapy (and onions) (page 287).

★ **Oceanopolis:** This aquarium is one of the best in France (page 293).

★ **Les Ateliers des Capucins Brest:** These 19th-century shipbuilding warehouses have been converted into a world-beating multimedia center, complete with a library, games room, and recreation area. Entirely free, it is a triumph of public investment (page 295).

★ **La Jument:** Famous around the world for a photo snapped of its keeper in the midst of a storm by Jean Guichard in 1989, this lighthouse is not much to look at in itself, but seen from the Île d'Ouessant, the westernmost point in France, this lighthouse has become representative of the edge-of-the-world feel of the island (page 302).

★ **Hiking the Crozon Peninsula:** This landscape of dramatic bays and coves with the color and texture contrast dialed up to 11 is also crisscrossed by a seemingly endless number of hiking paths (page 312).

★ **Marché Couvert Concarneau:** A center of Brittany's fishing industry, the town's covered market is the place to go for a flavor-led lesson in marine biology (page 332).

With Brest, meanwhile, Finistère boasts one of Brittany's most lively, outward-looking urban centers. It may not have the elegance of some other towns (it suffered mightily during the Second World War), but a strong local economy linked to seafaring and well-executed public spending have led to a palpably happy city, unrepentantly modern, and comfortable in its own skin. Just a few miles north, meanwhile, with a character that seems to separate it from urban France by at least a century, is the Île d'Ouessant: a rocky island, pounded by the Atlantic, where modern Europe itself feels like a forgotten dream.

A land of extremes, Finistère is packed with rewards for travelers who voyage this far.

HISTORY

In ancient times, Finistère was home to the Celtic Britons, whose ancient stone constructions still dot the landscape. The Romans conquered the region in the 1st century BC and established a number of Roman garrisons along the coast to protect against foreign raids. Back then, this area must have seemed almost unimaginably remote for the soldiers sent here—the great Atlantic Ocean literally appearing as a sea without end. Among these garrisons was a settlement that would eventually grow into modern-day Brest, established in around the 3rd century AD.

Power over the region was reclaimed by native Britons at the beginning of the 5th century. From then on, it was run from the town of Quimper, where a bishopric was established in 495, functioning under Frankish influence until the rise of the Duchy of Brittany in the 10th century.

Following two centuries of independence, Brittany was eventually invaded and conquered by King Henry II of England in the mid-12th century. After that, there followed a period during the Hundred Years' War where the French and English fiercely fought for under whose influence it would lie. The French were the eventual victors in this struggle, and Brittany became subsumed into the French state around the beginning of the 16th century.

Throughout this time, the value of Brest, which had grown into a large military port, cannot be overexaggerated. Indeed, a common phrase began to circulate: "He is not the Duke of Brittany who is not the Lord of Brest." When Claude, the daughter of Anne of Brittany, married Francis I of France, this lordship, and the rest of Brittany, passed definitively to the French crown.

Finistère became sorted as a department of France during the French Revolution in 1790, and saw its borders expanded into Morbihan somewhat in 1857. The populace of Finistère also widely supported Napoleon III's coup d'état in 1851.

In the 20th century, the region became an important base for Nazi submarine operations during the Second World War. Its direct access to the Atlantic made it the ideal location for Hitler's war against transoceanic trade. Wresting back control of Brest in 1944 resulted in almost the entire city being destroyed, and the port was rendered inoperable in the infamous and bloody Battle for Brest, where the Allies lost almost 10,000 men. Such was the Pyrrhic nature of this victory that it changed Allied strategy for the rest of the war; they would now only surround German-occupied port towns rather than directly try to reclaim them.

ORIENTATION

Consisting of the entirety of the westernmost portion of Brittany, Finistère could almost be characterized as looking something like the head of a great craggy monster, its jaws agape, roaring into the Atlantic Ocean, with the central Crozon Peninsula its barbed tongue.

Despite the savagery of its landscape, much of the region is well connected, with an

Previous: colorful shutters on the back streets of Brest; hiking along the Presqu'ile de Crozon; La Jument lighthouse

extensive series of decent-size roads linking its major towns and cities. As with elsewhere in Brittany, though, the rugged crenellations of the coastline itself often mean that the fastest route between any two coastal locations is to head inland for a bit to use the highway, rather than taking the seemingly more direct road between them.

Roscoff is the biggest town on the north coast, and connects to **Brest** via the D788, or the more arterial N12. Brest itself, to continue the metaphor of the monster's head, sits along its upper row of teeth, relatively sheltered on what is a vast natural harbor. Follow the D789 west from here, toward the monster's overbite, and you reach Le Conquet, from whence you can take the ferry to the **Île d'Ouessant,** which sits lonely and windswept offshore, the farthest west it's possible to get in metropolitan France.

The **Crozon Peninsula,** as mentioned, is like a barbed tongue, and despite its apparent proximity to the land both in the north and the south still is most easily accessed from either by driving back east and entering where it connects with the rest of Finistère. There is also a foot-passenger ferry that leaves from Brest to Le Fret in Crozon, run by a company called **Le Brestoâ** (http://lebrestoa.com). This takes about an hour and costs around €16 (see Crozon Transport section for more details). The farther west in Crozon you go, the smaller the roads and the slower going.

Quimper, meanwhile, sits firmly inland in the center of the bottom jaw. With its own ring road, it is well serviced from all directions and can be reached from Brest by driving south for about 50 miles (80 kilometers) along the N165, or from Rennes by driving west for about 135 miles (217 kilometers) along the N24, then the N165. **Concarneau,** home to some of the best seafood anywhere in France, is about seven miles (11 kilometers) southwest of Quimper, on the coast.

PLANNING YOUR TIME

With more activites than out-and-out sights, Finistère is best suited for a holiday that doesn't involve a massive amount of moving around. Rather, it's better to pick a particular area of this fascinating peninsula and really get to grips with it—hike its bays, explore its coves, learn to sail on its seas—than rush around ticking off one churchyard after another. At the very least, try to stay in one of its more rural coastal areas overnight, as it'll give you a chance to see the many almost otherworldly lighthouses in action—nowhere is this more the case than the **Île d'Ouessant.**

Also, while none of Brittany fully escapes from tourism, this is one of the region's less-invaded areas, which has the effect of making locals less cynical and more willing to welcome you into their customs. Finistère is thus an excellent region in which to crash a ***fest-noz,*** a traditional Breton village fair, complete with dancing, crepes, and cider. They take place throughout the year, and an extensive list of them can be found at www.tamm-kreiz.bzh.

Otherwise, **Quimper** and its immediate surrounds make for a great city break of a long weekend to five days, while **Brest** makes for a very welcoming and comfortable place to base a holiday, even if the town itself is not exactly overflowing with things to see and do.

Finistère

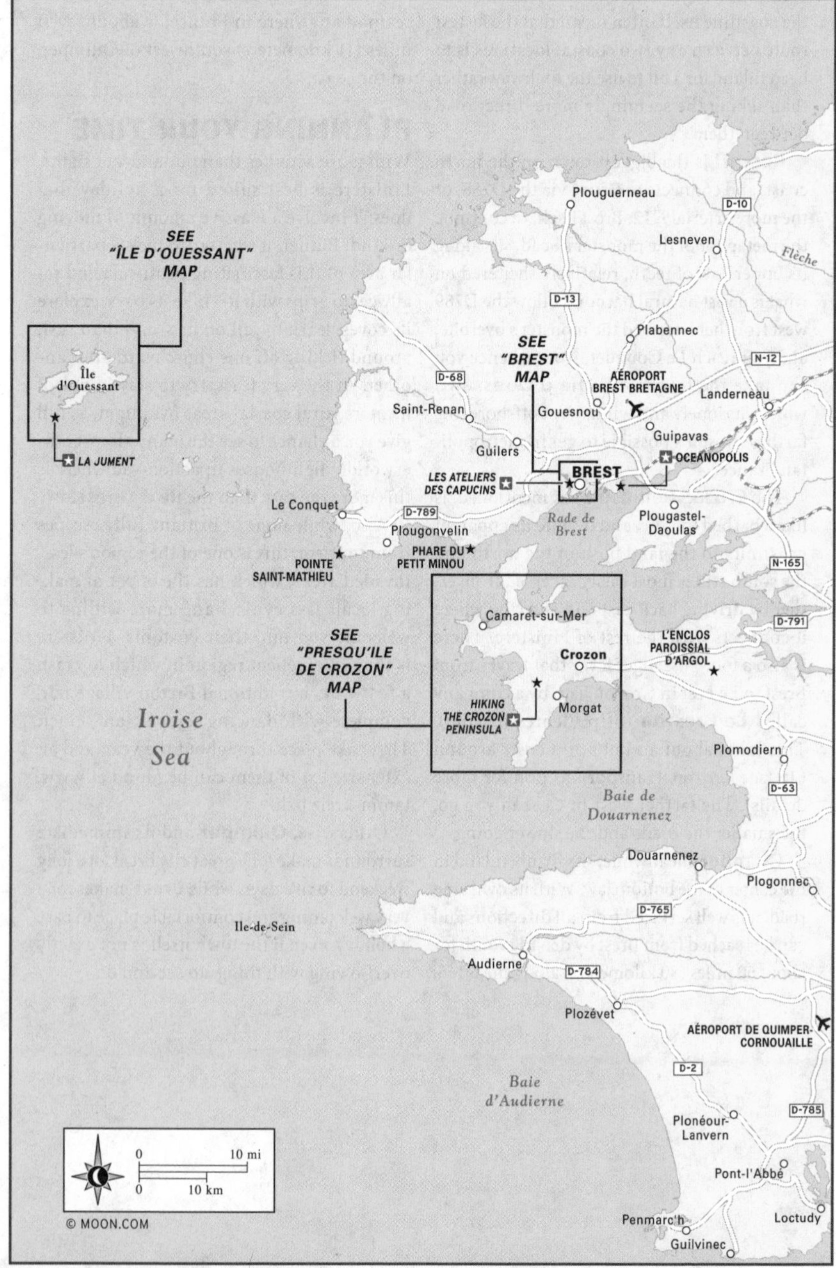
SEE
"ÎLE D'OUESSANT"
MAP
Île
d'Ouessant
LA JUMENT
Plouguerneau
D-10
Lesneven
Flèche
D-13
Plabennec
SEE
"BREST"
MAP
N-12
D-68
AÉROPORT
BREST BRETAGNE
Landerneau
Saint-Renan
Gouesnou
Guipavas
Guilers
OCEANOPOLIS
LES ATELIERS
DES CAPUCINS
BREST
Le Conquet
D-789
Rade de
Brest
Plougastel-
Daoulas
Plougonvelin
PHARE DU
PETIT MINOU
POINTE
SAINT-MATHIEU
N-165
Camaret-sur-Mer
D-791
SEE
"PRESQU'ILE
DE CROZON"
MAP
L'ENCLOS
PAROISSIAL
D'ARGOL
Crozon
Morgat
HIKING
THE CROZON
PENINSULA
Iroise
Sea
Plomodiern
D-63
Baie de
Douarnenez
Douarnenez
Plogonnec
D-765
Ile-de-Sein
Audierne
D-784
Plozévet
AÉROPORT DE QUIMPER-
CORNOUAILLE
D-2
Baie
d'Audierne
D-785
Plonéour-
Lanvern
0
10 mi
0
10 km
Pont-l'Abbé
Penmarc'h
Loctudy
Guilvinec
© MOON.COM

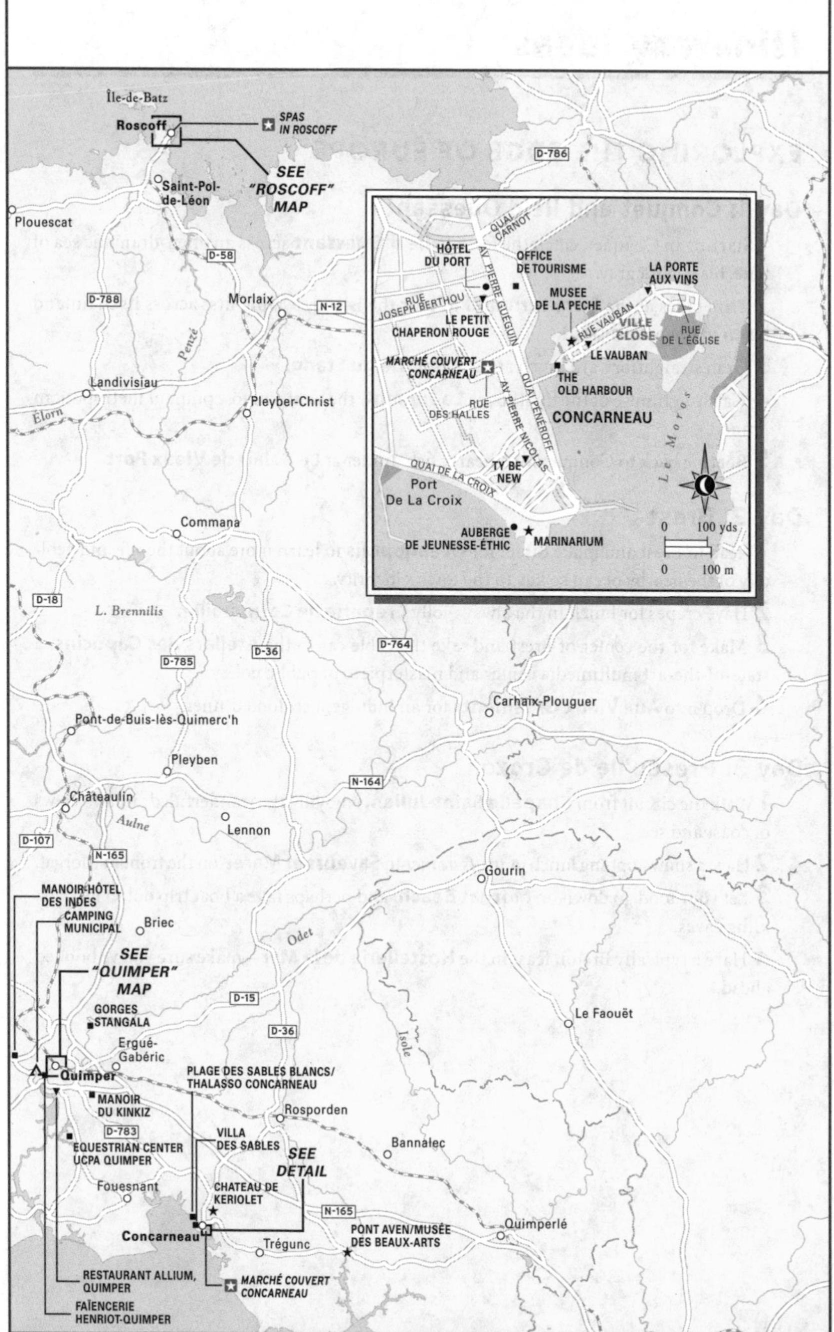
Île-de-Batz
Roscoff
SPAS IN ROSCOFF
SEE "ROSCOFF" MAP
Saint-Pol-de-Léon
Plouescat
D-786
D-58
D-788
Morlaix
N-12
Penzé
Landivisiau
Pleyber-Christ
Élorn
Commana
D-18
L. Brennilis
D-36
D-764
D-785
Carhaix-Plouguer
Pont-de-Buis-lès-Quimerc'h
Pleyben
N-164
Châteaulin
Aulne
Lennon
D-107
N-165
Gourin
MANOIR-HÔTEL DES INDES
CAMPING MUNICIPAL
Briec
Odet
SEE "QUIMPER" MAP
D-15
GORGES STANGALA
D-36
Le Faouët
Ergué-Gabéric
Isole
Quimper
PLAGE DES SABLES BLANCS/ THALASSO CONCARNEAU
MANOIR DU KINKIZ
Rosporden
D-783
EQUESTRIAN CENTER UCPA QUIMPER
VILLA DES SABLES
SEE DETAIL
Bannalec
Fouesnant
CHATEAU DE KERIOLET
N-165
Concarneau
Quimperlé
PONT AVEN/MUSÉE DES BEAUX-ARTS
Trégunc
RESTAURANT ALLIUM, QUIMPER
MARCHÉ COUVERT CONCARNEAU
FAÏENCERIE HENRIOT-QUIMPER
QUAI CARNOT
HÔTEL DU PORT
OFFICE DE TOURISME
LA PORTE AUX VINS
RUE JOSEPH BERTHOU
AV. PIERRE GUEGUIN
MUSEE DE LA PECHE
LE PETIT CHAPERON ROUGE
RUE VAUBAN
VILLE CLOSE
RUE DE L'ÉGLISE
LE VAUBAN
MARCHÉ COUVERT CONCARNEAU
THE OLD HARBOUR
RUE DES HALLES
AV. PIERRE NICOLAS
QUAI PENEROFF
CONCARNEAU
Le Moros
TY BE NEW
QUAI DE LA CROIX
Port De La Croix
AUBERGE DE JEUNESSE-ÉTHIC
MARINARIUM
0 100 yds
0 100 m

Itinerary Ideas

EXPLORING THE EDGE OF EUROPE

Day 1: Conquet and Île d'Ouessant

1 Starting in Conquet, catch the ferry to **Île d'Ouessant** across an often-dramatic sea of blue, black, and gray.

2 Hire bikes at the **ferry terminal** to tour the island, cycling first across its mainland heath to town, **Lampaul.**

3 Grab straightforward lunch at the **Crêperie du Stang.**

4 Catch a glimpse of the lighthouse **La Jument,** the westernmost point of metropolitan France.

5 Boating back to Conquet for a hearty fish dinner at **Le Relais de Vieux Port.**

Day 2: Brest

1 Head to Brest and make direct for **Oceanopolis** to learn more about the life and geology of the nearby ocean so key to the town's identity.

2 Have crepes for lunch in the always-jolly **Crêperie de Cornouaille.**

3 Make for the center of Brest and take the cable car to the **Ateliers des Capucins,** a state-of-the-art multimedia center and masterpiece of public policy.

4 Drop into **Aux Vieux Greements** for an indulgent seafood dinner.

Day 3: Presqu'ile de Crozon

1 Walk the circuit from **Chapelle Saint-Julien,** enjoying the wonderful, dramatic views of coast and sea.

2 Have a showstopping lunch of *fruits de mer* in **Saveurs et Marée** on the front in Morgat.

3 Let your food go down on **Morgat Beach,** and perhaps take a boat trip out to its sparkling caves.

4 Have a typically Breton feast in the **Hostellerie de la Mer**—make sure you've booked ahead.

Itinerary Ideas

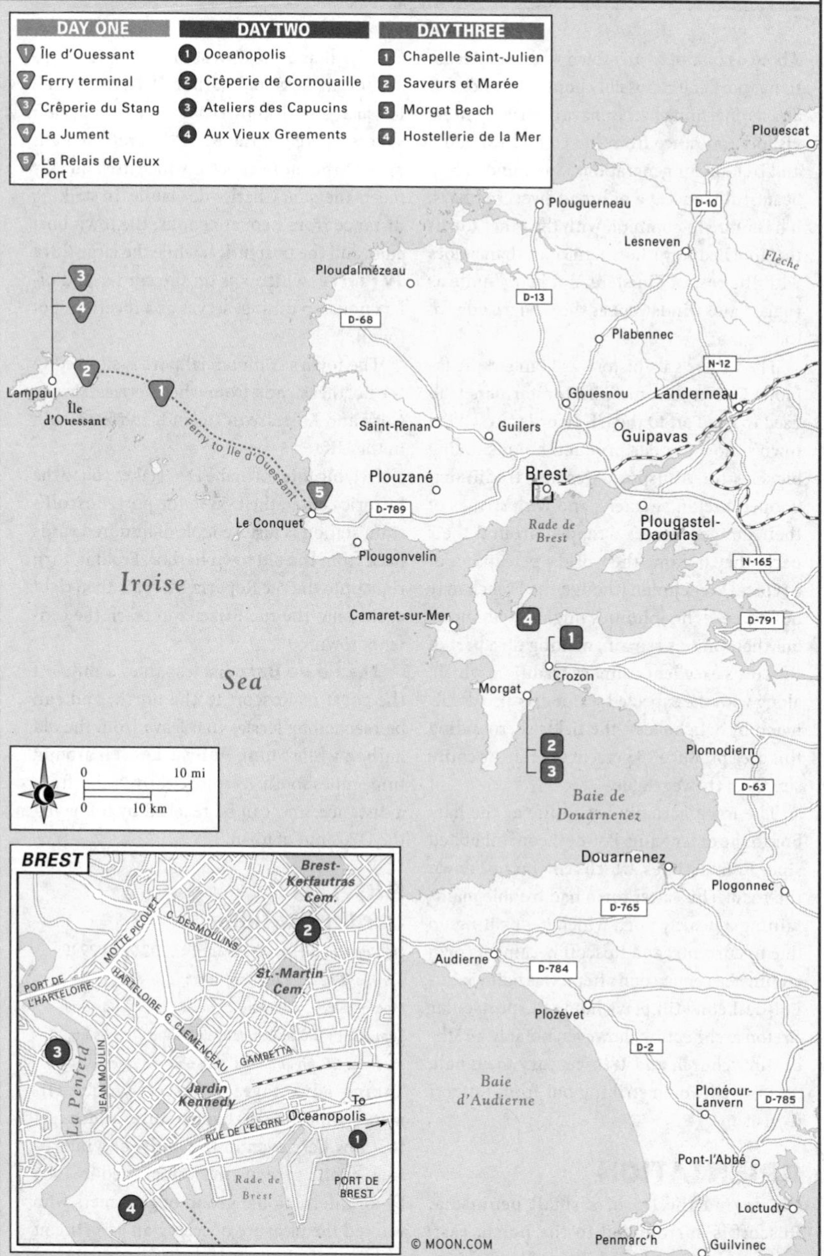

Roscoff

About as quaint as any town with an international port could possibly hope to be, Roscoff and its charming harbor have been welcoming visitors to France from the United Kingdom and Ireland for generations. Surrounded by a beautiful landscape of broad sweeping bays, it has more in common with the other towns that line Brittany's northern coast than it does with the rest of Finistère, not being quite as rugged and windswept as the western edge of the region.

Then there's its history as home to the famous Onion Johnnies, Breton farmers who used to head off to the UK in order to sell the town's most famous product: onions. Using bicycles for transport, wearing traditional hooped Breton sweaters, and with strings of their pungent wares wrapped around their neck, they became the world's perception of a typical Frenchman (though the French may not agree). The Johnnies might be no more, but their onions remain, making up a part of Roscoff's excellent culinary tradition, which, along with the expected seafood, is also dominated by artichokes—the fields surrounding this area produce 90 percent of France's entire supply of the vegetable.

The town actually began life as the harbor to the older Saint-Pol-de-Léon, inhabited since Roman times, which remains just down the road. This latter town had trouble maintaining a nearby port, which kept silting up due to currents, and Roscoff became its own commerce center soon after it was built. Saint-Pol-de-Léon still plays home to spectacular Breton architecture, however, notably a 15th-century church and 18th-century town hall, and is well worth striking out from Roscoff to visit.

ORIENTATION

Occupying the tip of a small peninsula, Roscoff is surrounded to the north, east, and west by the sea. Its historic "center" is to the north and northwest of town and wraps around its large old harbor. Relatively small for such a well-known port town, its busiest spot is where the rue Amiral Réveillère joins up with the rue Gambetta, which itself quickly meets the quai Charles de Gaulle. In striking distance from here are banks, the town boat club, and the post office, while the large **Café Ty Pierre,** which sits on the corner and offers nonstop dining, serves as a meeting spot for all.

The town's commercial port is situated to the northeast, and from where ferries leave to Cork and Rosslare in Ireland, and Plymouth in the UK.

Driving into town the D769 takes you to the historic center, the D58 to the port. Roscoff's train station is just a couple of hundred yards back from the old town harbor. From it, turn right onto the rue Ropartz Morvan, then right again onto the rue Brizeux to reach the center of town.

The **Île de Batz** sits less than a mile off the coast of Roscoff to the north, and can be reached by ferries that leave from the old harbor, while **Saint-Pol-de-Léon** is around three miles south, its spire clearly visible from a distance, and can be reached by following the D769 out of town.

SIGHTS

Jardin Exotique

Lieu-dit Roc'h Hievec, Roscoff; tel. 02 98 61 29 19; www.jardinexotiqueroscoff.com; 2pm-5pm daily Mar. and Nov., 10:30am-6pm daily Apr.-June and Sept.-Oct., 10am-7pm daily July-Aug.; adults €6, students €5, children 8-17 €3, under 8 free

Taking advantage of Roscoff's microclimate—which means temperatures seldom get that low here even in the midst of winter—this "exotic garden" was established in 1986 by an international group of gardeners who wanted the pleasure of seeing an assortment of subtropical plants in Brittany's distinctly

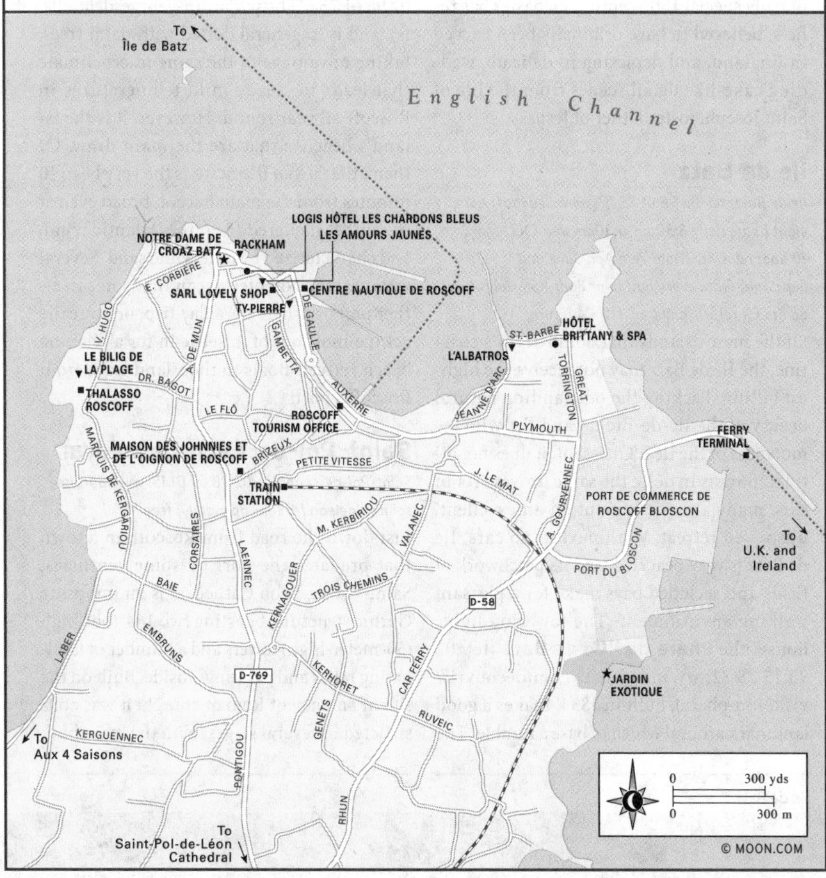

northern climes. A landscape of cacti, agaves, and aloes was the result, punctuated by man-made waterfalls, ponds, and rockeries, with some excellent panoramic views out across the Bay of Morlaix. Many of the plants are well labeled, in French and English, with information about their natural qualities and sometimes the history of their discovery. Fairly small in size, a visit here shouldn't take much more than an hour, though should you feel like lingering there's plenty of space to do so.

Notre Dame de Croaz Batz

2 rue Albert de Mun, Roscoff; tel. 02 98 69 70 17; 9am-6pm daily; free

This Gothic and Renaissance church, built of granite and consecrated in the late 16th century, features an opulent, classically Breton bell tower. Its building was financed by shipowners of Roscoff, which explains the three images of ships sculpted into its exterior stonework. Inside is particularly opulent, hinting at the impressive wealth of Roscoff in years gone by. There are several altarpieces on display, including ones depicting Saint Peter and Saint Genevieve, and another of Our Lady of Guadalupe, recalling Roscoff's trade links with the New World. Perhaps most impressive of all, though, is the church's "Alabaster Chapel," in which is housed a series of truly special 15th-century alabaster bas reliefs, believed to have originally been carved in England, and depicting in delicate, wedding cake-like detail scenes from the life of Saint Joseph, foster father of Jesus.

Île de Batz

Île de Batz; tel. 02 98 61 75 70; www.iledebatz.com; eight boats daily 8:30am-6:30pm mid-Oct.-Mar., 10 boats daily 8:30am-7pm Apr.-June and Sept.-mid-Oct., every half hour 8am-8pm July-Aug.; adults €9 return, children 4-11 €4 return

Of the many islands that dot Brittany's coastine, the Île de Batz may not receive the highest billing. Lacking the outstanding natural beauty of the Île-de-Bréhat and the wild remoteness of the Île d'Ouessant, it does not attract tourists in quite the same droves. Yet in this, many are missing out on an excellent, unspoiled retreat. With next to no cars, Île de Batz is very peaceful, and its patchwork of fields and secluded bays make for a pleasant walking environment. The towering lighthouse, the **Phare de l'Île de Batz** (tel. 02 98 15 78 32; www.iledebatz.com/découvrir/visite-du-phare), built in 1834, makes a good landmark around which to base a ramble. The island also boasts its own exotic garden, the **Jardin Exotique Georges-Delaselle** (tel. 02 98 61 75 65; http://jardin-georgesdelaselle.fr), and is in general dotted with palm trees, taking advantage of the same microclimate that leads to steady mild temperatures in Roscoff all year round. However, it is the island's beaches that are the main draw. Of them, the **Grève Blanche** is the very best: 10 minutes from the main harbor, broad even at high tide, sheltered from the Atlantic wind, and characterized by pure white sand. Several restaurants and hotels mean that you can either pop over here for a day trip, or, to really get the most out of it, settle in for a relaxing beach retreat. Boats to the island leave from Roscoff's port.

Saint-Pol-de-Léon Cathedral

Saint-Pol-de-Léon; tel. 02 98 69 01 15; www.paroisse-saintpoldeleon.fr; 9am-6pm daily; free

Just down the road from Roscoff, in a town that predates the port by some centuries, Saint-Pol-de-Léon Cathedral is an imposing Gothic structure, boasting two 164-foot-high (50-meter-high) towers and a number of fascinating relics and paintings inside. Built on the site of an ancient Roman church, it was constructed in several stages, with the main bulk

Île de Batz

of the building having gone up in the 13th-century. Today, as well as making an impact through its impressive size, there are plenty of artifacts in its interior that will encourage visitors to linger for more time than they might in a regular church. These include the remains of Saint Paul Aurélien's sacred bell; 32 boxes containing skulls, exhumed from the church graveyard in the 19th century; the tomb of a 17th-century mystic; and, supposedly, a thorn from Christ's crown at the crucifixion, among other things. Overall, it's well worth a trip out of Roscoff to see.

ENTERTAINMENT AND EVENTS

Festivals

FÊTE DE L'OIGNON DE ROSCOFF

48 rue Brizeux, Roscoff; tel. 02 98 61 12 13; www.roscoff.fr/Fete-de-l-Oignon-de-Roscoff,343.html; Aug. 18-19; free

Celebrating Roscoff's most famous product—onions—and its history of exporting them to the UK, this is a festival that's bound to bring a tear to your eye, though not out of sadness. Centered around an onion market, selling the best examples of the vegetable you're ever likely to taste, the gathering also includes demonstrations of onion weaving, exhibitions of old farm equipment, and plenty of food stalls as well. Fun for all the family!

Nightlife

L'ALBATROS

Boulevard Sainte-Barbe, Roscoff; tel. 02 98 61 20 05; 4pm-1am Wed.-Sat., 3pm-7pm Sun.; cocktails from €5

Offering a nice, friendly ambience deep into the evening, this lively spot serves tasty cocktails and specializes in different flavored rums—another reminder that, through trade, Roscoff has long been connected to sunnier climes. Near Roscoff's old harbor, the interior is not unlike that of a British pub. Popular with locals, it fills up especially on weekend evenings or when they have live music, as they do intermittently throughout the year.

SPORTS AND RECREATION

★ Spas

THALASSO ROSCOFF

16 rue Victor Hugo, Roscoff, France; tel. 02 52 56 00 13; www.thalasso.com/thalasso/les-destinations/roscoff; 8:30am-8pm daily; day-long treatment from €194

Thalassotherapy, or seawater therapy, is commonly believed to have been invented in Brittany at some point during the 19th century. In its most essential form, it is based on the notion that the properties of seawater have natural healing benefits, thanks to its high mineral content, that can be absorbed directly through the skin. In this spa in Roscoff, however, it's also the massaging effects of jetted water, the heated pools, and the views out across the English Channel that are likely to do wonders for your well-being. A modern complex with attentive staff, treatments here include massages, exfoliations, and aqua aerobics. Packages of several days, which include accommodations on-site, are also available.

Water Sports

CENTRE NAUTIQUE DE ROSCOFF

Quai Charles de Gaulle, Roscoff; tel. 02 98 69 72 79; www.roscoff-nautique.com; 9am-6pm daily Mar.-Nov.; kayak rental from €13, a week of sailing lessons from €150

This friendly, centrally located water-sports center offers the full range of services from boat rental to sailing courses, plus tours of the surrounding seas as part of a crew in larger sailing boats and catamarans. Accommodating for those spending a whole holiday in Roscoff or those just passing through, it's the spot to rent or receive lessons in kayaks, catamarans, and small sailing ships. Stand-up paddleboards can be rented, too. Book ahead for lessons or tours; for renting it should be fine just to show up.

FOOD

Local Cuisine

RACKHAM

27 place Lacaze Duthiers, Roscoff; tel. 02 98 61 14 23; www.rackham-restaurant.com/fr; 12pm-1:30pm and 7pm-9:30pm Wed.-Sat., 7pm-9:30pm Tues.; menus €48-95

Located inside an old seafarer's house, and with views out to sea and the Île de Batz beyond, Rackham runs with the nautical, even partly piratical, theme just enough to inject fun and individuality into the dining experience, but not so much that it undermines what is essentially a high-end, tasteful establishment. The food is prepared by a team of young, though highly decorated, chefs, and aims both to delight and surprise. There's a great deal of excellent seafood on the menu, but it is not entirely dominant: There are plenty of terrestrial specialties, from duck to slow-cooked lamb, available as well. Book in advance to be sure of a table, and a few days in advance on the weekend.

Budget Options

TY-PIERRE

1 rue Gambetta, Roscoff; tel. 02 98 69 72 75; www.cafetypierre.fr; 6:30am-1am daily; mains €7.50-16

Boasting a layout and central location in Roscoff that could never not result in it becoming a pillar of the local community, Ty-Pierre is a real thoroughfare bar, restaurant, and café likely to be bustling from dawn until dusk. Located on a corner, it has windows that look out onto a couple of streets and a terrace that stretches toward the harbor. Popular with tourists and locals, it serves food crammed with bold local flavors (the mussels and fries are a particularly good choice), and comes served with a sauce that changes every day. Though busy, tables are constantly being freed up, so you shouldn't have to wait too long for a seat.

LE BILIG DE LA PLAGE

14 rue Victor Hugo, Roscoff; tel. 02 98 61 15 50; 11am-8:30 pm Thurs.-Tues., 11am-6:30pm Wed.; mains €8-15

A beachfront gem, specializing in crepes. It's very well priced and pretty basic inside, with a small terrace. The dishes are unpretentious and made mostly out of local ingredients, including freshly caught fish. There are also some tasty meat options available: They're unafraid to serve packed crepes with a whole sausage alongside, making for a filling and delicious distraction from the sea.

LES AMOURS JAUNES

18 rue Amiral Réveillère, Roscoff; tel. 02 98 61 19 04; 7:45am-7pm daily; mains €8-13

Serving up decent, straightforward crepes for a very reasonable price, Les Amours Jaunes is centrally located and does a busy lunchtime trade. Cider is served, as it should be, in ceramic cups, while the interior is colorful, the walls hung with local art. Come for the savory buckwheat crepes and stay for the desserts, which are of a very high, indulgent standard.

ACCOMMODATIONS

€50-100

LOGIS HÔTEL LES CHARDONS BLEUS

4 rue Amiral Réveillère, Roscoff; tel. 02 98 69 72 03; www.hotel-chardons-bleus.com; from €76 d

A comfortable, if somewhat basic, hotel, centrally located and in an old stone building. Its budget credentials may be a little too obvious for some, especially regarding the interior of its rooms, which, though clean and not-yet tired, look like they were styled about 30 years ago. However, internet is available in all the rooms, and the on-site restaurant comes highly recommended, serving rich, traditional food simply prepared to a high standard (menus €14-60).

€100-200

HÔTEL BRITTANY & SPA

22 boulevard Sainte-Barbe, Roscoff; tel. 02 98 69 70 78; www.hotel-brittany.com/fr; from €155 d

An extremely nice hotel that effortlessly blends old and modern elements into a bright, stylishly furnished design. As its name

Know Your Onions! The Bizarre Story of Roscoff's "Onion Johnnies"

A vestige of Brittany's once very close relationship with the United Kingdom and a reminder that the national boundaries of modern Europe are relatively recent things, Roscoff's famous Onion Johnnies are local farmers who have been crossing the Channel for almost two centuries in order to sell their wares. Usually wearing the traditional Breton hooped jersey, and, of course, garlanded by their eponymous onions—bound into tight strings to keep fresh—their image became firmly sunk into the British imagination as being typical of all French men. They were, after all, for a long time the only French people many in Britain would have seen.

The Johnnies could have brought their produce to Paris, but in the mid-19th century, getting to the French capital from Roscoff was a long and difficult trip. It was far easier to take a boat across the sea, where, as an added bonus, their very exoticism also helped them sell their vegetables. Interestingly, many Johnnies headed straight to Wales, cycling on their equally characteristic bicycles to where their native Breton language was similar to the local dialect, and many could make themselves understood.

Business boomed in the early 20th century, with almost 1,400 Johnnies from the Roscoff area importing over 9,000 tonnes (9,921 tons) of onions to the UK in 1929. Their continued success was delivered a one-two punch, however, first by the Great Depression and later by trade restrictions introduced after the Second World War. Today, very few remain cycling the British countryside, though out of the original enterprise was born **Brittany Ferries,** established following the success of the Johnnies transporting their onions across the Channel year after year.

Today, the full story of the Onion Johnnies can be seen in a Roscoff museum founded in 2004 and dedicated to their honor, **Maison des Johnnies et de l'Oignon de Roscoff** (48 rue Brizeux; tel. 06 40 15 87 53; www.roscoff.fr/-Maison-des-Johnnies-et-de-l-Oignon-.html).

suggests, there's an on-site spa boasting many Brittany-specific wellness therapies, including water jets and soaps made from the algae of the region's coasts. There's also an on-site restaurant with a Michelin star boasting wonderful-tasting and beautifully presented seafood, and some great views out to sea through timeless stone arches. Rooms vary considerably in style, size, and price depending on what part of the hotel they're in, being more traditional and smaller in the old part, and more modern, bigger, and more expensive in the new extension.

Camping

AUX 4 SAISONS

Allée des Chênes Verts, Roscoff; www.camping-aux4saisons.com; open Apr.-Sept.; pitch €17.90, cabins from €580 per week

A short drive west of the town center following Roscoff's bay, this is a straightforward, well-maintained campsite with plenty of space and a strong family feel in the summer months. Don't put too much store by the promise of WiFi, and as for the on-site restaurant, haute cuisine it is not. It is, though, located on a beach; there's a well-kept shower block and even a small library room with a TV if the weather takes a turn. It also has quite a high turnover, attracting a lot of Brits as they make their way back home via Roscoff's ferry port. Worth booking a week ahead in high season.

INFORMATION

ROSCOFF TOURISM OFFICE

Quai d'Auxerre, Roscoff; tel. 02 98 61 12 13; www.roscoff-tourisme.com; 9:30am-6pm Mon.-Sat.

A centrally located modern tourist office with information about things to do on Île de Batz and Saint-Pol-de-Léon, as well as in Roscoff itself. Given the number of visitors traveling through town on their way to the UK, English is widely spoken.

TRANSPORTATION

Getting There

BY CAR

Roscoff is set out on a small peninsula, and the fastest way in and out by car is along the same road, the D58. From Rennes (132 miles/213 kilometers, 2.5 hours), the journey first starts on the N12, which then linking to the D58 at Morlaix. a town that acts as something of an inland travel hub for the coast. From Paris (347 miles/560 kilometers, 5.5 hours), head south out of the city on the A10 and follow signs to Rennes—this is a toll road, which will cost about €25—and pick up the N12 from there.

In the other direction, from Brest (40 miles/65 kilometers, 1 hour), take the N12 to Landivisiau, then head along the D69 until it joins up with the D58.

Once you arrive in town, there are plenty of free parking spaces to be found just a few streets away from the center.

BY BOAT

Roscoff is one of the passenger ferry ports, **Gare Maritime** (Port du Bloscon, Roscoff; tel. 02 98 29 28 13) along France's northern coast, with its harbor Port de Bloscon about a mile east of the town center. **Brittany Ferries** (tel. 02 98 29 28 00; www.brittany-ferries.fr) provides a service from Plymouth, with 1-3 sailings a day, taking 5-9 hours and costing around €250 return with a car or €70 as a foot passenger; from Cork, Ireland, the journey takes 14 hours, one sailing weekly between April and October, costing similar amounts; and from Bilbao, Spain, the journey takes 21 hours, with one sailing weekly, and no boats mid-July-early August. This costs about €300 one way with a car, and €100 as a foot passenger.

Irish Ferries (tel. 01 70 72 03 26; www.irishferries.com), meanwhile, sail to the port from Rosslare in Ireland. This crossing takes just under 18 hours and there are five weekly, costing about €250 return with a car, and €70 return on foot.

BY TRAIN

Roscoff's station, **Gare de Roscoff** (rue de la Petite Vitesse, Roscoff; tel. 36 35; www.ter.sncf.com/bretagne/gares/87474635/ROSCOFF/pratique; 9:40am-12:20pm and 1:40pm-2:15pm and 3:15pm-6:15pm Mon.-Fri., 8:40am-12pm and 1:15pm-5:10pm Sat.) sits at the end of a branch line. It can be reached nine times a day by trains from Morlaix (35 minutes, €5). Morlaix, meanwhile, sits on the mainline between Paris and Brest. There are six trains a day that come here direct from the French capital (3 hours, about €70). From Brest (30 minutes-1hour, €10), there are around 13 trains a day. From Rennes (once an hour 6am-10pm, 1 hour 40 minutes, €30), there are trains running to Morlaix.

BY BUS

Reaching Roscoff by bus is a slower, though cheaper, option. Buses stop outside both the train station and the ferry port. From Brest, there are as many as four a day. The journey takes around two hours and costs €2. From Morlaix there are around 3-5 buses a day. The journey takes 40 minutes and also costs €2. The company running the bus service throughout Finistère is **Viaoo:** Details of all their routes can be found on www.viaoo29.fr.

Getting Around

The center of Roscoff is easily walkable. Moving between there and Saint-Pol-de-Léon or heading to campgrounds west of town, however, takes a little more planning or money as buses are not very regular—you can find schedules and routes on www.viaoo29.fr. There are numerous taxi companies, however, all charging the same rates. **Taxi Arno** is just one of them (tel. 06 74 89 40 79), with whom it should cost around €8 to get from the ferry port into the center of town—there is no bus service between the terminal and the town center.

Making things a little easier in the high summer months of July and August is the **Rosko** bus service. These run in a loop around the town, arrive around every 15 minutes, and are free to use. More information about them can be found at www.roscoff.fr/Les-Rosko-Bus.html.

Brest

If towns were judged on reputation alone, then Brest would hardly get a mention in this book. Nearly flattened by the fighting of the Second World War, it has since become thought of across France as little more than an industrial port, efficient but ugly; bordering a spectacular natural harbor, but more interesting for its surroundings than its own qualities. What's more, the town's location in France's far west, not to mention its lack of a passenger ferry port, means it attracts few incidental visitors. And because of all this, people are missing out. Big time.

Unpretentious, extremely convivial, and forward-looking, Brest is an excellent city to visit not so much for any one particular sight, but for the atmosphere you'll find when you get here. This can be seen in its rows of reconstructed stone houses, its restaurants (often focused on quality of produce more than presentation), and its bars filled with salty locals more than happy to chat. It's also there in the town's public funded spaces and municipal architecture: the great multimedia complex, for example, in the Atelier des Capucins—a colossal building built for shipbuilding in the 19th century that has now given over to public libraries, cinemas, and much more.

The second-largest administrative center in Brittany, Brest has also been an important military port since medieval times. A visit to the town's docks, while not the most aesthetically attractive tour, makes for a fascinating insight into maritime industry. Well worth visiting, though, is the Oceanopolis aquarium and research institute, one of the largest institutions of its type in France, which offers both an educational and visceral experience.

ORIENTATION

A large city with architecture on a far grander scale that you'll find in most of the rest of Brittany, Brest's center is nevertheless still relatively compact. The city sits on the northern shore of the Rade de Brest, and is split by the wide Le Penfeld river, with its downtown on the left (eastern) bank. This area is constructed on an easy-to-navigate grid system, the central road of which, the rue de Siam, is also the main shopping district, connecting the river with the place de la Liberté, where Brest's town hall is located. Brest's main train station Le Gare de Brest, is also in this part of town, following the avenue Georges Clemenceau southeast of the town hall.

On the river's right (western) bank, you'll find Les Ateliers des Capucins complex, as well as the rue Saint-Malo, practically the city's only surviving prewar street.

On foot, there are two ways of crossing Le Penfeld in the town center, either via the Pont de Recouvrance, or the spectacular Téléphérique cable car system that links directly to Les Ateliers des Capucins.

The docks, as well as lining the banks of Le Penfeld, are in the southeast of the city, just beneath the downtown. There they bite into the water in a series of toothy quays, which also boast a few restaurants and fishmongers. Oceanopolis is a little out of town, at the far eastern end of the docks, and can be reached on the No. 3 bus via the D165 as it heads east, back toward the hinterland.

SIGHTS

Tour Tanguy

Square Pierre Péron, Brest; tel. 02 98 00 84 60; 2pm-5pm Mon., Wed., and Thurs., 2pm-6pm Sat.-Sun. Oct.-May 10am-12pm and 2pm-6pm daily June-Sept.; free

A rare remnant of Brest's medieval past, this squat and sturdy tower was likely built during the Breton War of Succession in the 14th century. It was designed to guard against enemy troops trying to cross the banks of the Penfeld River—though exactly who that enemy would have been, it's hard to determine: The tower

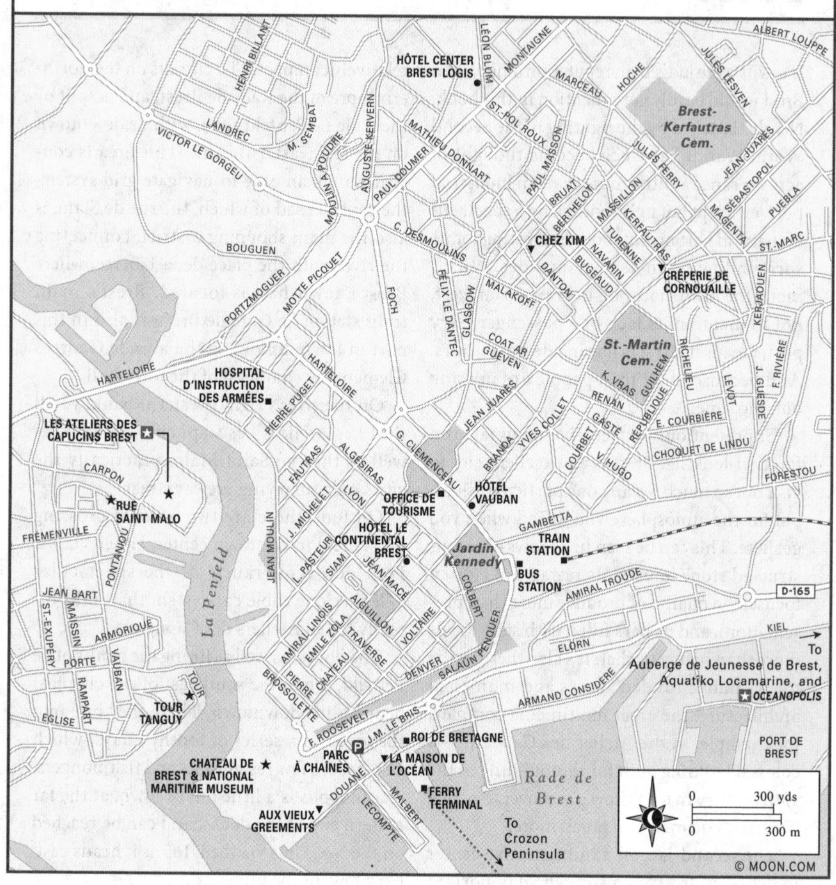

could have been built by the English, when they occupied the city, or the French-Breton leader Lord Tanguy du Chastel.

In any case, it was purchased in 1862 by an architect who turned it into a house, and its interiors retain a domestic feel despite its needing significant restoration after the Battle of Brest in 1944. It is now a museum, dedicated to how Brest was in the past, its surprisingly 19th-century-style interior filled with old prints, black-and-white photographs, and scale models of the former town. Given how little of this version of Brest remains today, the museum is very important for really coming to an understanding of the town. Visits shouldn't last much more than an hour.

Rue Saint-Malo

Rue Saint-Malo, Brest; www.vivrelarue.net

A street unique in all Brest, this cobbled stretch, defined today by trendy cafés and free concert venues, is far more than just a well-preserved road spared by the Allies' bombs. It's a veritable X-ray of the old city. Many of the buildings just back from the main thoroughfare remain in ruins, though these have been cleaned up and are well maintained, full of life, and can be thoroughly explored. The road itself is set in a small valley just down from the Capucins plateau. Stairways climbing the sides of walls now offer views down into buildings that have had their old roofs blown off, or are hardly more than a couple of teetering walls.

Historically home to a convent for "sinful women" (code for a prison for prostitutes), the houses that remain here date from the 17th and 18th centuries. They soon found themselves surrounded by naval buildings and became home to bars for sailors putting ashore. Damaged, like the rest of Brest, during WWII, their continued existence was down to an association called Vivre la Rue, who took over maintenance of the street in 1989 and have since turned it into one of the most vibrant, colorful places anywhere in the city. Come here in the day to look around, or check out the Vivre le Rue website to find out when evening concerts are happening. These are often by trendy local musicians, attracting a young, alternative crowd. The atmosphere is relaxed, friendly, and feels very safe.

Phare du Petit Minou

Plouzané

Of all the lighthouses in Finistère, surely this is one of the most poetic, not so much for its looks, but its location. Around five miles (eight kilometers) to the west of the town center, it occupies the northern side of the entry to the Rade de Brest, the massive natural harbor on which the city resides. It is the main marker of the naval entranceway to the city, telling arriving ships from the unpredictable wilds of the Atlantic Ocean that they have reached safe harbor and are home.

First lit in 1848, it was automated in 1989. Tricky to get to, unless you're driving or riding a bike (there is at least a free parking lot on-site), the lighthouse provides an evocative central point to a beautiful location. Though you can walk right up to it by means of an attractive stone bridge, visitors are no longer allowed inside. It's particularly impressive to see at sunset or in the midst of a storm.

★ Oceanopolis

Port de Plaisance du Moulin Blanc, Brest; tel. 02 98 34 40 40; www.oceanopolis.com; hours change regularly throughout the year; generally 9:30am-6:30pm daily during peak times, 10am-5pm daily in the off season, closed Jan. 7-Feb. 8 (consult website for more precise details); adults €21, children 14-17 and students €16, children 3-13 €13.35

Oceanopolis expands on the traditional aquarium offerings with a marine science center and multimedia displays. The diversity of its exhibits and the sheer number of individual tanks (50!) quickly made it Brest's biggest draw. In addition to the spectacle of seeing live fish inhabit realistic re-creations of their natural habitats, there are various multimedia displays aiming to educate visitors as well.

The center is divided into three pavilions corresponding to three different environments: temperate, polar, and tropical—housing a staggering 10,000 animals in total. Among the highlights are the touch tank, where you're invited to get up close to the flora and fauna of the deep, such as corals and sea stars; the extensive penguin colony; and a 10,000-cubic-foot (1,000-cubic-meter) shark tank, which will terrify, delight, and educate all at the same time.

It's a museum that requires almost a whole day, and for many is worth the trip into Brest all by itself. On-site restaurants cater to day-trippers.

Château de Brest and National Maritime Museum

Château de Brest, Boulevard de la Marine, Brest; tel. 02 98 22 12 39; www.musee-marine.fr/brest; 10am-6:30pm daily Apr.-Sept., 1:30pm-6:30pm Oct.-Mar.; €7

In many respects, the history of Brest is the history of its château. The Rade de Brest, on which the city sits, is one of the largest natural harbors in the world, and has been of strategic naval importance for almost as long as strategic naval importance has been needed.

A castle at the mouth of the Penfeld River was therefore erected before the town itself. The site of its current iteration, meanwhile,

1

2

3

has over 1,700 years of continuous history, with the oldest identifiable tower here dating from the 1200s. The mainstay of its current appearance, however, was the result of its defenses being "modernized" in the 17th century. Hence, the walls were designed to be thick enough to withstand a galleon's canon bombardment, meaning it's hardly the most attractive building, still looking squat and medieval, form given over to function. And indeed, it's a function that the château continues to serve, remaining as it is occupied by some offices of the French Navy, making it the oldest continually serving castle in the world.

There are other parts of the building open to the public, holding a number of collections from France's maritime museum, including scale models of ships, dramatic paintings of naval battles, and some striking ship figureheads. The real draw, though, is the castle itself, the history of which can be revealed to you by an audioguide at no extra cost. Consider taking a couple of hours to do it justice.

★ Les Ateliers des Capucins Brest

25 rue de Pontaniou, Brest; tel. 02 98 37 36 00; www.capucinsbrest.com; 10am-7pm daily; free

If there's anywhere that most exemplifies the spirit of modern Brest, then surely it's this remarkable collection of old factory buildings, previously owned by the French Navy, converted into a multimedia culture center and public space that would be the envy of any city in the world.

Originally the location of a Capucine convent, Brest's arsenal was moved here in the 19th century and the workhouses built that give it its current form. Like so much of the city, they were badly damaged in the war, though they were reconstructed in their original form by the navy and continued to produce machinery for ships until the 1980s. They were eventually sold to the City of Brest in 2009, and the municipality set about converting the 53,000 square feet (5,000 square meters) of high-ceilinged space they offered into the vast cultural space we see today.

Still retaining its industrial design, Les Ateliers des Capucins is made up of several large open spaces boasting polished concrete floors, which on the weekend are filled with young and old locals at leisure. Either they are Rollerblading, practicing dance moves, rehearsing theater, or simply hanging out in the main atrium, or they are in the vast Mediatheque Francois Mitterand: a state-of-the-art library filled with books, video games, and board games, all of which can be read and played on-site, in considerately designed settings. To cap it all off, the area is linked to Brest's downtown via the Téléphérique, a cable car offering spectacular views across the city. This is run by the city's urban transport company **Bibus** (www.bibus.fr) and can be taken with a regular tram or train ticket, costing €1.60.

A real family space, it's an area of utopian urban design, worth visiting for many reasons—not least as a testament to how effective public spending can be.

1: one of the houses on rue Saint-Malo 2: Les Ateliers des Capucins Brest 3: Oceanopolis aquarium in Brest

ENTERTAINMENT AND EVENTS

Festivals

INTERNATIONAL MARITIME FESTIVAL

Port de Brest; http://brest2020.fr; every four years in July, next taking place in 2020; free

Though it only takes place once every four years, this spectacular, week-long maritime festival is worth the wait. Offering a sight unlike anything you're likely to see anywhere else, more than 2,500 boats from around the world descend on the town to fill Brest's vast natural harbor. These include modern tall ships, replicas of famous craft from years gone by, and sleek sailing yachts, a dazzling display of maritime pageantry. Meanwhile, the banks of the Penfeld are overrun by live music shows and exhibitions about different aspects of sailing and street performers, while every night, boats assemble for a parade. The festival is also known as Tonnerres de Brest (the Thunder of Brest), after the cannon that used to signal the opening and closing of the city's arsenal every day.

Nightlife

CHEZ KIM

21 rue Danton, Brest; tel. 02 98 43 48 81; 9am-2am Tues.-Sat.; beers from €4

The sheer anarchic madness of this bar cannot be stressed enough. Its walls are covered floor-to-ceiling in beer mats drawn on by customers, its party atmosphere doesn't really hit full swing until after 10pm, and its barman/owner (the outlet's eponymous Kim) also provides the evening's entertainment. With an acoustic guitar always ready to go behind the bar, Kim frequently slings the instrument over his shoulders to perform cheesy pop classics, almost at the same time he's serving drinks. The regulars know to sing along, and there's even the chance to take the guitar yourself if you fancy leading the chorus. Cheap and as unfancy as it gets, attracting a young crowd, Chez Kim offers the kind of night where anything can, and frequently does, happen.

SHOPPING

ROI DE BRETAGNE

12 quai de la Douane, Brest; tel. 02 98 46 87 67; www.roidebretagne.com; 9am-9pm Mon.-Sat.

Poised somewhere at the apex of stores dedicated to Breton merchandise, here you'll find everything from hooped jerseys to artisanal sea salt, from blue and white crockery to quaint models of lighthouses. It's not even for tourists. These are not cheap knockoff goods made miles from here, but mostly authentic local products. And real Breton people really buy this stuff, as you'll see should you ever be lucky enough to be invited into one of their homes.

SPORTS AND RECREATION

Water Sports

AQUATIKO LOCAMARINE

247 rue Eugène Berest, Brest; tel. 02 98 87 95 95; www.locamarine-watersports.com; 10am-12pm and 1:30pm-6:30pm Tues.-Sun.; Jet Ski rental from €80

Very much at the motorized end of the watersports industry, this business specializes in boats, Jet Skis, and the improbably futuristic Flyboard hire. It's a very different way to experience time on the waves than the majority of other places along the Brittany coastline, which tend to concentrate on wind and paddle power. For the flyboards and Jet Skis, you don't even need a license. That said, they do also offer examinations for getting boat licenses, which to pass you will need a decent amount of practical experience already. Get one of these, though, and you can take more powerful craft onto the sea.

FOOD

Local Cuisine

AUX VIEUX GREEMENTS

145 quai Éric Tabarly, Brest; tel. 02 98 43 20 48; www.aux-vieux-greements.fr; 12pm-2pm and 6pm-10pm Mon.-Sat., 12pm-2pm Sun.; menus €28-40

With starched white tablecloths, smartly dressed staff, and a modern wood-paneled dining room, this is a restaurant with the feel of a formal restaurant on a cruise liner. Thus, it is likely to appeal a slightly older crowd. The food is of a decent quality, with fish and seafood the clear specialty: This comes without too much interference from the chef, allowing its freshness to stand for itself. It's frequently busy, and booking is recommended but not always necessary. Be aware if you're arriving by car that finding a place to park in its harborfront location can take a few minutes. It also has a terrace, which gets busy at lunchtime and on warm evenings.

LA MAISON DE L'OCÉAN

2 quai de la Douane, Brest; tel. 02 98 80 44 84; www.restaurant-fruit-mer-brest.com; 12pm-2pm and 7pm-10pm daily; menus €20-46

A high-quality, unpretentious seafood restaurant with a covered terrace on Brest's marina. Its gray interior may feel a bit cold for some tastes, but the produce is excellent, beautifully presented and served in generously sized portions—the mussels are a real crowd pleaser. Frequently very busy, it nevertheless specialized in a rapid turnover and is big enough that even showing up at peak times you should not have to wait too long for a table—even so, if you can, booking never hurts. Near to Aux Vieux Greements, it can be equally tricky to find a parking space nearby if you're arriving by car, so give yourself a few extra minutes to get there on time.

Crêperie

CRÊPERIE DE CORNOUAILLE

9 rue Saint-Marc,Brest; tel. 02 98 80 01 91; 11:30am-2:15pm and 6:30pm-10pm Tues.-Sat., 6:30pm-10pm Sun.; from €3.70

Often busy, with a jolly interior and friendly staff, this is one of the best among Brest's veritable galaxy of *crêperies*. OK, so there might not be anything wildly exceptional about the food; it's just very good, and that's kind of the point. It's fresh, comes in decent-size portions, and is inexpensive. That, coupled with a few bowls full of local cider, ought to be enough to keep most satisfied for the length of a lunchtime or evening meal.

ACCOMMODATIONS

Under €50

AUBERGE DE JEUNESSE DE BREST

5 rue de Kerbriant, Brest; tel. 02 98 41 90 41; www.aj-brest.org; beds from €20

A convivial and uncommonly stylish youth hostel situated just outside the center of Brest, not far from the Oceanopolis center, this is a good way to do the city on a budget. As well as its trendy common spaces, decorated with minimalist "Scandi" wooden tables and paneling, there's a decent-size garden, which is peaceful and a good place to hang out and meet other guests. Meals can be bought on-site and are both tasty and substantial. The rooms are typical dorms, lacking the style of communal spaces, while bathrooms are shared. WiFi is available throughout the property.

€50-100

HÔTEL LE CONTINENTAL BREST

Square de la Tour d'Auvergne, 41 rue Emile Zola, Brest; tel. 02 98 80 50 40; www.oceaniahotels.com/h/hotel-le-continental-brest/presentation; from €67 d

Centrally located, this hotel has the kind of

a typical Brest street corner

art deco interior that anywhere else could be described as having seen better days. The difference is that here, in Brest, it all seems as new as when it was built, and stepping into the large lobby, surrounded by imposing marble pillars, feels like stepping back in time. The attention to art deco detail extends to the rooms themselves, making for an overall excellent value experience. WiFi is available throughout, some rooms have private terraces, and all have flat-screen TVs. There's also a 24-hour reception and an on-site bar.

HÔTEL VAUBAN

17 avenue Georges Clemenceau, Brest; tel. 02 98 46 06 88; www.hotelvauban.fr; from €70 d

Named after the famous military architect who had such an impact on both France's and Brest's history, this is a straightforward, though very pleasant, classic hotel. In fact, it's so classic, it's the kind of place a location scout might choose for a film set in a typical midrange French hotel. Cases in point: the large wooden reception desk, complete with a concierge bell; the many cozy rooms lined with either rugs or carpets; and its welcoming on-site restaurant and bar, serving hearty French food and decked out in an inexpensive though still traditional brasserie style. Staff are friendly, it's centrally located, there's a 24-hour front desk, and WiFi is available throughout.

HÔTEL CENTER BREST LOGIS

4 boulevard Léon Blum, Brest; tel. 02 98 80 78 07; www.hotelcenter.com; from €90 d

This midrange establishment, complete with a decent on-site restaurant serving local food, is popular among business travelers. Its style could not really be described as either modern or traditional, more just blandly comfortable. Along with its central location, the other draw of this hotel is that it has its own fitness area and spa rooms. Questionably decorated some of these may be—see the hot tub from which you look out on a tropical island trompe l'oeil—but they're a great addition for a hotel of this price. Modern conveniences such as WiFi and flat-screen TVs come as standard.

INFORMATION

OFFICE DE TOURISME

8 avenue Georges Clemenceau-Place de la Liberté, Brest; tel. 02 98 44 24 96; www.brest-metropole-tourisme.fr; 9:30am-7pm Mon.-Sat., 9:30am-1:30pm Sun.

An extensive tourist office, complete with plenty of information and fliers about things to do in Brest and the surrounding area, set inside an ugly modern building just across from the town hall on the central place de la Liberté. English is spoken by most of the staff, who are happy to advise on hotels and local activities.

SERVICES

HOSPITAL D'INSTRUCTION DES ARMÉES

rue Colonel Fonferrier, Brest; tel. 02 98 43 70 00; www.hopital-armees-brest.fr/topic/index.html; ER open 24 hours

On the right bank of the Penfeld River, this is Brest's most central hospital. A teaching hospital for army doctors, it is nevertheless open to the public and has a full range of modern departments. The emergency department is open 24 hours, and though it does not offer English language as a service, most doctors can speak it to a comprehensible level.

TRANSPORTATION

Getting There

BY AIR

As the major town in Brittany most distant from Paris, Brest is one of the few locations in this book that might be considered worth flying to from the French capital. Its airport, **Aéroport Brest Bretagne** (Guipavas; tel. 02 98 32 86 00; www.brest.aeroport.bzh/accueil), is serviced by both domestic and international flights. This includes Air France routes from Paris, London, Nice, and Lyon. Ryan Air, meanwhile, connects the town with Marseille in the south, and Chalair Aviation to Caen and Bordeaux. There are also companies connecting Brest with Crete, Barcelona, and Fez in Morocco, farther afield. More destinations are added during vacation times. Prices, as with all airlines, are subject to availability and how far in advance you book. From Paris, flight time should be about an hour.

The airport is roughly five miles (eight kilometers) northeast of the center and connected to the city via a shuttle service run by Bibus (www.bibus.fr, €1.50). Tickets can be purchased onboard, and it runs to Tram line A at Porte de Guipavas. Taxis to the center should cost around €22 during the day and €32 at night.

There are several car rental firms with offices in the main terminal, from **Avis** (www.avis.fr/services-avis/location-voiture/europe/france/brest/aeroport-de-brest-bretagne) to **Europcar** (www.europcar-bretagne.fr/villes/location-voiture-Brest-aeroport.aspx). Prices should start from about €60 per day.

BY CAR

Though out on something of a promontory, as a major city Brest is well connected with the rest of France. From Paris (365 miles/587 kilometers, 6 hours), head south out of the French capital on the A10 and follow signs to Rennes—this is a toll road, which will cost about €25. From Rennes, the journey is about three hours on the N12.

From Nantes, it's about three hours and 180 miles (290 kilometers), hugging the coast along the N165.

With its whole southern side on the sea, Brest does not have a ring road. Rather, the D205 runs in a horseshoe shape around the north, east, and west of the city.

BY BOAT

Despite its status as a major port, Brest is not in fact a passenger ferry terminal for any international routes. The only way of reaching the town by boat is from **Le Fret** on the Crozon Peninsula (twice daily Tues.-Sun. Apr.-Sept., €9.50 adults, €7.50 children) or from the **Île d'Ouessant** (once or twice daily, €27.90 adults, €17.90 children). Both arrive in **Port de Commerce** (1er Eperon, Brest; www.pennarbed.fr). More details can be found on the port website.

BY TRAIN

The terminus of the train line from Paris, **Brest station** (Place du 19ème Régiment d'Infanterie, Brest; tel. 36 35; www.gares-sncf.com/fr/gare/frbes/brest; 4:50am-12am Mon.-Thurs., 4:50am-12:55am Fri., 4:50am-11:10pm Sat., 7:20am-12:10am Sun.) is serviced by trains from the French capital around 10 times a day. Expect to pay around €75-90 depending on how early you book; the journey takes about 3.5 hours. This train runs via Rennes, and if you pick it up there, tickets cost around €28-40 for the two-hour journey.

There are also 16 trains arriving from Morlaix (40 minutes, €10.50), which is a transport hub that can be reached from Roscoff.

Nine trains/SNCF bus services run every day from Quimper (1.5 hours, €9).

BY BUS

Brest's **bus station** (2 place du 19eme Régiment d'Infanterie, Brest; www.viaoo29.fr), located just outside the town's train station, serves as a major terminus for the whole Finistère region, making the bus, run by **Viaoo** (www.viaoo29.fr), a good way of reaching the town from more out-of-the-way places. At the other end of these bus lines are towns such as Le Conquet (six buses daily, 45 minutes, €2) and Roscoff (four buses daily, 1.5 hours, €2).

Getting Around

Downtown Brest is a relatively walkable area, with the only major sight that may lead you to taking public transport being Oceanopolis. Specifically, it is serviced by Bus Line 3, which leaves from outside the train station. This, along with all other metropolitan bus lines and the trams, is run by **Bibus** (www.bibus.fr). A single ticket costs €1.60 and is valid for multiple journeys over the space of one hour. Also covered by such a ticket is a ride on the Téléphérique cable car that connects to the Ateliers des Capucins—one of the best-value bits of entertainment offered anywhere in the city!

Île d'Ouessant

TOP EXPERIENCE

It doesn't get more Finistère than this: an island, adrift in the Atlantic, windswept and battered by waves, its seemingly indestructible granite cliffs surrounded by lighthouses, populated by taciturn sailors and hardy sheep. Ouessant holds an important place in the French imagination. It is the country's most westerly point, famous for centuries as a way marker, for its treacherous seas, and for the battles and shipwrecks that occurred off its shores. It was also the last outpost of French territory ever seen by Napoleon as he was carried away to his final exile on Saint Helena; it's said the emperor spent several hours on the deck of the British ship *HMS Bellerophon* watching the island recede into the distance.

Today, it is a place of pilgrimage for French tourists wishing to stand at the very edge of their country. People come to see untamed nature in all its savagery: from vast weather fronts that blow in across cobalt blue seas to fearsome rollers breaking against jagged rocks. The common practice is to come for a day, in which there is easily enough time to cycle around the entire island, then depart. For the full experience, though, try to spend a night here, in one of the island's low-slung hardy stone cottages, for only then will you get a chance to see the many vast, powerful lighthouses in action, their rays raking like some man-made aurora borealis across the Atlantic sky.

Ouessant is most commonly reached from **Le Conquet,** a charming Breton village of stone houses and plenty of tourist infrastructure, having cashed in on being the main port from which boats leave for the end of the world.

ORIENTATION

Ouessant is at once small and easy to navigate simply, and also offers the chance for many hours, if not days, of exploration off its more beaten paths. Almost all visitors will arrive in the ferry port, **Port du Stiff,** in the east of the island, with a smattering of buildings, plus several bike-hire companies competing for your business. There are also free maps being distributed, allowing you to get straight on with exploring.

The main road, the D81, crosses the island east to west in the direction most will head, toward Ouessant's only town, **Lampaul,** which resides in a bay in the west of the island. Here you'll find the majority of hotels and restaurants, as well as the tourist office and the offices and repair shops for all the bike-hire companies. Most of Ouessant's sights and points of interest are found around the island's coastlines, including its lighthouses, the lighthouse museum, and the impressive natural features. By bike, it's not always possible to circle the island, so be prepared to backtrack on occasion. When the cycle paths run out, get off and walk: It's both easier in the long run and more respectful to the fragile landscape.

Le Conquet, meanwhile, is a small town on the southern bank of a river mouth in the west. The town center of stone houses, bars, and tourist shops is just back from this. Outside of this, there's not much to see.

SIGHTS

The Fromveur Passage

Île d'Ouessant

A sight that is in some respects not a sight at all, the Fromveur passage is the area of sea just south of the Île d'Ouessant. Its edges are skirted on the approach to Port du Stiff from the Île Molene, and it can be looked at from the southern coast of the island. On the surface, it appears simply as a stretch of turbulent ocean, though underneath the waves, forces are at work that have set even the hardiest sailors' nerves on edge for centuries. For this passage is home to some of the strongest currents anywhere in Europe, and was once part of the

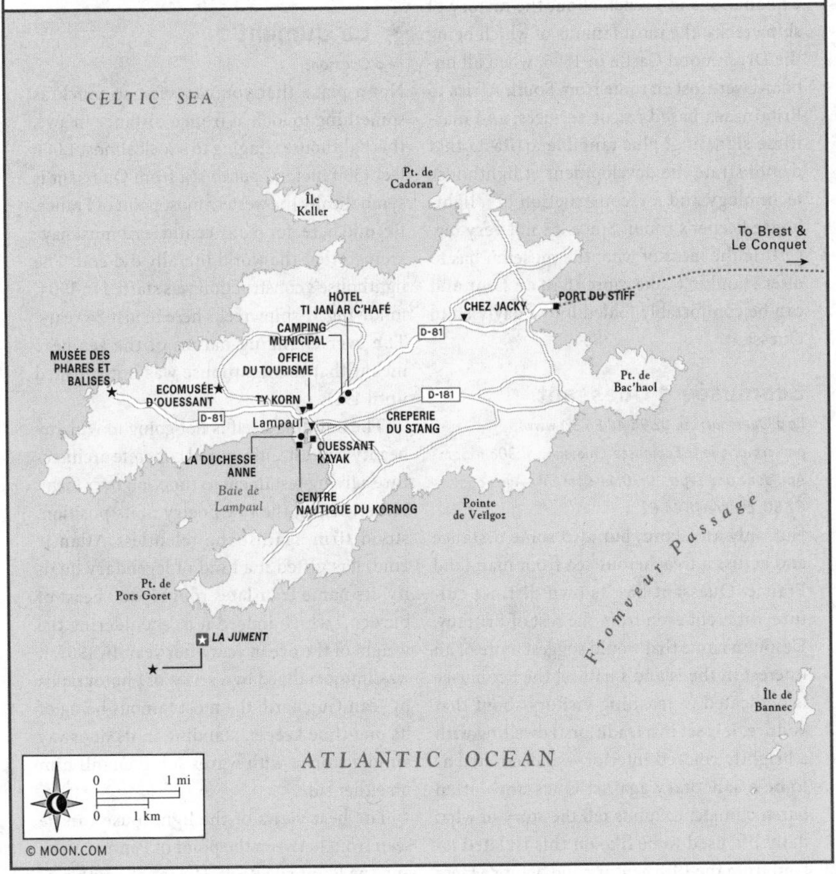

busiest shipping lanes in the world. As such, it has been the site of countless shipwrecks and is the progenitor behind an old mariner saying: "No one has passed through Fromveur without knowing fear." There are plenty of places on Ouessant where you can stand and contemplate the dark terrors and peril of the sea, but the island's cliff-lined southern shore, particularly the **Pointe de Veilgoz,** looking at the Fromveur passage, knowing its history and the powers at work beneath its surface, is perhaps the most poignant of them all.

Musée des Phares et Balises

Le Créac'h, Île d'Ouessant; tel. 02 98 48 80 70; www.pnr-armorique.fr/Visiter/Musees-maisons-a-themes/Musee-des-Phares-et-Balises; 11:30am-5pm Apr.-June and Sept., 10:30am-6pm July-Aug.; adults €4.30, children 8-14 €3

Dedicated to lighthouses and beacons, this is probably the number-one museum of its type anywhere in France. Part of that is no doubt its location. The **Créac'h lighthouse** is a Breton icon, with the most powerful beam in Europe. Built in 1863, it's considered an entrance post to the English Channel, while its black and white paintwork makes it look as archetypal as a kid's drawing. The museum is located in the lighthouse's old machine room. There are explanations in French about the history of shipwrecks, the most famous of which being the Drummond Castle in 1896, when all on-board were lost en route from South Africa to Britain; sea-based rescue services; and maritime signaling; plus tangible artifacts that demonstrate the development of lighthouse technology and a reconstruction of a lighthouse keeper's room. Since it's not very big, getting the most of what the museum has to offer shouldn't take more than an hour and can be comfortably folded into a day-visit to Ouessant.

Ecomusée d'Ouessant

Île d'Ouessant; tel. 02 98 48 86 37; www.pnr-armorique.fr/Ecomusee-Ouessant; 11:30am-5pm Apr.-June and Sept., 10:30am-6pm July-Aug.; adults €2.80, children 8-14 €2

Not only an island, but also some distance and across a treacherous sea from mainland France, Ouessant has its own distinct culture, different even from the rest of Brittany. Despite a name that would suggest more of an interest in the island's nature, the Ecomusée is dedicated to teaching visitors about that culture. It is set in a traditional dwelling with a brightly colored interior—so decorated as to be a sanctuary against Ouessant's often harsh climate. Exhibits tell the story of what daily life used to be like on this isolated island from the 19th century and before, where often as not men spent their time at sea, leaving women to work the fields and ensure the survival of the family. The team that works here is dedicated to preserving the culture of the island as much as they are displaying it, spending time ferreting out old stories, words, songs, practices, and beliefs. Monthly meetings are held in which visitors get a chance to discover some of these more intangible facts about island life, which include wool spinning and the building of a traditional hay heap (which remains on the museum grounds for weeks afterwards). In general, visits here should last less than an hour and can be easily folded into a general day-trip exploration of the island.

★ La Jument

Île d'Ouessant

Not a place that you can visit so much as something to look at from a distance in awe, this lighthouse clinging to a rock almost 1,000 feet (300 meters) out to sea from Ouessant is symbolically the westernmost point of France. Beyond here, for many centuries it must have seemed that the world literally did end. The lighthouse's construction was started in 1904, following 31 shipwrecks here in just 26 years. The ever-changing nature of the sea here meant that the lighthouse was not finished until 1911.

The building itself is not going to win any beauty contests, its poured concrete architecture a living testament to function over form. Nevertheless, the raw poetry of its position, stood firm against the relentless Atlantic void, has gifted it a kind of legendary quality. Its name translates roughly to "beast of burden," which indeed it is, shouldering the weight of the ocean year after year. In 1989, it was immortalized in a series of photographs by Jean Guichard, the most famous being of its one-time keeper, standing in its doorway amid a storm, with waves set to engulf him on either side.

The best views of the lighthouse can be seen from between the point of Penn ar Viler and the Pointe de Roc'h Hir in the southwest of the island.

SPORTS AND RECREATION

OUESSANT KAYAK

Cleuz de Porsnoan, Ouessant; tel. 06 47 27 32 14; http://brevalcrenn.wixsite.com/ouessant-kayak; 1pm-7pm daily Apr.-Sept.; kayak rental from €7

The island's dramatic coastline makes it an excellent place to explore from the water, and

1: the Créac'h lighthouse 2: waves thrash the island's rugged coastline 3: The view from just outside of Lampaul is one of many picturesque vistas on Ouessant.

PHARE
CR ACH
1
2
3

sea kayaks are a great way to do that, even for people of little to no experience. A number of options are offered by Ouessant Kayak, from renting to lessons to a two-hour guided tour by a well-trained professional (prices for this vary depending on the number of people you have and the season, but expect to pay around €30 per person). Reservations can be easily canceled should the weather turn.

CENTRE NAUTIQUE DU KORNOG

Port de Lampaul, Ouessant, tel. 06 56 88 21 29; http://cnkornog-ouessant.jimdo.com, May-Aug.

Unpredictable weather conditions mean that Ouessant is not a common destination for vacationers looking to learn sailing or windsurfing over a long period—kayaking is more suited to these waters. However, to try these more advanced water sports, Centre Nautique du Kornog specializes in small sailboats and catamarans.

FOOD

Île d'Ouessant

CHEZ JACKY

Mes Kerbel, Frugullou, Ouessant; tel. 02 98 48 83 69; 8am-9:30pm daily (kitchen open for mealtimes); mains from €17

There's a faint irony about Ouessant's most famous dish: It's actually lamb ragout, not seafood as you might expect, with the island surrounded by some of the world's most bountiful seas. The fame comes, though, thanks to the unusual cooking method used to make the dish: Because of the Ouessant's paucity of trees, this ragout is slow-cooked under heated clods of earth, making for an extraordinarily rich, rustic-tasting meal. Short of getting an invite to a local's kitchen, Chez Jacky is perhaps the best place to get this on the island. It's a bar and restaurant with an old-fashioned interior and food that is the very definition of home-cooked. Oh, and there are a few seafood options on the menu for those of a less openly carniverous bent. Great for a slow lunch or dinner if you're spending the night on the island.

TY KORN

Le Bourg, Ouessant; tel. 02 98 48 87 33; 11am-3pm and 5:30pm-1am Tues.-Sat.; mains from €24

Stepping into the Ty Korn, you're presented with what seems a good old-fashioned local pub, of the kind that would seem more at home on the British Isles than in France. There's a decent selection of beers, and given that it's the only establishment of its type on the island, it's as popular with locals as it is with tourists. What comes as a surprise is its food, served in a small upstairs dining area. Local seafood flavors are dressed and presented with haute cuisine flair. Arguably, this can be a bit jarring given the surrounds, and some people walking through the door would probably expect more straightforward, not to say less expensive, rustic grub, but there can be no arguing with the taste.

CRÊPERIE DU STANG

Le Bourg, Ouessant; tel. 02 98 48 80 94; 11:30am-8:30pm daily Mar.-Oct.; from €9

A lot of people visiting Ouessant won't feel they have time for a drawn-out lunch. For them, a quick bite at this solid traditional *crêperie* will be the best option. Being an island, there are a number of tourist-trap restaurants on Ouessant, where prices are a little higher than they should be and the quality a little lower. Avoid them and head to the Crêperie du Stang instead. Its interior is basic, but the food is reasonable and very tasty, particularly the scallop crepe with a seaweed sauce, a local specialty, and delicious, despite how it might sound!

Conquet

LE RELAIS DU VIEUX PORT

1 quai du Drellach, Le Conquet; 02 98 89 15 91; www.lerelaisduvieuxport.com; 12pm-9:30pm Sun.-Thurs., 12pm-10pm Fri.-Sat.; menus from €31

Housed within an old-fashioned stone building, this unpretentious seafood restaurant on the port of Le Conquet excels in serving up freshly caught local produce in generous portions. The tables have paper tablecloths and wooden chairs; it's the kind of establishment that it's hard to imagine having changed much in 30 years. Bustling for lunch and dinner, booking ahead wouldn't hurt, though it is the kind of restaurant where if you just show up they'll probably be able to squeeze you in somewhere after a short wait. The lobster comes highly recommended.

ACCOMMODATIONS

Île d'Ouessant

LA DUCHESSE ANNE

Bourg Lampaul, Ouessant; tel. 02 98 48 80 25; www.hotelduchesseanne.fr; from €55 d

Located in an old building with a modern extension, this hotel offers some quite spectacular views of Lampaul Bay and the vast Atlantic beyond. Its nine rooms are reasonably priced, with five of them being sea-facing. Their interiors are hardly lavish, but they are well-kept and insulated against the island's weather. There's also a decent on-site restaurant, also with excellent views, serving solid local cuisine. Set just outside of Lampaul village, all of Ouessant's main amenities are just a short walk away.

HÔTEL TI JAN AR C'HAFÉ

Kernigou, Ouessant; tel. 02 98 48 82 64; www.tijan.fr; open Feb. 15-Nov. 11; from €99 d

A modern-style guesthouse with colorful rooms and a small garden in which to relax after a long day exploring the island. The communal areas feel like being inside someone's house, while the bedrooms are self-contained with en suite bathrooms and free WiFi. Breakfast can be ordered at an additional €10 cost, but there's no on-site restaurant. Fortunately, Lampaul is just a short walk down the road.

CAMPING MUNICIPAL

Bourg, Ouessant; tel. 02 98 48 84 65; open Apr.-Sept.; from €7.80 pp

For the braver visitors to Ouessant, this is the only campsite on the island. Only open in the summer months, it's fairly basic, with no cabins on offer as are found elsewhere in France. Indeed, the shower block and toilet facilities are pretty much the only nods to amenities. That said, it's a great way to really get in touch with the raw nature of the island, not to mention experience the strange spectral presence of Ouessant's various lighthouse beams flashing through the night sky. Its unique quality means it can get busy, especially in the summer months, so booking ahead is a good idea.

Conquet and Vicinity

AUBERGE DE KERINGAR

15 route de Keringar, Le Conquet; tel. 02 98 89 09 59; www.keringar.fr; from €75 d

Inside a charming old stone house in the village of Lochrist, just between Le Conquet and the striking promontory Pointe Sainte Mathieu, this reasonably priced hotel boasts a very cozy traditional interior. Its rooms have a slight nautical theme, and an on-site restaurant serves rich local food in front of a roaring fire—where local folk musicians sometimes set up to entertain the diners. Despite its old-fashioned trappings, this hotel also offers free WiFi throughout the property, has en suite bathrooms, and is generally well insulated against Finistère's changeable weather.

HOSTELLERIE DE LA POINTE SAINT-MATHIEU

7 place Saint-Tanguy, Plougonvelin; tel. 02 98 89 00 19; www.pointe-saint-mathieu.com; from €150 d

Billing itself as a luxury hotel clinging to the edge of the world, the Hostellerie de la Pointe Saint-Mathieu sits right on the edge of Finistère and looks out toward Ouessant across the waves. Deliberately designed to allow as much light in as possible, the rooms "bring the landscape indoors"—which is another way of saying they have great views. No luxury hotel these days is complete without a spa, and the one here offers extreme comfort while watching Atlantic gales lash the windows. Focused around an old building with modern extensions, there are also two restaurants on-site—one traditional and formal, the other a more laid-back brasserie.

INFORMATION

OFFICE DU TOURISME

Bourg de, Ouessant; tel. 02 98 48 85 83; www.ot-ouessant.fr; 9:30am-6:15pm Mon.-Sat., 10:15am-12:15am Sun.

A relatively busy tourist office in the center of Lampaul, which offers free leaflets on the island's flora and fauna. It's also a good place to pick up a map of the island in case you missed out on getting one just off the boat.

TRANSPORTATION

Getting There

Most visitors arrive at Île d'Ouessant by ferry. Le Conquet, accessible by car or bus, is the closest departure point for boats to the island.

BY CAR

Le Conquet is a 16-mile (25-kilometer) drive to the west of Brest, taking the D67. It should take around 30 minutes.

The great majority of parking in Le Conquet itself only allows stretches of no more than four hours. Outside of town, there are several parking lots, and if you're planning on visiting Ouessant, these are effectively the only places you can leave your vehicle. The most popular and convenient of these lots is the **Parking des Îles,** just off from the Route de Brest at the town entrance. Parking here costs €9 for the day and includes a free shuttle bus to the ferry port—walking takes about a half hour. From November 15 to April the parking here is free, but there is no shuttle bus. It's recommended that you arrive in town a good hour before the ferry departure just to guarantee you have enough time to get from the parking lot to the port. Note: If you decide to walk in from Parking des Îles, the footpath straight along the D789 is better than trying to walk along the banks of the river, which though picturesque can only be accessed via this route at low tide.

If you're leaving for Ouessant by boat from Brest, there are a couple of parking lots where it's suggested you leave your vehicle. The **Parking Parc à Chaînes,** situated just below the city ramparts, next to the avenue Franklin Roosevelt, is good for day trips, being free and having 317 spaces. For longer stays, park just off the rue Jean Marie le Bris, **by La Carène venue,** which is also free and offers 60 spaces. Should you choose this latter option, it's a good idea to drop your bags off at the ferry terminal first, so you don't have to lug them the 1,500 feet (500 or so meters) from your car.

Leaving from Camaret, there are two free parking lots less than a five-minute walk away from the ferry port.

BY BOAT

Most visitors come to Ouessant by boat, using the ferry company **Penn Ar Bed** (Port du Stiff, D81, Ouessant; www.pennarbed.fr), which services all the islands of the Finistère coast. From April to September, there are three departure points: Brest, Le Conquet, and Camaret. From May to August, there are an average of around four sailings per day between Le Conquet and Ouessant; otherwise, it's about one per day during the other months and from the other ports. Schedules can change depending on the day and the month, so it's worth consulting the timetable before travelling.

From **Brest,** boats leave at 8:20am throughout the year, departing the city's commercial port. Crossing usually takes around 2.5 hours, pausing at La Conquet and at Molène Island. The boat leaves **Le Conquet** (Port Gare Maritime, Ruse Sainte-Barbe, Le Conquet) at 9:45am throughout the year and can be boarded here if you feel like a shorter crossing or a longer lie in. The crossing from here takes about 1.25 hours. (Le Conquet can also be reached from Brest by bus the morning of departure in time for the 9:45am sailing.)

From **Camaret,** boats leave every Thursday at 8:15am, mid-April-June. Then, in the first three weeks of July departures happen Mondays, Tuesdays, and Saturdays, also at 8:15am. Through the end of July until the last week of August departures take place every day apart from Sundays. Departure times can change in this latter period, so keep an eye on the website for details.

Ferries leaving Ouessant depart at 5pm most days.

Prices are the same regardless of the journey: Return tickets for adults are €27.90 in low season and €34.90 in high. For children, they are €17.90 in low season, €24.90 in high. Booking a day or so in advance, especially in high season, is strongly recommended.

BY BUS

The gateway to Ouessant, Le Conquet can be reached by bus from Brest several times a day throughout the year. The bus to take is number 11, run by **Viaoo 29** (www.viaoo29.fr), which leaves from outside the town's train station and deposits you just outside of Le Conquet's Marie. The journey lasts about 40 minutes and costs €2. Most importantly, buses run every day apart from Sunday, arriving on time for the 9:45am sailing. In the other direction things are less certain, with the last bus leaving Le Conquet for Brest at around 6:30pm. Most days this coincides well with the final sailing from Ouessant, but there are some days it does not. Consult the ferry timetables before traveling.

GETTING AROUND

The central area of Le Conquet is effectively very walkable, and getting into town from one of the exterior parking lots can be accomplished via a free shuttle bus, which runs several times during peak ferry arrival and departure hours.

On the Île d'Ouessant, meanwhile, the moment you step off the ferry you'll be assailed by bike-hire companies, all of which push more or less the exact same deal (around €14 per day), so don't worry about choosing between them.

In any case, keep in mind that cycling is not the only way to see Ouessant. The island is sufficiently small that in a day of dedicated walking you should be able to see a good deal of it, and at a more evocative pace. The only thing to keep in mind, then, is time management: The ferries will not wait, and while on a bicycle you can dash back from pretty much anywhere within less than 20 minutes, when walking you'll have to work a return journey into your itinerary, leaving at least an hour to get back to the port on time.

There is also a minibus service, **Ouessant Voyages** (tel. 06 73 87 82 28), running between Port du Stiff and Lampaul, costing €2 per passenger, timed to coincide with ferry arrivals and departures. These can get very full in summer months, though, and are worth reserving a space on before you arrive. This company also offers two-hour minibus tours of the island, costing €15 per person.

Presqu'île de Crozon

Presqu'île is French for peninsula, though its literal translation is "nearly an island." There are few peninsulas that match this latter description, in terms of their distinct character and sense of isolation from the mainland, quite as well as the Presqu'île de Crozon. Resembling a cross thrust out between the Rade de Brest and the Baie de Douarnenez, the surroundings become more windswept, the buildings more rudimentary, and the people more independent the moment that you cross through the hamlet of Saint-Marie-du-Ménez-Hom—Crozon's traditional access point. As the sea rushes in to enclose you on all sides, there's a sense you are entering another land.

Perhaps one of the reasons for the Presqu'île de Crozon's feeling like a peninsula on steroids is because it is effectively several peninsulas in one. Its strange shape, meanwhile, results in a great variety of landscape, with the coastlines it has facing the Atlantic bruised and battered by millennia of fierce waves (and the waves here hardly get fiercer anywhere in

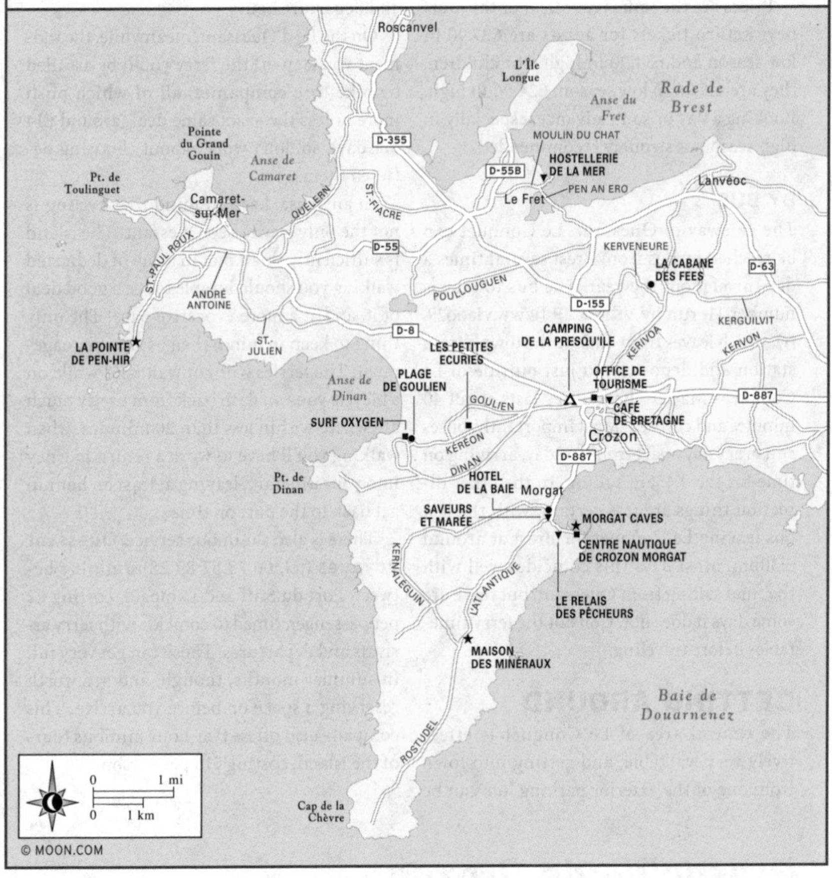

Brittany), while on the other side sheltered bays taper gently from sandy beaches into lush woodland. The combination makes for a paradise for water-sports enthusiasts and hikers alike. Spring to early autumn the area begins to fall with salty outdoors types, and there's an almost limitless supply of sailing clubs, kayak rentals, and walking paths to cater to them.

ORIENTATION

There's something a little disorienting about Presqu'île de Crozon. As mentioned, it's not really one peninsula, but several, barbing out different directions into the sea. Also somewhat confusing is that there is a town upon it called Crozon, which is where most road signs you need to follow will be pointing you rather than at the landmass as a whole. In fact, Crozon the town is really just a gateway to the peninsula. Head north of there and you're on a spit of land centered around the village of Roscanvel, looking out toward the Rade de Brest; go west and you reach Camaret-sur-Mer, the peninsula's second-biggest commune, with a picturesque harbor and some nice, easy nearby walks. It's also from here that ferries leave for the Île-de-Sein and Ouessant. Head south, meanwhile, and you're in Morgat, its sheltered, land-facing beach offering some excellent swimming opportunities for the whole family.

Getting in and out of Presqu'île de Crozon is most easily accomplished on either one of two roads, the D887 to the south, which heads toward Châteaulin, or the D791 to the north, which crosses some spectacular coastal scenery and is the fastest way to get to Brest.

Be aware that the shape of Crozon defies easy circuits of travel, and don't be surprised if you find yourself needing to retrace your steps. Cul-de-sacs—albeit beautiful ones—abound.

SIGHTS

L'Enclos Paroissial d'Argol

Église Saint-Pierre-et-Saint-Paul, rue Saint-Guénolé, Argol; tel. 02 98 27 07 92 (Crozon tourist office); open on request, subject to caretaker availability; free

The only "parish close"—one of Brittany's famous walled churchyard complexes—on the Presqu'île de Crozon, this church and its surrounding buildings are a fine example of the Breton tradition, which has its roots back in the region's pagan past. The Argol Parish Close was started in 1575 and had various elements added to it over the centuries—the church's Gothic spire and rectangular base, for example, date from 1585. As with other parish closes, there's a wide area to wander around, which feels like a veritable playground of religious architecture: There's an ossuary, several impressive statues, and a particularly grand triumphant arch, built in the 17th century, composed of fluted columns, pinnacles, and a lavishly decorated cross. The grounds are always open and free to wander, but to be let inside the church you'll have to find the caretaker; instructions for doing so are on an information board outside its gates, though don't expect him to always be about—it's worth calling the tourist office ahead of time to guarantee entry. Getting a chance to see the church's evocative wooden statue of Saint Peter, still colored and dating from the 16th century, is one of things that would make this worth your time. The need to go through a caretaker also means that when you get inside, the experience of the church is an intimate and private one.

La Pointe de Pen-Hir

Camaret-sur-Mer

Offering some of the best walking on the peninsula, this rocky promontory to the southwest of Camaret-sur-Mer has great views out to sea, with some of its cliffs rising over 260 feet (80 meters) above sea level. On a clear day looking south you can see the Pointe du Raz from here, and west the islands of Sein and Ouessant. Immediately below, six separate rock heaps stretch out to sea like an ellipsis reaching toward the western horizon. The point is also home to a monument dedicated to the Bretons who fought for Free France during the Second World War. It takes the form of a cross, known as the Croix de Pen-Hir, and was inaugurated in the 1960s by General de Gaulle. Built in blue granite, it bears the inscription in Breton "Kentoc'h mervel eget em zaotra," taken from the regional motto "Rather death than defilement."

Morgat Caves

Quai Kador, Crozon-Morgat; tel. 06 60 93 97 05; http://sirenes.bzh; boat tours Apr.-Sept.; boat tickets for adults from €14, for children €9

These caves have been compelling visitors for almost 170 years, ever since Crozon's earliest days as a tourist destination, with their multicolored and shining rock formations, entered at sea level by boat. It's impossible not to feel like some kind of pirate, with your treasure the land itself. Even the company that arranges boat tours has a long heritage, having been established in 1933 by the great-grandfathers of the current skippers Antoine and Guillaume, who passionately share their knowledge about the geology, environment, and tides of the peninsula. While taking you through this naturally occurring geology museum, they'll point out the different strata of rock formations and the fossil traces that whisper of Brittany's even more distant

1

2

past. Unfortunately, the tour is only available in French; however, an information sheet in English is provided. There are several different tour options available, all run by a company called **Vedettes Sirènes** (see website above), but in general they should take between one and two hours. It's also possible to visit them under your own steam, on a kayak or stand-up paddleboard.

Île-de-Sein

Île-de-Sein; tel. 02 98 70 90 35; www.pennarbed.fr/en; 1-2 sailings a day, times change throughout the year, see website for details; adults €34.90 return, children 4-16 €24.90

This low-lying, treeless island has a beguiling history intertwined with legend. With its treacherous surrounding waters and legacy of local women who once wore the highest headdresses in Brittany arose the story that the island was once home to witches, who would entice passing sailors onto the rocks by magic. Only slightly more plausible, it was once believed to be home of a conclave of druidic priestesses, who travelers would come to consult as they might an oracle. Whatever the reality, the island today is home to a couple of megalithic structures and a population fiercely committed to their own independence and freedom. The one town on the island is home to charming narrow streets as well as several restaurants and hotels ready to cater to visitors. Beyond the town is moorland and a lighthouse, with the whole island easily walkable in less than a few hours. Particularly exposed to the sudden moods of the sea, quayfront in the midst of even a light storm at high tide is a thrilling, spectacular experience. And while the rest of the island may not be the most picturesque in Brittany, there's a beguiling strangeness to it that makes it well worth a visit, and even staying the night.

Maison des Minéraux

Rue du Cap de la Chèvre, Crozon; tel. 02 98 27 19 73; www.maison-des-mineraux.org; 10am-12pm and 2pm-5pm Mon.-Fri. and 2pm-5pm Sun. Apr.-June, 10am-7pm daily July-Aug., check website for hours during off-season; adults €5, reduced €4

The coasts of the Presqu'île de Crozon are unusually rich in all manner of different rock types and formations, from fluorescent minerals to metal. This museum, located in a former schoolhouse, displays a great variation of these, changing their exhibition every year and organizing nature walks and conferences (in French) throughout the summer season. The interior design may seem a little old-fashioned, but the exhibits are sure to delight those with a passion for geology.

1: The Argol Parish Close dates back to 1573. 2: treeless landscape of Île-de-Sein

BEACHES

TOP EXPERIENCE

PLAGE DE GOULIEN

Kernavéno, Crozon

Beautiful Goulien beach is situated on the sheltered southeast of the Crozon peninsula. As well as being a long sweep of sand great for swimming, it also has a great surf break and a surf school, Surf Oxygene, to help you get out there. It's possible to surf here regardless of where the tide is, because there's a sand plateau that never moves.

SPORTS AND RECREATION

Water Sports

CENTRE NAUTIQUE DE CROZON MORGAT

Port de Morgat, Crozon; tel. 02 98 16 00 00; www.cncm.fr; 8:30am-12:30pm and 1:30pm-7pm daily July-Aug., by request in off-season; kayak rental from €18, a week of sailing lessons from €200

It's hard to imagine a better location for a water-sports center. Tucked on Morgat Cove, this is ideal for all levels of seamanship and different kinds of waterborne activity. Beginners can get to grips with their crafts protected from the wind and prevailing currents, while more advanced sailors can head out beyond the natural harbor and experience the thrill

The Island That Stood against the Nazis

In 1940, the situation was dire. France had surrendered to Hitler, and Nazi troops were making their way through the country, demanding that all the French give up their arms and offer no resistance. The small Île-de-Sein, however, windswept and slightly mysterious, situated at the farthest reaches of the country, had longer than most places to consider whether to comply.

And there were still no Nazis in town when on June 21, 1940, a radio was placed on the windowsill of the Hôtel de l'Ocean (now closed down) and over 100 people from the island's population gathered around to hear General Charles de Gaulle deliver a speech from London, calling on the French to resist. Deeply impressed by the general's words over the next five days, 114 inhabitants took to their boats, small and large, leaving the Île-de-Sein for Great Britain, where they volunteered for the Free French forces and to carry the fight to Hitler. By the time the Nazis actually made it to the island in July, they found only women, children, and the elderly living there; its whole fighting force was gone.

The island's inhabitants gathered with other Free French volunteers, of whom, at the time, there were only around 300 in total in front of de Gaulle himself in Empire Hall, London. When the general inspected his troops, even he expressed astonishment at how many had arrived from the Île-de-Sein. "It appears that the Île-de-Sein represents a quarter of our nation," he's said to have remarked.

The volunteers were assigned different tasks depending on their expertise, with most going into the Free French Navy. Twenty of them died in the service of their country, and after the war General de Gaulle presented the military medal the Cross of the Liberation to the island itself.

of big waves and high winds. Surfing is even an option here, with lessons available, too—there are some good waters for beginners, and also others such as the Spot de La Palue with some significant waves that should only be attempted by the experienced. Don't expect English to be widely spoken, however; the whole Presqu'île de Crozon is a predominantly French holiday destination, and the language skills of its sailing instructors reflect that.

SURF OXYGENE

Capitainerie de Morgat, quai du Kador, Crozon; tel. 06 45 18 12 79; www.surfoxygene.com; 9:30am-6pm Apr.-Oct.; one surfing lesson from €40, five from €150

Located on the Goulien beach, this surf school is protected from both winds and swells, but the waters abound in good waves. All in all, there are conditions here that suit surfers of all abilities, and the school runs introductory courses as well as lessons for more experienced surfers.

★ Hiking

Crozon is an excellent area both for serious hiking and more genteel walks. The peninsula's shape, with its many different coves, several villages, and at least half-decent public transport system, means there's always something different to look at, a number of places to refuel, and some opportunities to catch a bus back to where you've parked the car. Keep in mind that the lay of the land means a number of climbs and descents are inevitable. Also, that the whole area is crisscrossed by walking trails, so there's no specific wilderness area you have to head to. Below is just one of many options. For detailed maps and more hiking ideas, head to Crozon's **tourist office** (www.crozon-bretagne.com/tourisme/decouverte/littoral/randonnee-GR34.php), where they're more than happy to oblige.

THE POINTES OF PEN HIR, TOULINGUET, AND GRAND GOUIN

This is a decent-length walk—about 11 miles (17 kilometers), taking six hours—that offers a comprehensive tour of some of the Crozon peninsula's highlights, including dramatic cliffs, ocean views, sandy stretches, a fort, and even some megalithic alignments. It's a circuit, so feel free to park anywhere along its length. The parking lot near the Pointe de Pen Hir is just one starting point.

Starting at the Pointe de Pen Hir, head west, toward a memorial to Breton soldiers in WWII. When you reach this monument, make a right turn, following the red and white markers that show the GR34. Cross the sandy beach at Anse de Pen Hat, watching out for its shifting sands, and head up toward the French naval fort. Head around the perimeter of this building, joining the road on the right; walk for around 150 yards (137 meters), then cross the field to your left back to the shore. After about 400 yards (365 meters) walking along the shoreline, you have to turn back in again, and climb back upward. At the second junction you reach, there are black markers. Turn left here, through a residential neighborhood. This will take you to a main road, where you turn left, then right at the fork on the rue Saint-Rioc. Here you'll see the Lagatjar Alignments.

Make a right turn onto the rue Georges Ancey—there should be many Neolithic standing stones to your right. Eventually you'll get to the D8A, which you walk straight across, and likewise the D8, which comes after. By now, you will be walking down the rue de Kreisker in the direction of a small area known as Kremeur. From Kremeur you want to bear left in the direction of the Plage de Veyrac'h. From the parking lot of this beach, turn right, again picking up the red and white markers, that will lead you again toward the Pointe de Pen Hir.

Instead of starting at Pointe de Pen Hir, it's also possible to leave your car, and a picnic, inland, toward the central point of the walk, allowing you to do the trek as a figure eight, pausing for lunch halfway.

Horseback Riding

LES PETITES ECURIES

Ménez Kéréon, Crozon; tel. 02 98 26 12 42; open Mon.-Sat., call to book a time; an hour riding from €15.50

Riding horseback is excellent and different way to explore the various coves and cliff tops of the Crozon area. The horses from this stable are of small, solid stock, and the owner is happy to take you out whatever your experience. Groups can be of mixed skill levels, which can be frustrating for some riders. Try to call ahead to explain how much you know of riding horses to get a chance to go out with people with similar experience levels, that way you won't be forced to gallop on the beach if you've never sat in a saddle before, nor meander for too long behind a line of beginners if you're more of an expert.

FOOD

Local Cuisine

CAFÉ DE BRETAGNE

2 rue Anne de Mesmeur, Crozon; tel. 07 86 41 69 20; 7am-11pm daily; menus from €11.50

Offering basic but tasty food, this bar/restaurant is a good place to fill up your tank before heading off on a local walk or some other outdoors activity. Healthy most of its cuisine is not, with deep frying probably its favored cooking method. Nevertheless, its British-style fish and chips is as good as anything you could get this side of the Channel, and there's a laid-back friendly atmosphere, which is as good for drinking in as it is having a meal. The building is a traditional stone construction, its interior pub-like, and there's a pleasant small terrace with a view out to Crozon's church.

SAVEURS ET MARÉE

52 boulevard de la Plage, Morgat; tel. 02 98 26 23 18; http://saveurs-et-maree.com; 12pm-1:30pm and 7pm-8:45pm daily; menus €14-17.50

Among the number of restaurants on the front at Morgat, Saveurs et Marée is one of the best. It's frequently busy, especially in high season, and filled with a friendly buzz. The portion sizes are generous and the dishes

1

2

reasonably priced, mostly showcasing local flavors. With that in mind, the *fruits de mer* (seafood platter) is a showstopper in an otherwise unpretentious restaurant. The eating space, meanwhile, is bright and airy, even if it doesn't exactly brim with character.

HOSTELLERIE DE LA MER

11 quai du Fret, Crozon; tel. 02 98 27 61 90; www.hostelleriedelamer.com/restaurant; 12:15pm-1:15pm and 7:15pm-8:30pm daily; menus €29-76

In an area where there aren't that many high-end options for eating, the Hostellerie de la Mer stands out. With the same basic ingredients used in restaurants along the peninsula, from scallops to white fish, it crafts some genuinely special dishes, bordering on Michelin-star quality. The flavors are rich and varied—a lot of the sauces contain buckwheat, imparting a distinctly Breton flavor—and the presentation impeccable. The interior, meanwhile, is inoffensively modern and boasts large windows with great views out to sea. Unsurprisingly, it gets very busy, making booking in advance highly recommended to secure a table.

Budget Option

LE RELAIS DES PÊCHEURS

Quai Kador, Crozon; tel. 02 98 27 04 02; 10:30am-1am daily; sandwiches from €5

It's not a cast iron rule, but certainly a good rule of thumb that if a Breton restaurant is called Le Relais des Pêcheurs ("the fisherman's rest"), it'll be good, and likely attract locals. Reasons for this are unclear, but this harbor-front establishment is certainly no exception. Granted, it doesn't have much more on its menu than sandwiches, but they're generously sized and crammed with local ingredients, Plus, it's also a great bar, serving hoppy locally brewed beers, attracting a lively crowd, and hosting regular music events. The interior is pitched somewhere between old-fashioned and timeless, making for a great place to grab a quick and tasty lunch or to spend an evening.

1: a classic framing of a Breton beach, this one in Crozon 2: easy access to the waves in Morgat

ACCOMMODATIONS

€50-100

HÔTEL DE LA BAIE

46 boulevard de la Plage, Crozon; tel. 02 98 27 07 51; www.hoteldelabaie-crozon-morgat.com; from €68 d

A budget establishment with a luxury location, the Hôtel de la Baie is a straightforward and affordable base for exploring the Presqu'île de Crozon. The interior is clean, if somewhat uninspired, though all rooms have WiFi and en suite bathrooms. Frankly, though, any shortcomings of the rooms themselves are more than made up for by their striking views out to sea. The hotel is literally on the beach, and its breakfast room is filled with light and overlooks the promenade. There's no on-site restaurant, but given that it's in the heart of town, there are plenty of places to eat out very close by.

LA CABANE DES FEES

Kervéneuré, Crozon; tel. 06 87 49 91 90; http://cavalys-la-cabane-des-fees.e-monsite.com; open year-round; treehouse for two €152

A luxury treehouse with its own swimming pool: If that doesn't swing it for you, it's hard to know what will. An entirely wooden structure hoisted in the canapy of Crozon's inland forests, it includes a balcony where breakfast is delivered to every morning, as well as barbecue and campfire facilities on-site. The treehouse is also fully plumbed with its own en suite bathroom, including a hot shower. The interior, meanwhile, is trendy and made enitrely of wood. Very popular in the summer months, it's just the one property, so if you're coming then, make sure to book well ahead.

HÔTEL RESTAURANT D'AR-MEN

Rue Fernand Crouton, Île-de-Sein; tel. 02 98 70 90 77; http://hotel-armen.net; from €70 d

To get the best out of any Breton island, particularly one as romantic and shrouded in mystery as the Île-de-Sein, you have to spend the night. The Hôtel d'Ar-Men is the perfect establishment for this. A storybook hotel stood at the edge of Île-de-Sein's main village, it wears its isolation evocatively and is a fortress of coziness against the winds and rain that batter the island. Its rooms are old-fashioned and basic, though all have en suite bathrooms and there is—in theory—WiFi throughout. Particularly recommended on a blustery night is the speciality lobster stew, served at their on-site restaurant, though you have to reserve it ahead of dining.

Camping

PLAGE DE GOULIEN

Kernavéno, Crozon; tel. 06 08 43 49 32; www.camping-crozon-laplagedegoulien.com; Apr. 14-Sept. 15; camping for two people €15.50, cabin €725 per week

Camping is one of the most popular ways people spend time on the Crozon peninsula, and thanks to that, the region has plenty of well-accommodated campsites. The one on the Plage de Goulien is among the best, boasting an on-site snack bar, grocery, and laundry, as well as an extensive toilet and shower block. Family-friendly in the extreme, there's also a playground, a mini-golf area, table tennis, and a bouncy castle in high summer. Above all this, however, its main draw is its proximity to Goulien Beach. **Surf Oxygene** surf school is only 20 minutes away on foot. This place gets very popular in the summer, so make sure to book ahead.

INFORMATION AND SERVICES

OFFICE DU TOURISME

Boulevard de Pralognan, Crozon; tel. 02 98 27 07 92; www.crozon-tourisme.bzh; 9:30am-12pm and 2pm-6pm Mon.-Sat.

A modern building situated in the town of Crozon providing information about things to do and see along the whole peninsula. This includes the distribution of leaflets about hiking treks, bike-hire companies, and ferry times, among others. Be aware that while there are a lot of French visitors, Crozon is not a particularly popular area among foreign tourists, so there are no guarantees that English will be spoken.

TRANSPORTATION

Getting There

BY CAR

As the Presqu'île de Crozon is a peninsula, it can only be accessed by car from one direction, the east. There are two main roads that feed into it: the D887 to the south, which is the

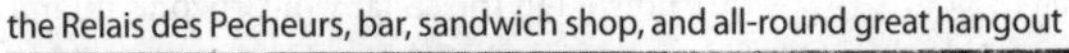

the Relais des Pecheurs, bar, sandwich shop, and all-round great hangout

way to get here from Quimper (30 miles/48 kilometers, 1 hour), or the D791 to the north, which crosses some spectacular coastal scenery and is the fastest way into Crozon from Brest (34 miles/54 kilometers, 50 minutes). Although the route from Brest is a longer distance than from Quimper, it goes down faster roads.

The drive from Paris to Crozon is about 360 miles (580 kilometers) and takes under seven hours total. Take the A11 to Rennes (about 220 miles/354 kilometers, taking 3 hours 40 minutes), which costs around €25 in toll charges. Then change to the N164 to reach Crozon (around 140 miles/225 kilometers, 3 hours).

Being effectively three peninsulas, driving around Crozon is virtually defined by finding yourself in cul-de-sacs. There's not much that can be done about this; just keep aware that it's almost always going to be faster to retrace your steps along main roads rather than taking the smaller, winding routes. Of course, if time isn't an issue, then the latter option is likely to yield some spectacular views.

BY BOAT

Reaching the Crozon peninsula by boat is something that can only be done in season, and these days is only an option for foot passengers. (There used to be a car ferry, but improved road links mean that is no longer an option.)

From April to September a company called **Le Brestoâ** (tel. 07 78 37 03 23; http://lebrestoa.com) runs two ferries a day, one at 9:30am, the other at 5:30pm (apart from on Mondays and Sunday mornings) between Brest and Le Fret. The trip takes about 30 minutes and costs €9.50 for adults, €4.50 for kids.

It's also possible to reach Crozon from the Île-de-Ouessant, though the boat service is hardly what anyone would call regular. From April 19th to June, and for the first two weeks of September, it runs once a week, leaving Ouessant at 6pm every Thursday. In July it runs Monday, Tuesday, Thursday, and Saturday, also leaving at 6pm, and in August it runs every day apart from Sunday, also leaving 6pm. The price is €25.10 for an adult and €16.10 for children between 4 and 16. This also includes the boat trip to Ouessant from wherever you plan to depart (Le Conquet, Brest, or Crozon's Camaret).

Please note, in the unusual case that you're planning a return journey from Ouessant to Crozon, the schedule is really set up for the opposite. Departures for Ouessant from Camaret happen the mornings of the Ouessant-to-Camaret sailing. This means in high season, you'd have to be prepared to spend at least a night on the peninsula, and in low season up to a week.

BY BUS

Presqu'île de Crozon can be reached by the Line 34 bus from Brest. This leaves from outside Brest train station 1-3 times a day—the earliest departure is at 8:55am, the latest 5:40pm, or 7:50pm on Sundays. The journey to Crozon takes about an hour, from whence the bus continues on to Camaret, taking another 30 minutes. All trips have a flat fee of €2. The full schedule can be found on Crozon's town hall website (www.mairie-crozon.fr/IMG/pdf/l34-6vol-ete2017-1.pdf).

From Quimper, Crozon can be reached by the Line 37 bus. There are likewise 1-3 services every day. Buses leave from Quimper train station, the earliest at 9:45am, the latest at 6:05pm, apart from on Fridays at 6:50pm and Sundays at 7:10pm. The journey takes about an hour to Crozon, then another half hour to get to Camaret. It costs a flat fee of €2. Full details of the schedule can be found at this address: www.cat29.fr/scripts/files/5af54f3f7150e0.74092688/l37-velovol-ete2018-0.pdf.

Getting Around

Getting around the Presqu'île de Crozon is really only easy if you have your own vehicle, or are prepared to take your time on foot: It's good hiking territory with many well-marked paths, and all told is not that huge. Walking between its two main towns, Crozon and Camaret, shouldn't take much more than a couple of hours if you go the most direct route—it's a little over five miles (eight kilometers).

Cycling is also a good way of getting around, with a number of hotels and campsites offering bike-rental services for an average of €8 a day. **Camping de la Presqu'ile** (tel. 06 83 36 84; http://camping-presquile-de-crozon.fr/fr/nos-offres/location-de-velos), just outside of Crozon, is among these, and it also offers various other pieces of sporting equipment for hire, should you want to get around the peninsula by stand-up paddleboard, say.

Bus services (www.cat29.fr, €2), meanwhile, run between Camaret and Crozon up to six times a day; look for Lines 34 and 37, which connect the peninsula to Brest and Quimper, respectively. Full schedules can be seen online.

Finally, you might find yourself wanting to take a taxi. There aren't many companies working on the peninsula, so be aware that you may have to wait to get picked up. However, most locations can be reached for €10-20. **GC Taxi** (tel. 06 33 72 06 64) is one company you might try, based near the northern commune of Lanvéoc.

Quimper

It may not be Brittany's biggest town—it's not even the biggest city in Finistère—but if Breton culture has a heart, then Quimper is where it beats. With an atmospheric old town, teaming with *crêperies* and traditional timber-frame buildings, the town was the capital of the ancient region of Cornouaille (which translates, incidentally, to Cornwall, the same as the English county with which it has strong ties) and is commonly regarded as the place where Brittany as we know it today began. A fierce local identity still defines the town. Quimper boasts perhaps the most famous festival in Brittany celebrating the region's culture, the Festival de Cornouaille, and the town's dedication to traditional Breton produce is second to none. You'd be hard-pressed to find better cider, crepes, or butter anywhere in the world.

The name comes from the Breton "kemper," referencing the fact that the town lies at the confluence of two rivers, the Steir and the Odet, the latter of which lends much of Quimper its character, with its flower-festooned banks and row after row of attractive bridges. Meanwhile, Saint-Corentin, the 12th-century cathedral, is commonly considered the finest example of Gothic architecture in Brittany. In the late 17th century, the town became known for its tin-glazed earthenware known as faience, the designs of which have now become famous across all of France.

"Living museum" is thrown about a lot in guidebooks, but there are few places for which it could be a more appropriate expression. The great thing here is that the people of this culture are not celebrating or making a display of it for tourists; they are doing it for themselves.

ORIENTATION

Capital of Finistère and the home of Breton culture it may be, but Quimper still isn't much bigger than an ordinary provincial town, which means it's easy to get around and unintimidating even for the first-time visitor. Its pair of rivers, the Odet and the Steïr, define the limits of the old town. Running west to east, the Odet draws a line under this historic area, while the Steïr runs north to south along the old town's western edge. The train station marks the eastern edge of the old town, within which sit the majority of buildings and museums visitors come to Quimper to see. This includes the incredible **Cathédrale Saint-Corentin,** just one block back from the Quai d'Odet, around which are clustered the **town hall, the Musée des Beaux Arts,** and the **Musée Départmental Breton.** A

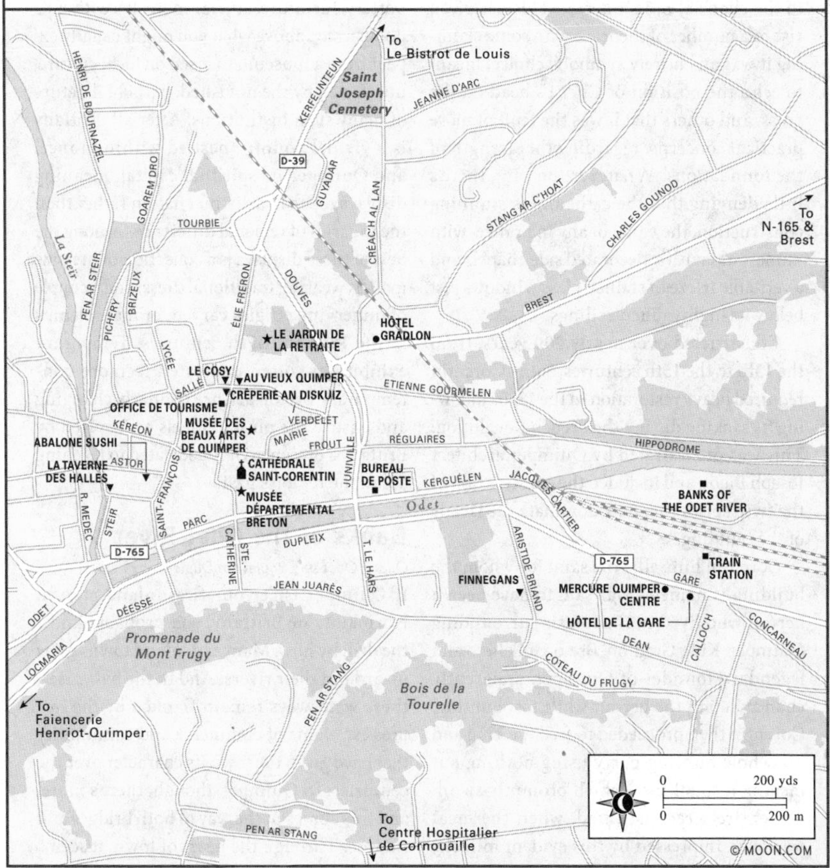

little north of here is the place au Beurre and, running from it, the rue du Sallé (essentially Butter Square and Salty Road), around which are a veritable theme park of *crêperies*, practically daring you to try as many as you can.

Quimper is very well connected to the rest of Brittany and has an effective ring road made up of a number of decent-size roads all connecting with one another from different parts of the country, meaning that arriving in the town is easy from any direction.

SIGHTS

Cathédrale Saint-Corentin

Place Saint-Corentin, Quimper; tel. 02 98 53 04 05 (tourist office); 9:45am-12pm and 1:30pm-6:30pm Mon.-Sat. and 1:30pm-6:30pm Sun. Sept.-June, 9:45am-6:30pm Mon.-Sat. and 1:30pm-6:30pm Sun. July-Aug.; free

A masterpiece of Gothic architecture, this is a building shrouded by much of the same myth and legend as Quimper itself. Its most instantly notable quality is how it bends somewhat in the middle, thanks to a lack of alignment between the chancel (the area around the altar and where the clergy sit) and the nave (the main section of the church, from entrance to the chancel) of its interior. This has given rise to a number of theories, with some claiming it was an entirely symbolic choice, meant to echo the position of Christ's head on the cross, and others that it was the fault of more practical concerns, regarding the strength of the foundations. Whatever the case, there's little denying that the cathedral is stunning construction, the equal of any in France, with numerous lavishly decorated side chapels and a veritable frieze of stained glass windows just below its high-vaulted ceilings.

Constructed over nearly 200 years, from the 13th to the 15th centuries, Saint-Corentin required heavy restoration in the 1850s following its sacking during the French Revolution. This was orchestrated by Quimper architect Joseph Bigot, and included the construction of the twin spires that now dominate the facade of the building.

Corentin himself—the saint for whom the building is named—was said to have been a hermit who lived in the forests surrounding Quimper. King Gradlon, Breton folk hero and legendary founder of Quimper, apparently chanced upon the hermit while lost hunting. Corentin then proceeded to feed the king and his whole hunting party using nothing but meat of a small fish, which promptly swum off, entirely reconstituted, when the meal was over. Impressed by this evident miracle, the king asked Corentin to become the first bishop of his kingdom.

Musée Départemental Breton

1 rue du Roi Gradlon, Quimper; tel. 02 98 95 21 60; http://musee-breton.finistere.fr/fr; 10am-7pm daily mid-June-mid-Sept., 9:30am-5:30pm Tues.-Fri. and 2pm-5:30pm Sat.-Sun. mid-Sept.-mid-June; adults €5, reduced €3, under 26 free

Located inside the old residence for the bishops of Quimper, close to the cathedral, this is surely one of the best places in the whole region to get to grips with the qualities that make Brittany so different from the rest of France. Despite its Gothic exterior, the museum is modern, with up-to-date exhibits dedicated to Breton craftsmanship, clothing, pottery, furniture, and far more. It's without a doubt a step above what you might usually expect from a museum focused on local culture, unaffected by the unvisited, parochial nature of many such institutions. After all, Brittany is a virtual country nestled within France, and Quimper its spiritual capital, meaning displays relate to a distinct nation rather than the vagaries of regional difference. Among the best of these displays is a collection of life-size models wearing traditional dress, and a couple of unnerving effigies carved for mausoleums in the 16th and 17th centuries. Temporary exhibitions, often dedicated to more contemporary Breton art, are regularly changing and ensure the museum feels as inspired by Brittany's present as it is dedicated to teaching about the region's past.

Banks of the Odet River

Quai d'Odet and Boulevard Dupleix

If Quimper isn't your first inland stop in Normandy or Brittany, you probably know the drill by now. Many old inland towns grew up around their rivers. And in the best cases, these waterways remain flanked by the impressive sights of commerce and community that have given the town its character over the centuries. In Quimper, though, there's more, and this comes in the way of both bridges and flowers. Through the heart of town, it seems there's a bridge stretching across the Odet every few footsteps, and every one of them is adorned by box after box of brightly colored geraniums, flashing in the wind and the light.

Walking east to west along the river from the train station, if you can tear your gaze away from the flowers, you'll see the spectacular **Max Jacob Theatre** on the Left Bank, designed in a palatial belle epoque style. Farther on, the Right Bank becomes dominated by the walls enclosing Saint-Corentin, and the south side of the old bishop's residence—now

1: Cathédrale Saint-Corentin 2: people in a café on a square in Quimper

1

2

the Breton Departmental Museum. Directly across the river from here are the local government buildings. Following the river farther, it's then nice to take a right turn at the confluence, walking along the banks of the smaller, though equally floral, Steïr River. The quai du Steïr, a part-pedestrianized street, leads to the extensive, modern **Taverne des Halles,** a covered market building bursting with local produce.

Musée des Beaux Arts de Quimper

40 place Saint-Corentin; tel. 02 98 95 45 20; www.mbaq.fr; 9:30am-12pm and 2pm-6pm Wed.-Mon. Apr.-June and Sept.-Oct., 9:30am-12pm and 2pm-5:30pm Wed.-Sat. and Mon., 2pm-5:30pm Sun. Nov.-Mar., 10am-6pm daily July-Aug.; adults €5, reduced €3

One of the most extensive art museums in western France, this repository includes French, Italian, Flemish, and Dutch paintings from the 14th century up to the present day. The Quimper museum came about almost incidentally, with many of its galleries decorated by the 1,200 paintings and 2,000 drawings left to it by Count Jean-Marie de Silguy in the mid-19th century. The building itself was designed by Joseph Bigot, the same local architect responsible for the reconstruction of the town's cathedral. Its neoclassical facade leads through to a series of light-filled, mostly modern gallery spaces. Whistler, Gauguin, and Corot are a few of the bigger-name artists whose work hangs on the museum's walls. As well as the international perspective on art that it offers, there are a number of images of distinctly Breton landscape. There is a whole room given over to Max Jacob, a Quimper native, and his turn-of-the-century contemporaries, such as Cocteau, Picasso, and Modigliani.

Le Jardin de la Retraite

35 rue Élie Freron, Quimper; tel. 02 98 98 88 87; 9am-7:15pm daily; free

As with much of Brittany, Quimper had a great exploratory tradition, with many sailors from the town embarking for the New World, then returning with unusual plant life to be rooted in native soils. Between the rue Elie Fréron and the rue des Douves, the Jardin de la Retraite pays homage to this. It is a small, protected garden closed in by walls with three distinct spaces: a palm garden, a space for tropical-leaved broad plants, and an area of grassland plants. Wandering from area to area, which are laid out on a number of levels connected by stairs and covered passages, can feel like crossing different latitudes, and, especially on a mild day, like being miles farther south than you are. The discombobulation of the experience is added to by the fact that some of the walls that surround the garden are the remnants of Quimper's 13th-century ramparts, including their only surviving tower, the Tour Névet.

ENTERTAINMENT AND EVENTS

Festivals

FESTIVAL DE CORNOUAILLE

Various locations; tel. 02 98 55 53 53; www.festival-cornouaille.bzh/fr; late July; free (some events ticketed, see website for details)

Quite simply one of the biggest festivals in Brittany, and the biggest for being a direct celebration of the region's culture. It began in the 1920s as a beauty contest, searching for the most beautiful woman in Brittany. Apart from during the war, a queen was crowned every year until 1947, when the election of a 16-year-old to the position drew widespread criticism from the Catholic church. This turned out to be a blessing in disguise, however, causing the festival to diversify. It became a celebration of Breton music, cuisine, dress, and much more, with all manner of different events, including parades and concerts, lasting for at least five days and culminating on the third Sunday of January. The beauty aspect remains an important part of the celebrations, too, though now there is no overall winner; rather, it's a number of "Breton Queens" who are praised. Unsurprisingly, the festival is more popular with Bretons than it is outsiders, allowing it to remain a deeply authentic expression of culture. Both family-friendly in the day and lively late into the evening, there's much to get involved in here for all-comers.

Nightlife

FINNEGANS

46 rue Aristide Briand, Quimper; tel. 02 90 41 71 02; www.finnegans.bzh; 11am-2:30pm and 6pm-1am Tues.-Fri., 11am-1am Sat., 5pm-1am Sun.; pints from €5

Even in Brittany, the French don't always get their pubs right. Not so in Finnegans, however, where cozy conviviality, the perpetual slight waft of beer, and a cool mezzanine level combine to form the kind of drinking establishment where you can lose hours and make friends for life. It boasts a decent selection of beers, particularly by the bottle, and offers hearty meals and bar snacks (of authentically variable quality) to keep you fueled into the early hours.

SHOPPING

FAIENCERIE HENRIOT-QUIMPER

2-4 place Berardier, Quimper; tel. 02 98 90 09 36; www.henriot-quimper.com; 10am-12:30pm and 2pm-6:30pm Mon.-Tues. and Thurs.-Sat.

This pottery workshop and school, the designs of which can be seen all over Brittany, was founded in Quimper in 1690. Faience is a hand-painted tradition, and its most famous image reoccurring on plate after plate is of the so-called "petit Breton," a representation of a Breton figure wearing traditional dress. This is often surrounded by an elaborately patterned border, and became popular with both Bretons and tourists in the late 19th century. It's still the most popular design, and you can even order personalized bowls that display it as well as your name—or whatever word you wish. All other manner of different earthenware can also be bought, from mugs to egg cups, as well as many more expensive, purely decorative pieces. Provided you can be confident of getting them home, these are some of the best souvenirs Brittany can offer.

This is also a shop with a museum attached. The historic workshops can be visited on a guided tour, starting at 10:30am, 11:30am, 2pm, 3pm, 4pm, and 5pm Monday to Saturday. The cost is €5 for adults, €4 for students, and €2.50 for children under 17.

MANOIR DU KINKIZ

75 chemin du Quinquis, Quimper; tel. 02 98 90 20 57; www.cidre-kinkiz.fr; 9am-12:30pm and 2pm-6:30pm Mon.-Sat.

Of course there's cider right across Normandy and Brittany, and of course much of it is good, artisanal produce. But the really luxurious stuff often requires going out of your way to source. Most of the time, cider is a cheap background drink, free-flowing and casually quoffable. At the Manoir du Kinkiz, however, it's elevated to a fine-wine-like status, as befits a place so close to Quimper, where everything that makes up Breton culture, including the region's most famed beverage, is bestowed maximum attention. The cider and the apple wine here are closely monitered at all the stages of their production and made from 21 different varieties of apples all picked by hand. Naturally, the drinks have won some of the most prestigious food prizes in all of France. Located amid its own orchards, Manoir du Kinkiz also invites visitors into their cellars, dark and mysterious, and to inspect the tools that have been used in cider-making for centuries past.

SPORTS AND RECREATION

Hiking

LES GORGES DU STANGALA

Route du Stangala, Quimper

One of the most extraordinary landscapes in Brittany, the gorges of Stangala follow the Odet River upstream of Quimper. They represent a geological curiosity, in parts reaching as high as 260 feet (80 meters) above the river thanks to tectonic activity in the distant past. The whole area has been thoroughly infiltrated by hiking trails that are well marked and stretch through woodland, cling to the slopes of the valley sides, and in places cross over the valley on pedestrianized bridges. It's also possible to ford the river using its large rocks when the water is low. Boasting deep folds in the landscape, overrun by thick vegetation and unusual bulbous rock formations, it's hardly a surprise that many legends have come to be associated with the gorges. Most of note is the one about a griffin, a creature with a lion's body and eagle's wings, which demanded a monthly sacrifice until it was slayed by a young man whose betrothed was due to be eaten.

You're unlikely to come across any griffins these days, even at the Pointe de Griffonez, where it was said to have lived. Indeed, getting lost is probably your main fear. To avoid that, either consult information about the Grande Route 38, which runs through the forest, or head to Quimper's tourist office for a map of shorter trails. Be aware, also, that as a valley much walking is across uneven, sloping ground, meaning most walks require a rudimentary level of fitness, and that it's not a place for baby strollers.

Horseback Riding

CENTRE ÉQUESTRE UCPA DE QUIMPER

1 chemin de Toulven, Quimper; tel. 02 98 54 84 02; http://quimper.ucpa.com; 9am-12pm and 2pm-5pm Sat. and Wed., 2pm-6:30pm Mon., Tues., and Fri.; hour-long trek from €25, a month of lessons from €390

Situated in the countryside just south of Quimper, these stables offer everything from horse-trekking to long-term lessons to show-jumping exhibitions and competitions on-site. With a stock of Shetland ponies, it's open to very young children as well as adults. Though it is an entirely French establishment without any official English-speakers, the friendly, welcoming group is happy to work around language barriers.

FOOD

Local Cuisine

ALLIUM

88 boulevard de Créac'h Gwen, Quimper; tel. 02 98 10 11 48; www.restaurant-allium.fr/fr; 12:15pm-1:30pm and 7:30pm-9:15pm Tues.-Sat.; menus €55-95

Just south of Quimper's center, this Michelin-starred restaurant sits in its own small gardens, offering diners plenty of space in its elegantly modern wood-floored and wood-tabled interior. Established thanks to an Internet crowd-funding campaign led by its head chef Lionel Hénaff, it offers modern takes on local dishes, with the "XXL crispy" langoustine served with hot mayonnaise, a house favorite. The floor-to-ceiling windows in the dining area ensure the space is always full of light. Booking is essential, and a few days ahead of dining for peak times.

LE BISTROT DE LOUIS

101B avenue de la France libre, Quimper; tel. 02 98 95 56 08; http://lebistrotdelouis.free.fr; 12pm-2pm and 6pm-10pm Tues.-Fri., 7pm-10pm Sat., 12pm-2pm Mon.; mains €14-21

This is a restaurant that resembles how people dream they will be eating all the time when they come to France. Reasonable, semiformal, and with good, honest, local food and excellently chosen wine, Le Bistrot de Louis may not look like much from the outside, and it is a bit out of town, but this is a real local gem. You can't go wrong choosing anything from the menu, which includes top seafood options as well as a fine line of terrestrial cuts. A good place to indulge a steak craving.

LE COSY

2 rue du Sallé, Quimper; tel. 02 98 95 23 65; 12pm-2pm and 7pm-9pm Tues.-Sat.; menus €16.50-21.50

Centrally located and serving dishes that both look and taste amazing, Le Cosy is unafraid to experiment with local flavors and present food in a stylish modern way. Though ostensibly a Breton restaurant, don't be surprised if you catch sushi or noodles on the menu. The interior is a trendy combination of stone walls with some white wooden fittings and white and black tables: stylish, but not overbearingly so. Indeed, if you consider the essence of good dining experience to rest in balance, then Le Cosy has that in spades. The only thing to keep in mind is that it is quite small, and very popular, so book ahead if you can especially for dinner.

Crêperies

CRÊPERIE AN DISKUIZ

12 rue Élie Freron, Quimper; tel. 02 98 95 55 70; 11:45am-2:30pm and 6:45pm-9:30pm Mon., Tues, and Thurs.-Sat.; €6-11

If the humble Breton crepe, the galette, has a spiritual home, then Quimper is it. And the Rue du Sallé (effectively Savory Street) sits at its heart. Granted, there are no statistics to bear this out, but it seems highly likely that this road and its immediate surrounds have the highest density of *crêperies* of anywhere in the world. With that in mind, it seems almost unfair to recommend only a couple. However, there not being space for more, the Crêperie an Diskuiz, on the corner of Rue du Sallé, but actually entered from Rue Élie Freron, is at least as good a one to suggest as any other. With a lively yellow interior, tiled floor, and wicker-seated chairs, it positively breathes authenticity. The crepes themselves are unpretentiously delicious—and how many restaurants of this size or price bracket boast a list of all their suppliers on the back of their menu? The locality of the produce is staggering.

AU VIEUX QUIMPER

20 rue Verdelet, Quimper; tel. 02 98 95 31 34; www.creperieauvieuxquimper.fr; 11:45am-2:30pm and 6:45pm-9:30pm Tues.-Sat.; €5-11

With decorative plates and spindly farmyard equipment on its walls, wood features, and a tiled floor, the aesthetic of this *crêperie* walks a line between adjectives: kitschy and twee sit on the one side, rustic and authentic on the other. What's under no debate whatsoever, though, is the quality of its food. The crepes are quite simply brilliant, with a wide-ranging menu composed of mainly local products. The flambéed crepes in particular are worth picking up for dessert.

International

ABALONE SUSHI

Halles Saint-François, Quimper; tel. 02 98 64 38 91; 11am-2:30pm and 5pm-7:30pm Tues.-Sat.; mains from €14

There's something oddly Breton about sushi. Most obviously it's the fish, but there's also something about its rawness, which connects to the Breton landscape, the subtlety in its preparation, and the way the sea seems to run through its every flavor. For those reasons and more, there are a number of excellent sushi joints around the region, and this one in Quimper's main food hall is no exception. Its location may be humble, but don't be fooled: This is no mere market stall. Well worth the price.

ACCOMMODATIONS

€50-100

HÔTEL DE LA GARE

17 avenue de la Gare, Quimper; tel. 02 98 90 00 81; www.hoteldelagarequimper.com; from €65 d

Granted, in charming old Quimper, this modern building with a distinctly some-expense-spared interior aesthetic may not be an obvious first choice. But it's well located and inexpensive. The rooms are also as comfortable as they need to be and well maintained. There are also the necessary modern conveniences at your disposal, such as WiFi, en suite bathrooms, and an on-site bar.

€100-200

MERCURE QUIMPER CENTRE

21 bis avenue de la Gare, Quimper; tel. 02 98 90 31 71; www.accorhotels.com/gb/hotel-1421-mercure-quimper-centre-hotel/index.shtml; from €111 d

This centrally located, midrange hotel is part of the Mercure hotel chain, with all the usual advantages and disadvantages that entails. A certain level of comfort and quality of service is guaranteed. The rooms are very well insulated against the noise and fluctuating temperatures, though perhaps also the character, of the outside world. A little corporate it may be, but for a trouble-free stay in Quimper it's hard to envision a better place. There's WiFi throughout, a decent always-fresh continental breakfast buffet, and an on-site bar.

MANOIR-HÔTEL DES INDES

1 allée de Prad ar C'hras, Quimper; tel. 02 98 55 48 40; http://manoir-hoteldesindes.com; from €120 d

On its own grounds just outside of Quimper, this eco-friendly luxury manor that takes its design cues from the subcontinent may have been an odd fit in the Breton countryside. But the foreign influence is handled dexterously and blends well into an excellent hotel, which comes complete with an uncommonly tasteful spa area, including—the pièce de résistance—an underground swimming pool surrounded by vaulted stone. Rooms are of sumptuous wood and all have en suite bathrooms, and there's WiFi throughout.

HÔTEL GRADLON

30 rue de Brest, Quimper; tel. 02 98 95 04 39; www.hotel-gradlon.fr; from €130 d

An old hotel that once-upon-a-time would have catered to those traveling by coach and horses, right in the center of town. The rooms are full of soft, floral furnishings and are well maintained, even if their interior design has a bit of an uninspired 1950s vibe. All rooms have en suite bathrooms, there's fast and reliable internet throughout the property, and there's a peaceful garden terrace to relax in after a day touring Quimper's streets.

Camping

CAMPING MUNICIPAL

Avenue des Oiseaux, Quimper; tel. 02 98 55 61 09; www.quimper.bzh/389-camping-municipal.htm; open year-round; tent for two people €9

Surprisingly close to the center of Quimper for a campsite—Saint-Corentin is only about half an hour's walk away—this is a basic establishment consisting of not much more than a cleared patch of the Séminaire Forest, with 74 pitches and a couple of shower and toilet blocks. It's an excellent choice if you want to visit Quimper for the Festival de Cornouaille, when prices can start to climb in the town center. Make sure to book well in advance, though, if that's something you're planning.

INFORMATION

OFFICE DU TOURISME

8 rue Élie Freron, Quimper; tel. 02 98 53 04 05; www.quimper-tourisme.bzh; 9:30am-6:30pm Mon.-Sat.

Despite not getting as many foreign visitors as some other parts of Brittany, Quimper's tourism game is strong. The tourist office here is large, central, and well-staffed—English is widely spoken. The adjoining website is also one of the best in the region, with plenty of suggestions of things to do, not just in Quimper but in the surrounding countryside as well.

SERVICES

CENTRE HOSPITALIER DE CORNOUAILLE QUIMPER

14 bis avenue Yves Thépot, Quimper; tel. 02 98 52 60 60; www.ch-cornouaille.fr; ER open 24 hours

This large hospital sits about a mile to the south of Quimper's center. The emergency department is open 24 hours (look for signs directing you toward *Urgences*), and while there are no promises made about speaking English, there will most likely be someone on staff with whom you can communicate, though not necessarily at the reception.

BUREAU DE POSTE

37 boulevard Amiral de Kerguélen, Quimper; www.laposte.fr/particulier; 9am-6pm Mon.-Fri., 9am-12pm Sat.

Post offices are remarkably standardized across the whole of France. This one, the most central in Quimper, is no different. Things can seem a little confusing when you first step in, but there are plenty of floating staff members ready to come and help you should you need to pick up or send a parcel. Don't expect much English to be spoken, but there's a system of color-coding for various sizes of mail, and with that plus hand gestures, most should be able to get by.

TRANSPORTATION

Getting There

BY CAR

Despite being a relatively small town, Quimper is well connected by road. From Paris (350 miles/563 kilometers, 5.5 hours), it's a straight shot down the A11 freeway via Rennes. It should cost around €25 in tolls.

From Rennes (160 miles/257 kilometers, 2.25 hours) to Quimper, take the N24 toward Lorient, then the N165. There are no tolls.

The N165 is also the fastest way to Quimper from its touristy neighboring town, Concarneau (20 miles/32 kilometers, 30 minutes).

From Nantes (180 miles, 290 kilometers, 2.5 hours), take the N165 heading via Vannes then Lorient. From Brest (50 miles/80 kilometers, 45 minutes), you head south on the N165 to reach Quimper.

Quimper itself is surrounded by an effective ring road made up of a number of decent-size roads all connecting with one another, meaning that arriving in the town is straightforward from any direction.

BY AIR

Quimper does have an airport, **Aéroport Quimper Bretagne** (Pluguffan; tel. 02 98 94 30 30; www.quimper.aeroport.bzh; help desk hours: 5:30am-10pm Mon.-Fri., 7am-8pm Sat., 9am-11:30am and 3:30pm-10pm Sun.), and its distance from Paris means that, unlike most places in this book, it can just about be worth taking a plane to get here. Thanks to a high number of connecting flights, prices are often as low as €30. Flights arrive from Paris every day, and from London's City Airport most days of the week.

BY TRAIN

Well connected by train, **Gare de Quimper** (1 place Louis Armand, Quimper; tel. 08 92 35 35 35; www.gares-sncf.com/fr/gare/fruip/quimper; 4:45am-12am Mon.-Thurs., 4:45am-12:45am Fri., 4:45am-11pm Sat., 8:30am-12am Sun.) is on several major lines. Quimper can be reached nine times daily from Paris (4.75 hours, €67-108). It is also possible to get here from Rennes, where there are 11 trains a day (2 hours, €35). From Nantes, there are three trains daily (2.5 hours, €40). There are also 11 trains/replacement bus services coming from Brest daily (1.5 hours, €9).

BY BUS

The **Viaoo 29** (www.viaoo29.fr) bus service, which runs throughout the Finistère region, runs a regular service from Brest (1.5 hours, €6). The same company also runs a bus from Concarneau (45 minutes, €2), and a bus from Camaret-sur-Mer on the Crozon peninsula (1 hour, €2). Buses stop just outside of Quimper's train station. Full details of routes can be found on the company's website.

Getting Around

With a small, walkable town center and the river to orient you, Quimper is an easy town to get around on foot for the most part. If you need to take a longer journey, the local bus company is called **QUB** (www.qub.fr), and details of their routes can be found on their website.

There are several taxi companies, all selling at the same prices. **Radio Taxi** (www.taxi-quimper.fr, tel. 02 98 90 21 21) is the most extensive, running a 24/7 service that can be contacted online, by phone or, indeed, hailed down in the street. Prices to and from Quimper airport are €15 in the day, €20 at night.

Concarneau

Close to legendary in its status as a tourist destination among the French, Concarneau also happens to be one of the country's most important commercial fishing ports. Its historic center, located on a long island stretching into the harbor, is characterized by a picturesque walled town of half-timber houses bursting with flowers. This used to be home to a shipbuilding industry, though now is mostly given over to souvenirs and restaurants. From its ramparts, however, the spectacle of modern Concarneau unfolds, as pleasure boats crisscross with fishing vessels and Atlantic catches are routinely brought in and hauled ashore.

The mainland town and its surrounds are characterized by tinning factories, marinas, and a number of pleasant, sandy beaches, which can get busy in the summer. The town's covered market, meanwhile, and its open-air markets on Monday and Friday mornings, are among the best in Brittany.

For all the town's conventional charms, one of its biggest draws is how close visitors are able to get to the historic fishing industry. Visiting fish auctions, helping deep-sea fishermen in with their catch, and even the possibility of heading out on a traditional fishing vessel are all on the proverbial menu; naturally, the literal menus of restaurants burst with the fruits of the sea. Also in this line is Le Festival des Filets Bleus, the Festival of the Blue Nets, a more than 100-year-old celebration of Concarneau's fishing culture that brings the town together every August.

ORIENTATION

The most striking thing about Concarneau's layout is the way its harbor, and effective town center, is dominated by an island, which is itself the home of a medieval walled town, the **Ville Close.** This area is distinct from the modern mainland town and consists of several streets dominated by tourist apparatus and ringed by scalable ramparts. It can only be entered by land on its western tip, where a short causeway, the rue Vauban, links it to the harbor. A local foot-passenger ferry leaves from the other side of the island, bridging the short distance to the harbor's eastern shore.

The harbor itself is given over to parking lots, pleasure marinas, and restaurants on its western side, and the town's commercial fishing industry in its north and east. Arrivals into town by bus stop in the northwest of this harbor—just where commerce gives way to industry. The twice-weekly market (on Mondays and Fridays) is held on the place Jean Jaures parking lot on the southwest of the harbor, directly opposite the causeway into the old town. This represents an extension of the town's **covered market,** open all week long, also on this square.

Concarneau rests in a sheltered inlet on the east of the Baie de la Forêt. Follow this bay out of town to the south or north and there are plenty of great beaches, with the **Plage des Sables Blancs** being the closest to the town center.

Just down the road from Concarneau is the quaint river town of **Pont Aven,** famous for its association with the post-Impressionist painter Paul Gauguin, who first came here in 1886, finding inspiration in what he saw as the rawness of the Breton landscape and its people. To get to Pont Aven, take the D783 southwest out of town.

SIGHTS

Musee de la Peche

3 rue Vauban, Concarneau; tel. 02 98 97 10 20; www.musee-peche.fr; 2pm-5:30pm Tues.-Sun. Feb.-Mar. and Nov.-Dec., 10am-6pm Tues.-Sun. Apr.-June and Sept.,10am-7pm daily July-Aug.; adults €5, reduced €3

Opened in 1961, this small though excellent museum dedicated to fishing has become a stalwart of Concarneau's tourism industry. Located in a former arsenal building in the

Ville Close, it offers numerous exhibits exploring the history of fishing and how technology has evolved over the years. Guests can check out detailed models and real-world artifacts, looking way back to coracles, the small, rounded, lightweight boats used in this part of Brittany centuries ago. The real highlight is a self-guided tour of a real fishing trawler, the no longer active *L'Hémérica*. You may not consider yourself that interested in commercial fishing, but there's no greater praise for this museum than that it makes you feel like you should be. A great way for adults and kids to pass an hour or so.

Château de Keriolet

Rue de Stang ar Lin, Concarneau; tel. 02 98 97 36 50; www.chateaudekeriolet.com; 10am-1pm and 2pm-6pm Sun.-Fri. June 6-Sept. 16; adults €6.50, children 7-15 €3.50

This striking 19th-century château was built in an ostentatious neo-Gothic style under the orders of Russian princess Zénaïde Narichkine-Ioussoupov, grandmother of one of Rasputin's assassins. She wanted a home for her young husband—a French artillery officer 30 years her junior who she had to leave Russia to marry. Designed by Joseph Bigot, who also led the reconstruction of Quimper Cathedral, it was sold to the city of Concarneau in the 1970s and is now open to the public. Visits take in the well-maintained public areas, full of heavy wooden furniture and grand fireplaces, as well as the château's particularly beautiful kitchen, covered floor-to-ceiling in exquisite hand-painted tiles. More striking than it is elegant, it's located just to the north of Concarneau. Exploring the château is a relaxing way to spend an afternoon, and there are plenty of events staged here throughout the summer season. Consult the website for details.

Marinarium

Quai de la Croix, Concarneau; tel. 02 98 50 81 64; www.stationmarinedeconcarneau.fr; 2pm-6pm daily Feb.-Mar. and Oct.-Dec., 10am-12pm and 2pm-6pm daily Apr., June, and Sept., 10am-7pm daily July-Aug.; adults €5, reduced €3

Boasting great views across the bay, this 19th-century marine institute is far more than your standard aquarium. It's a reminder, which sometimes seems necessary in Concarneau, that there's more pleasure to be gleaned from fish and marine life than simply eating it, and it was one of the world's first centers dedicated to the study of marine animals. Founded in 1859, it still functions both as a research institute, a museum, and an aquarium. As well as numerous educational exhibits, there are several aquariums and a large pool dedicated to local sea life. It may lack the pyrotechnics of some of the other aquariums along the Breton coast—it's no Oceanopolis, that's for sure—but this is a fiercely educational institution, which exists as much for the benefit of science as it does tourists. What that means is that the whole place is full of working researchers and academics, many of whom (if their English is up to the task) will be happy to answer questions about what they are doing and the center's various attractions. Signage, unfortunately, is in French.

Musée des Beaux-Arts

Place Julia, Pont-Aven; tel. 02 98 06 14 43; www.museepontaven.fr/fr; 2pm-5:30pm Tues.-Sun. Feb.-Mar. and Nov.-Dec., 10am-6pm Tues.-Sun. Apr.-June and Sept.-Oct., 10am-7pm daily July-Aug.; adults €8, reduced €6, under 18 free

Set in the picturesque riverside town of Pont Aven, this art museum houses an impressive collection. With the opening of the Paris-Quimper rail line in the 1860s, Concarneau began to attract artists who came looking for unspoiled Brittany; among them the most famous was Paul Gaugin, one of the fathers of the Expressionist movement. One hundred fifty years later, Pont Aven is still rustic in a way quite different from the sometimes resort-like coast, and it makes a good day trip from Concarneau, with a stop at this Beaux-Arts museum being a must. It features a number of original works by Gauguin and many by the contemporaries he inspired. Housed in an old building, it's been recently refurbished

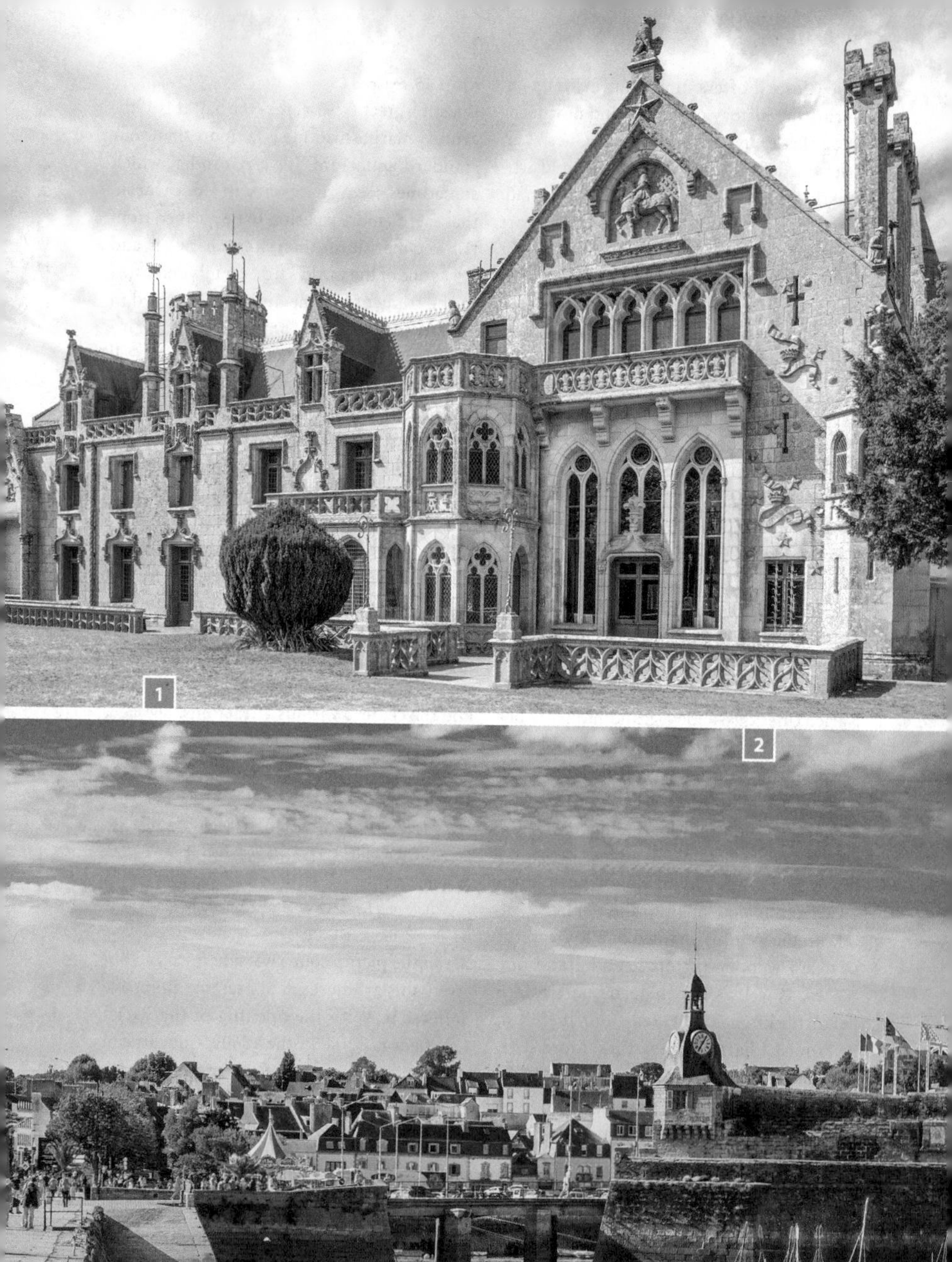
1
2

and now has a striking modern interior. It's not an enormous museum, but there's easily enough here to keep you busy for a morning or an afternoon. And more than that, because so many works were inspired by the Breton countryside and people, when you leave, you'll find yourself looking at the region in a new way.

ENTERTAINMENT AND EVENTS

Festivals

FESTIVAL DES FILETS BLEUS

Various locations; tel. 02 98 97 09 09; www.festivaldesfiletsbleus.bzh; mid-August; free (some events ticketed; see website for details)

The longest running festival in Brittany, established in 1905, the Festival des Filets Bleus was founded as a way of raising money for fishermen and their families following a sardine shortage at the turn of the 20th century. The party has moved with the times and today boasts a combination of live music and late-night dancing, as well more traditional features, such as a parade in traditional dress, an old-fashioned beauty pageant for the "queens" of the town. There's also, perhaps most notably, a march of bagpipers: no doubt great if you like that kind of thing! The festival lasts for around five days in the middle of August, during which time Concarneau reaches absolute maximum capacity. If you're planning on dropping in during this period, be sure to book accommodations well ahead.

SPORTS AND RECREATION

Fishing

SANTA-MARIA

2 rue du Verger–Kerléan, Concarneau; tel. 06 62 88 00 87; www.santamariapeche.com; 8am daily departures July-Aug., by reservation for groups the rest of year; adults from €37 for a half day, children under 12 from €22

An old sardine-catching vessel, the *Santa-Maria* offers groups and individuals the chance to take to the seas and spend a half day or full day in search of fish. It's a bit of a show—a bagpiper plays, and the atmosphere is convivial—so the whole experience is not a totally authentic representation of the perilous life on the waves. But a day aboard the *Santa Maria* is a great way to experience the lives of many Concarneau locals, with fishing professionals on hand to give you advice. For the fullest experience, choose the full-day excursion on Saturdays. All different types of fishing can be practiced onboard, including big game fishing: heading out to the Glénan Islands by day, people can even come back with sharks! Make sure to let them know the equipment and bait you need before you leave, all of which are provided at a very small extra cost (€1 per item).

Beaches

PLAGE DES SABLES BLANCS

Rue des Sables Blancs, Concarneau

Literally "white sand beach," this is the largest beach near Concarneau's center, and its name is a fitting description: It looks positively tropical when the sun is shining. This family-friendly beach is about a third of a mile (half a kilometer) long at low tide, though the southern section disapears when the sea comes in. As a result, it's at its busiest at its northern end, where there are also some nearby shops, restaurants, and cafés—it can get very busy in high season, so stay away if you don't like crowds. Monitored from July to August, there are also activities for very young children organized here at that time.

FOOD

Local Cuisine

TY BE NEW

13B avenue du Dr Pierre Nicolas, Concarneau; tel. 02 98 87 64 53; 12pm-2pm and 7pm-9pm Thurs.-Tues.; mains €7.20-14.60

A straightforward though very high-quality crepe restaurant on Concarneau's harbor, set just across the road from the town's Ville Close. Reasonably priced, with a pretty basic

---

1: the main facade of the De Keriolet castle 2: bridge and moat in front of Concarneau

interior, its specialty of the house is essentially a very thick crepe, used in a bread-like manner. It's a great option for anyone who doesn't feel quite filled by more traditional crepes. Right on the market square, it gets very busy Monday and Friday at lunchtime, but it's more a walk-in kind of joint than one that really takes reservations.

LA PORTE AUX VINS

9 place Saint Guenole, Concarneau; tel. 02 98 97 38 11; 11:45am-9pm Sun.-Fri., 11:45am-9pm Sat.; menus €20.90-26.90

Tourist traps abound inside the walls of Concarneau's Ville Close, but this place stands apart. Delivering straghtforward but decent, flavorful food in a pleasant traditional setting, it features a waitstaff who are very considerate to English speakers. Don't come expecting haute cuisine, with dishes mostly made up of quite distinct parts and fewer complex sauces than in other French restaurants, but if it's comfort food you're after, with the occasional Breton twist, then this is a good option.

LE VAUBAN

10 rue Vauban, Concarneau; tel. 02 98 97 34 93; www.levauban-restaurant.fr; 11:45-2pm and 6:45pm-9pm Tues.-Sun.; mains €21-40

A small, cozy seafood restaurant dedicated to some rich flavors. Set opposite the fishing museum in the Ville Close, it could almost be considered the museum gift shop, albeit one serving souvenirs in the shape of meals rather than anything you'd put on your mantel back home. As with many restaurants around here, the lobster is Le Vauban's real showstopper dish, but there's also a very tasty selection of white fish mains that won't break the bank.

LA TAUPINIÈRE

Rue de Concarneau-Croaz Sayé, Pont-Aven; tel. 02 98 06 03 12; www.la-taupiniere.fr; 12pm-2pm and 7:30pm-9pm Wed.-Sat., 12pm-2pm Sun.; menus €55-100

On the road between Concarneau and Pont-Aven, this restaurant in an old-fashioned building seems to date from another, more refined age, with pressed white tablecloths, wicker-backed chairs, and exceptional traditional Breton cooking. It is well worth a trip for a leisurely lunch or dinner. Langoustines are its speciality, though frankly everything from its—admitedly quite pricey—menu is likely to delight. It's at its best on a rainy Sunday lunchtime, when the open fire and warm atmosphere come into their own. Make sure to book ahead.

Crêperies

LE PETIT CHAPERON ROUGE

7 place du Guesclin, Concarneau; tel. 02 98 60 53 32; 12pm-2:30pm and 7pm-9:30pm Tues.-Sat.; €1.80-6.20

Serving mouthwatering crepes at mouthwatering prices, this fairy-tale *crêperie* on Concarneau's harbor is a truly terrific budget restaurant. The crepes in the region around Concarneau and Quimper have a quite legitimate claim to being the best in Brittany, and though inexpensive, Le Petit Chaperon Rouge does not let down. The interior is quaint, with a tiled floor, wood-paneled walls, and numerous wicker baskets hanging from the ceiling. The recipes, meanwhile, are standard *crêperie* fare, with egg, ham, and cheese crepes the staple.

Markets

★ MARCHÉ COUVERT CONCARNEAU

Les Halles, Marché Couvert, Concarneau; tel. 02 98 97 25 58; http://halles-cornouaille.com/halles-de-cornouaille/concarneau; 8am-1pm Mon.-Sat.

One of the more visceral manifestations of Concarneau's fishing industry open to the public, Concarneau's covered market houses 17 excellent food stalls. Stop by **Poissonnerie d'Armor Morelli Concarneau,** just one of the stalls, where the produce depends on the day's catch. Come here to buy lobster, crab, even shark—or just feast with your eyes at the shimmering spectacle of natural history, surrounded by chipped ice, looking utterly delicious. A map of the market is available on the website.

ACCOMMODATIONS

Under €50

AUBERGE DE JEUNESSE-ÉTHIC

Quai de la Croix, Concarneau; tel. 02 98 97 03 47; www.aj-concarneau.org/index.php; from €18 pp

You seldom find youth hostels with locations as good as this. Just a short walk from the harbor, perched on the rocks with a great view of the sea from most of its rooms, the Auberge de Jeuness-Éthic in Concarneau may be budget, but its scenery is top shelf. Beyond that, it's a fairly basic youth hostel, with sparse dorms and meals on offer, though not much else by way of on-site entertainment. Not that that matters with so much to do nearby, of course. The staff has a reputation for being fairly relaxed, which can be good or bad depending on your disposition.

€50-100

HÔTEL DU PORT

11 bis avenue Pierre Guéguin, Concarneau; tel. 02 98 97 31 52; www.hotelduport-concarneau29.com; from €56 d

Overlooking Concarneau harbor in a nice old building, this hotel could be on the postcard of a Breton port (minus the betting shop underneath). With a refurb, they could charge easily double the price. As it is, the interiors are a bit lackluster, neither quaintly old-fashioned nor stylishly modern. The views are great, however, and there can be little arguing over the location or the price. For these reasons, it gets booked up quickly in high season, so be sure to reserve a room a good few weeks in advance. WiFi and en suite bathrooms come as standard, and there's a continental breakfast served on the property.

€100-200

THALASSO CONCARNEAU

36 rue des Sables Blancs, Concarneau; tel. 02 98 75 05 40; www.concarneau-thalasso.com; from €128 d

This full-on luxury resort, just a short walk from the beach, features an on-site wellness center that sets the property apart. The rooms here are large and light-filled, and many have balconies and sea views. The biggest draw, the wellness center includes various types of thalassotherapy (seawater therapy), as well as indoor and outdoor swimming pools. The proximity of Concarneau is really just an added bonus to this place. It'd be perfectly possible to spend a whole holiday inside the grounds of the hotel and stay perfectly happy.

VILLA DES SABLES

12 boulevard Alfred Guillou, Concarneau; tel. 06 45 22 51 44; http://villadessables.fr; from €140 d

A thoroughly pleasant hotel, just back from Concarneau's most central beach. The black and white color scheme has been well handled, and the furniture in both the rooms and public areas is both modern and stylish. Indeed, the whole place could very nearly pass for a full-on luxury hotel, if not for some of the materials they've chosen and its slightly limited scale. But that keeps prices low enough that it's still affordable, even in high season. Like elsewhere in Concarneau, remember to book early in the summer months.

INFORMATION

OFFICE DU TOURISME

Quai d'Aiguillon, Concarneau; tel. 02 98 97 01 44; www.tourismeconcarneau.fr; 9am-6:30pm Mon.-Sat.

As befits a major tourist town, the Office du Tourisme in Concarneau is a well-used establishment on the harbor front. Filled with leaflets about things to do in the local area beyond the town itself, it's also a good place if you're interested in interacting more with the town's fishing industry. Tours of the morning fish auctions can be organized here, as can finding out when's best to see a catch being brought in. English should be spoken.

TRANSPORTATION

Getting There

BY CAR

A turn off the main road from Paris to Quimper, Concarneau is easy to reach by car. From the French capital (350 miles/563 kilometers, 5.5 hours), it's a straight shot down the A11 freeway via Rennes. It should cost around €25 in tolls. From Rennes (160 miles/257 kilometers, 2.25 hours), take the N24 toward Lorient, then the N165. There are no tolls.

From Quimper (15 miles/24 kilometers, 30 minutes), the N165 is the fastest way to Concarneau. From Nantes (180 miles/290 kilometers, 2.5 hours), take the N165 heading via Vannes, then Lorient. From Brest (50 miles/80 kilometers, 45 minutes), you head south on the N165 via Quimper.

BY BUS

Despite its popularity among tourists, Concarneau is not the easiest place to reach by public transport. Most visitors will have to come via Quimper, with its major train station, then take a bus run by **Viaoo29** (www.viaoo29.fr), which runs regularly from the train station, costs €2, and takes about 45 minutes. It will deposit you on Concarneau port.

There are also several bus companies that run between Lorient and Concarneau, including national carrier **Ouibus,** which leaves roughly three times a day from outside Lorient train station, taking about an hour and costing €5.

A final option is taking the train from either Lorient or Quimper to Rosporden, which is the closest train station (about eight miles/12 kilometers away) to Concarneau itself. From there, there are regular SNCF buses into town costing €3.70, or if you're feeling particularly energetic, you can walk.

Getting Around

With the town center concentrated around a relatively small area, Concarneau is easily walkable, even between the beaches. This is particularly true if you keep in mind the foot passenger ferry at the east end of the Ville Close, which effectively means you can traverse the entire harbor straight across and not have to take the long way round. The ferry runs regularly from 8am-12:30pm, then 2pm-7:30pm, from April-June and September; from 8am-11pm in July and August; and from 8am-6:30pm at all other times, with slighly reduced hours on public holidays and Sundays. It costs €1.

Connecting the areas immediately surrounding Concarneau is the **Coralie bus service** (tel. 02 98 60 55 55; www.coralie-cca.fr), which stops all over town. Line 43/47 takes you to Pont Aven. Tickets cost from €1.

There are also several taxi companies in town, of which **ace taxi** (tel. 02 98 97 13 82) is just one. Most have fairly similar pricing—it should cost about €15 to get from Concarneau to Pont Aven, for example, though at peak hours, especially during the summer, demand can exceed supply, so don't automatically assume taxis are the fastest way of getting somewhere unless you've booked in advance. If you're driving between Concarneau and Pont Aven yourself, take the D783, then the D70 north out of town, until you reach N165, on which it's a straight shot east. This is the fastest route, based on the usual traffic. It should take about 25 minutes, and is roughly 15 miles (24 kilometers).

Gulf of Morbihan

One of the great natural wonders of France, this enormous gulf is a veritable inland sea. Boasting a constellation of beautiful islands, hidden coves, and sandy beaches, it offers more to do and see per square inch than just about anywhere else in beguiling Brittany. Equally compelling, the surrounding area boasts a landscape crowded with relics of history and pre-history, from elegant abbeys to mysterious Neolithic remains, most notably the massed ranks of standing stones of Carnac, the most expansive collections of which cover what could be multiple end-to-end football pitches, and are the biggest sights of their kind anywhere in the world.

As though that weren't enough, the Gulf of Morbihan is also a land of exceptional oysters and artisanal salt, perfect for titillating the

Highlights

Look for ★ to find recommended sights, activities, dining, and lodging.

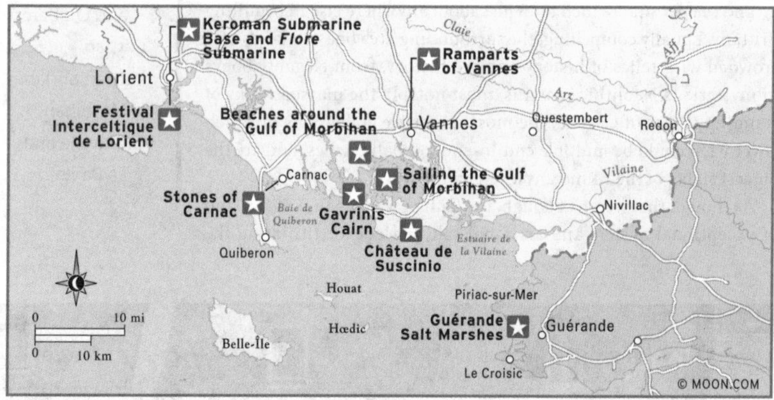

★ **Beaches around the Gulf of Morbihan:** With long stretches of sandy coastline, there's a beach for everyone here (page 340).

★ **Keroman Submarine Base and the *Flore* Submarine:** Take a fascinating look at Brittany's naval wartime past at this WWII-era German U-boat base that is now home to a French submarine from the 1960s, which is open to the public (page 344).

★ **Festival Interceltique de Lorient:** Join in the good cheer and raucous fun at the largest and most rollicking festival dedicated to Celtic culture on the planet (page 345).

★ **Stones of Carnac:** Wander among the hundreds upon hundreds of Neolithic standing stones, the largest collection of its kind anywhere in the world, and feel their mystic power (page 364).

★ **Ramparts of Vannes:** Walk atop these perfectly preserved medieval walls of one of the Gulf's most important towns (page 373).

★ **Gavrinis Cairn:** This ancient burial mound is home to some of the best Neolithic carvings in Brittany (page 383).

★ **Château de Suscinio:** Visit this fairytale castle and former residence of the Dukes of Brittany and imagine the days gone by (page 385).

★ **Sailing the Gulf of Morbihan:** The natural harbor and its islands are best explored from the water, with the sun warming your face and the fresh salty air filling your lungs (page 386).

★ **Guérande Salt Marshes:** This spectacular artificially constructed landscape is where much of Brittany's famous salt is produced. Don't leave without a taste (page 389).

palate, and warm microclimates, which make for bluer skies and higher temperatures than many other places this far north. No wonder it can get crowded in the high season—fortunately there's no scarcity in accommodations, which come in all shapes and sizes, sure to meet various budgets and tastes.

With such a density of sights and activities, a holiday around the Gulf of Morbihan can be different things to different people. Boating enthusiasts can while away days exploring its waters, and those in search of luxury treatment can indulge in many seawater spas. For people after a party, the small town of Lorient holds one of the biggest fairs in all of France, the Festival Interceltique de Lorient, which lasts almost two weeks every August and draws various Celtic cultures from around the world. Bagpipe and cider enthusiasts could hardly ask for anything more!

ORIENTATION

The Gulf of Morbihan looks like a hole punched out of the southern Breton coastline. It is roughly 44 square miles (114 square kilometers), and 13 miles (21 kilometers) across at its widest point. It is dotted by rocks and islands, the two largest of which are the Ile-aux-Moines and the Ile-d'Arz; most of the rest are in private hands and cannot be visited. The passage linking the gulf to the ocean is in its southwest, and it's important to note that there is no regular car ferry bridging this gap. The walled town of Vannes, sits just up from the Gulf's northern shore.

Follow the arterial N165 west of Vannes to Auray, then split south on the D768, which carries on all the way down to the narrow strip of land that is the Quiberon peninsula. This leads into the Atlantic, with Belle-Ile directly below it, like the oversized point to a geological exclamation mark.

Farther west still of Auray along the N165 is the town of Lorient (about 35 miles/56 kilometers west of Vannes in total), which sits on the western bank of the mouth of the Blavet River.

East of Vannes along the N165, then south along the coast on the D774, a total of about 40 miles (64 kilometers), sit Guérande and the restort town of La Baule.

PLANNING YOUR TIME

With so much to see and in such a compact area, the Gulf of Morbihan can tempt travelers to try and fit everything into a single visit: boat tours, hikes, Neolithic sightseeing, and so forth. While it is true that dedicated tourists might be able to tick most of Morbihan's boxes without totally exhausting themselves, such a dedication to planned activity almost negates the magic of the place.

For while the stones at Carnac are truly unmissable, and should be given at least a day to explore in full, perhaps the Gulf's greatest asset is that you could almost set out in any direction with no plans beyond a picnic basket and be sure to stumble across something worth seeing: a beach to pause on, or a charming local event to experience. Such a travel strategy also fits well with the laid-back atmosphere of the region. Be prepared to let incidental encounters guide you around, and welcome being pleasantly surprised.

All this said, trips to the offshore islands, particularly Belle-Île, are very much their own thing, and should be planned accordingly. Indeed, Belle-Île, Brittany's largest island, is easily big enough to accommodate a holiday all of its own. Since there's no way of crossing the harbor mouth by car, for these outings advanced planning only helps.

It's also hard to really say you've been to the Gulf of Morbihan if you haven't spent at least some time on its waters. There are plenty of boat tours to help accomplish this; those that include lunch are the most recommended. When considering how you'd like to experience this lovely region, do rank a water experience at the top of your list.

Previous: Port of Sauzon at Belle-Île; the French submarine, *Flore,* at the Keroman Submarine Base in Lorient; view of Vannes' ramparts, garden, and tower

Gulf of Morbihan

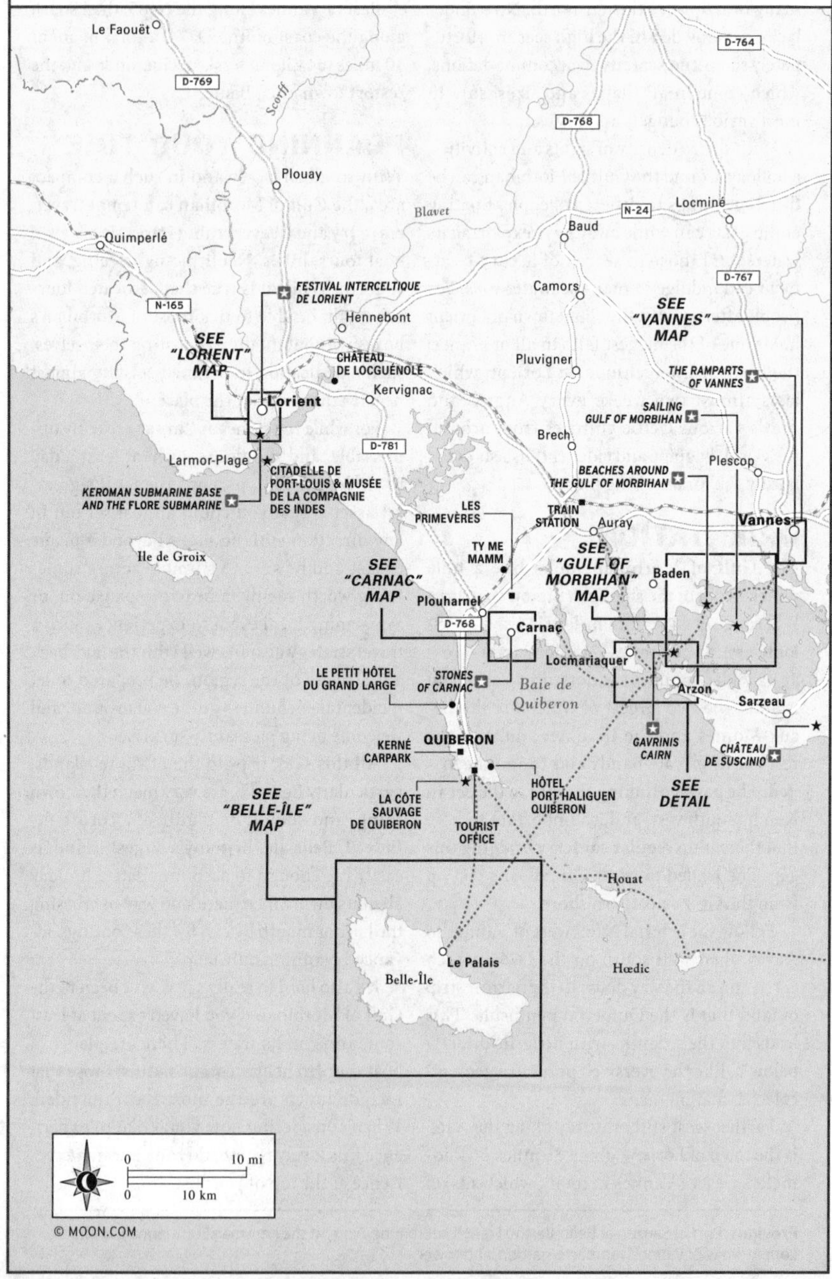

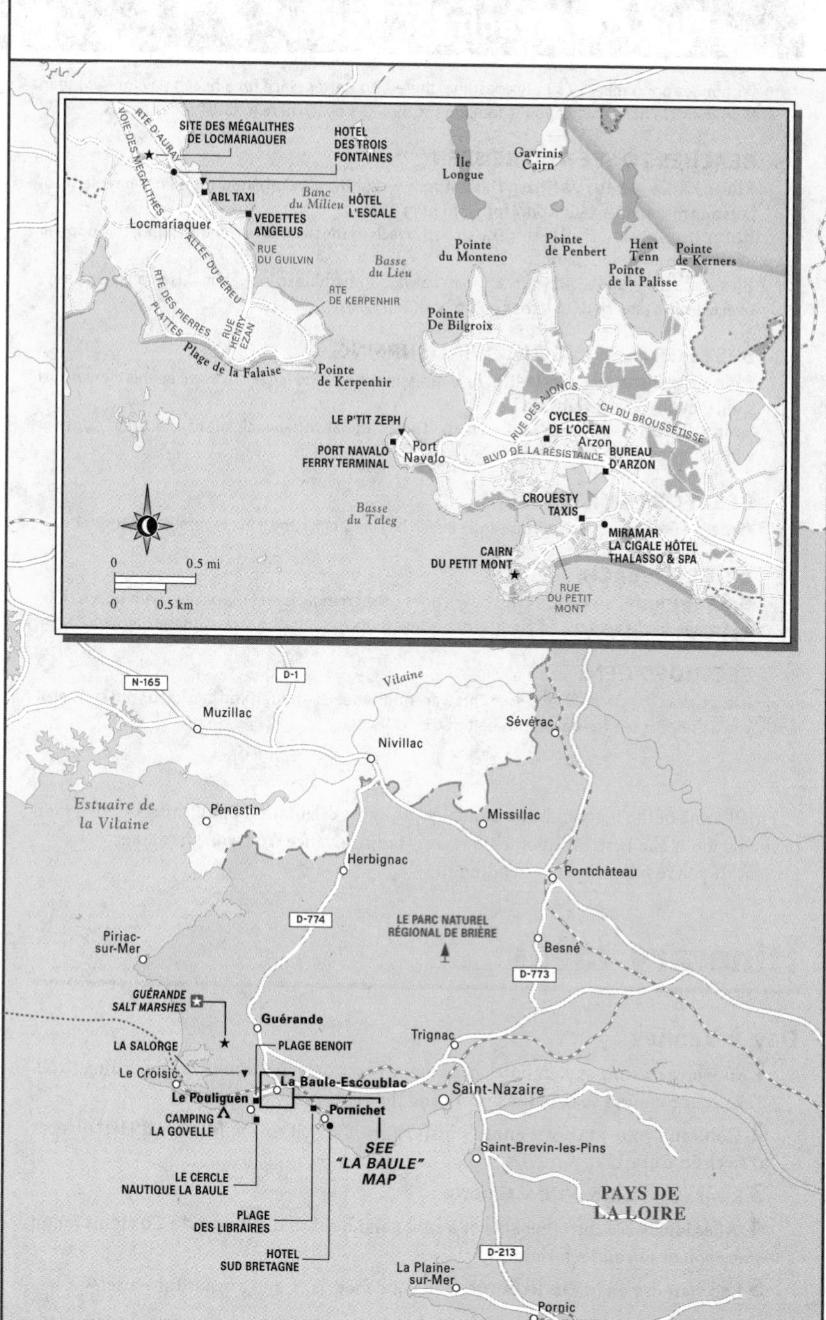
SITE DES MÉGALITHES DE LOCMARIAQUER
HOTEL DES TROIS FONTAINES
RTE D'AURAY
VOIE DES MÉGALITHES
ABL TAXI
HÔTEL L'ESCALE
VEDETTES ANGELUS
Banc du Milieu
Locmariaquer
RUE DU GUILVIN
ALLÉE DU BEREU
RTE DES PIERRES PLATTES
RUE HENRY EZAN
RTE DE KERPENHIR
Plage de la Falaise
Pointe de Kerpenhir
Île Longue
Gavrinis Cairn
Basse du Lieu
Pointe du Monteno
Pointe de Penbert
Hent Tenn
Pointe de Kerners
Pointe de la Palisse
Pointe De Bilgroix
RUE DES AJONCS
CH DU BROUSSETISSE
LE P'TIT ZEPH
PORT NAVALO FERRY TERMINAL
Port Navalo
CYCLES DE L'OCEAN
Arzon
BLVD DE LA RÉSISTANCE
BUREAU D'ARZON
CROUESTY TAXIS
MIRAMAR LA CIGALE HÔTEL THALASSO & SPA
Basse du Taleg
CAIRN DU PETIT MONT
RUE DU PETIT MONT
0 0.5 mi
0 0.5 km
N-165
D-1
Vilaine
Muzillac
Sévérac
Nivillac
Estuaire de la Vilaine
Pénestin
Missillac
Herbignac
Pontchâteau
D-774
LE PARC NATUREL RÉGIONAL DE BRIÈRE
Piriac-sur-Mer
Besné
D-773
GUÉRANDE SALT MARSHES
Guérande
LA SALORGE
PLAGE BENOIT
Trignac
Le Croisic
La Baule-Escoublac
Saint-Nazaire
Le Pouliguen
Pornichet
CAMPING LA GOVELLE
SEE "LA BAULE" MAP
Saint-Brevin-les-Pins
LE CERCLE NAUTIQUE LA BAULE
PAYS DE LA LOIRE
PLAGE DES LIBRAIRES
HOTEL SUD BRETAGNE
D-213
La Plaine-sur-Mer
Pornic

★ Find the Beach for You

With miles upon miles of sandy coastline, there's no better place for a beach day (or two) than Morbihan. No matter what you're looking for, there's a beach here to satisfy your needs.

BEACHES TO SEE AND BE SEEN

Plage de Conleau, Vannes: This hot spot in slightly more urban surroundings has plenty of bars and restaurants, plus a pool for swimming.

Ramonet Beach, Belle-Île: The closest beach to the main town on the island, this popular beach is hip and happening.

Plage de la Falaise, Île-d'Arz: There's always something to look at on this popular and busy beach, from oyster beds to ferries going back and forth.

BEST FOR SURFING AND WINDSURFING

Plage du Donnant, Belle-Île: Its impressive dunes and large waves make this a great surf spot, though it can get crowded.

Saint Colomban Beach, Carnac: The winds at this beach make it a great spot for windsurfers.

BEST FOR FAMILIES

Grande Plage, Carnac: This sandy beach has lifeguards and a lively, family-friendly vibe.

BIGGEST BEACH

Grande Plage, La Baule: This beach goes on seemingly forever, is packed with beach clubs and water-sports centers, and is one of the best spots to sunbathe and swim the day away.

SECLUDED GEM

Plage du Dotchot, Belle-Île: This wild, nudist beach (though you can keep your suits on if you'd prefer) is hidden away and sheltered by cliffs.

Finally, one of the biggest draws annually to the region is the Festival Interceltique de Lorient. If you're planning on attending the August celebration of all things Celtic, plan far in advance. You won't be alone.

Itinerary Ideas

Day 1: Vannes

1 After breakfasting at your hotel, head to the **ramparts** in **Vannes** for a morning stroll. Take your time and soak in the history and the views of the old town.

2 Continue your tour of Vannes's history with a visit to the **Musée d'Histoire et d'Archéologie.**

3 Savor a light lunch at **L'îlot Galette.**

4 After lunch, see the other side of Vannes and head to the **Plage de Conleau** for an afternoon of sun and relaxation.

5 End your day on **le Piano Barge** with good food, jazz, and a beautiful sunset.

Itinerary Ideas

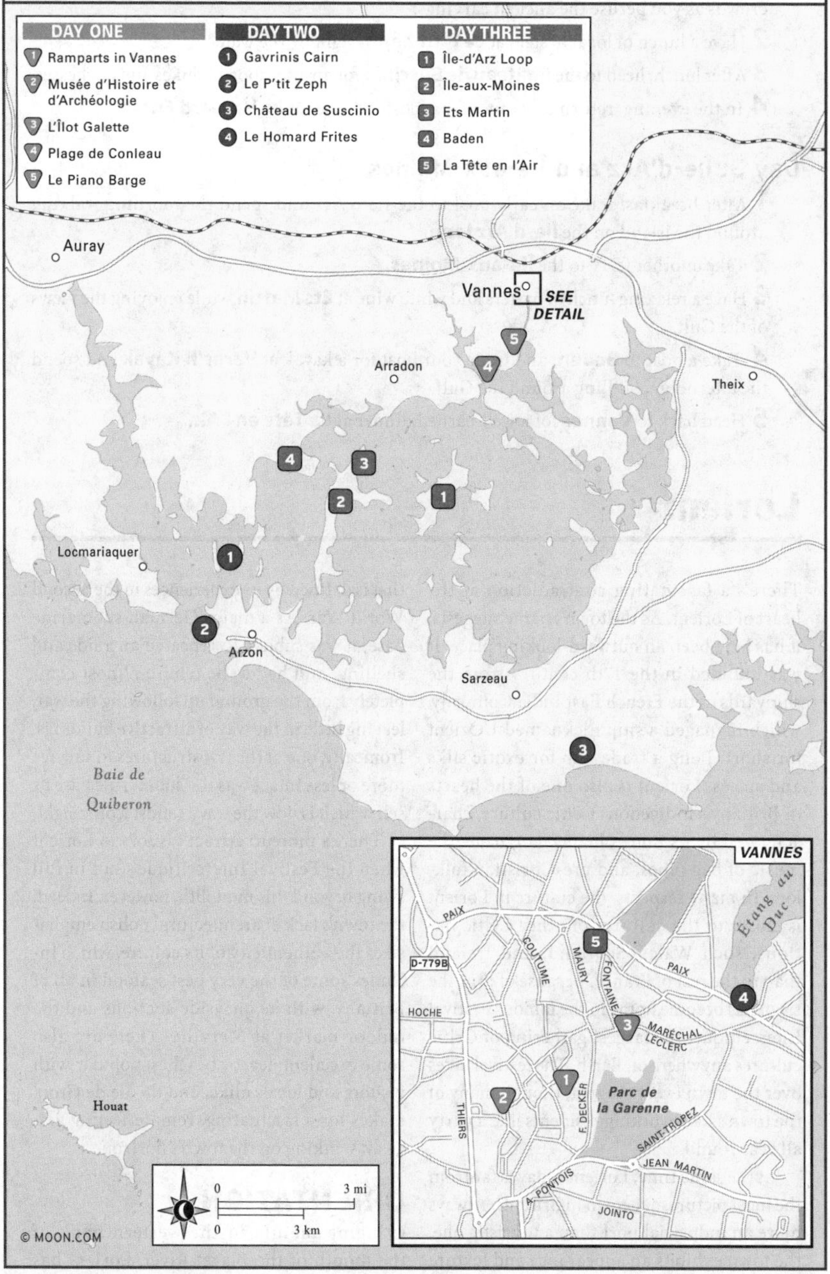

DAY ONE

1. Ramparts in Vannes
2. Musée d'Histoire et d'Archéologie
3. L'Îlot Galette
4. Plage de Conleau
5. Le Piano Barge

DAY TWO

1. Gavrinis Cairn
2. Le P'tit Zeph
3. Château de Suscinio
4. Le Homard Frites

DAY THREE

1. Île-d'Arz Loop
2. Île-aux-Moines
3. Ets Martin
4. Baden
5. La Tête en l'Air

Auray
Vannes
SEE DETAIL
Arradon
Theix
Locmariaquer
Arzon
Sarzeau
Baie de Quiberon
Houat
0 3 mi
0 3 km
© MOON.COM

VANNES
PAIX
D-779B
COUTUME
MAURY
FONTAINE
Étang au Duc
HOCHE
MARECHAL LECLERC
THIERS
F. DECKER
Parc de la Garenne
SAINT-TROPEZ
JEAN MARTIN
A. PONTOIS
JOINTO

Day 2: Around the Gulf

1 Head out bright and early to the first tour of the day of the **Gavrinis Cairn,** to avoid the crowds as you peruse the ancient carvings.

2 Have a lunch of local oysters at **Le P'tit Zeph,** right by the water.

3 After lunch, head to the **Château de Suscinio** for an afternoon of dukes and duchesses.

4 In the evening, return to Vannes for a lobster dinner at **Le Homard Frites.**

Day 3: Île-d'Arz and Île-aux-Moines

1 After breakfast, take an early boat to the Île-d'Arz and spend the morning walking around the island on the **Île-d'Arz loop.**

2 Take another ferry to the **Île-aux-Moines.**

3 Have a relaxing lunch of oysters and white wine at **Ets Martin** while enjoying the views of the Gulf.

4 Take a boat to **Baden,** and trade your boat for a kayak at **Varec'h Kayak** and spend the afternoon paddling around the Gulf.

5 Head back to **Vannes** for a well-earned dinner at **La Tête en l'Air.**

Lorient

There's a fascinating contradiction at the heart of Lorient. As the town's name suggests, it has long been an outward-looking place: It was founded in the 17th century from the shipyards of the French East India Company, which managed a ship nicknamed L'Orient for short. Long a trade hub for exotic silks and spices, Lorient is also one of the hearts of Brittany's indigenous Celtic culture, characterized by its non-romance language, the music of bag pipes, and pre-Christian folklore. In many respects, the culture in Lorient is closer to the cultures of other Celtic nations, such Wales, Scotland, and Ireland than to the rest of France. Because of this, the town has become home to the famous Festival Interceltique, the largest gathering of Celtic cultures anywhere on Earth. The festival takes over the town every August, though many of the town's hardworking residents like a party all year round.

At the same time, Lorient today is far from the most picturesque town in Brittany. Always more an industrial port than a touristic one, the town exhibits an appearance and texture that is defined by its experiences in the Second World War. As a major German submarine base, it was subject to repeated air raids and shelling, and had to be rebuilt almost completely from the ground up following the war, leaving little in the way of attractive buildings. Ironically, one of the few structures to survive more or less intact was the submarine base itself, which is now the town's most iconic sight.

There's more to attract visitors to Lorient when the Festival Interceltique's not in full swing beyond this monolith, however. Indeed, the town's lack of architectural polish emphasizes the authenticity of its culture, which includes some of the very best seafood in all of Brittany, with its quayside auctions and the indoor market at Merville. There are also some excellent nearby beaches, popular with visitors and locals alike, and the Île de Groix makes for a fascinating, remote-feeling getaway, winking on the town's horizon.

ORIENTATION

Clinging mainly to the western bank of the mouth of the Blavet River, Lorient has

Lorient

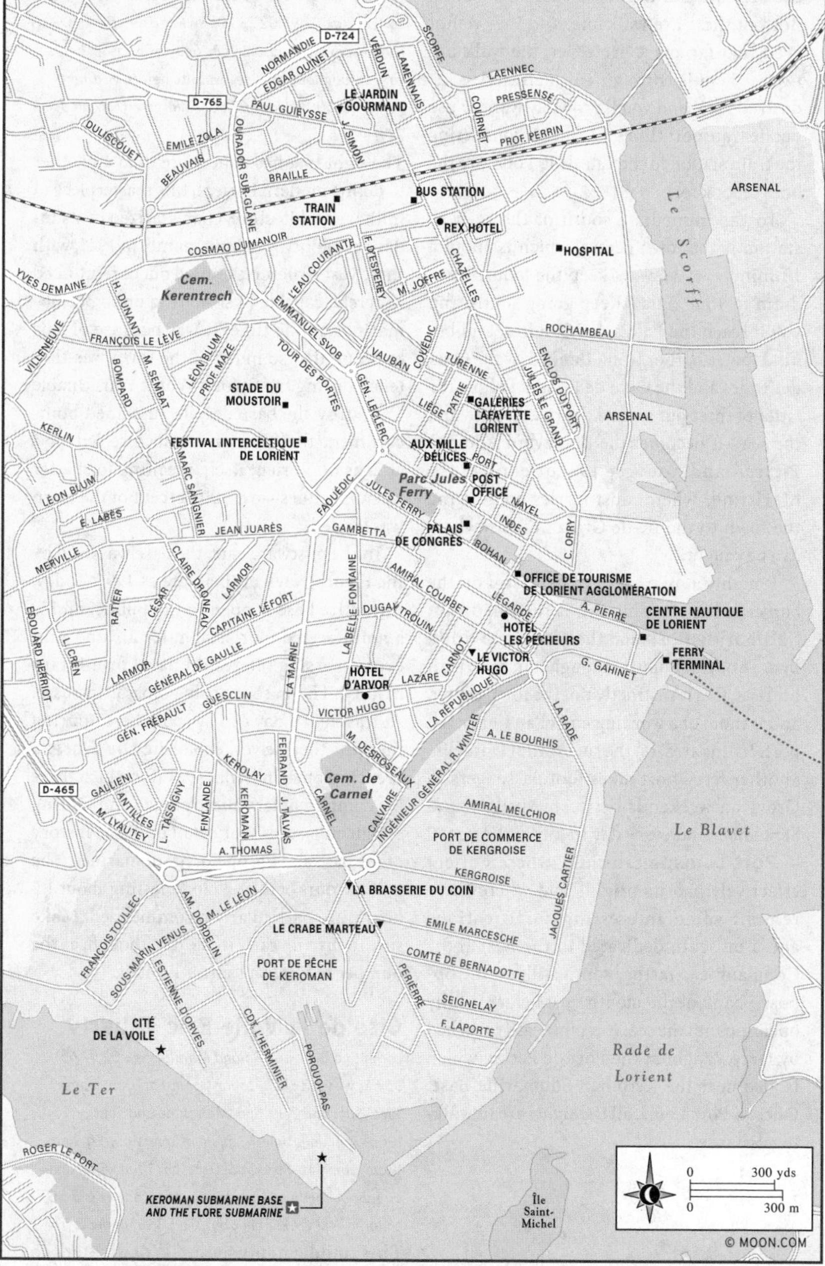
D-724
NORMANDIE
EDGAR QUINET
VERDUN
LAMENNAIS
SCORFF
LAENNEC
PRESSENSÉ
COURNET
PROF. PERRIN
D-765
PAUL GUIEYSSE
LE JARDIN GOURMAND
J. SIMON
DULISCOUET
EMILE ZOLA
BEAUVAIS
OURADOR SUR-GLANE
BRAILLE
BUS STATION
TRAIN STATION
REX HOTEL
HOSPITAL
ARSENAL
Le Scorff
COSMAO DUMANOIR
L'EAU COURANTE
F. D'ESPEREY
CHAZELLES
M. JOFFRE
YVES DEMAINE
H. DUNANT
Cem. Kerentrech
EMMANUEL SVOB
ROCHAMBEAU
VILLENEUVE
FRANÇOIS LE LÈVE
LÉON BLUM
M. SEMBAT
PROF. MAZE
TOUR DES PORTES
VAUBAN
COUÉDIC
TURENNE
ENCLOS DU PORT
JULES LE GRAND
BOMPARD
STADE DU MOUSTOIR
GÉN. LECLERC
PATRIE
LIÈGE
GALERIES LAFAYETTE LORIENT
ARSENAL
KERLIN
FESTIVAL INTERCELTIQUE DE LORIENT
MARC SANGNIER
AUX MILLE DÉLICES
PORT
Parc Jules Ferry
POST OFFICE
FAUDÉDIC
JULES FERRY
NAYEL
LÉON BLUM
E. LABÈS
INDES
C. ORRY
JEAN JUARÈS
GAMBETTA
PALAIS DE CONGRÈS
BOHAN
MERVILLE
CLAIRE DRONEAU
LARMOR
AMIRAL COURBET
OFFICE DE TOURISME DE LORIENT AGGLOMÉRATION
CÉSAR
RATIER
CAPITAINE LEFORT
LA BELLE FONTAINE
DUGAY TROUIN
LÉGARDE
A. PIERRE
CENTRE NAUTIQUE DE LORIENT
HOTEL LES PÊCHEURS
EDOUARD HERRIOT
L. CREN
LARMOR
GÉNÉRAL DE GAULLE
LA MARNE
CARNOT
LE VICTOR HUGO
FERRY TERMINAL
G. GAHINET
HÔTEL D'ARVOR
LAZARE CARNOT
GÉN. FRÉBAULT
GUESCLIN
VICTOR HUGO
LA RÉPUBLIQUE
LA RADE
INGÉNIEUR GÉNÉRAL R. WINTER
A. LE BOURHIS
KEROLAY
FERRAND
M. DESROSEAUX
Cem. de Carnel
D-465
GALLIENI
ANTILLES
M. LYAUTEY
L. TASSIGNY
FINLANDE
KEROMAN
J. TALVAS
CARNEL
CALVAIRE
AMIRAL MELCHIOR
Le Blavet
A. THOMAS
PORT DE COMMERCE DE KERGROISE
JACQUES CARTIER
KERGROISE
LA BRASSERIE DU COIN
FRANCOISTOULLEC
AM. DORDELIN
M. LE LÉON
SOUS-MARIN VENUS
LE CRABE MARTEAU
EMILE MARCESCHE
COMTÉ DE BERNADOTTE
PORT DE PÊCHE DE KEROMAN
ESTIENNE D'ORVES
PERIÈRRE
SEIGNELAY
CITÉ DE LA VOILE
CDT. L'HERMINIER
PORQUOI PAS
F. LAPORTE
Rade de Lorient
Le Ter
ROGER LE PORT
KEROMAN SUBMARINE BASE AND THE FLORE SUBMARINE
Île Saint-Michel
0
300 yds
0
300 m
© MOON.COM

basically two key areas where visitors are likely to find themselves: the town center and the area around Keroman submarine base. Both of these are walkable, and they're not even that far apart. However, the walk between them is through an unattractive industrial area, and you'll probably want to use public transport (lines T2 and 13, connecting the train station to the Cité de la Voile, are the ones to look for).

To the immediate south of the railway station is the town center, which is about a 10-minute walk away (keep the football stadium to your right). Keep going south, and you'll reach the Palais des Congrès, and behind that, a harbor front, flanked by the Quai des Indes and the Quai de Rohan. Follow the latter of these out toward the river mouth and the sea—it becomes the Boulevard Adolphe Pierre—and you get to Lorient's **Gare Maritime,** where most ferries connecting the town to the Île de Groix and elsewhere can be caught.

Roughly a mile south of here, still on the banks of the river mouth, is the **Keroman Submarine Base** and the **Cite de la Voile Éric Tabarly.** Popular though it may be with tourists, this is distinctly not the town center, and is more of a working end of an industrial port. In this area, on the rue Amiral Dordelin, another ferry port takes foot passengers to Groix on weekends between April 20 and September and every day in July and August.

Port-Louis, meanwhile, where Lorient effectively had its origins and where there remain some interesting fortifications and a museum dedicated to the East India Company, sits farther south still, on the opposite bank of the mouth, just before it fully opens up into the sea. It is most easily reached by ferry, caught at the Port de Peche, which is also near the Keroman Submarine Base. Once in Port-Louis, all the sights are in walking distance.

SIGHTS

★ Keroman Submarine Base and the *Flore* Submarine

Lorient; tel. 02 97 02 23 29; www.la-flore.fr; 10am-8pm high season, 2pm-6pm low season, hours vary throughout year, see website before visiting; adults €9.50, reduced €7.60, children 7-17 €7, under 7 Free

The sight that has done more than any other to define modern Lorient, this masterpiece of military architecture, characterized by its indestructability, was built mainly in 1941, with three vast structures crafted out of reinforced concrete, capable of sheltering up to 30 submarines at one time. It was because of this building that so much of the town was flattened during the Second World War. Unable to destroy the base despite sustained bombardment, the Allies eventually directed their attacks on Lorient itself, meaning to shatter its supply lines—over 90 percent of the town was leveled.

In the postwar years, the base was used by the French Navy until as late as 1997. Today, the entire base is open to the public, and is a multifaceted tourist sight for anyone with even a passing interest in naval or military history. The base is truly colossal in scale. At least half a day can be spent here, touring the pens themselves, exploring **the *Flore,*** a French submarine from 1961 (for which there is a complimentary audio guide), and visiting on-site museums that detail both the history of the base and life on board submarines. The guided tours of the K3 block, lasting about 1.5 hours, are particularly recommended. Make sure to turn up early in the day, though, as the number of English tours is limited.

Cité de la Voile Éric Tabarly

Lorient La Base, rue Roland Morillot; tel. 02 97 65 56 56; www.citevoile-tabarly.com/en; 10am-6pm Tues.-Sun. and 2pm-6pm Mon. June and Sept., 10am-7pm daily July-Aug., 2pm-6pm Mon.-Fri. and 10am-6pm Sat.-Sun. Oct.-Dec. (but 10am-6pm daily on school holidays), closed Jan.-May; adults €12.50, children 7-17 €9.30, children 3-6 €3.10, under 3 free

This modern museum is dedicated to

exploring the practicalities and history of sailing through interactive, multimedia exhibits. Named after the record-breaking French yachtsman Éric Tabarly, the museum was renovated as recently as 2015 at the cost of €2.2 million. Exhibits include videos on boat and sail design and primer displays explaining the basics of how to sail. Aspiring boaters can take advantage of hands-on chances to learn how to steer a yacht. There's enough to do here, even for a non-sailor, to keep you busy at least a couple of hours.

Île de Groix

Île de Groix; tel. 02 97 84 78 00 (tourist office); www.groix.fr

A 45-minute ferry ride from the mainland, the Île de Groix is Brittany's second-largest island and home to a few small towns. It's a great place for bird-watching, with a wide variety of seabirds dropping in at different times of the year on the grass-covered cliffs of Pen Men-Beg Melen. Distinct from the mainland right down to its geological make-up—more than 60 different types of minerals can be found here—it's a place of contrasts, with high cliffs to its north and sandy beaches to the south. It's well worth dropping by for at least a day, if not passing a whole holiday here.

Perhaps Groix's most distinguishing feature, according to the islanders anyway, is that it is home to the only convex beach (i.e., one that bulges into the ocean, rather than a bay) anywhere in Europe, Les Grands Sables. This peculiar feature is manipulated by the changing tides and has actually been moved by sea currents a third of a mile (half a kilometer) west over the last 15 years.

Previously France's main center for tuna fishing (note the tuna fish decorating the church belltower in the island's largest village), Groix now gets most of its income from tourism. As with most Breton islands, it's best explored by bicycle, with several hire companies immediately evident the moment you step off the boat—all offer similar rates (around €11 a day).

Citadelle de Port-Louis and Musée de la Compagnie des Indes

Avenue du Fort de l'Aigle, Port-Louis; tel. 02 97 82 56 72; www.musee-marine.fr/port-louis; 10am-6:30pm daily May-Aug., 10am6:30pm daily Sept., 1:30pm-6pm Wed.-Mon.Oct.-Apr.; adults €8, reduced €6.30

Another heavily fortified naval base instrumental to Lorient's history, the Citadelle de Port-Louis effectively led to the town's formation. Originally built by the Spanish during the 16th century, it later changed hands and was heavily fortified by the French. Eventually it became the headquarters of the French East India Company, and was used to protect its ship-building yards, which subsequently led to the founding (and naming) of Lorient itself. The current structure is a fascinating piece of military engineering from a previous age, characterized by star-like fortifications from which there are excellent views back across to Lorient and of the sea. It's a great place, especially for kids, to imagine themselves defending the harbor entrance, there are even a few rusting old canons still bristling from its battlements. For those wanting to understand more, the fortress is now home to a museum dedicated to the history of that company as well as Lorient itself. Exhibits consist mainly of models and maps, though there's very little in English. It's seldom too overrun by visitors and you should expect a visit to take an hour or so of your time.

FESTIVALS AND EVENTS

★ FESTIVAL INTERCELTIQUE DE LORIENT

Various locations; tel. 02 97 21 24 29; www.festival-interceltique.bzh; Aug. 2-Aug.11

A week-long celebration of Celtic culture and one of the biggest festivals in France, the Festival Interceltique de Lorient in August attracts participants from Celtic communities all over the world—from Scotland to Galicia and beyond. During its length, all of Lorient is infected by its spirit. The streets wail day

1

2

to night with the sound of bagpipes, the air smells of cider, and traditional costumes abound.

Events take place across the city, with the largest ones being staged in the town's **Parc du Moustoir** football stadium. Things are kicked off with a traditional seafood supper served in the harbor district and devoured to the sounds of old sailor's songs. Not to be missed after that is the Grand Parade of Celtic Nations, in which over 3,500 musicians from all different backgrounds march and play their way through the city streets.

There are also plenty of unofficial side events, from sailing races to music workshops and concerts that thrum from Lorient's bars and restaurants. The general atmosphere is one of excess, tinged with a slight madness, and the town is entirely overrun for the festival's duration. With that in mind, accomodations can be tricky to find during this period, so be sure to book up early if you can. Also, attending for the whole length of the festival is likely more partying (and certainly more bagpipes) than most people really need. Being there for around three days is probably enough, with the beginning and the weekends its liveliest and most hectic times.

SHOPPING

AUX MILLE DÉLICES

41 rue du Port, Lorient; tel. 02 97 21 84 84; www.auxmilledelices.fr; 2pm-7pm Mon., 10am-7pm Tues.-Fri., 10am-1pm and 2pm-7pm Sat.

Though only founded in 1998, this store specializing in spices and other exotic produce has definite links with Lorient's more distant past. Given the town sprung up because of the French East India Company, the spice trade has been big here for almost 400 years. Aux Mille Délices is simply the latest in a long line of establishments to take advantage of that fact. It's a great place to stock up on nonperishable foodstuffs to take home for friends and family, who may never have guessed that such exotic flavors should play a part in Breton culture. For those with more European tastes, a number of homegrown preserves also line its wooden shelves.

1: the Keroman Submarine Base **2:** Île de Groix, Brittany

SPORTS AND RECREATION

Water Sports

CENTRE NAUTIQUE DE LORIENT

Quai Eric Tabarly, Lorient; tel. 02 97 84 81 30; www.cnlorient.org; 9am-1pm Tues., Wed., and Sat., 10am-1pm and 2pm-6pm Thurs. and Fri..; from €20 for a stand-up paddleboard lesson to €200+ for sailing courses

Centrally located and using Lorient's busy harbor for many of its activities, this is one of the most "urban" water-sports clubs in Brittany. It offers a full range of lessons from stand-up paddle boarding to sailing, though it is more set up to deal with locals and visitors returning year after year than it is casual tourists. It boasts a strong community presence and puts on lots of events, though with few concessions to English-speakers; getting involved with this club takes a degree of confidence. If you're planning on being in Lorient for a while, however, you'll reap rewards.

Spectator Sports

STADE DU MOUSTOIR

Rue du Tour des Portes, Lorient; tel. 07 83 24 48 13; billetterie.fclweb.fr; open match and event days Aug.-May; match tickets from €5

The central location of this stadium, home to FC Lorient, makes it a large part of life in the town. As accessible and friendly a place to experience top-flight French soccer as you're likely to find anywhere in Brittany, it's got a capacity of just over 18,000 people, and if you're here on match day, joining the crowds is a great cultural experience, even if you're not too interested by the sport itself (there should always be a few tickets stiil available on match days). Other events are also held here throughout the year, most notably during the inter-Celtic festival, when large-scale parades and bagpipe displays take place throughout the week. You can also shop in the **FC Lorient**

Boutique (10am-12pm and 2pm-6:30pm Tues.-Sat.).

FOOD

Local Cuisine

LE JARDIN GOURMAND

46 rue Jules Simon, Lorient; tel. 02 97 64 17 24; www.tropmad.com; 12:15pm-1:30pm and 7:30pm-9:30pm Wed.-Sat.; 12:15pm-1:30pm Sun.; mains €27, menu €46

This eccentric, excellent restaurant has been serving the people of Lorient since 1990. Founded by husband-and-wife team Nathalie and Arnaud Beauvais, Le Jardin Gourmand is dedicated to Breton flavors from fresh-as-can-be seafood to crepes, which are not often seen in such a refined setting, to arranging food beautifully on your plate. You can even take the experience home with you in the form of the various Trop Mad recipe books associated with the restaurant and by attending their cooking lessons, in French, starting at €75. And while this may sound like a ploy to lure in tourists, the restaurant remains popular with visitors and locals alike.

LE VICTOR HUGO

38 rue Lazare Carnot, Lorient; tel. 02 97 64 26 54; http://restaurantlevictorhugo.com; lunchtimes and evenings Tues.-Sat.; lunch menu €19, evening menus €30.50-38

Traditional and a little old-fashioned (it feels a bit stuck in the 1980s), this restaurant nevertheless offers very tasty, local food with friendly service. The scallops are a definite highlight. They are unafraid to go rich with their sauces, so come with a big appetite, or for a holiday blowout.

LE CRABE MARTEAU

34 avenue de la Perrière, Lorient; tel. 02 97 59 40 71; http://crabemarteau.fr; 12pm-2pm and 7pm-10pm Tues.-Sat.; mains €17-22

Dedicated to crabs and other crustaceans, this fun restaurant is actually part of a small chain, though it retains plenty of idiosyncratic vibes, many of which give it a New England-like feel. Tablecloths are made from that day's newspaper, while the food comes with wooden mallets to crack your way in and zingy homemade condiments. You'll find unpretentious good fun for a family evening, provided of course that shellfish is to everyone's taste—there's not much else on the menu.

Budget Options

LA BRASSERIE DU COIN

9 avenue de la Perrière, Lorient; tel. 02 97 37 10 68; 10am-9:30pm Mon.-Sat.; menus €13.50-19

It may not look like much from the outside, and the interior is some distance from what most people would consider charming, with plastic chairs and a grey-pink color scheme, but this restaurant is an excellent example of the adage that beauty is more than skin deep. If you're on a real budget but still want to try Breton cuisine beyond the humble crepe, this is a great choice. The full bevy of local seafood flavors (as well as some other very good terrestrial dishes) is on offer here; it's a great place to snap up a crab for almost half the price as you'll find elsewhere.

ACCOMMODATIONS

Under €50

HÔTEL LES PECHEURS

7 rue Jean Lagarde, Lorient; tel. 02 97 21 19 24; www.hotel-lespecheurs.com; from €39 d

Right in the center of town, this is a great-value budget hotel, which comes with plenty of amenities that you'd usually expect at a significantly higher price bracket. There's a terrace, plus a restaurant and bar on-site. Interiors may be basic and dominated by cheap plastic materials, but they're also stylish enough to feel pleasantly up-to-date. Yes, the cheaper rooms do have shared bathroom and toilet facilities, but that's a small price to pay for such a small price! There's free WiFi throughout, and if you pay a little extra you can even find rooms with balconies.

HÔTEL D'ARVOR

104 rue Lazare Carnot, Lorient; tel. 02 97 21 07 55; www.hotel-darvor-lorient.com; from €47 d

This basic but perfectly servicable hotel

dates back to 1936. Don't expect somewhere quaint and old-fashioned, though. Most of the rooms are now decked out with modern fittings rather than period details. Nevertheless, there's a family-friendly atmosphere to the place that connects to Lorient's past, and it's very reasonable. All rooms have en suite showers and TVs, though some of the cheapest mean sharing a toilet. WiFi is available throughout, and continental breakfast is served Monday-Saturday in a light-filled dining room and terrace.

€50-100

REX HÔTEL

28 cours de Chazelles, Lorient; tel. 02 97 64 25 60;, from €77 d

A decent three-star establishment with comfortable, clean rooms. The interior design may be a little uninspired, with no real centralizing "theme" to speak of, but the rooms are perfectly serviceable for a couple of nights, and there's a pleasant communal lounge with some welcoming leather chairs to unwind in after a long day. All rooms have TVs and en suite bathrooms, and there is WiFi available throughout the building. Well located close to Lorient's center, it's also on a surprisingly quiet road and boasts an inside courtyard and picnic area. Continental breakfast is available on-site for an added €11.

€100-200

CHÂTEAU DE LOCGUÉNOLÉ

Locguenole, Kervignac; tel. 02 97 76 76 76; www.chateau-de-locguenole.com; from €150 d

A little outside of Lorient, this destination hotel is situated over an 18th- and 19th-century complex of buildings on the shores of Le Blavet river mouth. Its charming rooms remain fitted with largely period detail, with real dedication given to communal spaces that feel like stepping back in time. A particular mention goes to its period flooring, so often overlooked by such establishments, but that here completes the illusion of a hotel from another age (an illusion happily broken by the TVs, en suite bathrooms, and free WiFi in every room). The on-site restaurant offers a superb formal dining experience based around local Breton flavors worth a trip all of its own (expect a whole meal to cost between €40-100).

INFORMATION AND SERVICES

Tourist Information

OFFICE DE TOURISME DE LORIENT AGGLOMÉRATION

Quai de Rohan, Lorient; tel. 02 97 84 78 00; www.lorientbretagnesudtourisme.fr; 10am-12pm and 2pm-5pm Mon.-Sat.

Located in central Lorient along the quay, this is the main office of a well-connected and organized tourist network with several outposts around Lorient and one on the Île-de-Groix. Unusual for France, this is great for planning and executing a trip around the whole Lorient region. Used to large numbers of tourists, especially during the Celtic festival, English is widely spoken here.

Post Office

9 quai des Indes, Lorient; tel. 36 31; 8:30am-6pm Mon.-Fr. (closed 11:45am-2pm Tues.), 8:30am-12pm Sat.

The most central of Lorient's many post offices. Sending or receiving mail in France can seem intimidating at first, but the system is actually very well run, and though English is seldom spoken by staff, a color-coded system of different parcel types makes it possible to muscle through with a bit of determination. If you're picking up mail, be sure to bring a passport. Picking up someone else's mail for them, meanwhile, is almost impossible unless they've specified this as a plan to the post office before sending.

Medical Services

HOPITAL DU SCORFF

5 avenue Choiseul, Lorient; tel. 02 97 06 90 90; www.chbs.fr; emergency room open 24 hours

This general hospital to the northeast of town has a 24-hour emergency department. English is not officially spoken, but many doctors in

France are proficient with the language, so you should find someone with whom you can communicate. Be aware that things can get very busy here during the Celtic festival, so any comparatively minor injuries may result in a long wait.

TRANSPORTATION

By Car

Lorient is a major town and well-connected by roads to the north, south, and west. From Paris (total 310 miles/499 kilometers, 5 hours), first take the A11 to Le Mans and then the A81 to Rennes; up to Rennes, there are toll charges on the roads costing around €25. From Rennes (100 miles/160 kilometers 1.75 hours), it's the N24 all the way.

The journey from Nantes (100 miles/160 kilometers, 2 hours) is a straight shot northwest along the N165. Travelers from Carnac (30 miles/48 kilometers, 40 minutes) will also use this road.

Coming from the opposite direction, from Brest (80 miles/128 kilometers, 1.5 hours) and from Lorient's close-by neighbor Quimper (40 miles/64 kilometers, 45 minutes), take the N165.

There is plenty of free parking for short stays in central Lorient, with several underground parking lots if you want something more secure or longer-term. Longer stays can be negotiated for as little as €25 for a week. Among the most central of these parking lots is the **Parking Place d'Armes** (rue de l'Enclos du Port, tel. 02 97 02 23 21).

By Train

Lorient has a major national train station, the **Gare de Lorient** (place Francois Mitterrand; tel. 36 35; www.gares-sncf.com/fr/gare/frlrt/lorient), which is serviced by Paris eight times a day—a trip taking around 3 hours 40 minutes. Normal tickets should be around the €100 mark, but if you book in advance you may be able to shave some off that price.

There are more than 10 trains daily serving Lorient from Vannes (45 minutes), from Quimper (35 minutes), and from Rennes (1 hour 35 minutes). All these journeys should cost €15-30, depending on deals and how far ahead you book.

An average of five trains daily service Lorient from Nantes. Journey times tend to hover around the two-hour mark, and tickets cost about €30.

Reaching Lorient by train from Carnac, meanwhile, requires making a connection to the Vannes-Lorient line at Auray. There are roughly five opportunities to do this throughout the day and it costs about €10, with journey times of 1-3 hours.

By Bus

Lorient is serviced by several national bus companies, including **Flixbus** (https://flixbus.com), **Ouibus** (fr.ouibus.com), and **isilines** (www.isilines.com). From Paris, each of these carriers leaves once a day, taking 6-9 hours to reach the town's bus station, **Gare d'échange de l'Orientis** (cours de Chazelle), which is right next to the train station. It may not be the most comfortable way to travel, but it's certainly cost-effective, at a price of €15.30, provided that you book at least a day in advance. Each carrier offers a pretty much identical travel experience, so unless you're fond of a particular color scheme (Flixbus is green, Ouibus blue, and isilines red), then price should be your only concern. Tickets purchased at the bus station on the day of departure can go up in price significantly.

These same buses pass through Rennes, where it's possible to board them for as little as €5 to make the remaining two-hour trip to Lorient. (Note, prices can rise to as high as €20 for this journey, so if you're at all flexible, make sure to shop around a little before buying.)

The same bus companies also link Brest to Lorient. Likewise, each run on average about once a day, with the journey taking 2-3 hours. You should be able to grab tickets for €5, though again, prices can spike, so shop around. In the opposite direction from Nantes, there tend to be more buses running every day to Lorient (as many as five). They cost €5.20 and take around 2.5 hours. From Quimper there are 3-5 buses a day, costing €5.10. Journey time is just under an hour.

Surprisingly, there are no buses from Carnac to Lorient. From Carnac, head up toward Vannes first, from where several buses leave every day at a cost of around €57.

In town, the central harbor of Lorient is small enough to walk around, but there are some places to which you might consider taking the local bus service, the **CTRL** (www.ctrl.fr). The most obvious places you might want to use this to reach are the submarine base and nearby sailing museum, which can both be reached on the No. 20 bus in about 15 minutes from the town center—it stops on both the Quai des Indes and Quai de Rohan, and costs €2. The No. 2 bus is also useful, linking Lorient train station with its port—a journey of about 10 minutes (take the No. 3 bus on Sundays).

By Ferry

There are two ferry companies that link Lorient with the Île-de-Groix. The main one, **Compagnie Océane** (www.compagnie-oceane.fr), runs five or more sailings a day year-round in large ferries with a capacity of almost 300 people and up to 16 cars. These depart from Lorient's main passenger ferry port, the **Gare Maritime** (2 rue Gilles Gahinet), close to the center of town. The crossing time is around 50 minutes, and round-trip tickets are €35 in high season.

If you are driving, you may not want to bring your car across to the island, as costs rise to €150 and up with a car. Frankly, unless you're seriously lacking mobility, it will likely turn out to be an unnecessary expense—the island is small enough that it can easily be explored by bike in a day. You can leave your car in one of Lorient's parking lots, like the **Parking Place d'Armes** (rue de l'Enclos du Port; tel. 02 97 02 23 21). Be aware, though, if you do plan to go with this option, give yourself plenty of time before departure to secure your car, then make it to the port.

On weekends between April 20 and September, and every day in July and August, the ferry service **Escale Ouest** (tel. 02 97 65 52 52; www.escal-ouest.com) runs to Groix twice a day from just outside Lorient's submarine base on 7 rue Amiral Dordelin. This service is only for foot passengers, and costs €28 return. The journey time for this is 40 minutes.

There is also a shuttle boat for foot passengers that crosses between Lorient and Locmiquélic, and between Lorient, Port-Pouis, Gâvres, and Riantec. These run regularly, leaving from Lorient's **Gare Maritime**; they take about 15 minutes, and should be thought of as an extension of the city bus service. Tickets are €2.

Belle-Île and Quiberon

Brittany's largest island, and every bit as beautiful as its name suggests, Belle-Île has been attracting vacationers for more than a hundred years. They come for its isolation and its beaches, its traditional stone houses, and its dramatically spiky coastal formations. Every summer the island's population near doubles, for many wealthy French people have second homes here, and when they arrive, they bring their urbane culture with them. It's not for nothing that Belle-Île is host to the largest opera festival in the west of France.

Life here was not always so rosy, however: During the Seven Years' War in the 18th century, despite excessive fortifications that still dominate the island's main harbor to this day, Belle-Île fell to the British, leading to almost half its native population abandoning their lands. It was only handed back at the end of the war, in exchange for the island of Menorca. In the 19th century Belle-Île became

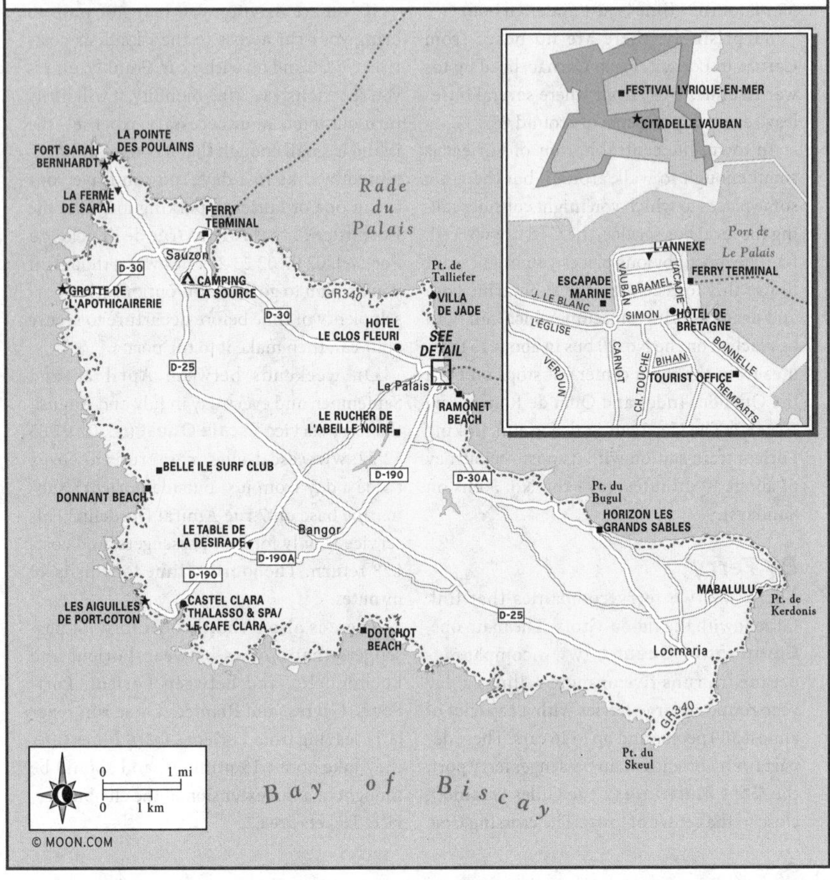

popular with artists and writers, many of whom helped to immortalize it in their work. The paintings Claude Monet completed here had such an impact that the first time his fellow artist Auguste Rodin saw the ocean from Brittany he declared, "It's a Monet."

Directly above Belle-Île, meanwhile, dangles the Quiberon peninsula, another popular holiday hot spot crammed with picturesque buildings and housing a thriving tourist industry. However, it's not only the promise of good food and warm hospitality that lures people here. There is a wildness to the landscape of Quiberon, particularly along its west-facing Côte Sauvage, which, when storms bluster in, has a striking elemental beauty worth a trip all of its own.

ORIENTATION

On a map, Belle-Île appears as an oversize dot that together with the Quiberon peninsula resembles an exclamation point stamped into the Atlantic, emphasizing the sentence of coastline that came before it. On the ground, it's easy enough to navigate. The main town, where most ferries arrive, is called **Le Palais.** It's characterized by a small harbor, with houses and commerce on the southern side and the imposing hotel/museum/former fortress looming over the other. The main roads on the island loosely form a cross, most passing its middle.

The second port of Belle-Île is **Sauzon,** a little farther to the west. From this picturesque village, it's possible to walk out into the wild-feeling Pointe des Poulains, the far northwest of the island, where French actress Sarah Bernhardt had her house.

The entire island is around 32 square miles (83 square kilometers), and roughly three times longer than it is thick. The coasts in the southwest are notable for their angry-looking rock formations, such as the Aiguilles de Port-Coton, while the northeast is made up of gentle beaches, including the Grands Sables.

SIGHTS

Belle-Île

LES AIGUILLES DE PORT-COTON

Lieu-dit Goulphar, Bangor

A series of jagged Gothic-looking sea stacks dominate an inlet on the south coast of the island. The name of the bay in which they reside is in reference to how the water here can be whipped to foam when storm fronts roll in: It's said that this foam resembles cotton. Inspiring to anyone who sees them, Les Aiguilles were a particular muse to the Impressionist artist Claude Monet, who lived for a time in Kervilahouen, just a short walk away. The artist had come originally to Belle-Île for just a couple of weeks, but was so taken by its landscape that he ended up staying for two months, making 39 paintings of its weather and coastline in all. Of these, his paintings of Les Aiguilles became the most famous, making them a sight as interesting for art lovers as they are for outdoor enthusiasts. The stacks are easy to reach, with the D190 road leading to a parking lot just above them, offering good views out across the stacks.

CITADELLE VAUBAN

Le Palais; tel. 02 97 31 85 54; www.citadellevauban.com; 9:30am-6pm daily Apr.-Jun. and Sept.-Oct., 9am-7pm daily Jul.-Aug., 9:30am-5pm daily Nov.-Mar. (closed Nov. 15-Dec. 15); adults €6, children 10-16 €3.50, under 10 free

Looming dramatically over the entrance to Belle-Île's port, the Citadelle Vauban today represents an interesting layer cake of different tourist activities and sights. On the most obvious level, it's a striking historic edifice, engineered primarily by the famous French military architect Sébastien Le Prestre de Vauban, whose distinctive star-like fortifications are a common feature of the French coastline. This one is even more forboding than most, with walls rising over a series of terraced levels, though the large inner courtyard has a neatly cropped lawn and ornamental trees tended with military precision, which lend the whole space an unlikely air of slightly starched luxury. Unfortunately, the most notable incident of the building's history was its being overrun by the British during the Seven Years' War. Returned to the French with the Treaty of Paris in 1763, it was later used as a prison, holding a number of high-profile inmates.

There is today, unsurprisingly, a museum on the site, dedicated to the building itself and its history. The interiors have been very carefully restored, meaning to wander around its many rooms with their austere stone walls and wood beams is a real chance to step back in time and glimpse how it must have felt to man such an outpost in the 18th century—the arsenal in particular is fascinating. Less usual, a large part of the building has been transformed into a luxury hotel, with a top-end restaurant attached. Even though a former prison and military fortress may seem odd foundations for such an establishment, the combination works, in part due to the inherent majesty of the building and in part to do with its great views of Le Palais harbor.

GROTTE DE L'APOTHICAIRERIE

D30, Belle-Île

An enormous sea cave formed of two connecting caverns, the Grotte de l'Apothicairerie used to be enough to draw visitors to Belle-Île all on its own. Unfortunately, the glory days of this particular natural wonder are paused at the moment: The steps cut into the rock that lead down to the cave are now considered too dangerous for public use. (The steps remain, but you're strongly advised not to use them, especially in rough weather, as slipping into the sea around these rocks could easily result in death.) The name originated from the many birds that used to roost along its walls, their nests reminiscent of jars in an apothecary shop. However, these birds were decimated by early visitors, who used to hunt them. Even though it's no longer possible to get up so close and personal with the cave, the sight still lingers large in the collective imagination of Belle-Île. There also are some great views of waves sucking in and out of the cave's entrance from the cliffs above, which are easy to reach from the road.

FORT SARAH BERNHARDT

Sauzon; tel. 02 97 31 61 29; 10:30am-5:30pm Tues.-Fri. Apr.-Jun. and Sept., 10:30am-6pm daily July-Aug., 1pm-5pm Thurs.-Sat. Oct.; adults €5, children 7-12 €3, under 7 free

Arguably the most famous actress of her time, Sarah Bernhardt (1844-1923) starred in many of the most acclaimed plays of the 19th and 20th centuries. She was so well regarded, she even took on a number of male roles, including Hamlet—quite remarkable in otherwise socially conservative times. This converted military fort, surrounded by wildflowers, rocks, and the thrashing sea, was where she spent her summer holidays for the last 30 years of her life. A great champion of Belle-Île, the actress called the island "a precious pearl, a delicate emerald, a rare diamond reflecting the iridescent blue mixture of sea and sky." She came across the fort for sale while wandering the coast, and immediately decided to buy it to restore and convert into a house herself.

Today, it has become a museum to her memory and, by extension, to the world she inhabited. The interiors remain exactly as they would have been in the 19th century, and there are plenty of photographs, books, and clothes that belonged to the actress on display. This place is worth visiting for being a time capsule as much as it is a primer about Sarah Bernhardt and her life.

LA POINTE DES POULAINS

Near Fort Sarah Bernhardt

A peninsula on an island: no wonder La Pointe des Poulains feels so isolated and wild. Stacks and rocks pepper the waters around here in every direction, and at the very tip flashes a small lighthouse. Spangled in wildflowers, it's one of the most dramatic places on the whole of the Belle-Île and well worth a wander around, whatever the weather. Indeed, one of Brittany's most resiliant characteristics is how much the landscape can seem to change depending on the elements. At different times of day or year, there's always something different to see. The point is well-connected by roads, though the lighthouse at its tip can only be reached at low tide, becoming an island when the water rushes in. The lighthouse remains active, but is today automated and not open to go inside.

Quiberon Peninsula

LA CÔTE SAUVAGE DE QUIBERON

Boulevard de la Côté Sauvage, Quiberon

At the mercy of Atlantic swells, the western coast of the Quiberon peninsula is postcard Brittany. This is the kind of landscape Bretons like to imagine characterizes their souls. Wind and waves seem to pound here so ceaselessly, it's as though you can see the coast's craggy features being beaten out in real time. Caves, arches, and coves mottle its five-mile (eight-kilometer) length, while nature-rich dunes and heath cover the area just back from the sea. Visit for walks, bird-watching, and spectacular views all the way out to Belle-Île. Make sure to stay out of the water, though—the currents and rough seas can be deadly. Of course, for the full experience, you want to catch it in the midst of a storm, when the waves rise high

1: Citadel Vauban at Belle-Île **2:** beautiful scenic area of Belle-Île with lighthouse at Pointe des Poulains

1

2

and the elements make you small—and you get some cracking photo opportunities!

FESTIVALS AND EVENTS

FESTIVAL LYRIQUE-EN-MER

Le Palais, Belle-Île; tel. 06 86 74 31 90; http://festival-belle-ile.com; first two weeks of Aug.; concerts €27-80

A popular holiday destination for France's urbanites, many of whom have second homes here, Belle-Île plays host every summer to an appropriately cosmopolitan festival of opera, the Festival Lyrique-en-Mer. Attracting some of the world's finest classical musicians, it stages shows over a two-week period in a number of different locations around the island, with the citadel a stunning focal point. Founded in 1998, the festival normally revolves around one central production taken from the canon of great operas, with numerous shows and events taking place in smaller venues at the same time. For the weeks that the festival is on, Belle-Île is at its busiest, so even if you're not planning on attending, keep an eye on its dates; any accommodations at this time, particularly those in the top end, will require booking far in advance.

SHOPPING

LE RUCHER DE L'ABEILLE NOIRE

Borgrouager, Le Palais, Belle-Île; tel. 06 25 46 21 63; www.lerucherdelabeillenoire.com; 6pm-7:30pm Mon.-Sat. Apr.-Oct., 5pm-6:30pm Mon.-Sat. Nov.-Mar.

Le Rucher de l'Abeille Noire is an apiary that sells some of the finest honey, and honey-based products, that you're likely to find anywhere in Brittany. While sales (on-site and to other concerns on the island) are its prime reason for existing, the on-site shop is only officially open briefly in the day, and the business, which sits in the suburbs of Belle-Île's main port, also offers hands-on information sessions (in French) about beekeeping. There's a lavishly decorated yurt on the property in case you want to sleep among, or at least close to, the bees.

BEACHES

There are more than 60 beaches large and small along the coasts of Belle-Île and Quiberon. Head to the local tourist offices to pick up a leaflet and map detailing them all. Below are three of the highlights, all on Belle-Île.

PLAGE DU DONNANT

Route de Port Donnant, Belle-Île

On the southern "wild coast" of Belle-Île, this extremely pictureqe beach is characterized by impressive dunes and large waves, making it a great surf spot and home to some interesting plant and bird life. Despite its relative isolation it can get quite full in the summer, when its only downside is how its access route can become something of a traffic bottleneck. If you can, cycling or walking is an easier way to get here. Amenities are minimal.

PLAGE DU DOTCHOT

Route de Calastren, Bangor, Belle-Île

This is a nudist beach, though one where you won't be made to feel unwelcome if you decide to keep your swimming gear on. Loomed over on both sides by cliffs, the atmosphere is one of seclusion, and it's a characterful, picturesque spot. Possibly because of the shelter provided by these cliffs, the water and sands here tend to remain warmer for longer than many other places along the Belle-Île coasts. Access is a little scary down a steep rope descent, and be aware that once you get here, it's effectively just a wild beach with no amenities.

RAMONET BEACH

Route de Ramonet, Le Palais, Belle-Île

The closest beach to Belle-Île's main town and port is very popular, especially with the island's more urbane vacationers. This is a place to meet up and be seen. It can accommodate over a hundred people, and it often has to in the summer months. Nevertheless, the views out to the citadel and back toward the mainland are spectacular, and it gets the sun late into the day. Despite its popularity, amenities are scarce.

SPORTS AND RECREATION

Water Sports and Surfing

HORIZON LES GRANDS SABLES

Plage des Grands Sables, Locmaria, Belle-Île; tel. 02 97 31 54 71; http://belleile-voile.fr; 9am-6pm May-Sept., lessons available July and Aug.; sea kayak rentals from €16 to week-long sailing lessons from €249

This water-sports center is geared up to help visitors of all ages get out on the waves. Based on Belle Île's largest beach, the Plage des Grands Sables, the club offers a full menu of water-based activities for a variety of levels and prices. Primarily, of course, it's a sailing club, and its week-long courses are an excellent way to keep kids occupied for the duration of a holiday. Unfortunately, there's no promise that the instructors will be able to speak English. Hiring of equipment, including sea kayaks and paddleboards, is also an option.

★ BELLE ÎLE SURF CLUB

Plage du Donnant, Belle-Île; tel. 06 77 12 37 80; www.belleilesurfclub.fr; July-Aug.; fkids' course €30, intensive course €265

All around Brittany there are great waves for surfing, but the waters around Belle-Île are particularly good for those just getting started or who have yet to fully find their feet. Belle Île Surf Club is there to guide such beginners, and it excels at doing so. The instructors are very friendly, with everyone working together toward a shared sense of accomplishment at the end of a course. English is not really spoken, but the club is willing to make the effort to communicate, and usually nonverbal instruction is clear enough.

Boat Trips

ESCAPADE MARINE

Port de le Palais, Belle-Île-en-Mer; tel. 06 48 49 94 69; http://escapademarine.org; tours from €39 pp

What better way to see the coasts of Belle-Île and Quiberon than on board a small powerboat, skimming across the water at speed, with an informed guide pointing out sights of interest and notable seabirds? This company offers a variety of different tours, starting with sizable group-based excursions, right down to bespoke trips including a midday picnic and watching the sunset from the waves, aperitif in hand.

FOOD

Belle-Île

LE CAFÉ CLARA

Port Goulphar, Bangor; tel. 02 97 31 84 2; 12:15pm-2pm and 7:30pm-9:30pm daily; mains €29-56

When the sun shines, a meal at Le Café Clara is an aesthetically impeccable dining experience. With a terrace looking straight out across the Aiguilles de Port-Coton, the smart design allows the landscape to speak for itself. The seafood buffet is a real highlight and matches the setting perfectly. If you've never tried sea urchin before, this is the place to do so! Not only are they wonderfully fresh, but their spiny, glistening exteriors seem a direct mirror of the jagged sea stacks far below.

LE TABLE DE LA DESIRADE

Le Petit Cosquet, Bangor; tel. 02 97 31 70 70; www.hotel-la-desirade.com/fr; 7:15pm-9pm daily; menus €34-79

Family-run and on its own grounds on Belle-Île, this restaurant serves some excellent local food, characterized by its fresh high-quality presentation. With starched white tablecloths and a brightly lit interior, it's a fairly formal atmosphere, and its menu is suited for blowouts and occasion dining. The rich mussels in saffron-flavored curry is a real highlight. Booking ahead is a good idea.

LA FERME DE SARAH

Pointe des Poulains, Sauzon; tel. 02 97 29 12 21; 10am-10pm Thurs.-Tues.; mains €10-25

Its name might suggest something rustic, but La Ferme de Sarah bursts with modern design features, has almost haute-cuisine levels of presentation of its food, and looks out across a golf course as much as it does farmland. What it does offer, though, is food with a close connection to the land and sea surrounding it; everything is pleasantly fresh and local. A decent informal place to pop into after a walk or a visit to the nearby Sarah Bernhardt museum, the restaurant offers continual service all day long into the night.

MABALULU

Port Andro, Locmaria; tel. 02 97 52 57 29; 10:30am-10pm Tues.-Thurs.; mains €9-19

This straightforward seafront bar and restaurant on Belle-Île is proof that some of the very best things in this world needn't come with a hefty price tag attached. Excellently located, overlooking a sandy cove, Mabalulu can easily feel like a Caribbean setting when the sun is shining. The quality of its food, meanwhile, even while it lacks sophistication, is far higher than it need be. The burgers in particular have a gourmet quality. The only trouble is they are so filling that after eating one you'll probably want to give it an hour or so before going for a swim.

L'ANNEXE

3 quai de l'Acadie, Le Palais; tel. 02 97 31 81 53; lunch Fri.-Tues. and dinner daily Apr.-June and Sept.-Dec., lunch and dinner daily July-Aug.; mains €10-25

Despite not boasting the most exciting interior in the world, this inexpensive crêperie offers great value and very tasty food, bolstering their crepes with local seafood ingredients and cooking up some really indulgent desserts of caramelized pear. It's an unpretentious place, where borders between the kitchen and dining room are broken down—so you can see exactly what the chef is up to.

Quiberon

★ LE PETIT HÔTEL DU GRAND LARGE

11 quai Saint-Ivy, Saint-Pierre-Quiberon; tel. 02 97 30 91 61; 12:30pm-1:30pm and 7:30pm-8:30pm Thurs.-Mon. (closed Sun. evening); menus €60-95

In the running certainly for the best restaurant in all of Brittany, this harbor-front place on the Quiberon peninsula manages to mix tradition expertly with modernity, both in the flavors it offers and its fresh well-lit interior. Dishes are inspired by local cuisine and generally revolve around seafood, while there's also a strong Japanese influence, keeping things light, sharp, and surprising. Menus tend to come with a lot of different courses, making any meal here a kind of journey. It may look pricey, but for a two-Michelin-star restaurant, this is actually a very good value. No wonder you have to make sure to reserve your table a good week in advance at high season.

ACCOMMODATIONS

Belle-Île

HÔTEL DE BRETAGNE

Quai de l'Acadie, Le Palais; tel. 02 97 31 80 14; www.hotel-de-bretagne.fr; from €75 d

With a great location right on Belle-Île's port, this is a good-value place to stay on the island, especially for people-watchers in the summer season, when the coming and going of visitors is almost constant. The room decorations are hardly what you might call inspiring, being a good couple of decades off trend, and the rooms are not especially large. At the same time, there's something faintly charming about this slightly tired quality, and the views from many of them, especially those facing the harbor, are great. There's an on-site restaurant and café pushing decent Breton food, WiFi throughout the property, and en suite bathrooms in all the rooms.

HÔTEL LE CLOS FLEURI

Route de Sauzon Lieu-dit Bellevue, Le Palais; tel. 02 97 31 45 45; www.hotel-leclosfleuri.com; from €110 d

Not far from the center of Le Palais on Belle-Île, this hotel feels a lot like a private house. Rooms are comfortable and clean, filled with bright colors and a combination of modern and antique furniture. A number have their own private gardens. There's also an on-site bar and a communal area heated by an open fire when the temperature starts to dip. En suite bathrooms, flat-screen TVs, and WiFi throughout are standard, while the beach is less than a 15-minute walk away.

VILLA DE JADE

Lann Platt-Taillefer, Le Palais; tel. 02 97 31 53 00; www.villadejade.com; from €180 d

This B&B in a beautiful large villa sits perched atop a promontory overlooking the sea. The rooms have some quite spectacular views, as well as dark wooden flooring, plush old-fashioned furniture, and private bathrooms. Just north of Le Palais, the villa is also a just above a secluded cove that can be easily accessed by walking. Perhaps the highlight, though, is the elegant dining room, where organic breakfast is served, included in the price. There is also a free shuttle service to take you into town.

★ CASTEL CLARA THALASSO & SPA

Port Goulphar, Bangor; tel. 02 97 31 84 21; www.castel-clara.com; from €180 d

A luxury modern hotel in a fantastic location overlooking the Aiguilles de Port-Coton. Rooms have subtly tasteful interiors letting in plenty of light, with some excellent views out to sea. There are also several top-end restaurants on-site of varying levels of formality, all serving excellent local food. There are both indoor and outdoor swimming pools here, as well as a sauna and a hot tub, while massages and other beauty treatments can be booked through reception. The opposite side of the island to Le Palais, there's a sense of seclusion, too: This is a place for a long weekend of "getting away from it all." Of course, all rooms have WiFi and their own bathrooms, which deserve a special mention for their fresh design.

CAMPING LA SOURCE

Le Vallon du Port aux Plages Belle-Île, Sauzon; tel. 02 97 31 60 95; www.belleile-lasource.com/fr; camping for two people €12, a week in a mobile home €504-630

Toward the northwest of the island, this is a pleasant if not quite top-end campsite, complete with its own swimming pool and extensive shower and toilet facilities. A family-friendly place, it offers spots to pitch a tent plus several different kinds of mobile homes and cabins to rent. It's situated in a good walking area near the Sarah Bernhardt museum, and the staff are helpful, and only too happy to suggest excursions around Belle-Île.

Quiberon

HÔTEL PORT HALIGUEN QUIBERON

10 place de Port Haliguen, Quiberon; tel. 02 97 50 16 52; www.hotel-port-haliguen.com; from €80 d

Full of bold, bright colors, this harbor-front hotel in a large, traditional-looking building offers modern interiors (though not in-your-face modern) and is just a short walk from the beach. Clean and comfortable, it's not trying to make statements, just doing its best to be a pleasant place to lay your head. All rooms have their own bathroom and flat-screen TV, while a high number have sea views. There's also a terrace on which to take breakfast on sunny days.

TOURIST INFORMATION

OFFICE DE TOURISME DE BELLE-ÎLE-EN-MER

Quai Bonnelle, Le Palais; tel. 02 97 31 81 93; www.quiberon.com; 9:30am-12:30pm and 2pm-6pm Mon.-Wed. and Fri.-Sat., 9am-1pm Thurs.

Right on the ferry port in Belle-Île's Le Palais, this is an obvious first stop, particularly for those only planning on spending a day on the island—their detailed maps to the various sights and advice on what to prioritize can be useful if you're trying to max out on a limited amount of time here. It can get busy immediately after ferry disembarkation, so consider either rushing to the front of those stepping ashore, or pausing for a coffee before going, if you don't want to hang around waiting for someone to talk to. English is widely spoken.

OFFICE DE TOURISME DE QUIBERON

14 rue de Verdun, Quiberon; tel. 02 97 50 07 84; www.quiberon.com; 9:30am-12:30pm and 2pm-6pm Mon.-Sat.

Located toward the tip of the Quiberon

peninsula, this is a large, modern tourist office that can hook you up with hotels, restaurant suggestions, and general advice on things to do in the immediate area, including boat trips. English is widely spoken.

TRANSPORTATION

Getting There

BY CAR

Belle-Île can only be reached by car on the ferry from Quiberon. The peninsula, meanwhile, is attached to the mainland via the D768, which runs out of Plouharnel. This is the town you should be aiming for whichever direction you're coming from, in order to access Quiberon and later Belle-Île by car.

From Paris (total 300 miles/483 kilometers, 5.5 hours), first take the A11, which splits at Le Mans into the A81 to Rennes; after that, it's the N24 until Ploërmel, then the N166 toward the coast and Plouharnel. Until Rennes, there are toll charges on the roads costing around €25. Just coming from Rennes is a journey of just over 100 miles (160 kilometers) and should take about two hours.

The journey from Nantes (100 miles/160 kilometers, 2 hours) is northwest along the N165, via Vannes and Auray.

Coming from Brest (110 miles/177 kilometers, 2 hours) in the opposite direction, travel along the same road (the N165), going via Lorient and Quimper.

Once in Quiberon, there are plenty of parking spaces. Zones are color-coded in blue, for normal paid public parking; green, for paid and guarded public parking; and red, for free public parking limited to four hours. Obviously, which one you chose will depend on your needs. If you're planning on leaving your car in Quiberon while you head over to Belle-Île, for example, the guarded green parking lots are probably for you; try either **La Sémaphore** (route de Kernavest, Quiberon; tel. 02 97 30 59 45), with 1,100 spots, or **Kerné** (route de Kerniscob, Quiberon; tel. 06 86 62 69 18) with 300 spots. Expect to pay about €14 per day, with prices going down the longer you stay.

Be aware, also, that because there's only one real way in and out of Quiberon, traffic can get bad, especially at the end of the day in the summer, when everyone is leaving the beach at the same time.

BY FERRY

The **Compagnie Océane** (tel. 02 97 35 02 00; www.compagnie-oceane.fr) runs a regular ferry service between **Port de Quiberon** in Quiberon and **Port de le Palais** on Belle-Île.

marina and main street of Le Palais

There are five round-trips a day in low season (Oct.-Apr.), then up to 12 in high season; check the website for the schedule. It should cost €14 one-way for adults and €7 for children. If you're taking a car across, prices start at €65 in low season, €85 in high, and go up according to the size of your vehicle. If you are planning on doing this, be aware that space for vehicles on the ferries is considerably more limited than that for foot passengers, and that booking a few weeks ahead is highly advised. The ferry trip takes around 45 minutes.

Another excellent way of getting to Belle-Île is by ferry from Vannes, the spectacular walled town on the Gulf of Morbihan. As well as being an easier way of getting to the island if you don't have your own transport, this is a picturesque route through the romantic waters of the island-strewn gulf. There are three companies that run this two-hour trip: **Compagnie du Golfe** (tel. 02 97 67 10 00; www.compagnie-du-golfe.fr), **Navix** (tel. 02 97 46 60 00; www.navix.fr), and **Les Vedettes du Golfe** (tel. 02 97 44 44 40; www.vedettes-du-golfe.fr). Prices are all pretty similar, being roughly €30 return for adults and €20 for children. Each company usually only runs one service a day maximum; none operate October-March, while in the run-up to the main season (April-June and September), sailings are mostly confined to weekends and school holidays. Be sure to check their websites before planning a trip.

BY PUBLIC TRANSIT

Quiberon is not on a main train line. The closest major station is the **Gare d'Auray** (place Raoult Dautry, Auray; tel. 36 35; www.gares-sncf.com/fr/gare/frxuy/auray), which sits roughly 20 miles (32 kilometers) north from the tip of the peninsula.

From Paris to Auray, there are six direct trains a day here, costing around €80 depending on how far in advance you book, and taking around three hours. From Rennes, there are 11 direct trains a day, costing around €30 and taking around 1 hour 20 minutes. From Brest, there is one direct train a day, costing around €40 and taking around 3.5 hours—it's also possible to reach Auray from Brest, making a change at Quimper, from where there are around 12 trains every day. From Nantes, meanwhile, there are four direct trains a day, costing around €30 and taking around 1 hour 20 minutes. From nearby Vannes or Lorient there are trains throughout the day, costing around €5.

From the Auray train station, you can take the TIM No. 1 bus to the tip of Quiberon. It leaves from outside Auray train station around 12 times a day. The earliest departure is 7:25am and the latest is 7pm. It should cost €2, and the trip takes between 45 minutes and 1 hour 10 minutes (some buses go via Carnac; others are more direct). More details about the service can be found on the **Mobi Breizh** website (mobibreizh.bzh).

In the summer, there is a branch line that runs from Auray to the tip of the Quiberon peninsula, dubbed the Tire-Bouchon. This runs 6-8 times a day on the weekends in June and September, and every day throughout July and August. It costs €3.50 and the full trip takes about 50 minutes, offering some great views.

Getting Around

BY BUS

The **Mobi Breizh** (mobibreizh.bzh) TIM No. 1 bus serves the Quiberon peninsula, with tickets costing €2, or €15 for a packet of 10. Also available in the summer is the **Quib'bus**, which loops the base of the peninsula 18 times every day. It costs €1 for a day ticket, with which you can hop on or hop off whenever you want.

On Belle-Île, six public bus lines, the "Belle-Île bus" (www.belle-ile.com/organiser/se-deplacer-sur-lile/en-bus) run regularly April-late October/early November. Together they connect nearly all the villages, accommodations, tourist sites, and beaches on the island. Most lines route through Le Palais. Ligne 1 takes you west toward Fort Sarah Bernhardt, Ligne 2 across the island to Port Coton, and Ligne 3 east to Les Grands Sables.

All tickets are sold on the bus, costing €2.50 for a single journey. More details about hours and precise routes can be found online.

BY BIKE

As with most Breton islands, probably the best, and certainly the most popular, way to explore Belle-Île is on two wheels, under your own steam. There are several bike rental companies set up to help you do this, most crowding the port, looking for your business as soon as you step from the ferry. All companies offer a similar service and at more or less the same price (starting at around €10 for one day's rental). Most also give the option of tandems and electrically assisted bikes at a slightly higher cost. **Roue Libre** (5 quai Jacques le Blancs; tel. 02 97 31 49 81; www.velobelleile.fr) or **Location Reversade** (14 rue de l'Eglise; tel. 02 97 31 84 19; www.location-reversade.com) are both good if you feel the need to reserve bikes ahead of time—though that isn't really necessary, even in high season, unless you're part of a large group.

Once out on the island, suggested bike routes and circuits are well-signposted—look for the white signs with green lettering. Though the island is quite hilly, a tour shouldn't be too strenuous, particularly if you take things slowly.

On Quiberon, try **Cycles Loisirs** (32 rue Victor Golvan; tel. 02 97 50 31 73; www.cyclesloisirs.com) for renting bikes to explore the wild coast. Prices start from €12 for the day.

BY TAXI

There are several taxi companies on Belle-Île and more servicing the Quiberon peninsula. For the latter, try **A Bâbord Taxi** (tel. 07 85 06 80 31) or **ABACA Quiberonnais** (tel. 06 07 09 01 27). For the former, try **Taxile** (tel. 06 08 77 41 74) or **Taxi Passat** (tel. 06 82 10 34 22). The service and rates they offer are pretty similar. If you don't leave the peninsula or the island, most journeys are going to cost between €10 and €20.

Carnac

A place name that is close to a byword for "mystery," Carnac is known throughout France as home to the largest collection of free-standing Neolithic monuments anywhere in the world. Standing like some ancient petrified army, they are assembled rank on rank in the town's surrounding fields, covering an area of more than 2.5 square miles (four square kilometers), as striking as they are impenetrable. They have been drawing visitors here for generations, and experts still scratch their heads as to their original purpose.

But there's more to the town than mere prehistoric puzzles, for Carnac is actually a town split in two. There's Carnac-Ville, base to the tourist industry surrounding this ancient heritage, including museums and tour companies. This small town is made up largely of quaint stone houses, with a narrow, winding center. Then, just down the road, there's Carnac-Plage, a seaside resort characterized by multiple sandy beaches, 19th-century villas, and some excellent sailing, which has been drawing an entirely different kind of vacationer for generations. There's also a top-end center in the village for thalassotherapy (Brittany's own seawater therapy technique), ideal for relaxing in after a hard day traipsing among the stones. Overall the area around Carnac offers an excellent compact holiday package: Come for the prehistory, stay for the spa!

ORIENTATION

The main thing to keep in mind about Carnac is that it's effectively two destinations: the inland Carnac-Ville and the beachside Carnac-Plage, a third of a mile (half a kilometer) to its

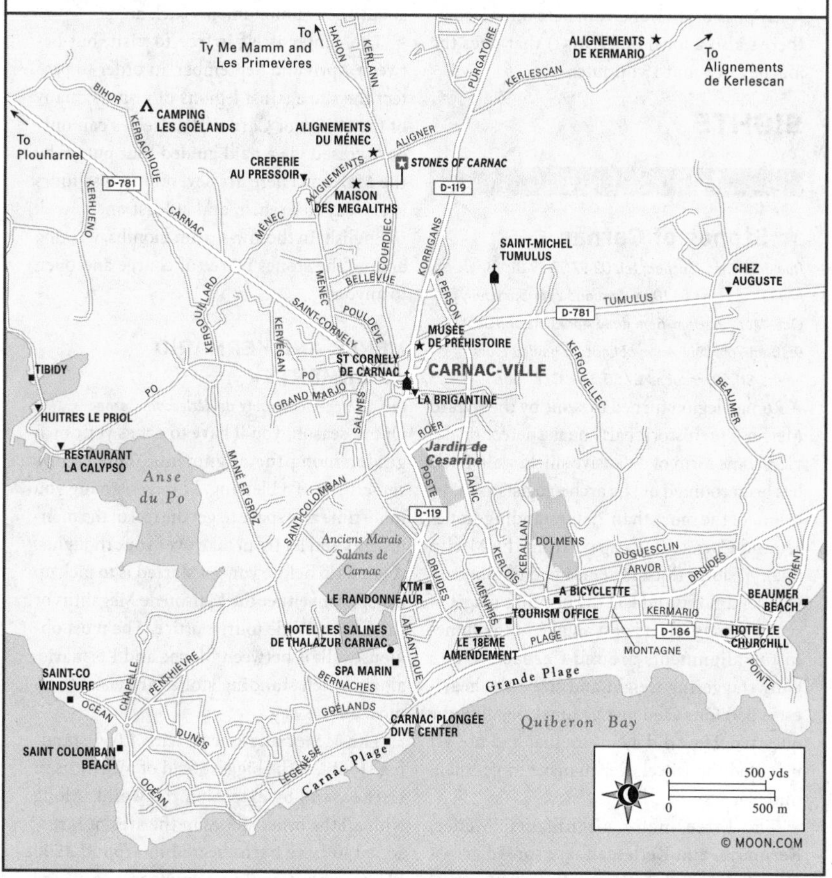

south. Both draw plenty of visitors, though for different reasons.

Carnac-Ville is the heart of the industry that caters to the megaliths, which themselves are located over a large area of land to the north and northwest of town. The **Maison de Megaliths,** which is the effective gateway to seeing them—particularly at high season, when many of the stones cannot be visited without a guide—is to the immediate north of the town center along the D196. Given its popularity among tourists, there are plenty of parking spaces in Carnac to go around: 1,500 for most of the year, with an extra 1,900 opened near the town center in high season.

Carnac-Plage, meanwhile, is more of a resort area. It has a long esplanade, Boulevard de la Plage, on its seafront, punctuated by hotels and restaurants, with what stands for its center—a lively crossroads of bars and commerce—located along the avenue Miln toward the west. A little farther from here is Carnac's famous thalassotherapy center. Follow the coastline around in either direction and you'll come to its many sandy beaches.

The closest train station to Carnac is the **Gare de Plouharnel-Carnac,** which is actually a couple of miles northwest of Carnac-Ville, in Plouharnel. While it is perfectly possible to walk from here into Carnac, there's also a local bus (No. 1) that does the journey in about 15 minutes.

SIGHTS

TOP EXPERIENCE

★ Stones of Carnac

Rue du Ménec, Carnac; tel. 02 97 52 29 81; www.menhirs-carnac.fr; 10am-1pm and 2pm-5pm daily Oct.-Mar., 9:30am-6pm daily Apr.-June and Sept., 9:30am-7pm July-Aug.; obligatory guided tours adults €11.50, reduced €7.50, free Oct.-Mar.

A Roman legion turned to stone by the wizard Merlin, a prehistoric earthquake detection device, some form of defensive shield wall: Little has been counted out by archeologists as to the origin of the more than 2,800 standing stones around Carnac (OK, apart from the Merlin one). Visitors flock here in huge numbers to wander among and feel the peculiar magic of such an unusual and vast a sight. Many stones in the alignments around Carnac are of a truly staggering weight and size—the heaviest is 330 tons (300 metric tons), begging the question: How did a culture that had not yet invented the wheel ever manage to get them into place?

The three major alignments, Ménec, Kermario, and Kerlescan, are spread across three fields, each within walking distance of one another, fanning northwest from Carnac's town center. Each one has its own unique features, and reasons you should visit.

Attempting to provide some answers to the questions about the standing stones, meanwhile, is the **Maison des Megalithes,** a visitors center and effective gateway to the sites. This sits just next to the Ménec Allignment, the closest group of stones to Carnac-Ville, and offers a general history about the site as well as a rooftop viewing deck that looks out across the stone-dotted fields. Completely refurbished in 2018, it now offers complete disabled access, and has a brand-new bookshop boutique onsite should you want to continue your learning about ancient monuments back home.

The center itself is free to visit, but between April and September, in order to protect the site against legions of visitors, many of the stones of Carnac themselves can only be accessed via a paid guided tour put on by the Maison. There are several of these tours every day in French, and at least one a week in English. In the low-season months, walking among the stones is free of charge and open to anyone.

MÉNEC AND KERMARIO ALIGNMENTS

Rue du Ménec and route de Kerlescan, Carnac

Out of season, you'll have to act as your own guide among the alignments. This can be something of a blessing, however, giving you more time and space to get the feel of the monuments and let them take over your thoughts. A good tip before you get started is to pick up a map from either the Maison de Megaliths or the Carnac-Ville tourist office. The most obvious walk is between Ménec and Kermario, along which standing stones are visiable almost all the way.

The Ménec alignment, with 1,050 standing stones, is the biggest field of megaliths in Carnac, and by extension the world. Along with all the other stones in the area, it is reasoned to have been erected in around 4500 BC, though it could be younger. For all the speculation about the original purpose of the standing stones, the most widely accepted hypothesis is that they served some form of religious function.

Following the D196, head northeast from Ménec for about a mile, crossing the D119, and you will reach the Kermario alignment, which is only marginally smaller, consisting of 1,029 stones. Parts of this field are open to the public and can be accessed without a guide all year round.

1: megaliths at Carnac **2:** Saint-Michel tumulus

1

2

Between April and September there are also seven buses a day running between these two sights, and to Carnac-Ville and Carnac-Plage beyond.

KERLESCAN ALIGNMENT

Route de Kerlescan, Carnac

The easternmost alignment, this is slightly smaller than the other two, consisting of just 555 remaining stones. It can be reached simply by continuing to follow the D196 east from Kermario. It's also notable for the **Dolmen De Kerlescan,** a prehistoric tomb (though who was once buried there is unknown) that can be found among the stones.

Perhaps the alignment's most impressive and evocative sight, though, is the **Manio Giant.** This single standing stone, located on a mound to the west of Kerlescan, is the tallest in all of Carnac at almost 20 feet (six meters) high—there's even speculation that it used to be taller but was struck by lightening. Nowhere in the whole area is the sheer amount of physical dedication that must have been needed to assemble much of Carnac more evident than it is here.

Musée de Préhistoire

10 place de la Chapelle, Carnac; tel. 02 97 52 22 04; www.museedecarnac.com; 10am-12:30pm and 2pm-6pm Wed.-Mon. Apr.-June and Sept., 10am-6:30pm Wed.-Mon. July-Aug., 10am-12:30pm and 2pm-5:30pm Wed.-Mon. Oct., 2pm-5:30pm Wed.-Mon. Nov. and Mar., also open. Tues. during school holidays; adults €7, reduced €3

Billing itself as the world's preeminent museum for megalithic culture, the Musée de Préhistoire takes visitors deep into Carnac's history. More than 6,600 objects are on display, with exhibits explaining how burial architecture developed and showing all kinds of tools people were using at that time, from jade axe heads to cooking pots. The ancient jewelry in particular is a highlight, including necklaces and bracelets, bridging the gap between our day and the distant past.

Housed in a large presbytery building since 1978, the museum is laid out chronologically, starting with exhibits about life in the Stone Age and moving to the more recentera of Roman Gaul. Information boards in display cases are only in French, but you can pick up folders in multiple languages to take around the exhibition. If this seems like a little too much effort, pictures and dioramas around many exhibits do help to get the essentials across. Expect to spend an hour or two here.

Saint-Michel Tumulus

Saint-Michel Tumulus, Carnac

At 410 feet (125 meters) long, 164 feet (50 meters) wide, and 32 feet (10 meters) high, this is the biggest megalithic grave mound in continental Europe. Effectively an ancient Breton pyramid, within it lies a central vault that when it was discovered in the mid-19th century boasted a veritable treasure-haul of Neolithic artifacts, including polished jade axes and a necklace of variscite pearls, dating back to 5000 BC. Unfortunately, it's not possible to enter the mound today, but it's easy to walk up, and the views from the top are excellent. There's also a small chapel that's been built to St. Michael (also usually closed). A very important historical sight, this one requires a certain leap of the imagination to truly appreciate.

SHOPPING

LES PRIMEVÈRES

Le Notério, Carnac; tel. 06 75 48 05 40; 7:30am-11am and 5:30pm-7:30pm daily Sept.-June, 7:30am-7:30pm daily July-Aug.

This ciderie in the Carnac countryside sells excellent artisinal cider, apple juice, and cider vinegar straight from the source. The product is great to then take with you on a picnic, or even home to uncork the taste of Brittany, but the ciderie is also a pleasant place to visit in its own right. This is especially true in springtime, when the apple orchards are in blossom and look almost as good as the products made from their fruit taste.

Every Stone a Story

Surely one of the most appealing qualities of the Carnac stones is how they act like magnets for the iron filings of myth. Their sheer, unyielding silence in the face of speculation means all sorts of bizarre tales have emerged to explain their presence. It's even been said that there are as many stories about the origins of the stones as there are stones themselves.

One of the more fantastical, though nevertheless most often told, regards Saint Cornelius, an early pope of the Christian church and latter Breton folk hero. Quite how the holy man ended up so far from Rome is unclear, but these were in the days when Christians were still being persecuted, so perhaps he was on a covert missionary endeavor, or perhaps he was simply in flight.

Whichever, the story goes that a whole Roman legion had picked up his trail and chased him to the coast. There, Cornelius hid in, of all places, a cow's ear, and waited for the legion to come marching past. Then, as they were surrounding him, in their regular Roman ranks, weapons no doubt devilishly glistening, Cornelius leapt out and using what was almost certainly holy magic turned them all to stone. And there they have remained ever since. What happened to the cow is anyone's guess. . . .

But if you don't like that story, then one of the wonderful things about Carnac is that you're utterly free to invent your own. There are few things we know less about in archeology than Neolithic standing stones—as recently as the 1960s, people were still allowed to camp among them, unaware that they had any historical significance at all. Perhaps one day there will be a breakthrough theory, but until then the Carnac stones are a license to dream.

BEACHES

GRANDE PLAGE

Boulevard de la Plage, Carnac

Carnac's main beach, sandy and just over a mile (1.6 kilometers) in length, stretches between the town's port and Churchill Point. Lifeguards are situated at its center, and there is disabled access here, too. The Boulevard de la Plage runs its whole length, so be aware of the proximity to this road if you have children. In general, though, it's a lively, family-friendly beach. It also has showers, public toilets, and plenty of parking nearby.

BEAUMER BEACH

Avebue d'Orient, Carnac

East of Churchill Point, this is another large sandy beach with some great views out to the Île de Stuhan. It's unsupervised, and swimming is only really possible here at high tide, though low tide exposes a big area of sand ideal for beach games (those that don't involve water, at least). There are also public toilets here, and the shops and restaurants of town are less than a 10-minute walk away.

SAINT COLOMBAN BEACH

Boulevard de l'Océan, Carnac

The farthest west of Carnac's beaches, this decent-size sandy stretch looks out toward the Quiberon peninsula, but don't think that makes it sheltered; it's actually open to prevailing winds, making it a popular spot for windsurfing. A little less busy than some of Carnac's other beaches, it's also a good place for swimming, provided you don't mind the waves. It has toilets, showers, and lifeguards in the summer months.

SPORTS AND RECREATION

Water Sports

CARNAC PLONGÉE DIVE CENTER

1 boulevard de Légenèse, Carnac; tel. 06 52 29 69 63; www.carnacplongeedivecenter.fr; 8am-6pm daily; tours €35, diving instruction courses €490+

An excellent professional dive center that caters to all levels throughout the year. The waters immediately around Carnac are filled with a veritable aquarium of life, including numerous wrecks that have gone down here thanks to its treacherous rocks, and which now shelter all manner of sealife. One of the most welcoming things about this dive center, though, is that instructors speak English (and Spanish, too), which, makes signing up less intimidating, especially for a beginner. Both lessons and guided tours of local wrecks are available.

SAINT-CO WINDSURF

1 allée de la Grève; 06 13 33 03 26; stcowindsurf.com; rentals from €20, courses from €210

Saint Colomban Beach is a popular place to go windsurfing, and Saint-Co Windsurf can get you out on the water with equipment rentals or lessons.

Spas

SPA MARIN

2 avenue de l'Atlantique, Carnac; tel. 02 97 52 53 54; www.thalasso-carnac.com; 9am-1:30pm and 2:30pm-8pm daily; €27 for an hour, weekend courses plus accomodations €290+

If people aren't coming to Carnac for its history, then chances are they're coming to unwind. This enormous spa complex, which covers more than a square mile (2.5 square kilometers) of relaxation and well-being, has been recharging people for years. Brittany's famous seawater therapy is its specialty, but there are also saunas, steam rooms, massage options, an on-site gym, and plenty of bespoke treatments to choose from. At such a size, it lacks the exclusivity of a certain kind of luxury, but then it's big enough that you can always carve out a space of your own. Everything from spending just an hour here relaxing to extended spa courses of a week are on offer, with accommodations included in their price.

FOOD

Local Cuisine

LE 18ÈME AMENDEMENT

9 allée du Parc, Carnac; tel. 02 97 58 44 41; 12pm-1am daily; mains €15-28

Trendy and modern, this restaurant boasts a cool light-wood interior and leather seats. The food is both tasty and well presented, with slices of vegetables such as radishes used to add both bite and color. Breton flavors are well represented in the form of fish and scallops, but as the restaurant name suggests, there's a clear U.S. influence to the menu—yes, the burgers are excellent. The restaurant is family- and vegetarian-friendly, and has a laid-back terrace.

RESTAURANT LA CALYPSO

158 rue du Po, Carnac; tel. 02 97 52 06 14; www.calypso-carnac.com; 12:30pm-2pm and 7:30pm-10pm Tues.-Sun.; mains from €30

Dinner *and* a show! Fresh-as-you-can-get seafood dishes are assembled in front of your eyes, then grilled to perfection for serving. This restaurant may look unassuming from the outside, but its kitchen is an open fire at heart and a preperation station packed with denizens of the deep. If you feel your bank balance can stretch to it, the lobster is highly reccomended. Be warned, it's by no means a cheap restaurant, and fish is sold by weight at the table, meaning it's easy to get upsold. Based on the quality of the food, it's a fine value, though some people may feel a little cheated paying so much in what might be described as an "eccentric" interior. After all, the place feels less top-end restaurant and more front room of a fisherman's cottage, which is essentially what it is.

LA BRIGANTINE

3 rue Colary, Carnac; tel. 02 97 52 17 72; 12pm-2pm and 7pm-9pm Tues.-Sat.; menus €35-68

The husband-and-wife team in charge of this small, family-run restaurant enjoy talking to their customers about their dishes, adding to the convivial atmosphere. La Brigantine features a tightly curated menu crammed with local products and decor with a pleasant nautical theme, including white wooden boarding on the walls and plenty of paintings of ships. If you're a fish lover, it's hard to go wrong ordering from the menu, though the bouillabaisse is particularly delightful. Best to book in advance.

Budget Options

CHEZ AUGUSTE

Lieu-dit Montauban, Carnac; tel. 02 97 58 24 84; 12pm-1:45pm and 7pm-8:45pm daily, closed Tues. and Wed. evening; mains €3-11

Here a fun, farmhouse-like interior connects to a kitchen specializing in burgers and crepes. There's nothing remotely pretentious here, but the food is of a high, comforting standard, and it's all very family friendly. For those with slightly more refined tastes, the scallop crepes are an excellent way to go. Such indulgent desserts, too!

CRÊPERIE AU PRESSOIR

Le Ménec, Carnac; tel. 02 97 52 01 86; www.creperie-au-pressoir-carnac.fr; 12:30pm-3:30pm and 7pm-11pm daily; €6-12

Poised somewhere between extremely authentic and tourist trap, this crêperie in and around a very rustic building is a good and popular place to pause while touring the Carnac stones. The crepes themselves are decent (though the variety of toppings is a little limited), but this place really comes into its own on warm days, when you can sit in its sunny garden. A worthy pit stop to an archaeological tour.

★ HUITRES LE PRIOL

165 zone Ostréicole Du Pô, Carnac; tel. 06 89 91 17 92; www.huitreslepriol.fr; 9:30am-10pm daily July-Aug., 10am-2pm and 5:30pm-9pm Sept.-June; one oyster €1

For those who like their food rough and ready, well, it doesn't come much rougher or readier than this. Not much more than a few wooden benches cobbled together outside a working oyster farm, Huitres le Priol hardly looks like a restaurant. In a way, though, that back-to-basics quality fits perfectly with the food it sells. After all, what could be more stripped back than an oyster? Eaten raw, and ideally unadorned, these shellfish are likened by many foodies to eating the sea itself. Here, you'll see them opened in front of you and served with bread, butter, and a bottle of cool Muscadet. Sea snails, crabs, langoustine, and lobsters are also all on the menu. It's best avoided by those who don't like shellfish, as there's nothing else to eat! Seating is exclusively outside.

ACCOMMODATIONS

€50-100

★ TY ME MAMM

Quelvezin, Carnac; tel. 02 97 52 45 87; http://tymemamm.com; from €80 d

A really excellent deal, this B&B in a converted farmhouse could almost be mistaken for a swanky hotel. Situated on its own extensive grounds, the pièce de résistance is its large on-site pool. However, the comfy, homey rooms also all have flat-screen TVs and private bathrooms. The shared living area is also a great boon, coming with an open fireplace, large table, and its own cooking facilities—perfect if you've been to a local market and want to try your culinary skills on fresh Breton produce. Continental breakfast is served in the morning around a large communal table.

€100-200

HÔTEL LE CHURCHILL

70 boulevard de la Plage, Carnac; tel. 02 97 52 50 20; www.lechurchill.com; from €120 d

A resort hotel right on Carnac beach, its rooms have a slightly hermetic quality, being soundproof, very well insulated, and fixed with temperature controls. They're extremely comfortable and spotlessly clean, if a little bland, and many have private balconies looking out to the sea. There's also a sauna, hammam, and heated swimming pool on-site, and Carnac's Grand Plage is literally just across the road. Breakfast, too, comes highly recommended, and there are plenty of restaurants within walking distance for dinner.

HÔTEL LES SALINES DE THALAZUR CARNAC

2 avenue de l'Atlantique, Carnac; tel. 02 97 52 53 00; https://hotel.thalasso-carnac.com; from €140 d

Directly connected to Carnac's Spa Marin, this hotel is an effective wellness retreat with all manner of luxury treatments just a telephone call to reception away. It's the kind of place you might stay in Carnac and barely leave the compound with its tennis courts, saunas, seawater spas, and more—who needs megalithic rocks when you've got heated stones? Rooms are just on the stylish side of bland, with modern furniture and large photographs of local sights. Many have excellent views either out across Carnac's salt marshes or toward the sea. An on-site restaurant offers themed buffets every night, mostly based on local cuisine, and live music entertains guests in the lounge bar on the weekends.

Camping

CAMPING LES GOÉLANDS

Plouharnel; tel. 02 97 52 31 92; www.camping-lesgoelands.com; tent pitch for two people €16, cabins €200 per week

Well-accommodated and reasonably priced, this campsite feels like it's situated at a crossroads for the Carnac region. Both the Quiberon peninsula and Carnac's beaches are within striking distance, but more appealing than that, it's in the midst of the megalithic landscape. If any magic rests within Carnac's stones, sleeping so close to them, and under the stars, is surely the way to find it! And while searching for that magic, there's a heated indoor pool, table tennis, and even an on-site spa to keep you occupied. A high-end campground, there are ample toilet and shower facilities, a snack bar, and WiFi throughout much of the site.

TOURIST INFORMATION

CARNAC OFFICE DE TOURISME

74 avenue des Druides, Carnac; tel. 02 97 52 13 52; www.ot-carnac.fr; 9:30am-12:30pm and 2pm-5pm Mon.-Fri., 2pm-5pm Sat.

Located in Carnac-Plage, this tourist office deals with all the various elements of the region and is worth approaching whatever your interest, from windsurfing to megalithic monuments. English is widely spoken. Keep in mind, though, that when visiting the Carnac stones, the Maison de Megaliths also serves something of a tourist-office function, being the gatekeepers to tours of the stones in the high season. In addition to this beach office, Carnac tourism also sets up an information post in the center of Carnac-Ville from April to September.

TRANSPORTATION

Getting There

BY CAR

From Paris (total 300 miles/483 kilometers, 5 hours), Carnac can be reached first via the A11, which splits at Le Mans into the A81 to Rennes, then after that by N24 until Ploërmel. Until Rennes, there are toll charges on the roads costing around €25. Just coming from Rennes, the journey is about 100 miles (160 kilometers) and should take about 1 hour 45 minutes.

The journey from Nantes (100 miles/160 kilometers, 2 hours) is northwest along the N165, then turning off at Auray to head south for the coast.

Coming from the opposite direction, from Brest (100 miles/160 kilometers, 2 hours), travel along the N165.

Arriving in Carnac, there should be plenty of parking spaces. Though it can get very busy, the town council and local sights are prepared, and parking capacity doubles in the summer.

BY PUBLIC TRANSIT

There are no trains that take you directly to Carnac-Ville or Carnac-Plage. The closest main train station is the **Gare d'Auray** (place Raoult Dautry, Auray; tel. 36 35; www.gares-sncf.com/fr/gare/frxuy/auray), about eight miles northeast of Carnac.

From Paris, there are six direct trains a day to Auray, costing around €80 depending on how far in advance you book, and taking around three hours. From Rennes, there are 11 direct trains a day, costing around €30 and taking around 1 hour 20 minutes. From Brest, there is one direct train a day, costing around €40 and taking around 3.5 hours—it's also possible to reach Auray from Brest making a change at Quimper, from where there are around 12 trains every day. From Nantes, meanwhile, there are four direct trains a day, costing around €30 and taking around 1 hour 20 minutes. There are trains throughout the day from nearby Vannes (10-minute journy) and Lorient (20-minute journey), both costing around €5.

From Auray, TIM No. 1 bus run by **Mobi Breizh** (mobibreizh.bzh) leaves from outside the train station around 12 times a day. The earliest departure is 7:25am, and the latest is 7pm. It costs €2 and takes about 35 minutes to the Carnac tourist office. More details about the service can be found on the Mobi Breizh website.

Getting Around

BY BUS

The TIM No. 1 bus serves the area in general (see the Mobi Breizh website), with tickets costing €2, or €15 for a packet of 10. Beyond that, it is perfectly possible to walk a lot of the area around Carnac.

BY BICYCLE

Cycling is probably the best way to see as many of Carnac's monuments as possible in a short space of time. Bicycle rental **KTM Le Randonneur** (20 avenue des druides; tel. 06 70 75 42 13) is open year-round and offers a wide variety of different modes of pedal-powered transport, with costs starting from around €11 a day. On the same street, there's also **A Bicyclette** (93 bis avenue des Druides; tel. 02 97 52 75 08; www.velocarnac.com), which similarly has plenty of bicycle options available, costing from €10 for eight hours.

BY TAXI

There are several taxi companies around Carnac, including **Allo Carnac Taxi** (tel. 02 97 52 75 75) and **Allo Bonin Taxi** (tel. 02 97 52 12 11). The service and rates they offer are pretty similar: expect a trip from Auray train station to Carnac-Plage to cost around €24. Taxis are in high demand in the summer season and at peak times (i.e. when a train arrives), so to be sure you're not waiting around, try to book ahead if you can.

Vannes and the Gulf of Morbihan

Brittany often feels like a land touched by magic, and there few places where that is truer than the Gulf of Morbihan itself. Legends have it that this inland sea was created by the tears of fairies chased from the Brocéliande forest. A Breton saying goes that there are as many islands in the Gulf of Morbihan as there are days in the year. This is a slight exaggeration—there are in fact between 30 and 40, depending on what you're counting as an island—but the fact remains that the Gulf sparkles with a constellation of small cut-off worlds. Most of these islands are, unfortunately, privately owned, though the largest two, Île-aux-Moines and Île-d'Arz, are not, and are home to many excellent walking trails and mysterious ancient burial mounds, stone circles, and standing stones.

The undisputed architectural highlight of the Gulf of Morbihan, Vannes is a walled city that can date its heritage back almost 2,000 years. Characterized as it may be by charming timber-frame houses and ancient ramparts, as capital of the Morbihan region Vannes is far more than just a museum town. Thriving artistically, it's also home to many unexpectedly trendy bars and restaurants, and beyond the historic center are tree-lined quaysides, which are an excellent gateway onto the rest of the Gulf.

Today, it's both an excellent highlight to any tourist itinerary around the Gulf of Morbihan and a great base from which to venture forth and explore, especially for travelers without

Vannes

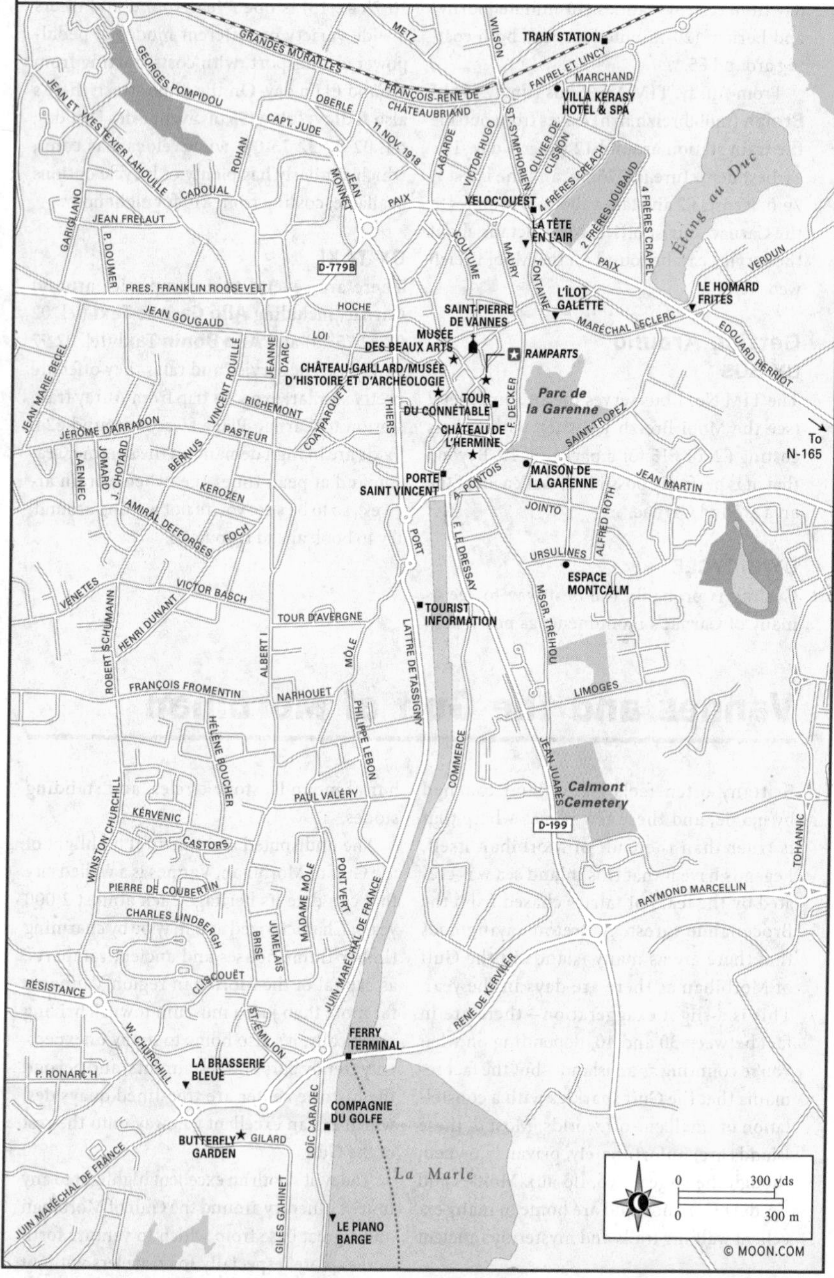
TRAIN STATION
VILLA KERASY HOTEL & SPA
VELOC'OUEST
LA TÊTE EN L'AIR
L'ÎLOT GALETTE
LE HOMARD FRITES
SAINT-PIERRE DE VANNES
MUSÉE DES BEAUX ARTS
RAMPARTS
CHÂTEAU-GAILLARD/MUSÉE D'HISTOIRE ET D'ARCHÉOLOGIE
TOUR DU CONNÉTABLE
CHÂTEAU DE L'HERMINE
PORTE SAINT VINCENT
MAISON DE LA GARENNE
Parc de la Garenne
Etang au Duc
To N-165
ESPACE MONTCALM
TOURIST INFORMATION
Calmont Cemetery
FERRY TERMINAL
LA BRASSERIE BLEUE
COMPAGNIE DU GOLFE
BUTTERFLY GARDEN
La Marle
LE PIANO BARGE
D-779B
D-199
0
300 yds
300 m
© MOON.COM

their own vehicles. Home to much of the area's tourist infrastructure, Vannes is the easiest place to grab a boat from and organize expeditions out on the famous inland sea, or indeed just to relax in, and indulge in a dash of cosmopolitanism amid an otherwise rural area.

Morbihan is a vacationer's dream, with an embarrassment of wonderful beaches and some excellent water sports. Unsurprisingly, the whole area gets very full in summer, but that's no bad thing, particularly on the Gulf itself, where a veritable carnival of different kinds of boats descends, and the sun blazes from blue waters to white sails to red kayaks in a riot of color that dazzles the eye. This said, it's worth booking accommodations well in advance just to be on the safe side.

ORIENTATION

One of the most distinctive landscapes anywhere in Brittany, the Gulf of Morbihan resembles nothing less than a fantasy landscape. It's a place where the sea has infiltrated the land, and taken a bite out of it in a manner that almost seems to contravene the natural order of things.

Starting at the mouth of the Gulf, **Locmariaquer** sits on the eastern shore, **Arzon** to the west. The latter commune is also home to one of the Gulf's busier ferry ports, **Port Navalo.** Despite their proximity, these towns occupy different administrative areas and the short distance between them is not bridged by car ferry. For drivers, both are cul-de-sacs!

Arzon, though, is at least connected by a major road, the D780. Head east along this and you reach **Sarzeau,** where the Château de Suscino is located. The road then horseshoes around, eventually reaching north of the Gulf in **Vannes**, the Gulf's biggest town with a train station and where the majority of ferry journeys can be booked in order to explore the waters.

Southwest of Vannes, not connected by such major roads, is **Baden,** from where it's possible to easily cross onto the **Île-aux-Moines.** This cross-shaped island, along with the slightly smaller **Île-d'Arz,** dominates the center of the Gulf. The two are surrounded by an archipelago of private islands, but as well as being the largest, d'Arz and Moines are the only two that can really be explored. Baden's small neighbor to its west, **Larmor-Baden,** is the access point to one of the most popular sights in the Gulf, Gavrinis Cairn.

VANNES

A town with two faces, Vannes is both its walled medieval center and its port. The former can be seen from the rue Francis Decker, which curves around the outside of its ramparts and their adjoining gardens. Inside of these walls, the town has a classic winding medieval quality, complete with half-timber houses, and the slightly boxed-in Cathedrale Saint-Pierre de Vannes at its bustling heart.

The port, meanwhile, requires a trip directly south of the center, following the banks of the Marle river, which eventually opens out into the Gulf of Morbihan. Before that though, at the start of the allée Loïc Caradec on the river's west bank, you can catch boats to the islands and farther out into the Atlantic. Farther south from here, and tapering away from the river briefly along the avenue Maréchal Juin Maréchal de France, you'll reach the Conleau peninsula, home to Vannes's beach, popular among tourists and locals alike.

Sights

★ RAMPARTS

4 rue des Vierges, Vannes; tel. 06 79 74 30 29; open daily; free

Vannes's defining quality, the town's ramparts are some of the best-preserved in all of Brittany and represent several remarkable layers of history. Strategically important since Gallo-Roman times, the oldest section of the walls (the section between the Tour Joliette and the Porte Prison) date from the end of the 3rd century. Many expansions and improvements have been made since then, most in response to the various conflicts that have swept through Brittany in the past.

Today, a walk along the walls is an absolute

must for visitors. Start at the 17th-century **Porte Saint-Vincent,** named after the city's patron saint, and make a circuit—the walk is just over half a mile and should take about 45 minutes to complete, given all you'll be wanting to look at on the way. Highlights include the **Tour du Connectable,** the highest part of the walls, built in the 1400s as a defensive structure and a residence; the 19th-century washhouses known as **The Lavoirs,** distinctive by their chimney stacks; and the rampart gardens, a comparitively recent addition, formal in the French manner and first planted in the 1950s. From here, the most iconic vista of Vannes's ramparts can be glimpsed.

MUSÉE DES BEAUX ARTS

15 place Saint-Pierre, Vannes; tel. 02 97 01 63 00; www.mairie-vannes.fr/vannesloisirs/musees/musee-des-beaux-arts; 1:30pm-6pm daily June-Sept., 1:30pm-6pm Tues.-Sun. Oct.-May; adults €6.50, reduced €4.50

Situated in an impressive timber-framed building in Vannes's historic old town, this art museum has been given a trendy refit with gallery spaces that expertly combine its stone-wall heritage with contemporary design. Arguably, its permanent collection is more of local than artistic interest, with few big-name painters to speak of, aside from one Delacroix and a Picasso print. There are, though, an interesting range of paintings depicting life around Morbihan in centuries gone by (mainly the 19th), as well as some good contemporary work. Keep an eye on the visiting exhibitions, as well, for they often include works by better-known artists. It's not a huge place, so don't expect to spend more than two hours here.

SAINT-PIERRE DE VANNES

22 rue des Chanoines, Vannes; tel. 02 97 47 10 88; www.cathedrale-vannes.fr; 8:30am-7pm daily; free

Vannes's cathedral is a Gothic structure that was slowly cobbled together piece by piece from the 15th to the 19th centuries, built over a Romanesque base. The first impression most visitors get of it, the 19th-century neo-Gothic façade, looms over a statue of Saint Vincent, a traveling priest from Valencia in the 1400s whose preaching had a great impact on Vannes, and who is now its patron saint. Inside, probably the most interesting feature are the numerous tombs, including that of Saint Vincent and of "the blessed" Pierre René, under its alter.

Aside from this, look for the chapel of Saint Anne, Brittany's patron saint, which is particularly impressive, illuminated by a stained glass window depicting events from her life. The treasury, too, constructed in the 18th century, is well worth seeing thanks to its woodwork and paneling.

CHÂTEAU DE L'HERMINE

5 rue Porte Poterne, Vannes; tel. 02 97 68 31 10; 10am-12pm and 2pm-6pm daily during exhibitions, closed between times; free

A striking neoclassical château built into Vannes's city walls, this site was once the main residence of the Dukes of Brittany between the 14th and 15th centuries. The building from that era was dismantled in the 17th century, then replaced with the current structure. Regardless of this outward change, it remains an important spot for Vannes's identity.

With a charming garden in front of it, the château is well worth visiting just for its outward elegance. It also hosts regular exhibitions, mostly of local artists, which provide a good opportunity to glimpse its interior as well.

MUSÉE D'HISTOIRE ET D'ARCHÉOLOGIE

2 rue Noé, Vannes; tel. 02 97 01 63 00; www.mairie-vannes.fr/vannesloisirs/musees/musee-dhistoire-et-darcheologie; 1:30pm-6pm daily June-Sept., 1:30pm-6pm Tues.-Sun. Oct.-May; adults €6.50, reduced €4.50

A fine example of the historical wealth of the Morbihan region, this archeology museum is itself located on a site of impressive heritage: the **Château Gaillard,** a 15th-century mansion, which simply blends into Vannes's impressively old streets. The collection is not vast, though at the same time, how many Neolithic axes do you really need to see? What it does, though, is orient visitors to the surrounding area's distant heritage. There's so much evidence of medieval life in Vannes, it's easy to forget the far more ancient culture. The jade jewelry and Roman coins are particularly impressive.

The Château-Gaillard itself, meanwhile, was once home to the parliament of Brittany, with some interiors that make a fine distraction from the archeology. The museum is located over the space of three rooms.

BUTTERFLY GARDEN

15 rue Daniel Gilard, Vannes; tel. 02 97 40 67 40; http://jardinauxpapillons.com; 11am-5:30pm Apr.-June and Sept., 10am-5:30am July-Aug.; adults €11.50, children 3-11 €8, under 3 free

Offering something entirely different and entertaining for the entire family, this is a great place to see and enjoy cascades of colorful, nonindigenous butterflies, housed in heated buildings full of exotic tropical plant life. There's also a hatchery on-site, so you can see butterflies progress from larval stages into the beautiful creatures providing the main attraction. It may seem a somewhat incongruous attraction for a trip to Brittany, but in fact there's something about the magic and the color of the place that makes it an excellent fit. There are exotic birds to spy, too, and some simple butterfly-spotting games for kids.

Beaches

PLAGE DE CONLEAU

Presqu' île de Conleau, Vannes

A well-sheltered sandy beach on a peninsula about three miles (five kilometers) south of Vannes's town center, this tourist hot spot has plenty of nearby bars and restaurants, plus a seawater pool for swimming. It can get quite busy in the summer, being popular with locals and visitors alike, though somehow the beach's slightly more urban surroundings mean that all the people give it a good holiday atmosphere rather than make it feel overcrowded. There's plenty of nearby parking, as well as showers, toilets, disabled access, and lifeguards on duty in the high season.

Boat Trips

COMPAGNIE DU GOLFE

7 allée Loïc Caradec, Vannes; tel. 02 97 67 10 00; www.compagnie-du-golfe.fr; departures 8:45am, 10:15am, and 2:15pm Apr.-Sept.; Gulf cruises from €23

Plenty of boat companies in Vannes offer tours of the Gulf of Morbihan and straightforward trips to the islands. Which one you pick is likely to depend on availability based on where and when you're departing. The Compagnie du Golfe offers three basic cruises: a nonstop boat trip (2-3 hours), one with a stop on one island (7-8 hours), and one with stops on two islands (10-11 hours). It's also possible to catch boats farther afield, to off-shore islands beyond the Gulf, such as Belle-Île, Houat, or Hoedic. It almost goes without saying, but no trip to Vannes is really complete without a Gulf tour, as the brilliant blue waters and constellation of islands are unique in Brittany, if not the world.

Festivals and Events

JAZZ EN VILLE

Multiple locations, Vannes; tel. 02 97 01 62 30; late July; free

Every July a remarkable change comes over Vannes as the town becomes less a historic destination in Brittany and instead swings to a distinctly New World rhythm. Attracting jazz musicians from around France and the world, this four-day-long festival is, remarkably, free. Multiple locations are set up across town, and from 1pm to 1am the air vibrates to clarinets, trumpets, and saxophones of all stripes, with visitors welcome to drop into whichever show they choose. The stage constructed in front of the ramparts, though, is doubtless the most impressive, offering an unlikely but spectacular backdrop to the visiting bands. Unsurprisingly, it's a very popular festival, so be aware that hotels can get booked up around the time, and restaurants can heave with customers. Plan ahead for a relaxed experience.

1

2

Food

LE PIANO BARGE

Allée Loïc Caradec, Vannes; tel. 02 97 47 76 05; www.pianobarge.com; 12pm-3pm and 7pm-12am Tues.-Thurs., 12pm-3pm and 7pm-1am Fri., 7pm-12am Sat.; menus €36.50-44.50

It's a restaurant, but also a jazz club on a boat, and that probably tells you most of what you need to know about the Piano Barge. Located outside of Vannes's old town, it offers atmosphere both laid-back and friendly, and can really swing if you get the right entertainment—bands play belowdecks, not in the restaurant itself, and usually are ticketed at about €5. The food is jazzily presented and tends to be a little lighter than you'll find in most places in this part of France, with a few zingy Asian touches to its flavors. It's best on a warm summer night, when you can take full advantage of the deck terrace, then listen to jazz as the sun goes down. Check the website to make sure there's music the night that you go.

LA BRASSERIE BLEUE

91 rue Winston Churchill, Vannes; tel. 02 97 46 40 39; www.brasserie-bleue.fr; 12pm-2pm and 7pm-10pm Mon.-Thurs.; 12pm-2:30pm and 7pm-11pm Fri.-Sat., 12pm-2:30pm and 7pm-9:30pm Sun.; menus €25-45

A modern restaurant with a no-nonsense attitude toward Breton flavors, La Brasserie Bleue has one of those menus where simply everything looks good. Try the brochette gambas (prawn kebab); it's both great to look at and delicious. The interor design is not quite as classy as it likes to think it is, but it is comfortable, and there's a charming terrace. Book ahead to be sure of a table.

★ LA TÊTE EN L'AIR

43 rue de la Fontaine, Vannes; tel. 02 97 67 31 13; www.lateteenlair-vannes.fr; 12pm-1:30pm and 7:30pm-9:30pm Thurs.-Fri. and Sun.-Mon., 7:30pm-9:30pm Sat.; lunch menu from €19, evening menus €47-65

This Aladdin's cave of gastronomy is tucked away in Vannes's old town, in a simple unpretentious interior. The food is all tasting menus of local flavors tweaked and played with in wonderfully refreshing ways. Tell the waiter if there's any food you don't eat—then the meal comes, course after course of colorful dishes that are expertly balanced with unexpected flavor combinations. For great value, drop in for lunch, where a more traditional two- or three-course meal is on offer. Be sure to book ahead!

LE HOMARD FRITES

5 place de Stalingrad, Vannes; tel. 06 60 21 65 28; http://lehomardfrites.com; 12pm-2pm and 7pm-10pm Tues.-Sat., 12pm-2pm Sun.; mains €20

In case you haven't realized it in your Brittany travels, *homard* is French for "lobster," and *frites* for "fries" (you probably know that one). Unsurprisingly given its name, this restaurant does both, and very little else. Such dedication of purpose means that they can keep the price down on what is usually a luxury ingredient, and they have worked out how to prepare the dish to perfection. The fries are thin, curling, and golden-crisp, while the rose-pink lobster is fresh as they come, given minimal preparation, tasting of nothing but its own brilliant lobsterness. Also on the menu are oysters (for starters) and surf-and-turf burgers (for the adventurous), plus a selection of standard French desserts. The interior design is basic, but pleasant, and of course there's the all-important lobster tank, filled with nervous looking crustaceans, unaware of their own deliciousness.

L'ÎLOT GALETTE

13 place du Général de Gaulle, Vannes; tel. 09 81 23 67 89; lilot-galette.business.site; 12pm-10pm Mon. and Wed., 12pm-10:30pm Thurs.-Sun.; €8-12

A straightforward Breton crepe place—which of course implies a high standard of well-prepared crepes using local ingredients where they can. Just outside the walled city, it's a couple of steps from the beaten path, meaning it has to tempt customers with its quality, and it does a such a good job that it is frequently

1: the ramparts of Vannes with the château **2:** colorful medieval houses in Vannes

busy. The interior is cheerful, bordering on twee, and there's a decent-size terrace for sunny days. Continuous service throughout the day means you'll probably be all right without booking, as long as you don't mind a bit of a wait.

Accommodations

★ ESPACE MONTCALM

Rue des Ursulines, Vannes; tel. 02 97 68 15 68; www.montcalm-vannes.org; from €40 d

Offering both a great deal on accommodations and something of an experience, the Espace Montcalm is a religious institute housed in the grand House of the Diocese of Vannes. There are a staggering 177 very reasonably priced rooms on offer, including ones for up to six people. It may be thin on luxury—if you had to label the school of interior design they follow, it would be "wipe-down"—but there's usually a lot of life in the building, religious and otherwise, with its numerous function rooms often in use. Rooms have sinks, but toilets and shower facilities are shared, and you have to bring your own towel. There are free internet hot spots throughout the building, and a continental breakfast is €5 extra.

VILLA KERASY HÔTEL & SPA

20 avenue Favrel et Lincy, Vannes; tel. 02 97 68 36 83; www.villakerasy.com; from €100 d

Asian-themed hotels may not be why most people come to Brittany, but this tastefully decorated spa just about manages to earn a shred of authenticity; its rooms are styled after the various French East India Company trading ports, which, once upon a time, would have been reached by ships sailing out of Vannes and its surrounds. In real terms, this means a lot of dark wood fixtures, Persian rugs, and Mogul arabesques on the picture frames. There's also a Japanese garden, a bar, and yoga classes offered on-site, and then of course there's the spa, which provides a steam room and India-inspired Ayurvedic treatments.. All rooms have WiFi and en suite bathrooms. The Asian theme doesn't quite cover breakfast, which is continental.

MAISON DE LA GARENNE

2 rue Sébastien de Rosmadec, Vannes; tel. 02 97 67 00 31; www.maisondelagarenne.com; from €147 d

With its large garden and outdoor swimming pool, this luxury establishment manages to trick guests into thinking they're in the countryside, even when in reality it's located barely 300 feet (100 meters) from Vannes's walled old town. The building itself is the kind of attractive 19th-century property found all over France, and it has retained a smattering of original features, including parquet floors in some rooms and an elegant wooden staircase. How well the modern additions fit into this is a matter of personal taste, with trendy floral wallpaper used to create feature walls in most of the airy, bright suites. WiFi, flat-screen TVs, and private bathrooms come as standard, and then there's the on-site spa. Continental breakfast is included in the price and is sourced from local providers.

Camping

CAMPING SITES ET PAYSAGES DE PENBOCH

9 chemin de Penboch, Arradon; tel. 02 97 44 71 29; www.camping-penboch.fr; Apr.-Sept.; two people and tent €35, cabins from €111

Here's the kind of camping site that offers a holiday all on its own. Boasting an extensive indoor and outdoor swimming pool complex, it's also right on the Gulf of Morbihan itself. It has its own little food shop, plus a bar for the evenings. About three miles (five kilometers) south of Vannes, it is a different world from the town, and really is a good launchpad for multiple directions. The shower and toilet blocks are clean and well maintained, and there's internet access near the main site buildings.

Information

The main branch of **Golfe du Morbihan Vannes Tourisme** (quai Éric Tabarly, Vannes; tel. 02 97 47 24 34; www.golfedumorbihan.bzh; 9:30am-12:30pm and 1:30pm-6pm Mon.-Sat.) is located in a purpose-built one-floor building on the banks of the Marle in Vannes. There are plenty of screens and leaflets giving information, and English is widely spoken.

Transportation

Vannes serves as the main entrance and exit point to the area surrounding the Gulf of Morbihan.

BY CAR

The journey to Vannes from Paris (total 300 miles/483 kilometers, 4.5 hours) first starts via the A11, which splits at Le Mans into the A81 to Rennes. Then after that, it's the N24 until Ploërmel, then the N166 toward the coast. Until Rennes, there are toll charges on the roads costing around €25. Just coming from Rennes, the journey of just over 100 miles (160 kilometers) and should take about 1.5 hours.

The journey from Nantes (80 miles/128 kilometers, 1.5 hours) is northwest along the N165.

From Brest (120 miles/193 kilometers, 2 hours), the journey is along the same road (the N165) but from the opposite direction, going via Lorient and Quimper.

Within Vannes and around the Gulf of Morbihan, driving is not the ideal mode of transport; walking or riding a bike is more suited to exploring this town.

BY TRAIN

Vannes has a major train station, the **Gare de Vannes** (rue Favel et Lincy, Vannes; tel. 08 92 35 35 35; www.gares-sncf.com/fr/gare/frvne/vannes), and thus is very well connected to the rest of France.

From Paris to Vannes there are nine direct trains a day, costing around €80 depending on how far in advance you book and taking around 2.5 hours. From Rennes, trains run very regularly throughout the day (sometimes more than two an hour), cost €20-30, and take around an hour. From Brest, there is one direct train a day, costing around €40 and taking about three hours—there are several more that require a change at Quimper. From Nantes, meanwhile, there are four direct trains a day, costing around €30 and taking around 1.5 hours. From nearby Lorient, there are trains throughout the day, costing around €5 and taking around 30 minutes.

BY BUS

The **TIM bus service** stops just outside Vannes train station and is serviced by around eight buses daily from Carnac, costing €2 and taking about 1 hour 20 minutes, and Quiberon, also €2, about 1 hour 45 minutes.

Local buses in the Gulf of Morbihan area are run by **Kiceo** (www.kiceo.fr), although their frequency and hours change almost daily and finding their stops can be unintuitive. In Vannes, the most useful line will likely be Line 3, which leaves from the town's central Place de la Republique and gets you to Plage de Conleau in about 15 minutes. Most journeys will cost around €2.

BY BOAT

The port in Vannes (Allée Loïc Caradec, Vannes) is one of the main ports serving Gulf destinations. Ferries between Vannes, Îles-aux-Moines, and Île d'Arz, are provided by several companies, including **Vedettes du Golf** (tel. 02 97 44 44 40, www.vedettes-du-golfe.fr) and **Navix** (tel. 02 97 46 60 00; www.navix.fr). They run regularly throughout most of the year, except during the deep winter months. Be aware, though, that many trips are designed as Gulf tours or cruises, rather than as mass transit. The price depends on the course you choose; for example, Vannes to Île-d'Arz costs about €18.

ON FOOT AND BY BIKE

Vannes itself is a small and fairly walkable town, but if you're planning on seeing more of the Gulf (which is recommended), renting a bike for your stay is a great way to go, especially since around the Gulf by car is difficult. It's well worth hiring a bike for several days, then paying the extra fare to get it onto ferries, crossing to islands, or opposite sides of the Gulf. There are plenty of bike-hire businesses in town, and they offer similar prices and services. One place to rent wheels is **Veloc'Ouest** (2 bis avenue Saint-Symphorien, Vannes; tel. 06 73 58 72 33; www.velocouest.fr).

BY TAXI

In Vannes, there are several cab companies, with **Radio Taxi Vannestais** (tel. 97 54 34 34; www.radiotaxisvannetais.com) being the most central.

ÎLE-AUX-MOINES

This narrow, cross-shaped island is the largest of islands dotting the Gulf of Morbihan and one of the few that are not privately owned. There are dolmens and stone markers of various sorts scattered about the island, which you will no doubt come across during any walk around the island, but the main attractions here are the island's natural beauty and the gorgeous views of the Gulf—perhaps best enjoyed over a plate of oysters and a glass of white wine.

Beaches

LA GRANDE PLAGE

Île-aux-Moines

Located on a narrow spit of land near where ferries dock in the north of the Île-aux-Moines, this thoroughly excellent beach is sandy, picturesque, and sheltered. Swimming is possible here at both high and low tide, while along its length are a number of colorful beach huts, backed by elegant villas. It's unsupervised and there are no amenities apart from the public toilets nearby.

Boat Tours

IZENAH CROISIÈRES

Le Port, Île-aux-Moines; tel. 02 97 26 31 45; www.izenah-croisieres.com; 7am-7:30pm Sept.-June, 7am-10pm July-Aug.; adults from €17.50, under 12 from €9.50

As well as offering a direct ferry service between the mainland and the Gulf's two main islands, Izenah Croisières is one of the least expensive ways to tour Morbihan's waters. Buy a ticket to or from Île-aux-Moines and/or Île-d'Arz and the ferry takes a roundabout route to your destination. They also offer other types of excursions, including several in which you are served a picnic or larger meal as part of the package. The food is mainly local, and includes a fruits de mer (seafood platter) selection if you feel like indulging.

Food

RESTAURANT LES EMBRUNS

Rue du Commerce, Île-aux-Moines; tel. 02 97 26 30 86; www.restaurant-ile-morbihan.com; 12pm-2pm and 7:30pm-9pm Wed.-Mon. Sept.-June, 12pm-2pm and 7:30pm-9pm daily July-Aug.; menus €20.50-29.50

This restaurant is something of an anomaly. Located on Île-aux-Moines, which for all its natural beauty can feel entirely given over to tourism, it retains a strong, uncompromising local vibe. Furthermore, in a place where speed of service is often high on people's priorities, given they often have ferries to catch, it is dedicated to the languorous, indulgent pace of true French dining. If you don't like the sound of this, give it a wide berth, for it is a place that turns the "customer is always right" trope emphatically on its head. At the same time, the food is rich and traditional, and an excellent value given the restaurant's location. Come for a slow Sunday lunch and you won't be disappointed, though be sure to book ahead.

BARA PITA

Rue du Commerce, Île-aux-Moines; tel. 06 84 29 84 73; 11:30am-7:30pm Fri.-Sun.; mains €7

An unlikely find on the Île-aux-Moines, this is an above-average Lebanese take-out joint, with service throughout the day of freshly prepared food, including kebabs and veggie options. The flavors are zingy and come straight from the Mediterranean, and the owner is friendly and speaks excellent English. A good antidote to those suffering crepe fatigue—just don't tell the Bretons!

★ ETS MARTIN

Beg Moussir, Île-aux-Moines; tel. 02 97 26 31 56; www.huitres-ileauxmoines.fr; 11:30am-5:30pm daily; one oyster €1

Though it's little more than a shack selling oysters, with a small garden and tent for shelter overlooking the beds from which they were farmed, this unpretentious spot delivers perhaps the best way to eat the mollusk, which thrives off lack of adornment. The food comes on minimalist white plates with nothing more than a lemon at their center and a basket of dense brown bread on the side. There are also drinks available, though everyone knows ice cold dry white wine is the only real option. The views out across the Gulf are spectacular. It almost goes without saying, though, that the quality of experience here is quite weather dependent. On a good day, however, there can't be many better places to pause for lunch in all of Morbihan.

Accommodations and Camping

HÔTEL REST. LE SAN FRANCISCO

Rue Benoni Praud, Île-aux-Moines; tel. 02 97 26 31 52; http://lesanfrancisco.com; from €110 d

It may be leaning over to the expensive end of what you can get for the price on this island, but this hotel is still basically a good value, well set up on a harbor with some excellent views out across the Gulf. The rooms are comfortable, clean, and tasteful, with plenty of smooth pine surfaces and windows letting in a lot of light—the one with the balcony is pretty special. WiFi is available throughout, all rooms have en suite bathrooms, and there's a good on-site restaurant, which attracts a lot of business and does an excellent lobster.

CAMPING MUNICIPAL

Le Vieux Moulin, Île-aux-Moines; tel. 02 97 26 30 68; www.mairie-ileauxmoines.fr/accueil/decouverte/camping_municipal; Apr. 28-Sept. 23; two people in a tent €15, furnished heavy canvas tents from €77

Municipal campsites are the very best way to see France on an ultra-shoestring budget, and it's refreshing to know that they can exist even on such potential tourist magnets as the Île-aux-Moines. With 41 pitches, sheltered by trees, and less than 1,000 feet (300 meters) from the beach, this is a great place to spend a holiday. Granted, amenities are pretty limited, but there is a shower block and toilets. Good for a short or extended stay. Make sure to book ahead in high season. Note: There's no electricity for campers.

Information

The **Île-aux-Moines Tourist Office** (rue Benoni Praud, tel. 02 97 26 32 45; www.golfedumorbihan.bzh; 9:30am-1pm and 2pm-5:15pm daily) is located near the port and will help you plan your time and find accommodations. English is spoken.

Transportation

BY BOAT

The only way to get to the island is by boat. The main ferry terminal on the island is Le Port, and there are various ports around the Gulf with departures to Île-aux-Moines. The main ones are **Baden** (l'Embarcadere, Port Blanc, Baden), to the west and the closest to the island; Vannes (Allée Loïc Caradec, Vannes); Port Navalo in the southeast (La criée, Rue du Général De Gaulle, Arzon), and Locmariaquer in the southwest (Port du Guilvin, Locmariaquer). Several boat and ferry companies serve the islands from these ports, including including **Izenah Croisieres** (tel. 02 97 26 31 45, www.izenah-croisieres.com), **Vedettes du Golf** (tel. 02 97 44 44 40, www.vedettes-du-golfe.fr), **Navix** (tel. 02 97 46 60 00; www.navix.fr), and **Vedettes Angelus** (tel. 02 97 57 30 29; www.vedettes-angelus.com). Be aware that many of their trips are billed less as a form of practical transport and more as pleasure cruises. Expect prices to start at around €4 for the shortest crossings, like Baden to Île-aux-Moines, and be around €18 for the longer ones.

ON FOOT AND BY BIKE

At about six kilometers at its longest, Île-aux-Moines is best explored on foot or on a bicycle. On the Île-aux-Moines, **Location de Vélos P'tit Louis** (rue Benoni Praud, Île-aux-Moines; tel. 02 97 26 35 21; http://locationdevelosptitlouis.com) rents out bikes from €8.50 per four hours.

ÎLE-D'ARZ

Slightly smaller than Île-aux-Moines, this island also affords a beautiful setting and can be well explored on a half- or full-day trip.

Beaches

PLAGE DE LA FALAISE

Avenue du Gal de Gaulle, Île-d'Arz

The first beach most people are going to come across when they land by boat on the Île-d'Arz, this is therefore the island's most popular one, too. It's got advantages and disadvantages—certainly there are more unspoiled places to swim if you persevere into the island—but if you need things to keep you occupied on a beach, then this is the place. Everywhere you look in high season there's something happening, from oyster beds to the back-and-forth of ferries to views of the Île-aux-Moines. There are also showers and public toilets, and the beach has disabled access, making it the most civilized on the island.

Hiking

ÎLE-D'ARZ LOOP

The coastal walk around the Gulf's second island is easy (because it's almost completely flat), beautiful (thanks to its rugged shores), and almost impossible to get lost on (it's pretty much just a simple loop). Starting and ending at the ferry terminal, the entire walk is about 10 miles (16 kilometers), but should take less than four hours on account of the easy terrain. There are also plenty of well-signposted paths that can be followed to cut it short. Don't miss the views across the water of **Moulin à Marée de Berno,** a tidal mill on a causeway to the island's west, less than a mile south along the coast from its ferry port that has been impressively restored in recent times. There are several bars and restaurants in the island interior if you want to break up your walk for refreshments.

Accommodations

L'ESCALE EN ARZ

Cale de Béluré, avenue Charles de Gaulle, Île-d'Arz; tel. 02 97 44 32 15; www.restaurant-escale.com; from €80 d

This two-story building sits in an absolutely stunning location, on the water just back from Île-d'Arz's wharf. Accommodations in such a unique setting tend to be more, well, unique in itself, but this offers a fairly basic setup of comfortable, inoffensive modern rooms and a decent on-site restaurant on its terrace serving local cuisine and continental breakfast in the morning. The best thing about all this is the price, reasonable enough for even budget travelers to drop in. Rooms have en suite bathrooms, and there's WiFi throughout.

Transportation

BY BOAT

The only way to get to the island is by boat, which land at Embarcadère Île-d'Arz. There are various ports around the Gulf with departures to the island. The main ones are Vannes (Allée Loïc Caradec, Vannes), Baden (l'Embarcadere, Port Blanc, Baden) to the west, Port Navalo in the southeast (La criée, Rue du Général De Gaulle, Arzon), and Locmariaquer in the southwest (Port du Guilvin, Locmariaquer). Several boat and ferry companies serve the islands from these ports, including **Izenah Croisieres** (tel. 02 97 26 31 45, www.izenah-croisieres.com), **Vedettes du Golf** (tel. 02 97 44 44 40, www.vedettes-du-golfe.fr), **Navix** (tel. 02 97 46 60 00; www.navix.fr), and **Vedettes Angelus** (tel. 02 97 57 30 29; www.vedettes-angelus.com). Be aware that many of their trips are billed less as a form of practical transport and more as pleasure cruises. Expect prices to start at around €4 for the shortest crossings, and be around €18 for the longer ones, such as Vannes to Île-d'Arz.

ON FOOT

Exploring Île-d'Arz on foot is easy—the perimeter walk is 10 miles (16 kilometers) over mostly flat terrain, and you can cut across the island at different points to make the walk even shorter.

AROUND THE GULF

The towns of Locmariaquer, Baden, Arzon, and their neighbors are not only jumping-off points for exploring the islands of the Gulf, they also have Neolithic sites and other attractions in their own right.

Sights

SITE DES MÉGALITHES DE LOCMARIAQUER

Route de Kerlogonan, Locmariaquer; tel. 02 97 57 37 59; www.site-megalithique-locmariaquer.fr; 10am-6pm daily May-June, 10am-7pm daily July-Aug., 10am-12:30pm and 2pm-5:15pm Sept.-Apr.; adults €6, reduced €5, under 18 free

A large megalithic site, this curiosity is just as interesting as anything you'll find at Carnac down the road. Fronted by a visitor center, the site is dominated by **La Table des Marchands,** a collective tomb mound from around 3000 BC. Unlike many such structures in the region, it's actually possible to go inside the tomb, which resembles a stone igloo. Being in such an ancient structure is enough to induce a kind of historical vertigo as you imagine the impossibly distant lives of the people who first built it, and of the individuals who were then buried inside. Also very impressive on the site is the **Grand Menhir Brisé.** This vast obelisk is now on its side and broken into four parts, which have been dated to 4500 BC. When it was upright and in a single piece it would have been 65 feet (20 meters) tall and have weighed 350 tons (317 metric tons), making it the equal of monuments from other ancient cultures more renowned for their technology, such as the ancient Egyptians.

A short movie presentation at the visitors center suggests a few theories on how the site came to be built in the first place—watching this is a real must to help bring the whole place into context. As it's not a huge site, expect to spend between 30 minutes and an hour looking around.

CAIRN DU PETIT MONT

Site du Petit Mont, Le Crouesty, Arzon; tel. 02 97 53 74 03; www.morbihan.fr/petit-mont; 11am-6:30pm daily July-Aug., 2pm-6:30pm Tues.-Sun. Feb. 10-Mar. 11, Apr.-June, Sept., and Oct. 20-Nov. 4; adults €6, reduced €5, under 18 free

A veritable pyramid, this immense, tiered stone structure on top of a rocky promontory is surely as impressive as anything in Brittany. Formed out of hundreds of painstakingly laid dry stones, it was not built in a single go. Instead, it represents the work of many hands over many centuries, and still has a volume of 350,000 cubic feet (10,000 cubic meters), looming almost 7 meters tall at its highest point. In a bizarre twist to its history, the last people to add to it were the Nazis during World War II, when they converted parts of it into a bunker as part of Hitler's famous system of coastal defenses. The combination of concrete with dry stones gives it an almost sci-fi aspect.

The structure's setting alone, though, would make it worth a visit, with spectacular views out across the Gulf. It sits, after all on a Petit Mont (a little mountain). There's no need to get out your hiking gear, though, as emphasis should be on the little; it only stands 118 feet (36 meters) above sea level and is easy to walk to. There's a small visitors center, with a fairly limited amount of information, selling tickets and booking tours of the monument (unfortunately, only in French). Visitors are given remarkable freedom of access, however, being allowed to step inside its dark passageways and clamber to its peak to admire the view.

★ GAVRINIS CAIRN

Rue de Pen Lammic, Larmor-Baden; tel. 02 97 57 19 38; www.morbihan.fr/gavrinis; departures 9:30am and 1:30pm daily Apr.-Sept., 1:30pm Tues.-Sun. Feb. 10-Mar. 11 and Oct. 20-Nov. 4; adult return €18, children 10-17 return €8, under 10 free

An ancient burial mound, webbed through by

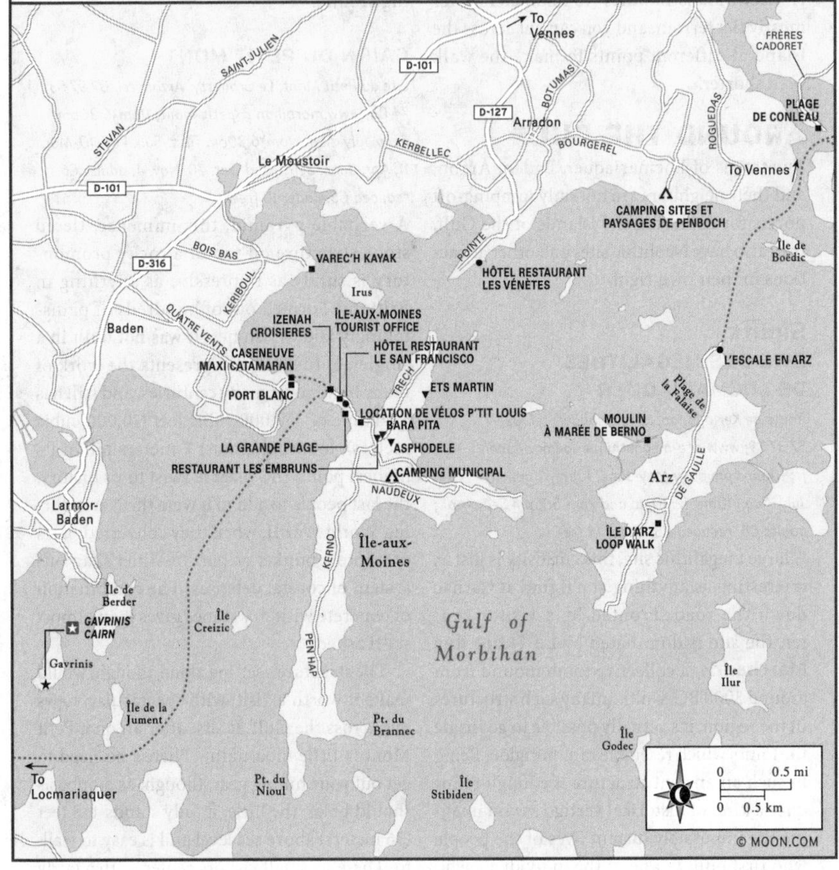

stone passages and covered in dry stone, the Gavrinis Cairn is home to what are some of the very best Neolithic carvings around the Gulf of Morbihan. These patterns of spirals and rings give the rocks here an almost organic quality; it's as though they contain the fossils of a culture, as unknowable as it is beguiling. Justifiably popular, the sight is located on its own island, which is part privately owned. Visits here can only be conducted as part of a tour that leaves from the port of **Larmor-Baden** and must be organized in advance. Even as part of a group, though, there's a sense of real adventure in having to set out across the water in order to get to such a beguiling sight, especially as you can see other, part-submerged Neolithic monuments cresting the waves on the approach.

Tours are only available in French and can feel a little mechanical since the guides often have large crowds to get through. Only 10 people are allowed inside the monument at a time, so also expect some waiting around. If you want to avoid the queues, book the first tour of the day. Nevertheless, there's plenty here that you don't need to be told anything about to appreciate, with intricate mysterious patterns carved into almost every rock inside the tomb. They are both aesthetically mesmerizing and giddying in the vastness of time they represent—the Cairn is said to date from 3500 BC.

ÎLE DE BERDER

Access via Larmor-Baden; www.larmorbaden.com/tourisme/sites-a-visiter/ile-berder; consult tidal charts; free

A small tidal island characterized by its Mediterranean vegetation, Île de Berder has been privately owned by a series of individuals who have left much of it open for visitors to come and enjoy its riches. A stroll around the public sections of the island should take 1-2 hours, along a rocky, forested coastline with plenty of intriguing distractions. These include an abandoned chapel, oyster farms, and a small shipwreck left entirely exposed at low tide. From the south of the island there's also a terrific view of Europe's second most powerful current, La Jument, which makes the sea churn.

It's a great, contained place to explore for a morning or afternoon as a family, particularly if you pack a picnic. Keep aware of the tides, though, as the island can only be reached when they are low (a period of roughly four hours a day), so you should make sure to check the local tourist office website to plan your time here.

★ CHÂTEAU DE SUSCINIO

Sarzeau; tel. 02 97 41 91 91; http://suscinio.fr; 2pm-5pm daily Jan. 8-Feb. 9 and Nov. 13-Dec. 25, 10am-6pm daily Feb. 10-Mar. and Oct.-Nov. 12, 10am-7pm daily Apr.-Jun. and Sept., 10am-8pm July-Aug.; adults €9.80, children 10-17 €4.90, under 10 free

This spectacular, imposing castle in the fairytale mold was built in the 13th century as a country retreat and hunting lodge for the dukes of Brittany. Further fortified in the 14th century as heirs to the duchy struggled against the French to retain their land, it's had its ups and downs since then, and fell into disrepair following the French revolution. In more recent years it was painstakingly restored to give visitors a clear glimpse of its history.

It's a very impressive building, consisting of high battlements, punctuated by fearsome towers, building to conical roofs, and surrounded by a moat. And while the rooms themselves are a little bare, there is a good audio guide (in English as well as French) that helps bring them to life. With their riveting views, the castle battlements in particular benefit from this treatment, and there's also an attempt to link the building with some of the stories of King Arthur, though in reality there was no connection. The castle makes a great day out for kids with lively imaginations, who will be convincing themselves they're back in the age of chivalry, slaying dragons and rescuing damsels (or "man-sels") in distress in no time!

Recreation

CASENEUVE MAXI CATAMARAN

Baden; tel. 06 82 69 38 13; www.anne-caseneuve.com; daily tours July-Aug., by demand rest of year; adults from €35, under 13 from €30, private group tours from €600

Journeys on a catamaran are an excellent way to explore the various islands from the water, and this large, professional company (which also has outlets in the Caribbean and Saint-Tropez) offers a wide variety of options, either as part of a group, or in your own private party. Trips usually take about three hours, and the most common one actually involves leaving the Gulf to sail around the Île d'Houat. Children are welcome on board, and the staff mostly speak English well.

VAREC'H KAYAK

70 rue de Bois Bas, Baden; tel. 06 03 32 35 67; www.bretagne-kayak.fr; 9am-7pm daily (call ahead out of season); €20 per two hours

Kayaking really is the easiest, most accessible water sport of them all, and a great way for all ages and levels to get what really is an essential experience of the Gulf du Morbihan: seeing it from the water, under your own steam. Varec'h Kayak lets you do this. Well-located

★ Sailing the Gulf of Morbihan

What could be better? The smell of the salty air, the pull of strange currents, the mysterious outline of Stone Age-era finds winking at you from beneath azure waters, and islands in every direction you turn, each one its own miniature world. The term "unmissable" is thrown around quite a lot in tourism, but here it's no overstatement. If you come to the Gulf of Morbihan, you simply cannot turn down taking to its waves.

But how best to do that? There are plenty of different ways to float these waters, from motorized ferries to kayaking under your own steam. Each has its advantages and disadvantages, and each appeals to different price brackets and states of physical fitness. There's also the question of how you want to spend your day: learning facts or quaffing chilled white wine? Choosing your own adventure or being taken by the hand? Maybe a mix of all? The suggestions below are aimed to make sure your experience of this unmissable activity is the best (for you) that it can be.

- **Varec'h Kayak** (70 rue de Bois Bas, Baden; tel. 06 03 32 35 67; www.bretagne-kayak.fr; 9am-7pm daily; from €20 per two hours): Needing almost no prior experience, kayaking is a wonderful, inexpensive way to tour the Gulf. Varec'h Kayak, well located in Baden for quick access to some of the most interesting parts of the Gulf, offers rentals and extensive tours.
- **Caseneuve Maxi Catamaran** (Baden; tel. 06 82 69 38 13; www.anne-caseneuve.com; tours in July and Aug. daily, rest of the year by demand; adults from €35, under 13 from €30, private group tours from €600): A more luxury company whose catamarans cut through the waves with silent ease, leaving you with the sensation that this was how water travel was always meant to be powered: by wind. Often they head beyond the Gulf to sail around the Île d'Houat. All experience levels are welcomed.
- **Compagnie du Golfe** (7 allée Loïc Caradec, Vannes; tel. 02 97 67 10 00; www.compagnie-du-golfe.fr; departures 8:45am, 10:15am, and 2:15pm Apr.-Sept.; Gulf cruises from €23): While a more basic boat tour company, this is a stress-free option, and unlikely to break the bank. They offer a variety of different trips, so you're bound to find one that suits your tastes and timeframe.

for quick access to the waves and easy exploration of interesting sights, it offers several services, including lessons, guided tours around the coasts, and rentals. If you rent, you could even pack a picnic, then go searching for some secluded cove on which to enjoy it. However, be sure to pay attention to the advice and charts given before you set out, for Morbihan has some very strong currents.

Food

★ LE P'TIT ZEPH

1 rue du Phare, Arzon; tel. 02 97 49 40 34; www.bar-ptitzeph.fr; 10am-2pm and 7pm-11pm Tues.-Sun.; mains €29

Another waterfront restaurant, this one boasts some lovely views of the channel leading into the Gulf of Morbihan. It specializes in seafood, which comes presented with an artist's eye, and it is a great place to try local oysters or fruits de mer. The interior is unpretentious, letting the spectacular location speak for itself. Worth booking ahead, especially in the summer, if only to secure a seat on its terrace. Dining inside in good weather is going to feel like missing out.

HÔTEL L'ESCALE

2 place Dariorigum, Locmariaquer; tel. 02 97 57 32 51; www.escale-hotel.com/hotel-locmariaquer-fr,cote-resto,2.html; 12pm-2pm and 7pm-11pm Mon.-Sat.; menus €17.90-24.50

Located directly on the water in an old building with an enviable terrace, this is a good-value slice of authentic Brittany. The food is not flashy, but it is tasty, and there enough local flavors to satisfy the more intrepid travelers, while solid French classics of unfussy steak and fries please those with less adventurous palates. Best when the tide's in and the water's lapping at the terrace walls.

Accommodations

HÔTEL DES TROIS FONTAINES

Route d'Auray, Locmariaquer; tel. 02 97 57 42 70; www.hotel-troisfontaines.com; from €90 d

This friendly, old-fashioned hotel, popular with an older clientele, is not quite on the Gulf itself, but it does have some excellent views out across the water. The rooms are about as far from hip as you're likely to get, but they are very comfortable. Situated in its own floral grounds, just a short walk from the shops, and run by a friendly couple, it's an excellent base to stay in for several nights. Continental breakfast is served on-site, and there is Wi-Fi throughout.

MIRAMAR LA CIGALE HÔTEL THALASSO & SPA

Port du Crouesty, route du Petit Mont, Arzon; tel. 02 97 53 49 00; www.miramar-lacigale.com; from €180 d

Looking something like a vast cruise ship that's run aground, though still facing the Atlantic, this is a modern luxury complex offering relaxation and well-being. Well-insulated with an on-site spa, gym, restaurant, and more, it's a holiday in and of itself, and certainly some guests are likely to see it like that. There's a little more character and taste to its interiors than many such places, though, and its large windows make the most of its beautiful surroundings. The staff are extremely attentive, of course, and all the expected five-star accoutrements are present, from very comfy beds to minibars to a very accommodating front desk. The restaurant, though good, is a little overpriced; food just as good can be found for cheaper if you leave the hotel.

Information

There are numerous tourist offices around the Gulf du Morbihan, with branches that include the the **Bureau de Sarzeau** (rue Père Marie Joseph Coudrin, Sarzeau; tel. 02 97 53 69 69; www.golfedumorbihan.bzh; 9am-12pm and 2pm-6pm Mon.-Sat.) and the **Locmariaquer Bureau de Tourisme** (1 rue de la Victoire; tel. 02 97 57 33 05; www.morbihan-way.fr/fr; 9am-12:30pm and 2pm-5:30pm Mon.-Sat.). The various tourist offices differ slightly, but will largely help you find the same stuff, including planning your time and find accommodations across the region. English should be widely spoken in all of them.

Transportation

The main entrance and exit point to the area surrounding the Gulf of Morbihan is the town of Vannes.

BY CAR

Cars are not the ideal transport for getting the most out of the Gulf du Morbihan. The reason for this, obviously, lies in the region's geography. While roads do loop the Gulf, there are no car ferries crossing it, meaning that journeys between locations that may be quite close together as the crow flies can actually take an annoyingly long time to complete. The most important of these to be aware of is that there is no car ferry between Arzon and Locmariaquer, which are split by the channel leading into the Gulf. Getting between the two in your own vehicle takes easily over an hour. Far better to park at one, then use the ferry to cross over.

That said, the major roads for getting around the Gulf of Morbihan are the D101 to the north west, and the D780 to the east. The arterial N165 runs just above the Gulf meanwhile. It runs through Vannes and is the fastest way to access the region. From Vannes to Larmor-Baden is around 10 miles (16 kilometers) and should take about 20 minutes down the D101, and to Locmariaquer it's about 18 miles (30 kilometers) via Auray along the N165 and should take 30 minutes. In the other direction, from Vannes to Sarzeau is about 16 miles (27 kilometers) and should take about 25 minutes, and to Arzon is around 22 miles (37 kilometers), both down the D780.

There are, at least, plenty of places where

you can park around the Gulf, leaving your car while you set off to explore its waters. If not free, then expect to pay about €1 an hour for parking privileges. Check the specifics of the parking lot, though, as some are meant for longer, others for shorter stays.

BY BOAT

There are few better ways to appreciate the Gulf du Morbihan than to travel by boat. Several ferry services, including **Izenah Croisieres** (tel. 02 97 26 31 45, www.izenah-croisieres.com), **Vedettes du Golf** (tel. 02 97 44 44 40, www.vedettes-du-golfe.fr), **Navix** (tel. 02 97 46 60 00; www.navix.fr), and **Vedettes Angelus** (tel. 02 97 57 30 29; www.vedettes-angelus.com) can help you do this, and they run regularly throughout most of the year (less regularly in the deep winter months). It's via these that you can access the two major islands, as well as bridge the vital channel between Arzon and Locmariaquer.

The main ports of the Gulf are in Vannes (Allée Loïc Caradec, Vannes), Baden to the west (l'Embarcadere, Port Blanc, Baden), Port Navalo in the southeast (La criée, Rue du Général De Gaulle, Arzon), Locmariaquer in the southwest (Port du Guilvin, Locmariaquer), and those on the two islands of Île-d'Arz (Embarcadère Ile D'Arz, Ile D'Arz) and Île-aux-Moines (Le Port, Île-aux-Moines). Be aware that linking between all these destinations using just one ferry company is not always straightforward, particularly in the winter months—many of their trips are billed less as a form of practical transport and more as pleasure cruises. It should be possible, however, provided you're not too pressed for time.

Expect prices to start at around €4 for the shortest crossings, like Baden to Île-aux-Moines, and be around €18 for the longer ones, such as Vannes to Île-d'Arz.

BY BUS

Run by a company called **Kiceo** (www.kiceo.fr), there are extensive local bus networks linking up much of the Gulf du Morbihan, though it can take some perseverance to be confident using them, given the way timetables fluctuate daily and depending on the season, and how stops are not always obvious to the non-local—in many places they won't be much more than a sign on a single pole, with the stop name and the line numbers that stop there written on it. (They're easier to track down with Google Maps than on the Kiceo website.) Indeed, you might find yourself wondering if any bus will actually come, and if it does, will it stop? But they will.

Buses are cheap—most journeys won't cost any more than €2—and reliable: Ignore the doubt that can easily set in at rural bus stops! Also, the website explaining the various routes is comprehensive and user-friendly, even if you don't speak French.

If you plan well, then buses can sometimes even be a better way of getting around the area than by car, offering more freedom to leap on and off ferries and cross the Gulf more directly than having to drive around its entire coastline.

ON FOOT AND BY BIKE

The wealth of things to see over a relatively small area, and the difficulty of getting around the Gulf by car, mean that getting around by bike is a great way to go, not just on the islands, but all over. It's well worth hiring a bike for several days, then paying the extra fare to get it onto ferries, crossing to islands, or opposite sides of the Gulf. It's no surprise then that there are plenty of bike-hire businesses all over the gulf, all of which offer pretty similar prices and services, from normal bikes to electric bikes to bikes pulling baby carts.

Wheels can be hired in Arzon at **Cycles de l'Ocean** (50 rue Centrale, Arzon; tel. 02 97 53 74 19; www.cycles-ocean.com; 9:30am-7pm daily high season; from €5 per four hours) and in Sarzeau **Abbis bike rental** (7 allée des Ducs de Bretagne, Sarzeau; tel. 06 47 04 28 99; www.abbis-location.fr; from €10 per four hours), two reliable options.

BY TAXI

If you're not driving, taxi can be another way to get around the Gulf of Morbihan. In Baden **Taxi du Golf** (tel. 06 61 16 56 56; www.taxi-du-golfe-56.com), in Arzon **Crouesty Taxis** (tel. 02 97 53 94 06), and in Locmariaquer **ABL Taxi** (tel. 02 97 57 31 17; abl-taxi.fr) are reliable.

Guérande and La Baule

It hardly seems possible for a place to be both a generations-old resort town frequented by the glamorous, and yet at the same time, be practically unknown by international tourists. But this is precisely what you have in La Baule. Located on a stunning natural bay, sandy from Pornichet to Pouliguen, and overlooked by sparkling five-star hotels and venerable belle epoque villas, it's been a hit with France's chattering classes ever since the late 19th century. But unlike comparable towns such as Saint-Tropez and Deauville, it's little talked about in the wider world.

The whys and wherefores of this anomaly are for sociologists to ponder; all foreign visitors need do is take advantage of it: the stunning scimitar-cradling open ocean, the Lucien Barrière casino-hotel-sports complexes akin to those of Deauville, and the top-end restaurants lining the bay. Sharing all this mainly with French vacationers gives a sense of what it must have been like to visit the country in the past, and indeed, perhaps more than anything else, it's this sense of bygone glamour that is La Baule's stock in trade.

Then, just down the coast is a town that has done more to contribute to the overall flavor of Brittany than pretty much any other—literally. Guérande is home to the region's famous salt marshes, a briny patchwork of more than seven square miles (18 square kilometers) that's been being harvested since medieval times. Both a natural wonder and the heart of a centuries-old industry, it's a fascinating destination that's a world away from the glitz of La Baule. Though, of course, none of the fries, fish, or other fantastic food served in the latter's classy restaurants could taste the same without it.

ORIENTATION

Defined absolutely by its long bay, La Baule is an easy enough town in which to orient yourself. Its main commercial street is the avenue du General de Gaulle, which starts just south of the train station and runs a little less than half a mile directly to the beach. Arriving facing the sea, take the esplanade Francois Andre to your right to reach the **Hôtel Barrière** and its casino—besides the bay, probably the most definitive aspect of this town.

As written above, go far enough west and you're technically in the town of Pornichet; head to the east and you reach Pouliguen. The distance is about five miles (eight kilometers), but the beach remains the same.

Guérande, meanwhile, is about 10 minutes northwest of La Baule's center, while its famous salt marshes bloom out to the west. Head directly into them, rather than into the town, to organize a tour. The **Terre de Sel,** the main museum and visitors center, is about a mile south of Guérande proper.

SIGHTS

★ GUÉRANDE SALT MARSHES

Terre de Sel, Guérande; tel. 02 40 62 08 80; www.terredesel.com/eng; 10am-6pm daily spring and autumn, 9:30am-7:30pm daily summer, 10am-12:30pm and 2pm5pm daily winter; adults €9, children €4

One of the most striking examples of human activity impacting on a landscape anywhere in all of France, let alone Brittany, La Guérande's salt marshes have been being farmed for thousands of years. Looking like a vast but fractured mirror and blazing different colors throughout the day and the different seasons, they can be visited by a guided tour put on

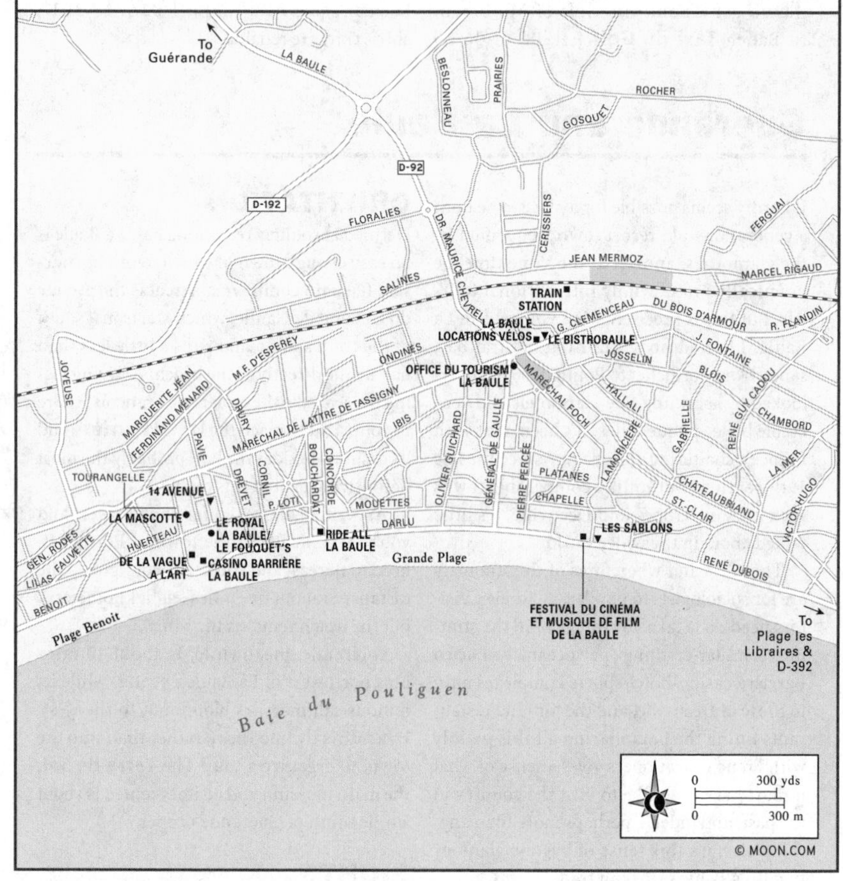

by a company called **Terre de Sel.** The tour wends its way along the ancient mud banks, teaches about the different grains of salt and its history as one of the modern world's building-block products, and lets you peer into the lives of the individuals still working the land today. As always, Guérande salt continues to be harvested by hand. Tours are mainly in French, though some are in English, and although the location is arguably impressive enough on its own—especially if you're interested in wildlife, which abounds—it's worth consulting the website or calling ahead to find out when English-speaking guides are available, as getting to know the history and techniques of salt production adds a remarkable dimension to any visit. The tour lasts a little under an hour, while there's a fairly basic museum to look around as well, full of old pictures and the tools used to extract salt.

As well as the sheer beauty of the sight, plus its fascinating history, there's also superb interactive quality to a visit. For in few other places are you really offered the chance to taste the landscape quite as you are here, both in the (slightly pricey) museum shop and throughout the nearby town. From butter caramel chocolate to fleur de sel, considered "the caviar of salt products," souvenirs are seldom so evocative. And what with one of salt's key qualities being how well it travels, it hardly matters how far you have to take it home.

LES REMPARTS DE GUÉRANDE ET LA PORTE SAINT-MICHEL

Rue Saint-Michel, Guérande; tel. 02 40 15 60 40 (Hôtel de Ville); year-round; free

Still characterized by the winding alleys of its medieval heyday, Guérande's highlight is its ramparts, which are some of the best preserved in France. Its structure doesn't seem to have changed a bit in hundreds of years, though the town is now dominated by souvenir shops. Guérande's signature salt industry was once extremely big business, generating plenty of wealth (Fun fact: the word "salary" is derived from the word "salt"). One thing about having lots of money? Others want it; hence perhaps why the defenses of Guérande are so extensive. Mostly erected in the 15th century by the Dukes of Brittany, following the city's sacking by Louis of Spain in 1342, they consist of 4,200 feet (1,300 meters) worth of wall, four gates, and six towers. A wander around them is a great way to imagine yourself back into the medieval past, and offers some great views over the town itself. The most imposing thing about them, though, surely is the Porte Saint-Michel, a hulking edifice of twin towers that dates back to the 1350s. Given the good state in which it remains, surely it was worth its salt.

LE PARC NATUREL RÉGIONAL DE BRIÈRE

Saint-Joachim; tel. 02 40 91 68 68; www.parc-naturel-briere.com; year-round; free

The second-largest area of marshland in France, and just inland from La Baule, the Brière is a remarkably diverse area of flora and fauna, which has been attracting curious tourists for decades. Once a veritable mine for the indiginous Bretons, who used the area as a source of reeds and peat, it's now crisscrossed by canals plyed by flat-bottomed chaland boats of bird-watching enthusiasts, who come to see the migratory species for which this is a popular stop off on the way between Northern Europe and Africa. These tours are run by several local companies—see below for details. Also worth seeing here are the several well-preserved villages, such as Saint Joachim and Kerhinet, where there are still traditional thatched buildings, and which sell the kinds of products, from pottery to eels, that have been consumed here for generations. Prepare to spend a whole day or more exploring these backwaters. There are places to stay among them, should you need.

ENTERTAINMENT AND EVENTS

Festivals

FESTIVAL DU CINÉMA ET MUSIQUE DE FILM DE LA BAULE

4 boulevard René Dubois, La Baule-Escoublac; www.festival-labaule.com; early Nov.; adults €49, under 25 €30

Despite the fact that a stylish French seaside resort without a film festival might seem to be missing a limb, La Baule's Festival du Cinéma et Musique de Film was only founded in 2013. Nevertheless, it fits so well, it already feels like a decades-old tradition, offering the town a much-needed bump of off-season glitz in the midst of November chill. A program of new films and shorts compete for jury prizes every year, and there are screenings of classics all based on a theme—in 2018 this was "the sea." In keeping with the festival being dedicated in part to film music, there are also several concerts to attend. Some big-name movie stars and directors do turn up every year, but keep aware that it's a pretty French festival, which includes the stars and the language of most of the films.

Casinos

CASINO BARRIÈRE LA BAULE

24 espl. Lucien Barrière, La Baule-Escoublac; tel. 02 40 11 48 28; www.casinosbarriere.com/fr/la-baule.html; 9am-3am Sun.-Thurs., 9am-4am Fri.-Sat.

In case you feel you're not spending money fast enough, there is, naturally, a casino in

1

2

3

La Baule to help you out. Part of the Barrière Group, its existence is in fact instrumental to the character of the town, having been built to complement the Barrière hotels and other concerns in La Baule, rendering the place a wealthy person's theme park of much the same stripe as Deauville in Normandy. Housed in a fairly bland modern building, the casino is not as glamorous as could be hoped for, but there's a full stable of table games on offer, from roulette to blackjack, as well as Texas hold 'em poker games to be dealt into. A buffet restaurant with sea views is on offer to sustain you between hands.

SHOPPING

As a popular haunt for wealthy big-city types, La Baule has many of the top-end clothing stores where they like to shop. Brands from Maje to Lacoste stand well-tailored-shoulder to well-tailored-shoulder along the length of the avenue du General de Gaulle. A browse among them is an excellent way to spend an afternoon, and a lot of cash.

DE LA VAGUE A L'ART

Passage du Royal, Esplanade François André, La Baule; tel. 06 76 28 77 34; www.delavaguelart.com; 10am-7pm daily

Refreshingly small-scale and artisan among so many big-name brands, this gallery represents a collective of 28 local artists displaying their paintings year-round, and every month invites an outside guest to display four or five pieces as well. A good place to pick up a locally crafted image of La Baule, with so many works being inspired by the town and its surrounding landscape.

BEACHES

GRANDE PLAGE

La Baule

Welcome to one of the most epic beaches in France. This four-mile stretch of sand curving elegantly from Pornichet in the east, where it is known as the **Plage des Libraires,** to Pouliguen in the west, where it is called the **Plage Benoit,** is more than just a beautiful bit of shoreline; it's the reason La Baule exists: such a perfect bay is positively crying out for a resort! It fills out in the summer months, with beach clubs and water-sports centers pocking its length, their colorful denizens spangling the blue waves with sails, paddleboards, and more. There are also plenty of lifeguard monitoring stations staffed throughout the summer, and the beach is well equipped for reduced mobility. It's a splendid place to swim, sunbathe, and see and be seen. The main thing to keep in mind if coming here on a day trip is parking: It can be a nightmare. Best is to park away from the beach itself, then hire a bike to get here: there's a bike path stretching from one end of the beach to the other.

WATER SPORTS

LE CERCLE NAUTIQUE LA BAULE

77 rue François Bougouin, Le Pouliguen; tel. 02 40 42 32 11; www.cnbpp.fr; 9am-6pm daily; courses from €100

Excellently located on the headland just beyond the far western end of La Baule's Grande Plage, in the satellite town of Pouliguen, this is a classy, professional yacht club that was founded in the 19th century. It runs multiple short courses for all ages throughout the summer and on weekends, and is active throughout the year. Lessons on ordinary sailing boats, catamarans, and stand-up paddleboards are all offered. The only downside is that there's no guarantee that the instructors will be able to speak English.

FOOD

Local Cuisine

LE FOUQUET'S

6 avenue Pierre Loti, La Baule-Escoublac; tel. 02 40 11 48 48; 12:30pm-2pm and 7:30pm-9:30pm Sun.-Thurs., 12:30-2pm and 7:30-10pm Fri.-Sat.; menus from €49

On a survey of the question "Where do most visitors to La Baule hail from?" year after year, Paris is the answer; it's no surprise that they've

1: salt marsh in Guérande **2:** medieval town walls **3:** Château de Suscinio in the Gulf of Morbihan

started to bring their restaurants with them. Le Fouquet's is an on-sea outlet of a famous Champs-Élysées bistro of the same name. Linked to the ubiquitous Barrière Group, it's formal and elegant, and serves rich, traditional French food. As part of a big international hotel chain, the waiters are also well disposed to dealing with foreign guests, meaning a decent amount of English is spoken, and that unlike in some French establishments, the customer is always right. It's always a good idea to book ahead, particularly in summer, if you want to get a table on the sea-facing terrace.

14 AVENUE

14 avenue Pavie, La Baule-Escoublac; tel. 02 40 60 09 21; www.14avenue-labaule.com; 12:30pm-2pm and 7:30pm-10pm Wed.-Sat., 12:30pm-2pm Sun.; menus from €41

It may not look like that much from outside, and its interior teeters on being tacky, but this is a truly excellent seafood restaurant. All the produce is straight-off-the-boat fresh, and talked up wonderfully by the place's passionate owner, who bustles from table to table conjuring meals with her words before you even get to taste anything. Follow her advice as to what's best that day, then sit back and enjoy. Fairly small and justifiably often very busy, don't even think about trying to eat here for dinner without a reservation.

LE BISTROBAULE

15 avenue Georges Clemenceau, La Baule-Escoublac; tel. 02 40 61 09 22; 12pm-2pm and 7pm-10pm Thurs.-Mon.; menus from €15

Unusual for a town famous for its luxury and sophistication, this working man's bistro is one of the best restaurants in La Baule, with almost no display of pretension whatsoever. The cheerful frontage gives way to a stripped-back though still comfy interior, and the chef is not afraid to serve up copious fries with expertly cooked slices of meat, often served without sauce and allowed to speak deliciously for themselves. A further boon is that the manager speaks excellent English. Frequently bustling, it's well worth booking a table in advance.

Budget Options

LA SALORGE

12 rue de la Croix Serot, Guérande; tel. 02 40 15 14 19; 12pm-3pm and 7pm-9:45pm daily; €3-10

A classic Breton crêperie with a decor slightly less twee than usual, with a large, high-ceilinged restaurant space and a terrace onto its garden out back, it can handle a large number of diners and feels very lively when full. The dessert crepes come particularly recommended.

LES SABLONS

6 boulevard René Dubois, La Baule-Escoublac; tel. 02 40 11 36 11; 10am-12am Thurs.-Mon.; €5-15

On the seafront, this straightforward eatery is one of the most popular restaurants in La Baule. It partly markets itself as a crêperie, but really it's the seafood that keeps people coming back. With a charming terrace that really packs people in during summer, the food here is uncomplicated, tasty, and inexpensive. Make sure to book for an evening meal in the summer, or you can just turn up late: Service continues until midnight.

ACCOMMODATIONS

€50-100

MAISON D'HÔTES "LA GUÉRANDIÈRE"

5 rue Vannetaise, Guérande; tel. 02 40 62 17 15; www.guerandiere.com; from €80 d

This hotel gives off some remarkably English vibes, both in terms of the 19th-century granite building it's housed in and the plush interiors, which borrow heavily from "shabby-chic" British style. Inside Guérande's medieval quarters, all rooms are individually decorated and have their own private bathrooms. There are also some pleasant public areas, including a garden terrace. Continental and buffet breakfasts are served in a conservatory, surrounded by flowers. WiFi is available throughout.

LA MASCOTTE

26 avenue Marie Louise, La Baule-Escoublac; tel. 02 40 60 26 55; www.la-baule-hotel.com; from €80 d

Most recommended because of its positioning, this hotel sits right in the midst of things, allowing you to take advantage of many of La Baule's attractions, such as its casino or thalassotherapy center, without the exorbitant accommodation fees of places nearby. This is not just a budget property, however; its interiors are characterized by monochrome modern style, which is more comfortable than it sounds. There are a couple of public areas, WiFi throughout, and private bathrooms in the rooms. There's also a highly recommended on-site restaurant, Bellis Garden, which serves both Breton and Mediterranean food—entrées from €25.

€100-200

HÔTEL SUD BRETAGNE

42 boulevard de la République, Pornichet; tel. 02 40 11 65 00; hotelsudbretagne.fr; from €150 d

There's a slightly unhinged quality to the interiors of Hôtel Sud Bretagne: If there were a single unifying theme to the hotel (which there isn't, really), it would be "Bond villain chic." Lavishness abounds, as do clashing textures, colors, and patterns, but against the odds, it all just about works. Private bathrooms, WiFi access, and flat-screen TVs provide the main continuity between the rooms, coming standard in all of them. There's also an on-site restaurant, a pool, and a pool table. Body massage treatments can be arranged at an extra cost.

Over €200

★ LE ROYAL LA BAULE

6 avenue Pierre Loti, La Baule-Escoublac; tel. 02 40 11 48 48; www.hotelsbarriere.com/fr/la-baule/le-royal.html; from €220 d

Barrière Group hotels are veritable monuments along the Normandy and Brittany coastlines, and for good reason: Many of them represent the very essence of the towns in which they occur. The Royal is such an institution, with a thalassotherapy center on-site, a direct connection to the Barrière casino, and complementary access to a golf course, windsurfing, tennis courts, and more. The hotel is the effective nexus of the resort that is La Baule.

The place itself, naturally, exudes luxury. There are sea views, rooms with crisp, plush furnishings, a terrace, two on-site restaurants, and a bar that tinkles to the classy sound of live music. The staff are bend-over-backward efficient, and there are the all-important robes and slippers provided in all the rooms, so that you can loaf louche-as-you-like through the hotel interior on your way to the spa.

Camping

CAMPING LA GOVELLE

10 route de la Govelle, Batz-sur-Mer; tel. 02 40 23 91 63; www.labaule-guerande.com/camping-la-govelle.html; pitch for two €23

It's not particularly flashy, but given not everyone can afford to stay at Le Royal, this pleasant campsite practically on the sea makes a fine budget choice. It's a little to the west of La Baule itself, but the location is good. It's clean and well maintained with toilets, showers, and laundry facilities. Shops for buying supplies are about a mile away, so if you're getting here under your own steam, be sure to stock up before arriving.

TOURIST INFORMATION

La Baule is so overflowing with hotels and other private concerns guiding you through the town and suggesting activities and restaurants that state-run tourist offices can hardly seem necessary. But the **Office du Tourism La Baule** (8 place de la Victoire Baule Escoublac; tel. 02 40 24 34 44; www.labaule-guerande.com; 10am-12:30pm and 2pm-6pm Mon.-Sat.) is here and worth dropping into for directions, pamphlets, and ideas about how to spend your time in town that you can be sure aren't backed by any agenda. In Guérande, the **Bureau d'Information Touristique de Guérande** (1 place du Marché au Bois, Guérande; tel. 02 40 24 96 71; www.labaule-guerande.com; 10am-12:30pm and 2pm-6pm

Mon.-Sat.) can help you plan visits to the salt marshes or trips around the old town. English is widely spoken.

TRANSPORTATION

Getting There

BY CAR

The fastest way to La Baule from Paris is via Nantes. This means heading south out of the capital on the A10, then connecting to the A11. From Nantes, you join up with N171, which takes you more or less directly to the resort. From Paris the total journey length is about 280 miles (450 kilometers), and it ought to take a little under 4.5 hours. Just from Nantes, it's around 50 miles (80 kilometers) and can be reached in just over an hour. Note: The trip from Paris to Nantes is a comparatively speedy one, but that's because it's along toll roads all the way; this will cost you around €40.

From Rennes (100 miles/160 kilometers, 1.75 hours), there are no tolls. Just head south on the N137.

From Brest (200 miles/321 kilometers, 3.5 hours), you take the N165. This passes through Quimper (114 miles/183 kilometers from La Baule, 2.5 hours), Lorient (76 miles/122 kilometers, almost two hours), and Vannes (42 miles/67 kilometers, one hour).

There are plenty of **parking lots** in town, which are your best choice if you want to find a space and aren't staying at a hotel with its own parking. Street parking starts from €2.60 for two hours and can be difficult to find in high season on account of the town's popularity. Resign yourself before you arrive to the fact that you probably won't be able to park close to the beach and you'll have a better, less frustrating, time.

In Guérande there are several parking lots outside the city walls. Most of the year these are free, though in July and August you may find yourself having to pay €1.60 an hour for the privilege of using them. Parking on the streets and inside the city walls is possible, costing €1.60 at any time of year, but it's far better to save yourself the hassle.

BY TRAIN

From Paris to La Baule's train station, **Gare de la Baule Escoublac** (Place Rhin et Danube, La Baule Escoublac; tel. 08 92 35 35 35; www.gares-sncf.com/fr/gare/frjee/baule-escoublac; 4:40am-9pm Mon., 6:10am-9pm Tues.-Thurs., 6:10am-11:30pm Fri., 5:40am-9pm Sat., 7:10am-9:40pm Sun.), there are three direct trains a day, costing around €80 depending on how far in advance you book and taking around 3 hours 40 minutes. It's also possible to transfer at Nantes, which dramatically ups the number of trains you can take, to almost one every hour.

There are usually 11 trains a day from Nantes to La Baule, and they cost about €20. The journey takes one hour.

From Rennes, you have to go transfer at Nantes. Tickets cost around €30 and there are around 10 trains a day that you can catch to make the connection. Total journey time is 2-3 hours, depending on how long you have to wait in Nantes.

Similarly, there are no direct trains from Quimper, Lorient, or Vannes. To get to La Baule from any of these places you have to transfer at Savenay. There are 4-5 trips from each of these towns every day that let you do this, and they will cost €20-50 and take 2-4 hours, depending on connection time.

From Brest, the fastest route is to connect at Nantes. There are one or two chances to do this every day. They cost around €50 and take 4-5 hours. It's also possible to go via Quimper, if you're really desperate, but this requires two changes and can take upwards of 5.5 hours.

Getting Around

BY CAR AND TAXI

By and large, La Baule is easier to walk or cycle around than drive, but to get between it and Guérande, take the D213. The journey is less than 10 minutes and well-signposted. If you'd prefer not to drive yourself, you can call a cab with **TAXI La Baule SUPIOT Maxime** (tel. 06 07 06 89 34; www.taxi-labaule-supiotmaxime.fr) or **Taxi Presqu'île la Baule** (tel. 06 80 84 55 30).

BY BUS

The bus service around La Baule and Guérande is run by a company called **LILA** (tel. 02 40 62 32 33; www.lilapresquile.fr). There are 10 lines in total, with bus Nos. 1 and 4 connecting Guérande with La Baule. The latter leaves from La Baule's SNCF station, and the former from a place called Les Salines, just a couple of minutes' walk north of the fish station.

BY BIKE

There are several bike rental firms in La Baule, including **La Baule Locations Vélos** (11 avenue Georges Clémenceau, La Baule; tel. 06 14 64 02 27; www.velocouest.fr; 10am-7pm daily) and **Ride All La Baule** (41 espl. François André, La Baule-Escoublac; tel. 02 40 60 18 85; www.ride-all.com; 10am-12:30pm and 2:30pm-7pm daily). Two wheels is a good way of getting up and down the beach—there's even a cycle path—as well as getting between the town and Guérande and exploring some of the marshy hinterland. Prices are fairly similar between companies, roughly €10 a day.

Nantes and Inland Brittany

As well as being a region of dramatic coasts, Brittany possesses the archetypal "mysterious interior." It's a land of myth and legend, where Christianity has melded to the old stories; even the chapels here have a whiff of paganism to their decoration. It's also stunningly beautiful, green country with all manner of hills and water courses, as ideal for ramblers and rowers as it is for fans of King Arthur, whose legend still thrives in the Paimpont Forest.

Farther south, and technically only in "historic" Brittany (despite once being the region's capital), is the city of Nantes: bustling, built-up, and bohemian. In many respects it's an antithesis of the shrouded hinterland, but easygoing Breton culture is as strong here as anywhere else, making Nantes a great gateway either in or out of the region.

Highlights

Look for ★ to find recommended sights, activities, dining, and lodging.

★ **Les Machines de l'Île de Nantes:** Become a kid again exploring this utterly unique menagerie of steampunk animal sculptures and rides (page 407).

★ **Château des Ducs de Bretagne:** Look out across modern Nantes from the battlements of the magnificent seat of power for rulers of Brittany until the 16th century (page 411).

★ **Château de Josselin:** Connect with Brittany's living past in this fairy-tale castle owned by the same family since the 13th century (page 421).

★ **Merlin's Tomb:** Pay your respects at the reputed final resting place of the legendary wizard (page 427).

★ **Rennes Old Town:** Rennes boasts the most extensive collection of medieval dwellings anywhere in the region (page 433).

★ **Rennes's Marché des Lices:** Spend a morning marveling at the full breadth of the Breton table in one the best produce markets in France (page 435).

★ ***Festoù-noz*:** Swill cider and watch locals dancing to the bagpipes at these traditional "night festivals" in villages across Brittany (page 440).

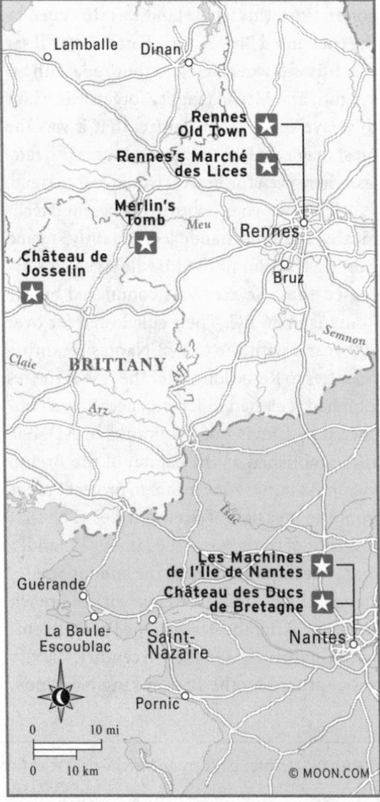

Finally, there's Rennes, Brittany's relaxed, earthy, modern-day capital. Often bypassed by travelers, this is one of the most vibrant party towns anywhere in France, with the region's largest weekly market, plus some beautiful municipal architecture. It's worth a couple of days of anyone's time, particularly because it's probably on the way to where you're going anyway.

HISTORY

Archaeologists will tell you the facts about prehistoric inland Brittany: how it was home to tribes who used flint tools, and kept domesticated animals, and erected mysterious stone monuments that we still don't know the function of to this day. The Bretons themselves, however, might be inclined toward the more esoteric, explaining that once, in some forgotten time, this whole land was shrouded by the enchanted Brocéliande Forest. They'll say that this was where King Arthur rode with his knights, and Merlin taught Morgan le Fay how to weave spells from nature; that it was the most magical place in Europe, lousy with fairies, where even the bravest would fear to tread.

Whichever you choose to believe (and technically, the Brocéliande legends only started gaining traction in the Middle Ages), it's accepted that the area was conquered by the Romans in 56 BC. Their rule lasted for over 500 years, with the city of Nantes retaining close ties to Rome long after the rest of the region had regained independence. It was conquered by Clovis I of the Franks in AD 490, and established as the capital of the Breton March—a buffer zone meant to protect France from the invasion of Breton tribes. The first governor of the city was the famous Roland, a character immortalized in the famous *Song of Roland*, the earliest surviving work of French literature. After the death of the Frankish emperor Charlemagne in the 9th century, the city was captured by the Breton king Nominoe, who became the first Duke of Brittany, making Nantes his capital.

Needless to say, the French didn't leave things at that, with Nantes and the rest of Brittany becoming a battleground for the next several centuries. Various noble families with different geographical bases vied for power over the region. Throughout this, though, Brittany effectively managed to retain its independence until the late 1400s. Nantes remained its capital until the marriage of the region's Princess Anne to France's Charles VIII in 1491 heralded the beginning of the end. Following an official unification between the two countries in the early 1500s, the French government opted to make Rennes the regional capital. Nevertheless, Nantes still achieved one final moment on the grand stage of history, when the Edict of Nantes was signed there in 1598, legalizing Protestantism in France and bringing an end to the bloody Wars of Religion.

The area was affected by the French Revolution as much as anywhere in France, meanwhile; Nantes perhaps more so, with one of its most prosperous economies, the slave trade, decimated by the country's abolition of slavery. Even so, this vile practice limped on in some corners, reestablishing itself in the first 20 years of the 19th century: It's the biggest stain on Nantes's history that the city was the last French port to give up the illegal trade of human cargo, which it did only in 1827.

Following large-scale damage in the Second World War, modern times have seen Nantes, Rennes, and the rest of inland Brittany rebuild themselves as successful cultural, agricultural, and industrial centers for France. And while the old forest of Brocéliande may have shrunk back, so that now it covers just the small area known as Paimpont, legends of myth and magic persevere. These attract thousands of visitors a year who want to explore the forest's maybe-enchanted rocks, valleys, and

---

Previous: Nantes city center; Marché des Lices; Château des Ducs de Bretagne

waterways, and use them to peer somehow into another kind of time.

ORIENTATION

Inland Brittany boasts a large, mostly similar landscape of rolling fields, still marked in places by small swatches of forest. Rennes represents the gateway city to almost the entire region. Look at it on a large-scale road map and you'll see the Breton capital as the neat center of a veritable web of roads. It could almost be compared to the spider, with spindly legs of freeways (though there are nine, rather than eight) extending out toward all the points of the compass.

Nantes is 70 miles (112 kilometers) almost directly below Rennes, with the two cities linked by the N137. A line drawn along this axis represents the base of a triangle that tapers into the Breton peninsula.

Paimpont and Josselin, meanwhile, are consecutively to the west of Rennes, and can be reached along the N24, which runs all the way to the coast. Of the callouts in this chapter, meanwhile, the Blavet Valley can be found slightly north of the N24 thoroughfare, west of Josselin, while Vitre is a 20-mile (32-kilometer) drive directly east of Rennes.

PLANNING YOUR TIME

There are without doubt some significantly different ways visitors choose to explore this part of Brittany. More than anywhere else, with the exception of perhaps Saint-Malo, it lends itself to long weekends or city breaks rather than extended holidays. That's not to say that you won't want to experience the latter here, just that they might not be the kinds of trips a region that boasts two bustling urban centers immediately inspires.

In short, there's easily enough in Nantes to keep visitors occupied from a Friday to a Monday, and even longer if you decide to explore the surrounding countryside. Rennes is not quite so cosmopolitan, and though there's still plenty to see, an extended stay here will almost certainly see you branching out to nearby sights and towns. Fortunately, both Vitre and the Paimpont Forest are less than a hour from its center, and well worth exploring.

A stay in Paimpont, meanwhile, can easily be extended. There are many bike paths and hiking trails to explore, and it's easy to look beyond the sights and just relax, letting the background magic of the place take hold over the course of a week or two. A trip to Josselin makes a fascinating addition, provided you've got your own transport to get there.

Inland Brittany

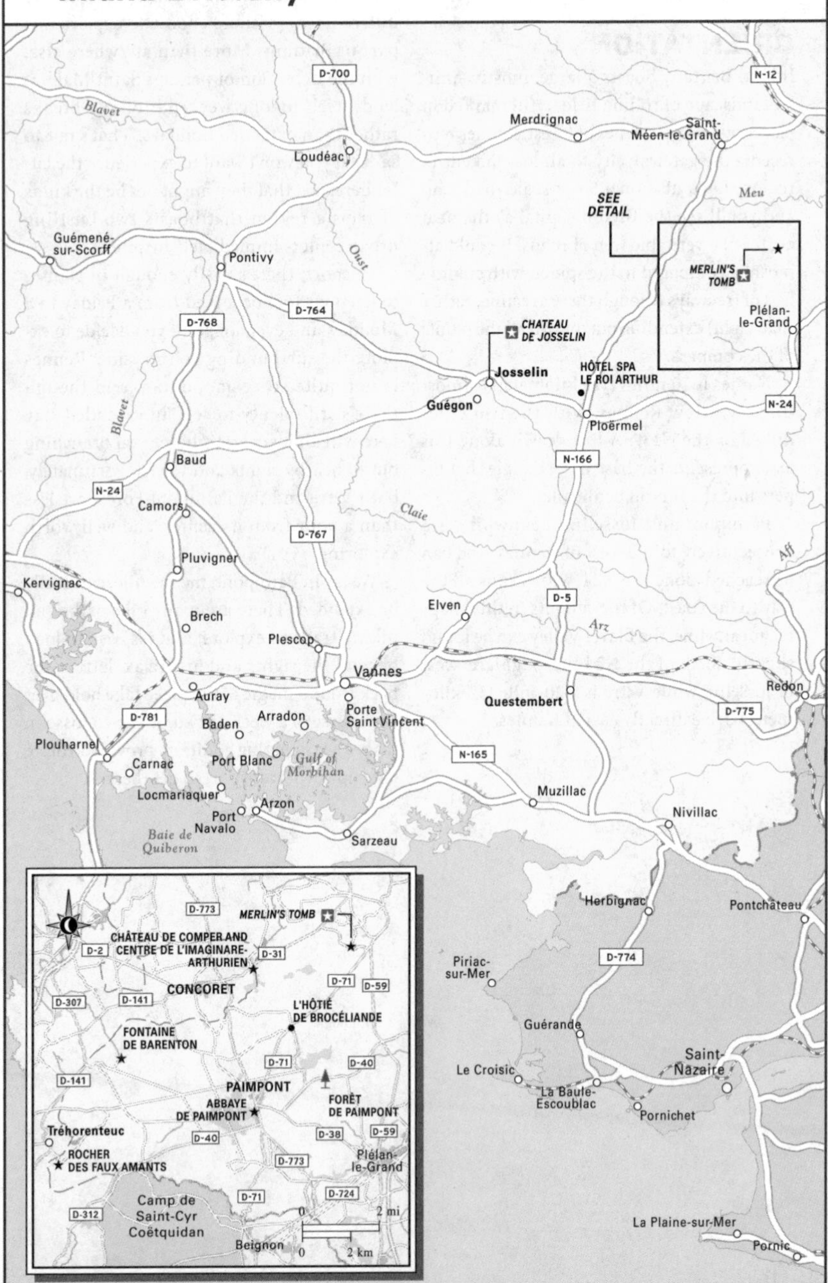

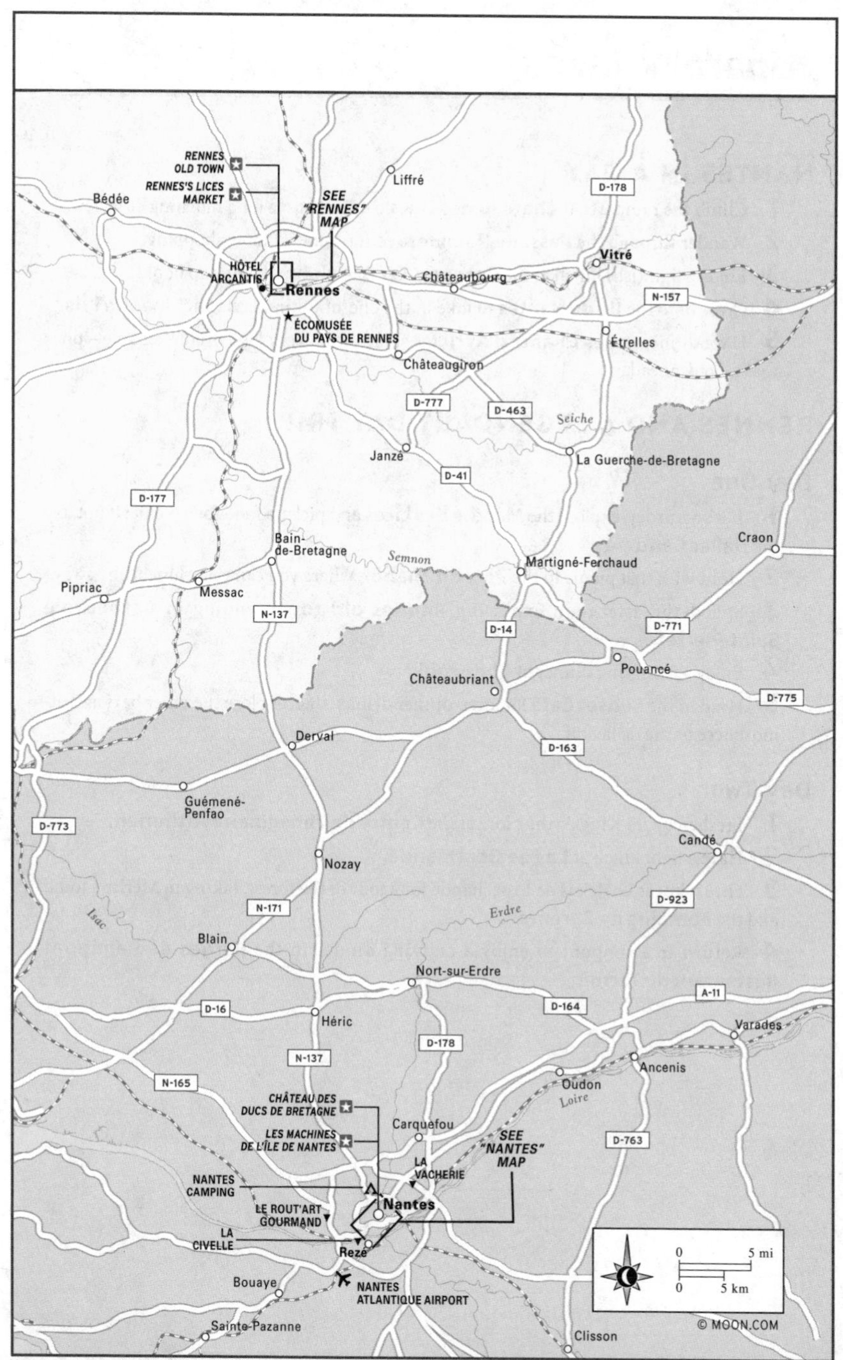

RENNES OLD TOWN
RENNES'S LICES MARKET
SEE "RENNES" MAP
Liffré
Bédée
D-178
Vitré
HÔTEL ARCANTIS
Rennes
Châteaubourg
N-157
ÉCOMUSÉE DU PAYS DE RENNES
Étrelles
Châteaugiron
D-777
D-463
Seiche
Janzé
La Guerche-de-Bretagne
D-41
D-177
Craon
Bain-de-Bretagne
Semnon
Martigné-Ferchaud
Pipriac
Messac
N-137
D-14
D-771
Pouancé
Châteaubriant
D-775
Derval
D-163
Guémené-Penfao
D-773
Candé
Nozay
N-171
D-923
Isac
Erdre
Blain
Nort-sur-Erdre
A-11
D-16
D-164
Héric
Varades
D-178
N-137
Ancenis
N-165
Oudon
Loire
CHÂTEAU DES DUCS DE BRETAGNE
Carquefou
LES MACHINES DE L'ÎLE DE NANTES
D-763
SEE "NANTES" MAP
LA VACHERIE
NANTES CAMPING
Nantes
LE ROUT'ART GOURMAND
LA CIVELLE
Rezé
0
5 mi
0
5 km
Bouaye
NANTES ATLANTIQUE AIRPORT
Sainte-Pazanne
© MOON.COM
Clisson

Itinerary Ideas

NANTES IN A DAY

1 Climb the ramparts at **Château des Ducs de Bretagne** for a morning city view.

2 Wander through the **Passage Pommeraye** for some window shopping.

3 Enjoy a light(ish) lunch at the **Crêperie Ker Breizh**—make sure to book!

4 Cross onto the **Île de Nantes** to take in the one-of-a-kind **Les Machines de l'Île.**

5 Have dinner at **Les Chants d'Avril** for some of the very best Breton cuisine—once again, book ahead.

RENNES AND A LEGENDARY DAY TRIP

Day One

1 If it's Saturday, explore the **Marché des Lices** and pick up food for a picnic; if not, try the **Halles Centrales.**

2 Head with that picnic to the **Parc du Thabor,** where you can relax lunchtime away.

3 Spend the afternoon exploring **Rennes old town,** ending in **Cathédrale Saint-Pierre.**

4 Enjoy a fortifying dinner at **Chez Paul.**

5 Head to the **Sunset Café** for after-dinner drinks, then explore the other bars and atmosphere of rue de la Soif.

Day Two

1 Freshen up on King Arthur lore at the **Centre de l'Imaginaire Arthurien.**

2 Have a light lunch at **La Fée Gourmande.**

3 Hire bikes at Le Relais de Brocéliande for a tour of the forest, taking in Merlin's tomb and the **Fontaine de Barenton.**

4 Return to Paimpont to enjoy a reviving dinner in the **Forges de Paimpont Restaurant du Terroir.**

Nantes Itinerary

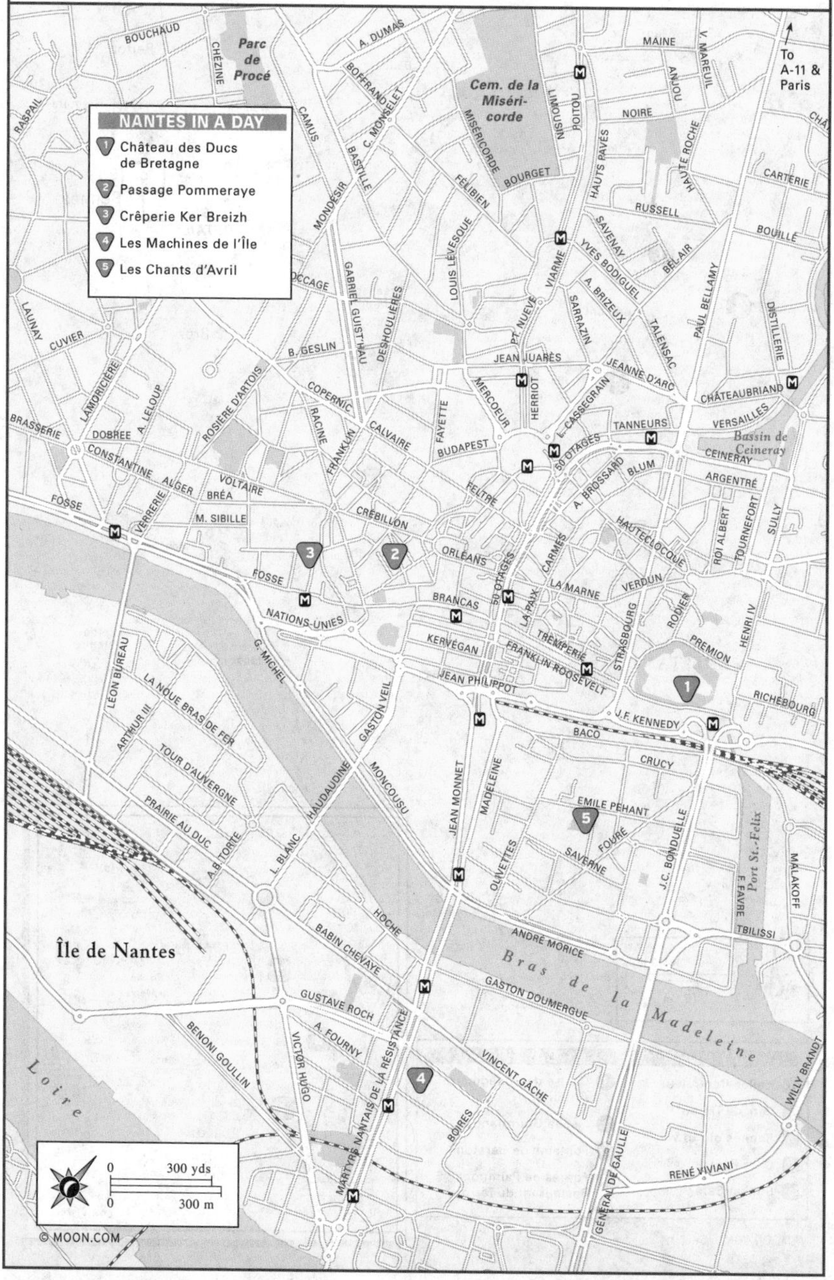

NANTES IN A DAY

1. Château des Ducs de Bretagne
2. Passage Pommeraye
3. Crêperie Ker Breizh
4. Les Machines de l'Île
5. Les Chants d'Avril

Île de Nantes

0 300 yds
0 300 m

Rennes and a Legendary Road Trip

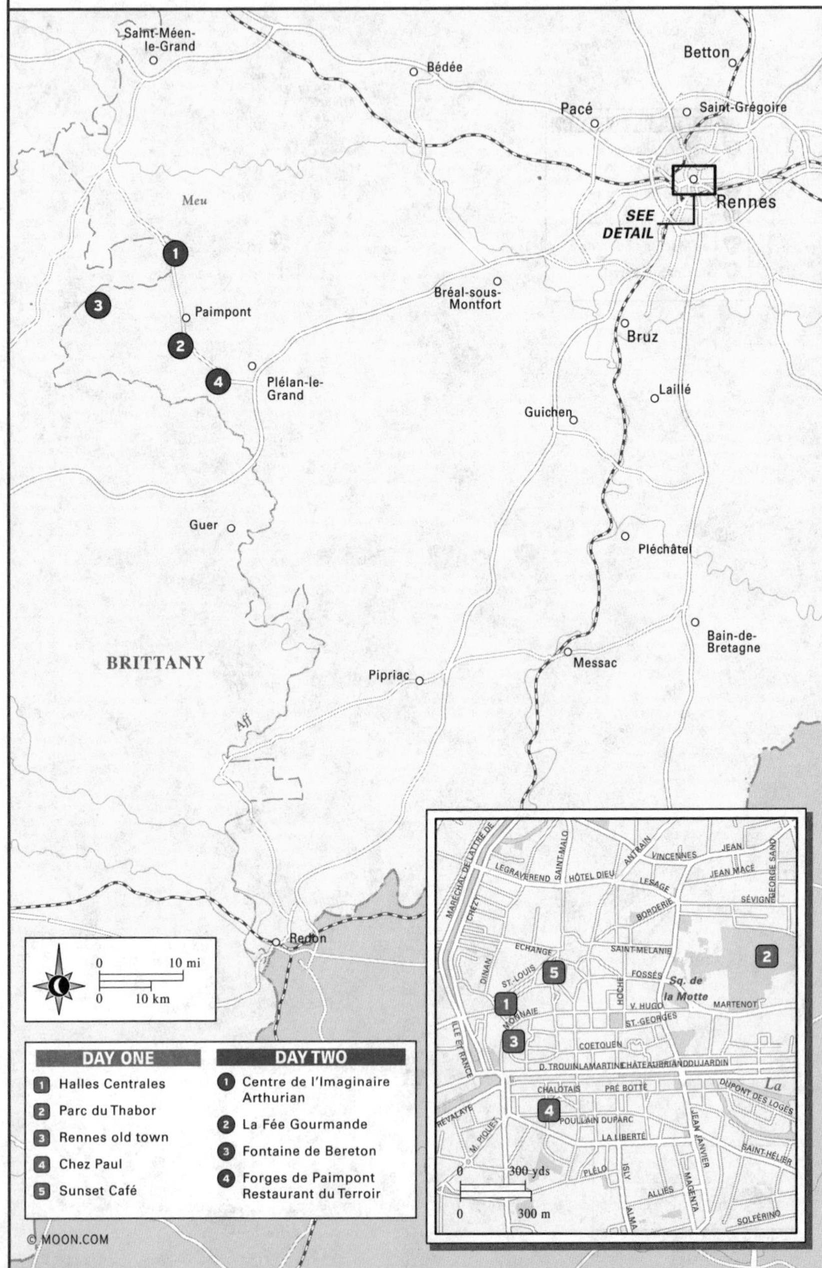

Nantes

There's nowhere in France quite like Nantes. For a start, there's the implicit paradox of its identity, in that it's both the spiritual capital of Brittany but technically no longer in Brittany at all. The 15th-century castle of the Breton Dukes dominates its heart, and still, a distinctly Breton attitude energizes its streets. The more casual approach to drinking, friendship, and art is unlike anywhere else in France. But mostly, this is an incredibly creative city, something evident in nearly every bar and restaurant, in its street art—such as the Voyage a Nantes, a festival of open-air works of art by famous names set up across the city every summer—and in the fashion sense of its people. The urge to create is everywhere, which is why the city's most representative attraction is probably the Machines de l'Île, a new sculpture park unlike anything else in France, taking the form of a menagerie inspired by the visions of Jules Verne.

Nantes is also a great culinary city. Close enough to the coast that its restaurants are busy with traditional Breton seafood flavors, it's also got one eye pointed toward the Loire hinterland, where the food is more oriented toward red meat and, of course, local wines. This passion for terroir flows into another feature of the Nantes's cityscape: its relationship with nature. Nantes is one of the greenest cities in all of France, with 613 square feet (57 square meters) of green space per inhabitant. It's also been made very easy, through a system of cycle paths, to escape the city center under your own steam and head into the beautiful countryside of the Loire Valley beyond.

An excellent destination both as a city break on its own or as a staging post into the rest of Brittany, Nantes has a lot to offer. Elegant but never fussy, it charms, delights, and leaves you with the thought of how nice it would be to live here.

ORIENTATION

Nantes was founded on the confluence of the rivers Loire and Erdre. Its approximately one-square-mile **old town** sits on the north bank of the Loire and the west bank of the Erdre. Most of the activity is concentrated in three large squares that sit almost parallel to each other: the place Graslin, which is the farthest west; then the place Royal, nearing the Erdre; and the place du Commerce. Streets get progressively more winding and medieval the farther east you stray, until the town spills out onto the imposing **Château des Ducs.** Nantes's main train station is just east of this.

The Île de Nantes, which lies south of the old town, in the middle of the River Loire, is a former industrial hub, which is now a trendy district full of bars and restaurants. The must-see **Machines de l'Île** sculpture park is also on the island, in its west.

SIGHTS

TOP EXPERIENCE

★ Les Machines de l'Île de Nantes

Parc des Chantiers, boulevard Léon Bureau, Nantes; tel. 08 10 12 12 25; www.lesmachines-nantes.fr; 10am-5pm Tues.-Sun., 10am-6pm Sat.-Sun. and school holidays Apr.-June and Sept.-Oct., 2pm-5pm Tues.-Sun., 2pm-6pm Sat.-Sun. and school holidays Feb.-Mar. and Nov.-Dec., 10am-7pm daily July-Aug.; adults €8.50, reduced €6.90

"Unique" is an epithet thrown about with casual abandon these days, especially in the tourism industry, but Les Machines de l'Île de Nantes earns it, and then some. For a start, what even is it? A sculpture park? A theme park aimed as much at adults as it is kids? A steampunk menagerie? It's all these things and more.

The stated inspiration behind the park is the imagination of Jules Verne meeting the

Nantes

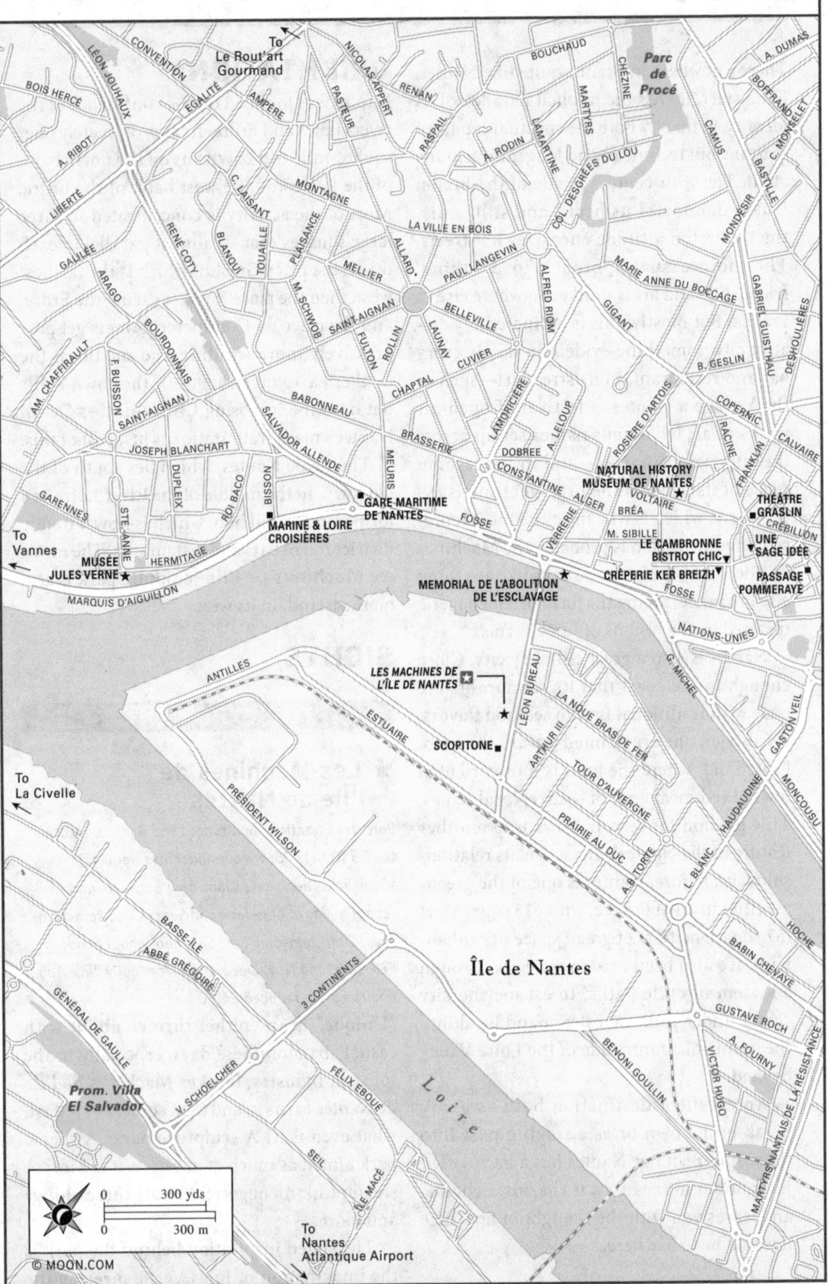
To Le Rout'art Gourmand
Parc de Procé
NATURAL HISTORY MUSEUM OF NANTES
THÉATRE GRASLIN
GARE MARITIME DE NANTES
MARINE & LOIRE CROISIÈRES
To Vannes
MUSÉE JULES VERNE
LE CAMBRONNE BISTROT CHIC
UNE SAGE IDÉE
CRÊPERIE KER BREIZH
PASSAGE POMMERAYE
MEMORIAL DE L'ABOLITION DE L'ESCLAVAGE
LES MACHINES DE L'ÎLE DE NANTES
SCOPITONE
To La Civelle
Île de Nantes
Loire
Prom. Villa El Salvador
To Nantes Atlantique Airport
0 300 yds
0 300 m
© MOON.COM
LÉON JOUHAUX
CONVENTION
BOIS HERCÉ
EGALITÉ
AMPÈRE
NICOLAS APPERT
PASTEUR
RENAN
RASPAIL
BOUCHAUD
CHÉZINE
MARTYRS
LAMARTINE
A. RODIN
COL. DESGRÉES DU LOU
A. DUMAS
BOFFRAND
C. MONSELET
CAMUS
BASTILLE
A. RIBOT
LIBERTÉ
C. LAISANT
MONTAGNE
LA VILLE EN BOIS
MONDÉSIR
GALILÉE
RENÉ COTY
BLANQUI
TOUAILLE
PLAISANCE
MELLIER
ALLARD
PAUL LANGEVIN
ALFRED RIOM
MARIE ANNE DU BOCCAGE
GABRIEL GUISTHAU
DESHOULIÈRES
ARAGO
BOURDONNAIS
M. SCHWOB
SAINT-AIGNAN
FULTON
ROLLIN
LAUNAY
BELLEVILLE
GIGANT
CUVIER
B. GESLIN
AM. CHAFFRAULT
F. BUISSON
SAINT-AIGNAN
BABONNEAU
CHAPTAL
LAMORICIÈRE
A. LELOUP
ROSIÈRE D'ARTOIS
COPERNIC
RACINE
CALVAIRE
FRANKLIN
JOSEPH BLANCHART
SALVADOR ALLENDE
BRASSERIE
DOBREE
CONSTANTINE
VOLTAIRE
ALGER
BRÉA
GARENNES
STE-ANNE
DUPLEIX
ROI BACO
BISSON
MEURIS
FOSSE
VERRERIE
M. SIBILLE
CRÉBILLON
HERMITAGE
MARQUIS D'AIGUILLON
FOSSE
NATIONS-UNIES
ANTILLES
ESTUAIRE
LÉON BUREAU
LA NOUE BRAS DE FER
ARTHUR III
G. MICHEL
GASTON VEIL
MONCOUSU
TOUR D'AUVERGNE
HAUDAUDINE
PRAIRIE AU DUC
A.B. TORTE
L. BLANC
PRÉSIDENT WILSON
HOCHE
BABIN CHEVAYE
BASSE-ÎLE
ABBÉ GRÉGOIRE
3 CONTINENTS
GUSTAVE ROCH
A. FOURNY
GÉNÉRAL DE GAULLE
BENONI GOULLIN
VICTOR HUGO
MARTYRS NANTAIS DE LA RÉSISTANCE
V. SCHOELCHER
FÉLIX EBOUÉ
SEIL
ÎLE MACÉ

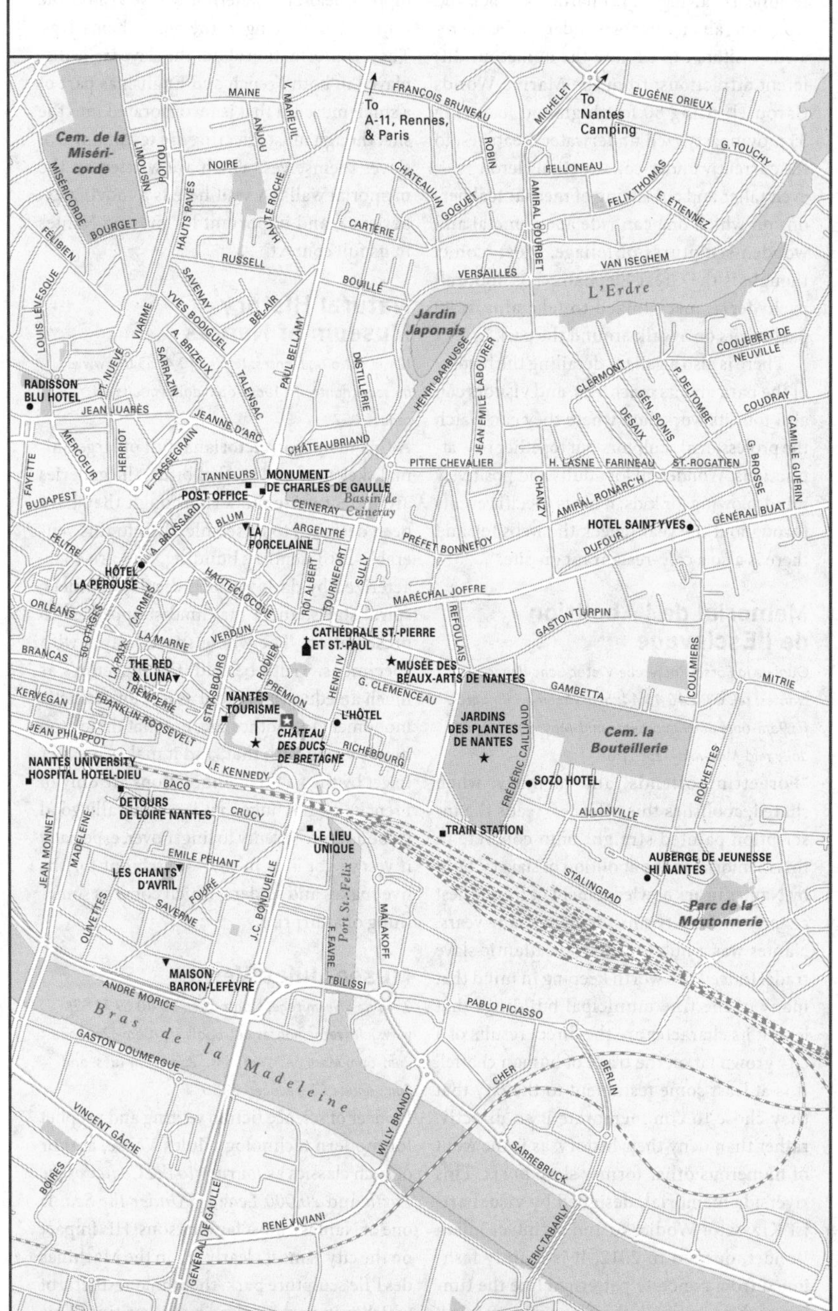

MAINE
V. MAREUIL
To A-11, Rennes, & Paris
FRANÇOIS BRUNEAU
MICHELET
To Nantes Camping
EUGÈNE ORIEUX
Cem. de la Miséricorde
LIMOUSIN
POITOU
ANJOU
ROBIN
G. TOUCHY
MISÉRICORDE
NOIRE
HAUTE ROCHE
CHÂTEAULIN
FELLONEAU
HAUTS PAVÉS
GOGUET
AMIRAL COURBET
FELIX THOMAS
E. ÉTIENNEZ
BOURGET
CARTERIE
FELIBIEN
RUSSELL
VAN ISEGHEM
VERSAILLES
BOUILLÉ
SAVENAY
L'Erdre
LOUIS LEVESQUE
YVES BODIGUEL
BEL-AIR
Jardin Japonais
VIARME
A. BRIZEUX
PAUL BELLAMY
DISTILLERIE
HENRI BARBUSSE
JEAN EMILE LABOURER
COQUEBERT DE NEUVILLE
PT. NUEVE
SARRAZIN
TALENSAC
CLERMONT
RADISSON BLU HOTEL
P. DELTOMBE
GÉN. SONIS
COUDRAY
JEAN JUARÈS
DESAIX
CAMILLE GUÉRIN
JEANNE D'ARC
MERCOEUR
HERRIOT
CHÂTEAUBRIAND
L. CASSEGRAIN
PITRE CHEVALIER
H. LASNE
FARINEAU
ST.-ROGATIEN
G. BROSSE
FAYETTE
TANNEURS
MONUMENT DE CHARLES DE GAULLE
POST OFFICE
Bassin de Ceineray
BUDAPEST
CEINERAY
CHANZY
AMIRAL RONARC'H
GÉNÉRAL BUAT
BLUM
LA PORCELAINE
HOTEL SAINT YVES
A. BROSSARD
ARGENTRÉ
PRÉFET BONNEFOY
DUFOUR
FELTRE
HÔTEL LA PÉROUSE
ROI ALBERT
TOURNEFORT
SULLY
HAUTECLOCQUE
MARÉCHAL JOFFRE
ORLÉANS
50 OTAGES
CARMES
REFOULAIS
GASTON TURPIN
LA MARNE
VERDUN
CATHÉDRALE ST.-PIERRE ET ST.-PAUL
BRANCAS
LA PAIX
ROGIER
MUSÉE DES BEAUX-ARTS DE NANTES
THE RED & LUNA
STRASBOURG
HENRI IV
G. CLEMENCEAU
GAMBETTA
COULMIERS
MITRIE
KERVÉGAN
TREMPERIE
PREMION
FRANKLIN ROOSEVELT
NANTES TOURISME
L'HÔTEL
JARDINS DES PLANTES DE NANTES
FRÉDÉRIC CAILLIAUD
Cem. la Bouteillerie
JEAN PHILIPPOT
CHÂTEAU DES DUCS DE BRETAGNE
RICHEBOURG
ROCHETTES
NANTES UNIVERSITY HOSPITAL HOTEL-DIEU
J.F. KENNEDY
BACO
SOZO HOTEL
DETOURS DE LOIRE NANTES
ALLONVILLE
CRUCY
JEAN MONNET
MADELEINE
LE LIEU UNIQUE
TRAIN STATION
EMILE PEHANT
AUBERGE DE JEUNESSE HI NANTES
LES CHANTS D'AVRIL
STALINGRAD
FOURÉ
J.C. BONDUELLE
Port St.-Felix
MALAKOFF
OLIVETTES
SAVERNE
Parc de la Moutonnerie
F. FAVRE
MAISON BARON-LEFÈVRE
TBILISSI
ANDRE MORICE
PABLO PICASSO
Bras de la Madeleine
GASTON DOUMERGUE
BERLIN
CHER
VINCENT GÂCHE
WILLY BRANDT
SARREBRUCK
BOIRES
GÉNÉRAL DE GAULLE
RENÉ VIVIANI
ÉRIC TABARLY

technical drawings of Leonardo da Vinci, and from this, all manner of wonder has been created. Visitors can explore the numerous different attractions: from the Marine Worlds Carousel, rising 80 feet high and featuring 35 moving, stylized underwater creatures, to the currently under-construction Heron Tree, even taller and consisting of mechanical herons on which one can ride above metal and wooden sculptures of foliage. Most iconic, though, is the Great Elephant: a 39-foot-tall pachyderm, mechanized to take almost 50 passengers on a walk around the park.

There is also a gallery detailing the history of the park and its machines, and visitors can also tour its workshop where they can watch the professional sculptors put together new attractions. Wonderful for adults and positively mind-blowing for kids, it hosts specific events throughout the year (check the website), and there is also a café-restaurant on-site.

Memorial de l'Abolition de l'Esclavage

Quai de la Fosse, Passerelle Victor-Schoelcher, Nantes; tel. 08 11 46 46 44; http://memorial.nantes.fr; 9am-6pm daily mid-Sept.-mid-May, 9am-8pm daily mid-May-mid-Sept.; free

"Forgetting offends, and memory, when shared, abolishes this offence," reads the inscription painted straight onto concrete in this memorial to the abolition of slavery, built by Nantes in acknowledgement of the darkest chapter in the city's history. For many years, Nantes was a hub for the transatlantic slave trade. Indeed, it's worth keeping in mind that many of the fine municipal buildings that lend it its character are the direct results of a city grown fat on the trade of human chattel. It is at least some testament to the city that they chose to commemorate it so directly, rather than deny their history, as is the wont of numerous other former slave ports. This riverside memorial, designed by visual artist Krzysztof Wodiczko and architect Julian Bonder, opened in 2012. It is mainly fashioned from concrete patterned like the timber of ships in which the slaves were carried, dipping below the waterline to give visitors the impression of being in the boats themselves. There's information about the slave trade displayed in both French and English as part of a small museum that is incorporated into the site, though most affecting are testimonies of slaves themselves, which are written on the memorial walls. A visit here is a moving experience, and important for putting Nantes in its full context.

Natural History Museum of Nantes

12 rue Voltaire, Nantes; tel. 02 40 41 55 00; www.museum.nantes.fr; 10am-6pm daily; adults €4, reduced €2

A fine temple of Victoriana, full of large animal skeletons and stuffed birds, the galleries are in fact quite modern, though they have been designed to fit seamlessly into this venerable 19th-century building, and are characterized by dark wooden display cabinets, spiral stairs, and a maximalist approach to presentation. The whole space heaves with specimens. Truth be told, the museum's as much an educational tool as it is an aesthetic monument to another age, not that there's too much wrong with that, and it makes it easier to get by the fact that annotations are only in French. It's not huge, but it is generally good value as there's plenty to linger over, especially if you've got kids in tow—watch out for the live snakes and spiders, which come as something of a surprise.

Musée Jules Verne

3 rue de l'Hermitage, Nantes; tel. 02 40 69 72 52; www.julesverne.nantesmetropole.fr; 10am-12pm and 2pm-6pm Mon. and Wed.-Sat., 2pm-6pm Tues. and Sun.; adults €3, reduced €1.50

Pioneer of science fiction writing and prophet for modern technology, Jules Verne, author of such classics as *Journey to the Center of the Earth* and *20,000 Leagues Under the Sea*, is one of Nantes's most famous sons. His impact on the city is most clearly felt in the Machines des l'Île sculpture park, the whole aesthetic of which is in part inspired by his writing. This museum dedicated to his works and memory is for visitors who want to go deeper. Situated in a 19th-century house overlooking the Loire, it is filled with the ephemera of his life as well as many scale models inspired by his work. As you might be able to guess by the price, this is not the biggest museum, and it should be cautioned that the house has no direct connection to Verne himself, save for its age. Perhaps for that, and because the writer's imagination has steeped enough into general world consciousness, this museum is likely to satisfy people with only a passing interest in Verne's work, rather than die-hard fans, who may be left wanting more.

★ Château des Ducs de Bretagne

4 place Marc Elder, Nantes; tel. 02 51 17 49 48; www.chateaunantes.fr/en; courtyard 8:30am-7pm Tues.-Sun. Sept.-June, 8:30am-7pm daily July-Aug., museum 10am-6pm Tues.-Sun. Sept.-June, 10am-6pm daily July-Aug.; château free, museum €8

Even for those who have been in France a while, and have seen châteaus from Nice to Brest, this monumental building is a standout. This is true thanks to both its historical significance and its raw aesthetics. The seat of power in Brittany between the 13th and 16th centuries (the current building is mainly a 15th-century construction), it then became the Breton residence of the French monarchy. Accordingly, it was among some of the earliest monuments in all of France to receive the country's vaunted *monument historique* status.

Resembling nothing less than an authentic fairy-tale castle, it is an entirely walled structure surrounded by a moat channeled from the nearby Loire. Just observing from the outside is impressive enough, but there are various levels a visit can take. It's free to explore the château grounds and to walk around its ramparts, from which there are great views down into the central courtyard and across the city. Inside the palace, meanwhile, is the **Musée d'Histoire Urbaine** (the Museum of the City of Nantes), which can be visited for a small fee. This is decorated with unexpectedly modern flourishes. There are 850 exhibits, including both historic artifacts and multimedia displays that guide visitors through the city's history, right from its origins as home to the Breton dukes up to its modern-day status as a center of art and culture for France. The audio guides are only in French, but each room contains information booklets in English for the committed visitor. Expect to spend a good two to three hours to get the most out of this interesting sight.

Cathédrale Saint-Pierre et Saint-Paul

7 impasse Saint-Laurent, Nantes; tel. 02 40 47 84 64; http://cathedrale-nantes.fr; 8:30am-7pm daily summer, 8:30am-6pm daily winter; free

Even by the standards of Gothic cathedrals, this one took a long time to complete. Construction on the church started in 1434, and it was not declared finished until 1891. The main portal was constructed in 1481, the towers in 1508, and the flying buttresses not until the 1600s. After that, construction was delayed to await the demolition of the walls of the old city, which stood in the way of the planned location of the choir for the cathedral.

Despite this straddling of different periods, the cathedral builders remained committed to its Gothic roots, giving it a surprising continuity of style. Thanks to recent restoration work, meanwhile, much stone in the cathedral appears white, making a visit thereby quite distinct from many other similar buildings—for those interested in fantasy literature and movies, there's something of Lord of the Rings's Gondor to the interior. The most interesting artifact inside is the tomb of Francois II, Duke of Brittany, and his wife Marguerite de Foix, parents of the region's favorite daughter, Queen Anne. This sits just to the side of the altar and is guarded by a whole retinue of biblical and allegorical figures.

1

2

Musée des Beaux-Arts de Nantes

10 rue Georges Clemenceau, Nantes; tel. 02 51 17 45 00; http://museedartsdenantes.nantesmetropole.fr; 11am-7pm Fri.-Mon. and Wed., 11am-7pm Thurs.; adults €8, reduced €4

As a major center of French culture, Nantes is home to a world-class art museum. Founded in the 1800s, under the same laws that opened Paris's Louvre to the general public, the Musée des Beaux-Arts de Nantes has been added to repeatedly across its lifespan, both architecturally and in its collection, making the current institution a wonderful crossroads of styles and artistic periods. There are works from the 13th century here, through artists like Rubens and Tintoretto, up to Pablo Picasso and sculptures from the modern day.

The neoclassical facade of the building dates from the late 19th century, though much of its interior is newly designed—an overhaul that lasted five years before the museum reopened in 2017. The cool plain whites of the interior walls combined with the retained grandeur of the building help to make all the art there seem relevant and vital. There's also a trendy café you can drop into after your visit. The only downside is that there isn't much information in English about the exhibits. Nevertheless, there's enough to keep even casual art lovers interested for hours.

Jardins des Plantes de Nantes

Rue Stanislas Baudry, Nantes; tel. 02 40 41 90 00; 8:30am-8pm daily Feb.-Oct., 8:30am-6pm Nov.-Jan.; free

As well as being one of the more satisfyingly named places in this book—go on, say it, Jardins des Plantes de Nantes—this English-style botanical garden has a surprisingly long heritage, being able to trace its origins way back to the 17th century. It's gone through plenty of iterations since then, starting to approach its current form when it was restyled in the mid-1800s with the addition of several ponds and an artificial "mountain." A beautiful late-Victorian-style palm house was constructed in the 1890s.

With over 11,000 different plant species covering 17 acres (7 hectares), the garden is a haven for botanists, but also very pleasant for the casual visitor, with winding paths crisscrossing its various waterways; a collection of fun contemporary sculptures, many incorporating plant life; and fabulous greenhouses. There are also plenty of places to sit down and relax and to observe the abundant wildlife. Meanwhile, the recent "Dépodépo" playground in the garden's north, made out of giant plant pot sculptures, is sure to delight any kids you bring along.

ENTERTAINMENT AND EVENTS

Festivals and Events

LE VOYAGE A NANTES

Various locations throughout Nantes; tel. 02 72 64 04 79; www.levoyageanantes.fr; July-Aug.; free

Transforming the cityscape every summer, dozens of artists from disparate backgrounds set up installations across Nantes, which visitors and locals are invited to explore and discover in whatever way they see fit. It's perhaps the strongest manifestation of the artistic spirit of the city, as the streets become a veritable playground in the name of creativity. More than just sculpture, many exhibits are of an interactive scope, and include concerts as well as sporting activities. Attractions tend to be based in, or planned by, established sights or restaurants, often offering a new spin on visitor experiences of these places, particularly in the case of large pop art murals, transforming otherwise unassuming walls, or the large-scale installation art along the banks of the Loire, from a villa balanced precariously on top of a chimney stack to a house in the river that looks poised to sink.

1: the Great Elephant at Les Machines de l'Ile de Nantes conceived by Pierre Orefice and Francois Deleroziere; **2:** aerial view of Nantes

SCOPITONE

Stereolux, Nantes; tel. 02 40 43 20 43; www.stereolux.org/scopitone-2018; late Sept.; concerts tickets free-€32

Spread across the city, and involving the coming together of different art forms, Scopitone is a September festival aiming to celebrate music, imagery, live shows, and the digital arts. Large electronic concerts by international acts in the industrial Nefs space on the Île de Nantes represent the festival's main attraction, but there are also installations and roundtable discussions about art (in French), some involving the festivals main music acts, going on elsewhere in the city across the five days. Scopitone's name, incidentally, refers to a hybrid jukebox from the 1960s, which also showed small music video clips with the songs it played.

Performing Arts

LE LIEU UNIQUE

1 rue de la Biscuiterie, Nantes; tel. 02 51 82 15 06; www.lelieuunique.com; 8am-12am daily, concerts year-round; free entry, paid exhibitions from €6, paid concerts from €12

A former biscuit factory, the Lieu Unique is Nantes's national center for contemporary arts, providing a space right in the middle of town for artists to meet and trade ideas about their work. To this end, the building is a veritable department store for creatives, although instead of shops, there are spaces to practice and perform, plus a bar, a restaurant, a bookstore, a nursery, and even a hammam for gathering. The minds behind the enterprise called it a "factory for producing the imaginary"—the design has been left accordingly industrial. It's a great place to drop in on to soak up the creative atmosphere, or to come and watch some eclectic concerts or shows.

THÉÂTRE GRASLIN

Place Graslin, Nantes; tel. 02 40 69 77 18; www.angers-nantes-opera.com; season from Sept.-June; tickets €5-25

With so many of its main creative projects only having been inaugurated since the year 2000, it's possible to believe Nantes's reputation as a center of creativity is a relatively recent phenomenon. The Théâtre Graslin says otherwise. This majestic opera house was first constructed in the late 18th century (though had to be rebuilt about 30 years later following destruction by fire). Built in an imposing neoclassical style, it offers a regular roster of world-quality opera and other concerts for impressively reasonable prices.

SHOPPING

PASSAGE POMMERAYE

20 Passage Pommeraye, Nantes; www.passagepommeraye.fr; 8am-8pm; free

A shopping experience that's worth having even if you don't intend to buy anything, the Passage Pommeraye is an early example of a shopping mall, being a covered alley boasting multiple levels. Built in the 1840s, its details are more like those of a cathedral or a palace than anything usually associated with mere commerce. It's characterized by extravagant Renaissance-inspired architecture and sculptures, as well as a fabulous flight of stairs, and is flooded by natural light thanks to its glass roof. Within the passage are a variety of around 30 outlets and restaurants, including a high-end sweet shop, perfumers, jewelers, handbag sellers, and more.

SPORTS AND RECREATION

Boating

MARINE & LOIRE CROISIÈRES

Gare Maritime, quai Ernest Renaud, Nantes; tel. 02 40 69 40 40; www.marineetloire.fr; Apr.-Oct.; from €25

Once a major trading port, Nantes's main river, the Loire, is an essential element of its history and character. Taking a boat trip into its estuary is both a pleasurable day out and a good way to better understand the town. The 2.75-hour journey, on a decent-sized boat with a couple of outdoor observation decks, takes passengers to Saint-Nazaire on the coast, where they're free to explore for a time before returning. En route, expect to see riverside sculptures, ex-submarine pens built by the

Nazis, and much of the fascinating industrial architecture of the shipping industry. Expect the round-trip to take a full day—you might consider taking the boat in one direction, then returning by some other form of transport. Boats depart at 10am daily in the summer and about every other day in the spring and fall.

Cycling

With 292 miles (470 kilometers) of bike paths crisscrossing its center and the wider metropolitan area, Nantes is far and away a bicycle-friendly city. There are plenty of route suggestions and maps available from bike-hire firms and the Nantes tourist office.

ALONG THE RIVER ERDRE

One of the most accessible of these bike paths, and one that is appropriate for nearly all levels of fitness, is the 23-mile (37-kilometer) route up along the River Erdre. The trip takes you through a largely wooded environment following the riverbends and ends in the town of Sucé-sur-Erdre, which is picturesque and fun to wander around.

Finding your way really is very simple. Start at the Monument Charles de Gaulle in Nantes's town center and head north along the quai de Versailles. Follow the river north, bulging away from it briefly as you go through the Université de Nantes. Then take the route de la Joneliàre, which passes through a number of sports fields. From here you join up with the D39, which is a fairly main road, but there's a bike path running alongside it. This turns into the D69, which takes you to the center of Sucé-sur-Erdre. If you want to cut the trip down a little, it's also possible to cross the river just after the Université de Nantes, and follow the tow path back into Nantes center along the other side. It's very hard to get lost on this ride, so as long as you're following the river you should be OK.

DETOURS DE LOIRE NANTES

Allée de la Maison Rouge, Nantes; tel. 02 40 48 75 37; https://detoursdeloire.com; half-day bike rental from €10

A bike-hire firm for both day trips around Nantes and taking off into the surrounding countryside of the Loire Valley. There's a wide selection of well-maintained bikes on offer, from classic touring rides to electricity-assisted bikes to racers. They'll also give you plenty of advice and maps for where to go, and there's a selection of guided tours on offer. Prices start at €10 for a half-day on the most basic bike.

FOOD

Local Cuisine

★ LES CHANTS D'AVRIL

2 rue Laennec, Nantes; tel. 02 40 89 34 76; www.leschantsdavril.fr; 12pm-1:30pm Mon.-Wed., 12pm-1:30pm and 8pm-9:15pm Thurs.-Fri.; lunch menu €22.50, evening menu €28.50

This kind of eating seldom comes at such a low price. The chef constructs the menu daily, which takes its cue from traditional French flavors which are completed with modern twists. Intended as a mystery, what comes out of the kitchen is a complete surprise—it's only revealed when it's on your plate in front of you! Just come in, explain any dietery restrictions, and you're away (but note that they don't speak much English, so if you have serious needs, make sure you can explain them in French). The "mystery menus" are designed to build upon each other elegantly; each one is a culinary journey, and they look as beautiful as they taste. The interior is surprisingly traditional for what might otherwise be considered a high-concept restaurant. Book ahead, as it's popular.

MAISON BARON-LEFÈVRE

33 rue de Rieux, Nantes; tel. 02 40 89 20 20; www.baron-lefevre.fr; 12pm-2:30pm and 7:30pm-9:30pm Tues.-Sat.; lunch menu €18.50, evening menu €28

With a trendy, industrial-chic design and semi-open kitchen, this large restaurant serves surprisingly traditional food. It's an exciting place to be when it's busy, and it's good for large groups—there's a whole room that can be booked privately. The place is also big enough that they'll probably have room for you if you turn up without reserving. The scallops are particularly recommended, and the desserts are quite indulgent.

UNE SAGE IDÉE

15 rue Jean Jacques Rousseau, Nantes; tel. 02 51 84 15 15; http://unesageidee.fr; 12pm-2:30pm and 7pm-11pm Mon. and Wed., 12pm-2:30pm and 7pm-12am Thurs. and Sat.; menus from €24.90

Urbane, but with a hint of eccentricity (see the model giraffe out front), Une Sage Idée serves fresh, light food, artfully presented. Its interior is characterized by black ceilings and other fixtures, which contribute to an intimate air: It's the kind of restaurant that's great for a date. (Whether you need such a place on holiday in Nantes may be immaterial, but you never know.) Prices are pretty reasonable for what you get.

LE CAMBRONNE BISTROT CHIC

6 rue de l'Héronnière, Nantes; tel. 02 40 47 36 42; www.lecambronne-bistrotchic.fr; 12pm-2pm and 7pm-10pm daily; menus from €24.50

Serving excellent food with a slightly more formal vibe than some of the other places recommended here, this restaurant's interior is all sleek, dark colors with some trendy black and white tiling and wooden panels lending it timeless class. The inspiration behind the dishes is local with some Asian flourishes, such as bok choy in place of cabbage, and wasabi as an accent to some of the seafood. There are also a couple of terraces, which prove popular during the summer months. Booking ahead is recommended.

LA VACHERIE

3 rue Albert Londres, Nantes; tel. 02 51 13 13 13; www.lavacherie.fr; 12pm-2pm and 7pm-10pm Mon.-Thurs., 12pm-2pm and 7pm-11pm Fri.-Sat., 12pm-2pm Sun.; mains €16.50-22

You can fuss around all you like with painstakingly reduced sauces or delicately poached fish, but sometimes all you want is a steak, and nothing but a steak will do. La Vacherie is here to provide for just such moments, flame-grilling a variety of perfectly sourced and aged beef cuts, and serving them in a straightforward restaurant with a modern, though folksy, wood interior. It's a little out of the town center, granted, but this is a gem if you happen to be headed out of town by car. Prices are satisfyingly reasonable, and yes, there are other things on the menu for those not so carnivorously inclined.

LA CIVELLE

21 quai Marcel Boissard, Rezé; tel. 02 40 75 46 60; www.lacivelle.com; 9:30am-12am daily; menus from €31

Here's one of the many restaurants in Nantes's trendy Trentemoult district, which lies on the southern bank of the Loire and is most easily reached by boat. The interior is full of industrial-chic touches, and there are some great views out across the river, with a terrace that is very popular on warm days—particularly on weekends, when this area becomes a day-trip destination for locals. Be sure to book ahead. The food is traditional with a strong sense of seasonality, and includes a colorful, hearty vegetarian option—the kind of thing that isn't always easy to find in Brittany.

International

LA PORCELAINE

14 rue Léon Blum, Nantes; tel. 02 55 58 16 46; https://la-porcelaine.business.site; 12pm-3pm and 7pm-11pm Tues.-Thurs. and Sat., 12pm-3pm Mon., 7pm-11pm Fri.; menus from €20

At La Porcelaine, the food is zingingly delicious and surprising. The restaurant is also beautifully designed, with bold blue feature walls, trendy modern furniture, and yes, artfully laid out porcelain. As good for lunch as it is for dinner, this is the kind of place that big cities excel at, but which are rare in the Breton hinterland. Book ahead to be sure of a place.

THE RED & LUNA

7 rue de la Juiverie, Nantes; tel. 09 83 77 62 48; http://theredluna.business.site; 12pm-2:30pm and 7pm-10:30pm Thurs.-Mon., 7pm-10:30pm Tues.-Wed.; mains €6-18

Competing for best Japanese restaurant in Nantes, The Red & Luna offers a classic menu of dishes from the Land of the Rising Sun, including some excellent sushi—there's an interesting crossover between this cuisine and Breton food in general, so it's hardly a surprise. The dining area riffs on modern Japanese style, which can come as something of a surprise given the traditional half-timber building in which it's located. There's both a small street-side terrace and an outdoor eating area in the back.

Budget Options

CRÊPERIE KER BREIZH

11 rue de l'Héronnière, Nantes; tel. 02 40 69 80 20; 12pm-2pm and 7:30pm-9:30pm Sun.-Thurs., 12pm-2pm and 7:30pm-10pm Fri.-Sat.; from €5.70

A reminder, if one were needed, that despite legal borders saying otherwise, Nantes is very much a Breton city, with the cuisine to prove it. The Crêperie Ker Breizh is commonly regarded as serving the best crepes in town. Trendier than many of its country cousins, its interior design is more hipster than it is chintzy. The food is reliably traditional, though, with a few sexy specials bolstering its urbane credentials: The scallops with curry sauce is a real highlight. Book well ahead, for the place is both small and very popular.

LE ROUT'ART GOURMAND

Various locations, Nantes; tel. 06 47 09 68 30; www.leroutartgourmand.com; 12pm-2:30pm Mon.-Fri.; menus €10.50-13.50

Are there any food trends more emblematic of modern big city living than the food truck? Building from fast-food roots, this business, which crops up mainly in the Nantes outskirts (check their website on any given day for their location and hours), sells some really excellent, often surprisingly healthy dishes made with top-end ingredients at welcome low prices. The "Black Burger" with gravlax is a real showstopper, but there are also more traditional choices, too. Its non-central locations make it a good place to aim for if you're planning on an extended day's cycle through the city's green spaces. It's better than most picnics can offer.

ACCOMMODATIONS

Under €50

AUBERGE DE JEUNESSE HI NANTES

2 place de la Manu, Nantes; tel. 02 40 29 29 20; www.hifrance.org/auberge-de-jeunesse/nantes.html; dorm room bed plus breakfast from €22

Located in the premises of an old tobacco factory, this hostel could, in theory, offer the kind of cool credentials that match the city in which it's found. In reality, the interior, with its unupdated furniture and decor, is a little tired. However, it's close to the center of town and has friendly staff. It offers rooms with 3-6 beds, and a simple continental breakfast is included. There is also an independent kitchen and hang-out space complete with table tennis and pool tables. Internet access is available throughout.

€50-100

HÔTEL SAINT YVES

154 rue Général Buat, Nantes; tel. 02 40 74 48 42; from €70 d

This is one for the traditionalists. Among all the trendy minimalism and industrial-chic of Nantes's other restaurants and hotels, this centrally located hotel is as soft and welcoming as a countryside cottage. There remain modern conveniences, such as flat-screen TVs, en suite bathrooms, and WiFi, but this is also a hotel you'd be happy to take your grandmother to. Breakfast is traditional French, and the staff are very friendly.

L'HÔTEL

6 rue Henri IV, Nantes; tel. 02 40 29 30 31; www.nanteshotel.com/fr; from €80 d

While its name may stray a little on the bland side—not to mention potentially prove confusing to taxi drivers—this is a good-value trendy hotel. Its style is all plush modern colors, but it's fairly minimal in furniture, with most rooms getting their own individual design. Rooms either have views out to the Château des Ducs or of the hotel garden, making the train station walking distance, as well as most of Nantes's other major sights.

There's a buffet breakfast, bar service, and a 24-hour reception. Internet access is available throughout the property.

HÔTEL LA PÉROUSE

3 allée Duquesne, Nantes; tel. 02 40 89 75 00; www.hotel-laperouse.fr; from €90 d

The concept is high with this one. The architecture of the Pérouse's purpose-built structure is box-like and intensely modern, and perhaps not for everyone. Inside, things are a little more classically tasteful: rooms are minimalist and boast an attractive combination of white fabric and unpainted wood. They're also soundproof, well insulated, and comfortable. En suite bathrooms come as standard, while the breakfast, which is €16 extra, is a real cut above the usual, being composed entirely of fair trade, organic produce. It's well located in the center of town.

€100-200

SOZO HÔTEL

16 rue Frédéric Cailliaud, Nantes; tel. 02 51 82 40 00; www.sozohotel.fr; from €130 d

Hotels rarely come with more character than this one built in the interior of a former church. The 19th-century ecclesiastical architecture has been left as intact as possible, though the actual furniture, carpets, and other decor is all ultra-modern—think bucket chairs under vaulted ceilings and crisp white sheets spangled by light thrown from stained glass windows. Features include Nespresso machines, private bathrooms, and free WiFi, and the hotel bar stays open until 2am. There's also a wellness area (read: mini spa) on-site.

RADISSON BLU HÔTEL

6 place Aristide Briand, Nantes; tel. 02 72 00 10 00; from €130 d

This extraordinarily grand property is set inside a vast neoclassical courthouse in the center of town. Public spaces are cavernous, colorful, and full of modern, arty details. Rooms are all curves and smooth surfaces, with a largely dark color scheme, designed by Jean-Philippe Nuel. It also overflows with amenities and top-end services, including the standard WiFi throughout, en suite bathrooms, and flat-screen TVs in all the rooms. There's also 24-hour room service—great for those midnight snacks, which you can work off in the affiliated fitness center nearby.

Camping

NANTES CAMPING

21 boulevard du Petit Port, Nantes; tel. 02 40 74 47 94; www.nantes-camping.fr; open year-round; two people with a tent €25, cabin €79

About 10 minutes north of the city center and surrounded by a lush green estate, this top-end campsite boasts a swimming pool, a restaurant, and mini golf, as well as a variety of different accommodation types, from simple tents to quite luxurious cabins (requiring a minimum of three nights). There are also extensive shower blocks and toilets, plus a laundry service. Its position also makes it well placed if you want to explore the countryside around Nantes as well as the center. Bikes are rented on-site to make this easier.

INFORMATION AND SERVICES

NANTES.TOURISME

9 rue des États, Nantes; tel. 08 92 46 40 44; www.nantes-tourisme.com/fr; 10am-6pm Mon.-Sat., 10am-5pm Sun.

Just outside the Château des Ducs, this is a decent-size tourist office where English is widely spoken. It's good with figuring out trips in the surrounding area as well as in town, particularly for cyclists—a number of cycle path maps and other brochures are available.

NANTES UNIVERSITY HOSPITAL

Hotel-Dieu, 1 place Alexis-Ricordeau, Nantes; tel. 02 40 08 33 33; www.chu-nantes.fr; 7:30am-8pm Mon.-Fri., 10am-8pm Sat.-Sun., ER open 24 hours

A big city hospital with multiple departments, and a 24-hour ER. Though English is not officially spoken, you should be able to find some doctors with whom you can communicate.

BUREAU DE POSTE

3 rue du Moulin, Nantes; www.laposte.fr/particulier; 9:30am-6pm Mon.-Fri., 9:30am-12:30pm Sat.

One of the more central of Nantes's many post offices. It's unlikely you'll find English speakers, and post office workers in France are among the worst for demonstrating their country's sometimes over-fondness for bureaucracy. However, the color-coded system of parcels is pretty intuitive, and the system is surprisingly sleek, when it works.

TRANSPORTATION

Getting There

BY AIR

A real gateway airport to Brittany and the Loire, **Nantes Atlantique** (Bouguenais; www.nantes.aeroport.fr/fr) is the third-largest airport in the west of France. Flights arrive here from all around France and the rest of Europe, including ones from Brussels, Geneva, Milan, Madrid, and many more. The main airlines serving the airport are Hop!, Volotea, Transavia, and EasyJet. The last of these flies in from London-Gatwick and London Luton. Expect these flights to cost around €40 one-way, obviously depending on availability.

From Paris, the airport is only served by Air France, pushing the price up a little to around €80 one-way, also subject to availability.

For getting into Nantes center from the airport, there is a shuttle bus. This runs every 20 minutes from Monday to Saturday and every half an hour on Sundays. It takes about 20 minutes to get to the city center and should cost around €9. If you have a little more time, however, it's possible to save money by taking the shuttle just to Neustrie bus stop, then taking the tram. This journey should only cost €2. It will take almost 40 minutes.

If you'd prefer just to grab a taxi, though, the main rank is outside Hall 3. It should cost between €30 and €35 to get to the center.

BY CAR

A major hub in France's northwest and a gateway town to the rest of Brittany, Nantes is well connected by multiple major roads. From Paris (240 miles/386 kilometers, 4 hours), it's a straight shot along the A11. Because you are traveling on toll roads all the way, expect to pay about €40.

From Rennes (70 miles/112 kilometers, 1.5 hours), head south on the N137. From Brest (183 miles/294 kilometers, 3.25 hours), you follow the N165, which takes you along a route near the coast. This coastal route goes via Quimper (142 miles/228 kilometers, 2.5 hours), Lorient (100 miles/160 kilometers, 2 hours), and Vannes (65 miles/104 kilometers, 1 hour 20 minutes).

From Caen (180 miles/290 kilometers, 3 hours), you take the A84 to Rennes, then continue along the N137. From Rouen (240 miles/386 kilometers, 4 hours), take the A28 to Le Mans, then transfer to the A11 to Nantes; this journey should cost about €15 in tolls.

Arriving in Nantes, there is a wide ring road, which is by far the most effective way of getting to the part of the city you need. There are plenty of parking lots in the center of town, many close to major monuments. Parking prices are quite high in the short term, but more reasonable the longer you stay: €3.10 for an hour, €17.30 for the day.

BY TRAIN

Nantes main train station, **Gare de Nantes** (27 boulevard de Stalingrad, Nantes; tel. 08 92 35 35 35; www.gares-sncf.com/fr/gare/frnte/nantes; 4:20am-12:15am Mon.-Thurs., 4:20am-12:45am Fri., 5:15am-12:45am Sat., 6:15am-12:45am Sun.), is a through-station rather than a terminus, connected directly with many of the major cities in France, and much of the rest of Brittany. Aligned on an east-west axis, it can be entered both from the north and south sides. These entrances are described separately as Gare Nord and Gare Sud, which can give the impression that they are distinct stations. This is not the case—they are linked by an underground walkway, and you can access all platforms easily from both. The north side, though, is closest to the Line 1 of Nantes tram service, while the south side is where you'll be left or picked up by the airport shuttle.

Getting to Gare de Nantes from Paris, there are around 18 trains a day, leaving from the capital's Gare de l'Est, Gare du Nord, and Saint-Lazare. All take 2-3 hours and cost €40-90, depending on how early you book tickets.

Getting there from the modern-day Breton capital, Rennes, there are around 11 trains a day, taking 1-2 hours and costing about €20.

From Brest, there is only one direct train a day, which takes about four hours and costs around €50—there are, however, 10 opportunities to get to Nantes from Brest by transferring at Rennes. This is roughly a five-hour journey.

From Quimper, there are around four direct trains a day, taking just under three hours and costing around €30.

From Bordeaux directly to the south, meanwhile, there are around three direct trains a day. This journey is 4 hour and 40 minutes and costs around €30-90, depending on how far in advance you book.

Getting Around

BY BIKE

Nantes is a quite astoundingly bike-able city—it's been ranked no less than the seventh-best city for cyclists in the entire world. The main reason for this is the extensive system of bike lanes, which thread everywhere in the city and its suburbs. Beyond that, there are also numerous bike-hire companies to help budding cyclists, even those without their own wheels, to explore them. This includes **Bicloo** (tel. 08 10 44 44 44; www.bicloo.nantesmetropole.fr/home), a municipal bike station service, for which there are 103 stations and 883 bikes available around Nantes in total.

These are perfect for short trips. It's a self-service system, in which you pick up a bike at one station then leave it at another. After sign-up, the first half hour of riding is free, then it's €0.50 for every additional half hour after that. There's a tourist deal, available at the tourist office, which allows you to sign up for three days for €3. All you need is a credit card. The system is available 24 hours.

BY PUBLIC TRANSPORT

There are three tiers of public transport in Nantes operating on something called the **TAN network** (tel. 02 40 44 44 44; www.tan.fr): tram, bus, and river bus. They operate extensively around the city and across its river. One ticket for €1.60 permits you use of the system for one hour.

Probably the two most useful lines to know are tramline 1, which runs on the city's east-west axis, and tramline 3, which travels north-south across the island. These intersect at the north side of Nantes's main train station.

The **Navibus** runs every 20 minutes between the Gare Maritime de Nantes on the north bank of the Loire to Trentemoult on the south bank. The crossing takes 10 minutes.

BY TAXI

Several taxi companies service Nantes and its suburbs; some companies to try include **Allo Taxi Nantes Atlantique** (tel. 02 40 69 22 22), **ABC Taxis** (tel. 02 40 65 59 00) and **Oh-Taxi** (tel. 02 28 00 00 82). There is also a large taxi stand to the south of Nantes's train station. Most trips around town are not going to set you back much more than €10, while a trip from the center to the airport will be about €30-35.

Josselin

Today, it's known for its castle, one of the most impressive sights in all of the Breton hinterland. But before Josselin attracted visitors for this feat of architecture, before people came to explore its surrounding forests, or indulge on its hearty, honest cuisine, they came here as pilgrims. Because way back in the almost-forgotten mists of the early 9th century, a local farmer discovered a statue of the Virgin Mary in a bush of brambles.

As the legend goes, he took it home with him, only for it to disappear and, the next day, reappear in the bush. This happened again and again, until the farmer recognized what was happening as a miracle. Instead of taking the statue home, he prayed to her where she always found her way back to: the bush. The next day, his daughter was cured of blindness. Before long, word of this miracle had spread, and the statue was attracting Christians from far and wide. Even Saint Malo, whose name would become linked with one of Brittany's most enduring and enigmatic ports, found his way to the spot.

She's no longer there, the statue; burned during the French Revolution, all that remains of her is a fragment, which is saved at the Basilique Notre Dame du Roncier. Nevertheless, in many respects, it was her existence that led to the building of the mighty château: Josselin was drawing in money thanks to the pilgrimage, which made it an excellent place to establish a stronghold. This building continued being added to across the ages, with formal gardens from the 14th century and a vast library from the 17th just two of its highlights. The town, meanwhile, remains characterized by the kind of half-timber buildings common throughout this part of the world, and is home to a small section of the famous Nantes-Brest canal. A commune of barely more than 2,000 people, Josselin nevertheless offers much to do and see.

ORIENTATION

The town of Josselin is sandwiched in between the route Nationale 24 to the north and the River Oust to the south. The town center is small and sits closer to the river than the main road: It's around here that you'll find more of the historic half-timber houses plus the tourism infrastructure, with the main hub being the area around the town square next to the Notre Dame du Roncier. The château itself is a little farther south still, on the river itself, within its own extensive grounds. The Bois d'Amour, meanwhile, fringes the east of town.

SIGHTS

★ Château de Josselin

Place de la Congrégation, Josselin; tel. 02 97 22 36 45; www.chateaudejosselin.com; 2pm-6pm daily Apr.-mid-July and Sept., 11am-6pm daily mid-July-Aug., 2pm-5:30pm Sat.-Sun. and school holidays Oct.; guided Château visit: adults €9.40, children €5.60, museum visit: adults €8.40, children €5.40, combined visit: adults €14.90, children €8.90

This is easily one of the most impressive châteaus in Brittany, if not all of France, with three towers regally surveying the Oust Valley and a Flamboyant Gothic facade. The interiors boast an extensive 17th-century library with more than 3,000 volumes and many valued portraits. Also, there is the 16th-century fireplace, and even the actual table on which was signed the all-important Edict of Nantes, which effectively brought the Wars of Religion conflict to an end. The gardens, meanwhile, offer some excellent views of the château and a wonderful array of horticultural designs, from the French- and English-style ones created by landscape architect Achille Duchêne at the beginning of the 20th century to a more recent rose garden constructed in 2001.

Besides its architecture or location, though, perhaps the most fanciful quality to the château is that the same family, the Rohans, have owned it for around 600 years. As a throwaway fact this already sounds impressive, but is even more so when you consider the ravages of history the family had to endure in that time to hold on to their ancestral home. These included recriminations from Cardinal Richelieu in the 1600s and the ever-present threat of the guillotine during the French Revolution. Throughout their history, many members of the Rohan family have been involved in the governance of both Brittany and France, with the current duke having served as the regional President of the Brittany region from 1998 until 2004.

A visit to the chateau today can include wandering the grounds of the castle independently, where a number of information signs in English give context to what you're seeing. Or, join a guided tour to look around the interior. (Note: These are only available in English in July and August; outside that time you'll have to follow a French tour guide, though they will make sure you get an English pamphlet on the château's history.)

There is also a small museum dedicated to dolls in the castle's old stables (**Musee de Poupees,** 3 rue des Trente, Josselin; tel. 02 97 22 36 45). This collection, which belongs to the Rohan family, costs €7 to see and can be toured in about 30 minutes. Somewhat self-evidently, this is the kind of place that is really fascinating if you feel you have an interest in old toys, but may leave those that don't a little cold.

Bois d'Amour
(Lover's Wood)

Rue de la Carrière, Josselin; year-round; free entry

An unusual but utterly arresting public park, this takes the form of a small, planned forest. It's ideal for a wander along its many paths, which take you past rhododendrons, bamboo, and all manner of sculptures under a canopy of trees. Great for picnics, for kids, or for walking your dog, the whole place is a fascinating example of how something so painstakingly maintained can still feel quite wild and natural. There's a fun circuit to follow called *au fil de l'eau* ("over the water"), which actually starts outside the wooded area. Themed on the subject of water, you leave from the washhouse at the foot of the château, go past information boards about the history of the Nantes-Brest Canal, and follow signs into the woods and toward the Millennium Clock surrounded by a fountain. This walk should take about 1 hour 30 minutes.

Château de Josselin

Basilique Notre Dame du Roncier

Rue Olivier de Clisson, Josselin; tel. 02 97 22 20 18; 9am-5:30pm daily; free

A Gothic church with its oldest elements dating from the end of the 12th century, this has long been home to the famous Virgin of the Brambles. Sadly, this statue, which was credited with a number of miracles in the 9th century, was burned during the French Revolution, though a fragment was saved from the flames and placed in the church reliquary. Supposedly, it retains its holy properties, and the basilica remains noted as a place of miracles and is the center of a pilgrimage that still takes place every September.

Besides the statue fragment, the church boasts several other treasures, including the opulent tomb of Olivier de Clisson and his wife, Marguerite de Rohan; some magnificent stained glass windows (also depicting the couple); and some remarkable antique furniture dating from the 16th century. Probably the quality that will draw most visitors, however, is that they are still allowed to venture up the church bell tower, which still rings out after services, and is open every day from Easter (the start of spring) to All Saints (mid-fall), offering excellent panoramic views of the surrounding country.

SPORTS AND RECREATION

Hiking

POPINETTES TRAIL, QUESTEMBERT

Beginning and ending the center of Questembert; www.france-voyage.com/outings/popinettes-trail-questembert-4251.htm; year-round; free

Lying a little to the south of Josselin, this 8-mile (13-kilometer) circuit trail is a wonderful way to spend an afternoon, working up an appetite for a hearty local dinner—it should take most walkers about 3.5 hours. Beginning and ending at the town of Questembert, it takes walkers along the banks of a creek, past the 12th-century Chapelle Saint-Jean, and through woodland that shimmers in spring with blooming asphodels. These ghostly flowers are referred to by locals as *popinettes,* giving the trail its name. Full details and a map of the walk can be found by visiting the website. It's a hike suitable for moderately fit walkers.

FOOD

LA TERRASSE

55 chemin Glatinier, Josselin; tel. 02 97 22 20 35; 7:30am-7pm Mon.-Fri.; menus from €12.20

With a colorful frontage and busy interior characterized by old farm and kitchen equipment hung on its ceiling and walls, this is the kind of traditional French bistro that isn't so common anymore. The food is simple, but comprised of rich local flavors, including hearty meat and potato dishes, which are great to enjoy with cider. There's also a floral garden that overlooks the canal, while the owner is something of an eccentric: An artist in metal work, he's also a motorbike enthusiast and often only too happy to show visitors his collection. More than anything, though, this place is a great value.

LA TABLE D'O

9 chemin Glatinier, Josselin; tel. 02 97 70 61 39; https://latabledo.eatbu.com; 12pm-1:15pm and 7:30pm-8:45pm Tues.-Fri., 12pm-1:15pm and 7:30pm-9pm Sat.; menus €24-34

An elegant interior and some great views out toward the Château Josselin, combined with some refined locally sourced food, from juicy steaks to expertly baked river fish, makes this restaurant a great place for a formal holiday meal. The menu may not offer the widest selection, but that means they can focus on doing whatever dishes are on it that week to the highest quality—and the presentation is often top notch. A slight word of warning: Portion size of any individual course is not huge, but the arc of a full meal should be sufficiently filling.

★ HÔTEL RESTAURANT DU CHÂTEAU

1 rue du Général de Gaulle, Josselin; tel. 02 97 22 20 11; 12pm-1:45pm and 7pm-8:45pm daily; menus

Detour: The Blavet Valley

A little farther to the west of Josselin, running north of the N24, is the Blavet Valley. As lush and green as anywhere you're likely to find in Brittany, it's an area famous for two things: horses and chapels.

HORSES

You'll find the horses at **Haras National** (rue Victor Hugo, Hennebont; www.haras-hennebont.fr), one of Brittany's two national stud farms. Here, visitors are invited to get up close and personal with some incredibly fine animals on guided tours, or if they're lucky, check out one of the events that take place here throughout the season, displaying both the horsemanship of the people who regularly ride here and the spectacular tricks performed by the horses themselves. The season is late April to the end of August, and there are further shows during the Christmas holidays.

CHAPELS

The chapels, meanwhile, dot the valley, representative of a far simpler kind of Christianity than the one seen in the mammoth Gothic architecture of many places elsewhere in France. There are 25 in total, dating from the 15th century, often built near springs of water, hearkening back to pagan beliefs in the element's healing properties. They are humble, earthy places of worship, though no less affecting for that fact. The most impressive is Saint-Gildas chapel, lurking underneath a massive overhang, supposedly marking the place where the missionary Saint Gildas once took shelter in the 6th century.

Recognizing what they've got in the chapels, and attempting to convince the public to visit more than one despite their wide spacing, every July to September local authorities run an initiative to fill each one of these religious spaces with contemporary art (www.artchapelles.com). Suddenly the 15th-century interiors come alive in an entirely unexpected way with sculpture, painting, and sometimes recorded sound. With the exhibitions changing every year, visiting them makes for a well-structured wander through the countryside, with the juxtaposition of art with the chapels a clear visual suggestion of the interesting blend of paganism and Christianity in this part of the world.

INFORMATION

For more information about the chapels and the Blavet Valley area in general, check out the tourist office website of the nearby town of Pontivy (www.tourisme-pontivycommunaute.com).

€22.50-48.50

There's something quite Germanic about this restaurant's large, open-plan dining area. The fireplace, the replica medieval weaponry hanging from the walls, the heavy wooden details: All make you feel when you look up as though you could be in Bavaria, dining at the pleasure of some local count. However, the food is reliably French, and utterly delicious. There's a rustic weight to many of the dishes here, though they have been made with care and skill. There's also a terrace overlooking the river, which has some great views of the château directly opposite.

ACCOMMODATIONS

€50-100

HÔTEL DU CHÂTEAU

1 rue du Général de Gaulle, Josselin; tel. 02 97 22 20 11; from €91 d

Yes, its rooms could probably do with a bit of an update, still languishing as they are with interiors straight from the 1990s, but this is a very well-positoned hotel, cozy and comfortable, and above all reasonably priced. There are TVs in all rooms, plus WiFi and en suite bathrooms, and then there's the excellent on-site restaurant as mentioned above. Being immediately opposite the château, some of its rooms have quite spectacular views.

€100-200

HÔTEL SPA LE ROI ARTHUR

Le Lac au Duc, 1 rue de la Fée Viviane, Ploërmel; tel. 02 97 73 64 64; www.hotelroiarthur.com; from €188 d

Around three miles (4.8 kilometers) outside of Josselin, the Roi Arthur is a modern spa hotel with a heated swimming pool and direct access to a local golf course. Possessed of so many luxury facilities, it should come as little surprise that the hotel's rooms are comfortably plush and well insulated, with blend-into-the-background, mostly traditional interiors. They have a full roster of modern conveniences, plus some lovely relaxing views of the Lac du Duc, on which the hotel sits. Surrounded by countryside, with a large garden and an on-site restaurant, Les Chevaliers, a retreat here can be fully contained. A meal should set you back about €50-70 each, without wine.

Camping

CAMPING DOMAINE DE KERELLY

RN 24, Guégon; tel. 02 97 22 22 20; www.camping-josselin.com; pitch for two people in high season €14, cabins from €65

A clean and efficiently run midrange campsite complete with 55 pitches, plus 12 cabins and three heavy canvas permanent tents. There's a small swimming pool surrounded by a deck area, and direct access to the River Oust. There's also an on-site snack bar, a convenience store, bike hire, and theme nights during the summer.

INFORMATION

Despite being only a small town, there are two tourist offices in Josselin. The **Office de Tourisme de Ploërmel Communauté—Site de Josselin** (21 rue Olivier de Clisson, Josselin; tel. 02 97 22 36 43; www.broceliande-vacances.com; 10am-12pm and 2pm-5pm Tues.-Fri) is an outpost of the Ploërmel tourist board. The other **tourist office** (Place Alain de Rohan, Josselin, tel. 02 97 22 24 17; www.josselin.com; 2pm-5:30pm Mon., 9am-12:30pm and 2pm-5:30pm Tues.-Thurs., 9am-12:30pm and 2:30pm-5:30pm Fri., 9am-12pm Sat.) is more directly connected to the town itself. Both are particularly good for suggesting walks to go on in the local area, are staffed by English speakers, and are full of leaflets about nearby restaurants and activities. The only issue is to keep aware of their opening hours—the Ploërmel tourist board outpost is not open at all at weekends, while the other shuts Saturday afternoons and Sundays.

GETTING THERE

By Car

It's easy to reach Josselin by car. From Nantes (80 miles/130 kilometers, 2 hours), follow the N165 route that runs parallel to the coast, then making a right to turn inland when you reach the N166. From Rennes (50 miles/80 kilometers, 1 hour), it's an even more straightforward trip west down the N24. From Lorient (50 miles/80 kilometers, 1 hour), this is an almost identical trip, also along the N24, just from the opposite direction. From major towns west of here (Brest and Quimper), the fastest route is via Lorient.

From Vannes (30 miles/48 kilometers, 50 minutes), drive north on the D778. Despite Vannes being the closest major town to Josselin, journey times are a touch longer than you'd expect on account of the smaller roads connecting the two.

Once you're in Josselin there's plenty of free parking, though much of it is for a limited amount of time—keep aware of signs instructing you of specific rules. The town can get pretty busy in the summer, but there are a number of parking lots to cater for it. It may take a few minutes to find a space, but stay confident and you should be fine.

By Bus

With no train station, the only public transport into Josselin is by bus from either Rennes or Vannes.

The buses from Rennes are run by the SNCF and leave seven times a day from the city's train station. The journey takes about 1 hour 20 minutes, and should cost about €15.

From Vannes it's necessary to go via local transport on the Line 4 bus route to Ploermel. This is a stopping service, but the easiest place to catch it is the Vannes train station. At Ploermel, change onto the SNCF service, which stops outside that town's tourist office. There are normally services making this journey three times a day, with an average of about an hour wait in Ploermel. Buses stop in place du 18 Juin 1940 in Josselin. The upside of this slightly tricky journey is that it's cheap, costing just €4 in total. With wait time included, it should take an average of two hours. (Note: There is a fourth local bus that leaves from Vannes after 7pm, but it will not get you into Ploermel in time for a changeover. Ploermel is less than 10 miles/16 kilometers from Josselin, so you might consider a taxi from that point.)

GETTING AROUND

A small town, Josselin itself is wholly walkable. You may, however, want to go cycling in its surrounding greenery, in which case you can rent from **Guého Roblin** (tel. 06 10 96 54 14; from €4 an hour), based on the banks of the river, near the lock.

Alternately, taxis are a good way of getting out to more rural restaurants, hotels, and to the slight transport hub that is Ploermel. Try **Taxi du Lac** (tel. 06 61 25 32 36), based out of Ploermel. Expect a journey between the two towns to cost around €20.

Paimpont Forest

Once upon a time, forest used to cover all of Brittany. Thick and mysterious, it gave birth to all manner of superstition, and was renowned throughout Europe as a place of myth and magic. The trees have shrunk back now, and Paimpont Forest is all that remains. Perhaps its endurance can be explained because this is where the magic was always strongest. Vitally linked to the stories of King Arthur and his knights since the early Middle Ages, Paimpont is alive with sites of legendary significance: from the tomb of Merlin to the fountain of eternal youth.

Unsurprisingly, Paimpont has been cashing in on its reputation for many years, luring countless visitors in search of the supernatural since the 19th century, if not before. It's well set up to guide visitors through the landscape of Arthurian legend, with the byways and specific places of the stories now clearly demarcated with modern signs and information boards. At the heart of it all, the Château de Comper has been transformed into a practical Arthurian theme park, where the tales are retold, exhibitions are put on, and events are staged.

Despite the apparent commercialization, much of the spirit of the place lives on. Forests are places of wilderness and myth, sure to spark our imaginations, and when you have one with place names like the Valley of No Return, where some of the very building blocks of our storytelling DNA are said to have been first laid down, modern signage and easy-access paths can only do so much to allay the magic.

SIGHTS

Château de Comper and Centre de l'Imaginaire Arthurien

Château de Comper, Concoret; tel. 02 97 22 79 96; http://centre-arthurien-broceliande.com; 10am-5:30pm Wed.-Sun. (daily during school holidays) mid-Mar.-June and Sept.-Oct., 10am-7pm daily July-Aug.; adults €7, reduced €5

The perfect place to begin an exploration of Paimpont, this château, the oldest parts of which date back to the 13th century, has been set up as an effective visitors center for the region, first offering a refresher on many of the Arthurian myths, then bringing them to life, and finally providing a reflection on what they mean for us today. The château itself is on the shores of not just a lake, but *the* lake: that is, the home to the legendary Lady of the Lake, the sorceress fairy who gave Arthur Excalibur, his legendary sword, and who lived here in a crystal city built by Merlin the Magician.

As a museum dedicated to something as ephemeral as stories, the château's offerings can seem unusual at first. Its exhibition spaces are in parts a little more like an art gallery than something directly informative, with various eclectic cultural artifacts used to get at the essence of King Arthur as well as to tell a story. Make sure to grab one of the English-language explainer pamphlets on entry so you don't find yourself scratching your head. In the high season between March and October, the museum also offers storytelling sessions, workshops—in which you can even learn to sword fight!—and a reconstruction of King Arthur's camp, complete with as many as 50 costumed actors lending it character. In the off season, visit **la Petite Maison des Legendes** (9:30am-12:30pm and 2pm-5pm Tues.-Fri. Oct.-Mar. (closed Dec. 23-Jan 9), where there's a small bookshop full of Arthurian-focused literature, some Paimpont inspired artwork, and staff happy to tell you more about the forest, though only some of them speak English.

The center also offers guided tours, in English, of the key Arthurian sights around Paimpont Forest, which are highly recommended in order to really bring the area to life.

★ Merlin's Tomb

Sur la Landelle, Paimpont; year round; free

Some tourist sights are made special more by what people can bring to them rather than by what they offer in themselves. There's a literal truth to this about "Merlin's tomb," where for many years visitors have been making all sorts of offerings. Ostensibly just three slabs of reddish rock in a forest clearing, the tomb has been layered with meaningful ephemera from its many visitors, praying for miracles from the spirit of the dead wizard.

In a more figurative sense, what you get out of this sight depends on how much feeling you imbue it with. It helps to know the story (or at least one of them) of how Merlin ended up here. Like so many tragic tales, it began because he fell in love with a princess. This princess, usually referred to as Nimue, told the wizard she could never love him back unless he taught her all his magic. Utterly smitten, Merlin did this, though secretly Nimue was always disgusted by the old man's desire. Once she had learned enough and the two of them were traveling through Paimpont, they paused for the night in this old tomb. While Merlin was sleeping, Nimue cast a spell on him so that he could never leave it, causing his death. Nimue is also, incidentally, the famed Lady of the Lake.

There's a small parking lot nearby, and access is easy for both wheelchairs and strollers. There's also a short, signposted walk (under 30 minutes) you can do around the area to see a modest waterhole dubbed the Fountain of Youth. Allegedly, this was used as a kind of baptismal font in Druidic custom, though the evidence for this is pretty scant.

Fontaine de Barenton

Parking Fontaine de Barenton, Folle Pensée Paimpont; year-round; free

This small font in a forest clearing is another example of a sight that may seem unremarkable in itself but has been the subject of so many legends, and so much human attention over the centuries, that it possesses a power that goes way beyond its physical appearance. Since perhaps even before the Arthurian legends, the water here was said to be a cure for madness. The people who used to live around here dedicated it to the worship of Belenos, a god of healing. Latterly, it became the place where Merlin was said to have first met and fallen in love with Nimue, Lady of the Lake. It was here that he taught her magic, standing on its nearby stone slab, known as the Perron de Belanton. Legend also says that if water is brought from the fountain and sprinkled on the slab, then it will bring rain—though this

1

2

being Brittany, the odds of rain at some point during any given day are already pretty high.

It's reached by a walk through the forest—a wide track leads from the parking lot into the forest, slowly becoming narrower and more winding, which can be trying with a stroller or a wheelchair. This certainly lends magic to the place, however. It takes about twenty minutes, and by the time you reach the fountain, it feels as if you have arrived in a different realm.

Rocher des Faux Amants

Rue Neuve, Tréhorenteuc, year round; free

The "rock of false lovers," also known as the Val Sans Retour ("the valley of no return"), appears in legend as the place where for 17 years the sorceress Morgan le Fay would imprison knights who had been unfaithful in love. At one point there were said to have been 253 knights trapped here, and it's something of a Monty Python-esque image to think of them all lounging bored on its various rocks or on the shores of its babbling stream.

A beautiful secluded place to wander through, this valley sinks deep into the landscape, where trapped moisture lets the trees grow strong and tall. At its entrance is a beautiful still lake, called the Miroir aux Fées. In Celtic legend, water was always seen as a boundary, and passing this it can feel as though you really are entering another more magical reality, given how its stillness so reflects the sky and the forest that surrounds it. Search, too, for the *Arbre d'Or*, a sculpture of a golden tree built in 1991, which now sits at in the valley's heart—appearing without explanation, it truly looks like a place where the landscape has been touched by magic.

In case you're wondering why there are no remnants of the 253 knights, ultimately they were said to have been liberated by Lancelot, who had the power to do so because of the strength of his commitment and love for Queen Guinevere (who, of course, was technically King Arthur's wife, but it seems Morgana let that one slide).

1: Merlin's Tomb **2:** Paimpont Abbey

Abbaye de Paimpont

3 espl. de Brocéliande, Paimpont; tel. 02 99 07 84 23 (tourist office); www.abbayedepaimpont.org; 9am-6pm; free

When it comes down to it, what really makes this 7th-century abbey special is the way it has used wood. It's almost so obvious as to be unexpected, but its location in the heart of Brittany's most famous forest has given it direct access to this highly pliable resource for its entire history. Indeed, the abbot was given the right to take freely from the trees of Paimpont from the 12th to the 18th centuries.

The exposed wooden vaults of its ceiling and the pews are the most obvious features, but beyond that, there are opulently carved picture frames, statues, and altarpieces. Give yourself up to an hour to inspect these features in detail. A major religious hub since its conception, the oldest sections of its architecture now date from the early 1200s, while its extensive treasury includes objects from the next 300 years after that. There's also the reliquary of one of its founders, Saint Judicael, to intrigue.

Nicely situated on the Étang de Paimpont, there's also a well-signposted lake walk if you want to extend your visit.

SHOPPING

ARMORIA

23 rue du Général de Gaulle, Paimpont; tel. 02 99 07 23 05; www.armoria.com; 11am-12:30pm and 2pm-6:30pm Tues. and Thurs.-Sat., 2pm-6:30pm Wed. and Sun.

Specializing in pagan, Viking, and fairy ephemera, this is a store where you can purchase some of the perceived magic of Paimpont to take home with you. Artifacts include Gothic goblets, replica skulls, amulets, and scale models of sexy cartoon fairies. Not for all tastes, to be sure, but it's well suited to many of those who come to the forest for spiritual reasons.

SPORTS AND RECREATION

Cycling

The Paimpont Forest is latticed with bike paths, and there can be little disputing that pedal power is the best way to get to grips with its delights. Part of this is down to the fact that most people don't come to Paimpont for a specific attraction, but rather to connect with its overall spirit of mysticism and history. The sights, as they are, are more akin to prompt cards, hinting at this other realm. They're best when they take a little effort to get to, when you've the time to admire the natural beauty of their surroundings, and when you have time to contemplate after leaving them, hence a bike!

The Paimpont tourism website (http://tourisme-broceliande.bzh/activite/circuits-velo-vtt-vtc) has several suggestions of routes, and lots of leaflets with maps detailing them are on offer, both in the tourist office and at bike-hire companies.

LA BOUCLE DES HINDRES

Esplanade de Brocéliande, Paimpont

This 22-mile (35-kilometer) route is a good general tour. It starts on the esplanade de Brocéliande in the village of Paimpont itself, then heads north past the Abbaye de Paimpont, and up into the forest. It then bears east up toward Merlin's Tomb—you can look for signs for this, or for Saint-Malon-sur-Mel. Have a picnic around the tomb area, where there are benches, running water, and toilets, then head directly south, following signs to Plélan-le-Grand, and from there back to Paimpont, passing the village forges as you go. The entire journey is should take 3.5 hours to complete.

BROCÉLIANDE BIKE

2 rue des Forges, Paimpont; tel. 06 45 41 59 88; http://broceliande.bike; 9am-6pm daily; two-hour rental from €14, one-day rental for €25

A decent-size, well-used bike-hire company based in Paimpont, they rent a wide variety of two-wheeled transport, including electricity-assisted bikes, kids' bikes, and bike trucks. They also have maps on-site, with plenty of different route suggestions, and are happy to give personal advice. There are also mountain bikes on offer, which can be used on the forest's many well-signposted off-road paths.

Hiking

There are a quite staggering number of hiking trails to go on around Paimpont. This can be something of a relief to those hikers used to rambling around Brittany's coasts, which for geographical reasons don't always allow for such freedom in creating your own path. The official tourist website for Paimpont (www.broceliande-vacances.com/en/things-to-do/walking-and-riding-trails-in-broceliande/by-foot) makes the most of this, with an excellent list of suggested trails that come with themed names and can be selected in terms of length and by destination. There are simply loads to choose from, and the website even includes an app, which means maps and route instructions can be easily downloaded to your phone.

AU PAYS DES FÉES

Paimpont; www.broceliande-vacances.com/en/things-to-do/walking-and-riding-trails-in-broceliande/by-foot/1-au-pays-des-fees; year round; free

Au Pays des Fées ("in the Land of the Fairies") is a fairly midlength trail that reaches up in a circle, starting in the village of Paimpont. It passes the village of Mauron, which was the site of a battle between Anglo-Breton armies and the French in 1352; then the Oak Guillotin, a hollow oak tree inside which the Abbot Guillotin hid from revolutionaries (presumably to escape the guillotine—no relation), and finally loops back past the Barenton Fountain, where Merlin is said to have schooled the Lady of the Lake in the magical arts. It's a roughly seven-mile (11-kilometer) walk and should take about three hours.

FOOD

LA TERRASSE DE L'ABBAYE

2 avenue du Chevalier Ponthus, Paimpont; tel. 02 99 07 81 12; 12pm-10pm daily; mains €4.40-15

Granted, it's nicer on warm days, but this restaurant located under a tent is well set up to take maximum advantage of its lakeside position, and there are effective heaters for when the mercury drops. The food is straightforward and cheap, and generally better than you might expect just by the look of the place. The steaks, particularly, are very generous, and an excellent value. There's also a fine offering of cocktails at the bar.

LA FÉE GOURMANDE

16 avenue du Chevalier Ponthus, Paimpont; tel. 02 99 07 89 63; 7pm-9pm Fri., 12pm-2:30pm and 7pm-9pm Sat., 12pm-6pm and 7pm-9:30pm Sun., 12pm-2:30pm and 7pm-9pm Mon. and Wed.-Fri. during school holidays; menu €20 (includes drinks)

A smashing location on the lake in a traditional stone building with a garden and terrace that can be taken advantage of on warm days, this is a decent *crêperie* that does a fine line in meat toppings and cream. The local cider they serve with everything is great. With plenty of seating, the atmosphere here on warm summer days can be really excellent. Vegetarian and health-conscious options are also on the menu if that's more your speed.

FORGES DE PAIMPONT RESTAURANT DU TERROIR

Les Forges, Plélan-le-Grand; tel. 02 99 06 81 07; 12pm-1:45pm and 7pm-8:45pm Wed.-Sat., 12pm-1:45pm Sun.; menus €23-35

This more traditional restaurant features views out over water. The dining room is decorated with hunting trophies and paintings of hunting trophies (admittedly, it just about works). There's a roaring fire, which some meats are cooked over, with the food almost the platonic ideal of concepts such as rustic and hearty. If you can resist ordering one of the fire-grilled steaks, the game dishes are truly excellent, all being locally caught, and, as this restaurant's name would have it, representing the terroir of the region. Good for a long formal meal, and at its very best in the autumn, it's worth booking to be sure of a seat.

ACCOMMODATIONS

€50-100

LE RELAIS DE BROCÉLIANDE

5 rue des Forges, Paimpont; tel. 02 99 07 84 94; relais-de-broceliande.fr; from €90 d

It's a rare thing when a midrange hotel comes with its own on-site spa, but the Relais de Brocéliande does, and this easily raises it from its competition. Besides its well-being attributes, this is a large, comfortable hotel in a traditional-style stone building on Paimpont's lake. Clean, with plenty of soft furnishings, its interiors may come across as a bit bland, but the flipside to that is that they're also highly inoffensive. The carpeted rooms are nice and cozy throughout the year and come complete with en suite bathrooms, satellite TVs, and WiFi, and there's a decent on-site restaurant dedicated to local produce served at reasonable prices.

€100-200

L'HÔTIÉ DE BROCÉLIANDE

La Chesnais Telhouët, Paimpont; tel. 07 60 50 10 06; www.hotie-de-broceliande.com; from €110 d

This guesthouse, deep in the forest just a few short miles from Merlin's tomb, is a snug retreat for travelers who are really coming to Paimpont to feel on their own. The interiors largely match the architecture of this traditional building, though they contain a few hints toward the pagan culture that charges this part of the world. There's a private garden for relaxing in, WiFi throughout, and a private bathroom in every room. The owner is both very helpful and friendly. Continental breakfast is served on-site.

Camping

CAMPING MUNICIPAL DE PAIMPONT

Rue du Chevalier Lancelot, Paimpont, tel. 02 99 07 89 16; https://camping-paimpont-broceliande.com;

open year-round; pitch for two in high season €13, cabin €520 per week

Boasting 90 pitches and six fully equipped (kitchen, bathroom, washing machine) holiday cabins, this is an excellent and popular choice for those wishing to experience the Paimpont Forest on a budget. It's a municipal campsite, so don't expect too many luxury amenities, but there is a shower block, a space for dish-washing, and a laundry. Plus, there are plenty of shops and restaurants nearby in the village of Paimpont itself, which is just a short walk south.

INFORMATION

OFFICE DE TOURISME DE BROCÉLIANDE

1 place du Roi Saint-Judicael, Paimpont; tel. 02 99 07 84 23; http://tourisme-broceliande.bzh; 9:30am-12:30pm and 2pm-6pm daily

In the village of Paimpont, this is a busy, efficiently run tourist office, excellent for picking up maps of the forest hiking and bicycle trails. It also runs an expansive, very useful website, which has advice on the local bike trails and is compatible with mobile devices. English is spoken, and there are even a few souvenirs for sale.

GETTING THERE

BY CAR

Paimpont is easy to reach by car, with most routes coming from the east going via Rennes (30 miles/48 kilometers, 50 minutes), the Breton capital, driving southwest along the N24.

Coming from Brest (150 miles/240 kilometers, 2.5 hours), it's faster to take the main road along the coast (N165) than cut directly across the country. This goes via Quimper (106 miles/170 kilometers, 1 hour 50 minutes) and Lorient (68 miles/109 kilometers, 1 hour 20 minutes), where it joins up with the N24 toward Rennes.

From Vannes (45 miles/72 kilometers, 1 hour), the journey is north along the N166. From Nantes (70 miles/112 kilometers, 2 hours), head north along the N137.

The closest point of interest otherwise is Josselin (23 miles/37 kilometers, 30 minutes), which is just down the N24. If need be, you can do this by taxi, though be warned, it will end up costing €40-60.

BY BUS

Almost universally, the fastest and easiest way of reaching Paimpont by public transport is by heading to Rennes first. Even from Vannes or Josselin, which are the next closest major town and tourist hot spot, respectively, this is the best route. The Breton capital is well connected to just about every major town in the wider region. From there, catch Bus 1a run by **Illenoo** (www.illenoo-services.fr). It leaves from outside Rennes train station around eight times a day, with the earliest departure just before 8am and the last just after 7pm. It travels the 30-odd miles (48 kilometers) direct to Paimpont village, taking about an hour on average. The cost is €4.

GETTING AROUND

Paimpont is a great place to explore either on foot or two wheels. Both cycle paths and walking trails are well signposted, and there are plenty of maps and suggested routes on offer from the tourist office and bike-rental firms operating in the forest. The easiest place to start any exploration from is Paimpont village, which is where **Brocéliande Bike** (2 rue des Forges, tel. 06 45 41 59 88; http://broceliande.bike) is based.

Otherwise, you might consider using a taxi. **Taxis BCG** (tel. 06 18 20 27 60; www.taxi-bcg.fr), based out of nearby Guer, is among the most professional local companies. Expect a trip of five miles (eight kilometers) to cost around €10.

Rennes

Brittany's administrative capital is an often-overlooked authentic gem. It's a university town that because of its brilliant transport connections feels like the region's center. Rennes bursts with life, and treats its remaining medieval architecture with a shabby nonchalance that brings the past into the present in a way that some better-preserved, more tourist-centric towns do not: why not put a cheap fast-food joint in a half-timber building from the 17th century?

If you can tear yourself away from the student bars of the old town, Rennes also boasts one of the most elegant buildings in Brittany in the shape of the Palais du Parlement de Bretagne, the baroque parliament building constructed in the 1600s to mark the region's official reunification with the rest of France. Then there are the Thabor Gardens, a rolling public green space laid out in the English style with twisting paths and secluded corners that really does feel like a wilderness in the center of town.

Rennes also has some splendid state museums, which host much art and cultural artifacts from the rest of Brittany, making the town an excellent primer for the rest of the region. This is convenient, as it's a real gateway town—if you're headed anywhere on the west coast, either by car or train, chances are you'll pass through Rennes. So why not get out to have a look around? To cap it all off, its central market is one of the largest in France, pulsing with all the color, scents, and mineral joy of the Breton table, from butter to artichokes, oysters to salt.

ORIENTATION

Following the catastrophic fire that gutted it in the early 18th century, Rennes was built up again on a grid system, which makes it a very easy city to navigate still to this day. The Vilaine River has been guided into a canal here, the banks of which, running on an east-west axis in the city and passing under the place de la République, comprise effectively the dead center of the city.

Roughly half a mile south and slightly to the west of République is the city train station, which is also where intercity buses arrive in Rennes. Slightly to the northwest is the **old town,** where you'll find the proliferation of half-timber houses centered around the Cathédrale Saint-Pierre de Rennes, as well as the best drinking in the city—for the famous rue Saint-Michel, or, as it's more colloquially known, the rue de la Soif (the road with the most bars per foot anywhere in France), just keep heading north through the old town. The famous **Marché des Lices** takes place every Saturday on the place des Lices, which is right next door to here, just to the west. The **Park du Thabor** is about a third of a mile directly east of here.

The whole town is circled by the N136 ring road, which is excellent for heading off to other parts of Brittany or France, but not really necessary when it comes to getting around town, especially for tourists, most of whom will confine themselves to the center.

SIGHTS

★ Rennes Old Town

Rennes; tel. 08 91 67 35 35; www.tourisme-rennes.com/en; year round; free

It may come as a surprise to discover that there are more half-timber houses in Rennes than any other town in Brittany. Housing contemporary businesses and ordinary people, the medieval buildings blend so seamlessly into the present-day texture of the town that they can be easily overlooked. But behind the modern signage and surrounding the double-glazed windows is a historical marvel hiding in plain sight.

Rennes suffered massively from fire in 1720, but enough buildings still survive from before that date to make for a very distracting

Rennes

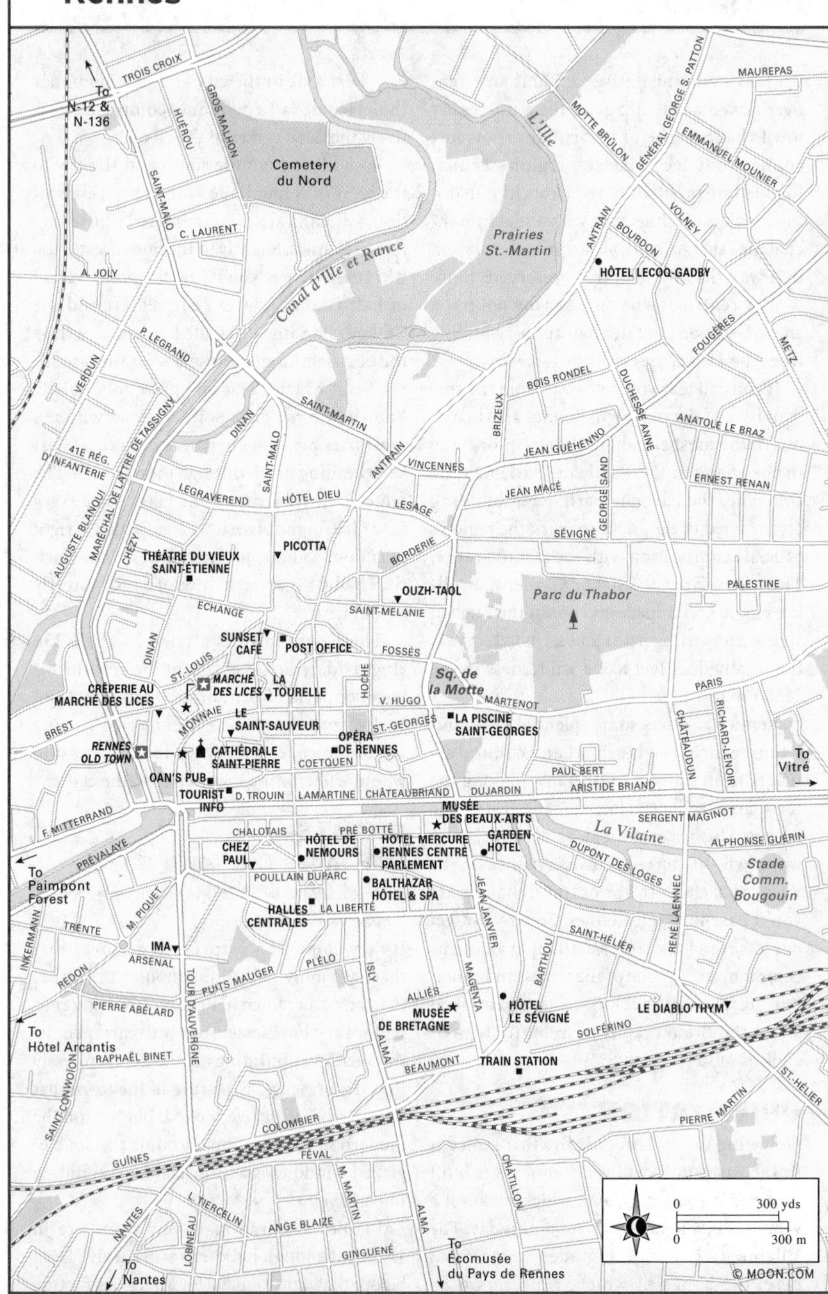
Cemetery du Nord
Prairies St.-Martin
Canal d'Ille et Rance
L'Ille
HÔTEL LECOQ-GADBY
Parc du Thabor
Sq. de la Motte
PICOTTA
THÉATRE DU VIEUX SAINT-ÉTIENNE
OUZH-TAOL
SUNSET CAFÉ
POST OFFICE
CRÊPERIE AU MARCHÉ DES LICES
MARCHÉ DES LICES
LA TOURELLE
LE SAINT-SAUVEUR
LA PISCINE SAINT-GEORGES
RENNES OLD TOWN
CATHÉDRALE SAINT-PIERRE
OPÉRA DE RENNES
OAN'S PUB
TOURIST INFO
MUSÉE DES BEAUX-ARTS
CHEZ PAUL
HÔTEL DE NEMOURS
HOTEL MERCURE RENNES CENTRE PARLEMENT
GARDEN HOTEL
BALTHAZAR HÔTEL & SPA
HALLES CENTRALES
IMA
MUSÉE DE BRETAGNE
HÔTEL LE SÉVIGNÉ
LE DIABLO'THYM
TRAIN STATION
La Vilaine
Stade Comm. Bougouin
To N-12 & N-136
To Vitré
To Paimpont Forest
To Hôtel Arcantis
To Nantes
To Écomusée du Pays de Rennes
TROIS CROIX
GROS MALHON
HUÉROU
SAINT-MALO
C. LAURENT
A. JOLY
P. LEGRAND
VERDUN
MOTTE BRÛLON
GÉNÉRAL GEORGE S. PATTON
MAUREPAS
EMMANUEL MOUNIER
VOLNEY
BOURDON
ANTRAIN
FOUGÈRES
METZ
BOIS RONDEL
BRIZEUX
DUCHESSE ANNE
ANATOLE LE BRAZ
SAINT-MARTIN
DINAN
MARÉCHAL DE LATTRE DE TASSIGNY
41E RÉG. D'INFANTERIE
AUGUSTE BLANQUI
VINCENNES
JEAN GUÉHENNO
JEAN MACÉ
GEORGE SAND
ERNEST RENAN
LEGRAVEREND
HÔTEL DIEU
LESAGE
SÉVIGNÉ
CHEZY
BORDERIE
PALESTINE
ECHANGE
SAINT-MELANIE
FOSSÉS
HOCHE
ST.-LOUIS
V. HUGO
MARTENOT
PARIS
BREST
MONNAIE
ST.-GEORGES
CHÂTEAUDUN
RICHARD-LENOIR
COETQUEN
PAUL BERT
D. TROUIN
LAMARTINE
CHÂTEAUBRIAND
DUJARDIN
ARISTIDE BRIAND
F. MITTERRAND
SERGENT MAGINOT
ALPHONSE GUÉRIN
CHALOTAIS
PRÉ BOTTÉ
PRÉVALAYE
DUPONT DES LOGES
POULLAIN DUPARC
LA LIBERTÉ
JEAN JANVIER
RENÉ LAENNEC
INKERMANN
TRENTE
M. PIQUET
ARSENAL
SAINT-HÉLIER
REDON
PUITS MAUGER
PLÉLO
ISLY
MAGENTA
BARTHOU
PIERRE ABÉLARD
TOUR D'AUVERGNE
ALLIÉS
ALMA
SOLFÉRINO
RAPHAËL BINET
BEAUMONT
SAINT-CONWOION
ST.-HÉLIER
PIERRE MARTIN
COLOMBIER
GUÎNES
FÉVAL
M. MARTIN
CHÂTILLON
L. TIERCELIN
ANGE BLAIZE
NANTES
LOBINEAU
GINGUENÉ
0 300 yds
0 300 m
© MOON.COM

wander, characterized by colorfully painted timber and beautiful, intricate carving—color was once expensive and thus a marker of social rank, while the carvings tend to be more prevalent on the older houses. The absolute highlight remains the **Maison Ti Koz** on the rue Saint-Guillaume: This is the oldest house in town, dating from the early 1500s. With red detailing, the house was originally constructed for the canons of Rennes Cathedral, though has played home to many different concerns in its long life, from a Michelin-starred restaurant to a *crêperie*. Unlikely as it sounds, the building is now a nightclub called **El Teatro** (06 31 35 42 55; www.elteatro.fr), and is only open to the public after midnight Thursday-Saturday, when it fills with revelers. The interior still boasts wood beams and stone walls, but is probably not sufficiently interesting in itself for most history buffs to tolerate the thumping bass, strobe lighting, and smell of spilled beer that today accompany an inspection. The exterior is well worth a look, though, iconic of Rennes, and with carvings of Saint Michael and Saint Sebastian looming above its door, originally meant as charms to keep away the plague.

Also worth your time is the **Hôtel de l'Escu de Runfao** on the rue de Chapitre. Its red and yellow coloring remains consistent with how it was designed in the 17th century, and it is a latticed feast for the eyes. Farther east, on the **place des Lices,** check out the Hôtel de la Noue and the Racapé de la Feuillee: twin half-timbered buildings from the late 1600s.

Cathédrale Saint-Pierre

Carrefour de la Cathédrale, Rennes; tel. 02 99 78 48 80; http://cathedralerennes.catholique.fr; 9:30am-12pm and 3pm-6pm daily; free

There's something a little different about the Cathédrale Saint-Pierre that you may not notice at once. For though its shape is the same as many of the Gothic churches around France, it's actually built in the entirely different neoclassical architectural style. There's been a church on this site since the 6th century, and in fact, a Gothic one *was* built in the 1100s. That almost entirely collapsed in 1490, however, leading to a slow and steady rebuilding program, which eventually resulted in the current construction.

Over the years, what had been conceived in fairly plain, austere terms was added to extensively with gilt, stucco, and paintings now dominating the interior, meaning that stepping inside now is to experience a riot of different imagery. The ceiling is particularly striking, being a beautiful long arch of golden details and sumptuous painted patterns. Adding to the experience, gentle organ music will often be playing in the background to accompany your visit.

★ Marché des Lices

3 place du Bas des Lices, Rennes; www.tourisme-rennes.com/en/discover-rennes/lices-market-rennes-Saturday; 8am-1:30pm Sat.

The third-largest market in France has a long pedigree, too. The first evidence of there being a market on this square can be traced all the way back to 1483. Of course, back then the place des Lices was mainly being used as a jousting field, and occasionally a spot for public executions. By the 1700s, though, it was largely only chickens having their necks wrung, when a more official poultry market was established on this site. Gutted by the 1720 fire, this was rebuilt as a hall to deal with all the incoming goods to the city.

The market reached something close to its current iteration around the mid-19th century, with the building of the current market pavilions in a classically elegant Victorian style. It remains incredibly vital today, attracting farmers from miles around and bursting with all the life of the city. It can almost seem hard to believe, but the Marché des Lices has absolutely nothing to do with attracting tourists. It's genuinely used week in, week out, by the people of Rennes, sourcing the freshest, most seasonable of produce. The whole Breton table is on offer here, and produce from some other French departments besides. Worth spending a morning in, even if you don't plan to buy anything, but even better if you're in self-catered accommodations, or planning a picnic. A couple of tips: If you're driving into town, make sure you come early, otherwise finding a parking space can be a nightmare; and bring your own bag, or, if you really want to blend in with the locals, a shopping trolley.

Musée des Beaux-Arts

20 quai Emile Zola, Rennes; tel. 02 23 62 17 45; https://mba.rennes.fr; 10am-5pm Tues.-Fri., 10am-6pm Sat.-Sun.; adults €6, reduced €4, under 18 free

This large and very reasonably priced museum houses an eclectic collection of paintings and sculpture from medieval to modern times, plus some interesting Egyptian, Greek, and Roman antiquities. As with many museums in France, it was founded during the Revolution, with the origins of its collection being the result of looting from Breton churches. Added to over the years, the museum now includes work from a number of important French painters as well as some big-name international artists, including Rubens, Gauguin, and Picasso; there are also sketches by Da Vinci, Michelangelo, and Dürer. The galleries themselves are fairly traditional, with parquet floors and gilded frames that will be familiar to anyone who has been to Paris's Louvre. Skim past the ground-floor "cabinet of curiosities" exhibition to get into the real meat of the place. Expect an average visit to take about two hours.

Musée de Bretagne

10 cours des Alliés, Rennes; tel. 02 23 40 66 00; www.musee-bretagne.fr; 12pm-7pm Tues.-Fri., 2pm-7pm Sat.-Sun. Sept.-June, 1pm-7pm Tues.-Fri., 2pm-7pm Sat.-Sun. July-Aug., 10am-7pm Tues.-Fri. during school holidays; adults €6, reduced €4, under 18 free

For many people traveling to Brittany, passing through Rennes is inevitable, either by road or train. And if you do decide to do a stopover in the city, this museum dedicated to Breton culture is an excellent primer on the region you're entering. It has artifacts big and small dating from pre-Roman times until almost the present day, from coins to furniture, spread over several floors in a modern, light-filled building. There's ample signage in English, which is a welcome change from a lot of museums, and means you can leave really feeling you've learned something. At the same time, it's quite a serious museum, suited to those with a real enthusiasm for history, and not a place that is going to keep kids occupied for that long. Expect visits to last about two hours.

Parc du Thabor

Place Saint-Mélaine, Rennes; tel. 02 23 62 19 40; 7:30am-8:30pm daily spring, summer, and fall, 7:30am-6:30pm winter; free

Redesigned by Denis Bühler in the 19th century, these gardens used to belong to the monks of Saint-Melaine Benedictine Abbey. Characterized by secluded sections and some steep inclines across 25 acres (10 hectares), there are plenty of different aspects to get lost in, including both an English-style landscaped garden and one designed along formal French lines. There's also a diverse rose garden, an aviary, and even a man-made cave. A popular hangout with the city's large student population, it's a great place for a long languorous picnic or just a wander—and you should usually be able to find some privacy.

Écomusée du Pays de Rennes

Route de Châtillon-sur-Seiche, Rennes; tel. 02 99 51 38 15; www.ecomusee-rennes-metropole.fr; 9am-6pm Tues.-Fri., 2pm-6pm Sat., 2pm-7pm Sun.; adults €6, reduced €4, under 18 free

One of Rennes's best qualities is that you never feel too far away here from the countryside. The Bintinais Farm on Rennes's southern limits is the largest producer in the town's immediate area, and has been open for visitors since 1987, when it established this on-site museum dedicated to explaining the history and processes involved in farming. Signage

1: the sun-dappled Parc du Thabor **2:** bars in Rennes Old Town **3:** classic scenes on the Place Sainte Anne in Rennes Old Town

1

2

3

A Day Trip to Vitré

Up there with Vannes and Dinan among Brittany's best-preserved towns, Vitré is barely 20 miles (32 kilometers) east of Rennes and has always sat right on the border between the region and the rest of France. It makes for an excellent day trip from the Breton capital. Just wandering around the streets here is enough to enchant, festooned as they are with Brittany's iconic half-timber houses, most dating back to the 15th and 16th centuries.

HALF-TIMBER HOUSES

The best examples of these can be seen on the **rue de la Baudière,** where they rise several stories from street level, inducing a mild inverse vertigo and causing one to wonder how they have remained standing for so many centuries. There are also some fascinating houses on the **rue de la Poterie,** many of which reach out over the sidewalks, forming arcade-like structures, which also give a good opportunity to spot medieval wood-carvings up close. Most, alas are private residences, so cannot be visited, though the ones that are being used as shops or bars offer a chance to see the wood beams of their interiors, albeit not always surrounded by period details.

THE RAMPARTS

Then there are the ramparts, a key feature of any well-preserved border town—if only because it's unlikely such towns would have remained so well-preserved without these city walls. Looming high, most of them can, unfortunately, no longer be climbed, but even the **Promenade du Val** that skirts just beneath their northern edge is high enough to provide excellent views of the surrounding countryside. Following this from east to west, then slipping into Vitré's center through the small side gate that leads onto the **Rue du Bas Val,** is a wonderful way of being transported back into the past.

CHATEAU DE VITRÉ

tel. 02 99 75 04 46; http://bretagne-vitre.com/les-musees; 8:30am-12:30pm and 2pm-5:30pm Mon.-Fri., 8:30am-12:30pm Sat.-Sun.; €6

What really attracts people to Vitré, though, is the town's magnificent 13th-century castle. Every inch the fairy-tale fortress, it's stunning from the outside, with pointing slate turrets that look primed for Rapunzel, or for a dragon to perch upon. Of course, reality saw neither of those things, but the Château de Vitré did play home to the Breton parliament a couple of times in the 16th century, when they had to escape the very real-world danger of plague, which had descended on Rennes. Exploring the inside is a fun distraction for an hour, even if the furniture is a little sparse and English guidance nonexistent. To get the most out of your visit, it's worth doing a bit of homework beforehand, just so you can put what you see in some historical context. The alternative is to forget the history entirely, and just make believe you've walked onto the backlot for *Game of Thrones*—surprisingly easy, given the surroundings.

INFORMATION

For other ideas how to spend your time here, drop into the **Office de Tourisme** (place du Général de Gaulle; tel. 02 99 75 04 46; https://bretagne-vitre.com; 2:30pm-6pm Mon., 9:30am-12:30pm and 2:30pm-6pm Tues.-Fri., 10am-12:30pm and 3pm-5pm Sat.).

and tours are almost entirely in French, but the exhibits are mostly self-explanatory. More than anything, it's great to wander around the farmland and interact with the animals under the watchful eyes of farmers. Though quite a way from the center of town, you can reach the museum fairly easily taking the Rennes metro to Le Triangle station, then walking the rest of the way. A word of warning: Come prepared with your own food and (particularly) drink, for despite the excess of produce being reared and grown around you, there's no on-site restaurant or café, at least for the time being. Also note that in the low season (October through March), the museum closes for lunch on weekdays 12pm-2pm.

THE ARTS

OPÉRA DE RENNES

Place de la Mairie, Rennes; tel. 02 23 62 28 28; www.opera-rennes.com; season Sept.-June; tickets €5-52

Rennes Opera directly faces the town hall and is characterized by a beautiful neoclassical frontage designed in the 1830s by Charles Millardet and Pierre Louise. With only 642 seats, it's one of the smallest opera houses anywhere in France, which is probably why in 2009 the city decided to open up its doors and move the show outside every other summer, performing opera directly on the place de la Mairie, attracting up to 8,000 spectators at a single time—the next will be in 2019. Outside of that, it runs a strong seasonal schedule, attracting companies from all over the world to perform both classic operas and concerts. Of course, trips to the opera can be expensive, but any unsold tickets are released an hour before every show for €5-10. With such a (relatively) small number of seats, though, there may not be many tickets left, and those that are go fast. If you want to risk this, it's best to call beforehand to check the relative popularity of the show you want to see.

THÉÂTRE DU VIEUX SAINT-ÉTIENNE

14 rue d'Échange, Rennes; tel. 02 99 78 29 19; www.ay-roop.com/theatre-du-vieux-st-etienne; productions year-round; tickets free to up to €16.50

What was once a 12th-century church has now been reclaimed as a performing-arts space and theater, attracting companies and musicians from both inside and outside Rennes to put on an eclectic schedule of performances throughout the year. Yes, the shows will almost universally be in French, but many are based on physical performance or music, which needs no translation. The actual performance space with its medieval vaulting is almost worth the price of admission in itself.

FESTIVALS AND EVENTS

TOMBÉES DE LA NUIT

Many locations, Rennes; tel. 02 99 32 56 56; www.lestombeesdelanuit.com/fr; Every Sun. throughout the year, plus the first week of July; events free to up to €20

Established in 1980, this is a festival dedicated to street art. For one week of the year, Rennes's squares, roads, and parks overflow with sculpture and performances by artists from around France and the world. The style is mostly contemporary—expect a lot of light shows. The real highlights, though, are the shows and installations inside public buildings. Some of these need to be paid for and others are free; consult the website for details and look out for fliers around festival time (available in the tourist office and many hotels) so you can better plan the night.

YAOUANK

8 rue Hoche, Rennes; tel. 02 99 30 06 87; https://yaouank.bzh; first weeks of Nov.; tickets from €15

Traditional Breton celebrations reach their apex with this, the largest *fest-noz* (night festival) in the world. While it's more usual for a *fest-noz* to involve a few families eating crepes and dancing to bagpipe music in a village hall, this is a full-fledged modern party with music that combines Breton folk tunes with modern beats. It centers around a massive concert in Rennes's exhibition park, which runs practically nonstop all the way through the night. Besides this main event, there's also a small cinema festival that springs up, playing both Breton movies and blockbusters from the United States. Intended to make Breton tradition relevant to the modern region, the festival absolutely achieves this goal. It's a great chance to immerse yourself in the local culture, being not at all exclusive. So what if you're not Breton? After six hours dancing to electrified bagpipes and drowning in local cider, you'll feel that you are!

TOP EXPERIENCE

Festoù-noz

The smell of strong cider, the wail of bagpipes, the percussion of feet shuffling in time across the shiny surface of a municipal hall, the taste of the best crepe you've ever eaten, the booming twang of Breton being spoken in family groups, kids dodging in and out between the legs of grown-ups, the black-and-white blur of people dancing in traditional Breton dress: This is a *fest-noz.*

Translated literally as "night festival," these parties take place in villages and towns across Brittany throughout the year and represent the essential heartbeat of the still-living local culture, so distinct from anywhere else in the world. They are emphatically not meant for tourists, but Breton hospitality being what it is, that doesn't mean tourists aren't welcome—so long as you're respectful, and don't try to join in with the dancing.

DANCES

Dancing is at the center of the festivities, and there are hundreds of different local dances across the region, many of which may be familiar to people who are familiar with traditional Scottish and Irish dancing—even so, out of respect, it's best not to dance unless you're invited. What remains constant is that the dances are performed in sets of three (suites), in between which there are breaks for socializing and snacking on local food.

FINDING A LOCAL FESTIVAL

Festoù-noz (as they are described in plural) come in all shapes and sizes, with the very biggest being Yaouank in Rennes, where bagpipes and folk-singing get overlaid by drum and bass, and the strong cider is swilled until the early hours of the dawn. It's still authentic and still intended primarily for Bretons, but if you want the real *fest-noz* experience, you have to get out into the countryside, steel your nerves, and walk into the kind of parties where attendees still think of the people in neighboring villages as being foreign.

A comprehensive list of *festoù-noz* can be found on the website www.tamm-kreiz.bzh, but it's also worth just keeping your eyes peeled for signs advertising them on public notice boards as you pass through rural Brittany—there are literally hundreds to choose from, with almost every commune boasting its own. Apart from Yaouank, which really is something different, trying to attend the "best" or the most famous, however, would totally miss the point. Most *festoù-noz* are local rites that would not survive if suddenly inundated by tourists. If you're just a small group of curious strangers, though, you're sure to be heartily invited in, and likely to have one of the best experiences that Brittany can offer.

BARS

Rennes is a drinker's paradise, positively bursting with excellent convivial bars, which are thoroughly well attended. The main concentration of these is on the rue Saint-Michel, more commonly known as rue de la Soif, or "Drinker's Alley." Not a very long street, it nevertheless plays home to 13 bars; this comes in at one every seven meters, and makes it the single booziest street in all of France. Unsurprisingly, it gets pretty rowdy in the evening, when it's best avoided if you've kids in tow.

SUNSET CAFÉ

22 rue Saint-Michel, Rennes; tel. 02 99 79 09 63; 12pm-1am Mon.-Sat.; pints of beer from €3.50

There's a degree to which the bars on the rue de la Soif all seem to merge into one another, particularly after you've had a few! Sunset Café is among the most popular, though, thanks largely to cheap drinks and a great atmosphere, which is served, cyclically, by its popularity. Primarily a student bar, it attracts a young crowd and is a great place to engage with Rennes's university culture. Be warned that you might find yourself standing, especially on student nights. Don't expect anything flashy—drinks are mainly beers and spirits.

OAN'S PUB

4 rue Georges Dottin, Rennes; tel. 02 99 31 07 51; 5pm-1am Sun.-Fri., 12pm-1am Sat.; pints of beer from €4

Objectively, Oan's Pub just looks like a dingy room, but filled with people its walls seem to bottle atmosphere. It's the kind of place where people laugh, set the world to rights, get wildly drunk, and then drink some more. There's nothing flashy about the drinks on offer, either—just your basic wine, beer, and shots—but somehow it all works, especially on nights when there's a local rock band playing. It's also not on the rue de la Soif, which means things are often not quite as crazy, and you can actually hear yourself think, if you sit on the terrace outside.

SHOPPING

HALLES CENTRALES

23 rue Jules Simon, Rennes; www.lacriee-marchecentral.com; 9am-7:30pm Mon.-Sat., 9am-1pm Sun.

Open every day, this covered food market is a great place to pick up high-quality local produce. Built between 1913 and 1926, its stylings are art deco, and under its roof it houses 28 small concerns, including top-end butchers, fishmongers, and cheesemongers—the prices of whom are all reassuringly expensive. You can also pick up top-quality wine, and some stalls are essentially small restaurants, cooking up great food in front of you for takeaway. It's a good place to go if you're not going to be in town for the Saturday market, but still want to sample the sharp end of Rennes cuisine.

SPORTS AND RECREATION

Swimming

LA PISCINE SAINT-GEORGES

2 rue Gambetta, Rennes; tel. 02 23 62 15 40; 12pm-2pm and 7pm-10pm Tues. and Thurs., 5pm-8pm Wed., 12pm-2pm Fri., 2pm-7pm Sat., 9am-2pm Sun.; adults €5, children €2.10

So much more than just a public swimming pool, this is one of Rennes's most iconic structures. Inaugurated in 1926 with an eye to improving the hygiene of the city's people, it was designed in a beautiful art deco style and spangled by mosaics, which are maintained to this day. And while it's still very much used for swimming, the pool has now developed a second life as an arts venue, with a regular turnover of different events: one time being transformed into a nightclub, another time being dominated by pieces of conceptual art, including a giant sculpture of the moon, which hung over the water and conjured a genuinely magical atmosphere, especially at night. With no specific website, to discover what unusual events are going on at the Saint-Georges, search for it on Twitter using the hashtag #piscinerennes.

FOOD

Local Cuisine

LE DIABLO'THYM

116 allée Saint-Hélier, Rennes; tel. 02 23 42 19 75; 12:30pm-1:45pm Mon.-Thurs., 12:30pm-1:45pm and 7:30pm-10pm Fri., 7:30pm-10pm Sat.; menus from €28

A little out of the center, this is nevertheless an excellent local hangout that does straight-up unfussy French food made with local ingredients. It's pretty small and run by just a small staff, who are friendly and efficient. They're not making any grand gestures with their interior, which is inoffensive, if a little unmemorable, but for good value, tasty meals, and a welcoming atmosphere, it's hard to beat. Adventurous diners should try the steak tartare (yes, the raw meat one), which comes served with sophisticated baked potatoes rather than the usual fries.

CHEZ PAUL

30 rue Poullain Duparc, Rennes; tel. 02 99 78 22 49; 12pm-2pm and 7pm-11pm Tues.-Sat.; mains €16-19

Understanding that good food doesn't have to involve reinventing the wheel, Chez Paul is how a lot of people might imagine French bistros to be, with wooden fittings, a tiled floor, and a homogenous style throughout. This, actually, makes it something of a rare gem: a traditional bistro that doesn't overdo the kitsch modern touches. The dishes are mostly unpretentious combinations of meat, legumes, and potatoes, often prepared in some sort of delicious fat. The house wine is eminently quaffable and the atmosphere usually bustling—so much so that you should make sure to arrive early for lunch to be sure of a table, and book for dinner.

IMA

20 boulevard de la Tour d'Auvergne, Rennes; tel. 02 23 47 82 74; http://ima.restaurant; 12pm-1:45pm and 7:30pm-9pm Wed.-Sat.; lunch menus from €30, evening menus €70-90

An open kitchen, Asian-influenced flavors, and an achingly cool interior characterized by dark colors, industrial-chic details, and stone—and it's got a Michelin star! This relatively young restaurant is quite unlike anything else in Rennes, and popular for it. The dishes look like minor works of abstract expressionism, and while it's true you might sometimes struggle to figure out exactly what you're eating, they're reliably delicious, full of surprise and zing. Best is to sit at the bar, where you can see the artist-chefs in action putting the food together. And if you're watching your wallet, it's well worth dropping in for a lunchtime meal, which at only €30 is one of the best deals in town. Book ahead to be sure of a place.

LA TOURELLE

7 allée Rallier du Baty, Rennes; tel. 02 99 78 23 53; http://latourellerennaise.fr; 7:30pm-12:30am Tues.-Sat.; menus €22-37

The deep red walls of this restaurant combine with its dark wood fittings and details to make for a very plush experience. It almost seems wrong not to order rich food here, and the menu is obliging—if you're feeling up to it, the side of beef to be shared between two people is terrific. Peaceful and intimate, it's a good date-night restaurant (though if that's why you're coming here, it's probably better to go for one of the lighter mains).

LE SAINT-SAUVEUR

6 rue Saint-Sauveur, Rennes; tel. 02 99 79 32 56; http://restaurant-lesaintsauveur.fr; 12pm-2:15pm and 7:30pm-9:30pm Tues.-Sat., 12pm-2:15pm Mon.; menu €27

Inside one of the city's half-timber buildings, the visible history in the shape of a latticework of wood beams is key to this restaurant's character. It's not at all pokey, however, with shiny wooden floorboards and fresh white tablecloths on all the tables. The food is lovingly prepared traditional French, and while the menu may not be massively extensive, it leans heavily and very well on local produce. There are a few tables on the street, but in general this is far more a place for cooler or rainy evenings than for when the sun is shining.

Budget Options

CRÊPERIE AU MARCHÉ DES LICES

3 place du Bas des Lices, Rennes; tel. 02 99 30 42 95; 12pm-2pm and 7pm-10pm Mon.-Sat.; crepes €7-10

A great *crêperie,* this looks a little like a farmhouse kitchen with its well-trodden wooden floorboards, and bustles thrillingly on the weekends—particularly market days. The crepes themselves are hard to fault, an excellent midday meal made with the freshest ingredients. There's also a small courtyard area for warmer days, although the decor outside unfortunately comes across as a little kitschy, and lacks the warm style of inside. Still, the food is just as good, and there's a wood fire that they light on winter days.

OUZH-TAOL

27 rue Saint-Melaine, Rennes; tel. 02 99 63 36 33; 12pm-2pm and 7pm-10:30pm Tues.-Sat.; crepes €8-10

Straightforward, inexpensive, and offering service with a smile, this has got to be one of the best crepe places in town. The staff are particularly knowledgeable about what they're serving and are sure to give you good advice—though if you're a seafood fan, the combined scallop and salmon crepe is a great place to start. It's got a colorful interior, well-suited for families. And it's popular: You might just about manage to squeeze in by turning up at lunchtime, but if you want an evening meal, be sure to book.

PICOTTA

20 rue Saint-Malo, Rennes; tel. 02 99 78 22 91; 12pm-2:30pm and 9pm-11pm Tues.-Sat.; menu €22, pizzas from €10

Here the flavors are international and the meals not always served in a traditional way. Picotta is a tapas restaurant, which does excellent pizza alongside its sharing platters. Recommended for its informality, this is great for a casual evening with friends: It could almost be mistaken for a great drinking establishment that also just happens to have fantastic food. Unlike many places in Rennes or Brittany in general, there are also plenty of decent vegetarian options, giving many a relief from having to ask for dishes off the menu. That said, they also grill steaks over a fire on the restaurant floor—it's considerate to the taste of vegetarians, but not necessarily their other senses.

ACCOMMODATIONS

Under €50

HÔTEL ARCANTIS

10 rue de Guébriant, Rennes; tel. 02 99 67 33 33; www.hotel-arcantis-rennes.fr; from €42 d

It's a little outside of Rennes's center, but this is an excellent value hotel, which is at the same time a little quirky, feeling like the kind of place you might run across in the American Midwest rather than the capital of Brittany. Kitschy 1950s ads plaster the walls of communal areas, and there's even a retro *Playboy* pinball machine. The rooms themselves are a little more conservative, verging on basic, while the staff are pure Breton. There's an on-site bar and breakfast buffet, TVs in all the rooms, en suite bathrooms, and WiFi throughout.

GARDEN HÔTEL

3 rue Jean Marie Duhamel, Rennes; tel. 02 99 65 45 06; www.hotel-garden.fr; from €44 d

Centrally located and self-catered (there's also an optional breakfast buffet), this hotel can feel like your own small apartment in Rennes, and is accordingly a great place to base an extended stay in the city. With pleasant treated wooden floorboards in some rooms and tastefully inoffensive interiors, it feels classier than many places twice its price. There's also on-site parking and a small outside public area.

€50-100

HÔTEL DE NEMOURS

5 rue de Nemours, Rennes; tel. 02 99 78 26 26; www.hotelnemours.com; from €60 d

Characterized by sleek monochrome colors, this is a remarkable value hotel right in the center of Rennes that gives the impression of executive class. The book-lined public areas come complete with stylish modern furniture and a shiny parquet floor, while the rooms boast elegant patterned wallpaper and fun wall art of quirky images in traditional frames. There's a good continental breakfast served in the mornings in a well-lit room with a view of the street, WiFi throughout, and en suite bathrooms in every room, complete with fancy Nuxe toiletries.

HÔTEL LE SÉVIGNÉ

47 bis avenue Jean Janvier, Rennes; tel. 02 99 67 27 55; https://hotellesevigne.fr; from €65 d

A well-insulated, well-maintained modern hotel near the train station. Granted, it's hardly overflowing with character, but there's an executive-style reliability here, the rooms having just enough nods to contemporary design. It's also all very clean and perfectly comfortable. Rooms have WiFi, TVs, and en suite bathrooms, and there's a continental breakfast served on-site.

HÔTEL MERCURE RENNES CENTRE PARLEMENT

1 rue Paul Louis Courier, Rennes; tel. 02 99 78 82 20; www.accorhotels.com/gb/hotel-1056-mercure-

rennes-centre-parlement-hotel/index.shtml; from €80 d

If you're a seasoned traveler, you'll have made your mind up as to whether chain hotels are for you or not. This branch of the Mercure group is fairly representative of their type, except that it's located in the building of an old printing press, making its external character at least quite unique. Inside, the design is modern and generically quirky, with executive levels of cleanliness. Every room has a TV and an en suite bathroom, and there's WiFi throughout, as well as an on-site fitness center and plus a continental buffet in the morning.

€100-200

★ HÔTEL LECOQ-GADBY

156 rue d'Antrain, Rennes; tel. 02 99 38 05 55; http://hotel.lecoq-gadby.com; from €120 d

A spa hotel about a mile away from Rennes center, set in an old-fashioned-looking wooden building. Rooms offer eclectic modern designs, and some come with balconies or terraces. The concept is eco-friendly, so expect a lot of wood, good insulation, and an organic breakfast. Rooms come complete with modern conveniences such as TVs and WiFi. The spa section, meanwhile, includes a swimming pool, a hammam, and a sauna—all of which cost extra.

BALTHAZAR HÔTEL & SPA

19 rue Maréchal Joffre, Rennes; tel. 02 99 32 32 32; www.accorhotels.com/gb/hotel-9170-balthazar-hotel-spa-rennes-mgallery-by-sofitel/index.shtml; from €150 d

This luxury hotel in an elegant stone building features rooms full of plush modern design characterized by cool monochrome colors, art deco-inspired furniture, and industrial-chic details. There are large and comfortable public areas designed in much the same way, including a bar and a high-end restaurant, which serves sophisticated takes on local Breton cuisine. The pièce de résistance, meanwhile, is its extensive spa and wellness center, including a hammam, all of which are available at an extra cost. Expect all the modern conveniences in the rooms and a 24-hour reception.

INFORMATION AND SERVICES

DESTINATION RENNES OFFICE DE TOURISME

11 rue Saint-Yves, Rennes; tel. 08 91 67 35 35; www.tourisme-rennes.com; 1pm-6pm Mon., 10am-6pm Tues.-Sat., 10am-1pm and 2pm-5pm Sun.

Rennes's tourist office is located on a quiet street in a traditional building. It offers a selection of brochures, and there are English-speaking staff happy to help you with all aspects of your stay in the city. The website is also especially good, particularly on the subject of the town's history, which is well covered on its pages. There's also a free exhibition here about the development of the city, organized thematically on the subjects of water, wood, stone, and metal.

HOSPITAL CHU DE RENNES

2 rue Henri le Guilloux, Rennes; tel. 02 99 28 43 21; www.chu-rennes.fr; ER open 24 hours

A university hospital in the northwest of the city with a 24-hour emergency department and full selection of other medical units. Though English is not officially spoken, you should be able to find a doctor who you can communicate with.

POST OFFICE

11 place Sainte-Anne, Rennes; www.laposte.fr/particulier; 9:30am-6pm Mon.-Fri., 9:30am-12:30pm Sat.

This centrally located post office is practical for both sending and receiving mail. French post offices are centrally run and can seem a little intimidating at first, especially if you don't speak the language. However, there's a fairly clear color-coded system at play, which is straightforward enough that you should be able to figure it out without too much trouble. If you're picking up a package, make sure to bring ID.

GETTING THERE

BY AIR

Saint-Jacques Airport is a minor international center, receiving a small number of flights from Ireland via Aer Lingus, the U.K. via Flybe, Spain via Vueling and Iberia Express, Switzerland via easyJet, and Belgium via TUI fly Belgium, and from all over France from a variety of companies. Most flights will cost between €40 and €120 provided you book at least several weeks in advance, with flights from the U.K., Ireland, and inside France usually the cheapest.

There are around three flights every day from Paris's Charles de Gaulle airport with a flight time of around an hour, though with all the accompanying rigamarole of getting to the airport and extra costs of flights, it's hard to see what this route offers above the train, unless you're already at the airport just connecting to it from another flight.

Saint-Jacque is at least quite close to the center of Rennes, meaning you don't have to rely on a shuttle bus to get you into the center of town. The regular city bus No. 57 does the route in about 20 minutes and runs one every hour. Its stop is the junction between avenue Joseph Le Brix and avenue Jules Vallès, about 400 yards (365 meters) from the terminal.

Taxis waiting outside the arrivals hall should cost about €18 into the town center, or €20 at night.

BY CAR

Just as it's a hub of the rail network, Rennes sits at the nexus of a number of large motorways, making it very easy to reach by road. It's also the town that you're likely to find yourself passing through on your way to many other places in Brittany, including towns on the coast.

From Paris (220 miles/354 kilometers, 3.75 hours), drive along the A11. This involves toll roads, which should cost about €30.

From Nantes (70 miles/112 kilometers, 1.5 hours), it's a straight shot up along the N137. From Brest (150 miles/241 kilometers, 2.5 hours), drive east along the N12. From Saint-Malo (40 miles/64 kilometers, 1 hour) drive south down the D137.

Mont Saint-Michel (50 miles/80 kilometers, 1.25 hours) is also close: take the A84 south. This is also the road you pick up to get to Rennes from Caen (115 miles/185 kilometers, 2 hours) away.

BY TRAIN

It's fair to say that Rennes might be the best-connected place in all of Brittany. A gateway to the region, and located just before it begins to taper into a peninsula, there are high-speed train links from the Rennes train station, **Gare de Rennes** (19 place de la Gare, Rennes; tel. 08 92 35 35 35; www.gares-sncf.com/fr/gare/frrns/rennes; 5am-12:30am Mon.-Sat., 6am-12:30am Sun.), to just about everywhere you might want to go. Indeed, whenever you crisscross the region, there's every chance that the fastest way will be to go via Rennes.

From Paris, trains leave from Montparnasse. There are around 24 every day, and the journey takes about 1.5 hours and costs €70-80. From Nantes, there are nine trains a day, costing about €18 and taking around 1 hour 15 minutes. From Quimper, there are 11 trains a day costing €30-40, taking two hours. From Brest, there are 10 trains a day, costing €30-40, taking about two hours. From Saint-Malo, there are around 12 trains a day, costing €15, taking about an hour.

From Caen, the great majority of trains go via Paris. This is a trip that can be taken many times a day, costing €40-50, and taking about four hours. However, Caen is sufficiently close to Rennes that it's faster and more cost effective to take a bus. From Mont Saint-Michel, there are two trains a day, costing about €30, and the journey takes about an hour.

BY BUS

Thanks to the emergence of national bus companies in recent years, there are now numerous routes running to Rennes every day. These include around 20 every day from Paris, run by operators such as **Ouibus** (www.ouibus.

com) and **Flixbus** (flixbus.com). Prices fluctuate, but expect it to cost around €25 to get here from the French capital, and the journey to take 4-6 hours. Traveling in the other direction, around four buses leave Brest every day for Rennes. This journey lasts 4-5 hours, and should cost about €15.

The other place it's well worth catching the bus from is Caen. From the Norman town, there are around four buses a day, taking about three hours and costing €5-15.

GETTING AROUND

BY CAR

Being right in the middle of things and relatively flat, Rennes is able to have a complete ring road in the shape of the N136, which while representing an efficient way of arriving in the right part of the city is too far from the center to be used in getting around the town. Indeed, you're probably better off not using a car at all to get around central Rennes, as it's fairly walkable anyway and has good public transport, not to mention that its old town area includes a lot of one-way streets and several roads that have been entirely pedestrianized. There are, however, numerous parking lots in town, for which prices start at around €2 an hour. Keep aware that finding a place anywhere near the Marché des Lices on market day is close to impossible.

There are many taxi companies in Rennes, such as **Taxi Rennes** (tel. 09 88 99 41 30), **Artisans Taxis de Rennes** (tel. 02 99 36 03 03; www.artisans-taxis-rennes.fr), and **MK Taxi Rennes** (tel. 06 50 61 90 10; www.taxis-rennes.fr/service-taxi-3/fiche-taxi-mk-rennes). Prices are much the same across the board.

BY BIKE

The streets of downtown Rennes are home to, at turns, a lot of car traffic and many pedestrians, meaning it's not quite as ideal a cycling city as that other Breton urban center, Nantes. However, there are a good number of bike lanes, and a bike-hire scheme that can be accessed by any tourist with a credit card. Just look for the **Star** bike stands (tel. 09 69 36 50 07; www.levelostar.fr). There are several around the city, and using them costs from €1 per hour. Just follow the instructions on their interface, which you can find in English.

BY PUBLIC TRANSIT

Rennes's public transit system is run by a company called **Star** (www.star.fr/accueil), which comprises buses and one metro line. The metro line crosses the city north to south with 15 stops, including the main train station. There are no fewer than 149 bus routes, which extend out into the surrounding countryside. A one-hour ticket anywhere on this system costs €1.50, and a book of 10 can be bought for €14.50.

Background

The Landscape

GEOGRAPHY

Normandy

Normandy is not an area of France historically defined by its geography but rather the former territory of the Norman nation, which encompasses what are today two different administrative areas, Haute-Normandie and Basse-Normandie (Upper Normandy and Lower Normandy, respectively), made up of wwa distinct number of geological areas.

The most recognizable of these is the **Alabaster Coast,** made up of

high chalk cliffs that stretch from Le Tréport in the east to the Hève cape, just above Le Havre in the west. The famous coastal arches of Étretat are part of their length. Beyond here, the coast gets less dramatic, with long stretches of low-lying sandy beach that proved an ideal landing ground for Allied forces during the D-Day invasion. Farther west still, the coast hardens to granite and juts out into the English Channel in the form of the Cotentin Peninsula, the western side of which is characterized by the longest **tidal reach** in Europe. It is on one of these extensive sandy areas that the region's most visited site is located. The Mont-Saint-Michel is a tidal island formed after sea levels rose in prehistoric times and its hard granite structure resisted the erosion that wore away many of the surrounding rocks.

Inland, the majority of Normandy is defined by the **Paris basin,** a low-lying region of plains and low plateaus centered around the River Seine, which here meanders gradually through a landscape of forests and farmland and, of course, the city of Rouen. Widening toward the sea, the estuary of the Seine is a significant natural barrier, which marks the clearest split between the two administrative regions of Normandy. Today it can be crossed by the magnificent Pont de Normandie, which opened in 1995 and links the towns of Le Havre and Honfleur.

The westernmost third of Normandy belongs to the Armorican Massif, the same geological region as all of Brittany. It is also typified by the **bocage,** a landscape that combines both woodland and pasture, the profuse foliage of which was an initial hindrance to invading Allied forces in the Second World War.

Brittany

The largest peninsula in France, all of Brittany is located on the **Armorican Massif,** which juts out into the Atlantic, bordered to the north by the English Channel and to the south by the Bay of Biscay. In total, Brittany has 1,780 miles (2,864 kilometers) of **coastline,** which accounts for a third of the total of all of France's coast. This may come as a surprise just casually looking at a large-scale map, but zoom in and you'll see the reason: the coastline is massively jagged and unforgiving. It is made largely of granite and is characterized by cliffs, capes, and deep coastal inlets. Stretch these out and the coastline statistic begins to make sense.

Among the region's more spectacular sections of coast is the **Côte de Granit Rose,** so named, understandably, for the distinctly pink color of its rock. Also very unusual is the **Gulf of Morbihan,** an enormous natural harbor almost entirely closed to the sea.

The granite makeup of the Breton coast also has lent itself to the formation of around **800 islands,** all of varying sizes and often distinct characters. The largest of these is the Belle-Île in the region's south, while the Île d'Ouessant is the farthest west that is still inhabited—indeed, it's the farthest west inhabited place in metropolitan France.

Inland, Brittany is characterized by hills, some of which are covered in areas of heathland and moors. The highest point in the whole region is the Roc'h Ruz in the western Monts d'Arrée, which even so reaches only 1,263 feet (385 meters). Unlike Normandy, meanwhile, the bocage in Brittany is almost nonexistent, having been systematically replaced since the 1960s in order to accommodate modern farming.

Historically, Brittany was covered by **forest.** This too was slowly demolished by human hands—indeed, it was mostly gone by the Middle Ages. That said, some patches remain, most notably the Paimpont Forest, which now is seen to personify the woodland that used to cover the peninsula.

There is also a significant amount of **marshland** in Brittany, mostly accounted for by the Briére, a large area north of the Loire estuary. Included in this are the salt marshes

Previous: the Alabaster Coast of Étretat

of Guérande, where the region produces its famous salt.

CLIMATE

Throughout France the weather in both Normandy and Brittany is something of a running joke: Both are famous for getting a lot of rain! This is only partly true, and no doubt stems at least as much from the fact that they belong to a large country that also has some comparatively very hot and settled areas (i.e., the Mediterranean coast) as it does from the on-the-ground reality.

The weather in both regions can be sorted into clear seasons, with a chilly, rainy winter and a warmer, drier spring and summer. Broadly speaking, though, things here are fairly mild and get a decent amount of rainfall year-round.

In Normandy, the hottest month is **July,** with average highs of about 68°F (20°C), while **February** is the coldest with average lows of around 39°F (4°C). **Rainfall** is fairly constant throughout the year, with around 1.5 inches most months, and a little more October-December.

The stats in Brittany are quite similar, though **August** just tops July as the hottest month, with highs of 71°F (22°C), and **January** is a little colder than February, with lows of 41°F (5°C). **Rainfall** is on average a little higher—expect perhaps two inches in a month, but Brittany doesn't tend to see the same early winter spike.

Spend any time in the regions, though, and you'll hear plenty of talk about microclimates (the locals are very proud of these) and how they make whatever area you are in, actually far warmer than you might expect for somewhere so far north. Brittany in particular gets warmed by the **Gulf Stream,** though the real benefit of this is that winters never get that cold.

If there's any real summing up of both Norman and Breton weather, it's that it's changeable. You really can have four seasons in one day here, which means a sensible tourist should travel prepared for rain and shine whatever the weather reports are saying and however the day begins.

ENVIRONMENTAL ISSUES

Both Brittany's and Normandy's naturally mild climates and generally unexceptional weather mean that, as yet, neither have suffered majorly from the effects of global warming. Indeed, with a relatively low population given its size, and a departmental respect for its traditional bocage landscape, human impact on Normandy in particular has been fairly minimal, especially in a global context.

Bocage Destruction and Chemical Runoff

The main environmental issue that has faced Brittany in recent years stems precisely from the region's lack of respect for its traditional structure. Throughout the 1960s, there was a systematic destruction of the bocage—literally the uprooting of lots of natural vegetation and woodland that previously divided Brittany's fields into fairly small concerns. This was part of a plan to grow the scale of farming, as more large agricultural business moved into the region. However, it's theorized that without the bocage to stop it, there has been excessive water run-off from the larger fields into the region's rivers.

In itself, this has caused some erosion problems in Brittany's rivers. Of more concern, however, is that the water is believed to have carried excess levels of fertilizer nitrates into the river system and latterly the sea as well. This in turn is said to have toxified patches of naturally occurring algae in Breton waters. This is harmless until it washes up on a beach, dries, and decomposes, leading to pockets of toxic gas becoming trapped under its crust. These toxic gases are said to have caused the deaths of a number of curious animals in recent years who have come to investigate. The best thing for visitors to be aware of in this regard is to not interfere with any dried algae clumps they see washed up on beaches.

There's absolutely nothing to worry about regarding the effect of these chemicals on the area's wonderful seafood, however. The toxifying of the algae only takes place ashore and is more to do with the unique way the chemicals affect how its decomposition.

Plants and Animals

TREES

Being in the path of bird migration routes, having a mild year-round climate, and receiving plenty of rain, Normandy and Brittany are home to a wide variety of both evergreen and deciduous trees. The latter of these, come autumn, burst into an array of burnished oranges and reds, which some years can rival New England in the fall.

The inland forests of both regions are predominated by typical North European species such as oak, chestnut, and beech. In Normandy, these species also occur in the famous bocage, the composite landscape of woodland and fields that is found in the west of the region. Near the coast, meanwhile, marine pine is among the most common of varieties.

If there's any species that both regions are best known for, however, it would probably be the **apple tree.** These are cultivated in orchards throughout both the Normandy and Brittany hinterland. They're best caught in springtime when blossoming, adding a sea of pale pink to the otherwise earthy colors of the landscape.

Also worth a mention are the numerous exotic trees, such as palms, that are able to prosper in Normandy's and Brittany's many microclimates. These have an impressive heritage in the regions, thanks to the many homegrown sailors and explorers who habitually brought tropical plants back from their travels.

FLOWERS

Ubiquitous along both the Normandy and Brittany coastlines is the **hydrangea.** Looking like large floral bushes, boasting dome-like heads of multiple petals, these popular, decorative flowers are seldom found growing wild, but occupy countless gardens and public flower beds throughout the regions. The color of their petals alternates between white, blue, and pink depending on the acidity level of the soil.

In terms of wild flora, on the coast at least, there's nothing you're likely to see more of than the **yellow lichen,** which shades rocks and roofing tiles from the Alabaster Coast to the Gulf of Morbihan—a result of the nutrient-rich water around this part of the world. Contributing to this richness is the profusion of **seaweed** off the shores here: The highest profusion of seaweed in the entire world, no less, can be found in the waters around Finistère. Frequently washed ashore by storms or great tides, this substance has been farmed by the people of this part of Brittany for generations.

Also common in Brittany is **heathland,** populated by yellow gorse and purple heather, reminiscent of more northern climes. And then there are the road verges, which in springtime especially dance with the multicolored exuberance of wildflowers, spread by frequent winds and given sustenance by regular rain. Among the most eye-catching of these, and certainly the most romantic, is the **poppy,** which of course earned itself an evocative reputation following the bloody battles on the western front of the First World War, which took place in a similar biological environment to the one that you'll find here.

Finally, as with the trees, you're also likely to find many different exotic, imported species, both thanks to the many microclimates of the regions and the overseas exploration that their people were famous for in the past.

MAMMALS

The hedgerows and forests of both Normandy and Brittany are home to a decent variety of large mammals. King among these is the **wild boar,** which is surprisingly common in both regions. Sizable creatures, the evidence of their activity can be spotted all over, in the worn lines across fields or through the underbrush. However, seeing one is still comparatively rare, and if you do, make sure to give these sometimes-dangerous animals a wide berth. A less intimidating large wild animal that you're more likely to stumble across is the **roe deer.** These sprightly, speckled creatures still frolic freely through Normandy and Brittany's wilder spaces. As for large carnivores, don't worry... yet. There haven't been wolves in either region for a number of centuries; however, conservationist programs in the south of Europe have contributed to the canine's spread throughout France in recent years, with reports in 2017 of their reaching the outskirts of Paris. At their current rate of spread, wolves could reenter the forests of Normandy and Brittany within a decade. If they do so, though, they're unlikely to pose a threat to humans.

Also worth keeping an eye out for is the **red squirrel,** more common in both regions than its gray counterpart, which is native to North America and has taken over much of the United Kingdom. These small tree-dwelling rodents are a frequent sight in any forest.

That said, it's the farmed species for which both Brittany and Normandy are most famous. All that cheese, butter, and cream can hardly be expected to come from nowhere, and sure enough, there are plenty of cows roaming the fields here. The **Normande cow** breed is the one you'll see most often: Large and usually with a speckled or red-blotched coat, they are famous for the high fat quality of their milk, which is ideal for making butter and cheese.

Look out, too, for **horses**—more than 70 percent of all French thoroughbreds and trotters are bred in Basse-Normandie—and sheep around the coastal, less fertile areas.

SEALIFE

It's hard, in many respects, to divorce an entry about Normandy and Brittany's sea life with one about their cuisine. Surely one of the defining features about the culture in this part of the world is that when presented with a new kind of organism that lives under the sea, their first question is likely to be, can we eat it? The second, does it go well with cream?

With that in mind, it's best to start with the few creatures that live in the sea around these parts that don't end up on local plates. These are dominated by **seals** and **dolphins.** Both are increasingly common the farther toward the Atlantic you get, spiking just west of the Cotentin Peninsula. The seals are of the gray or harbor variety, and are most commonly found lounging on the rocks of islands. Dolphins often come as more of a surprise, though they are remarkably numerous, and can often be spotted on boat trips, with many different species accounted for.

The waters of the English Channel around Normandy and Brittany play home to all sorts of marine life that one might think belong only to more expansive seaways: Sharks and whales of multiple stripes find their way here all the time, though they're highly unlikely to bother you when you're swimming. As for Brittany's Atlantic coast, meanwhile, it's literally the ocean, and a whole book would not be enough to catalog all the denizens that it contains.

As far as creatures that you are likely to come across in the shallows, the **blue mussel** predominates, clinging to rocks along both regions' coastlines. This is the case for **oysters,** too, though frankly you're more likely to see them in the copious man-made beds that take advantage of natural tides in order to nurture the thorny mollusks into a delicacy eaten all around France.

There are also numerous species of **crab** and **lobster** found in these waters, many of which also make for a tasty morsel. Large numbers of crabs tend to come in close to Brittany's shores around the early summer, when it's not uncommon to see their molted shells wash up on the beach.

It's worth emphasizing that this entry is not, nor could it ever be, exhaustive. The seas around Brittany, particularly, are almost miraculously diverse, and anyone wanting to find out more about what lives within them is best advised to head to one of the regions many excellent oceanography museums (**Oceanopolis** in Brest being the most extensive), or, failing that, go to a good seafood restaurant and take a deep read of the menu.

BIRDS

Brittany and Normandy's skies are almost as teeming in different forms of life as their seas.

Again, **Brittany** is the real haven in this regard, particularly along its northern coast, where sizable populations of puffins, guillemots, and razorbills can be seen, as well as more common seabird varieties from cormorants to gulls. This is especially true around the Sept-Îles, off the Côte de Granit Rose, where boat trips are on offer with the express intention of visiting the bird colonies. The Gulf of Morbihan, meanwhile, plays home to many wading birds, such as black-winged stilts, while the salt marshes of Guérande are also an ornithologist's candy store, with small, robin-like bluethroats and spindly-legged avocets in abundance.

Not to be totally outdone, there's also some excellent bird-watching around Mont Saint-Michel and up the western coast of the Cotentin Peninsula with pintail, teal, and whistler ducks all passing through between July and October, along with starlings, thrushes, finches, and many other common bird varieties.

The inland forests are also very dense in terms of bird life, particularly in the early spring. You'll hear the hoots and tweets of abundant common varieties, from tits to crossbills to nightingales, while the distinctive call of the cuckoo is one that will be in the ears of any outdoor enthusiast almost wherever they go, all summer long.

History

ANCIENT CIVILIZATION

Evidence of ancient cave paintings and fire pits suggest that both Normandy and Brittany have been inhabited by humans since distant prehistoric times. It is the megalithic monuments in the latter that are best known in the wider world, specifically the constellation of them found around the town of Carnac in Brittany's far east. These are reckoned to date from between 5000 BC and 2000 BC, though as to their use, archaeologists are still unsure.

The Celts are the first clear civilization that we know of in Normandy, with a large decent number of archeological finds, such as iron helmets, urns, and cremated remains, giving us tantalizing glimpses of their culture. The regions were then invaded by the Gauls—one of the more successful Celtic tribes—in a series of waves between the 4th and 3rd centuries BC.

These groups were then themselves conquered by the Romans about 300 years later. In one of history's small ironies, however, it was the writings of Julius Caesar, leader of those conquering armies, that give us most of our knowledge about Celtic culture today.

Following their victory, the Romans Romanized Normandy and Brittany in much the same manner as they had done for conquered provinces across Europe, building an infrastructure of roads, villas, and urban centers. It's said that the technique of half-timbering, seen across both Normandy and Brittany, originated in this period, with the ever-practical Romans using local materials to build their houses.

EARLY HISTORY

Christianity arrived in Normandy in around the 3rd century AD, which was when Saint

Mellonius was ordained as the first bishop of Rouen. This corresponded, in many respects, with the slow decline of the Roman Empire, as various tribes, including Saxons on the coast, began to harry the region's borders. The eventual fall of the Western Roman Empire is pinpointed as AD 476, with well-organized Frankish tribes, led by Lord Clovis, taking their place little more than a decade later.

It was just a little later than this that many churches and abbeys began to be founded. And though their buildings may have gone through different stages since then, the sites remain home to religious institutions, or the ruins of religious institutions, to this day. This was particularly the case along the banks of the Seine, with abbeys such as Fontenelle, Jumièges, and Pavilly all dating from this period.

A few years later still, in the 8th century, the first religious buildings were established on a former Gallo-Roman stronghold on a tidal island in the bay in the southwest corner of the Cotentin Peninsula. According to legend, this was the result of the archangel Michael appearing to the then bishop of Avranches, instructing him to build a church on the isolated outcrop: so were laid the foundations of Mont-Saint-Michel.

Brittany, meanwhile, was Christianized in the midst of the first millennium by seven semi-legendary missionaries, mostly from Wales, who today are referred to as the region's seven founder saints. They were part of a general exodus from the British Isle, of people seeking to escape from invading Saxons as the Roman Empire fell. The official union of the country as Brittany came about as a resistance of the now Breton-speaking people of the pensinula gathering together to resist Frankish incursions on their territory. A series of victories led by the first Breton king Nominoë established a borderland between Brittany and France just beyond the towns of Rennes and Nantes.

THE NORMAN CONQUESTS

Viking raids were common right across the north coast of France and along the banks of the Seine from the end of the 8th century. Frankish policies to combat them were muddled at best, which is what led to land gradually being yielded to the raiders, who nevertheless kept pushing on France's borders. Following a last stand defeat of the Vikings at the Battle of Chartres in 911, the Frankish king, Charles the Simple, signed the Treaty of Saint-Clair-sur-Epte, which ceded the area of present-day Haute-Normandie to the invaders in return for a truce. The now settled Vikings were referred to as Nortmanni, which means "men of the North." From this root, the terms Norman and Normandy originated.

Norman expansion continued over the next couple of centuries, despite the truce. However, Norman rulers still observed the ceremonial superiority of France, referring to themselves as Dukes of Normandy rather than kings. Quite possibly it was a desire for a more regal title that led one of them, Duke William, to set his sights on the realm to the north of Normandy, the other side of the channel: England.

The death of England's childless Anglo-Saxon king, Edward the Confessor, sparked competition for the English throne, with William one of several claimants. He marshaled an army and in September 1066 landed a Norman armada on England's southern coast. Victory at the Battle of Hastings, against the Anglo-Saxon Harold Godwinson, meant that William won the kingdom, and that Norman, English, and world history was forever changed.

This success, however, marked the high point of Ducal Normandy's power. Barely more than a century later, French forces under King Philip II had retaken Rouen, marking the beginning of the end of the Normans as an independent force.

THE HUNDRED YEARS' WAR

Neither lasting exactly 100 years, nor technically being a single war, the Hundred Years' War is in fact the name given to a number of conflicts that took place from 1337 to 1453 between the House of Plantagenet, rulers of England, and the French House of Valois, who would ultimately control France itself.

Normandy was essential to the conflict's origins, for since William the Conqueror, English monarchs had held multiple titles and lands in the technically French realm. These had already been a source of conflict for centuries, with the French long concerned with checking English expansion, flexing their political prerogative either by diplomacy or military force—such as the invasion of Rouen by King Philip II at the turn of the 13th century. English holdings in France oscillated quite a bit in the years following 1066, and at times were much bigger than the French kingdom itself. By 1337, Gascony was their only holding that remained.

Ultimately, a confusing, soap-operatic wrangling of dynastic succession led English king Edward III to officially declare war against the French, which would go on to suck in several surrounding kingdoms as allies, last for five generations, and go a long way to establishing the national identities of France and England as we see them today.

A subsidiary conflict of this war took place in Brittany. This was called the War of Breton Succession (1341-1365) and was fought over laws of dynastic succession—should it be de facto passed to male heirs, or should female heirs also get some claim. The belligerents were the house of Montfort, whose position that power should pass to a male heir was backed by the English, and the Blois, whose view that it should go to a more direct female heir was backed by the French. The Duchy of Brittany was the prize. After a great deal of back and forth, victory eventually fell to the Montforts, though they ultimately failed to declare homage for the English, leaving Brittany still as a duchy in the French realm.

The Hundred Years' War as a whole, meanwhile, was to rage on for another 88 years. A series of catastrophic French defeats at Crecy, Poitiers, and Agincourt pushed the French monarchy to the brink. It was only the visions of a lowly peasant girl in the ravaged French countryside that were to save the nation. In 1429, the 17-year-old Joan of Arc begged her way into the presence of the French king, and somehow managed to convince him that she should act as a standard bearer at the siege of Orleans, which she did, delivering a great victory that would go on to rally French troops across the country and ultimately drive the English out of France, bringing more than a century of conflict to an end.

Things ended badly for Joan, of course, captured by the English and burned as a heretic in Rouen, 1431—she was rehabilitated 25 years later by Pope Callixtus III.

JOINING FRANCE

While the reunification of Normandy with the rest of France was effectively subsumed by the English-French conflict of the Hundred Years' War, Brittany's submission as an independent nation was more distinct.

In 1488, Francis II, Duke of Brittany, died without a male heir, leaving his daughter, Duchess Anne, a prize for the various rulers of Europe. Her hand marriage represented the effective key to the whole Duchy of Brittany. By 1489, at the age of 11, she was indeed married, by proxy, to Maximilian I of Austria. Charles VIII of France saw this as a threat, however, and mounted a military campaign in Brittany to force her to renounce the marriage.

This Anne did, marrying Charles VIII in 1491. None of their children survived early childhood, however, and Charles died in 1498, passing the throne, and the hand of his wife, to his cousin Louis XII. Despite their somewhat unorthodox union, Louis actually fell in love with his new wife, giving Anne the opportunity to make a strong claim for Breton independence—she remains a folk hero in the region even to this day. In the end, though, she gave birth to only daughters, the younger of whom married her cousin, Francis of France, which paved the way to a definitive submission of Brittany to France in 1536.

THE FRENCH REVOLUTION

From 1789, all of France and its colonies were plunged into a state of upheaval as the people revolted against King Louis XVII, leading to the eventual collapse of the monarchy, execution of the king, and a period known as the Terror, in which large numbers of aristocrats and suspected counterrevolutionaries were put to death, often using the infamous guillotine.

These major affairs of state did not, comparative to other French regions, have an enormous impact on day-to-day life in Normandy, though the old region was split into five separate administrative departments. Normandy also provided shelter for a number of Girondins, a group who initially supported the revolution, but latterly began to feel alienated by its spiraling extremism. In Caen, they gathered an army of 2,000 volunteers, which attracted the attention of Charlotte Corday, who would go on to assassinate the firebrand journalist Jean-Paul Marrat. The movement itself came to nothing, however, with their march on Paris being routed at the Battle of Brécourt on July 13, 1793.

In Brittany, meanwhile, a lot of people retained a sympathy for the monarchy throughout the Revolution, even going so far as to plot a reestablishment of the old political system in the province. This went so far as to be aided by the British, and eventually had to be put down by Republican forces, who ended up executing numerous leaders in the counterrevolutionary movement, declaring them guilty of treason against the state.

As well as this, both Nantes in Brittany and Granville in Normandy were attacked during in the Vendée Revolt of 1793, a broadly counterrevolutionary uprising that originated south of the Loire River.

19TH CENTURY

The near constant political revolt that characterized France in the 19th century, from the First Empire to the Restoration, all the way through to the Third Republic, had remarkably little impact in Normandy. Rather, the region as a whole was more affected by more general societal trends impacting much of the western world in that period. These included the abolition of the slave trade, a general mechanization of factories, and a relative rural exodus, with many former peasants heading to the cities. The last of these led to an overall change in the farming culture of the region, with cattle taking a large precedence over cereal crops, thanks to their being less labor-intensive to husband. As a result, much of the large-scale cheese production, for which Normandy is justly famous, dates from this time.

For Brittany, meanwhile, the 19th century led to the region's reidentification as something somehow separate from France, albeit in a more modern context. There was always something of a mistrust of Breton soldiers in the French military, which intensified during the disastrous Franco-Prussian War (1870-1871). A fear of Breton separatists led to the interment of the region's soldiers in a particularly grim military camp, which, ironically, fed the cause of a new Breton nationalism. At the same time, while Brittany's reputation grew as a distinct and thoroughly traditional region, it was actually becoming more and more integrated with centralized power, and better known by bourgeois society as tourists began discovering the delights of its coast, as they also did in Normandy.

The late 19th century was also the era of the Impressionist art movement, a reevaluation of artistic subjects and techniques, characterized by paintings that offer just an "impression" of what the artist saw rather than its precise reproduction. Artists such as Monet, Degas, Renoir, and many others flocked to the countryside, with Normandy a particular muse. The paintings of the bucolic and coastal landscapes that the region proffered would eventually come to represent an archetype of all rural France.

WORLD WAR II

To many, Normandy is almost synonymous with the Second World War. And indeed, it was here that saw one of the most defining campaigns of that entire conflict. Initially escaping much of the fighting after the French capitulated in the early years of the war, the region was singled out by the Allies as the best access point from which to reestablish a foothold on the European mainland in 1944.

The D-Day landings, the largest sea-to-land invasion ever staged in the history of the world, took place along the sandy coastlines of the Basse-Normandie region. Following their success on the beach, the Allied armies launched a full-scale assault across Northern France. The Battle of Normandy, code-named Operation Overlord, lasted from June 6-August 30, and saw the almost full-scale destruction of many historic Norman cities, including Caen, Cherbourg, and Le Havre. The eventual result was an Allied victory, though the cost among ordinary Normans was extremely high, with between 25,000 and 39,000 civilian deaths estimated in the course of the campaign.

Brittany, meanwhile, was actually something of a frontline in WWII for longer than its neighbor, being the main base from which the Nazis orchestrated their role in the Battle of the Atlantic. The infamous submarine "wolf-packs" had their harbors in ports such as Lorient, from whence they were sent out on what became increasingly suicidal raids to disrupt the supply chain of shipping that kept Britain in the war.

Following D-Day, Brittany was also a major target of the Allied advance, with cities such as Brest and Saint-Malo near leveled by the fighting.

CONTEMPORARY TIMES

Postwar, the immediate history of both Normandy and Brittany is one of reconstruction. Industries had to reestablished and towns rebuilt. In some cases, such as that of Saint-Malo, this meant painstaking reconstruction; in others, Le Havre being the most obvious example, it provided an opportunity for reinvention: the harbor city was rebuilt as a modernist masterpiece of urban design by the Belgian city planner and architect Auguste Perret.

Aside from that, the latter half of the 20th century has been fairly quiet, and offered little but good news stories for both regions. They have become increasingly popular with tourists and have seen gradual improvements to their infrastructure, including many motorways and bridges—the epic Seine Estuary-spanning Pont de Normandie, which opened in 1995, being the most notable.

Government and Economy

ORGANIZATION

On the national level, France is run by a semi-presidential system, which consists of three separate branches of government: the Executive, run by the president and the government's ministers; the legislative, represented by a parliament comprised of two houses, the National Assemble and the Senate; and the judiciary, an extensive courts system.

Though the state government is ultimately supreme, France is divided into a number of administrative subdivisions. The largest of these are "regions." There are 18 of these in total, 13 in metropolitan France (their lines were redrawn as recently as 2016), and it is to their number that Normandy and Brittany belong.

Regions do not have legislative authority, so cannot write their own laws. However, they do levy their own taxes, while their budgets are managed by a regional government voted for in regional elections. The regional governments of Normandy and Brittany, therefore, have the power over much of their spending infrastructure, from education to public transit, assistance to local businesses, and so forth.

Below regions, in France's subdivision of power, are the "departments." Dating from 1790, the time of the French Revolution, these intended to make every local area in the country feel part of the national whole. In Normandy there are five (Manche, Eure, Calvados, Orne, and Seine-Maritime) and in Brittany four (Finistère, Côtes-d'Armor, Morbihan, and Ille-et-Vilaine). Their responsibilities include local roads, rural buses, and social and welfare allowances.

Underneath these are the "communes"—effectively town and village councils—of which France boasts, staggeringly, more than 36,000. These have no legislative powers, but function in an administrative capacity.

POLITICS

As with many other places in the world, the political scene in France has been in flux in recent years, with previously fringe parties rising to positions of unheard-of importance, and one entirely new political party taking power in 2017.

Until quite recently, the French government has alternated between two more-or-less stable coalitions: One led by the Republicans on the center-right, and one on the center-left led by the Socialist Party, which historically allied with the Greens and the PRG (the Party of the Radical Left).

These traditional parties seem to be on the decline, however, with a recent rise of the far-right in the form of the Rassemblement National (formally the Front National) and the populist left in La France Insoumise draining their fringes, and the current president, Emmanuel Macron's party *En Marche!* poaching from their center. Also worth a mention is the Breton independence party, which campaigns for Brittany to be recognized as an independent republic within the European Union. As yet, though, this receives only a small portion of the vote in local elections (about 4 percent). Though there is a great deal of Breton pride, the active separatist movement is fairly small and nonviolent.

In general, Normandy and Brittany have resisted the draw of the extremes of the political system; Normandy tends to favor center-right candidates and Brittany center-left. Politics in France saw a lot of volatility at the end of 2018, particularly with the *Gilet Jaune* or Yellow Vest protests, which began over hikes in gas prices and came to stand in for the general discontent of largely rural workers feeling neglected by urban elites. The movement was truly France-wide, with numerous marches large and small in both Brittany and Normandy. Though some of these erupted into violence, particularly in Paris and other big cities, protests in Normandy and Brittany were largely peaceful. The political landscape continues to be redrawn.

INDUSTRY AND AGRICULTURE

With large areas of green space, agriculture makes up a significant part of both Normandy's and Brittany's economies. Cattle breeding and cider production are two of the most noticeable agricultural industries throughout both regions, giving a clear character to their rural landscapes that is quite distinct from the rest of France.

Normandy, specifically, is well known for its horse studs and flax production. Brittany, meanwhile, is the largest region in France for producing vegetables. These include iconic varieties such as Roscoff onions and artichokes, but also many others that Brittany is less famous for, from tomatoes to potatoes. Much farming, especially in Brittany, is managed by very large estates.

Fishing, too, is important to Normandy, specifically in the Calvados and Manche areas, which provide 12 percent of all France's fish catch. It's an even bigger industry in Brittany, however, which, with the Atlantic on its doorstep, is the largest seafood-producing region in France.

Both regions have roughly a third to a quarter of their industries given over to food processing, though both also have large automotive and electronic device manufacturers located in their territories. Brittany remains a center of the French shipbuilding industry. Le Havre, Rouen, and Brest, meanwhile, number among France's biggest ports.

TOURISM

Tourism is of massive importance to the economies of both Normandy and Brittany, both in terms of French and international visitors. A brief look at French government statistics shows that in 2016 there were around 11.1 million overnight visitors to Normandy. Brittany received 12.7 million.

Most come to Normandy for its sights and its culture, from Mont Saint-Michel (1.25 million visitors in 2016) to Monet's garden in Giverny (630,000 visitors in 2016). The D-Day landing beaches, though, are the region's single-biggest draw (1.7 million visitors in 2016, which was not even a major anniversary year!). Brittany tends to be more popular among tourists for its landscape and outside activities: The region boasts no less than twice as many campsites as its neighbor.

Of course, though, these are generalizations: There's plenty of great outdoor space in Normandy, and Brittany overflows with fascinating culture.

People and Culture

DEMOGRAPHY AND DIVERSITY

Normandy's population is roughly 3.3 million people, with slightly more women than men, and an average age of 41 years, according to a 2014 survey. The largest cities are Le Havre, with nearly 200,000 inhabitants, and Rouen and Caen, which both have just over 100,000.

The French government notably doesn't keep statistics on ethnicity, though rural areas are largely white, with some North African and sub-Saharan communities in the larger cities. Foreign nationals make up 2.7 percent of the population.

Brittany's population is also roughly 3.3 million, with slightly more women than men and an average age of 41.6 years, according to a 2014 survey. Its largest cities are Rennes, with a population of around 213,000, and Brest, with a population of 141,000. Nantes, meanwhile, sits outside the modern administrative zone of Brittany, with a population of nearly 300,000.

As with Normandy, there are no statistics on Brittany's ethnic diversity, though the same applies that there tend to be more second- or third-generation immigrant communities in the bigger cities, and very few in the countryside. Foreign nationals make up 2.3 percent of the population.

SUBCULTURES

Much of traditional Norman culture has been pretty well imbibed into the rest of France, though there are still vestiges left around the region that can be glimpsed during cultural occasions, such as the wearing of traditional dress, which tends to consist of a lot of intricate embroidery and is often made from homemade raw material, such as linen, hemp, or wool.

Brittany, meanwhile, is famous throughout France for clinging to its local Celtic traditions, and the celebration of them still represents a thriving subculture throughout the region. Local festivals known as *festou-noz* occur in villages throughout Brittany year-round that involve traditional songs played on bagpipes, traditional dancing, and dressing in traditional clothes. Like their Norman equivalent, these clothes are characterized by embroidery and lace, and are best known for their impressive female headgear, known as *coiffe,* the differing designs of which designate the woman's stage in life: unmarried, married, with children, or widowed.

RELIGION

Despite the large number of impressive churches and abbeys throughout both regions, religion today plays a comparatively small role in most people's daily life. Though official statistics are forbidden, according to private surveys Roman Catholicism is the declared religion of around 60 percent of the two regions' inhabitants. One to two percent are Protestant, and about 1-3 percent are Muslim. Around a full quarter of the population lay claim to no religion at all.

Breton Catholic tradition is notable for a number of customs distinct from the main body of the church. These include penitential ceremonies known as pardons, and the veneration of the region's seven founder saints, missionaries mostly from Wales who brought Christianity to the peninsula in the Dark Ages. A very old pilgrimage called the Tro Breizh exists that involves walking between the graves of these saints.

There is also a strong neo-Pagan tradition that exists in Brittany, partly linked to the region's very present Celtic past.

LANGUAGE

The first language of both Normandy and Brittany is French, a Romance language descended from Latin.

Traditional Norman was, and is, really just a dialect of French, and when written on the page the two languages are indistinguishable. While it's not really spoken today, there are a number of words from its lexicon, different from the French, that remain in common use. It's not uncommon, for example, to hear local Normans refer to sheep as *berca* (from the Latin) rather than *moutons,* or use *floquet* (from the Scandinavian) for a small herd. Don't panic about this too much, however; using normal French terms for these things and others will make you perfectly comprehended.

The Breton language is still spoken across the peninsula. This is a Celtic language most closely related to Cornish and Welsh, and despite government policies against it in the 19th and 20th centuries persisted widely until around 1950. Today, it's reckoned there are only around 200,000 speakers, the majority of whom are over 60. Nevertheless, it's now taught in schools and appears on road signs across the region. Again, don't worry about being able to speak or understand any Breton to get by, but a couple of words of the language would go wonders in ingratiating you to locals.

LITERATURE

Normandy's rich heritage of monasteries in the Middle Ages led to it being a hub of European literary work, with monks and clergy some of the best-educated people of the age, and the whole region possessing higher literacy rates than much of the rest of the continent. The knowledge of history and legend contained within many of these monasteries was passed on to visiting travelers and traveling minstrels, inspiring a series of early Christian epics known as the *Chanson de Geste.* Indeed, it's even reckoned that the very first work of literature in the French language, *Le Chanson de Roland,* was by a Norman poet called Turold, whose name appears in its last line.

In more recent times, the best-known authors to have come out of Normandy are **Charles Alexis de Tocqueville** (1805-1859), who wrote the classic of political science *Democracy in America* and whose ancestral home was just outside of Cherbourg; **Gustave Flaubert** (1821-1880), a master of realism from Rouen, whose *Madame Bovary* reinvented the possibilities of the novel; and Flaubert's protégé, **Guy de Maupassant** (1850-1893), one of the greatest short story writers of all time, born just outside of Dieppe.

By far the best-known Breton author in the wider world is **Jules Verne** (1828-1905). Born

Arthur and His Knights

The sword in the stone, Excalibur, the Knights of the Round Table, Guinevere, Merlin, Lancelot, the Holy Grail: The touch points of Arthurian legend have sparked the minds of countless dreamers across the centuries and have been re-written countless times by some of the greatest authors to ever live.

No one knows how these legends originated, or even if the figure of King Arthur was based on a real person. There are some suggestions that the stories were first told in Wales, where the historical Arthur may have led a resistance movement against Saxon incursions. This, at least, would make for a good explanation of how they ended up in Brittany, and associated with so many Breton locations: The late Dark Ages saw a mass immigration to the peninsula by the Welsh.

LITERATURE

There was never single definitive story of Arthur and his adventures; however, it was simply a tradition gradually added to over time, most concretely first by Geoffrey of Monmouth in the 12th century and then as a work of indisputable literature by Thomas Mallory in his *Morte d'Arthur* in the 15th century. Reaffirming the French link, Arthur was also written about by Chrétien de Troyes in the 1100s, whose additions to the tale were essential in it becoming one of the most read works of literature at the time.

LEGENDS

The most enduring elements of the story, which are still retold today, speak of how Arthur proved his right to rule by being the only person who could draw a magic sword from a stone, how he was advised by the mysterious wizard Merlin, and later, how his bravest and most noble knight, Lancelot had an affair with his wife, the enigmatic Guinevere. The quest of his knights for the Holy Grail, the cup said to have been the cup at the Last Supper and the Crucifixion, has also long been one of the most iconic stories throughout European history.

Also common to Arthurian legend, is that it ends in Arthur's heroic death at the Battle of Camlann. After sustaining a mortal wound, the dying king requests his sword, Excalibur, be returned to the Lady of the Lake, another enchantress supposedly taught her magic by Merlin, who then appears in a barge to take Arthur to the legendary island of Avalon, where the sword was first forged.

in Nantes, he practically invented the genre of science fiction, with his iconic inventions and characters, from the *Nautilus* submarine to Phileas Fogg, still capturing the imaginations of children and adults to this day.

VISUAL ARTS

Few regions of the world, outside of maybe Tuscany, can be said to have been served better by the visual arts than Normandy. The region's proximity to Paris, its at turns picturesque then dramatic landscape, and its benign climate led to an entirely new form of painting for which artists left the studio and set up their easels in the open air.

Of the first artists to take this approach, one, Eugéne Boudin (1824-1898), was actually from Normandy himself, having been born in the historic harbor town of Honfleur. His paintings of the expansive skies around the Seine Estuary were to inspire a young Claude Monet to drop his caricature work in favor of landscapes, a move that ultimately led to one of the most important artistic movements of all time, Impressionism.

Though few Impressionists were actually from Normandy, the region provided their greatest inspiration, with the likes of Sisley, Renoir, and Pissarro all attracted by the frequently changing light and the lush, windblown colors that present themselves here. Monet liked it so much that he eventually moved to Normandy in 1881, calling the rural hamlet of Giverny home until his death in 1926.

Brittany also proved something of a muse

to this set of painters, though its greatest champion was the Expressionist Paul Gauguin (1848-1903), who took inspiration from what he saw as the elemental and raw qualities of both the region and its people to create paintings that burst with both color and emotion.

ARCHITECTURE

Churches

Much of the epic story of architecture in Normandy can be read in its oldest churches, which almost without fail have received additions to their structure across the centuries, and therefore boast several different design styles, often rubbing shoulder to shoulder.

In terms of what still survives today, the story begins with **Romanesque** architecture, dating mostly from the 11th and 12th centuries. This combines features of Roman and Byzantine building and is characterize by sturdy walls and semicircular arches, large pillars and decorative arcading, with buildings having clearly defined forms, built over a symmetrical pattern. It tends to look more simplistic than later styles. There aren't many pure examples of Romanesque to be found in Normandy, though the oldest sections of many churches in and around Caen and abbeys along the Seine are clearly often of the style.

Following on the heels of Romanesque in the 12th century was **Gothic** architecture. This style, conceived of in the Île-de-France, is commonly considered one of humanity's finest artistic achievements, with features such as the rib vault and the flying buttress allowing churches to reach heady heights, and allowing space for increasingly larger windows, which taken together give the impression of stone being made lighter than air. The Merveille buildings of Mont-Saint-Michel are as fine an example of this form of architecture as anywhere in the region.

The **Flamboyant** style, starting in the 14th century, came next, and often consisted of the touching up of preexisting buildings with ever more elaborate decorations, including vast rose windows and orgies of intricate carving. Rouen today is perhaps the world center for Flamboyant Gothic, with the church of Saint-Maclou one of its undisputed masterpieces.

Breton churches are mostly Gothic and Flamboyant in their heritage, often featuring even more elaborate decoration both inside and out. The most distinct examples of this in Brittany are the parish closes, dating from the 16th and 17th centuries. These buildings tend to be set within a walled compound consisting of multiple out-buildings, which hearken back to Celtic traditions of deeming whole clearings of forest as sacred spaces.

Half-Timber Houses

Common across all of Normandy and Brittany is the half-timber house. There's evidence that buildings like this have been constructed here since Roman times, but the oldest now in existence date from the 14th and 15th centuries, when the technique was particularly popular, taking advantage as it did of the abundance of wood as a cheap raw material. Conversely, stone could not be quarried from everywhere in the two regions, and these buildings were able to be made anywhere without it. Earth could be used to make both the foundations and the walls, while clay was mixed together to make cob, providing good insulation.

MUSIC AND DANCE

Truth be told, for all their other staggering artistic and cultural achievements, music and dance are not so well represented by Normandy and Brittany on the world stage.

Normandy's most impressive offerings stem from Rouen, wherein both the city cathedral and the Abbatiale Saint-Ouen boast very impressive organs, the latter of these having been designed by master organ builder Aristide Cavaillé-Coll in 1890. Described as "a Michelangelo of organs," it's also one of the few pieces by Cavaillé-Coll left entirely unaltered, meaning that it still sounds exactly as he would have intended. Of the cathedral, meanwhile, its choir was famous up to the French Revolution for singing from memory, and its first major organist was Jean Titelouze, the father of the French organ school.

Brittany, on the other hand, is best known for its folk tradition. The wail of bagpipes and literally hundreds of different dances, closely connected to those from both Ireland and Scotland, are a common sight and sound at the many village festivals known as *festoù-noz* that happen across the region throughout the year.

Essentials

Transportation

GETTING THERE

From the United States and Canada

In almost all cases, the most efficient and cheapest way to get to both Normandy and Brittany from either the United States or Canada is by flying into Paris. There are numerous international airlines that do this, with more than 30 North American cities connected directly to the French capital. Among them are New York (7 hours), Los Angeles (11 hours), Chicago (8 hours), Montréal (7 hours), and Vancouver (10 hours). This list is far from exhaustive, and all flight times are approximate for nonstop flights.

Among the carriers making these trips are several major national companies, including **Air France** (www.airfrance.com), **Delta** (www.delta.com), and **Air Canada** (www.aircanada.com). There are also a number of budget long-haul airlines such as **Wow Air** and **Norwegian Air.** For the best deals, use the flight comparison website skyscanner.net, and book well ahead of time.

Direct flights from the West Coast of North America should take around 11 hours, and from the East Coast around 8 hours. Prices, as anyone with experience flying will know, can vary enormously and depend on a number of factors, namely how far ahead you book, the frequency of flights from the airport you're leaving from, and whether you fly direct.

From Paris, most places in Normandy and Brittany are fastest and most practically reached by land. This is true of everywhere apart from the westernmost reaches of Brittany, such as Brest, Quimper, and Nantes. Adding a connecting flight from Paris to any one of these cities should cost in the region of €100-150.

From the United Kingdom and Ireland

BY AIR

Several major and regional airports in the United Kingdom and Ireland link up directly with towns in both Normandy and Brittany, though many flights will have to go through Paris first. Nevertheless, flying makes for an efficient way of getting to the regions, especially if you're just planning a short city break or intend to hire your own transport when you get there. This said, the small size of the planes flying these routes and their relative infrequency means that flights are often more expensive than you might expect to pay flying similar, or even farther, distances. If you're richer in time than money, flying from the United Kingdom or Ireland needn't be your first choice.

Easyjet connects London Gatwick and Manchester with Nantes. There are **Cityjet** flights from London City Airport to Nantes and Deauville, while **British European** flies from mutliple cities, including Manchester, Exeter, Southampton, Birmingham, and Southend to numerous locations in both Normandy and Brittany, including Rennes, Caen, Nantes, and Brest. **Ryanair** flies direct from London Stansted to Dinard.

Almost all flights from Ireland have to go through Paris, though there are some RyanAir flights chartered directly from Dublin to Nantes.

BY CAR

Having your own car in Normandy and Brittany is easily the best way to explore both regions, where regional public transport can be slow and intermittent. Unfortunately, there is as yet no road either over or under the English Channel, so bringing a car with you means loading it onto either the Eurotunnel train or a ferry.

The fastest and most efficient way of getting your car across the channel, the **Eurotunnel** (www.eurotunnel.com) is a train with space for motorists to drive on board. On the U.K. side, the train boards close to Folkstone on the M20 motorway, about two hours south of London. After parking on board, you are then invited to remain in your car (though there is space to walk around, and toilets if you need them) for the 35-minute crossing as the train dips under the sea and surfaces just outside of Calais.

The service continues around the clock with up to four departures per hour 6am-12am, and one per hour 12am-6am. Tickets are worked out on a per-car rather than per-passenger basis and can cost €60-170 one way, depending on how far in advance you book and time of year of travel.

Arrive at least 30 minutes before departure, and book ahead of travel—you can by tickets at the terminal, but to keep costs down and to be sure of getting on the train you want, it's always worth planning ahead.

Previous: medieval city of Dinan and its Gothic bridge

Keep in mind also that though Eurotunnel gets you to France, Normandy and Brittany are still some drive away. Dieppe is 117 miles (188 kilometers) down the A16, which takes about two hours, while Brest is a massive 445 miles (716 kilometers) away using multiple highways, taking seven hours.

BY TRAIN AND BUS

If you're traveling without a car, the closest you can get directly by train or bus from London to Normandy and Brittany is Paris.

The **Eurostar** (www.eurostar.com) train service takes travelers between London and the French capital in style and comfort with a journey time of around 2.5 hours. Prices fluctuate depending on the usual factors, but can get as low as €35 one-way with enough forward planning. A service called **Eurostar Snap** (snap.eurostar.com) lets you book tickets close to the date of travel, at nonspecific times, for the cheapest rates. You're informed of your train's precise departure time the day before travel.

Coach services **Flixbus** (flixbus.com), **Ouibus** (ouibus.com), and **Eurolines** (www.eurolines.eu) get you to Paris in considerably less comfort and style, and journey times are 8-11 hours, but they do get you there, often at a very low cost, even if you're booking just a day before depature. You'll pay around €20 one way.

BY FERRY

There are four ferry ports along the coast of Normandy and two in Brittany, all regularly serviced throughout the year, which provide motorists, foot passengers, and cyclists traveling from Ireland and the south coast of England a direct and romantic access to the regions. There is also the Dover-Calais crossing farther east along the coast, which is both cheaper than most of the Normandy and Brittany routes and takes less time (about 1.5 hours, with more than 30 sailings daily). However, this may also not be particularly close to your starting point, and as with the Eurotunnel, more driving will be required from here to reach Normandy and Brittany themselves.

There's also the fact that many of the ferries crossing direct into Normandy and Brittany are likely to be smaller, and a little more romantic, than the behemoths that make the Dover-Calais crossing.

The ports in Normandy are Dieppe, serviced from Newhaven by **DFDS** (U.K. tel. +44 208 127 8303; www.dfdsseaways.co.uk; 2 daily; 4 hours); Le Havre, serviced from Portsmouth by DFDS (1 daily; 5.5-8 hours) and **Brittany Ferries** (U.K. tel. +44 330 159 7000; www.brittany-ferries.co.uk; 1-2 most days Apr.-Dec.; 4-5 hours); Caen, serviced from Portsmouth by Brittany Ferries (2-3 daily; 6-8 hours); and Cherbourg, serviced from Poole by Brittany Ferries (1 daily; 4.25) and Portsmouth by Brittany Ferries (1 daily late-Apr.-mid-Sept; 5 hours).

The ports in Brittany are Saint-Malo and Roscoff. Saint-Malo is serviced from Portsmouth by Brittany Ferries (1 daily in summer, 3 weekly in winter; 10.75 hours); from Plymouth by Brittany Ferries (Thurs. Oct.-Mar; 10.5 hours); and from Poole (via Jersey or Guernsey) by **Condor Ferries** (U.K. tel. 0044 148 172 9666; www.condorferries.co.uk; 1-3 daily May-Sept.; 6.75 hours). Roscoff is serviced from Plymouth by Brittany Ferries (up to 2 daily summer, three times weekly winter; 6-11 hours); from Rosslare in Ireland by Irish Ferries (5 weekly; 18 hours), and from Cork in Ireland by Brittany Ferries (1 weekly Apr.-Oct.; 14 hours).

Prices can vary wildly depending on the usual factors of how far in advance you book, the season, and so forth. A car plus two passengers can range €100-400 one-way. Additional passengers are charged extra. Foot-passenger tickets are considerably less, starting from around €35 one-way, and passengers can often be picked up at the port on the day of sailing at little additional fee. It's also possible to book cabin space on many of these ferries—highly recommended if you're taking a night crossing—at around €50 for a berth.

In all seasons, but especially summer, it's well worth booking ahead to keep costs down and to avoid disappointment when you arrive at the port.

From Australia, South Africa, and New Zealand

As with the United States, the fastest way to Normandy and Brittany from farther afield is to go via Paris. There are no direct flights here from Australia or New Zealand, however; the distance is simply too far. It's possible to make the trip from the major cities of both countries multiple times every day. The cheapest tickets you will find should be around €1,000.

There are five direct flights from Cape Town every week and seven from Johannesburg. These are run by **Air France.** Flight time is 12 hours from the former, 11 hours from the latter. There are also numerous connecting flights from South Africa, a number of which require switching between carriers. Connecting flights tend to be an average of 15 hours in length. Prices vary widely, but can come in as low as €400 return, if booked out of season and ahead of time.

From Paris, it is possible to pick up a further connecting flight out to Normandy or Brittany, though this is seldom cost effective, and if you're coming from Australia or New Zealand may represent the breaking point of your stamina. It's probably best to give yourself a day's rest in the French capital. It is, after all, quite nice too.

GETTING AROUND

By Car

Driving is by far the best way to get the most out of the two regions. Normandy and Brittany are well connected by several highways, but the true depth of their charm lies in the many small roads that wind their way through every inch of the beautiful countryside. Indeed, taking the slow way between towns and even getting a little lost could not be more recommended. That said, the **Michelin road maps** of the regions are faultlessly accurate, easy to follow, and widely available, while **GPS** works even in Normandy and Brittany's most remote places (though reception can get a little patchy in the valleys in between headlands).

Gas stations are plentiful throughout Normandy and Brittany, even in the more rural areas, with most now being self-service with the use of a credit card, and open 24 hours. Average gas prices are around €1.50 per litre, or €5.90 per US gallon.

ROADS

Also, keep aware that many highways in France are **toll routes.** These are well maintained and make for a very speedy way of getting around—their speed limit is 80 miles per hour (130 kilometers per hour)—but expect to pay roughly €20 for every hundred miles you travel along them. The level of road below these are **dual carriageways,** with speed limits of 68 mph (110 km/h), and below them regular **main roads,** with speed limits of 56 mph (90 km/h). The limit is 30 mph (50 km/h) in towns, which incidentally, tend to be fairly easy to drive around. While you shouldn't expect a U.S.-style grid system, despite the two regions' medieval heritage, most inner-city streets are less winding and confusing than they are in Europe's south (the exceptions are the walled towns such as Saint-Malo, Vannes, Dinan, etc., the centers of which are best avoided).

ROAD RULES

It's perfectly acceptable to take to the road here with a foreign driving license, and remember to **drive on the right!** Note also that **French driving law** requires all cars to carry a warning triangle, spare bulbs for the lights, and the now famous reflective jackets, one for every occupant of the vehicle. All these items can be picked up cheaply at gas stations around the country, and rental cars should come with them included.

The **alcohol limit** is 0.2 grams per liter of blood for drivers with less than three years experience and 0.5 grams per liter for those with more. A "standard" drink, say a half pint of beer or small glass of wine, will raise your blood alcohol by about 0.2 grams per liter, though obviously this depends on your size and metabolism, and it's always better to err on the side of caution. Note that the police don't need an excuse to pull you over to check, and random tests are common, especially around Sunday lunchtimes and Friday and Saturday evenings. Don't assume that being in a rural spot means you won't be pulled over; if anything, these tests are even more common on country roads. Penalties can be severe.

PARKING

By and large, finding a place to park is seldom a problem in Normandy and Brittany. This is down to, on the one hand, the regions being largely rural and comparatively sparsely populated, and on the other, tourist hot spots and resort towns being long-established and well-accommodated for dealing with many visitors. Parking is free in the huge majority of villages, and even in towns, there are usually spaces in residential areas you can pull into without paying.

Otherwise, parking price tends to go up the closer to the town center you get, with color-coded zones indicating cost and how long you can stay in a particular place. Prices vary considerably, but expect an average of about €1 per hour, with rates decreasing slightly the longer you stay. Some very touristy places, such as Honfleur, Étretat, and Carnac have overspill carparks in the high season, set up just outside of town, charging around €4 for a whole day parking. This is a good deal, as the towns that use these are mostly not very big, and it's usually easy to walk from the overspill area to the sights. Just make sure to leave your valuables out of sight, as such places are not necessarily well policed and can attract thieves, even if they usually don't.

The only real parking nightmare that you're likely to face in Normandy and Brittany is Saint-Malo, where the many parking lots around the historic walled citadel fill up quickly in high season. To avoid hours of searching for a space, it's easier and cheaper to pull up somewhat away from the center, then catch a local bus to the beaches and sights.

Keep in mind, too, that many hotels will have on-site, free parking, which should be taken advantage of if you can.

CAR RENTAL

There are numerous international car rental firms at work throughout Normandy and Brittany, with **Europcar** (www.europcar.fr), **Avis** (www.avis.fr), and **Hertz** (www.hertz.fr) being the most visible and common. The great majority are based near major railway stations or in airports, with cars starting from around €50 a day. In smaller towns, it's well worth calling ahead or booking a car on their website before you arrive, particularly in high season. Only in the major cities, such as Rouen, Caen, Le Havre, Rennes, Brest, and Nantes, can you be sure of being able to turn up on the day and getting a vehicle. Of course, these car rental companies operate in Paris, too, where choice is much wider, and for an extra price, roughly equivalent to an extra day's rental, it's often possible to drop your car at a different garage from the one you picked it up at. However, if you have specific needs (a car with an automatic gearbox, say) reserving in advance is highly recommended no matter where you rent.

Taxi

There are taxi services throughout Normandy and Brittany with fairly standardized pricing—expect to pay roughly €10 for a 10-minute journey, depending on traffic. In rural areas, it's worth keeping in mind that demand can easily outstrip supply, and if you're depending on using a taxi at a key point in a journey, then book ahead to make sure that you're not waiting around for a long time. In the cities, this isn't such an issue.

At the time of writing, Uber has not really penetrated very deep into either region, with only the biggest towns boasting any drivers at all. Of course, that may be subject to change, but don't rely on your smartphone to help you get around.

Car Share

The French car share company **BlaBla Car**

(www.blablacar.fr) allows travelers to take up spare seats in the cars of ordinary people driving through the regions, which is an excellent and inexpensive way to get around (about a third of the cost of most rail travel). It is particularly useful for those not too pressed for time, and if you're lucky, it can be a good way of getting to hard-to-reach rural spots.

By Train

The French are justifiably proud of their intercity national train service, the **SNCF** (www.sncf.com), which is one of the fastest and most efficient in the world. But prices can be high, with last-minute fares from Paris to most places in Brittany easily topping €140 return. Booking just a week in advance can significantly reduce the price, however, and most of Normandy, being much closer to the French capital, is mostly cheaper to reach.

A further disadvantage of rail is that it is only larger towns, including Rouen, Le Havre, Caen, Saint-Malo, Rennes, Brest, and Nantes that are easy to get to. Branch lines reaching out to smaller destinations do exist as part of the SNCF's **TER** (Transport Express Regional) service, but they are slower and do not always connect to one another, apart from at major transport hubs.

Train stations are usually central in most towns, and they are often sure-fire places to catch regional and intercity buses as well.

By Bike

Both Normandy and Brittany are a cyclist's heaven, thanks to their small roads, the reasonably short distances between attractions, and the beautiful, mostly flat landscape. Given cycling's status as a national pastime, much of the region's infrastructure is cycling-friendly. You'll notice this particularly on the trains, where it's possible to load a dismantled or foldable bike for a small fee. See the SNCF website for more details: www.sncf.com/fr/offres-voyageurs/voyager-en-toute-situation/velo-a-bord.

On top of this, there are extensive cycle lanes around Nantes that are well worth exploring, and the increasingly popular "green route" (www.donaldhirsch.com/dieppeparis.html) that runs from Dieppe to Paris, avoiding as many roads as possible.

Finally, there are also many bike rental firms throughout both regions, including at most campsites and hotels—rates are usually about €9 for half a day. For some areas, including the Paimpont Forest and Brittany's many islands, hiring or taking your own bike is indisputably the best way to travel.

Regulations for cyclists in France remain fairly light. Only those under 12 years old are required by law to wear a helmet, and high visibility jackets are only obligatory at night or in low-visibility situations. Aside from that, it's necessary to obey many of the same road laws as other vehicles: Stop at stops signs, traffic lights etc., cycle on the right, and don't use the sidewalk. Fines are in place for all these infringements, as are those for cycling drunk: The same limit of 0.5 grams of alcohol per liter of blood applies (roughly two standard drinks).

By Ferry

Brittany especially is a region of islands. Many of these can be visited by local ferry services that run year-round, with more boats in the high season. These ferries are run by a variety of different companies, though the services and prices they offer are pretty similar everywhere, with average crossing costs to islands being about €15 return, both interior and outside spaces to sit in, and on the longer crossings rudimentary snack bars on offer, serving chips, sandwiches, and instant coffee.

A both practical and romantic way of getting to certain destinations, ferries are used by tourists and locals alike. With this in mind, it can be well worth reserving a place on these boats ahead of time to avoid getting stranded at the dock. Also, keep aware of tides: Just because a ferry has dropped you off in one place does not mean that it will pick you up in the exact same one. The tidal reach can mean you have to walk farther than you expect to catch a leaving ferry, so always give yourself at least 10 more minutes than you think you will need.

Almost all ferries, provided they have room, will let you bring your bike on board.

By Bus

Services such as Ouibus (www.ouibus.com) and Flixbus (www.flixbus.com) offer a skeleton service (usually one or two per day) between Paris and both regions' major towns at about a third of the cost of rail travel, provided you book at least a day in advance.

Local rural bus services linking villages and midsize towns run seldom, but are more reliable than their often-deserted stands and hard-to-read timetables might suggest. They are also extremely cheap, most of the time costing little more than a couple of euros for journeys that may be upwards of two hours.

A further disadvantage is the sheer number of bus companies, and the fact that different operators may not encroach on one another's territory. This leaves some small patches of no-man's-land between micro-regions that, if you're really determined to travel only by local bus, you will have to traverse by foot.

All this said, if you're not in a rush, buses represent a cheap way to see the country.

Visas and Officialdom

France is part of the Schengen area, a group of 26 countries in Europe with no border controls between them. A visa-waiver program to the area exists for travelers from the **United States, Canada, Australia, and New Zealand,** all of whom are permitted to stay in the region for up to 90 days within a 180-day period, provided they have a valid passport. In 2021, a pre-travel registration system (European Travel Information and Authorisation System or ETIAS) is expected to be implemented for entry to the Schengen area. Check with the state department or foreign affairs ministry in your home country for more information if traveling in 2021.

Travelers from **Ireland** and other **European Union** countries have it even easier and are allowed to travel the Schengen region for as long as they want without visas, though they should inform authorities if they plan to do so for more than 90 days at a time. **South Africans,** meanwhile, must apply for a Schengen visa, which can be done via French authorities, no more than three months and no less than 15 days before their date of travel.

After the U.K. exit from the European Union, travelers from the **United Kingdom** should check www.gov.uk/foreign-travel-advice/france/entry-requirements for updated information on entry requirements.

EMBASSY OF THE UNITED STATES

2 avenue Gabriel, Paris; tel. 01 43 12 22 22; https://fr.usembassy.gov; 9am-6pm Mon.-Fri.

EMBASSY OF CANADA

130 rue du Faubourg Saint-Honoré, Paris; tel. 01 44 43 29 00; www.canadainternational.gc.ca; 9am-12pm and 2pm-5pm Mon.-Fri.

EMBASSY OF AUSTRALIA

4 rue Jean Rey, Paris; tel. 01 40 59 33 00; https://france.embassy.gov.au; 9am-4pm Mon.-Fri.

EMBASSY OF NEW ZEALAND

103 rue de Grenelle, Paris; tel. 01 45 01 43 43; www.mfat.govt.nz/fr/countries-and-regions/europe/france/new-zealand-embassy; 9am-1pm Mon.-Fri.

EMBASSY OF SOUTH AFRICA

59 quai d'Orsay, Paris; tel. 01 53 59 23 23; www.afriquesud.net/index.php?lang=fr; 9am-5pm Mon.-Fri.

EMBASSY OF IRELAND

12 avenue Foch, Paris; tel. 01 44 17 67 00; www.dfa.ie/irish-embassy/france; 9:30am-12pm Mon.-Fri.

EMBASSY OF THE UNITED KINGDOM

35 rue du Faubourg Saint-Honoré, Paris; tel. 01 44 51 31 00; www.gov.uk/world/france; 9:30am-1pm and 2:30pm-5pm Mon.-Fri.

Recreation

HIKING AND TREKKING

Away from the main roads, Brittany and Normandy are a walker's paradise, with many small forests, a largely agrarian farming culture, and that fabulous coastline. There are a large number of official walking trails that allow visitors to take advantage of this natural beauty.

For the really serious, there are the *sentiers de grande randonnée,* or the GRs. These are long-distance walking trails that exist throughout France, are well marked with red-and-white signs, and offer frequent campsites and rest huts along their length. A full 21 of them run through and around Normandy and Brittany, with the best being the GR34, which is an epic journey running the full coast of Brittany—best taken along its northern stretch, dipping up and down along the coves and coastline of the Côte de Granit Rose—and the GR223, which links Granville to Mont Saint-Michel and is a terrific way of feeling like a real pilgrim to the ancient monument. The GR2 along the Seine Valley all the way to Le Havre is also highly recommended, being a little less popular and also, with the multiple abbeys along the way, providing great insight into the history of the Seine maritime region. As well as being well-signposted, there are detailed guidebooks to all the GRs, often available in local tourist offices. Granted, these guidebooks are usually in French, but they come complete with detailed maps on almost every page.

For less ambitious hikers, it's always possible to do small stretches of the GRs, and there are plenty of other smaller walking tracks that often create circuits throughout both regions. The Presqu'île de Crozon area of Finistère is particularly good for these, with sea and spectacular views on almost all sides, as is the Paimpont Forest on account of its density of history and legendary spots, and the Alabaster Coast, where vistas that inspired the Impressionists abound.

Precautions

Hiking is a pretty safe activity in both Normandy and Brittany, though stay well clear of large animals such as cattle and horses when crossing fields, and keep an eye out for wild boars in more forested spaces. Ticks are also present in the regions, some of which, though far from all, carry Lyme's disease, meaning that checking yourself after a walk, especially one through long grass or other foliage is a very good idea. Aside from that, make sure you know what tides are doing at all times—tidal reach on some of the coastline here, can be extremely long, so don't think that just because the sea seems miles away it won't at some stage come all the way up the beach. Cliff edges, especially in the Alabaster coast, where collapse is relatively frequent, are also best avoided, whether from on top of the cliff or below it. Finally, make sure to pack ample water and protection from the sun. Normandy and Brittany might have a reputation for frequent rain, but that doesn't mean you can't get dehydrated, and when the sun is out it can be deceptively strong.

CYCLING

As mentioned above, Normandy and Brittany, like much of France, are excellently suited and very well prepped for those wishing to cycle. A lot of this comes down to the general love that the French have for the humble bicycle: Cycling is a national pastime that lasts way beyond the Tour de France. Incidentally, that world-famous road race has made frequent use of both Normandy's and Brittany's undulating coastline and bucolic pastures.

Some of the best cycling includes the roads near Dieppe along the Alabaster Coast, running all the way to Étretat, thanks to that area's wide roads and excellent views; the Cotentin

Peninsula between Barfleur and Cherbourg, for similar reasons; and along the Seine from Rouen to Le Havre, where the roads are quiet, the landscape changes frequently, and you can always hop on a ferry if you want to avoid (or deliberately tackle) hills. Then, there's also Nantes, recently voted one of the top cities for cyclists anywhere in the world, with its extensive network of cycle lanes, reaching deep out into the surrounding countryside.

For less ambitious riders, there's also the cycling prevalent on almost all of Brittany's larger islands. If you've only got half a day to see Ouessant, for example, then a bike is the best way to do it, and there are always plenty of rental firms onsite to help with that (prices are usually around €9 per half day). Trains, hotels, and campsites are almost ubiquitously considerate of the needs of cyclists, and drivers are more likely to shout the encouraging expression *"Chapeau!"* rather than yell at you for taking up the road.

SAILING AND WATER SPORTS

With so much coastline, it's little surprise that sailing and other water sports are extremely popular in both Normandy and Brittany, with the latter, thanks to its Atlantic winds and many sheltered coves, considering such activities as essential to its regional identity. Indeed, there are so many places where sailing and water sports predominate west of the Cotentin Peninsula and along coastal Brittany as a whole that it's difficult to pick one out as a highlight.

The Crozon Peninsula, however, offers perhaps the greatest variation; thrust out into the Rade de Brest like a barbed tongue, it is excellent for both those wanting to brave the open waters and beginners just learning their craft, thanks to its more sheltered bays. Goulien Beach here is particularly good for surfers, being a long sandy beach that gets large waves but is not assaulted by particularly high winds or big swells. Surf Oxygene (www.surfoxygene.com) are the people to contact here for help with lessons.

For a milder experience, the Gulf of Morbihan is the place to be. Effectively an inland sea, thanks to its small inlet, the waters here are relatively calm (though there are some powerful tidal currents), while its constellation of islands make for a constantly arresting trip in a sea kayak, rentals of which can be organized through Varec'h Kayak (www.bretagne-kayak.fr).

In Normandy, the western edge of the Cotentin Peninsula is among the best areas, with higher winds than farther east along the coast and some fleeting glimpses of Mont-Saint-Michel in the distance. Granville is a good spot for this, with the Centre Régional de Nautisme de Granville (http://centre-regional-nautisme-granville.fr) the place to start.

Festivals and Events

SPRING

GRANVILLE CARNIVAL

Granville, www.carnaval-de-granville.fr, Feb.-Mar.

One of Europe's biggest Mardi Gras carnivals, where people fill the streets in the day then head to elaborate parties in the evening. Known for its *intrigues,* where locals don disguises to find out town gossip about themselves.

FÊTES JEANNE D'ARC

Rouen, www.rouentourisme.com/agenda/fetes-jeanne-d-arc-3431, May

A reserved celebration of France's most famous daughter, who was put to death in the center of Rouen. Parades take place through the town, and church services bookend the days.

SUMMER

D-DAY ANNIVERSARY

D-Day beaches, www.dday-overlord.com/en/normandy/commemorations, June

Commemorating the biggest sea-to-land invasion of all time, every year the roads around this otherwise quiet coastline rumble again to the sound of period tanks and aircraft, attracting people from all over the world. Bigger on landmark years.

TOMBEES DE LA NUIT

Rennes, www.lestombeesdelanuit.com, July

A festival dedicated to street-side art and performance. For one week of every July, Rennes's squares, roads, and parks are packed out by contemporary sculpture and performers from all over the world.

INTERNATIONAL MARITIME FESTIVAL

Brest, http://brest2020.fr, July

One of the biggest gatherings of sailboats anywhere in the world; literally thousands of vessels descend on Brest's natural harbor, creating a stunning spectacle once every four years.

FESTIVAL DE CORNOUAILLE

Quimper, www.festival-cornouaille.bzh, July

One of the biggest celebrations of Breton culture anywhere in the region, with parades, concerts, and a beauty contest at its heart.

FESTIVAL INTERCELTIQUE DE LORIENT

Lorient, www.festival-interceltique.bzh, Aug.

A week-long celebration of Celtic culture, attracting participants from across the Celtic world from Scotland to Galicia. The streets of Lorient wail with bagpipe music, its harbor swings to old sea shanties, and an atmosphere of excess tinged with slight madness pervades.

FALL

DEAUVILLE AMERICAN FILM FESTIVAL

Deauville, www.festival-deauville.com/pid1/accueil, Sept.

Showcasing both Hollywood productions and independent films, this is a veritable northern Cannes, drawing international celebrities and presenting more than 100 new films to audiences.

OUESTPARK FESTIVAL

Le Havre, www.ouestpark.com, Sept.

An inner-city rock music festival, bringing together groups from all around France. Small scale, but trendy and of high quality.

FÊTE DU VENTRE

Rouen, http://en.rouentourisme.com/the-festival-of-gastronomy-of-the-stomach, Oct.

Showcasing the startling depth and variety of Norman food, this "festival of the stomach" was founded in 1935, and sees farmers from across the region descend on Rouen, offering up what is surely some of the best food in the world.

WINTER

LES FÊTES DES HARENGS

Dieppe, www.normandie-tourisme.fr/a-voir-a-faire/gastronomie/fetes-gastronomiques-pour-tous-les-gouts/les-fetes-du-hareng-408-1.html, Nov.

A food festival dedicated to the humble herring, which migrate along the Norman coast at this time, that takes over Dieppe's harbor for a few days every November.

LA ROUTE DU ROCK

Saint-Malo, www.laroutedurock.com, Feb.

Attracting international rock stars from Patti Smith to Charlotte Gainsbourgh, this music festival plays off the fashion world with both summer and winter editions, and sets Saint-Malo's gray granite streets ablaze in the chilly months.

Accommodations

Being major tourist destinations, both Normandy and Brittany abound with hotels, B&Bs, and campsites to suit all budgets. Throughout most of the year, there are easily enough of these that as long as you're not choosy, you should be able to turn up in any town or tourist destination and find yourself a room for the night. Things get a little trickier in the very high season, during July and August, when it's not only other international tourists who flock to the regions but also the French themselves. During this period, booking in advance is close to essential, especially if you want your pick of places to stay.

HOTELS

Saying that the quality of hotels in Normandy and Brittany varies widely hardly does justice to the kind of variety on offer here. Even confining yourself to a particular end of the budgetary scale provides no end of difference.

For the less expensive places, there's everything from the achingly quaint family-run hotel, which is likely to have hardly changed in 50 years with wooden floorboards and antique furniture to the tired, polyester-duvet places that seem stuck in a more recent past. The latter types, while they may not be your first choice, can sometimes be found in good locations. There are also plenty of budget chain hotels, such as Budget Ibis or Formule 1, few of which have made it into this book, often at the edges of town—all right in a pinch, but not great to base a holiday from. For the very lowest budgets, there are also youth hostels, where for around €15-20 you'll be able to get a bed in a dorm for the night. Hostels are not, however, massively prevalent through Normandy and Brittany, only reliably cropping up in larger cities. In the countryside and even small towns, budget travelers are better off searching for municipal campsites.

In the midrange, you can be a little more certain of quality. Don't expect too much by way of climate control or insulation, as independent midrange hotels are frequently located in old buildings, and given the generally cool climate of Normandy and Brittany, air-conditioning is seldom among their priorities. Should you want a more reliable experience, there are also plenty of midrange chain hotels throughout both Normandy and Brittany, belonging to groups such as Mercure or Ibis. What these lack in local character they make up for in well-insulated comfort, and many have on-site gyms and swimming pools.

Top-end hotels might take the form of anything from renovated châteaus to seaside resorts. Some trade on the two regions' heritage as a place of rejuvenation: Thalassotherapy, or seawater treatment, is the star factor at their on-site spas. Among the number of these top-end places are the famed Barrière hotels, originating in the early 1900s and instrumental to the formation of resort towns such as Deauville and La Baule.

A very general rule with hotels in both Normandy and Brittany: For obvious reasons, you're likely to get more bang for your buck in inland destinations. Expect to have to pay a small additional charge for breakfast in most (but not all) hotels. This will usually be of the continental variety—croissants, French bread, and jam. If the establishment has onsite parking, however, it will almost inevitably come included in the overall price.

CAMPSITES

It's a little-known fact in the outside world, but camping is a major French institution. Every year, particularly during the months of July and August, the good people of French cities and towns flock to the countryside to spend several weeks under either canvas or the roof of their very own motor home, with many returning to the same campsite year after year.

While Normandy is a popular destination for this kind of holiday, Brittany is a veritable mecca. As such, campsites great and small dot the coastlines of both regions with an almost alarming regularity. Some are utterly spectacular, with beautiful views, sparkling facilities, and a pervasive sense of calm. Others are more like miniature theme parks, with elaborate waterslides, game rooms, and entertainment evenings. Others still are incredibly basic, but nevertheless a godsend to the true budget travel, where a night under canvas can cost less than €10.

The fastest way of telling them apart at a glance is via their star system. The five-star options are the most elaborate, practically small cities, often favored most of all by returning families in need of something to occupy their kids while they barbecue and drink local cider to their hearts' content. Truth be told, such places are unlikely to offer much to most international travelers, unless they've strong language skills and a real desire to throw themselves into the French tourist community. It's better to search instead for the places sold on their location, where joining in is more an option than an obligation. These tend to be three stars.

Also, don't immediately assume that because it's a campsite a stay there is going to mean camping. Yes, at the cheap end there will always be room for pitching your own tent, but many such locations come complete with prefab cabins, often with cooking equipment and toilets attached. These are generally rented by the week rather than the night, and can be an excellent budget option from which to base an entire holiday. Keep in mind, though, thanks to the aforementioned French obsession with camping, many such places book up early—sometimes as much as a year in advance. So, if this is how you want to spend your holiday, be prepared to plan way ahead.

When searching for campsites at the least expensive end, keep an eye out for signs for "Camping Municipal." These can be found in what can sometimes seem like every village in Normandy and Brittany. They don't come with much, but they are cheap, and there are usually basic facilities on-site like showers and toilet blocks—which means you'll leave them washed and rested, if nothing else! Sometimes you can luck out and find them in very good locations: see the sites in Paimpol and on the Île d'Ouessant as examples.

Food

With some of the best fishing and farmland in France, it's worth coming to Normandy and Brittany for the food alone. Some of the best restaurants in the whole country can be found here, many in unassuming rural locations. They range from ultra-traditional, where the food comes rich as a king, to supermodern restaurants specializing in inventive dishes, twisting old flavors into brand-new forms. Often as not, though, they are united by local produce, the highlights of which are listed below.

In general, there's a healthy crossover between Norman and Breton cuisines. As a vague guide, though, the former tends more toward the formal sophistication of sauces, while the latter leaves the produce to speak for itself. However, there are plenty of exceptions to this in both regions. Brittany and Normandy have long been in a dialogue, after all.

DAIRY

Brittany and Normandy are both lands of well-watered pastures home to legions of cattle, ruminating gently in the sea-salt wind and responsible for some of the tastiest **milk** and **cream** anywhere in the world. The latter of these is a fixture of countless sauces throughout both regions, often used to accompany white fish or in seafood dishes such as *moules a la crème* (mussels with cream). In Brittany, meanwhile, the former is famously churned to **butter,** which the Bretons are able to use their rich salt deposits to preserve. Norman **cheese,** then, is a perfect example of the phrase "necessity is the mother of invention," for lacking such a plentiful supply of salt the Normans had to turn to other means of preserving their dairy produce. This resulted in a veritable museum of culture and the development of world-renowned cheeses such as the tangy **camembert,** the almost fluffy, goat's cheese-like **Neufchâtel** (often sculpted into the shape of a heart), and the pungent, springy-textured **Livarot.**

SEAFOOD

Seafood is an essential element of both regions' terroir (the French term for the character of the land and the kind of food it produces) and almost as notable a feature of their coastal vistas as their plates, with farms and trawlers a near-constant sight on any seaward horizon. While the same basic ingredients appear in both regions, Normandy is perhaps marginally more famous for its **mussels,** or *moules,* which usually come served in either a garlic or cream sauce. The region is also known for its delicious ***marmite Dieppoise,*** a saffron-flavored fish and seafood stew from Dieppe, which hearkens back to the town's heyday as a key port for the spice trade. Breton seafood dishes tend to be saltier and more elemental, including **oysters,** which are eaten raw with just a dash of vinegar or lemon, and even **seaweed** regularly on the menu. A willingness to let good seafood ingredients stand on their own, often with no cooking in their preparation, sees a lot of Breton restaurants taking on Japanese influences—some of the best sushi in all of France can be found here.

Scallops, too, are found in both regions and come served in all manner of ways—flambéed in Calvados, poached in cream, or just lightly fried in butter—and all preparations are just as delicious. The real showstopping dish in seafood restaurants from Dieppe to Brest, though, is the ***fruits de mer.*** This cornucopia of denizens of the deep is served cold, usually with a **crab** as its centerpiece, surrounded by whelks, winkles, langoustine, shrimp, and oysters. Glistening and grand, it's a work of art straight from the natural world, a feast that is as much about ritual as it is flavor: from the initial presentation of it in the restaurant, inevitably catching the eye of other diners, to the slow, studied way it is eaten, requiring a veritable surgeon's table of instruments and a practiced hand. A first time with this dish is bound to be a game of trial and error, and some of its rewards are an acquired taste, but waitstaff are bound to applaud your attempt.

Also keep an eye out for ***soupe de poisson,*** the fish and shellfish soup served by most self-respecting Breton and Norman restaurants. Rich in flavor, though subtly different wherever you have it, it comes with croutons, mayonnaise, and grated cheese, which you are expected to assemble and set afloat in the dish, like tiny vessels of flavor.

CREPES

These savory pancakes, whose main ingredient, buckwheat, prospers in Brittany's acidic, low-fertility soils, have been a cheap food staple of the region for centuries. The most basic savory crepes are served with a fresh fried egg, ham, and liberal gratings of Swiss cheese, but this is truly just the thin end of the wedge. Across Brittany, crepes serve as the base for dishes of impressive complexity, often leaning on other local flavors. Scallop crepes are an excellent example of this.

DRINKS

Cider, the golden, apple-based alcohol, which is served fizzy and comes in both sweet and dry varieties, has been ubiquitous in both Normandy and Brittany for millennia. The orchards from which it's cultivated are an essential feature of their landscape. In Normandy, these apples are also used to make **Calvados,** a powerful brandy to round off heavy meals or served between courses, poured over sorbet as dishes called *le trou normand* (literally "a Norman hole"), aiding digestion and allowing the diner to make more space for the food to come.

Beer is also a more popular drink here than it is in the rest of France, with local breweries producing richly flavored hoppy drinks found in both regions—though there are more in Brittany. Be aware, however, that in the great majority of bars, you're likely to get only a small selection of low-quality international brands.

And an entry on the drinks of any regions in France would hardly be complete without a mention of **wine.** Normandy and Brittany are not traditional wine-producing regions, but that doesn't mean that the beverage is not consumed here. What could go better, after all, with a plate of traditional Norman cheese? The closest vineyards are in the Loire Valley, east of Nantes.

SET MENUS

Eating out most places in France is still considered something of an event, and it's usually expected that you sit down for several courses rather than just one. With this in mind, the huge majority of restaurants in both Normandy and Brittany offer set menus, from which you can combine a starter, main, and desert at a lower cost than you might ordering "a la carte" off the rest of the menu. The more indulgent of these also include a cheese course between main and desert—which to get maximum benefit from, you should try to save a little red wine to drink alongside. Throughout this book, pricing for most restaurants has been given with regard to these set menus, as they are what most people will order, offer the best deals, and are usually made from the freshest ingredients. They will also tend to include the "plat du jour," a dish that changes every day, often based on what is available at the market and seasonality. Set menus do not, unless otherwise stated, include drinks.

Conduct and Customs

Though by and large the Normans and particularly the Bretons are easygoing people, there are a few aspects of their cultures foreign visitors would do well to keep in mind in order to make the best impression.

RESTAURANT ETIQUETTE

Food is taken seriously here, and even at the smaller, less fancy restaurants, the chefs consider themselves artists. Travelers should not be surprised if asking for additional condiments or even precise dietary requests elicit confusion or mild rudeness from waiters. This remains especially true in less touristy areas.

CLOTHING

Some, though not all, restaurants, even those in seaside communities, may expect a certain formality of dress from customers—no shorts or beachwear. This has become less rigidly enforced in recent years, but nevertheless is still worth staying sensitive to. Attitudes toward public nudity on the beach, however, tend to be more relaxed than in most English-speaking countries, so do not be surprised to see women sunbathing topless.

BRETON CELTIC PRIDE

Though there are few serious demands for independence, many Bretons consider themselves culturally distinct from the rest of France, and certainly from Normandy. It's important to stay aware of this, particularly if attending cultural events such as *festoù-noz.*

LANGUAGE

The French tend to be prouder of their language than many other nations, meaning that visitors learning a few choice phrases, especially the basics of *merci* and *bonjour,* is greatly appreciated.

Health and Safety

Broadly speaking, Normandy and Brittany are very safe regions, particularly with regard to violent crime. However, there are several dangers to watch out for

TICKS

On account of deer in the two regions' large tracts of woodland and livestock raised in their fields, Lyme disease-carrying ticks are a very real concern for anyone spending an extended time outside. Vigilance, and frequent checking, is essential.

LIVESTOCK

Cows famously are responsible for more human deaths than any other large animal. Of course, the huge majority of bovine encounters pass without incident. But both regions are home to very large numbers of cattle, and it pays to be careful in their presence.

COLLAPSING CHALK CLIFFS

The chalk cliffs of the Alabaster Coast are liable to partial collapse. Keep a safe distance from them when on the beach, and don't approach their edges when looking from their heights.

TIDES

At several points along the coast of both regions there is an extensive tidal reach, which shortens with speed, and can easily trap the unsuspecting beachgoer. The area around Mont-Saint-Michel is most famous for this, but there are few coastal areas that are entirely exempt. To make matters worse, the threat of such conditions is not always clearly announced on the beaches themselves. It's best to check for such dangers with hotel staff or at tourist offices, and consult a tide chart before planning any beach excursions.

THE ATLANTIC

The wild fronds of Finistère reach out into the ocean, where conditions can fast grow significantly more intense than in the comparatively sheltered English Channel farther down the coast. Swimmers, surfers, and sailors should keep this in mind.

Practical Details

WHAT TO PACK

Normandy and Brittany are renowned for their capacity to experience all four seasons in one day, and with that in mind, it's only mild hyperbole to say that visitors to both regions should pack clothes appropriate for all weather whatever time of year they're traveling. Sure, you can probably afford to leave the T-shirt at home in the middle of winter and your heavy overcoat in summer, but decent and easily transportable **waterproofs** are an absolute must. An **umbrella** and **sunscreen** (that coastal sun can be deceptively vicious) are also highly advised. French electrical outlets take round, two-prong plugs, so you will want to bring an **adapter** or two for your devices. Many modern electronics can accommodate both U.S. voltage (110-120V) and European voltage (220-240V), but be sure to check your power supply before leaving to be sure. (Hairdryers are a common casualty of this difference.)

Apart from that, it really depends on the kind of holiday you're planning on having here. For those after beaches, pack swimming gear; for those interested in walking, sensible shoes. For people on a gastronomic tour, meanwhile, a belt with plenty of extra notches wouldn't go awry—it's also worth keeping in mind that many restaurants can be quite formal, so some smart clothes are a good idea if you want to blend in.

If you're driving your own car, make sure it has both a brightly colored, high visibility vest (recently made famous by the *gilet jaunes* movement) and a warning triangle—a free-standing reflective sign, which you can erect beside your car in the event of a breakdown: Both of these are required by law for those driving French roads. They can be picked up at practically all service stations.

In general, though, don't stress too much about packing everything you could possibly need before departure; both Normandy and Brittany are prosperous places, meaning anything you forget can always be picked up in situ. This is particularly the case for beach toys, which are copiously available anywhere that has even the sniff of the sea.

MONEY

Currency Exchange and Exchange Rates

France, along with 18 other European nations, uses the euro. Be aware that the United Kingdom is not among these. Currency can be exchanged at Bureau de Changes, which can be found in some major towns, though are no longer especially common across the region. They are still present, however, on cross-channel ferries.

Below is a list of the euro's exchange rates with several major currencies, though do keep in mind that these can be volatile.

- 1 euro (€) = 1.14 US dollar ($)
- 1 euro (€) = 0.90 Great British pound (£)
- 1 euro (€) = 1.56 Canadian dollar (CAD)
- 1 euro (€) = 1.62 Australian dollar (AUSD)
- 1 euro (€) = 1.71 New Zealand dollar (NZD)
- 1 euro (€) = 16.51 South African rand (ZAR)

Credit Cards and ATMs

ATMs compatible with foreign cards are plentiful throughout Normandy and Brittany, even in rural areas. Most will let you choose the language you want to proceed in at the start of the transaction. Making a withdrawal at an ATM is one of the easier ways to access euros in cash—and one of the most economical, even with the fees often charged by your bank and the ATM's bank.

Paying with a credit card at restaurants, cafés, and shops, and at museums and other attractions, is possible for the most part, albeit usually only above a certain amount (usually €5-10). Rural France is a long way from fully embracing a cashless economy, meaning it's still worth checking on payment options before you sit down to eat, but this could of course change in the future. If you have a choice to pay in euros or the currency in your home country, know that you may pay more if you choose your home currency, due to fees or a less favourable exchange rate.

Also note that while Visa and MasterCard are widely accepted, American Express is less so. And if your credit card has a PIN, you should try to memorize it before leaving—although most transactions will go through a signature, you never know when you will need it.

COMMUNICATIONS

Phones and Cell Phones

The international dialing code for France is 0033, which you will have to key in at the start of all numbers, as well as dropping their first 0 if you're dialing from abroad or a foreign phone. Should you be calling from a French phone, disregard the +33. As you will see in this book, Normandy and Brittany landline numbers start with 02, while French mobile numbers begin with either 06 or 07.

Your mobile should link automatically to local carriers, although beware of international data roaming charges if you don't have an international plan.

France uses the same emergency telephone number as the rest of the European Union, **112.** This connects you to an operator linked to police, fire, and ambulance services. However, the old emergency numbers of **15** for urgent medical calls, **17** for the police, and **18** for Pompiers (who are both firefighters and a paramedic service) are still in use.

Internet Access

The Internet in Normandy and Brittany is not quite yet the ubiquitous resource that it is in much of the rest of the western world. Most hotels will have WiFi, but for the less expensive ones it seldom feels like their first priority, and if you're on the top floor, say, you might find yourself too far from the router for it to count. Likewise, a lot of cafés and restaurants will shrug their shoulders and keep their WiFi passwords to themselves. It's not that the technology hasn't made it here; more that the culture is not geared toward the opening of laptops in restaurants or flicking through your phone at a bar.

All this being said, there are eating establishments where you *can* find WiFi access, but they probably account for less than half the total. If you're desperate to get online, make sure to confirm the WiFi password with the waitstaff, and that the system works, before you order.

Shipping and Postal Service

The French postal service, *La Poste*, with its bright yellow and blue branding, is evident throughout Normandy and Brittany. All medium-size towns will have at least one post office, and post boxes are everywhere and frequently emptied. Note that despite being a nationally run institution, opening hours for post offices can be idiosyncratic, differing from town to town. They're also frequently closed for lunch.

Inside the post office can feel intimidating at first, and post office staff are unlikely to speak much English, but there's also a well-designed, color-coded system at hand to help you select the size and weight of parcel and speed of delivery you're after. Provided you persevere, you should be fine.

You can buy stamps from post offices, but also from *tabacs* and newsagents (the shops with *Presse* written over the door). Stamps to send mail within France cost €0.88 each, to the rest of Europe €1.20, and to the United States €1.30.

OPENING HOURS

Once famous for their obstinacy when it came to opening hours, the French have recently been drawing more in line with consumer demands. Thus, the days of towns being entirely dead on Sundays or wholly closing their shutters for lunch are coming to be things of the past.

Such trends do persist in some parts, however, especially in more rural areas. At the very least, Sundays see reduced opening hours for most business concerns, including big supermarkets, so make sure to keep aware of what is and what isn't going to be open before venturing forth. Note that Mondays, too, tend to have reduced opening hours.

When it comes to eating, meanwhile, most restaurants keep fairly strict mealtime hours, with comparatively few having open all-day kitchens. As a very general rule, you can order lunch 12pm-1:30pm and dinner 7:30pm-9:30pm. These times tend to be more lax in bigger towns, and rigidly adhered to in the countryside: Don't casually expect a rural restaurant to serve you lunch if you turn up 15 minutes later than their last serving, and know that if they do, they are doing you a favor!

PUBLIC HOLIDAYS

The official public holidays in Normandy and Brittany are the same as they are in the rest of France (note the large number in May). These often lead to French people planning work holidays in between them, meaning beaches can be busy and some shops not open in this time. There's also a big tradition of pausing work for much of August. Tourists sights stay open—it's their high season, after all—but many of the cities clear out.

- **New Year's Day:** January 1
- **Easter Monday:** Between mid-March and mid-April (date varies)
- **Labor Day:** May 1
- **Victory in Europe Day:** May 8
- **Ascension Day:** Between April 30 and June 3 (date varies)
- **Whit Monday** Between May 11 and June 14 (date varies)
- **Bastille Day:** July 14
- **Assumption of the Blessed Virgin Mary:** August 15
- **All Saints' Day:** November 1
- **Armistice Day:** November 11
- **Christmas Day:** December 25

WEIGHTS AND MEASURES

France uses the metric system, which is altogether easier to get to grips with quickly than imperial measurements, with every quantity being divisible by 10 and certain measures linking up across categories. For example, one liter of water is exactly a kilogram. Note that all road signs deal in kilometers. Below is a conversion chart.

1 kilogram (1,000 grams) = 2.2 lbs
1 kilometer (1,000 meters) = 0.62 miles
1 liter (1,000 milliliters) = 2.1 pints
10 degrees Celsius = 50 degrees Fahrenheit

TOURIST INFORMATION

Tourist Offices

France has been in the tourist game for a long time and has an extensive system of tourist offices to prove it. Rare indeed is the town or village that does not have one, for they exist across both the macro and micro level. Tourism in France is organized rather like its government, with an overarching general tourist office, then underneath that, ones dedicated to each of its regions, such as Normandy (www.normandy-tourism.org) and Brittany (www.brittanytourism.com), and underneath them, offices dedicated to individual departments:

NORMANDY

- **Calvados:** www.calvados-tourisme.com
- **Eure:** www.eure-tourisme.fr
- **Manche:** www.manchetourisme.com
- **l'Orne:** www.ornetourisme.com
- **Seine-Maritime:** www.seine-maritime-tourisme.com

BRITTANY

- **Morbihan:** www.morbihan-tourism.co.uk
- **Finistère:** www.finisterebrittany.com
- **Côte d'Amour:** www.macotedamour.com
- **Ille-et-Vilaine:** www.bretagne35.com

Below these still are tourist offices for individual towns, villages, or definable tourist regions. These have physical outlets, which can be visited when you first arrive in a place for advice and assistance on spending your holiday, and for picking up often necessary local maps to help navigate between points of interest. English is almost universally spoken in these offices. To find them, look for the *Office de Tourisme* sign.

Entrance Fees

There is a wide variety of entrance fee prices for sights and attractions across Normandy and Brittany, with little in the way of standardization as to who is eligible for reduced ticket price. In this book, if reduced prices are purely a question of age then those ages have been listed. If there are several factors that may qualify for a reduction (for example, being a student, coming from an E.U. country, being a pensioner), then said price has been given simply as "reduced," and you should consult the listing website for further details or ask before paying.

One quite common reduction, usually on the bigger, government-funded attractions, is to offer free entry for E.U. citizens under the age of 26. If this includes you, it obviously pays to keep an eye out for this excellent deal.

Several sights also offer group reductions, which can be worth enquiring about if there are a number of you visiting at one time.

Maps

France is an incredibly well-mapped country. For road maps, the gold standard are those by Michelin, which can be found in service stations and bookshops across both Normandy and Brittany. For hiking, look for publications by the FFRP (Fédération Française de la Randonnée Pédestre). They bring out guides outlining all of the GR hiking routes, complete with detailed maps. These can usually be found in bookshops or service stations close to the trail that they are outlining, or can be ordered online before departure.

For finding your way around towns or small areas, there are usually plenty of small-scale maps on bus stops or signs around town. Tourist offices will also be able to provide maps of the area that highlight top sights and attractions.

Traveler Advice

OPPORTUNITIES FOR STUDY AND EMPLOYMENT

This is a big subject, and if you're serious about pursuing study or employment in Normandy or Brittany, there are plenty of books on the market or websites such as www.goabroad.com or www.transitionsabroad.com that can help you.

There are many universities and higher-education institutions across the two regions, including those in Caen, Rouen, and Rennes. Many of these run exchange programs and accept international students. Note that French universities are almost unimaginably cheaper than U.S. institutions and considerably less than U.K. universities, even for students from abroad. Most courses, though, will of course be taught in French.

Regarding work, keep in mind that this is much easier if you're from an E.U.-member state, which grants you the automatic right to employment in France. If you're from outside that block, things become trickier, and you'll have to apply for a work permit. If you're between 18 and 30, though, it's worth checking to see if your country has an agreement with France to grant a working holiday visa.

ACCESS FOR TRAVELERS WITH DISABILITIES

Though improvements have been made in recent years, France as a whole remains a destination only halfway geared to catering for travelers with disabilities. One significant reason for this is simply the lay of the land itself. Many towns in Normandy and Brittany have been built over medieval bones, with winding, cobbled streets and narrow stairways that are almost impossible to fix ramps to, and which are still waiting for lifts. Saint-Malo is a clear example of this, and even much of Mont-Saint-Michel is off limits for people with reduced mobility.

Nevertheless, investment and changes in the law do now mean that all hotels are required to adapt at least one room to be wheelchair accessible, taxi drivers are under legal obligation to assist you in and out of their vehicles, and the majority of SNCF train stations offer assistance to disabled travelers. Planning ahead is still the best way to go, however, contacting individual tourist offices to best work out what is available in any particular area. Most museums are disability-friendly.

In terms of getting to the regions, most transport companies will offer assistance and reserve spaces for disabled passengers. If you're coming from the United Kingdom, by far and away the most practical method, provided you have your own transport, is the Eurotunnel, given there's no obligation to get out of your vehicle.

APF, the French paraplegic organization (www.paratetra.apf.asso.fr), is the one of the best resources on the facilities available for disabled travelers around the country.

TRAVELING WITH CHILDREN

Normandy and Brittany are both excellent destinations if you're traveling with children. A large number of their top sights offer plenty of interactive, kid-friendly displays, from the touch tanks of Oceanopolis to simulations of parachute jumps on the D-Day beaches. Places like Mont-Saint-Michel, Saint-Malo, and the Paimpont Forest, meanwhile, are bound to set imaginations on fire for any kid who's ever pretended to be a knight in the age of chivalry or has watched *Lord of the Rings*!

More directly for kids, there are the beaches, with most water-sport centers offering courses for ages three and up, and a variety of theme parks across both regions—they might not be Disneyland, but they'll certainly keep eight-year-olds entertained for a few hours.

On the downside, the formality of some restaurants is not immediately suitable for all kids, and waiters may cast snooty looks if yours are thought to misbehave. This is certainly not true everywhere, but it does make it prudent to do some research before booking a table.

If you're really keen on building your holiday around your kids, then you could do far worse in Normandy and Brittany than booking into a top-end campsite. These places come with water parks, activities, and entertainment all included on-site, though your kids will have to be OK joining in with French children.

WOMEN TRAVELING ALONE

France is generally a safe country for solo women travelers—as far as any country can be, at least. Though it's worth keeping in mind that cat-calling, despite recent laws against it (indeed, women's rights are generally well protected in France), can be more prevalent than it is in Anglo-Saxon nations. Also, there is a strong "chat up" culture here, meaning a woman sitting alone in a bar is almost certain to be approached. This can seem aggressively forward to women traveling from the United Kingdom or United States, but it has a strong ritual element to it, and there's seldom any offense taken from resisting these advances.

SENIOR TRAVELERS

Normandy and Brittany represent popular destinations for senior travelers. There's a generally gentle pace of life here, plenty of sights likely to appeal to older tastes, and tour companies with their own transport for getting you from place to place. There are only two elements to watch out for here: First, that several sights require quite a lot of walking to do full justice to, whether this be Mont-Saint-Michel, Étretat, or some of Brittany's islands. True, the physical effort required is seldom excessive, but it pays not to be too ambitious and try to accomplish too much in a single day. Second, Breton and Norman food can be extremely rich: apple tart follows cheese follows cream in a number of dishes. This can prove trying on sensitive older stomachs, so be sure to know what you're taking on before you order.

LGBTQ TRAVELERS

Both Normandy and Brittany, like the rest of France, are laid-back in their attitudes toward sexuality and sexual relations, considering them a private matter. This means that LGBTQ travelers should not encounter aggravation, either in cities or tourist hot spots, where public displays of affection barely raise an eyebrow.

As is true around the world, more rural areas tend to be more conservative, meaning there may be some furtive muttering with regard to same-sex couples, though even here, most people would take more offense if you drank a coffee with your dinner than kissed your partner in public.

It's only really the larger cities, however, that have anything approaching an LGBTQ scene. For finding out more on this, the website www.gay-france.net is a good resource.

TRAVELERS OF COLOR

Normandy and Brittany are both relatively multicultural places and among two of the more liberal regions of France, where the days of overt racism are long gone. While it's true that people of color may find themselves in the minority in rural areas, hostility is rare. In some even less-visited, almost exclusively Caucasian areas, some sideways glances may be given by locals, but expect the majority of people to be pleasant and convivial.

Resources

Glossary

Below is a list of words that you're likely to see as you make your way through Normandy and Brittany: on menus, signposts, and so forth. The majority are in French, as these are the only terms you will really need to know, though there are also a handful in Breton, just to give you more idea of the names of some shops, festivals, and so on.

HOTEL

auberge de jeunesse: youth hostel
baignoire: bath
chambre: room
douche: shower
hôtel: hotel
laverie: laundry service
lit double: double bed
lit simple: single bed
réception: reception

AROUND TOWN

banque: bank
boulangerie: bakery
bureau de poste: post office
centre-ville: town center
église: church
gare: train station
hôpital: hospital
hotel de ville: town hall (note: *not* a hotel!)
marché: market
parc: park
pharmacie: pharmacy

ON THE ROAD

arrêt: stop
autoroute: highway
autre directions: other directions (literally, "all directions that are not otherwise signaled")
chaussée glissante: slippery road
diesel: diesel/gazole
essence: gas/petrol
passage piétons: pedestrian crossing
péage: toll road
ralentir: slow down
rappel: reminder (this is usually written under speed-limit signs)
sans plomb: unleaded
sens unique: one way
tout directions: all directions (when driving through a town, what this sign really means is "all directions that are not the town center")

EATING OUT

Restaurant Types

bistro: more casual and often less expensive than restaurants, usually serving a fairly narrow range of traditional French dishes: omelet, steak and fries, and (in Normandy and Brittany) *moules* (mussels)
brasserie: nowadays often interchangeable with *restaurant* or *bistro,* though technically referring to a brewery; there are some in Normandy and Brittany that still make their own beer, but it's certainly far from all
café: fairly interchangeable with the *bistro* or *brasserie,* though open for breakfast and often not dinner; drop in for a coffee at any time of day, though be prepared to be moved on if you're not eating around lunchtime
crêperie: a fairly cheap restaurant specializing in crepes

restaurant: a restaurant specializing in big meals and more formal dining

General Restaurant Terms

carte: menu
dégustation: tasting menu
déjeuner: lunch
dessert: dessert
dîner: dinner
entrées: appetizers
fromage: cheese
menu/formule: set menu
petit déjeuner: breakfast
plats: main courses

Food

crêpe jambon fromage: savory ham-and-cheese pancake
crêpe sucré: pancake with sugar (which often comes with butter as well)
crevettes: shrimp
escargots: snails
frites: fries
homard: lobster
huitres: oysters
legumes: vegetables
moules a la crème: mussels in cream sauce
moules mariniere: mussels in garlic and white wine sauce
pain: bread
poisson: fish
potage: soup
poulet: chicken
salade: salad
soupe de poisson: fish soup
steak: steak
steak haché: hamburger
tarte Normande: apple tart
torteau: crab
viande: meat

Drink

aprétif/apéro: pre-meal drink, often accompanied by light snacks
bière: beer
café: coffee
cidre: cider
jus: juice
thé: tea
vin blanc: white wine
vin rouge: red wine

BRETON WORDS

armor: sea
bran: hill
coat: forest
cromlech: stone circle
dolmen: stone table
ker: town
kreis ker: town center
penn: end
traez henn: beach
ty: house

French Phrasebook

PRONUNCIATION

For a lot of people in the English-speaking world, French is the first language they will be exposed to outside of their own, and coming to the country offers a great chance to dust off the basics of what was learned in school. Of course, French words are not pronounced the same way as they would be in English, and there are more sounds in French than there are letters in the Roman alphabet, but there is a consistency within the language and once you learn the ways in which individual letters should be said and how they can be combined to make new sounds, there are not going to be that many words that surprise you. In general, you pronounce all of a word's syllables as they appear (this is not a cast iron rule as it is in Spanish, say, but much more the case than it is in English).

Below is a general guide to how different letters are pronounced.

Vowels

a tends to be pronounced fairly short and sharp, somewhere between how it appears in "cat" and "bar." The sharpness is emphasized when it has a grave accent (à). It is also frequently seen with a circumflex (â), but this doesn't make much of a difference to how it is pronounced.

au is like the "o" sound in the British word "no"

e is usually short and sharp, like in "bet." It can also appear at the end of a word, often signifying the word is feminine. In this case, the "e" is left silent, but the final consonant becomes harder. When "e" appears with an acute accent (é), it means it should be pronounced more like in "way." This is the case if it appears at the end of a word as well, when it can indicate the past participle or adjective form of the verb. A grave accent or circumflex (è or ê) emphasizes the shortness, again like bet.

i is generally like "ee", as in "keep."

o this is either a close "o" sound as in "no," or as an open sound as in "rot." The former often appears with a circumflex (ô), the latter in syllables that end with a consonant, and always if the syllable ends in a double consonant.

oi is usually like a shortened version of the "aw" sound in the English word "squawk."

ou is a bit like the "oo" noise in the middle of the English word "food."

u is usually like the end of the English word "do".

Consonants

c pronounced "s" before "e," "i," or "y," pronounced "k" before "a," "o," or "u."

ç always pronounced "s" no matter what comes after it.

ch "sh," as in shut.

g before "e," "i," or "y," is pronounced soft, like the "g" in the word "message". Otherwise it's pronounced hard.

h not pronounced in French and is mostly treated as though it doesn't exist. *L'hôtel* (the hotel), for example, would be pronounced *l'ôtel.*

j pronounced like the "g" in the English word "message" wherever it appears.

ll mostly pronounced as an "ee" sound, though there are a couple of dozen words where this isn't the case and it's pronounced "l"—of these ville or village, meaning town or village are the ones you're most likely to encounter. It can also be pronounced like the "y" in "why," if preceded by two or more vowels.

qu mostly pronounced as a "k" sound, and only occasionally as a "kw" sound as it is in English, usually on Latinate words.

r a particularly tricky one to get perfect, not having an easy equivalent in English—it's probably most like the "ch" at the end of "loch" being mostly pronounced in the throat. It also has the ghost of a hard "r" in it, however. At the same time, don't sweat it too much: pronouncing it the English way, most French people will get what you mean.

s mostly pronounced in the same way as it is in English. However, when it appears at the end of a word making it plural, it's not pronounced, unless the word following begins in a vowel.

th pronounced like a hard "t."

w not a common letter in French apart from in imported words, with "website," or the neologism "wifi" being among the most likely ones you'll encounter. In those cases it's pronounced just like it is in English. Otherwise, the "w" sound is made at the beginning of words with an "ou," as in "oui," meaning "yes."

Tips

As much as reading how to speak the language can help, there's no substitute for time spent listening to it. Before you travel to Normandy and Brittany, it can be worth watching a few French films with subtitles, just to train your ear to the different sounds. If you're feeling particularly virtuous, try watching the French films with French subtitles, helping you to divide the sounds into different words. This is especially useful if you know already know the film well in English.

A final piece of advice: don't be afraid to really go for it! You know that exaggerated French accent you might put on when doing an impression of a French person speaking English? Use that when you speak French. It won't sound half as silly to the locals as you trying to pronounce their language in your own accent, and in fact, you're far more likely to be understood. Of course, make sure you are actually speaking French when you do this: saying "Pleaze caan ah 'ave ze bill," is not going to help anyone's comprehension.

PHRASES

Below is a very small selection of some key French phrases that may come in useful during your travels in Normandy and Brittany. Though in most places you should be able to get by with English, being able to use some of these is polite and will serve to ingratiate you with the locals.

General

Hello/Good day Bonjour
Hi Salut
Good-bye Au revoir
Have a nice day Bonne journée
Do you speak English? Parlez-vous anglais?
Please S'il vous plaît
Thank you Merci
Yes Oui
No Non
How are you? Comment allez-vous?
I would like... Je voudrais...
I want Je veux
Sorry Pardon
Where is the beach? Où est la plage?
I'm looking for... Je cherche...
Straight ahead Tout droit
To the left À gauche
To the right À droit
Where is the restroom? Où sont les toilettes?
I don't understand. Je ne comprends pas.
Speak slower Parlez plus lentement
How do you say "I'm just visiting" in French? Comment dit-on "I'm just visiting" en francais?
I'm just visiting. Je viens de visiter.
How much is it? C'est combien?
To pay Payer

Food

A table for two/three/four... Une table pour deux / trois / quatre...
Do you have a menu in English? Avez-vous un menu en anglais?
I'm/We're ready to order. Je suis / nous sommes prêts à commander.
I'm a vegetarian. Je suis un végétarien.
I can't eat shrimp. Je ne peux pas manger les crevettes.
gluten-free sans gluten
some water de l'eau
the check l'addition

Health

drugstore pharmacie
pain douleur
fever fièvre
headache mal de tête
stomachache maux d'estomac
toothache mal aux dents
cramp crampe
nausea la nausée
vomiting vomissement
medicine médicament
antibiotic antibiotique
pill/tablet pilule/comprimé
aspirin aspirine
I need to see a doctor. J'ai besoin de voir un médecin.
I need to go to the hospital. Je dois aller à l'hôpital.
I have a pain here... J'ai mal ici...
She/he has been stung/bitten. Elle/il a été piqué/mordu.
I am diabetic/pregnant. Je suis diabétique/enceinte.
I am allergic to penicillin/cortisone. Je suis allergique à la pénicilline/cortisone.

My blood group is…positive/negative. Mon groupe sanguin est… positif/négatif.

Numbers

0 zéro
1 un
2 deux
3 trois
4 quatre
5 cinq
6 six
7 sept
8 huit
9 neuf
10 dix
11 onze
12 douze
13 treize
14 quatorze
15 quinze
16 seize
17 dix-sept
18 dix-huit
19 dix-neuf
20 vingt
21 vingt et un
30 trente
40 quarante
50 cinquante
60 soixante
70 soixante-dix
80 quatre-vingts
90 quatre-vingt-dix
100 cent
101 cent un
200 deux cents
500 cinq cents
1,000 mille
10,000 dix mille
100,000 cent mille
1,000,000 million

Time

What time is it? Quelle heure est-il?
It's one/three o'clock. C'est une heure/ trois heures.
midday midi
midnight minuit
morning matin
afternoon après-midi
evening soir
night nuit
yesterday hier
today aujourd'hui
tomorrow demain

Days and Months

week semaine
month mois
Monday lundi
Tuesday mardi
Wednesday mercredi
Thursday jeudi
Friday vendredi
Saturday samedi
Sunday dimanche
January janvier
February fevrier
March mars
April avril
May mai
June juin
July juillet
August août
September septembre
October octobre
November novembre
December decembre

Suggested Reading

FICTION

Bradley, Marion Zimmer. *Mists of Avalon.* Tells the Arthurian story through the eyes of women at his court.

de Maupassant, Guy. *Normandy Stories.* Flaubert's protégé, de Maupassant is a master short-story writer, and this collection groups together tales of the author's native land.

Doerr, Anthony. *All the Light We Cannot See.* A Pulitzer Prize-winning book set partly in Nazi-occupied Saint-Malo.

Elkins, Aaron. *Old Bones.* A mystery taking place in and around Mont-Saint-Michel.

Flaubert, Gustave. *Madame Bovary.* Flaubert is considered among the greatest writers of literary realism to ever live. Set in the countryside around Rouen, this book, which scandalized the French public when it was published in 1856, tells the story of the infidelities and excesses of the title character as she tries to escape the banality of provincial life.

Malory, Thomas. *Le Morte D'Arthur.* The most famous work of literature about King Arthur and his knights, telling the classic stories about Lancelot, Guinevere, and the Holy Grail.

Simmonds, Posy. *Gemma Bovary.* A graphic novel that is a modern update of Flaubert's most famous work.

Verne, Jules. *20,000 Leagues Under the Sea* A book written by one of Brittany's most famous sons. Though not about the peninsula, the clear fascination with and respect for the sea that comes from its pages could hardly be more Breton.

HISTORY

Ambrose, Stephen E. *Band of Brothers.* An up close and personal history of the D-Day Landings and subsequent Battle of Normandy, following a particular U.S. parachute company's experience of the campaign, turned into the famous HBO series of the same name.

Balkoski, Joseph. *From Beachhead to Brittany.* A good history of the liberation of the peninsula.

Beevor, Anthony. *D-Day.* A more recent and historically in depth description of D-Day and its surrounding events. Also engagingly written.

Butler, Mildred Allen. *Twice Queen of France.* A fascinating insight into Breton history and the region's tussle with independence, focusing on Anne of Brittany.

Castor, Helen. *Joan of Arc: A History.* A manageable biography, concentrating only on the end of the war.

Howarth, David. *1066: The Year of the Conquest.* A history of the Norman conquests.

Robb, Graham. *The Discovery of France.* An overview of French history.

Ryan, Cornelius. *The Longest Day.* Among the best known and most lively retellings of the events of D-Day from multiple perspectives, later turned into the famous film of the same name.

Sumption, Jonathon: *The Hundred Years' War.* A history of the title war.

TRAVELOGUE AND MEMOIR

Fedden, Robin. *Chantemesle.* A lyrical evocation of a Normandy childhood.

Fermor, Patrick Leigh. *A Time to Keep Silence.* An excellent short chronicle of the author's time spent staying in French monasteries, including several in the Norman countryside.

Greenside, Mark. *I'll Never Be French (No Matter What I Do).* A book about the American author's experience of moving to a village in Brittany.

Kerouac, Jack. *Satori in Paris.* Tells the story of a road trip the author took to Brest to discover his roots.

Internet Resources

ACCOMMODATIONS

AIRBNB

www.airbnb.fr

Tending to offer cheaper and self-catering options, this website lets travelers stay in private homes.

BOOKING.COM

www.booking.com

A massively comprehensive website offering good deals on hotels, guesthouses, and B&Bs, which makes it easy to compare prices.

GÎTES DE FRANCE

www.gites-de-france.com/en

A mark of quality, linking travelers up with holiday home rentals and guesthouses across both regions.

LOGIS DE FRANCE

www.logishotels.com/en/

A federation of trustworthy midrange hotels across France and an institution of midrange travel in the country for the past 70 years.

HIKING

FFRANDONNÉE

www.ffrandonnee.fr

An extensive website informing hikers of all the major walking routes around France, from which you can download maps and order guides.

TIDES

TIDESCHART

www.tideschart.com

Tides are an important consideration for visiting a number of sights in Normandy and Brittany, and you can check low and high tide times here.

TRANSPORTATION

BUS VERTS

www.busverts.fr

One of the more extensive local bus services linking up the Calvados region.

FLIXBUS/OUIBUS

www.flixbus.com/www.ouibus.com

France's two main intercity coach services. The latter is a subsidiary of France's national rail network.

SNCF

www.sncf.com/fr

France's national rail service, for information about all train journeys around both regions and more.

TRAINLINE

www.thetrainline.com

A price-comparison website for train and coach journeys around France and beyond.

MEDIA

OUEST FRANCE

www.ouest-france.fr

A newspaper covering both local and national news, available in Brittany and lower Normandy.

PARIS NORMANDIE

www.paris-normandie.fr

The local newspaper for the Haute-Normandie region.

THE LOCAL

www.thelocal.fr

A useful resource, aggregating local French news in English.

LGBT COMMUNITY

FÉDÉRATION LGBT

http://federation-lgbt.org

A list of LGBT communities and their activities around France.

GAYVIKING

www.gayviking.com

A more informal site, focused mainly on LGBT activities in Normandy.

Index

D

E

F

G

H

N

O

P

QR

S

T

UV

WY

List of Maps

Front Map

Discover Normandy and Brittany

Giverny, Rouen, and the "Impressionist Coast"

Caen, Bayeux, and the D-Day Landing Beaches

Mont-Saint-Michel and West Cotentin

Saint-Malo and the North Coast

Finistère

Gulf of Morbihan

Nantes and Inland Brittany

Photo Credits

All interior photos © Chris Newens except: title page photo: © frederic hodiesne | dreamstime.com; page 6 (top left) © elenathewise | dreamstime.com; page 10 © jef wodniack | dreamstime.com; page 13 (top) © enrico della pietra | dreamstime.com; (bottom) © kateryna levchenko | dreamstime.com; page 14 (bottom) © jorisvo | dreamstime.com; page 16 © tatsiana hendzel | dreamstime.com; page 17 (top) © mike wakely | dreamstime.com; (bottom) © prillfoto | dreamstime.com; page 18 © plotnikov | dreamstime.com; page 19 (top) © matteo ceruti | dreamstime.com; (bottom) © jef wodniack | dreamstime.com; page 21 © photoprofi30 | dreamstime.com; page 24 © prillfoto | dreamstime.com; page 29 © rosshelen | dreamstime.com; page 30 © rosaline napier | dreamstime.com; page 35 © dmitry shishkin | dreamstime.com; page 47 (top right) © dmitry shishkin | dreamstime.com; (bottom) © fondation claude monet giverny - droits réservés; page 55 (top) © marius godoi | dreamstime.com; (bottom) © claudio giovanni colombo | dreamstime.com; page 59 © jorisvo | dreamstime.com; page 83 © philippehalle | dreamstime.com; page 104 (top left) © arndale | dreamstime.com; page 145 (top) © jorisvo | dreamstime.com; page 226 © vladimir zhuravlev | dreamstime.com; page 237 (left middle) © boris breytman | dreamstime.com; page 254 (bottom) © prillfoto | dreamstime.com; page 286 © saintho | dreamstime.com; page 294 (bottom) © dolby1985 | dreamstime.com; page 310 (top) © jakezc | dreamstime.com; (bottom) © saintho | dreamstime.com; page 321 (top) © franfoto | dreamstime.com; (bottom) © saintho | dreamstime.com; page 330 (top) © giuseppemasci | dreamstime.com; (bottom) © navarroraph | dreamstime.com; page 335 © musat christian | dreamstime.com; page 346 (top) © dennisvdwater | dreamstime.com; (bottom) © calinat | dreamstime.com; page 355 (top) © musat | dreamstime.com; (bottom) © cyrnam | dreamstime.com; page 360 © petunyia | dreamstime.com; page 365 (top) © amidala76 | dreamstime.com; (bottom) © aagje de jong | dreamstime.com; page 376 (top) © calinat | dreamstime.com; (bottom) © elenathewise | dreamstime.com; page 392 (top left) © maxironwas | dreamstime.com; (top right) © allouphoto | dreamstime.com; (bottom) © daliu80 | dreamstime.com; page 398 © rosshelen | dreamstime; page 412 (top) © daliu80 | dreamstime.com; (bottom) © dutourdumonde | dreamstime.com; page 422 © ed francissen | dreamstime.com; page 428 (top) © mailland tom | dreamstime.com; (bottom) © ed francissen | dreamstime.com; page 447 © stefano valeri | dreamstime.com; page 463 © tilo | dreamstime.com

MAP SYMBOLS

- Expressway
- Primary Road
- Secondary Road
- Unpaved Road
- Trail
- Ferry
- Railroad
- Pedestrian Walkway
- Stairs
- City/Town
- State Capital
- National Capital
- Highlight
- Point of Interest
- Accommodation
- Restaurant/Bar
- Other Location
- Information Center
- Parking Area
- Church
- Winery
- Trailhead
- Train Station
- Airport
- Airfield
- Park
- Golf Course
- Unique Feature
- Waterfall
- Camping
- Mountain
- Ski Area
- Glacier

CONVERSION TABLES

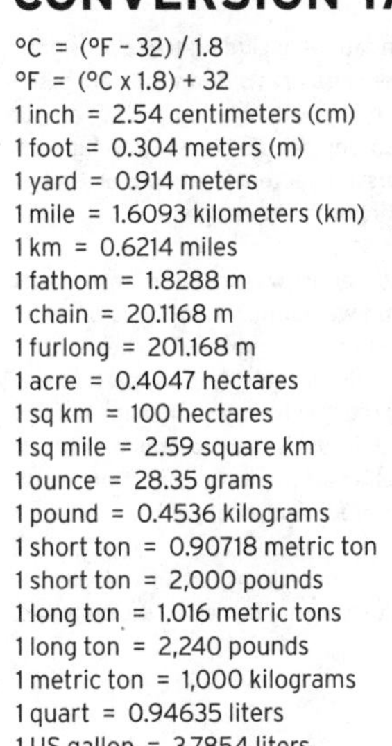

°C = (°F - 32) / 1.8
°F = (°C x 1.8) + 32
1 inch = 2.54 centimeters (cm)
1 foot = 0.304 meters (m)
1 yard = 0.914 meters
1 mile = 1.6093 kilometers (km)
1 km = 0.6214 miles
1 fathom = 1.8288 m
1 chain = 20.1168 m
1 furlong = 201.168 m
1 acre = 0.4047 hectares
1 sq km = 100 hectares
1 sq mile = 2.59 square km
1 ounce = 28.35 grams
1 pound = 0.4536 kilograms
1 short ton = 0.90718 metric ton
1 short ton = 2,000 pounds
1 long ton = 1.016 metric tons
1 long ton = 2,240 pounds
1 metric ton = 1,000 kilograms
1 quart = 0.94635 liters
1 US gallon = 3.7854 liters
1 Imperial gallon = 4.5459 liters
1 nautical mile = 1.852 km

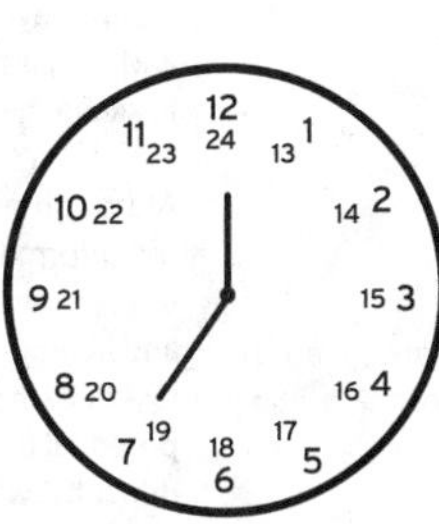

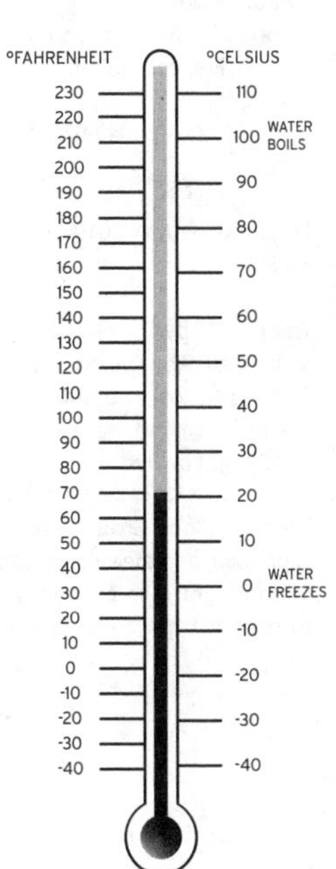

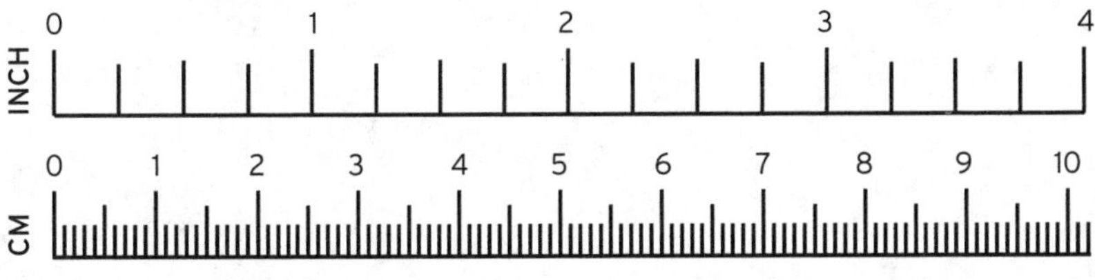

MOON NORMANDY & BRITTANY
Avalon Travel
Hachette Book Group
1700 Fourth Street
Berkeley, CA 94710, USA
www.moon.com

Editor: Ada Fung
Series Manager: Kathryn Ettinger
Copy Editor: Jessica Gould
Graphics Coordinator: Suzanne Albertson
Production Coordinators: Suzanne Albertson, Lisi Baldwin
Cover Design: Faceout Studios, Charles Brock
Interior Design: Domini Dragoone
Moon Logo: Tim McGrath
Map Editor: Albert Angulo
Cartographers: Albert Angulo, Karin Dahl, Andrew Dolan
Proofreader: Barbara Schultz
Indexer: François Trahan

ISBN-13: 978-1-64049-075-8

Printing History
1st Edition — May 2019
5 4 3 2 1

Front cover photo: Restaurants by Vieux Bassin at dusk © Danuta Hyniewska / Getty Images
Back cover photo: Mont Saint-Michel © Kyolshin | Dreamstime.com

Printed in Canada by Friesens